£15

JJ7421

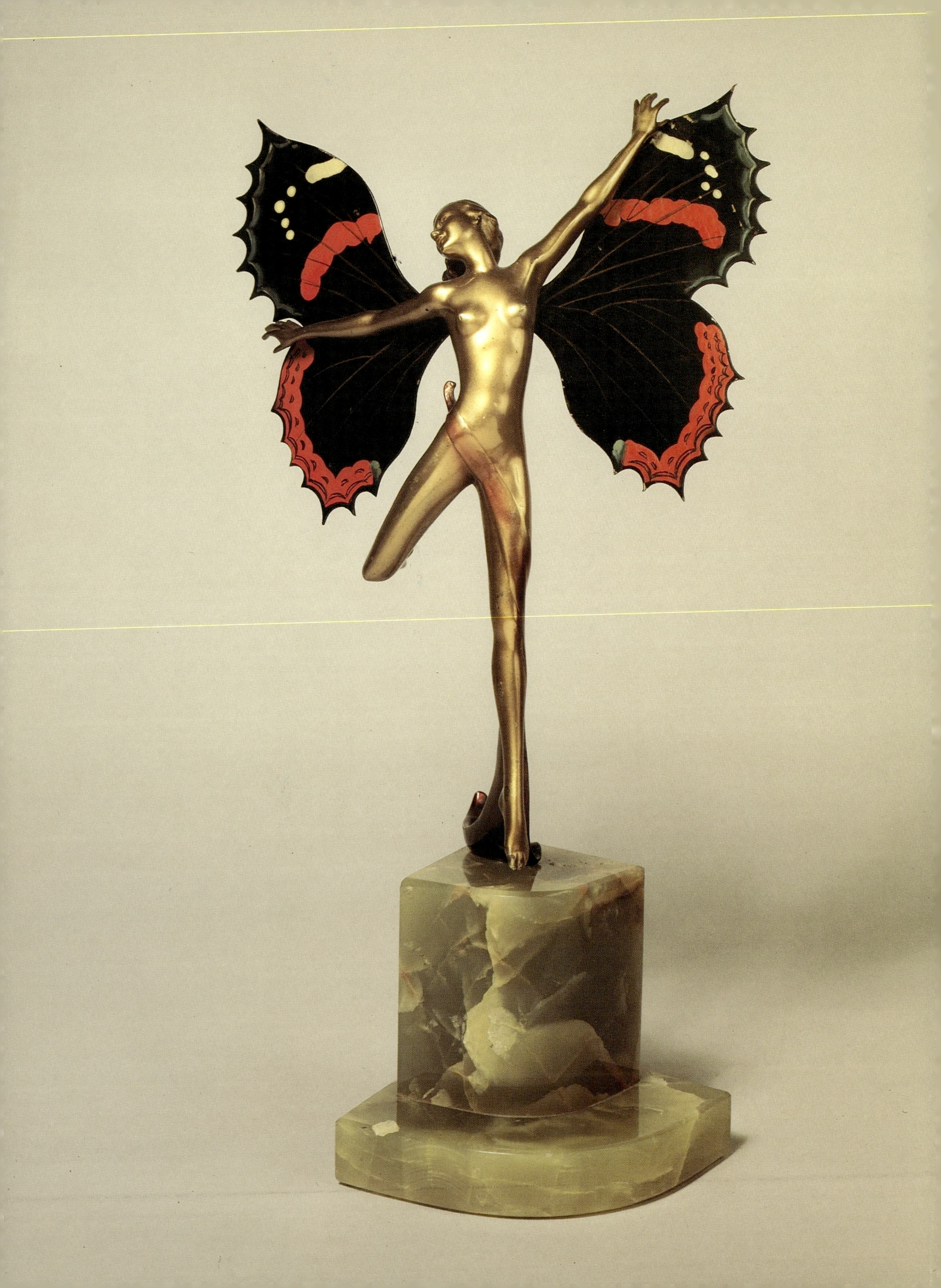

ART DECO and other FIGURES

Bryan Catley

Left. Adolph
A Butterfly Dancer
38cm:15in.

Antique Collectors' Club

ISBN 0 902028 57 X

Reprinted 1984
Reprinted 1985
Reprinted 1987
Reprinted 1989
Reprinted 1990

British Library CIP Data
Catley, Bryan
Art deco and other figures
1. Art deco 2. Figurines
I. Title II. Chancery House Publishing Co. Ltd.
731'.82'0904 NK789.5.A7

ISBN 0 902028 57 X

Published for the Antique Collectors' Club
by Antique Collectors' Club Ltd.

Printed in England by the Antique Collectors' Club Ltd.
5 Church Street, Woodbridge, Suffolk

THE ANTIQUE COLLECTORS' CLUB

The Antique Collectors' Club was formed in 1966 and now has a five figure membership spread throughout the world. It publishes the only independently run monthly antiques magazine *Antique Collecting* which caters for those collectors who are interested in widening their knowledge of antiques, both by greater awareness of quality and by discussion of the factors which influence the price that is likely to be asked. The Antique Collectors' Club pioneered the provision of information on prices for collectors and the magazine still leads in the provision of detailed articles on a variety of subjects.

It was in response to the enormous demand for information on "what to pay" that the price guide series was introduced in 1968 with the first edition of *The Price Guide to Antique Furniture* (completely revised, 1978 and 1989), a book which broke new ground by illustrating the more common types of antique furniture, the sort that collectors could buy in shops and at auctions rather than the rare museum pieces which had previously been used (and still to a large extent are used) to make up the limited amount of illustrations in books published by commercial publishers. Many other price guides have followed, all copiously illustrated, and greatly appreciated by collectors for the valuable information they contain, quite apart from prices. The Antique Collectors' Club also publishes other books on antiques, including horology and art reference works, and a full book list is available.

Club membership, which is open to all collectors, costs £17.50 per annum. Members receive free of charge *Antique Collecting,* the Club's magazine (published ten times a year), which contains well-illustrated articles dealing with the practical aspects of collecting not normally dealt with by magazines. Prices, features of value, investment potential, fakes and forgeries are all given prominence in the magazine.

Among other facilities available to members are private buying and selling facilities, the longest list of "For Sales" of any antiques magazine, an annual ceramics conference and the opportunity to meet other collectors at their local antique collectors' clubs. There are over eighty in Britain and more than a dozen overseas. Members may also buy the Club's publications at special pre-publication prices.

As its motto implies, the Club is an amateur organisation designed to help collectors get the most out of their hobby: it is informal and friendly and gives enormous enjoyment to all concerned.

For Collectors — By Collectors — About Collecting

The Antique Collectors' Club, 5 Church Street, Woodbridge, Suffolk

Foreword

Where possible the artist and correct title of each work is given. If the title is not known, a simple description or generally-known title is used.

Heights are given in centimetres and inches and include bases, unless otherwise stated. (When it is known that the figure was made in more than one height, other known heights are also given.)

It is impossible to illustrate every work of each artist. However, when an unsigned figure is found it is hoped, by reference to the examples illustrated here, that it will be possible to ascertain the name of the artist by the style of the figure.

Knowledge about art deco figures is growing all the time; 'new' works turn up; unknown artists are identified; titles are established. But many gaps still need filling and the author is always grateful to receive any information.

Acknowledgements

I am grateful to Joan Collins for allowing me to include photographs of some twelve works from her collection; also to the British Museum and the Victoria and Albert Museum for their assistance in researching details of the sculptors.

Many of the photographs are of items from my own collection and from the stock of Catspa Antiques of which I am a partner.

Contents

Introduction

In the early stages of researching for this book it seemed almost impossible to get hold of hard information about art deco figures and their artists since very few records are available. There are several reasons. In the first place the majority of original records and sales details were not preserved against the day when the figures would be collectors' items – indeed many of the figures when first introduced were not considered 'good taste'. This fact is easily appreciated since many were of poor quality and gaudy colouring. Then the destruction caused by the Second World War in European cities took its toll of many works and records. Anti-semitism in Europe, prior to and during the war, and the fact that many of the artists were Jewish, are yet further reasons why much related information has disappeared.

The scarcity of manufacturers' lists and sales records has inevitably meant that hearsay is one of the main sources of information and, while not filling factual gaps, this does make fascinating anecdotal material. One supplier gave an account of the damage caused to his premises after a severe bombing raid in 1942, and how more than a dozen broken works were swept up, the ivory thrown out and the bronze sent away as scrap metal to help the war effort.

General facts concerning the artists are that many were born in what is now the Eastern bloc, that Berlin and Paris were their study centres, with many of them making Paris their main base for the remainder of their lives – presumably because Paris had become the centre of the art world with several of the great exhibitions of the period being held in the Salon des Artistes Français and other salons. For instance, according to records kept by the salons, D.H. Chiparus was just one of the art deco artists who exhibited in Paris from 1914 to 1943. (*The Dictionary of Western Sculptors in Bronze,* by James Mackay, published by the Antique Collectors' Club has much useful information on some of the better known art deco sculptors.)

Much of the work of art deco artists came from Austria, in particular Vienna. One well-known Viennese bronze works illustrated two figures on its notepaper, one of which was sculpted by Lorenzl, the other by Zack, which leads one to presume that these artists worked, or at least had their works produced, in Vienna. The same firm produced work by Laurel in 1927.

From order forms which remain it is clear that there was a flourishing export of art deco figures from Austria in the 1930s and that these were not exported as single items – even by the dozen in some instances. Prices varied considerably from a few shillings to over £100 – a considerable sum in the 1920s and 1930s.

A common practice among artists was to use the same titles – each making their own interpretation of the subject – a practice which does not help in attributing works to artists and vice versa. It also seems that there was close cooperation between some artists, since the same work can be found several times, each one signed with a different name. This particularly applies to works by F. Preiss and Prof. Otto Poertzel – at one time it was thought they were one and the same artist.

To give an example of this confusion: two versions of a work known as 'The Aristocrats' are frequently found which are very similar in appearance except for the ears of the dogs which are inclined at slightly different angles; at first one version was attributed to one artist, the other to the other artist – inaccurately as it turns out, since both versions exist signed by *both* Preiss and Poertzel (see page 240).

Many of the earlier figures were classical or mythological subjects, but it was the social, political and topical events of the period which had the strongest influence on the choice of subject matter. Thus one finds works modelled on celebrities – Miss Ada May, who appeared in the 1930 C.B. Cochran review, modelled for 'Lighter than Air' by F. Preiss, who also produced 'The Airwoman' modelled, it is believed, by Amy Johnson. Ballet and dance subjects, always popular, probably became more so with the impact of the Ballet Russe. Fashion of the period, especially Erté's styles, is self-evident in many of the costumes of the figures.

The opening up of the Pharaohs' tombs in the early 1920s accounts for the many Egyptian dancers which were modelled, while the idea and ideal of a master race propounded by Hitler in the early '30s was reflected in numerous athletic figures and postures.

Children were, as always, ideal and therefore popular subjects. Many delightful studies were produced, especially D.H. Chiparus' figures of schoolchildren and the all-ivory, naked children by F. Preiss.

The combination of ivory and bronze, with the ivory representing exposed flesh and the bronze the clothing, had been well known for generations, but it was not until the 1920s and 1930s – the art deco period – that this combination was exploited to the full, mainly due to the surplus of ivory from the Belgian Congo which was made available at a very low cost and was considerably cheaper than bronze. In fact the more ivory in a piece the lower the cost – a fact which influenced some artists to produce all-ivory works which could sell at less than £5.

In order that the figures reached all social levels, a particular figure would be produced at various levels of craftsmanship and in a variety of materials or combination of materials as well as a variety of sizes. In top quality works gold and silver were used as decoration or in place of bronze and some even had precious or semi-precious stones. Better quality works were of bronze or ivory or a combination of the two. Medium quality was of spelter alone or with ivory, or in some instances a plastic composition known as ivorine, and an inferior type was produced of tin or other low grade metal.

Although reference has been made in particular to works being of metal and ivory, several works were made of porcelain and some versions are known where marble was used to represent the exposed flesh. Where ivory is included in a figure this may have been carved, at least in part, by machine. It seems almost impossible that all the carving was by hand in view of the numbers of each work which are to be found where the carving is almost identical – even down to the waves in the hair. In all probability such works were hand carved at the final stage.

The works were mounted on bases which varied considerably. Green Brazilian onyx was popular and was sometimes combined with black marble or onyx. This latter combination was frequently favoured by F. Preiss. Marble in its varied colours and combinations was used for many of the larger works and D.H. Chiparus provides us with some spectacular bases using various combinations. Inferior works were mounted on alabaster or, in some instances, wood.

It is worth repeating here that these works were not 'one off' works – similar or identical figures could be ordered, sometimes with slight variations in decoration and material or combination of materials. With this in mind it is very probable that numerous examples of the works must still exist in private collections or homes.

Perhaps the most popular period for these works was between 1931 and 1936, when Messrs. Phillips and MacConnel gave considerable space to such items on their stand at the Ideal Home Exhibitions held at London's Olympia during those years. In 1931 they had on display a magnificent example of the work by F. Preiss of 'St. George and the Dragon' at the staggering price, for that time, of £70 – for a work less than eight inches high. It was carved from a single piece of ivory and showed in great detail the subject and craftsmanship of the artist (see page 256).

To promote further interest in these works, a new method of decoration was suggested by one of the well-known suppliers of the day in one of their catalogues, which reads as follows:–

> "A new and very beautiful way of decorating a room is to form a niche in the wall and place therein a small piece of sculpture either in bronze or bronze and ivory; these can be had in silver or gilt bronze to match the electric fittings. The effect is greatly enhanced if the models are lighted up by a hidden globe placed above the figure. Or, better still, select one of those charming little figures already mounted upon hollowed out marble in which is placed a small electric bulb; the soft light showing through the opaque marble gives a charming effect when done in this way. The bulbs themselves can be had in several colours, which can be periodically changed as desired to coincide with any colour scheme that may be required.
>
> "The background of the niche should be lined with the same woods as the furniture of the room, or, if preferred, a matt black. If the background of the sculpture is desired to be seen, this can be done by having a mirror fixed behind."

It is interesting to note that the figures could be made to special order in any desired colour or to tone in with a special colour scheme. This especially applied in the case of a lamp where the colour of the shade and the figure matched or toned with the upholstery in a room.

Condition is the all-important factor: ivory, when used, must not be broken and should not have age cracks – lines running along the contours of the ivory; it should not be stained by age or yellowed by sunlight. With bronze, the patina should not be scratched in any way.

While on the subject of condition it should be remembered that on no account should an item be cleaned with an abrasive product if the patina is to be protected. It is wise to keep well dusted and maybe apply a light polish. In fact the best thing to do is to keep in a cabinet larger items and those items which will allow such display, when simple dusting only is necessary. One important thing is to keep figures which include ivory in a slightly damp atmosphere in order to prevent the ivory drying out and cracking. A small glass of water kept hidden behind the base of the item is ideal, or even a vase of flowers nearby will serve the same purpose.

The manner of assembly of the figures is fascinating and particular attention is drawn to works by F. Preiss in this respect. In each case there appears to be a master item which, rather like a Chinese puzzle, when removed allows the complete work to be taken apart.

In order to dismantle a work, for cleaning or packing purposes, it is first necessary to find this master component. Where the head is the master component a threaded bolt passes into the lower part of the neck, generally from the lower part of the body, or a similar bolt passes through the head from above with the hole in which the head of the bolt sits being closed by a plug. A good example is 'Con Brio' by F. Preiss (page 283). The feathered plume fits into a hole in the head; when the plume is removed, by a gentle pulling movement, the slotted head of a threaded bolt is disclosed. On removal of the bolt the head of the figure can be separated from the upper part of the body. The arms can then be removed by releasing a small nut from a threaded stud attached to each arm. Once the arms are removed a threaded bolt is revealed in the lower part of each arm socket which, on removal, allows the part of the body forming the brassiere of the costume to be removed. At this stage a centrally located head of a bolt is uncovered which, on being released, allows the ivory torso to be detached from the lower part of the costume. Each leg can then be removed by releasing a nut connected to the free end of a threaded stud attached to the upper part of each leg. (Anyone attempting to dismantle such a figure is advised to detach it from its base before proceeding.)

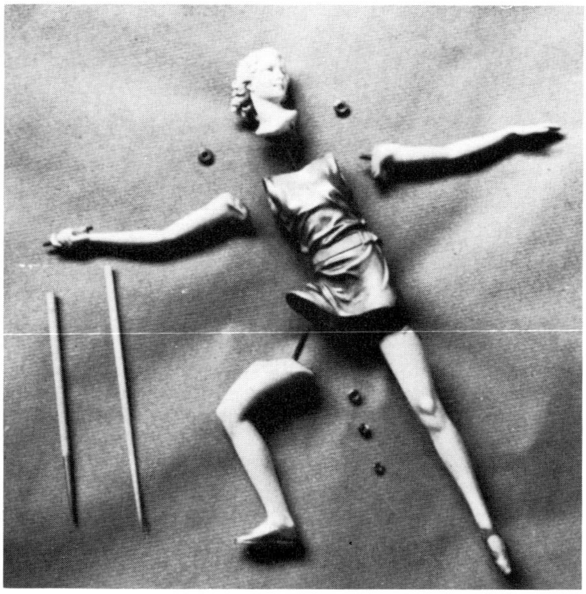

The component parts of 'The Javelin Thrower' by F. Preiss (page 264). As with 'Con Brio' described above, the head is the first part to be detached when dismantling the figure; it is held by a nut engaging the end of a threaded rod below the dress. The other parts are then dismantled as shown.

Nowadays art deco figures are very much sought after by collectors and command high prices in the salerooms. A point to note here is that not all works by the same sculptor fetch high prices; it is only those of good design, and especially those having movement or in a spectacular pose, that are really desirable. A good example is the 'Flame Leaper' by F. Preiss (page 277): a figure in perfect condition was sold for more than £5,000 in 1977; the same subject which, although complete, was in poor condition, sold for only £500 in the same year. These prices seem amazing when one realises that in the 1930s when Phillips and MacConnel held their annual sale they generally included several works to reduce their stock and many of the all-ivory models sold for less than £5. In 1931 the same firm sold a pair of schoolchildren by F. Preiss known as 'The Hoop Girl' and 'Sonny Boy' for about £14 each (page 267).

It is to be hoped that all those who are inspired to collect art deco figures will get the same pleasure from them as the author has had over the years. There is no doubt that they evoke an atmosphere and mood. Coming across one for the first time or seeing one again after a length of time, it is possible to catch a feeling of that lifelike quality (which so many of the figures possess), when it seems the figure is only waiting for a spell to be broken so its dance can continue.

Biographical details of some of the artists

(As already mentioned in the introduction, information on artists is difficult to come by. The following list does not, therefore, claim to be comprehensive. It lists details of some of the artists represented in this book as well as artists whose work is not illustrated here.)

Lucien Charles Edouard **ALLIOT**: Born in Paris on 16th November, 1877; he was a pupil of Barrias and Coutan, exhibited at the Salon from 1905 to 1939.

Armel Emile Jean **BEAUFILS**: Born in Rennes; member of the Salon.

Ary **BITTER**: Born in Marseilles; exhibited at the Salon for many years during the early part of the twentieth century.

Suzanne **BIZARD**: Born at Saint-Amand on 1st August, 1873; exhibited at the Salon from 1900 to 1936.

Antoine **BOFILL**: Born in Barcelona; exhibited in Spain and at the Paris Salons from 1902 to 1920s.

Marcel **BOURAINE**: Born in Pontoise; in the main he was self-taught. All his works are of sincere realism and drawn from life. Taken prisoner by the Germans during the 1914-1918 war, he so interested his captors that they gave him many works to execute. He was interned in Switzerland where he produced several monuments, of which one was for Lausanne. He exhibited at all the main Paris Salons.

Jean-Marie **CAMUS**: Born in Clermont-Ferrand; exhibited for the first time at the Salon in 1905, where he won an award.

Albert **CARRIER-BELLEUSE**: Born in Laon on 12th June, 1827; he was one of the masters of his generation and received many honours such as the Grand Prix de Rome, Prix d'Honneur and Hors Concours. His works are to be seen in many art centres throughout the world, among them the monument for independence in Costa Rica and several works in Paris including a ceiling in the Louvre. He died on 3rd June, 1887 when he was a director of the Sèvres factory.

Eugene **CARTIER**: Born in Arles; received a medal of honour from the Salon in 1926.

Thomas François **CARTIER**: Born in Marseilles; received many awards from the Salon, one of the first being in 1908.

Auguste J. Ch. **CARVIN**: Born in Sin-le-Noble; received many awards from the Salon, one of the earliest being in 1907.

Louis Albert **CARVIN**: Born in Paris; received a medal of honour from the Salon in 1894 and exhibited there frequently until 1933.

Demetre H. **CHIPARUS**: Born in Romania and lived in Paris studying under A. Mercier and J. Boucher. He exhibited at the Salon from 1914. His later works in the 1920s were influenced by the interest in Egypt after the excavation of the Pharaohs' tombs. He based many works on the ballet and the theatre, one particular theme being the Ballet Russe, from which resulted 'The Russian Dancers' depicting Nijinsky and Ida Rubinstein in their roles in *Schéhérazade* (see pages 85 and 89). Like many artists he had a particular gift for portraying children and his work in this field covers a whole range of childish pursuits.

Fernand **CIAN**: Born in Italy; exhibited at the Paris Salons from 1911 to 1928.

Juan **CLARA**: Born in Olot in Spain in 1875; exhibited at the Paris Salons.

Sylvestre **CLERC**: Born in Toulouse on 31st December, 1912; exhibited at the Salon with special merits in the 1920s.

Claire Jeanne Roberte **COLINET**: Born in Brussels; studied with Jef Lambeaux. Like so many artists she moved to Paris where she was elected to the Société des Artistes Français and exhibited in the Salon from 1913. She exhibited in the Salon des Indépendants from 1937. Her works were varied – from the usual conventional ballet poses of the period to a very magnificent work of a Valkyrie maiden on horse-back (page 111).

Joaquin **COSTA**: Born in Lezignan on 8th January, 1888; exhibited at the Salon during the 1920s.

Joseph **D'ASTE**: Born in Naples; exhibited in Italy and France in the early 1920s.

Sophie **DEBRY**: Born in Charleville; exhibited at the Salon in the 1920s.

Maurice **DELANNOY**: Born in Paris on 11th March, 1885; received in 1921 a medal of honour from the Salon and a first class medal in 1931.

Pierre François Fernand **DELANNOY**: Born in Paris; exhibited in 1921 for the first time at the Salon where his work gained him an honourable mention. Later exhibits at the same Salon were equally well received.

Louis **DELAPCHIER**: Born at Saint-Denis; exhibited at the Salon from 1904 until the late 1920s.

Jean **DESCOMPS**: Born in Agen on 14th May, 1852; studied under Falguière, worked in Paris and exhibited frequently at the Salon.

Joseph (Joé) J.E. **DESCOMPS**: Born in Clermont-Ferrand in the latter part of the nineteenth century; exhibited at the Salon.

Edouard **DROUOT**: Born in Sommevoire on 3rd April, 1859; exhibited bronzes at the Salon from 1889.

Jean Alexander Joseph **FALGUIERE**: Born in Toulouse on 9th September, 1831, and died in Paris on 19th April, 1900; won many awards from the Paris Salons from as early as 1857 and trained many well known sculptors.

Henry **FUGERE**: Born in Saint Mandé on 7th September, 1872; studied with Barrias, Cavelier and Puech. Exhibited at the Salon.

Amedeo **GENNARELLI**: Born in Naples; exhibited at the Salon, particularly in the 1920s.

Alfred **GILBERT**: Born in London on 12th August, 1854, and died on 4th November, 1934; studied in England and Paris. Received many awards and was knighted in 1932. Perhaps his best known work is Eros in London.

Geneviève **GRANGER**: Born in Paris on 1st February, 1877; received several awards from the Salon.

Henry Leon **GREBER**: Born in Beauvais on 28th May, 1855; received the medal of honour from the Salon in 1891 and several awards in following years.

Rene **GRÉGOIRE**: Born in Saumur on 4th June, 1871; received the Prix de Rome in 1899 which was followed by many other awards from the Salon.

Right. D.H. Chiparus
Oriental Dancer
40cm: 15¾in.; 31cm: 12in.

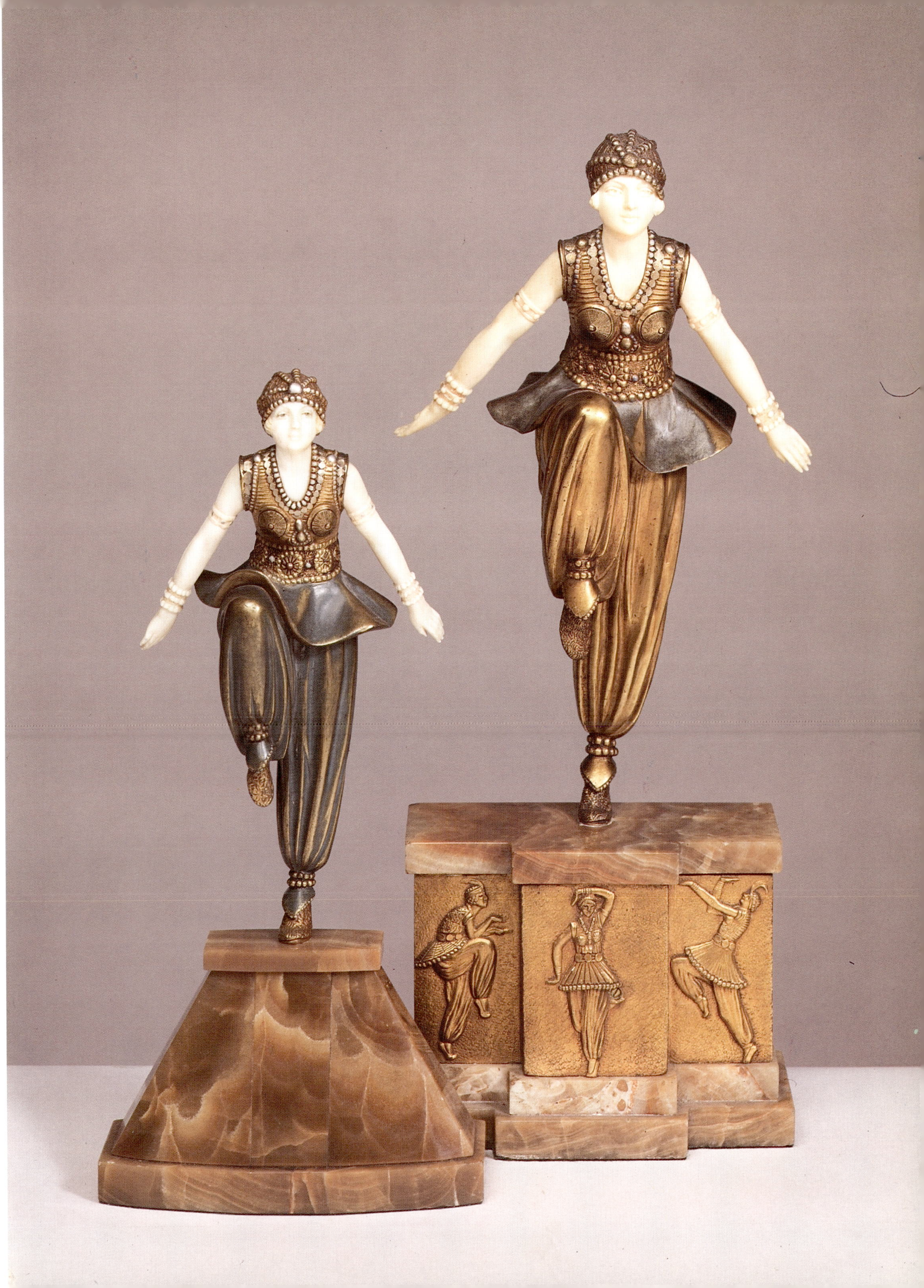

(Henri) Desire **GRISARD**: Born in Paris; exhibited at the Salon.

Samuel **GRUN**: Born in Reval, Russia; worked in London and Paris; exhibited at the Royal Academy and the Paris Salons during the 1920s and 1930s.

A. **GUERVAL**: Pupil of her husband Pierre Le Faguays; she exhibited several times in artistic circles, where her talents for portraying lifelike work were well received. Her first exhibition was in 1924 at the Salon where she showed a work entitled 'Dawn', which has been produced in many versions since, both draped and as a nude.

Maurice **GUIRAUD RIVIÈRE**: Born in Toulouse; became a member of the Salon where he exhibited during the 1930s.

Emmanuel **HANNAUX**: Born in Metz on 31st January, 1855; studied in Paris, received an award from the Salon in 1884, the first of many.

Rachel **HAUTOT**: Born in Fermanville (Manche) on 20th September, 1882; exhibited at the Salon.

Jean Antoine **INJALBERT**: Born in Beziers on 23rd February, 1845, and died in 1933; received the Prix de Rome in 1874 and many other honours in following years.

Alexander **KÉLÉTY**: Born in Budapest, in Hungary; studied sculpture at Toulouse with Imre Simay before studying in Paris where he exhibited at the Salons in the years between the wars.

Sylvain **KINSBURGER**: Born in Paris on 21st January, 1855; had great success from 1884 when he received the first of many awards from the Salon.

Joseph Marie Thomas (Jef) **LAMBEAUX**: Born in Antwerp on 13th July, 1852 and died in Brussels on 6th June, 1908; won many awards and trained Mme. C.J.R. Colinet.

Antonin **LARROUX**: Born in Toulouse on 3rd June, 1859; exhibited many times at the Salon.

Blanche **LAURENT**: Born in Paris; she was an exhibitor at the Salon from 1901.

Pierre A. **LAURENT**: Born in Montlucon on 8th July, 1868; studied under Barrias and won awards from the Salon from 1897.

George **LAVROFF**: Born in Siberia on 19th April, 1895; studied in Moscow and moved to France after the Revolution. Exhibited at all the main Paris Salons. Produced art deco styles similar to work by Lorenzl.

Pierre **LE FAGUAYS**: Born in Nantes; pupil of Vibert. He attracted the attention of the public at his first exhibition due to the originality he gave his dancing subjects which were inspired from the statues of Tanagra. He was a member of the Salon and of La Stele and Evolution groups. Medal of honour in 1927.

Charles **LEONARD**: Born in Lille; exhibited at the Salon from about 1891.

Henry Louis **LEVASSEUR**: Born in Paris on 16th April, 1853; received his first award from the Salon in 1882, and exhibited in all the main French Salons.

Clarisse **LEVY**: Born at St. Maurice on 31st July, 1896; won an award from the Salon in 1929.

Marcelle **LEVY**: Born in Abbeville; exhibited at the Salon.

Jacques **LIPCHITZ**: Born in Druskieniki on 22nd August, 1891; spent most of his life in France where he exhibited with great success. In 1941 he was forced to flee the country when he moved to the U.S.A. where again he had great success.

LORENZL, LOR and **RENZL**: All believed to be one and the same. Produced many works during the 1920s and 1930s, in bronze or the combination of bronze and ivory. It is known that Lorenzl designed ceramics for the Austrian firm of Goldschneider.

Samuel **LYPCHYTZ** (sometimes signs Lipchytz): Born in Russia; he was an excellent artist who specialised in ivory sculpture and was influenced by the statues at Tanagra as were many others. He exhibited at the Salon and elsewhere.

Alix **MARQUET**: Born in Oudan on 8th January, 1875; exhibited at the Salon and won many awards from 1903.

Rene Paul **MARQUET**: Born in Port Louis on 5th July, 1875; studied under Fontaine and Falguière; received an honourable mention from the Salon in 1909.

Jules Edward **MASSON**: Born in Paris on 3rd June, 1871; received a medal of honour from the Salon in 1890 and several awards in the 1920s.

Jacques **MERCULIANO**: Born in Naples; exhibited at the Salon from 1914, with great success in 1927.

Jean **MICH**: Born in Machtum in the Grand Duchy of Luxemburg; exhibited at the Salon from the early part of the twentieth century.

Henry Raphael **MONCASSIN**: Born in Toulouse on 3rd April, 1883; studied under Mercié, received a medal of honour in 1911 from the Salon and many other awards in following years.

Charlotte **MONGINOT**: Born in Paris on 18th December, 1872; received an honourable mention from the Salon in 1895. She gained many other awards in the following years.

Hippolyte François **MOREAU**: Born in Paris; received a medal of honour in 1886 from the Salon.

George Desire **MORICE**: Born in Paris on 11th November, 1899; received a medal of honour in 1927 from the Salon.

Raphael **NANNINI**: Born in Florence; exhibited at the Paris Salons in 1923.

Louis **OURY**: Born in Montauban; exhibited at the Salon with an honourable mention in 1898.

Germaine **OURY-CERF**: Born in Valenciennes on October 1889; received many awards from the Salon, the first being in 1921.

Roland **PARIS**: Born in Vienna in 1894; studied under Henry Van der Velde who founded, with others, the Bauhaus School.

Charles Theodore **PERRON**: Born in Paris on 16th October, 1862; studied under Falguière; received many awards from the Salon, the first being in 1896.

Raphael Charles **PEYRE**: Born in Paris on 1st June, 1872; studied under Falguière, Mercié and Barrias; received a medal of honour in 1894 from the Salon, which was followed by many other awards.

Paul **PHILIPPE**: Born in Thorn, in Poland; pupil of Larroux. He exhibited with success at nearly all the salons in Paris. Among his best works are 'Awakening' (page 250), 'The Challenge' (page 250) and 'The Russian Dancer' (page 251).

Evelyn **PHILIPPE-STANDEN**: Born in London; exhibited at the French Salons with some success.

Charles Philippe Germaine Aristide **PILLET**: Born in Paris on 20th July, 1869; received the Grand Prix de Rome in 1890 from the Salon and many other awards in following years including a medal of honour in 1923.

Prof. Otto. **POERTZEL**: Born at Scheibe on 24th October, 1876, he became one of the most prominent sculptors in Germany and was for many years under the special protection of the Duke of Saxe-Coburg-Gotha who gave him many orders for large monuments. The artist lived in the society of prominent actors, and under this influence created many well known works such as 'Snake Charmer' (Page 255) and 'Bacchanal'. Many of his earlier works were to be found in the salons of German royal courts and a few of the most beautiful were purchased by the late King of Bulgaria. It is possible that the confusion between figures by this artist and Preiss is due to the fact that their work is similar in a great many respects, which in turn may well be due to their sharing a studio in Berlin.

Johann Philipp Ferdinand (Fritz) **PREISS**: Born in Erbach-Odenwald on 13th February, 1882. Studied in Paris and worked with Prof. Poertzel in Berlin. This latter point may well have some bearing on the fact that several works by both artists are similar which has, in the past, led many to believe that they were one and the same person. Preiss worked to a great extent with ivory and used the combination of ivory and bronze with magnificent results. His models of children are exquisite, in particular those of all ivory. Another important aspect of his work is related to sport, and in this respect one must see the works as being based on the German ideals of youth and the so called master race, a fact which is particularly evident from the works produced during the Berlin Olympics of 1936.

Many of the works of F. Preiss have the monogram PK embossed in the bronze and this shows that the figure was produced by the firm of Preiss and Kassler. Walter Kassler and Ferdinand Preiss founded the firm in 1906 in Berlin and it continued to flourish until the death of Preiss from a brain tumour in 1943. It has been established that Preiss designed and worked on all his models and had many sculptors who worked for him. In this way he was able to produce many works though, as will be appreciated due to the numbers of each model, it was impossible for him to make each item entirely, although many are signed by him. It is presumed that each sculptor executed a particular component of each figure and that the various parts were assembled, in many cases by Preiss.

Edouardo **ROSSI**: Born in Naples on 20th September, 1867, and died on 1st May, 1926; exhibited at the Salon.

Anne Marie **ROUX**: Born in Nevers; received many awards from the Salon including a medal of honour in 1925.

Charles **ROUX**: Born in Paris; received a medal of honour from the Salon in 1922.

Constant Ambroise **ROUX**: Born in Marseilles on 20th April, 1865; received many awards from the Salon, the first being in 1892, and a medal of honour in 1930.

Fanny **ROZET**: Born in Paris on 13th June, 1881; she exhibited in the Salon from 1904 and received a medal in 1921.

Rene **ROZET**: Born in Paris on 14th May, 1859; received first award from the Salon in 1885, and many more in the 1920s.

Marius Joseph **SAIN**: Born in Avignon on 18th October, 1877; received many awards from the Salon, the earliest being in 1903 and several during the 1920s.

Paul Etienne **SAIN**: Born in Paris; exhibited at the Salon in the 1920s.

Charles M.L.J. **SARRABEZOLLES**: Born in Toulouse on 27th December, 1888; studied under Mercié and Marqueste. He became a member of the Salon where he won many awards including a Grand Prix in 1937.

Gustav **SCHMIDT-CASSEL**: Born in Cassel on 2nd November, 1867; studied under Herter; his chief work is that of Peter the Great in Riga.

Theophile François **SOMME**: Born in Nancy; received a medal of honour from the Salon in 1902 and then, after many other awards, the prize of the year in 1927.

Fredy Balthazar **STOLL**: Born in Switzerland of French parents; exhibited at the Salon and won a gold award in 1937.

Georges Lucien **VACOSSIN**: Born in Grandvilliers on 1st March, 1870; received many awards at the Salon from as early as 1904.

George **VAN DER STRAETEN**: Born in Ghent on 21st December, 1856; worked in Paris from 1883 to 1928 and lived for the latter part of his life in Ghent.

Jean **VERSCHNEIDER**: Born in Lyons; studied under Injalbert; received many awards from the Salon including a mention in 1909.

Serge **YOURIEVITCH**: Born in Paris in the latter part of the nineteenth century; he was Ancient Chamberlain to the Court of Russia but did not become a sculptor until he met Rodin, who became his initiator. He spent years of hard work in his ambition to become an artist and several of his works were sent to the Société Nationale. Frequently his work is considered as a continuation of Rodin's.

Gabriel Eugene Lucien **ZIMMERMANN**: Born in Paris on 22nd January, 1877; exhibited at the Salon.

ABELL

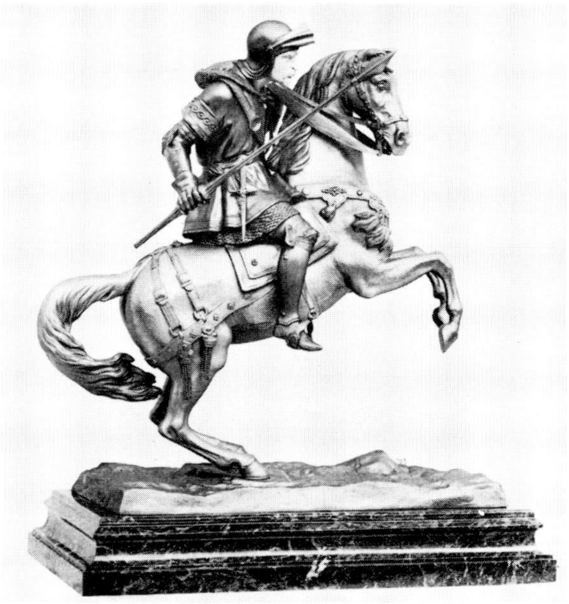

Tournament, 54cm:21¼in.

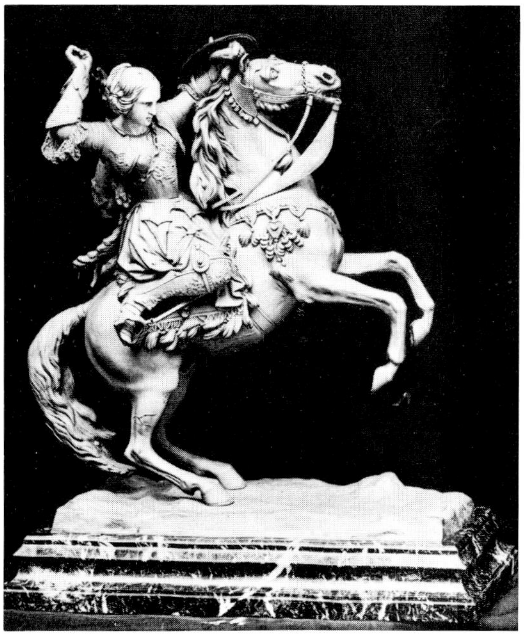

Victorious, 45cm:17¾in.

ADOLPH

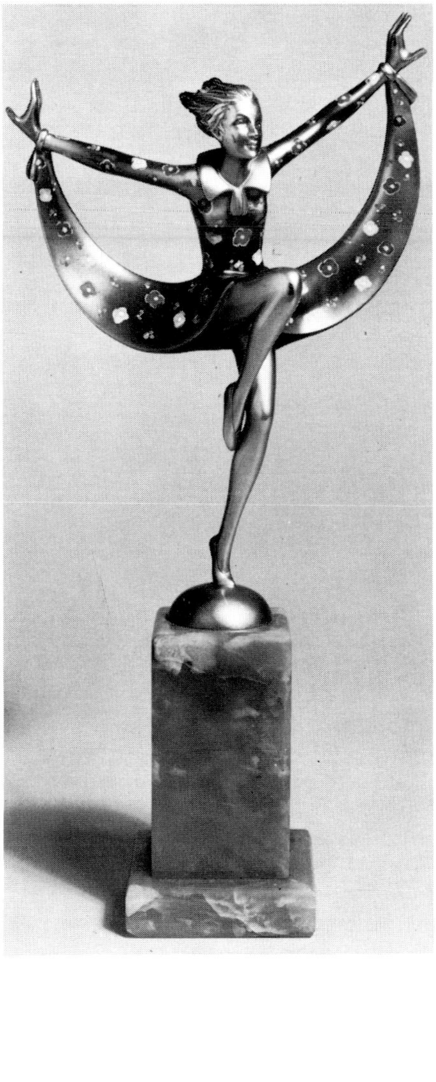

A Dancer, 24cm:9½in.

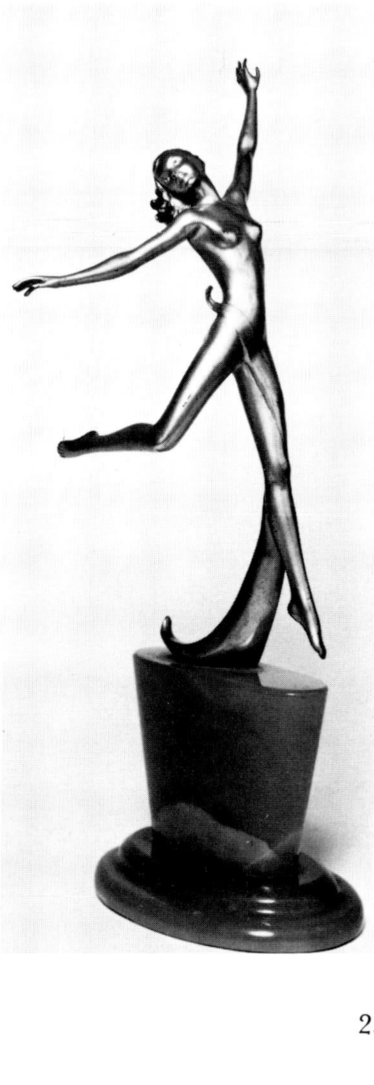

A Dancer, 36cm:14in.

L. ALLIOT

ALLMAN

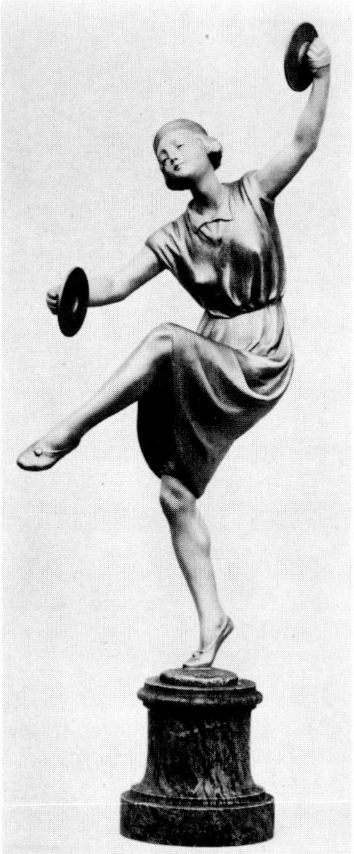

Cymbals Player
38cm:15in.
22cm:8½in.

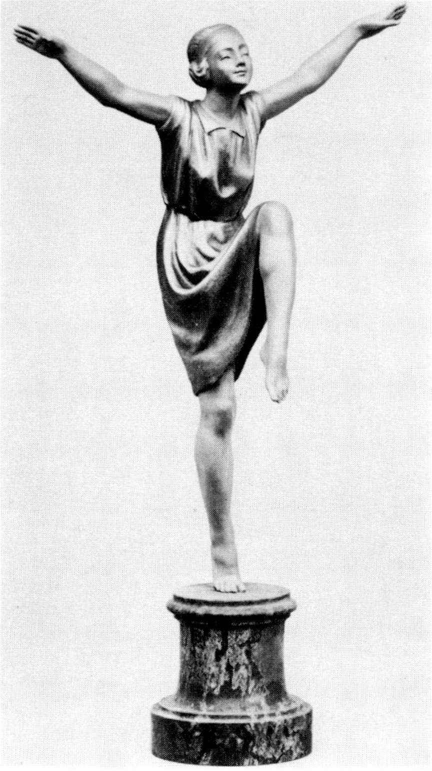

Sporting, 33cm:13in.; 19cm:7½in.

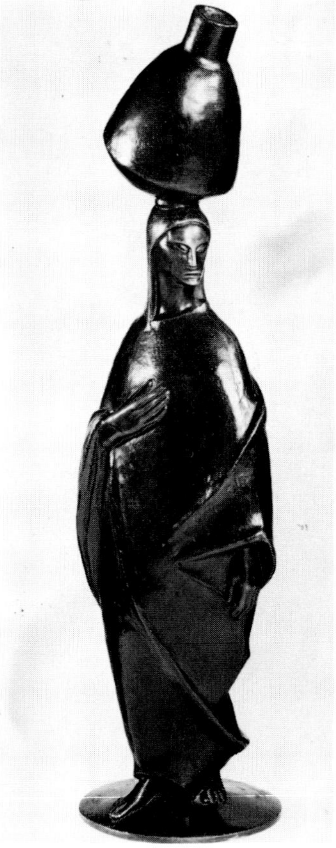

Water Carrier, 38cm:15in.

D. ALONZO

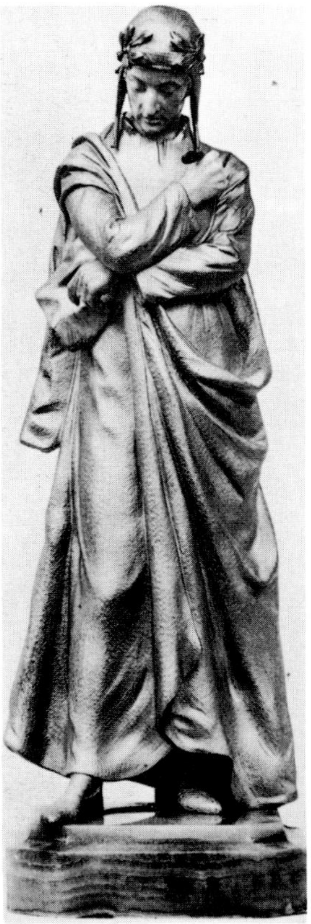

Dante, 31cm:12¼in.

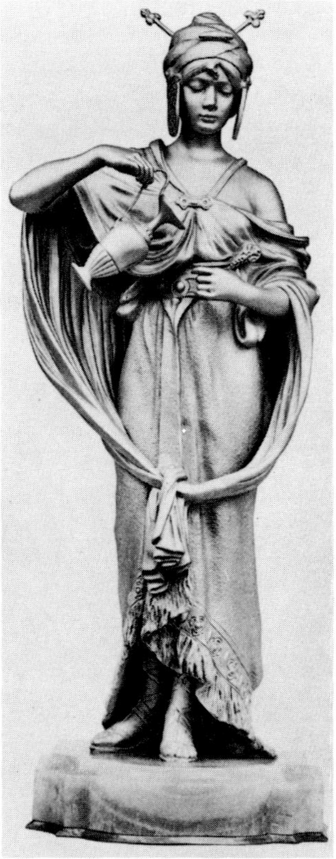

Rebecca, 42cm:16½in.

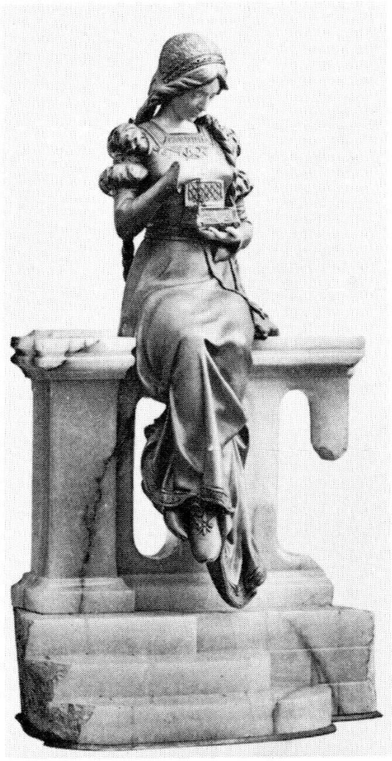

Marguerite, 40cm:15¾in.; 29cm:11½in.

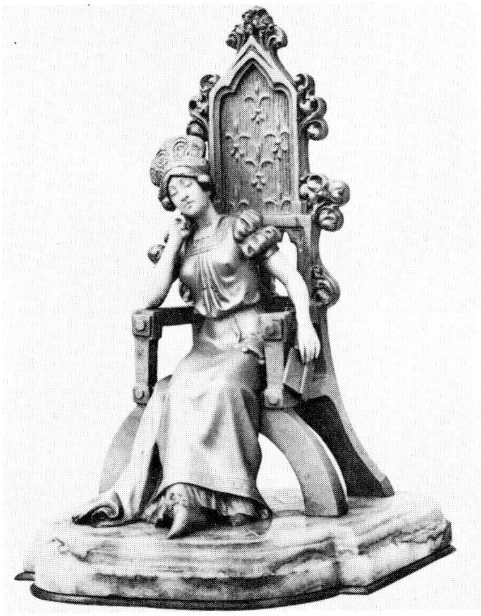

Reading in the Chair, 29cm:11½in.

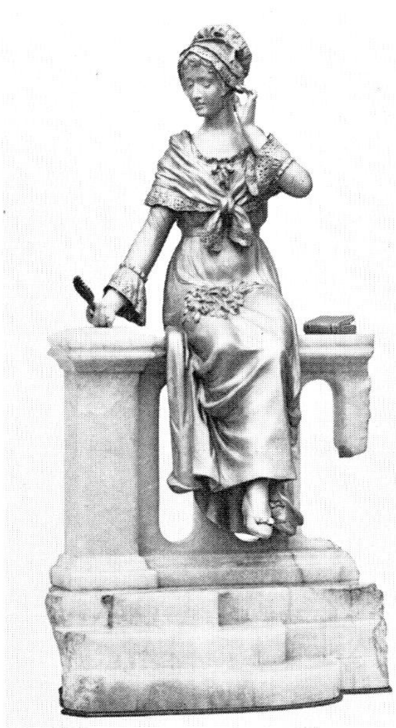

Looking Pretty, 41cm:16in.

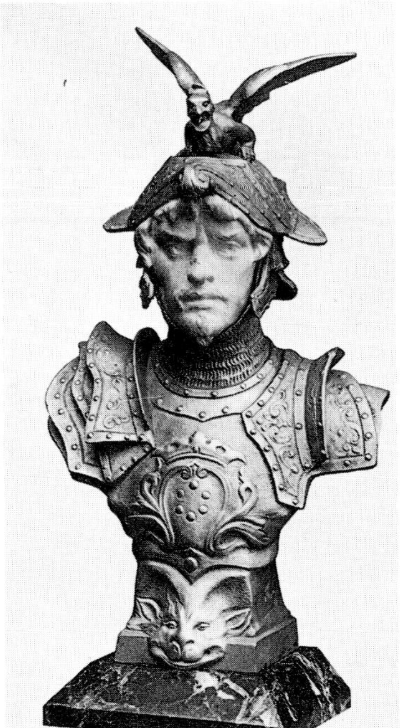

Trooper, 31cm:12in.

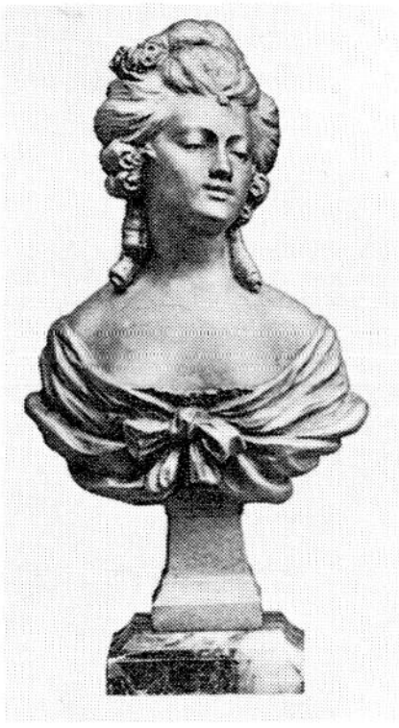

Marchioness, 17cm:6¾in.

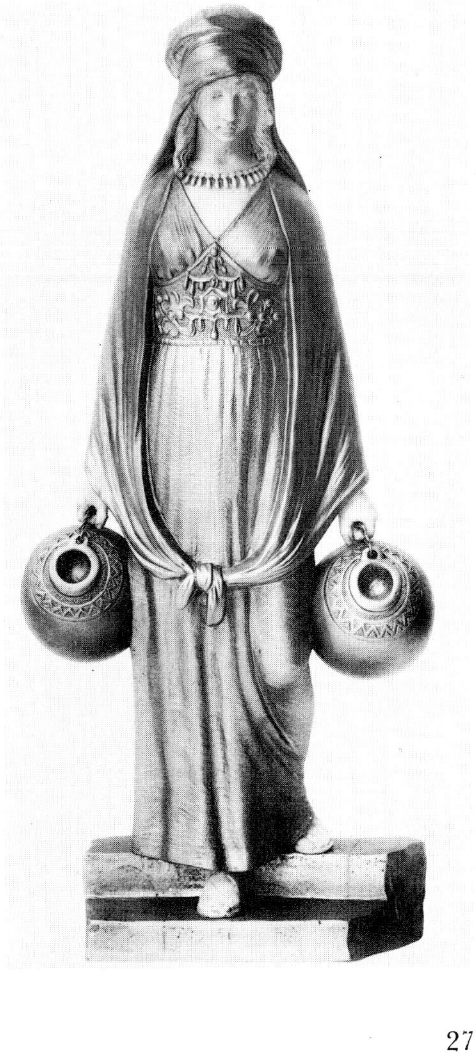

Oriental Water Carrier 33cm:13in. 20cm:7¾in.

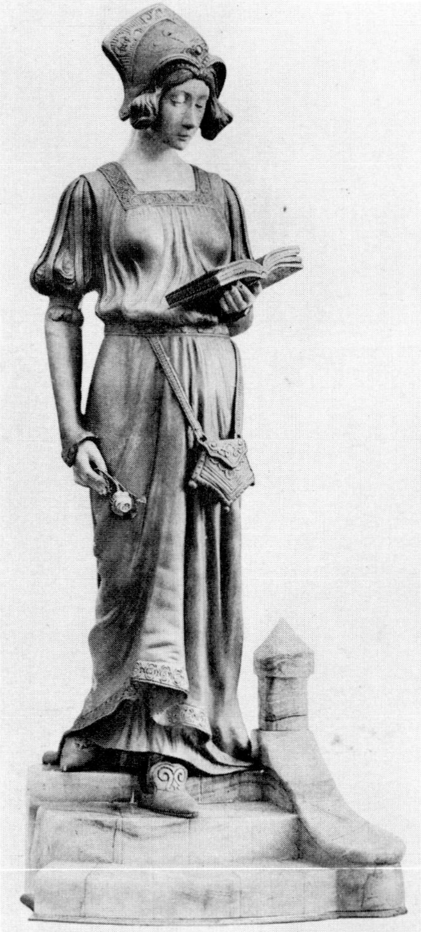

The Lecture
61cm:24in.
33cm:13in.
24cm:9½in.

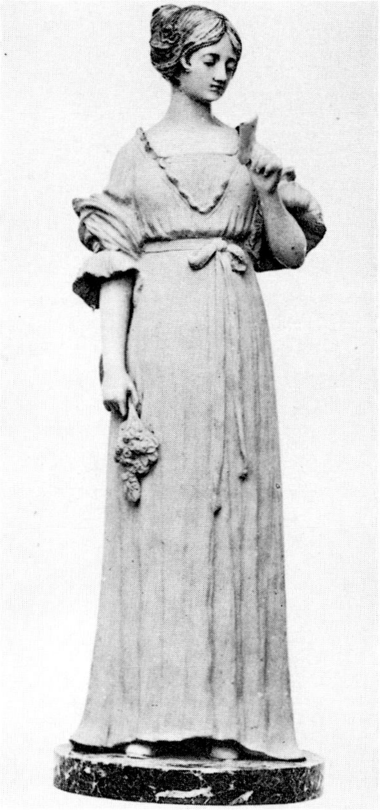

Good News
34cm:13½in.; 22cm:8½in.

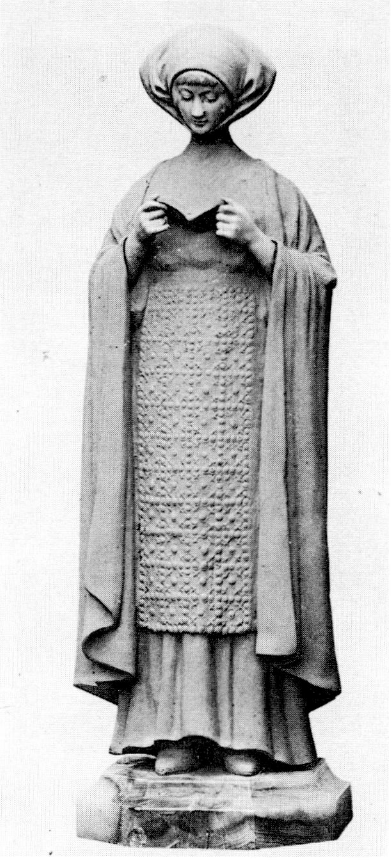

Gothic Reader
40cm:15¾in.; 22cm:8½in.

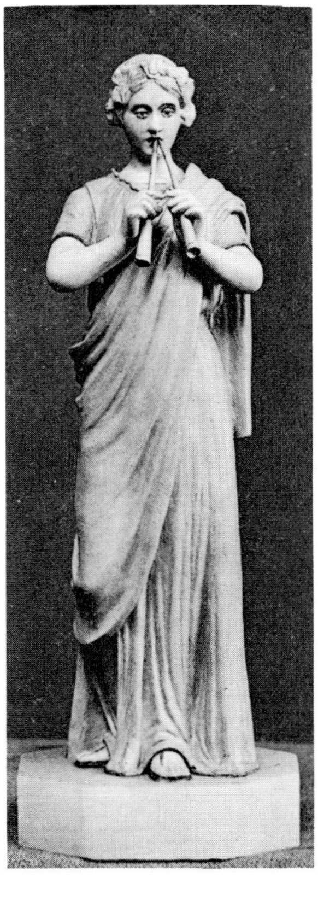

Flautist, 22cm:8½in.

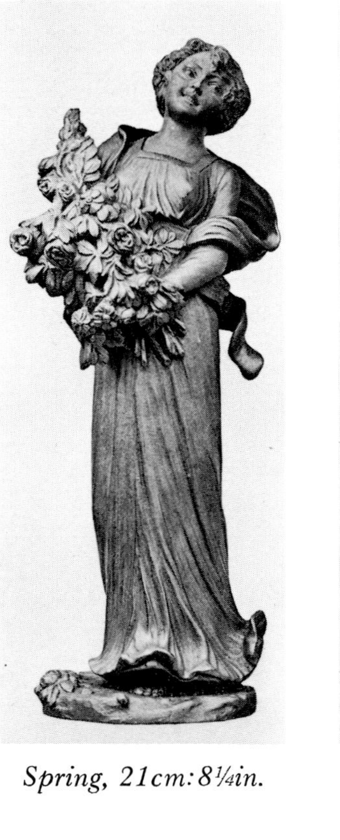

Spring, 21cm:8¼in.

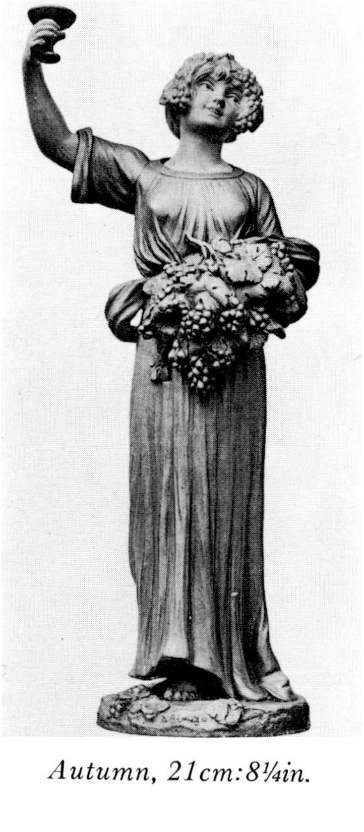

Autumn, 21cm:8¼in.

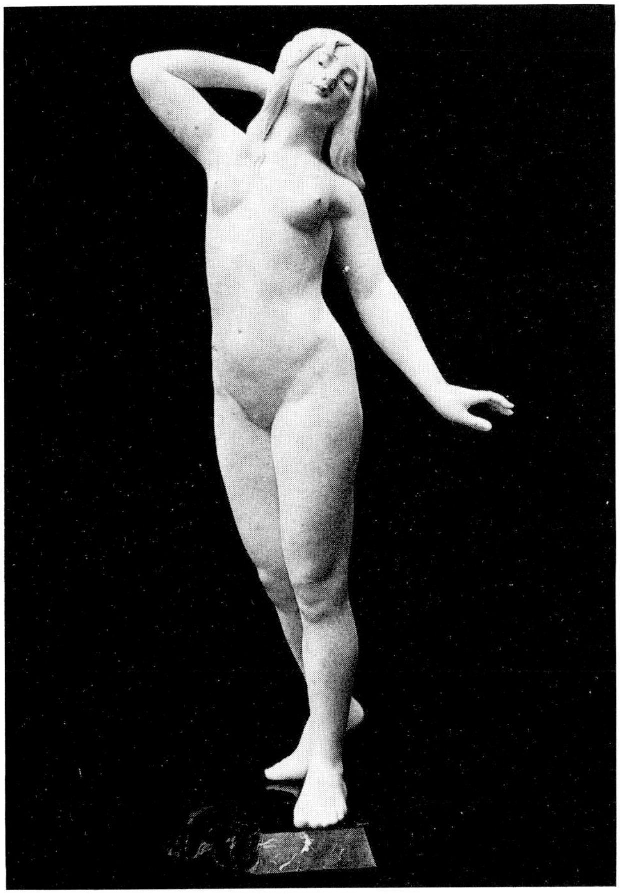

Dawn
80cm: 31½in.
60cm: 23½in.
45cm: 17¾in.

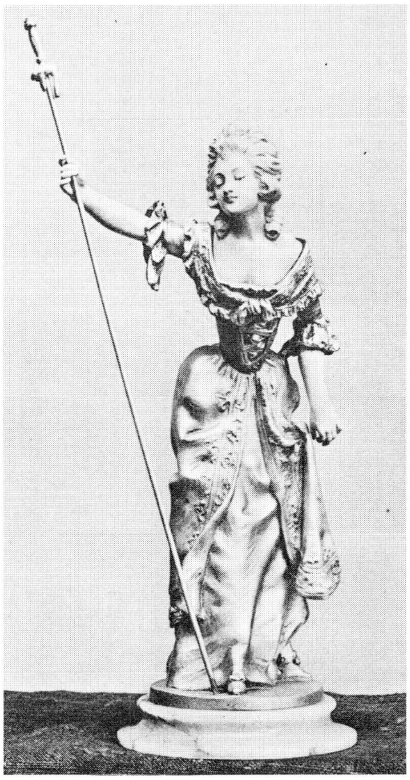

At the Court, 31cm: 12¼in.

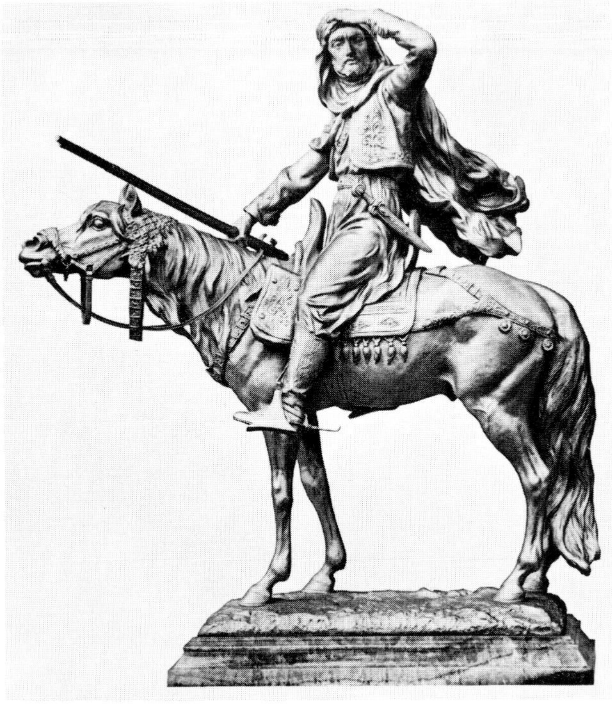

Arab Sentry, 43cm: 16¾in.

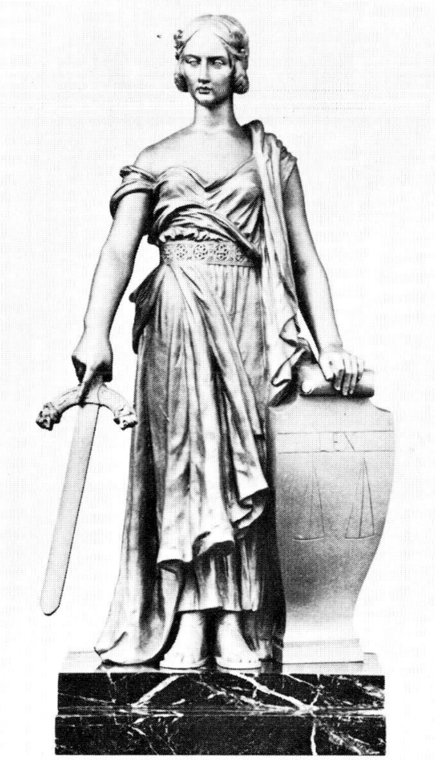

Justice, 64cm: 25in.; 46cm: 18in.

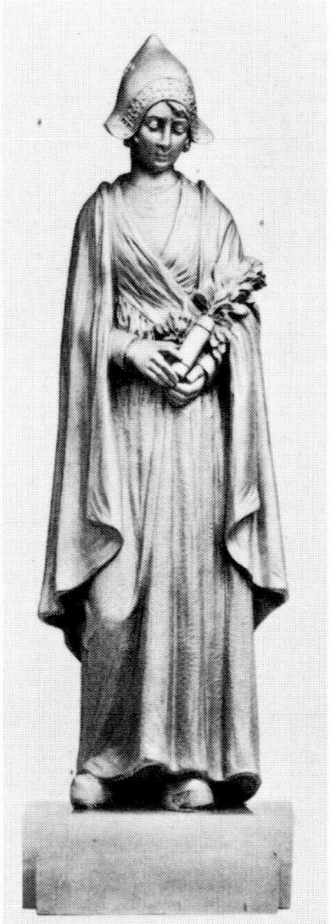

Palm Sunday
25cm:10in.

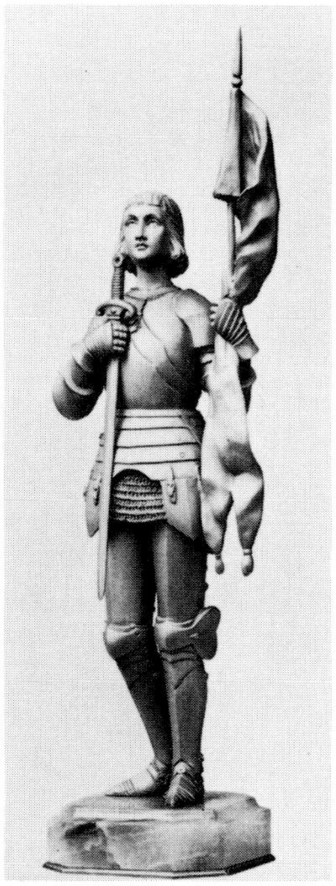

Joan of Arc
30cm:12in.

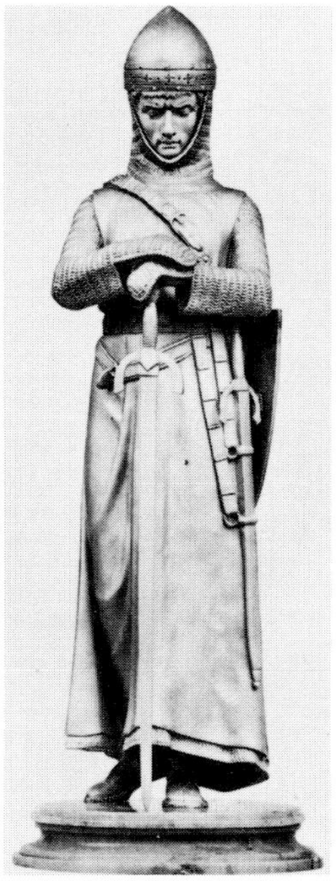

Crusader
48cm:19in.

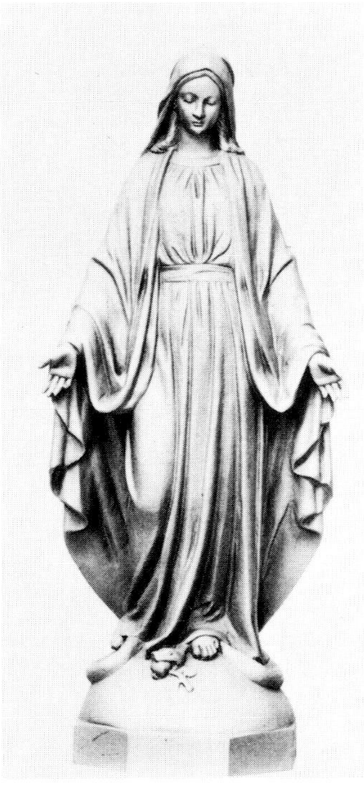

The Immaculate Conception
45cm:17¾in.
29cm:11½in.
19cm:7½in.

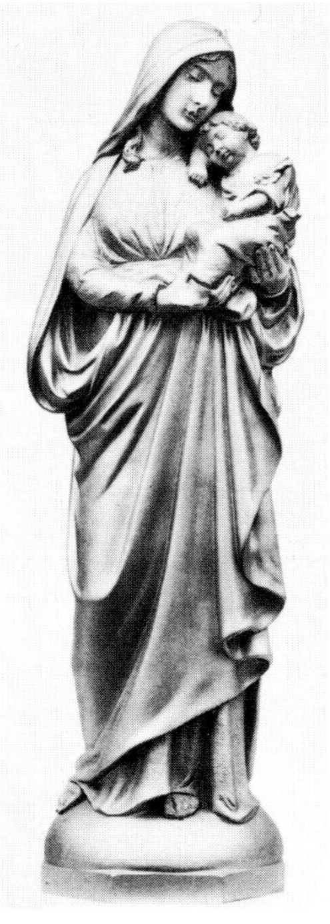

Virgin Mother
33cm:13in.

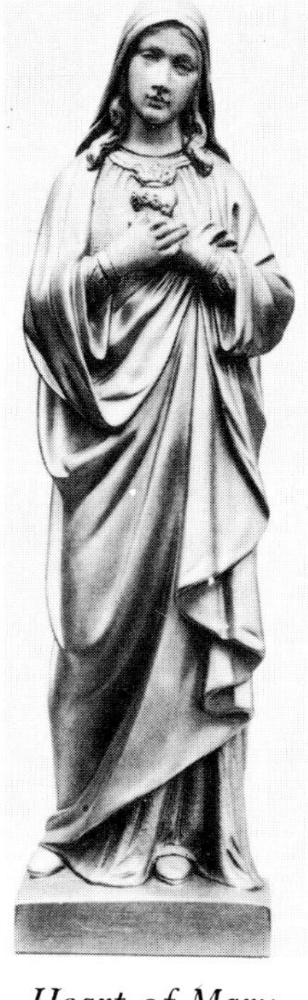

Heart of Mary
47cm:18½in.
32cm:12¾in.
20cm:8in.

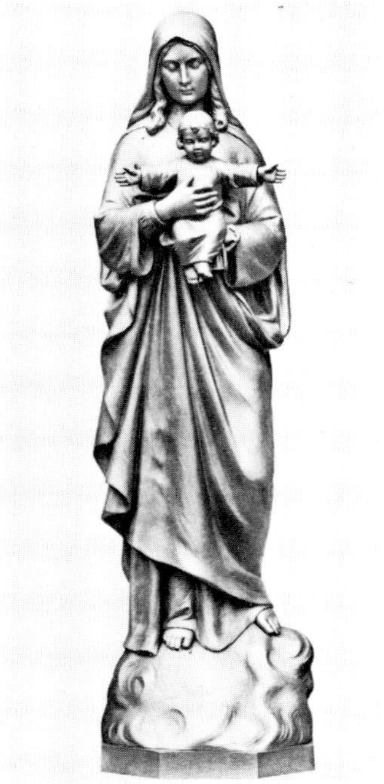

Virgin with the Child Jesus
36cm: 14in.

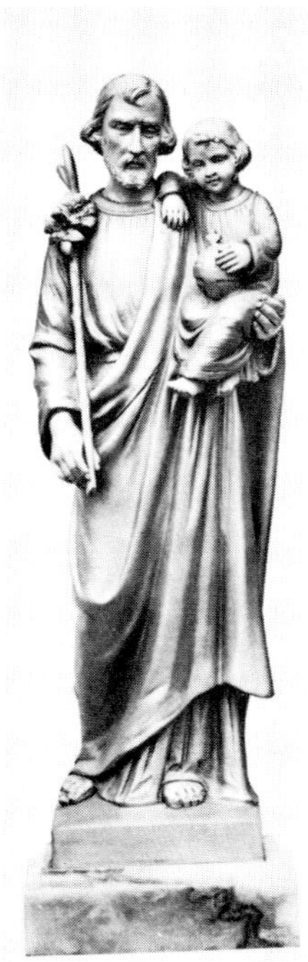

Saint Joseph
35cm: 13¾in.

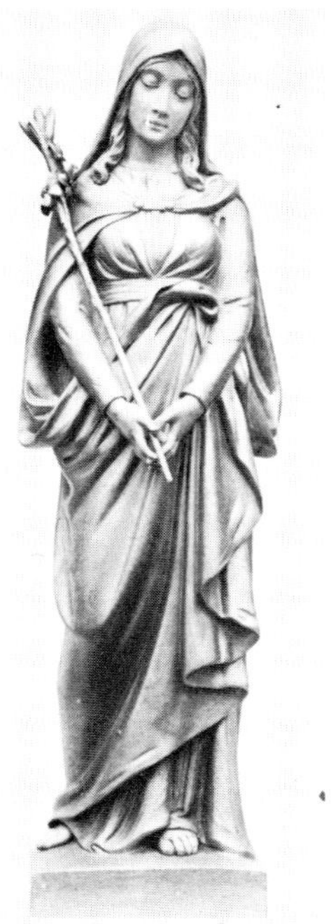

Virgin with Lily
31cm: 12¼in.

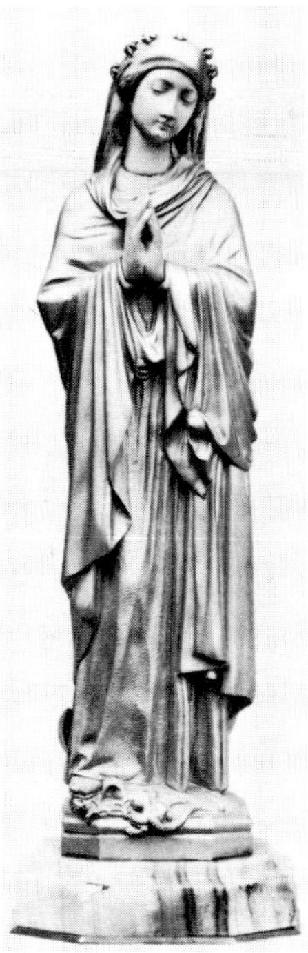

Virgin of the Stars
43cm: 17in.
32cm: 12½in.
22cm: 8½in.

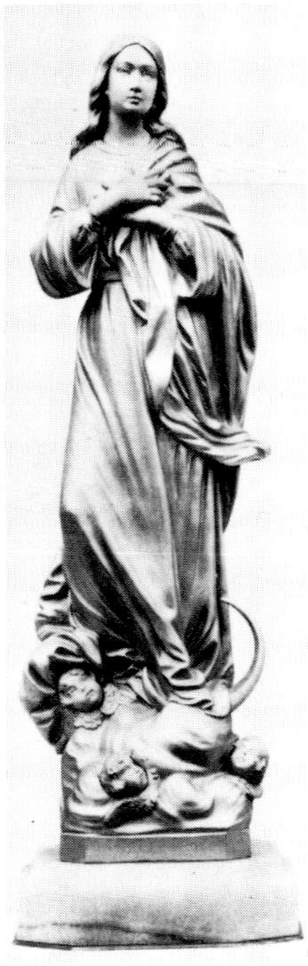

Virgin of Murillo
35cm: 13¾in.

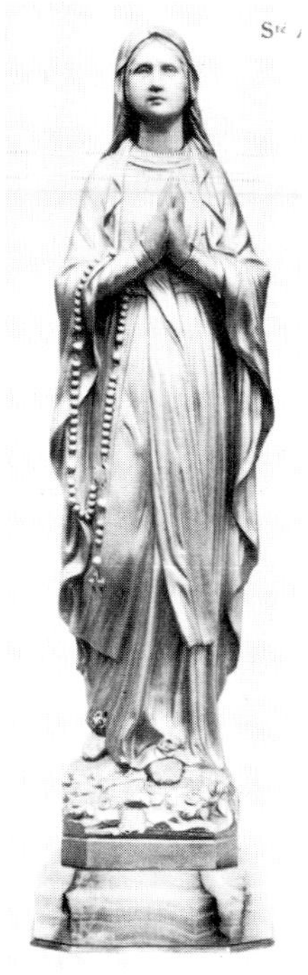

Virgin of Lourdes
31cm: 12¼in.
22cm: 8¾in.

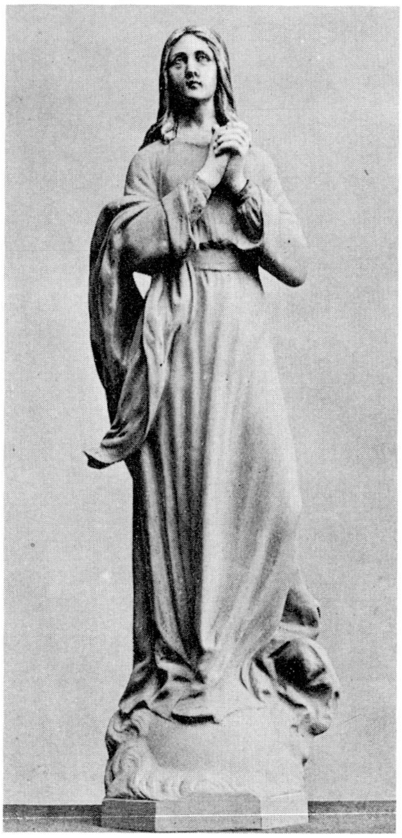

Virgin, 51cm:20in.; 35cm:13¾in.

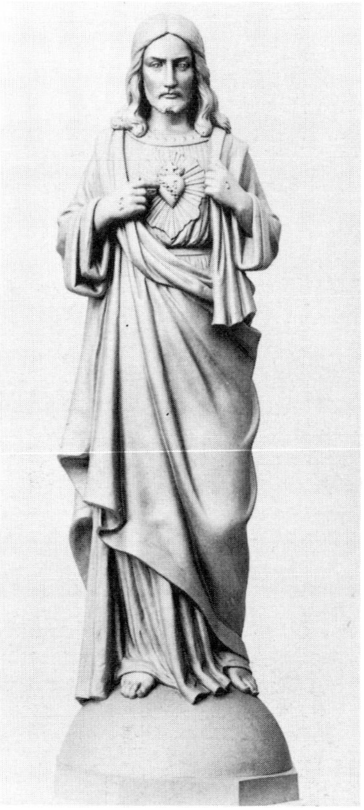

Sacred Heart
60cm: 23½in.
46cm: 18in.
29cm: 11½in.
20cm: 8in.

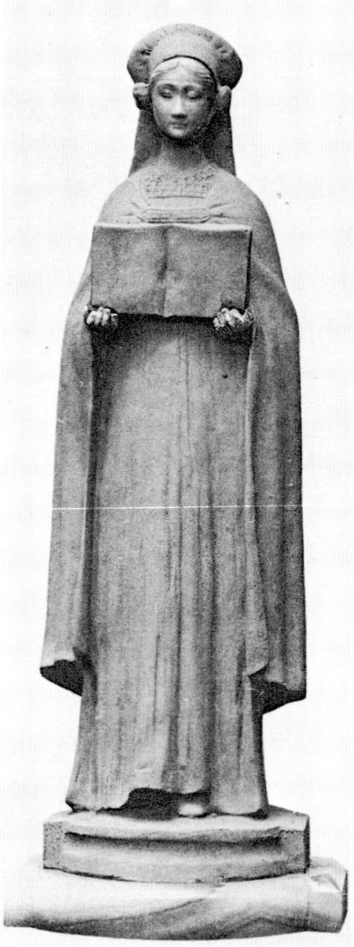

The Gospel, 26cm:10¼in.

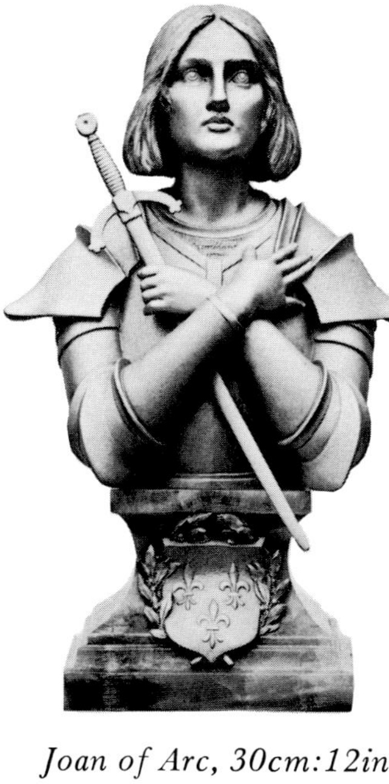

Joan of Arc, 30cm:12in.

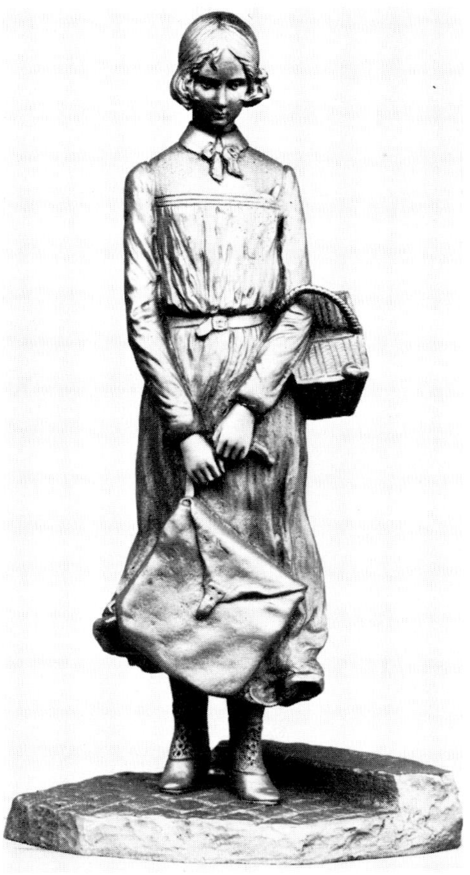

Claudine, 22cm:8½in.

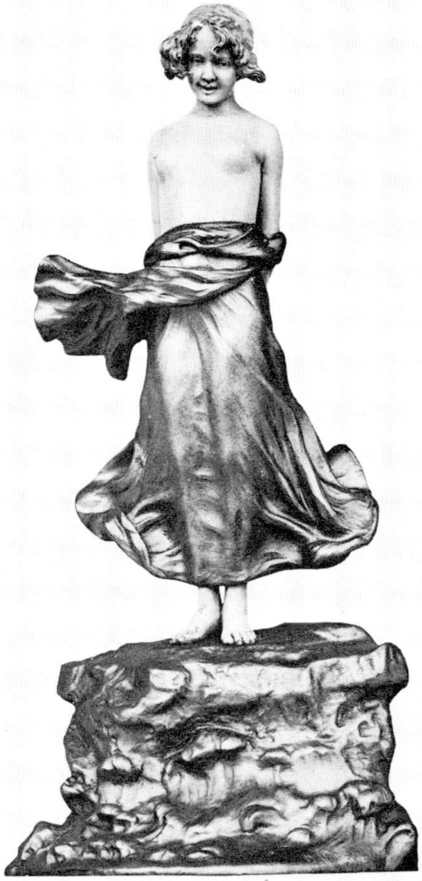

Young Girl, 20cm:8in.

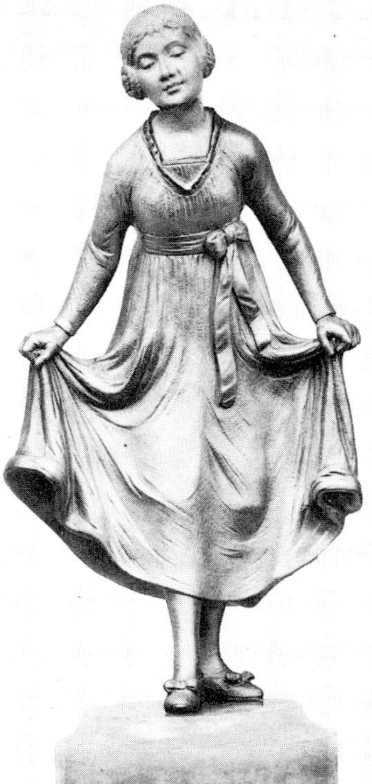

The Curtsy
21cm:8¼in.

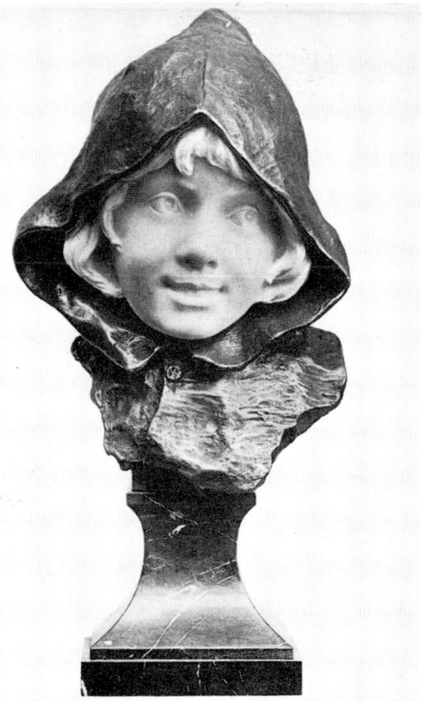

Urchin
41cm:16in.

D. ALONZO

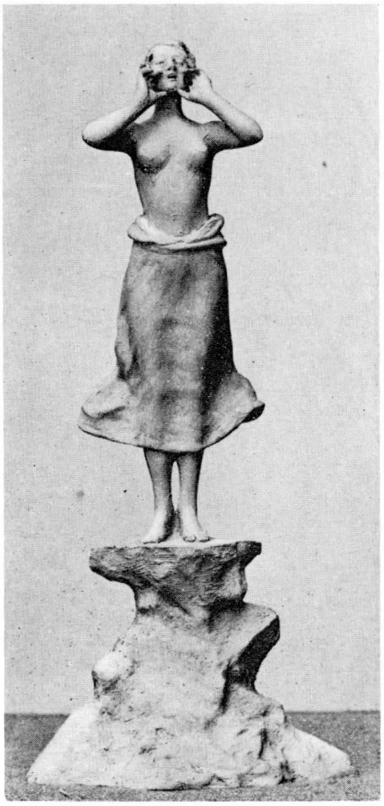

Right: Paris Sport or Newspaper Boy
64cm:25in.
46cm:18in.
35cm:13¾in.
24cm:9½in.
16cm:6¼in.

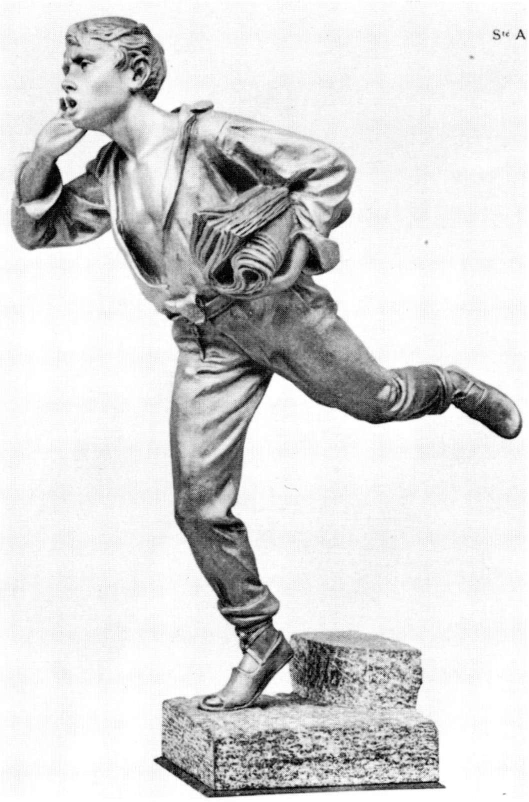

Hi There! 26cm:10¼in.

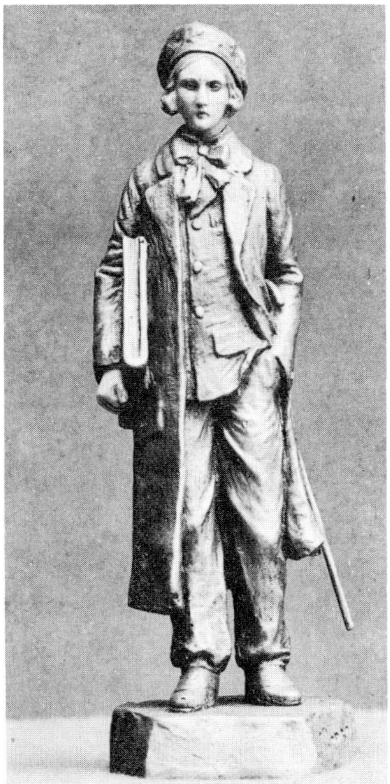

Student Painter, 22cm:8½in.

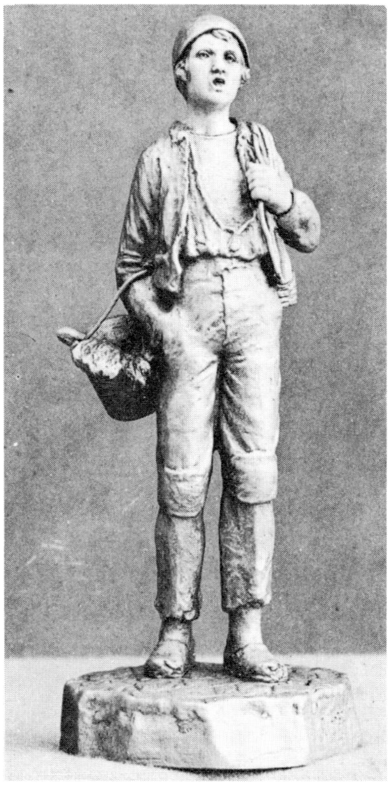

Sweep, 21cm:8¼in.

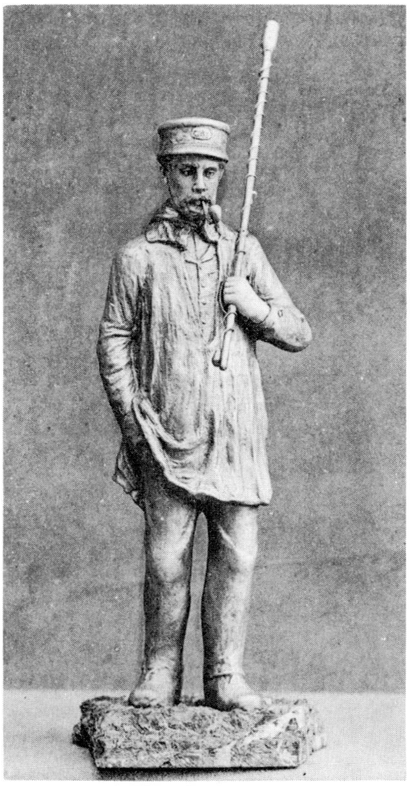

Lamp Lighter, 24cm:9½in.

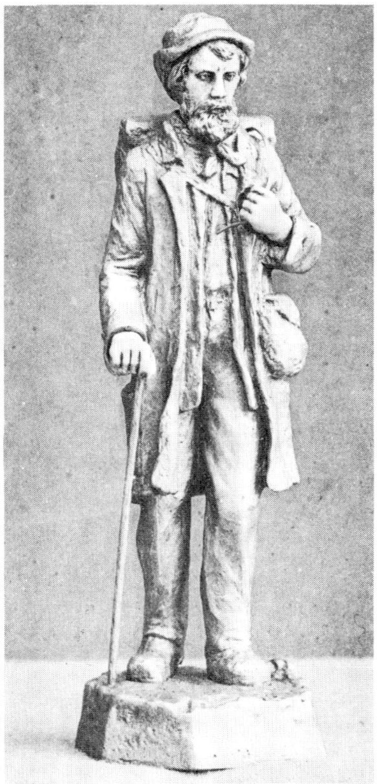

Tramp, 22cm:8½in.

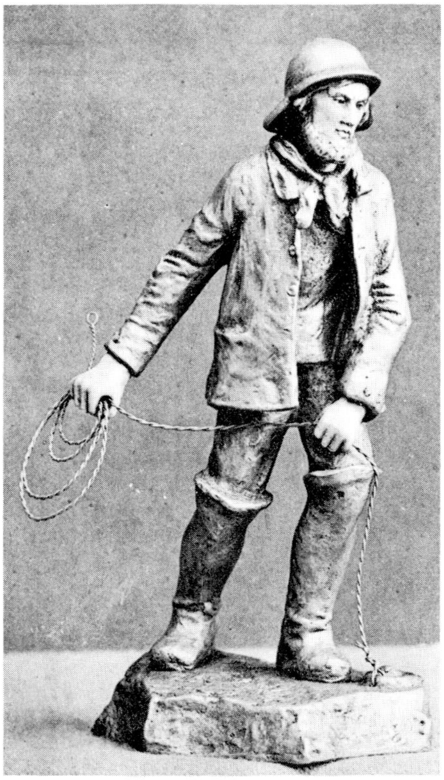

Life-Boat Man, 20cm:8in.

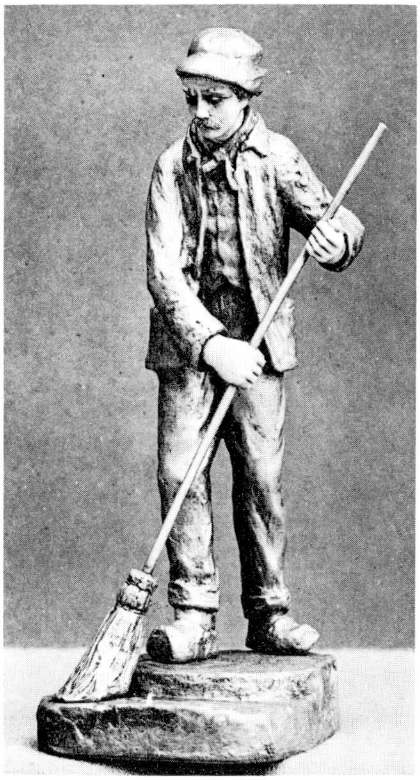

Sweeper, 22cm:8½in.

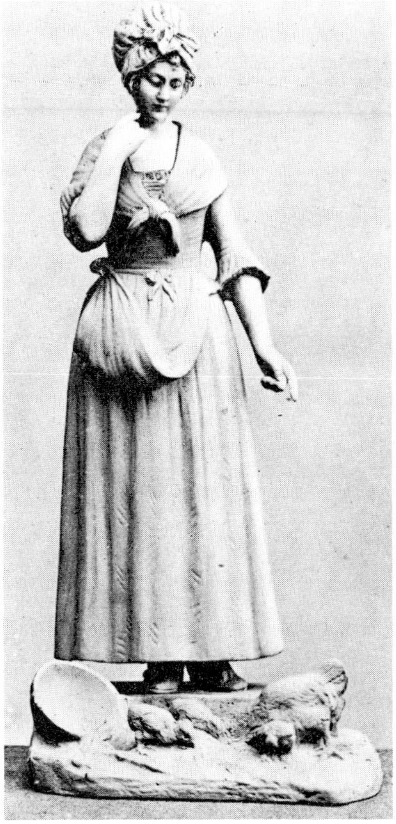

Left: Farmer's Wife
24cm:9½in.

Right: Miss
22cm:8½in.

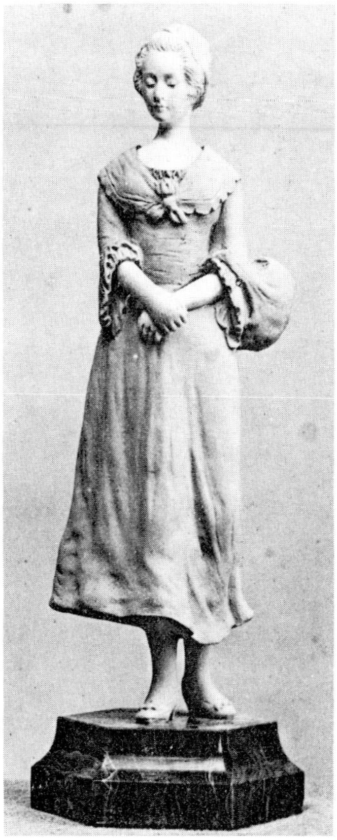

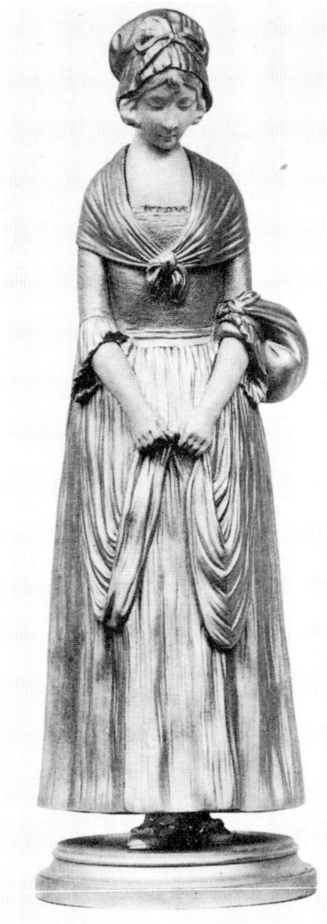

Off to Market, 22cm: 8¾in.

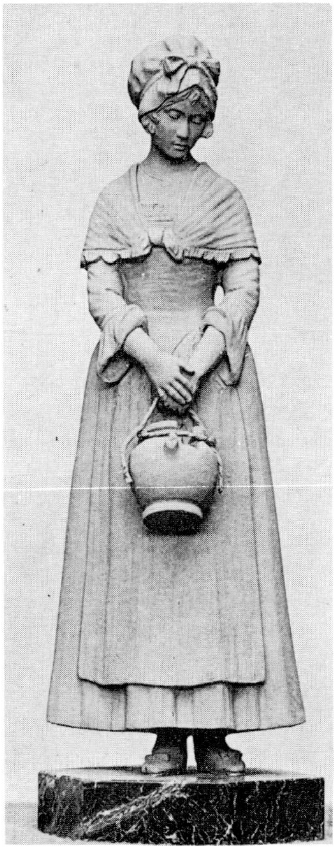

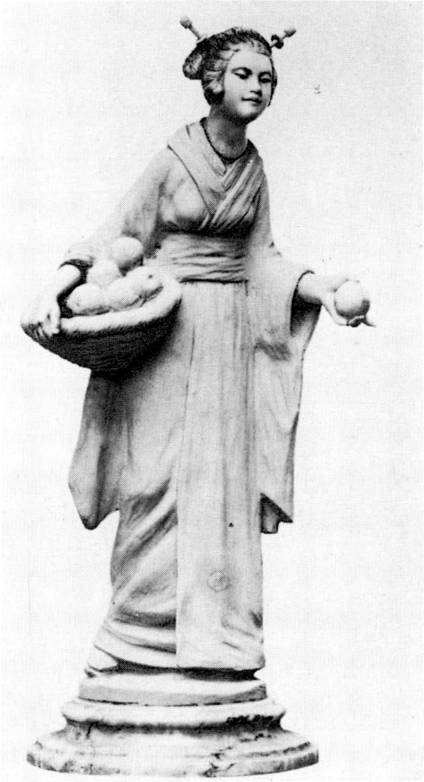

Orange Seller, 23cm: 9in.

The Broken Jug, 26cm: 10¼in.

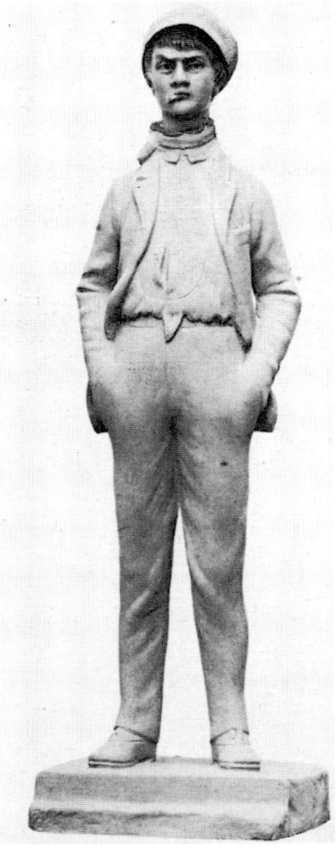

Gipsy, 19cm: 7½in.

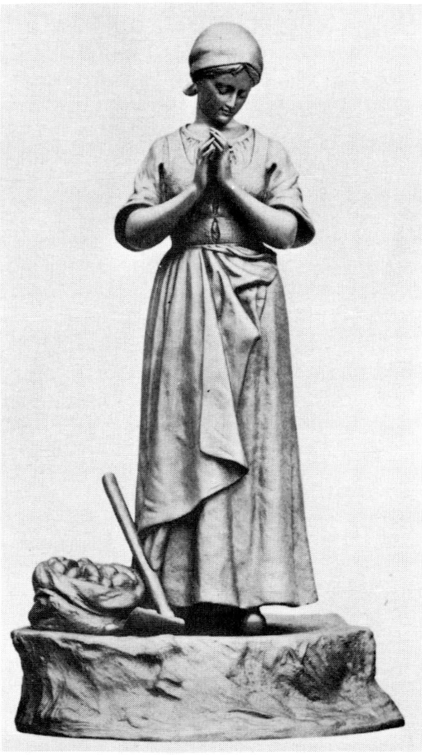

The Prayer, 39cm: 15½in.

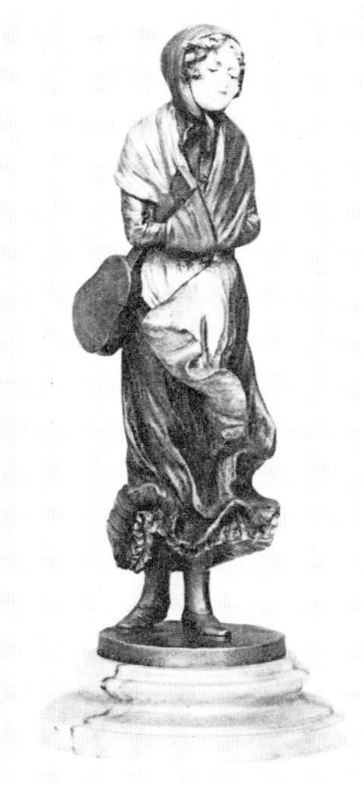

Cicada, 23cm:9in.

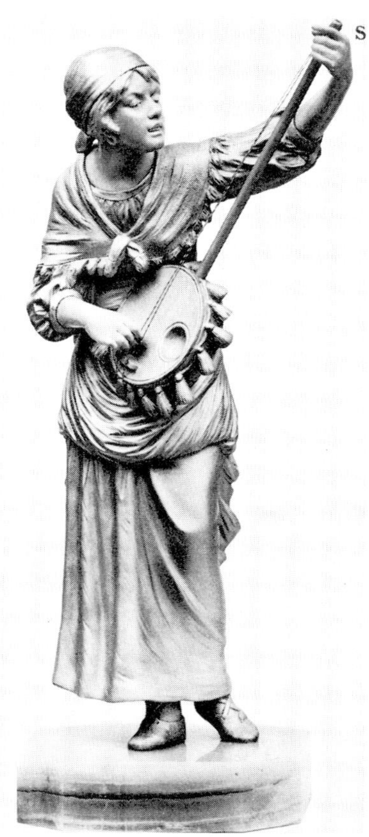

Gipsy, 33cm:13in.

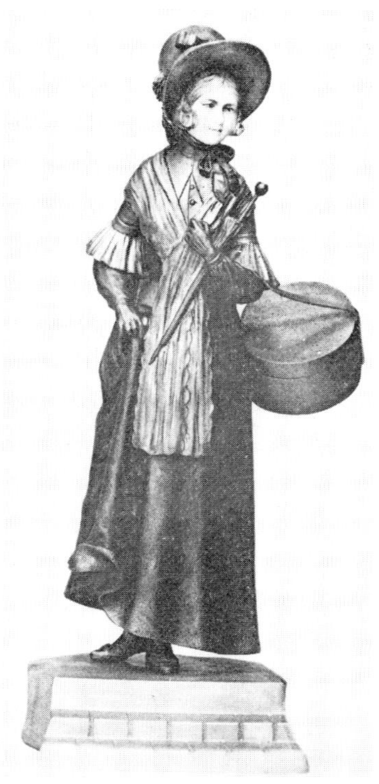

Modesty, 26cm:10¼in.

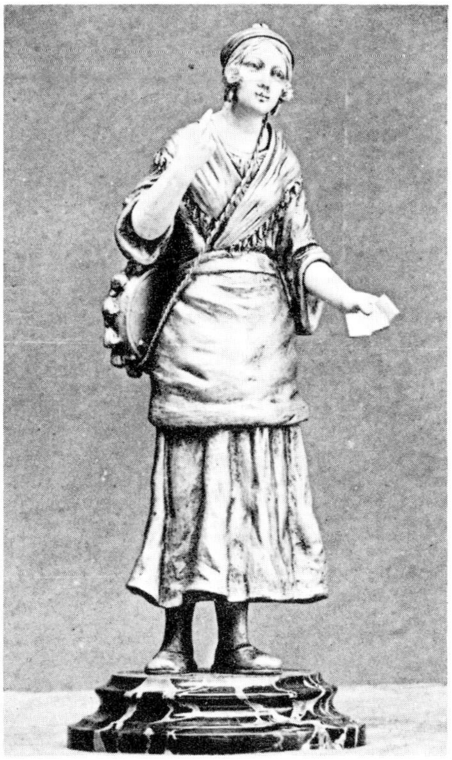

Gipsy, 23cm:9in.

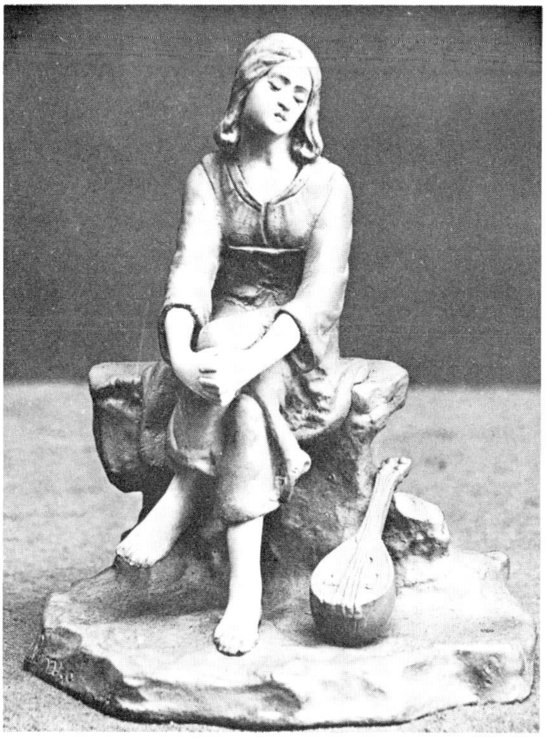

Pretty, 15cm:6in.

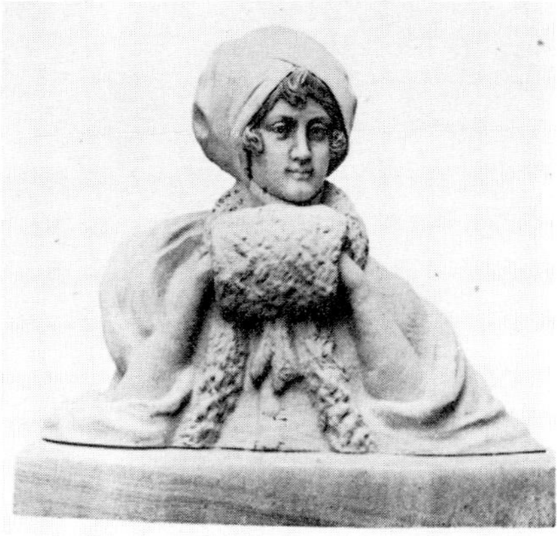

Chilly One, 15cm:6in.

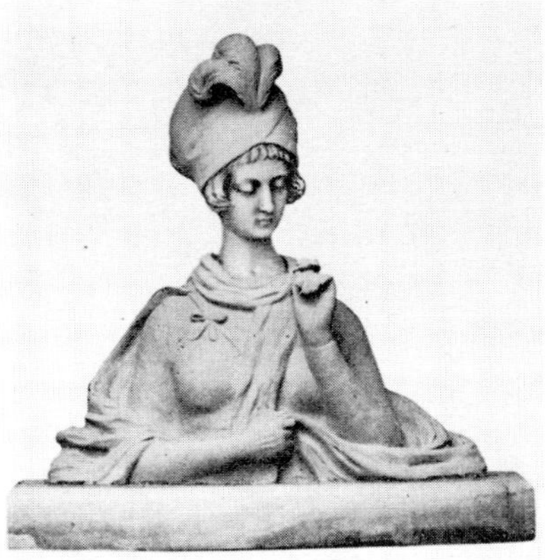

Fragrance, 18cm:7in.

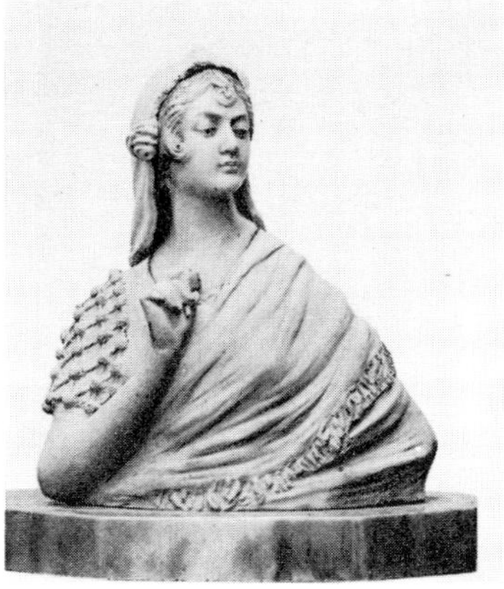

Carmen, 15cm:6in.

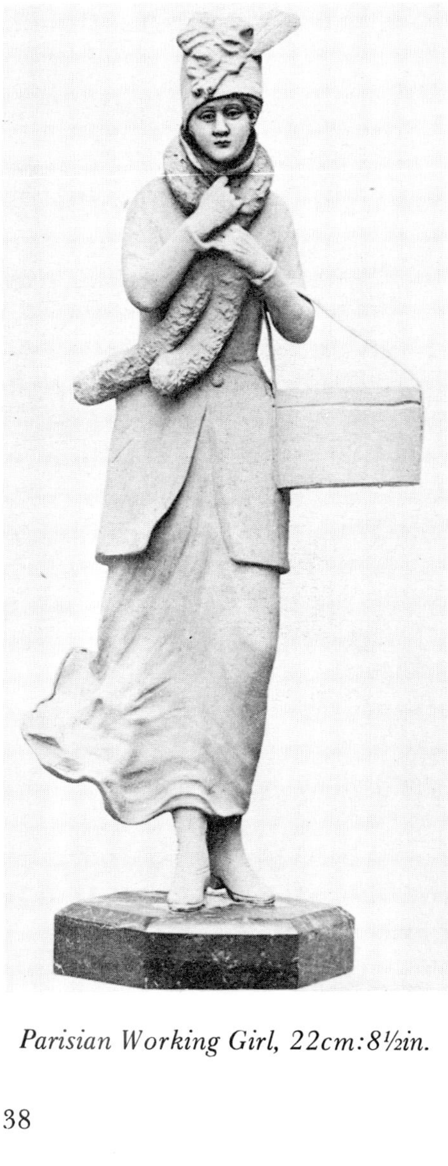

Parisian Working Girl, 22cm:8½in.

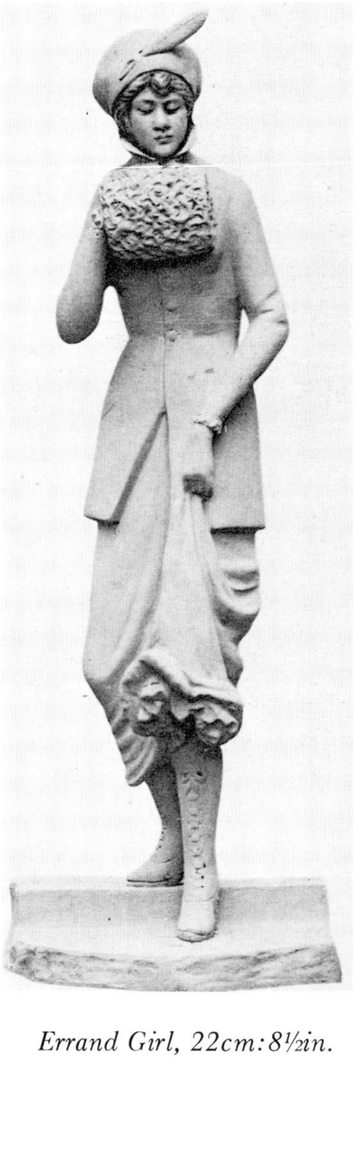

Errand Girl, 22cm:8½in.

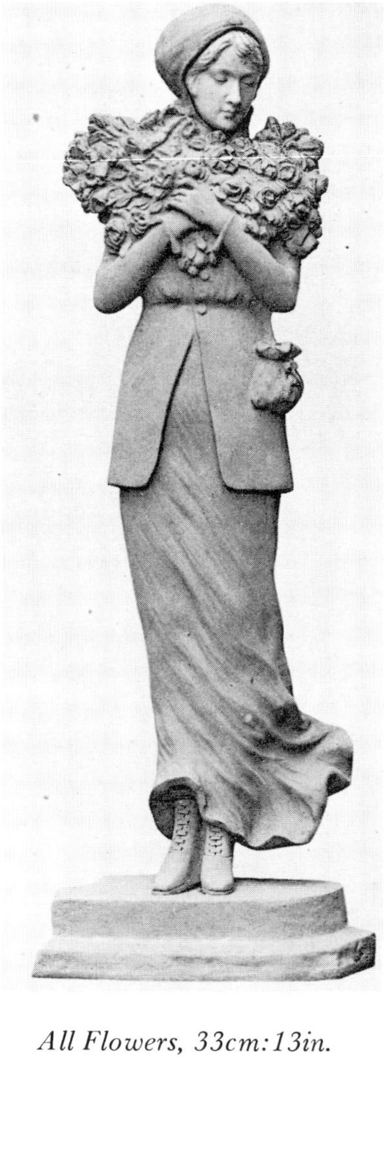

All Flowers, 33cm:13in.

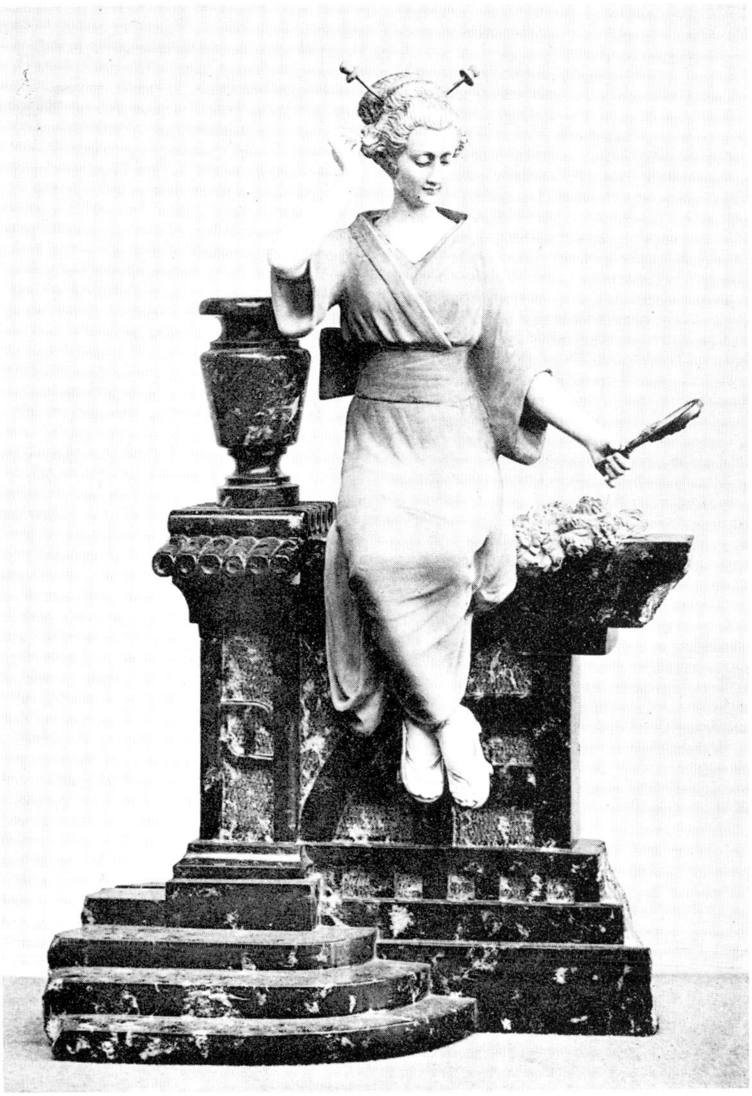

Chrysanthemum, 37cm:14½in.

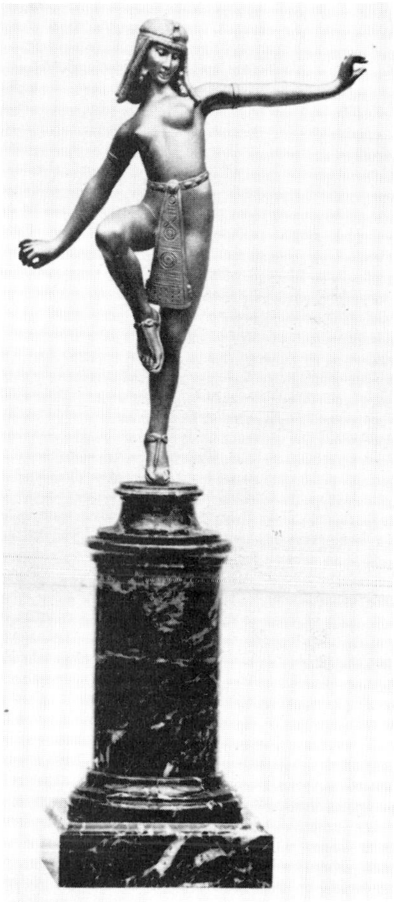

Egyptian Dancer, 33cm:13in.

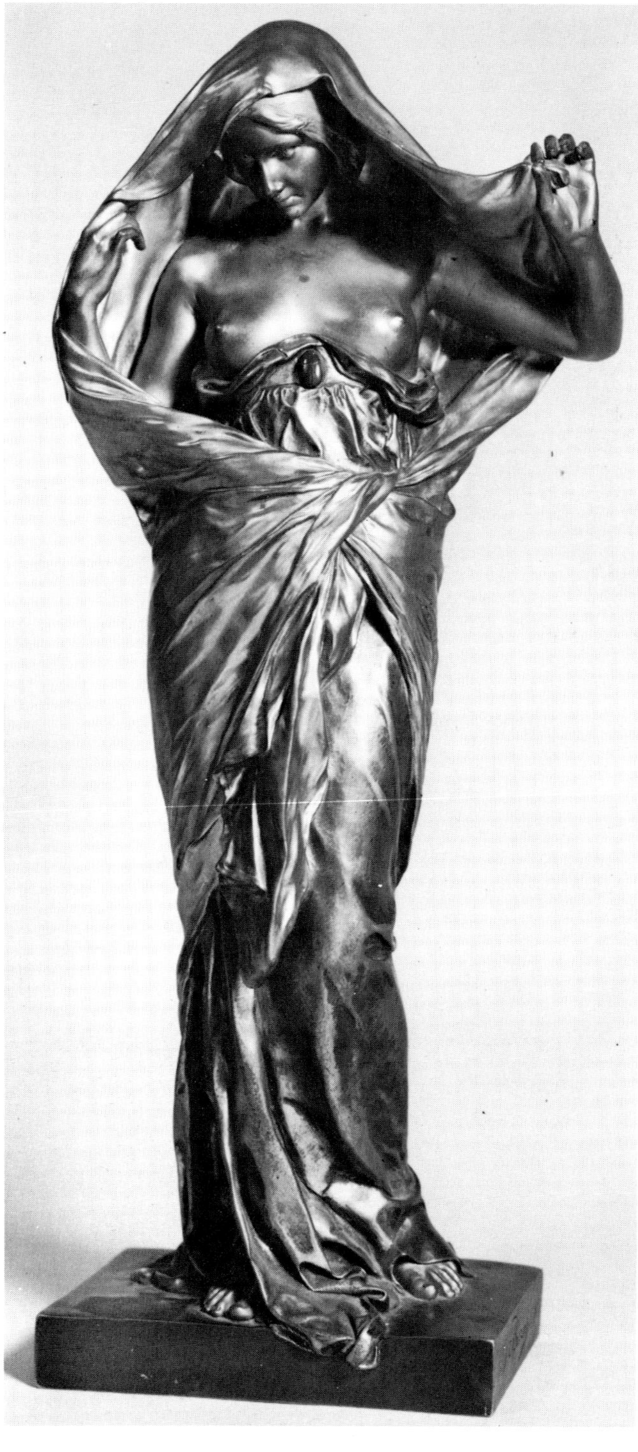

Nature Revealing Herself to Science
Various sizes and combinations of materials were produced

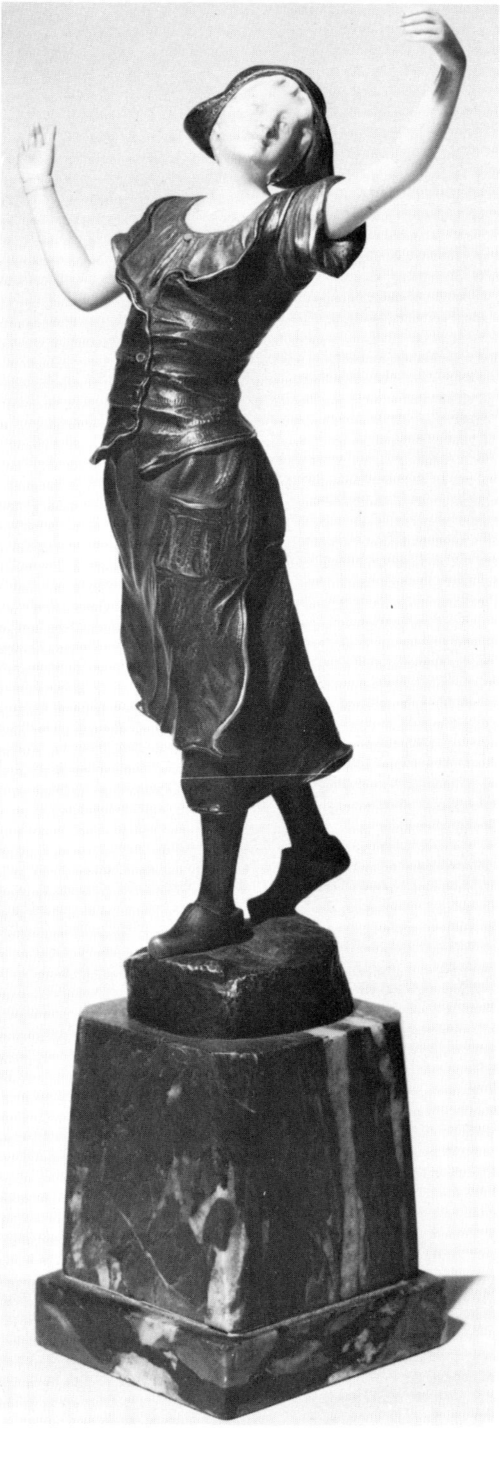

A Dancer, 38cm:15in.

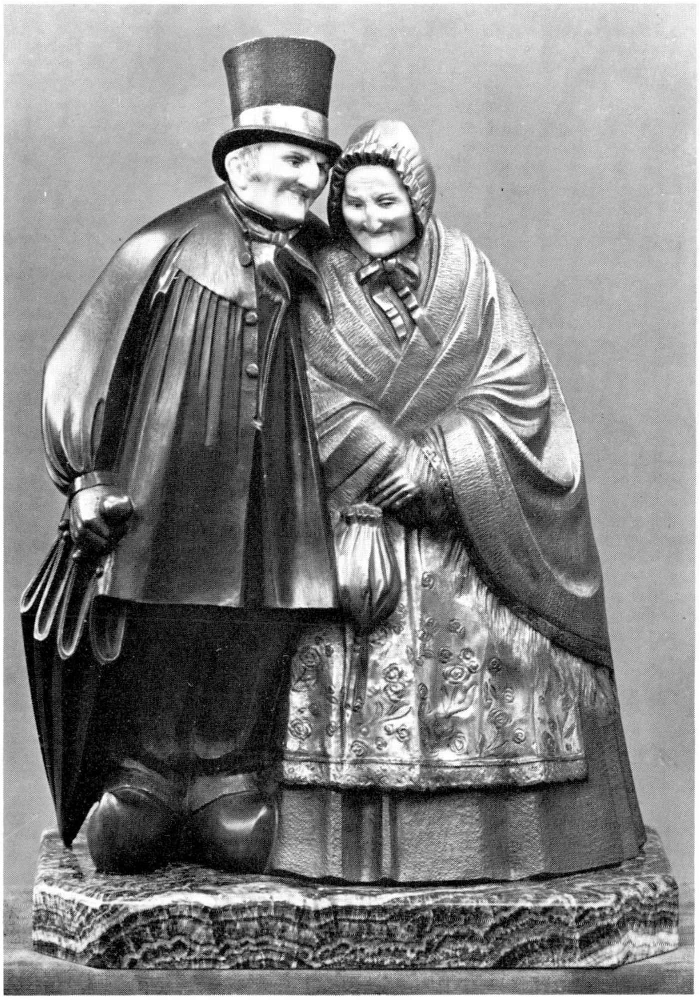

The Golden Wedding
38cm:15in.; 25cm:10in.

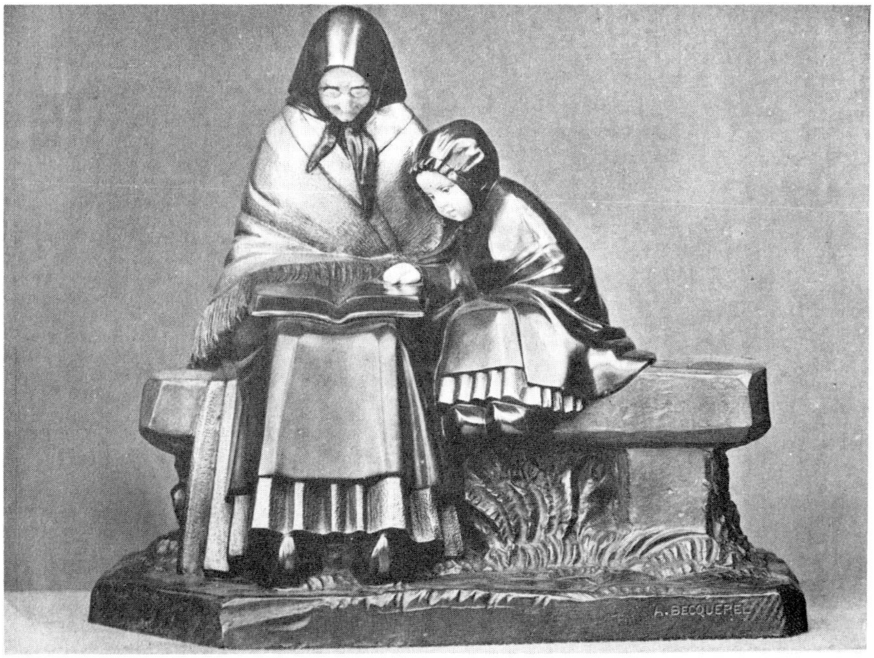

The Beautiful Pictures
32cm:12½in.

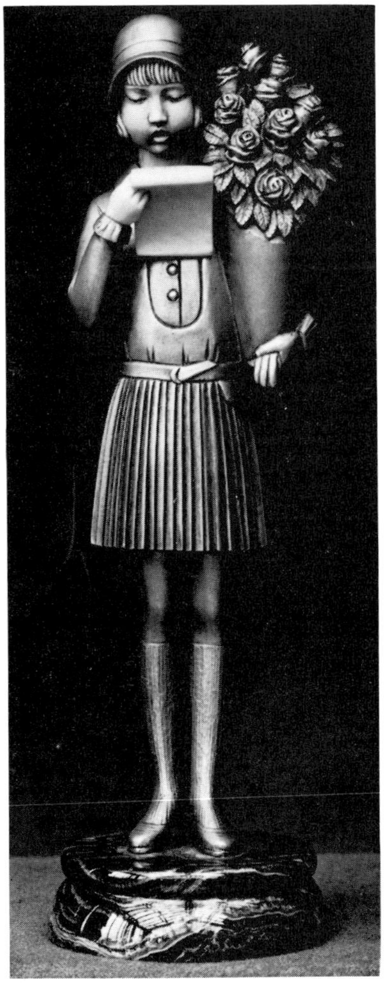

The Compliment
27cm:10½in.

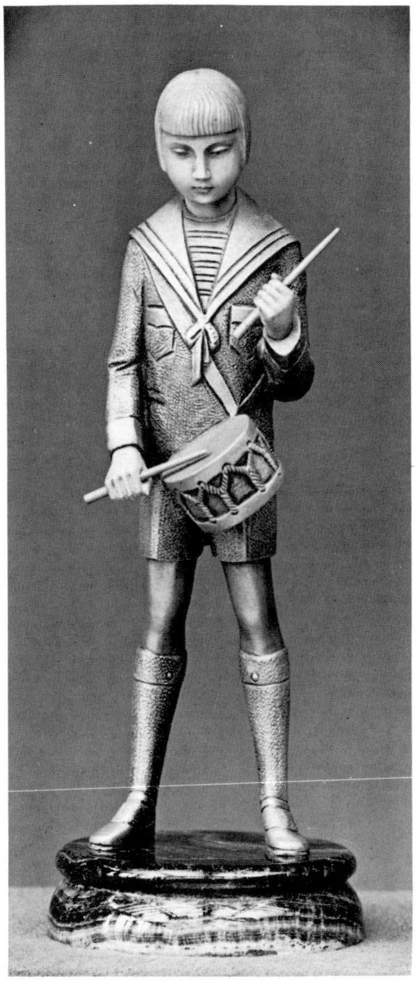

Child with Drum
25cm:10in.

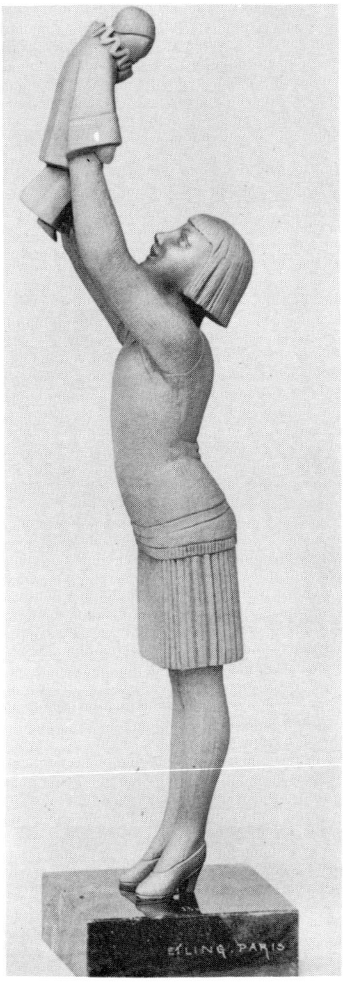

Girl with Doll
28cm:11in.

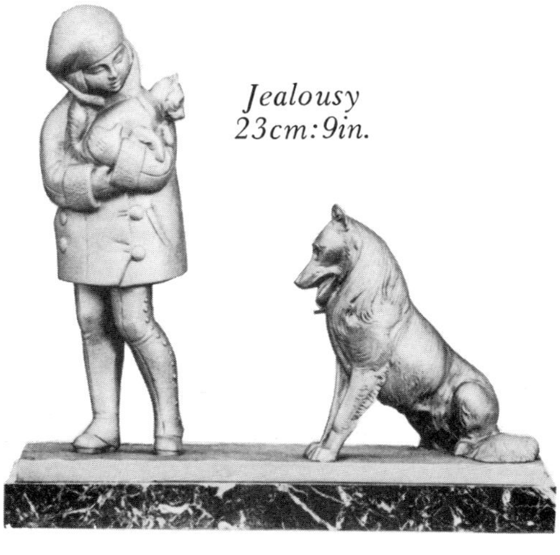

Jealousy
23cm:9in.

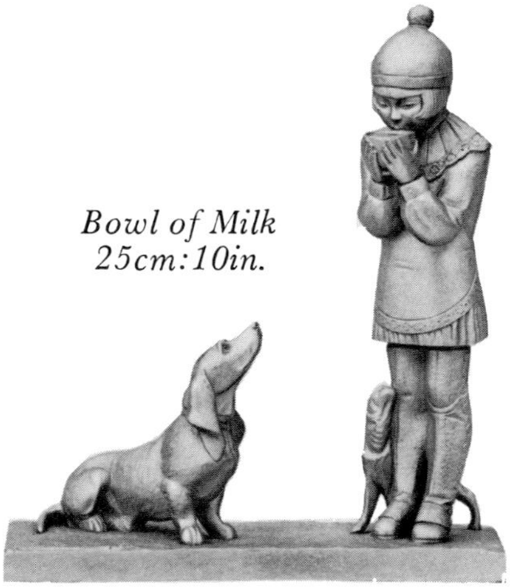

Bowl of Milk
25cm:10in.

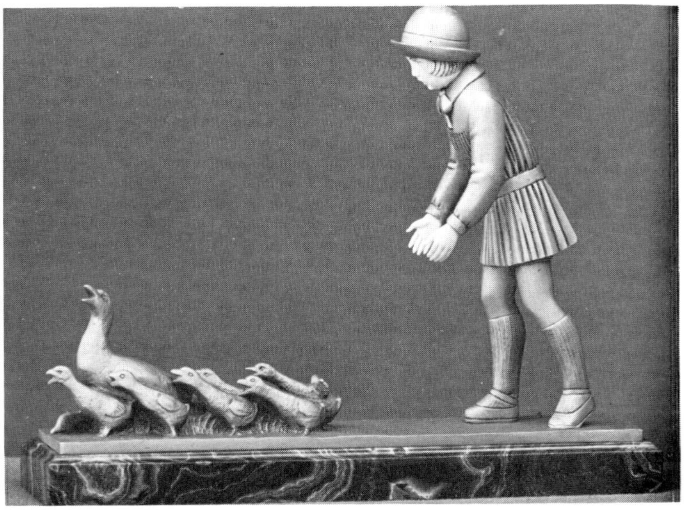

Peace of the Country, 25cm: 10in.

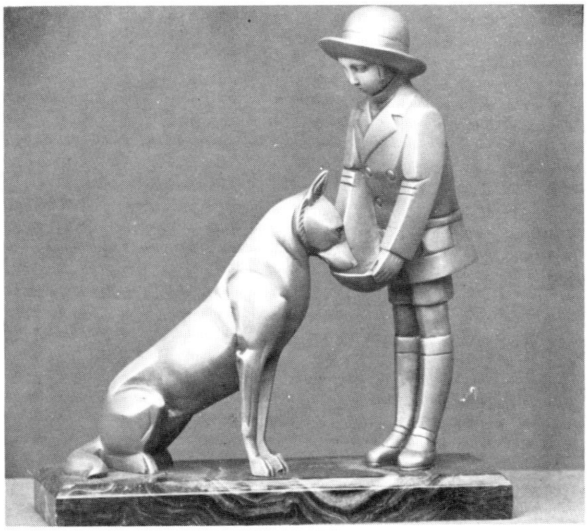

Lunch, 23cm: 9in.

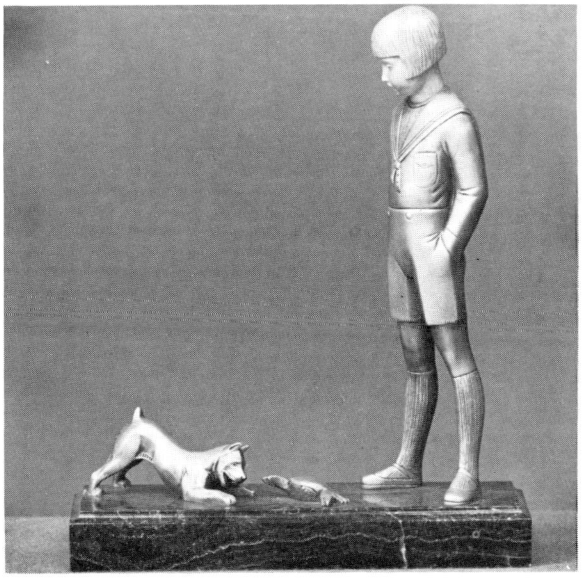

Child and Crab, 20cm: 8in.

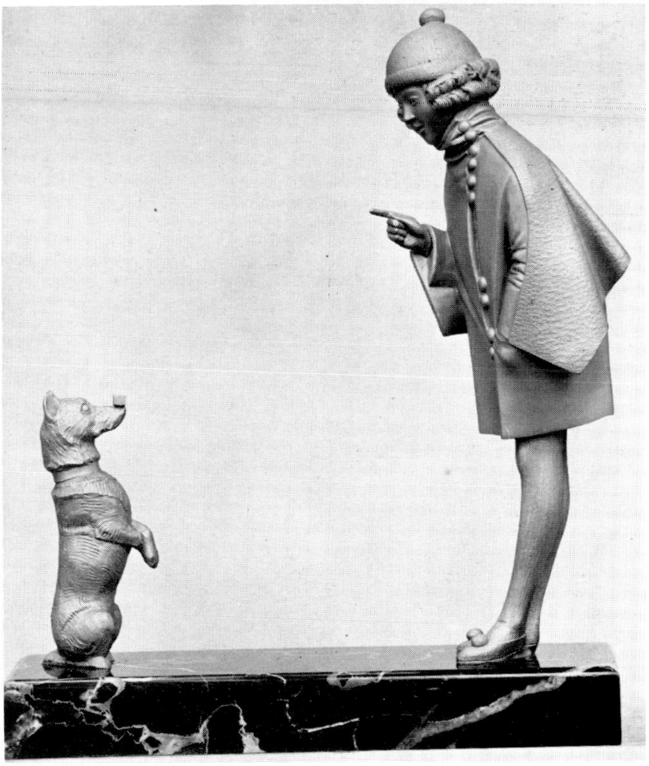

Little Girl with her Dog, 24cm: 9½in.

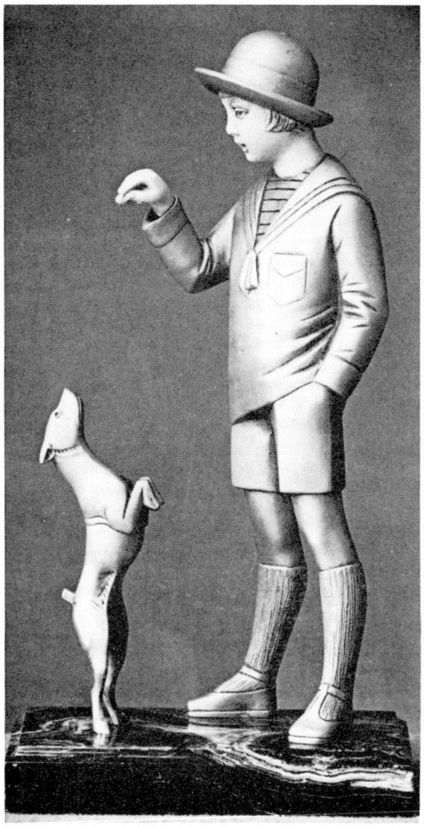

Piece of Sugar 29cm: 11½in.

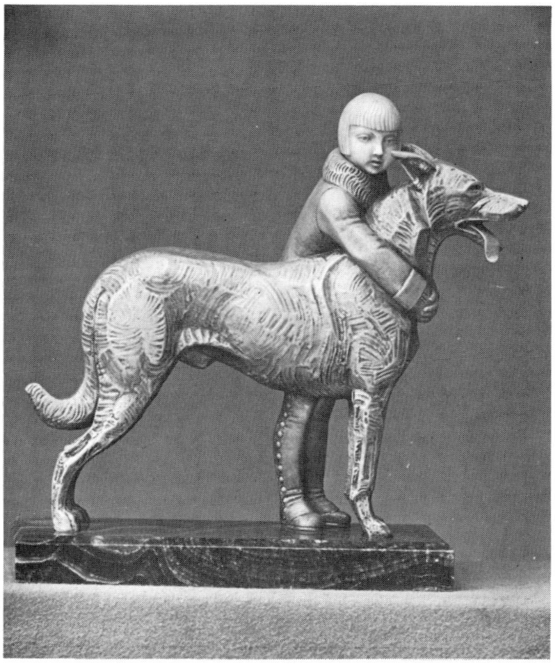

Docile, 20cm: 8in.

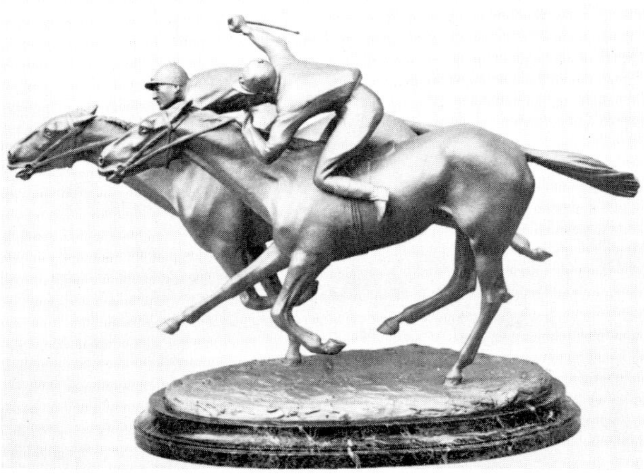

The Race, 43cm: 17¼in.

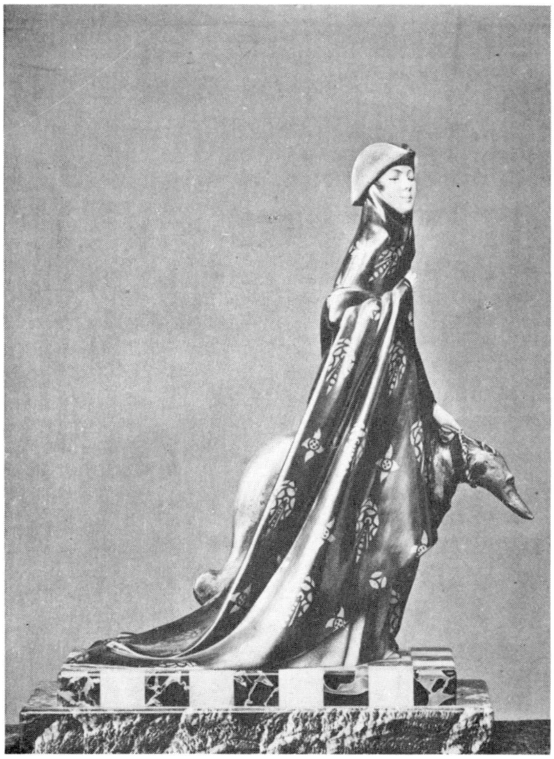

Venetian, 40cm: 15¾in.; 25cm: 10in.

L. BETTI

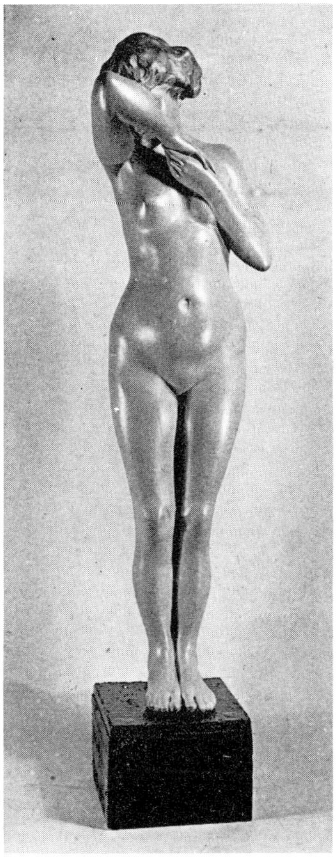

Coy
55cm:21½in.

BIANCHI

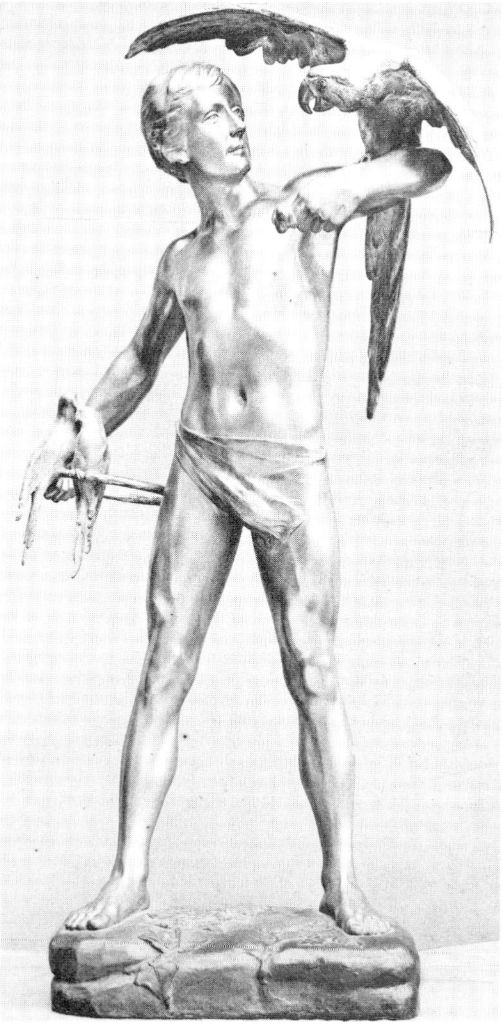

Bird Catcher, 93cm:36½in.

A. BITTER

Chloe
34cm:13¼in.
22cm:8½in.
15cm:6in.

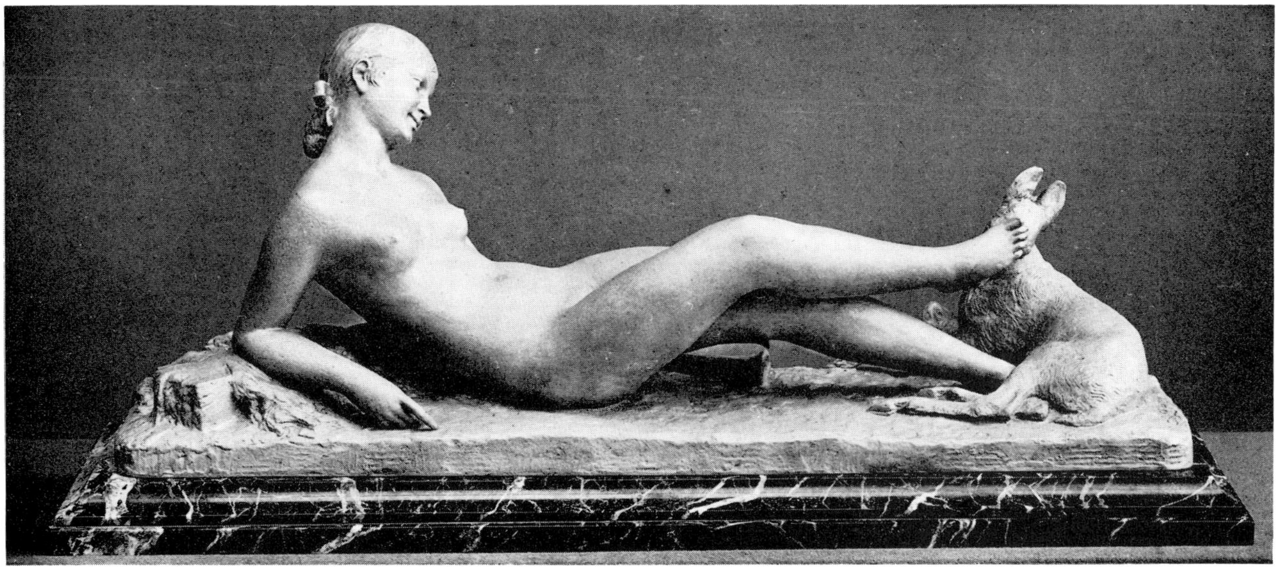

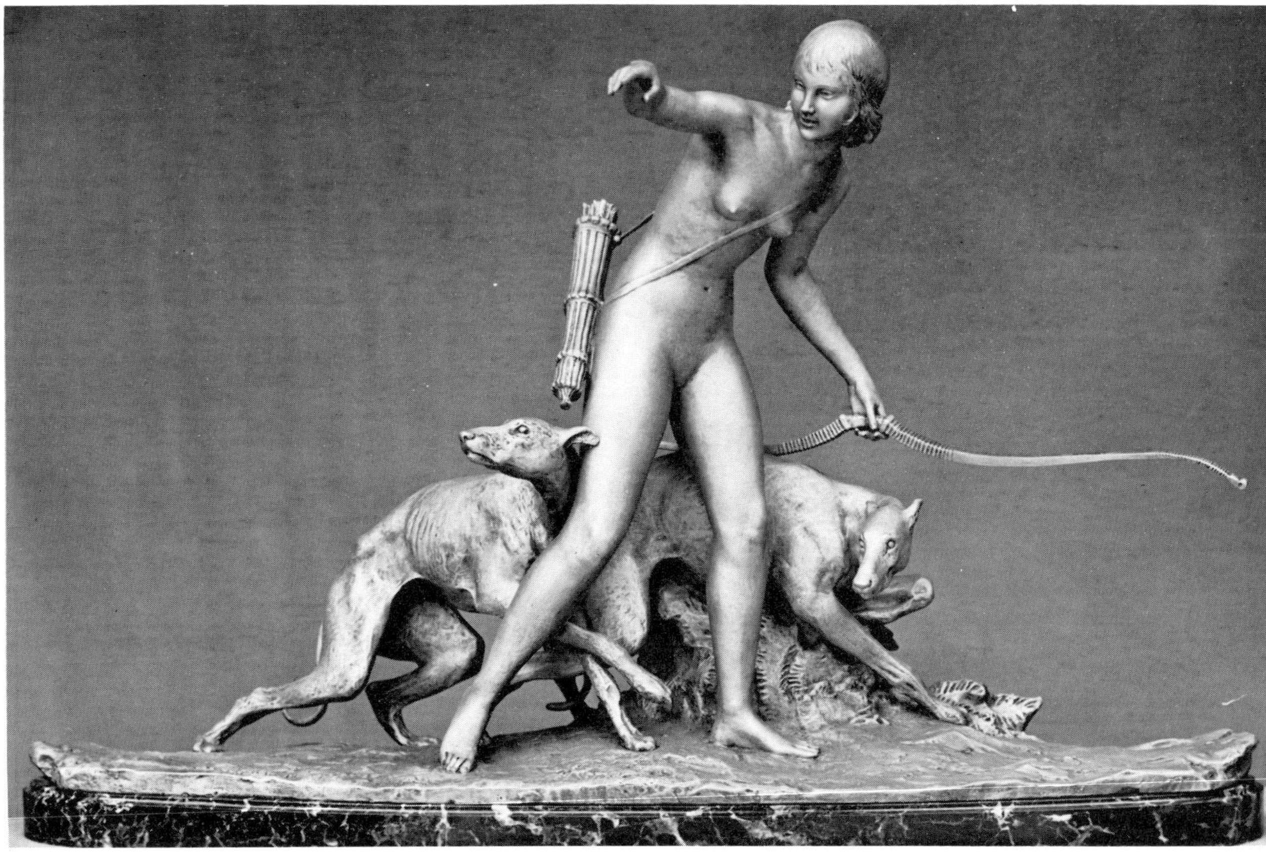

Diana the Huntress, 61cm:24in.

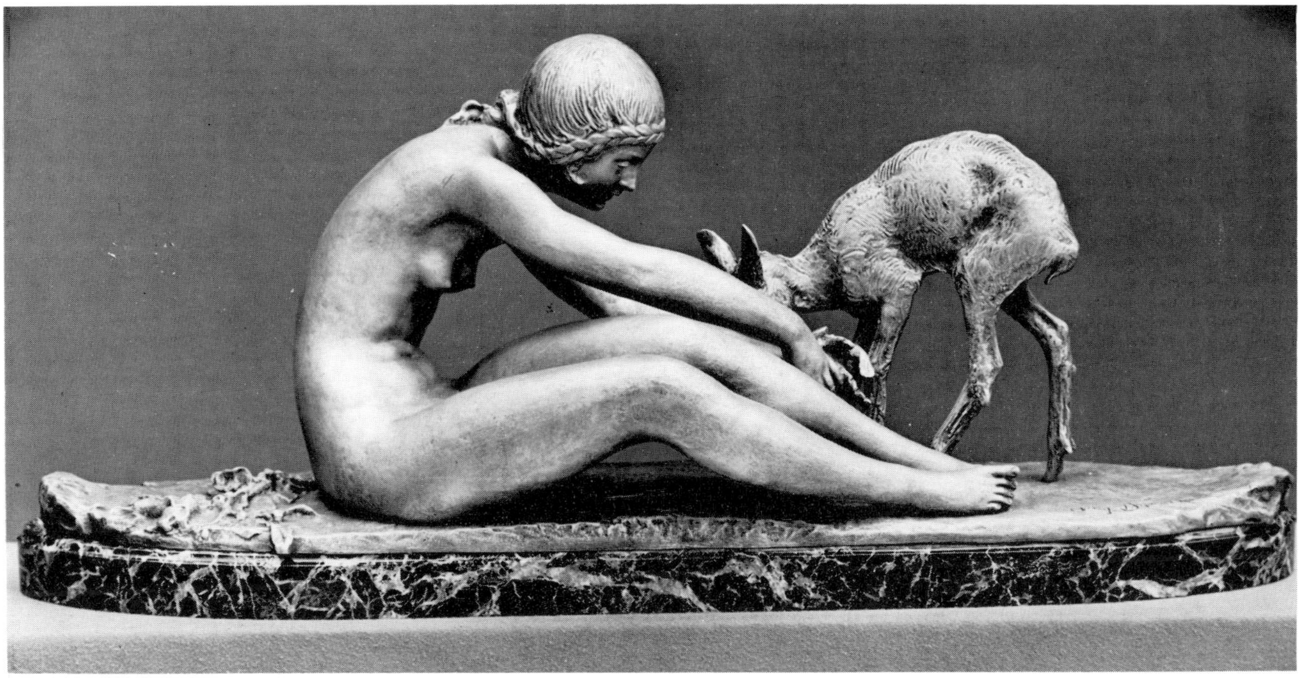

Gluttony, 36cm:14in.

A. BITTER

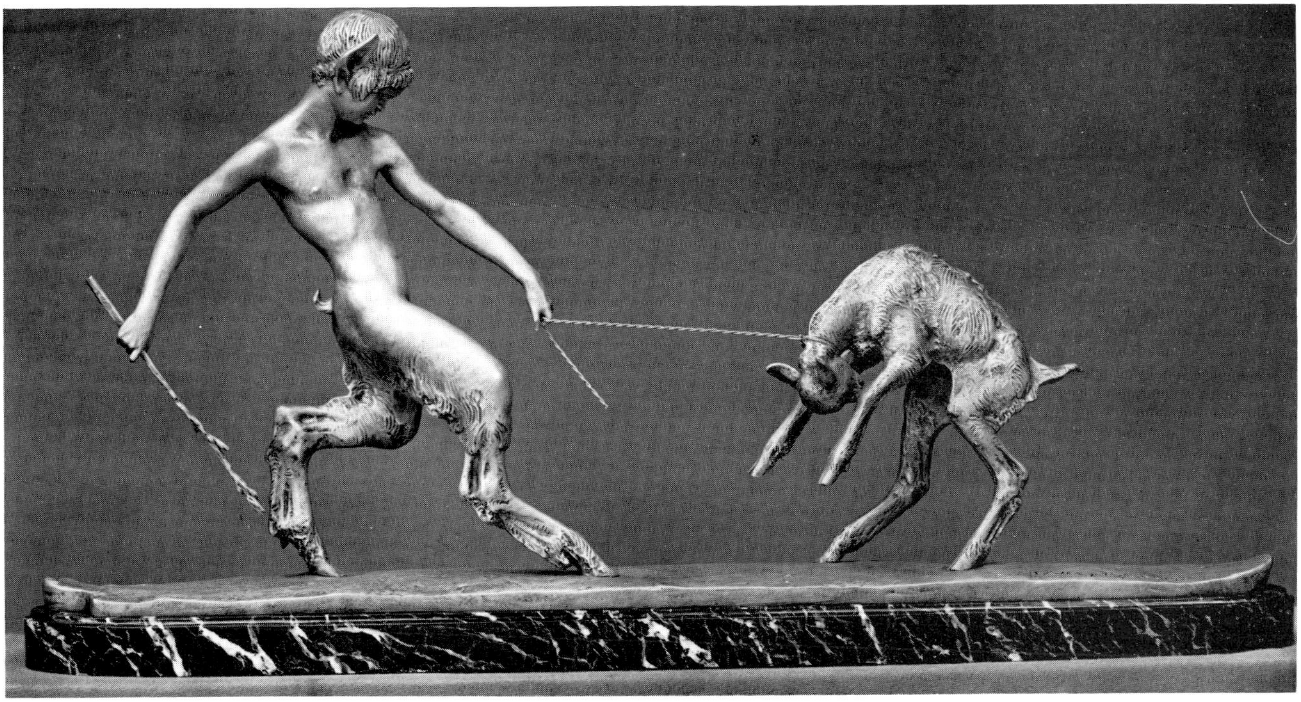

Capture, 18cm: 7in.

S. BIZARD

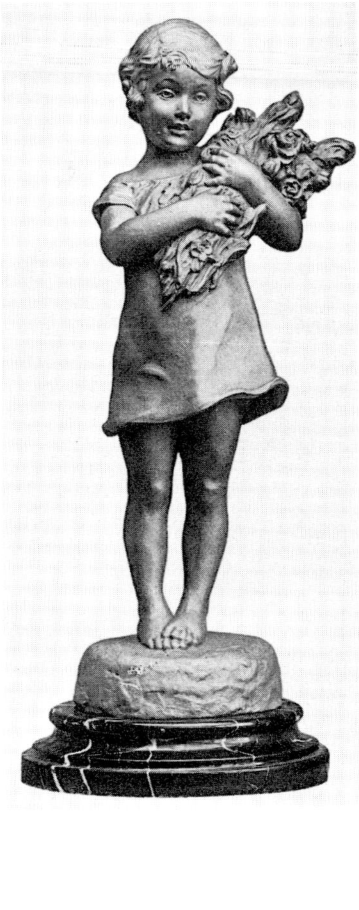

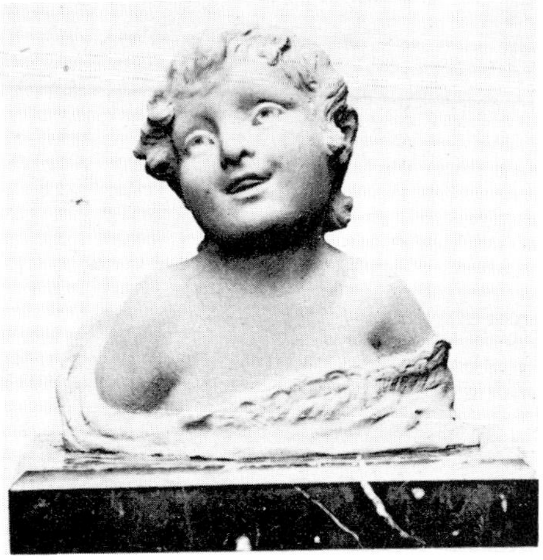

Bust of a Child Laughing
12cm: 4¾in.

Left: Happy Birthday, 26cm: 10¼in.

Right: Soap Bubbles, 27cm: 10½in.

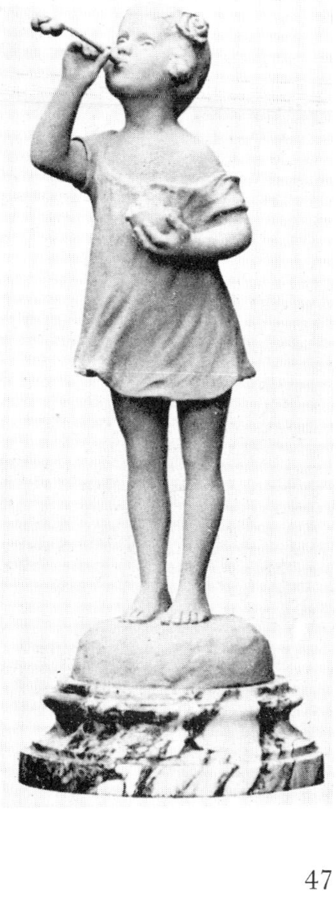

A. BOFILL

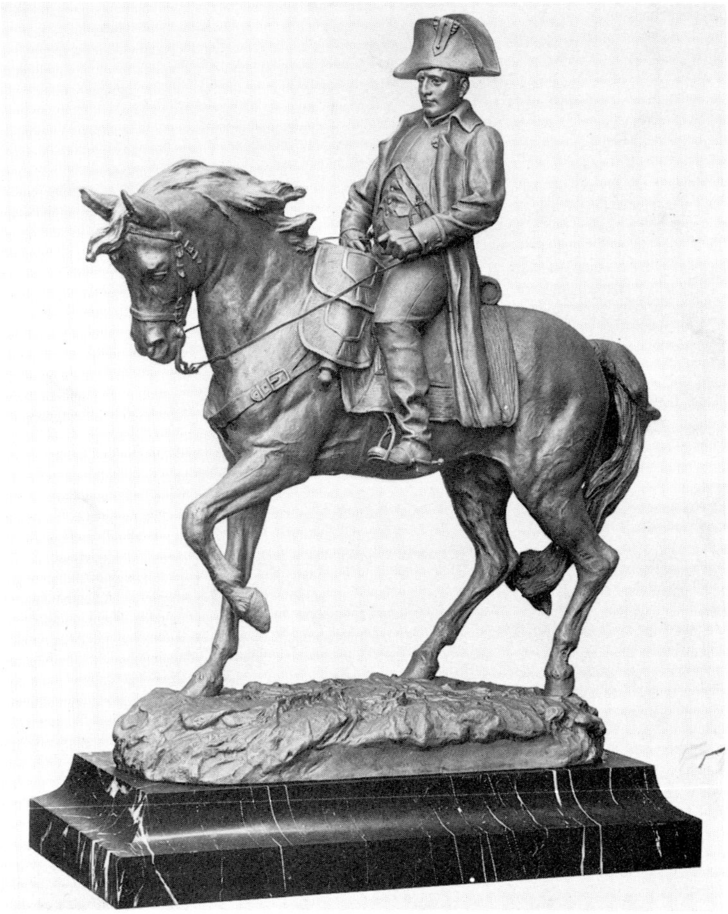

Napoleon, 71cm:28in.; 62cm:24½in.

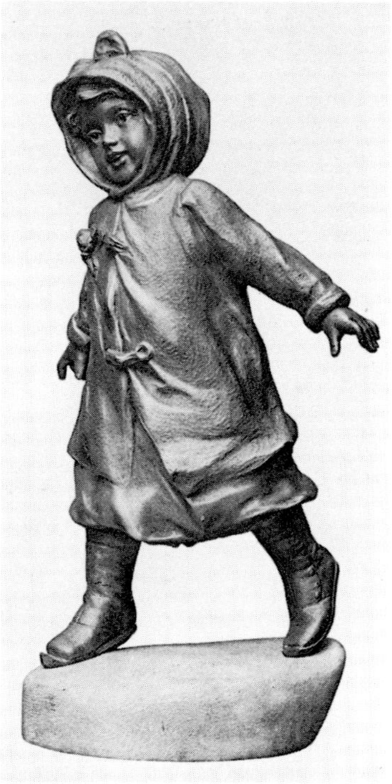

Skater
26cm:10¼in.

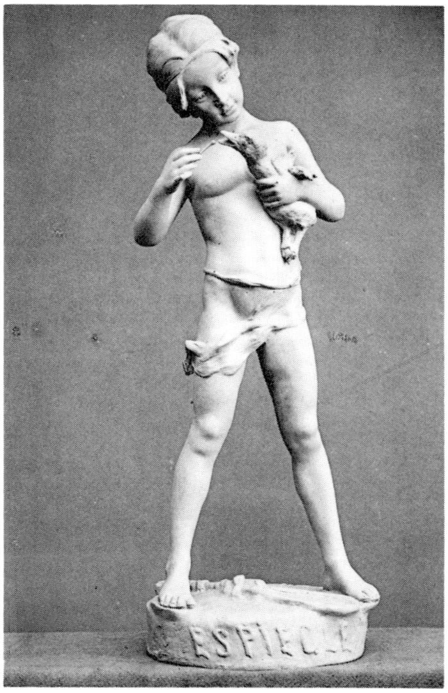

Frolicsome Child
55cm:21½in.

L. BOSSERT

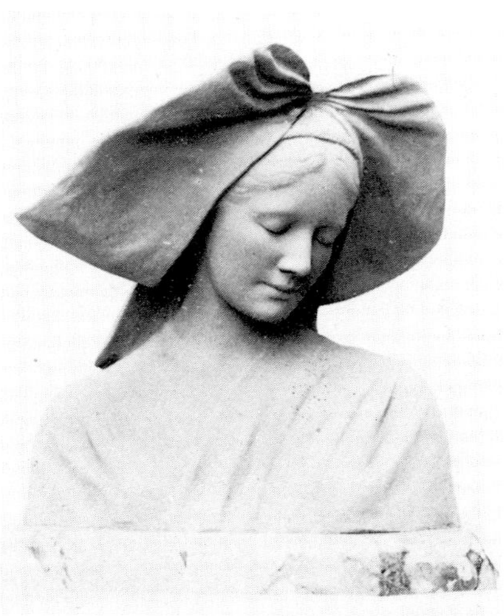

Bust of an
Alsatian Woman
29cm:10¼in.; 15cm:6in.

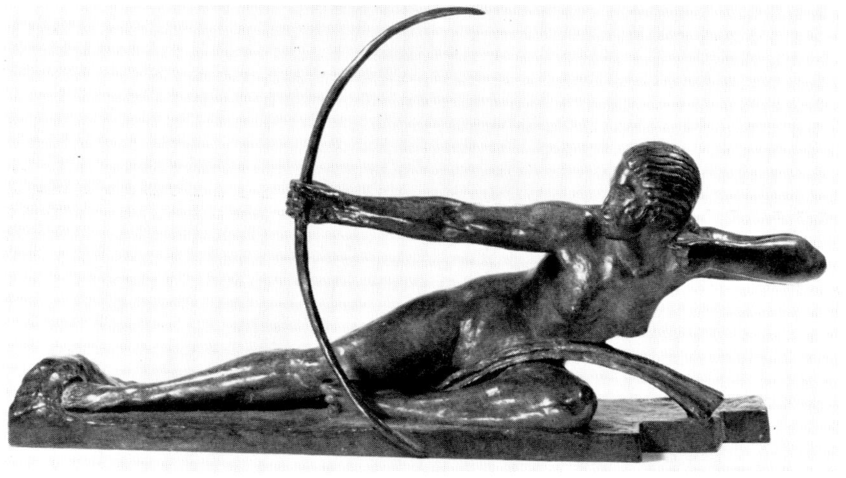

Penthesilia
Queen of the Amazons
26cm:10¼in.

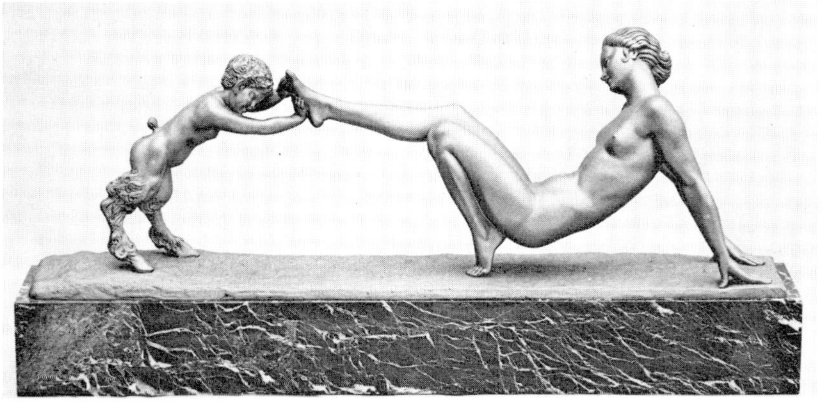

Playing with the Nymph
28cm:11in.

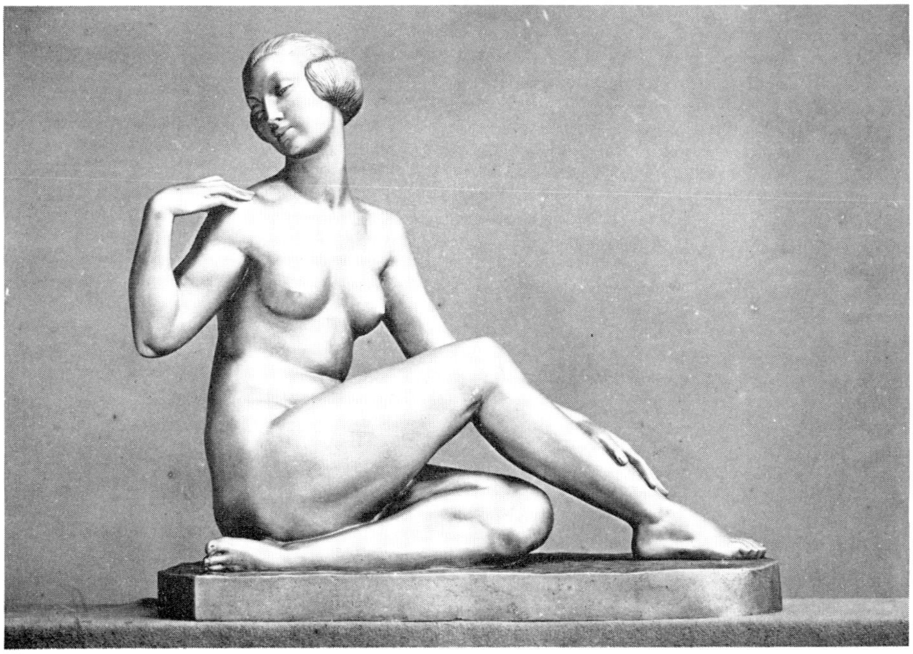

Awakening
54cm:21¼in.
36cm:14in.
20cm:8in.

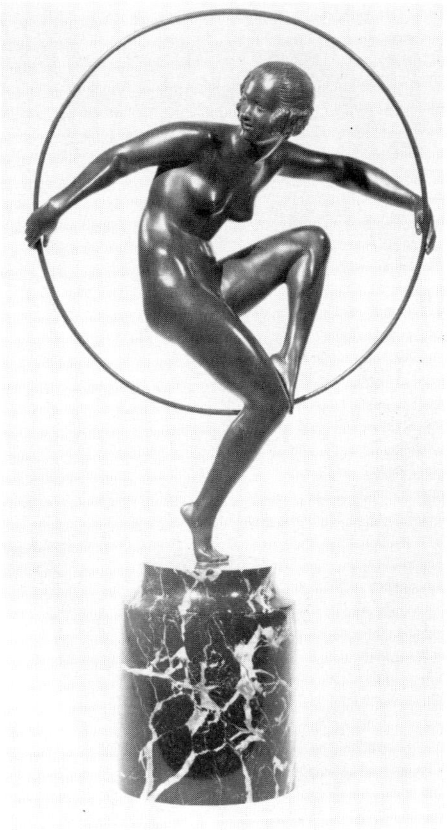

Girl with Hoop
45cm:17¾in.

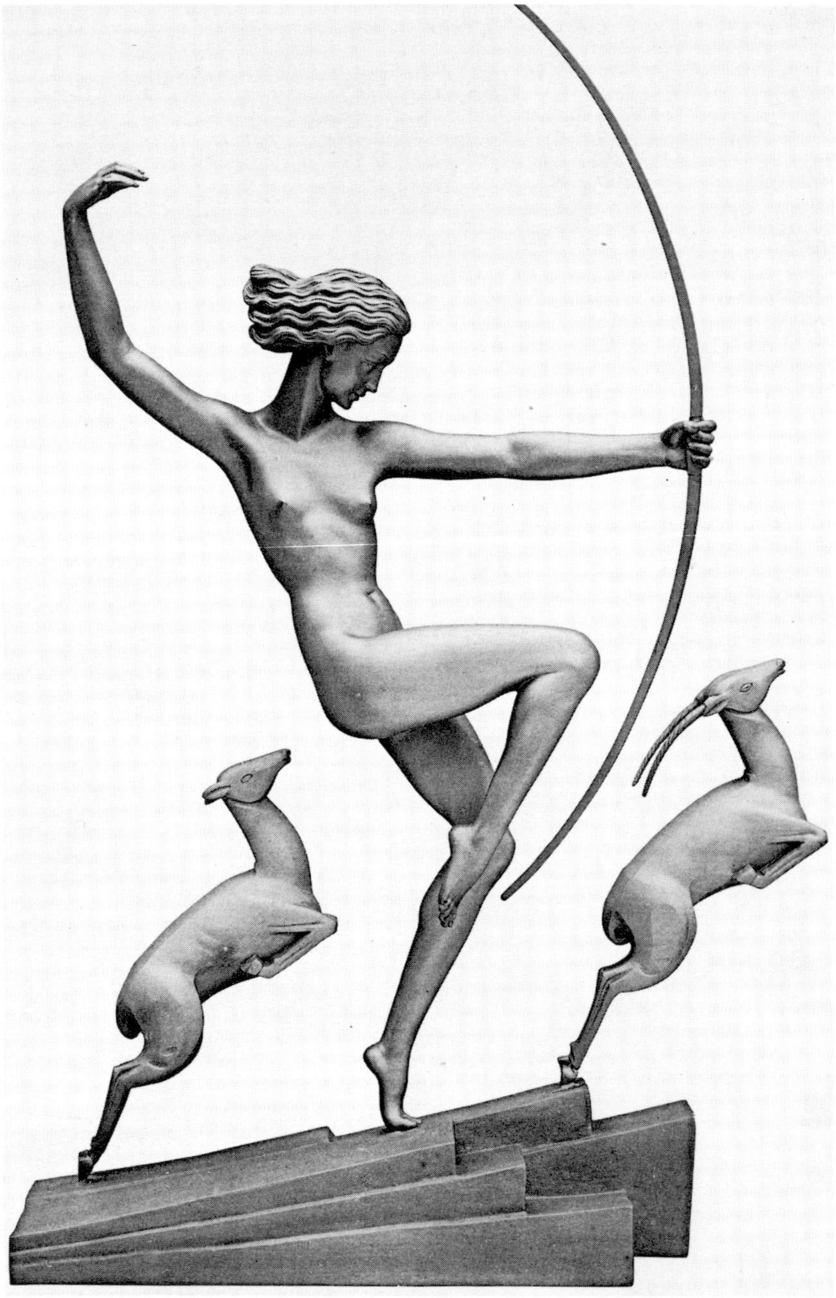

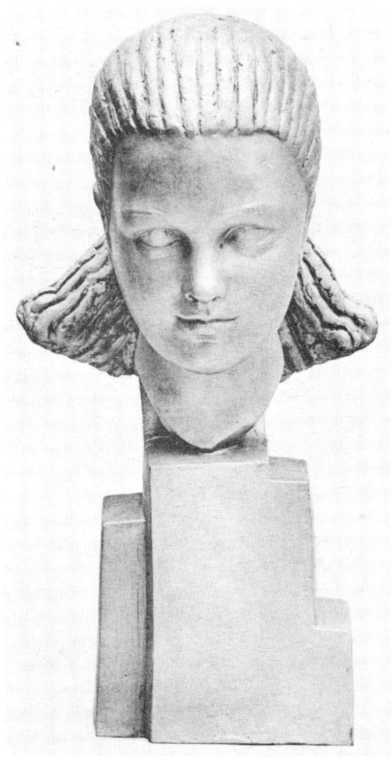

Diana with Fawns, 55cm:21¾in.; 25cm:10in.

Bust of Young Girl, 46cm:18in.
Exhibited 1925

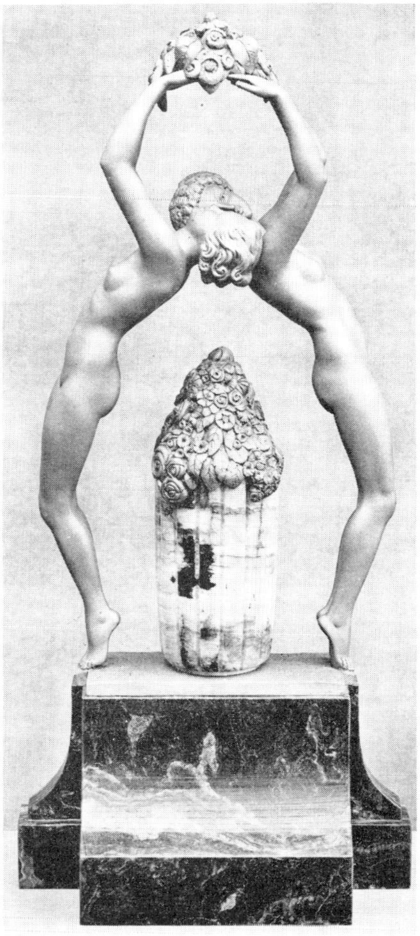

Floral, 66cm:26in.

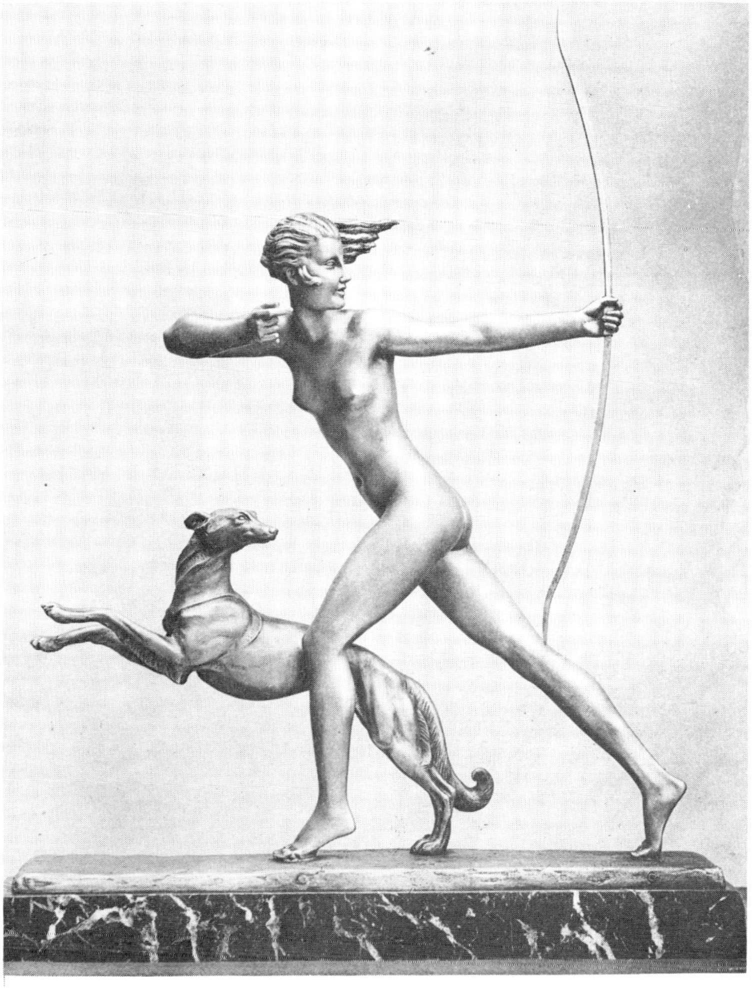

Last Arrow, 69cm:27in.

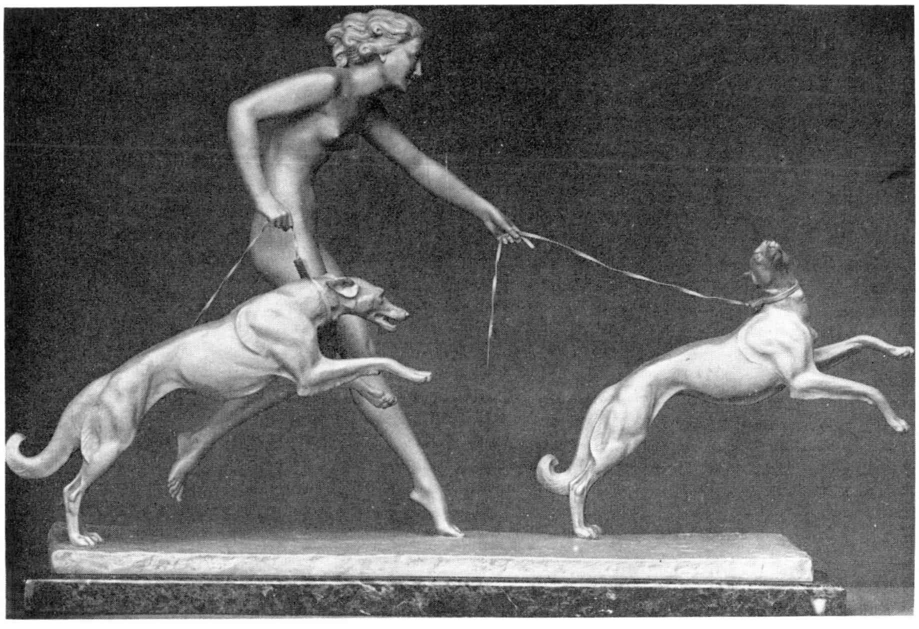

Spring Frolic 50cm:19¾in.

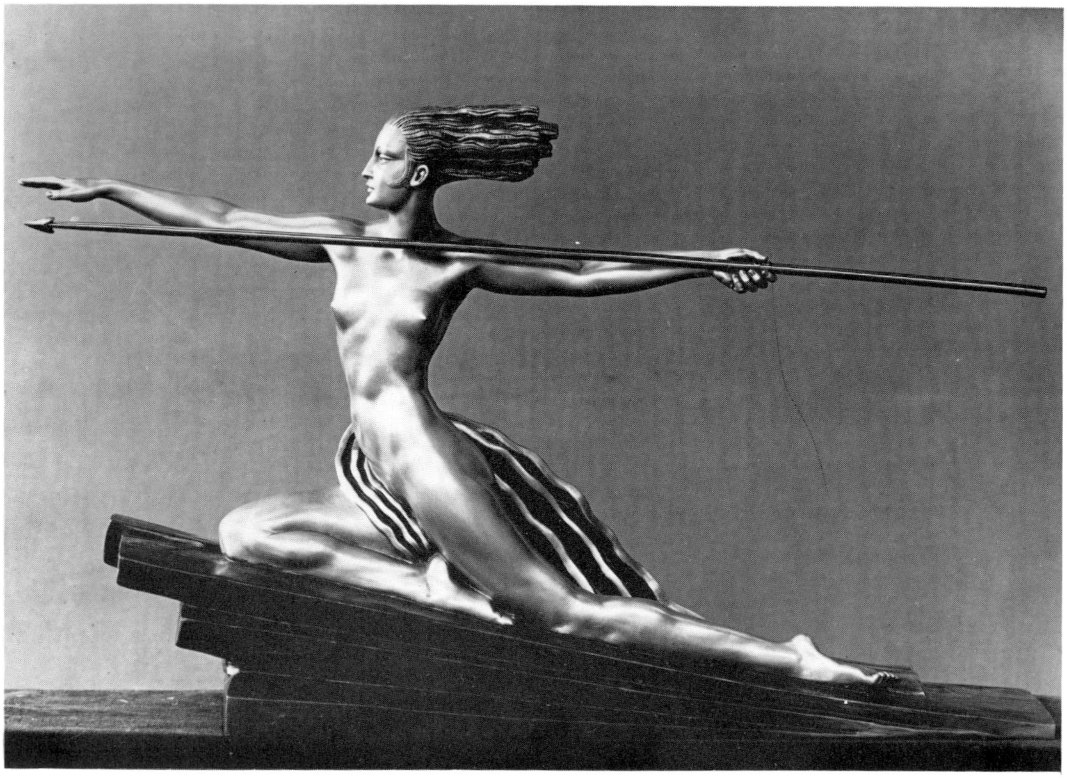

Amazon, 37cm:14½in.; 15cm:5¾in.

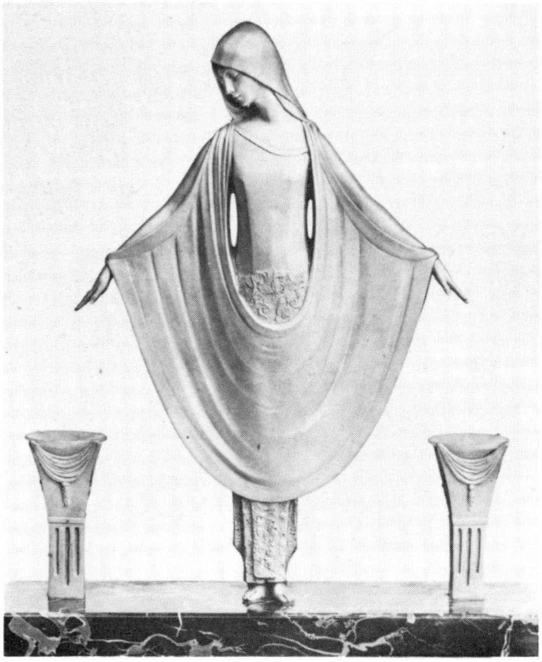

Vestal, 39cm:15½in.

Idol
50cm:19¾in.

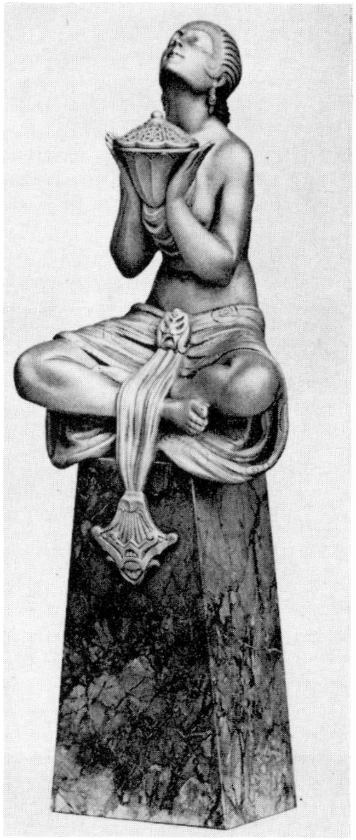

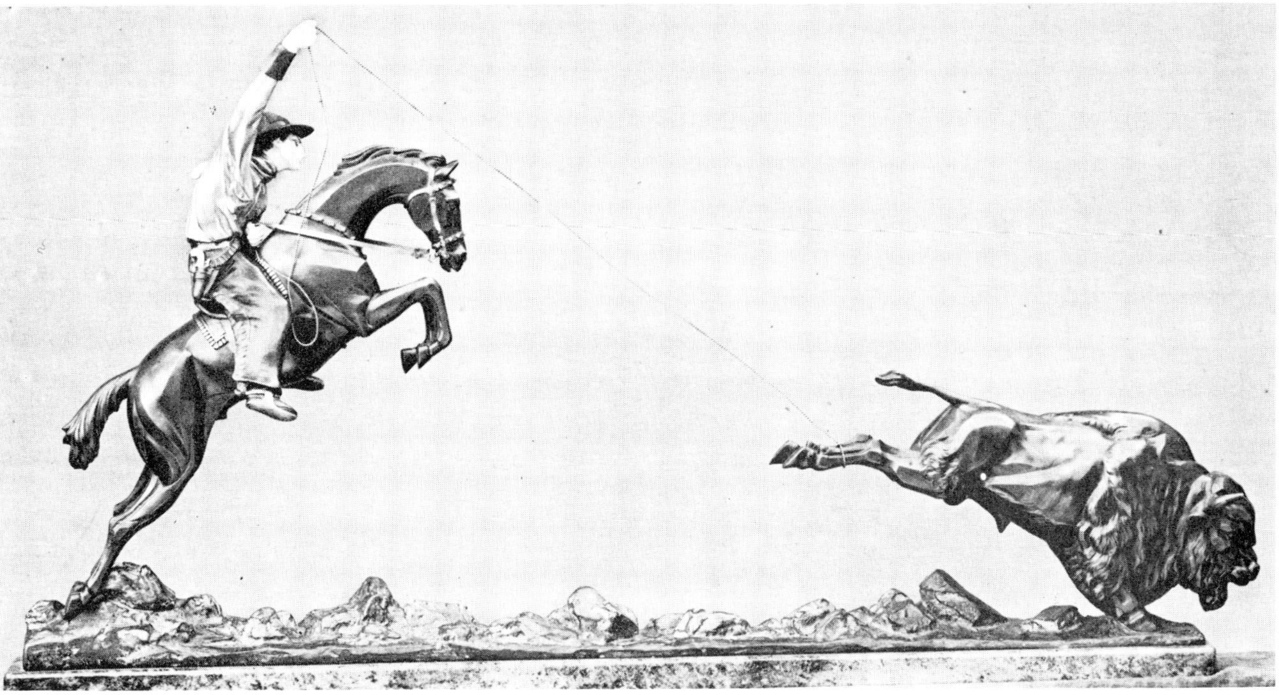

Chase of the Bison, 59cm:23¼in.

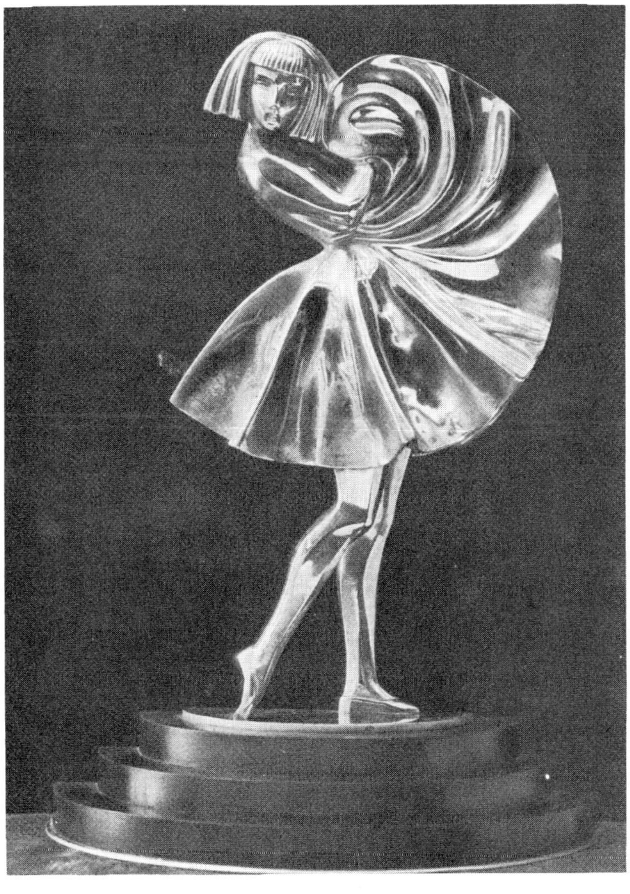

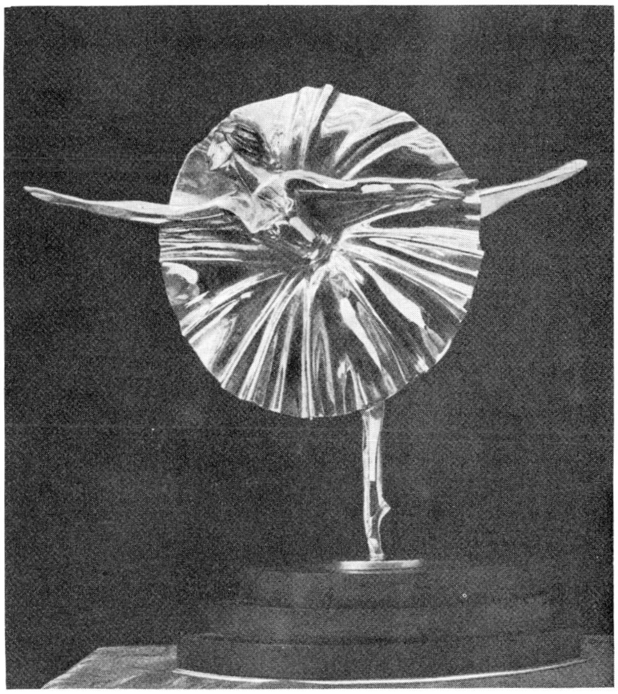

Above: Ballerina, 24cm:9½in.
Left: Dancing Girl, 32cm:12½in.

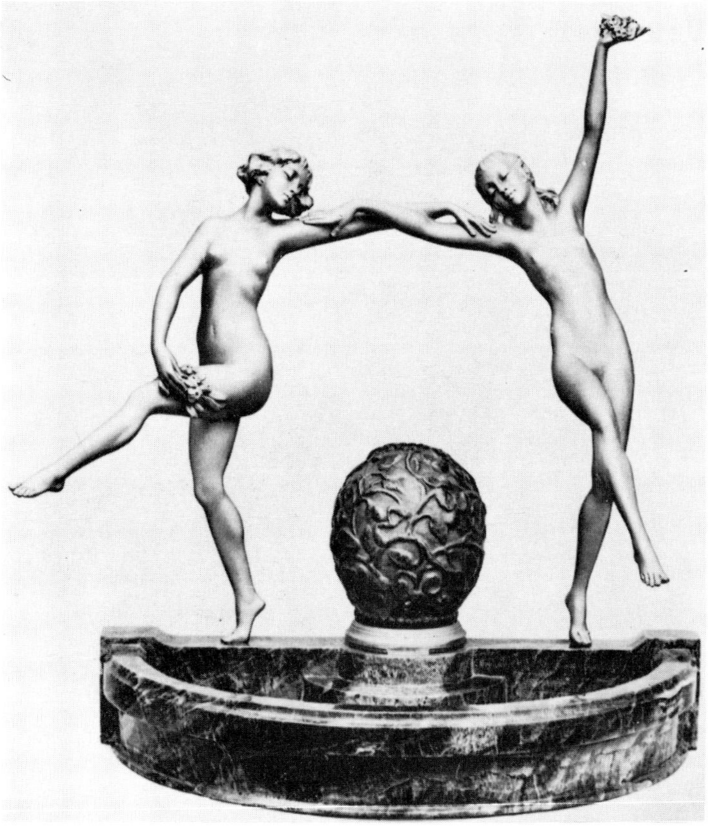

Spring, 40cm:15¾in.

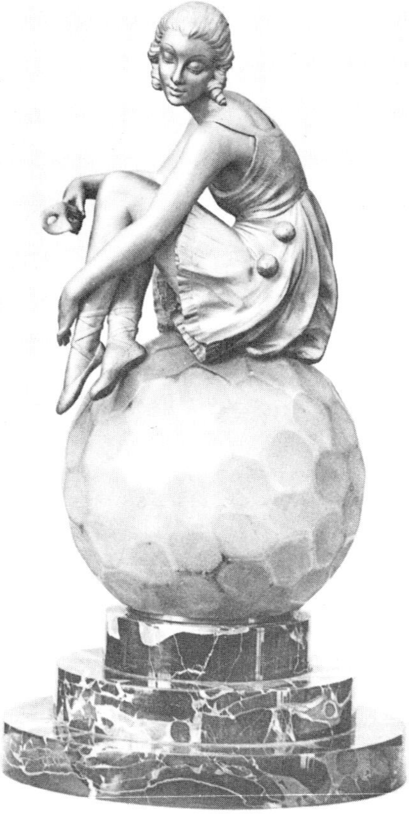

After the Ball
37cm:14½in.

Dance with Birds
35cm:13¾in.

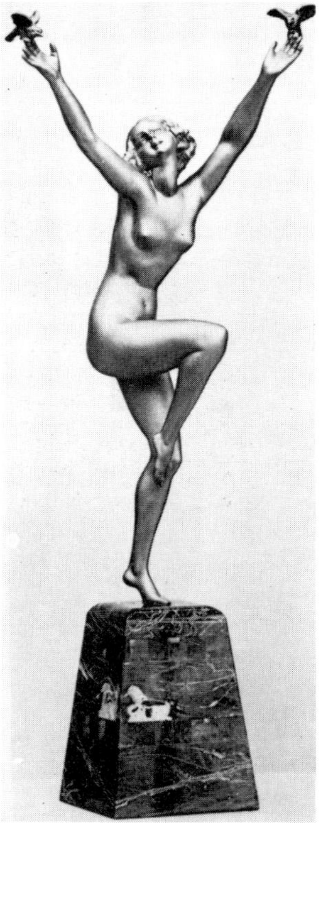

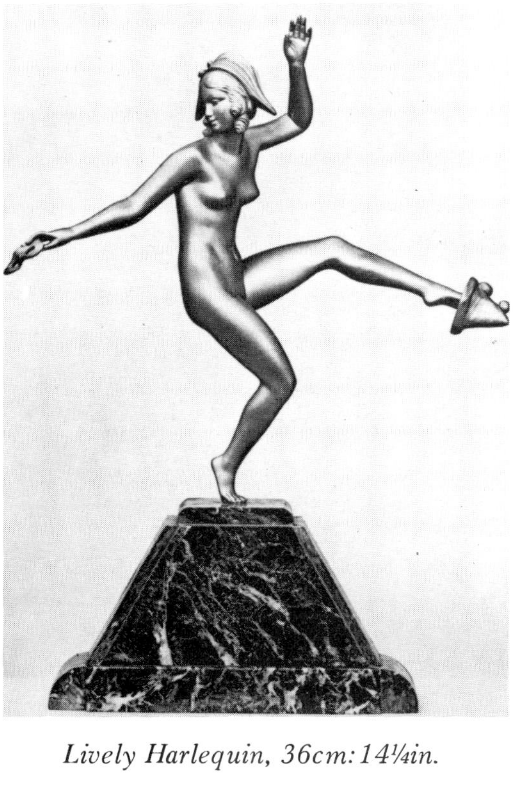

Lively Harlequin, 36cm:14¼in.

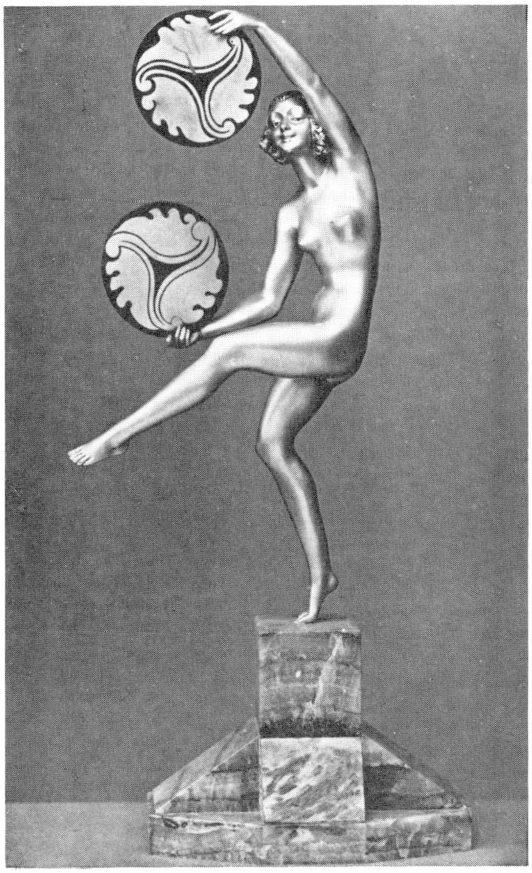

Dance of the Discs, 60cm:23½in.

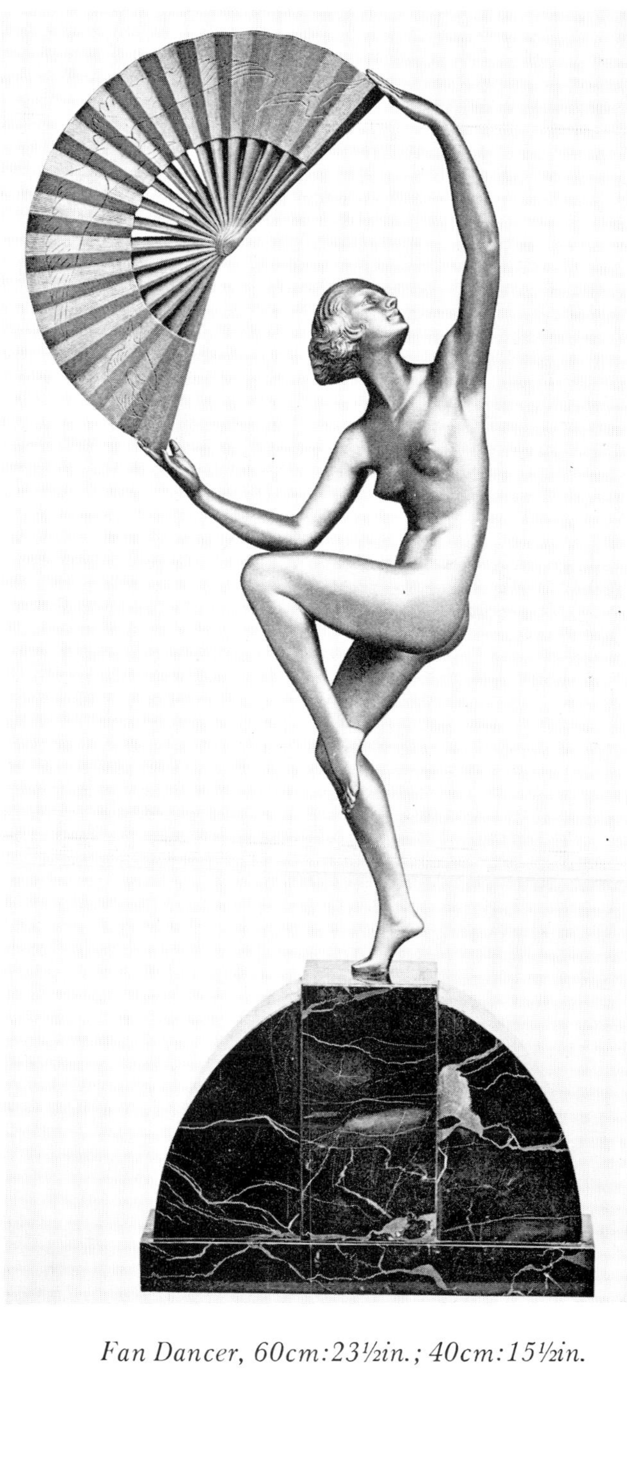

Fan Dancer, 60cm:23½in.; 40cm:15½in.

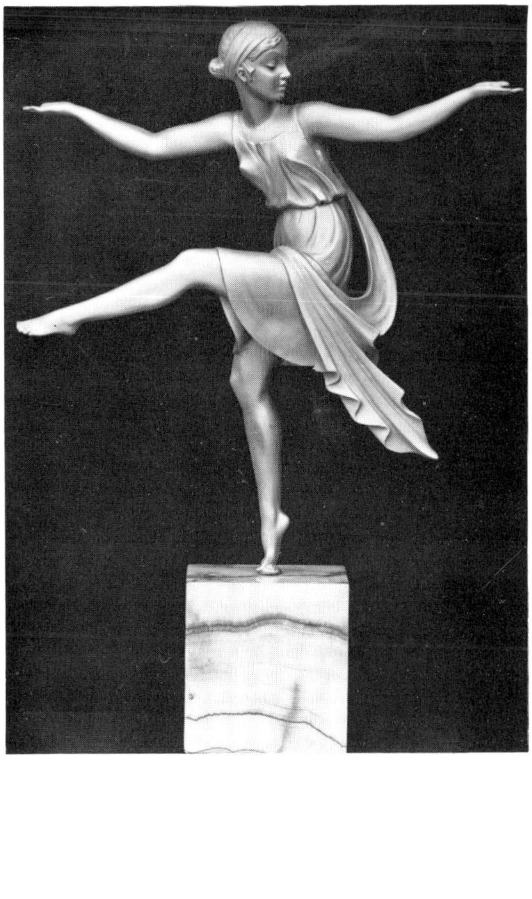

Dance of the Scarf, 44cm:17¼in.

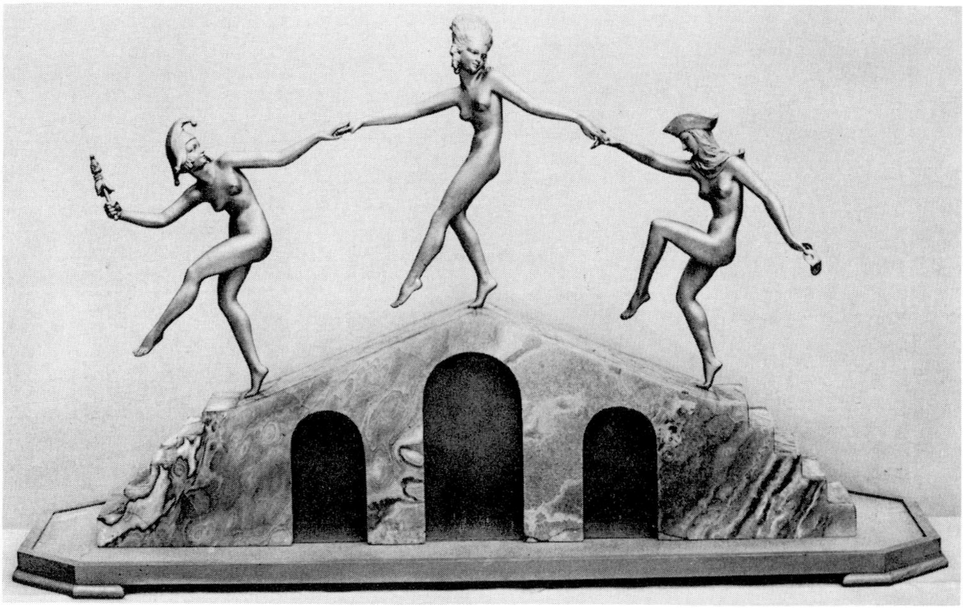

Evening of Madness

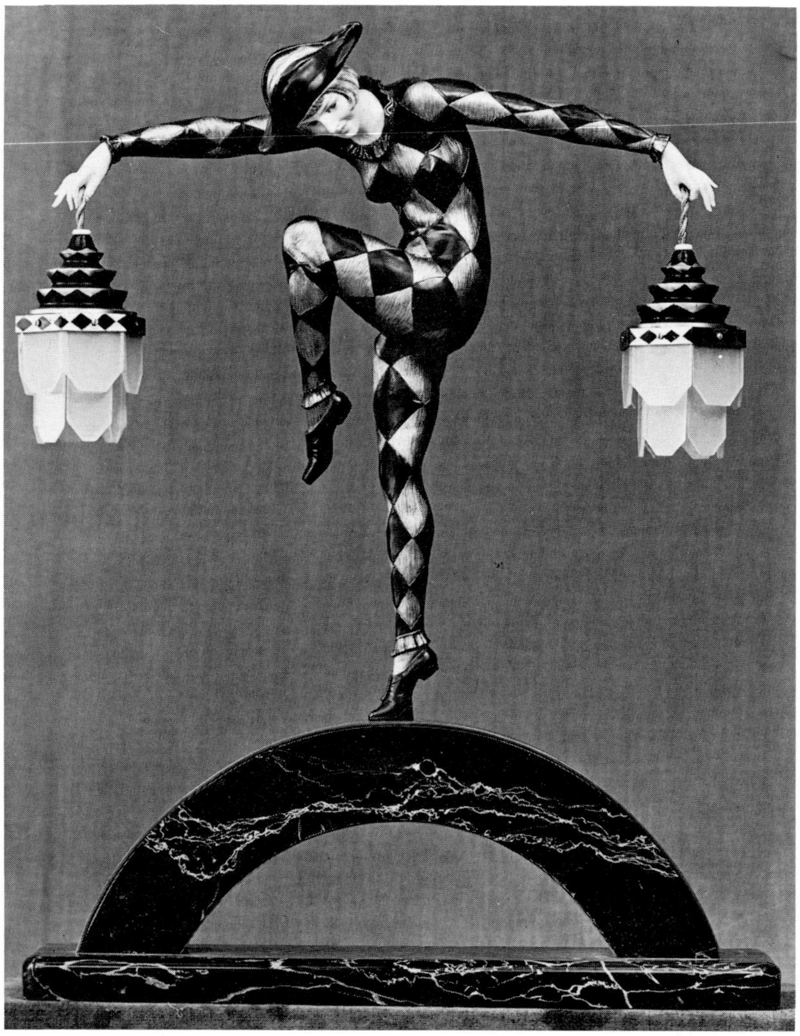

Harlequin
55cm:21¾in.
Wired as a lamp

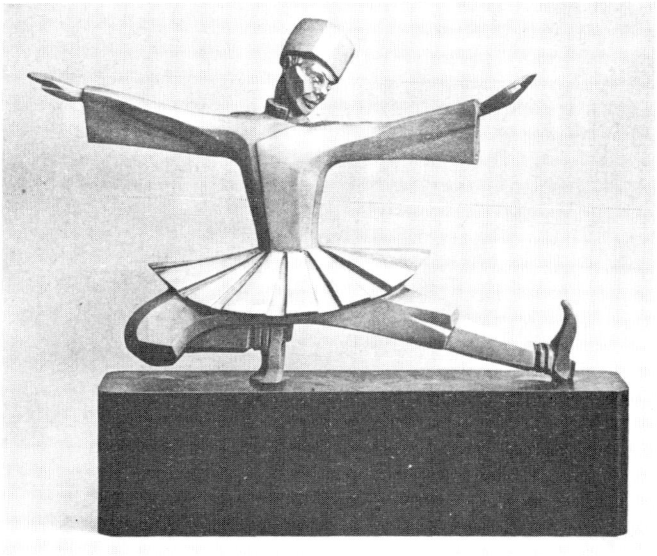

Russian Dancer, 27cm:10½in.

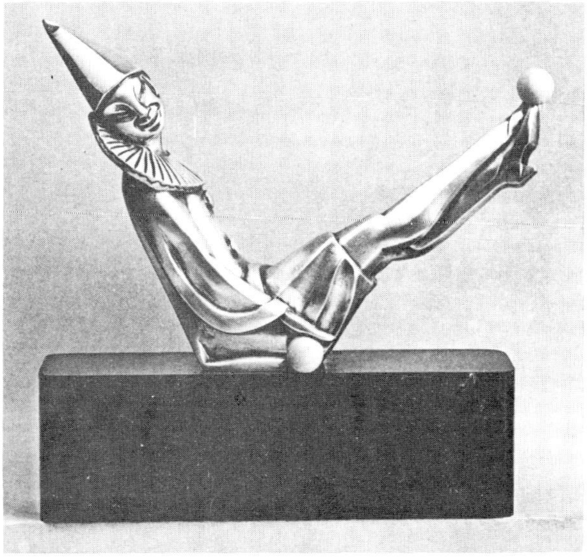

Clown with Balls, 27cm:10½in.

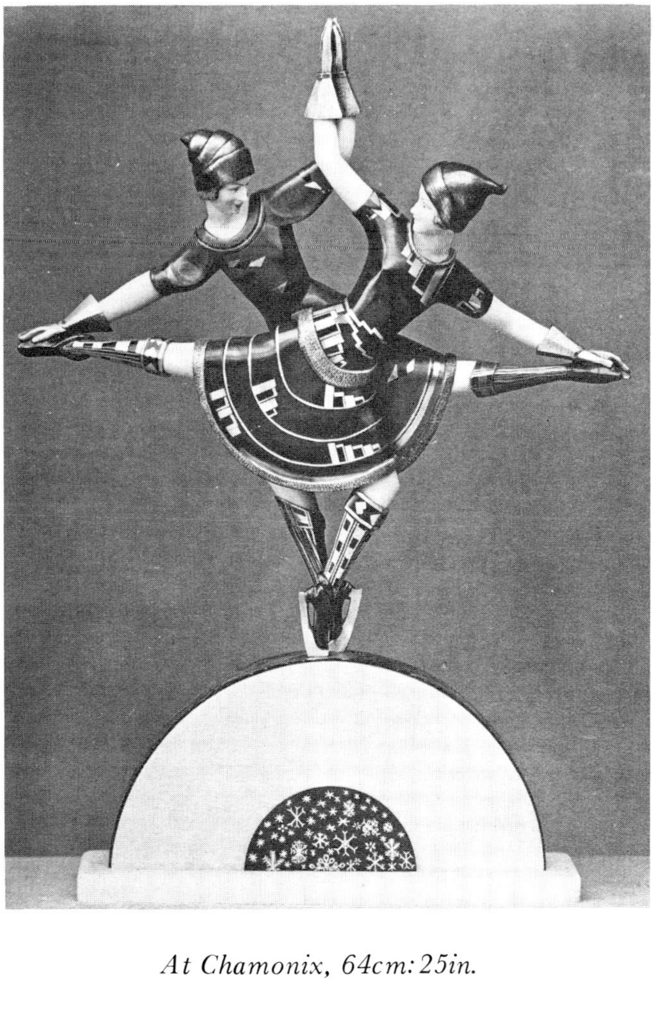

At Chamonix, 64cm:25in.

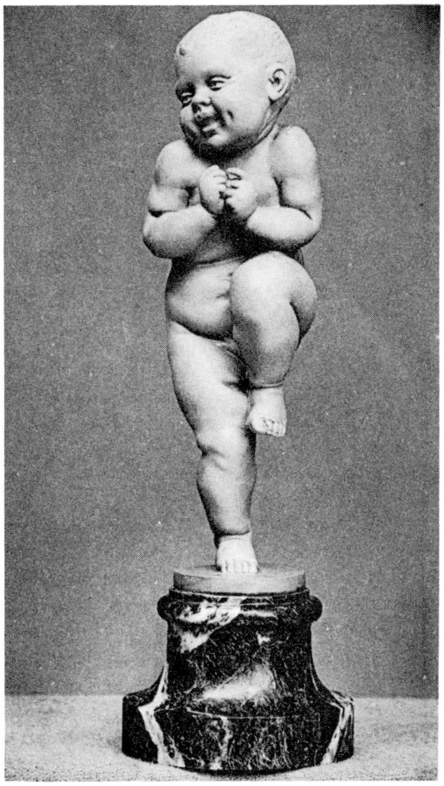

Child Laughing, 25cm:10in.

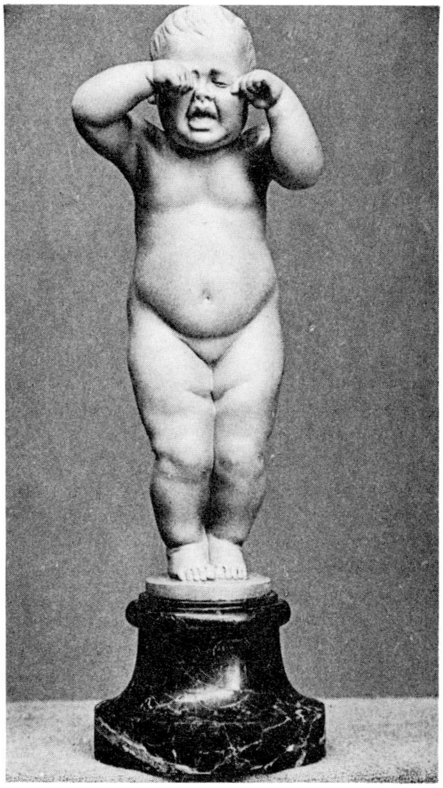

Child Crying, 25cm:10in.

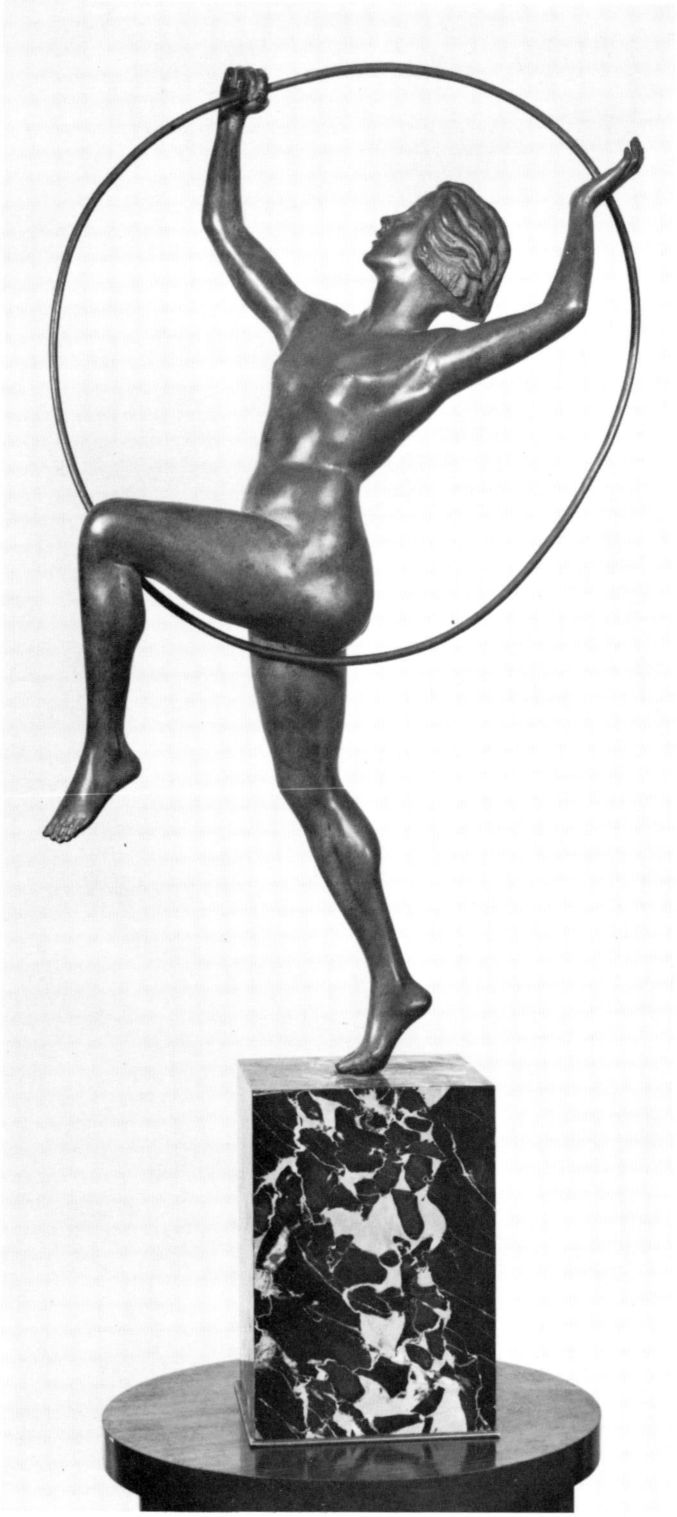

Dancer with Hoop, 79cm:31in.

MME. CALLENDER

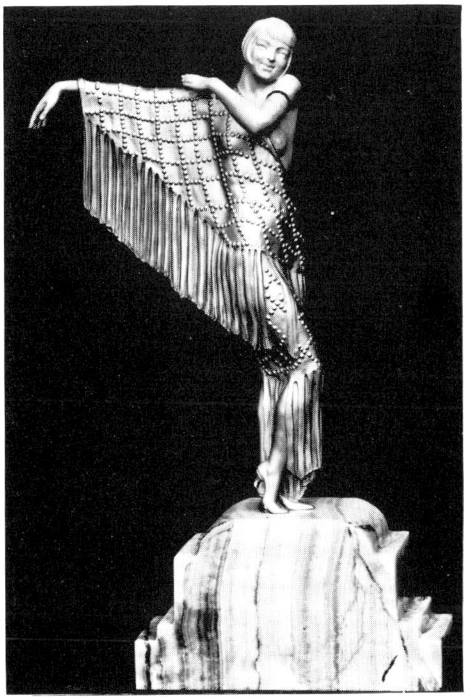

Anita, 42cm:16½in.

JEAN CAMUS

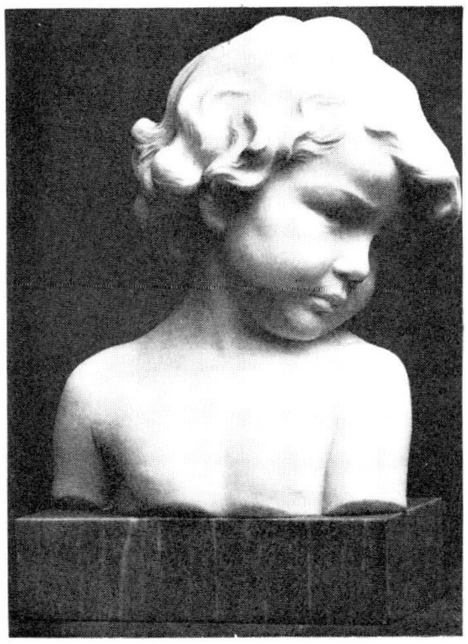

Child Sulking
40cm:15¾in.
25cm:10in.
11cm:4¼in.

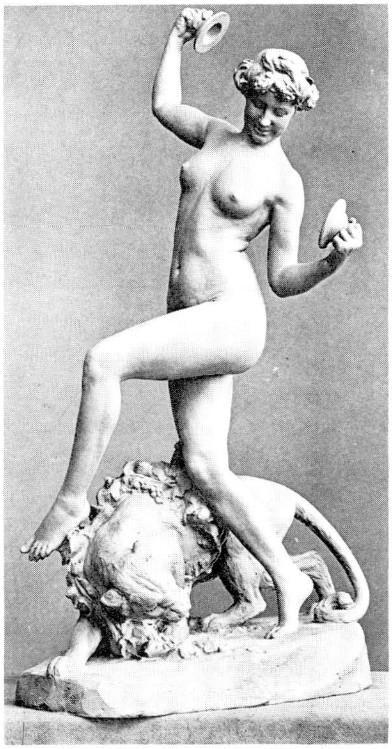

Bacchante and Panther
94cm:37in.; 60cm:23½in.

CANOVA

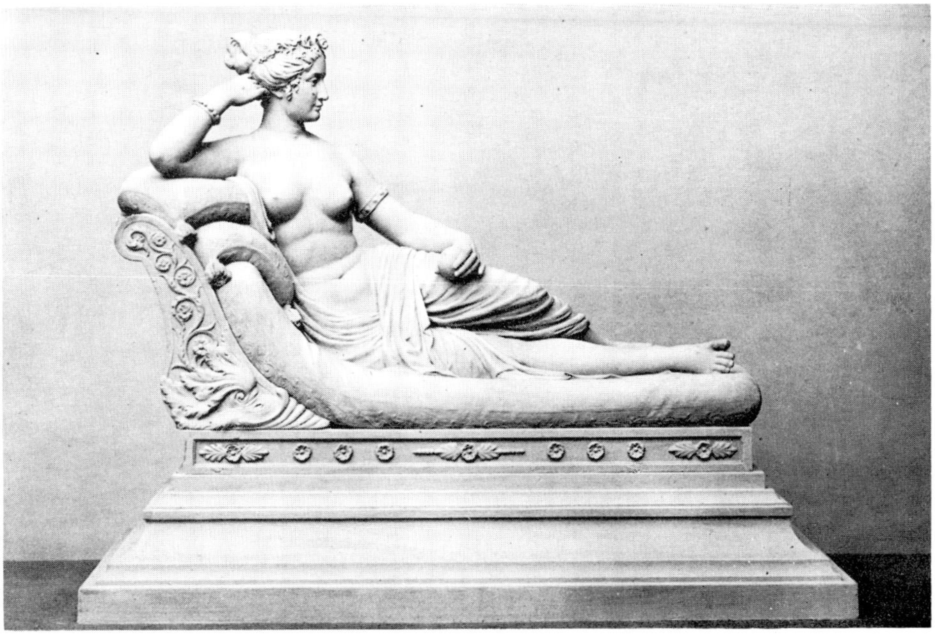

Pauline Borghèse, 46cm:18in.; 24cm:9½in.

ALBERT CARRIER-BELLEUSE

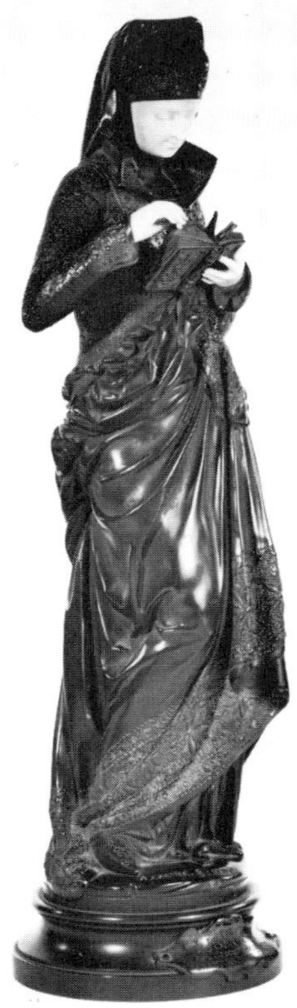

The Reader
61cm:24in. and
various smaller sizes

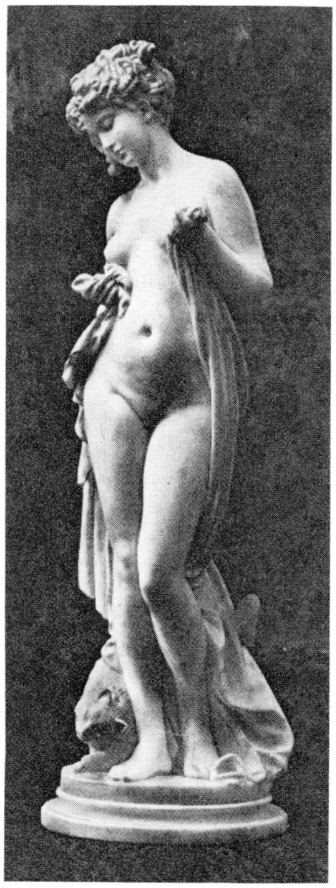

Dawn
81cm:31¾in.
65cm:25½in.
25cm:9¾in.

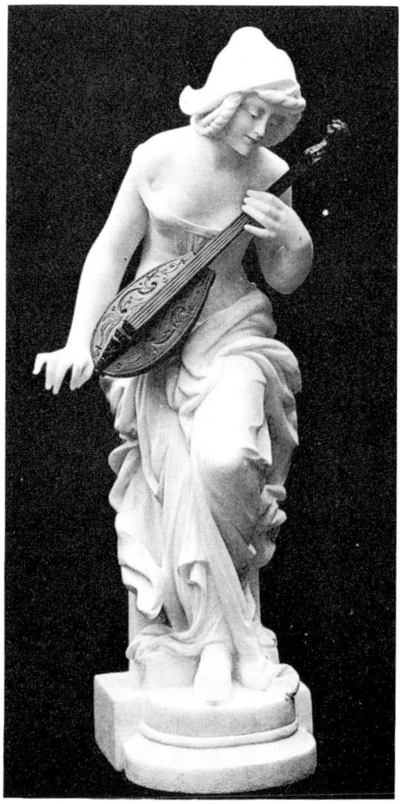

Musician
80cm:31½in.
60cm:23½in.

ADRIANO CECIONI

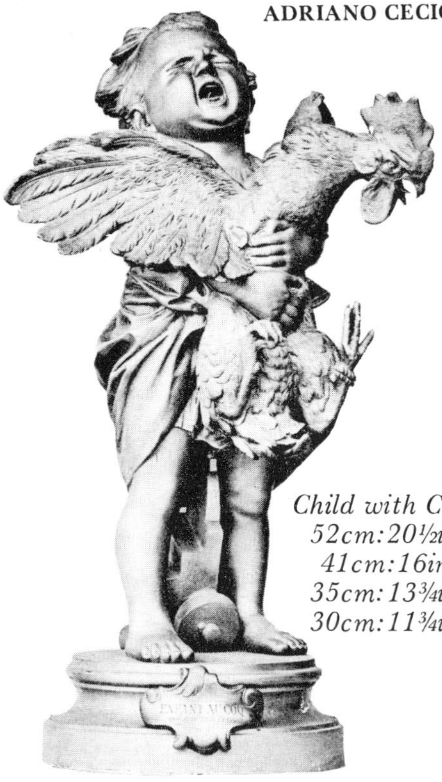

Child with Cock
52cm:20½in.
41cm:16in.
35cm:13¾in.
30cm:11¾in.

W.M. CHANCE

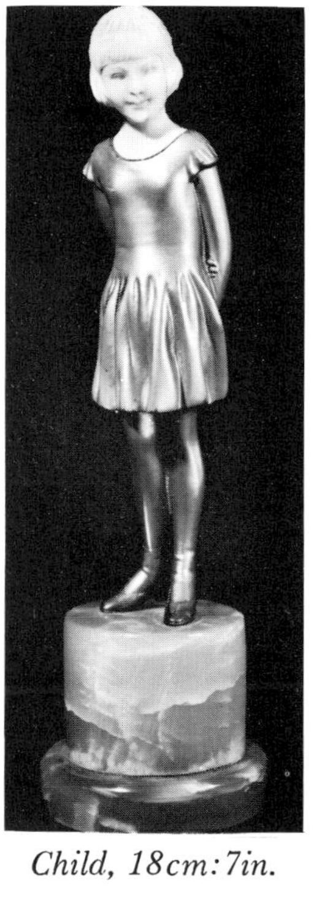

Child, 18cm:7in.

Right: Collection of works by D.H. Chiparus, with the exception of the top right-hand figure which is by Joé Descomps, showing the similarity between the styles of the two sculptors.

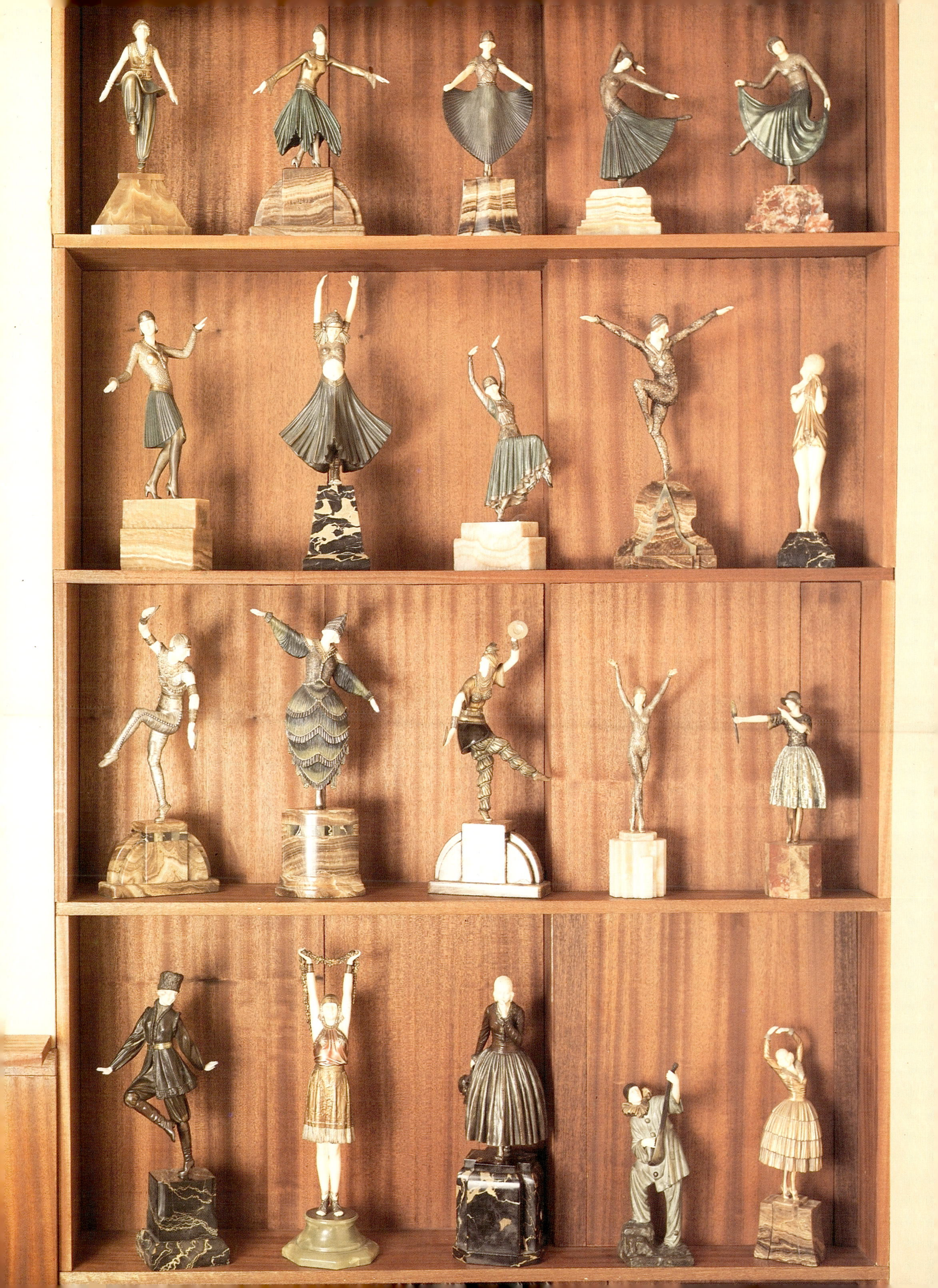

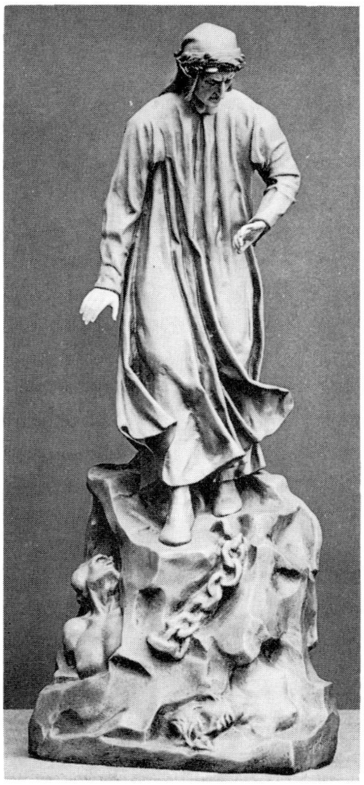

Dante
70cm:27½in.

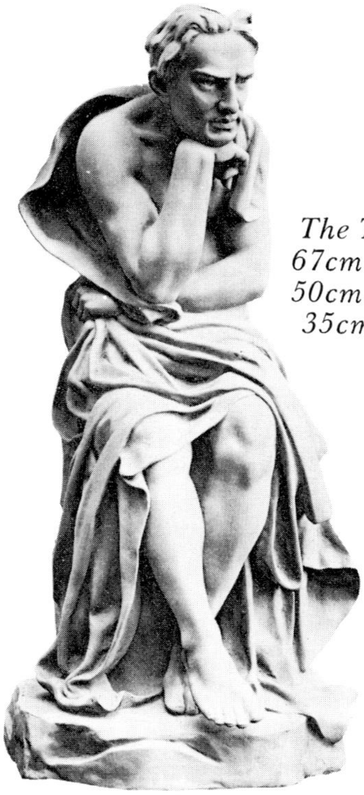

The Thinker
67cm:26½in.
50cm:19¾in.
35cm:14in.

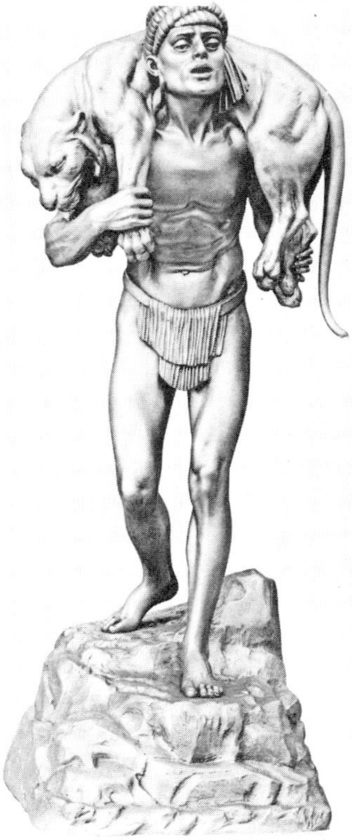

Return of the Hunter, 54cm:21¼in.

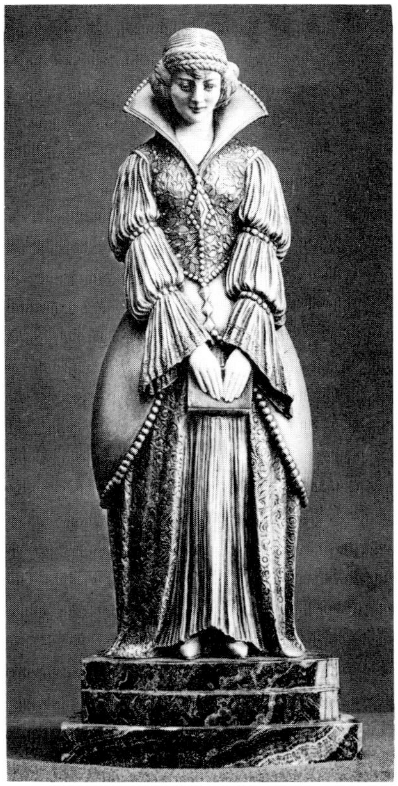

After Reading
37cm:14½in.
25cm:10in.

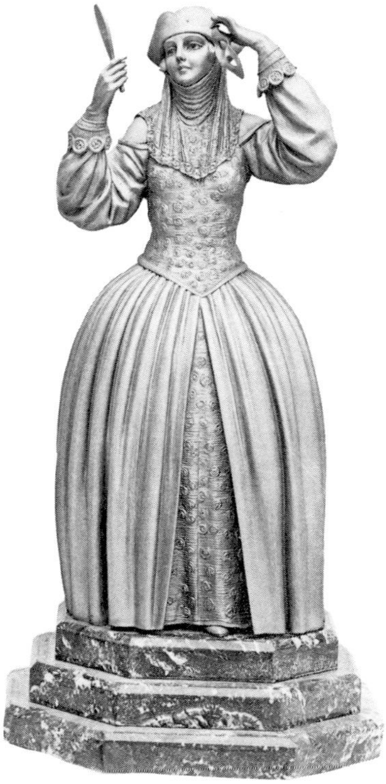

Venetian Lady
37cm:14½in.

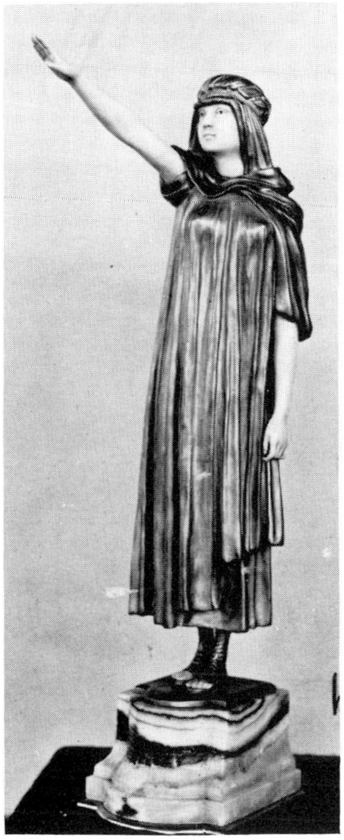

Adieu
36cm:14in.

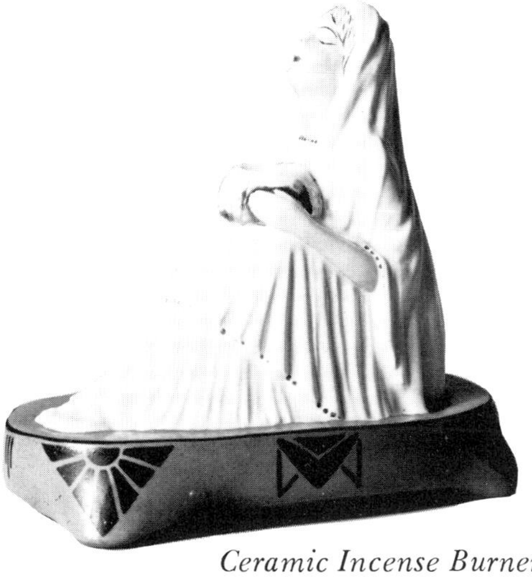

Ceramic Incense Burner
15cm:6in.

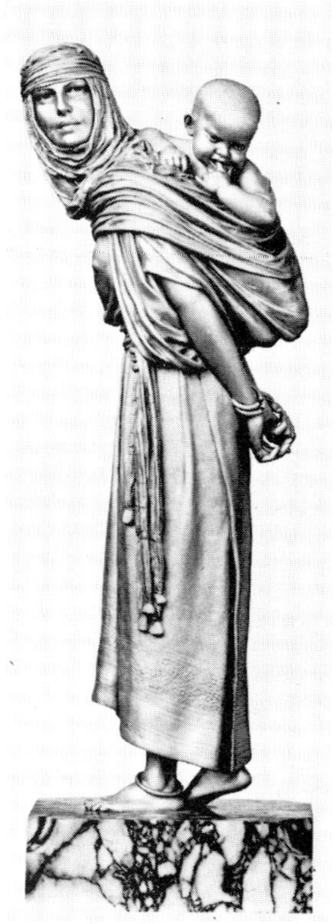

Arab Mother
90cm:35½in.
66cm:26in.
33cm:13in.

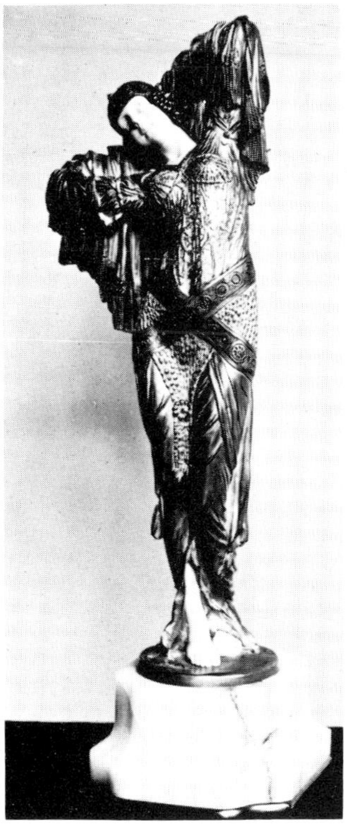

Odalisque
45cm:17¾in.

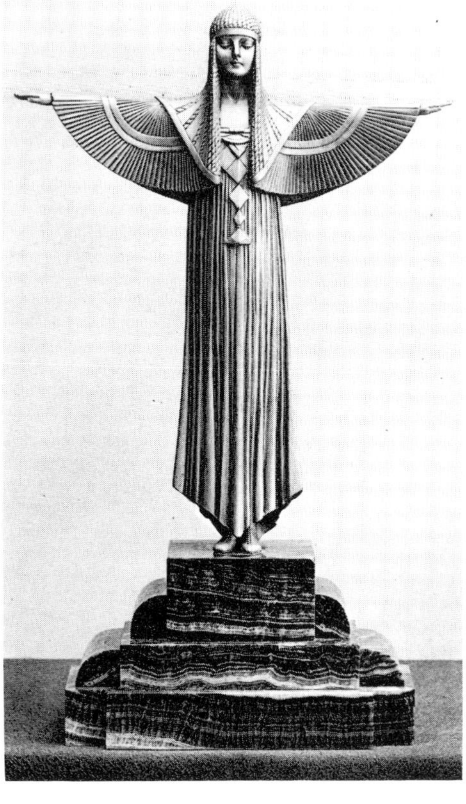

The Creed, 39cm:15¼in.

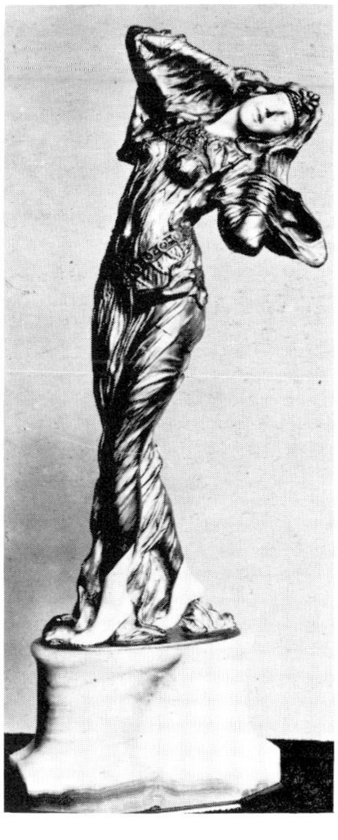

Favourite
45cm:17¾in.

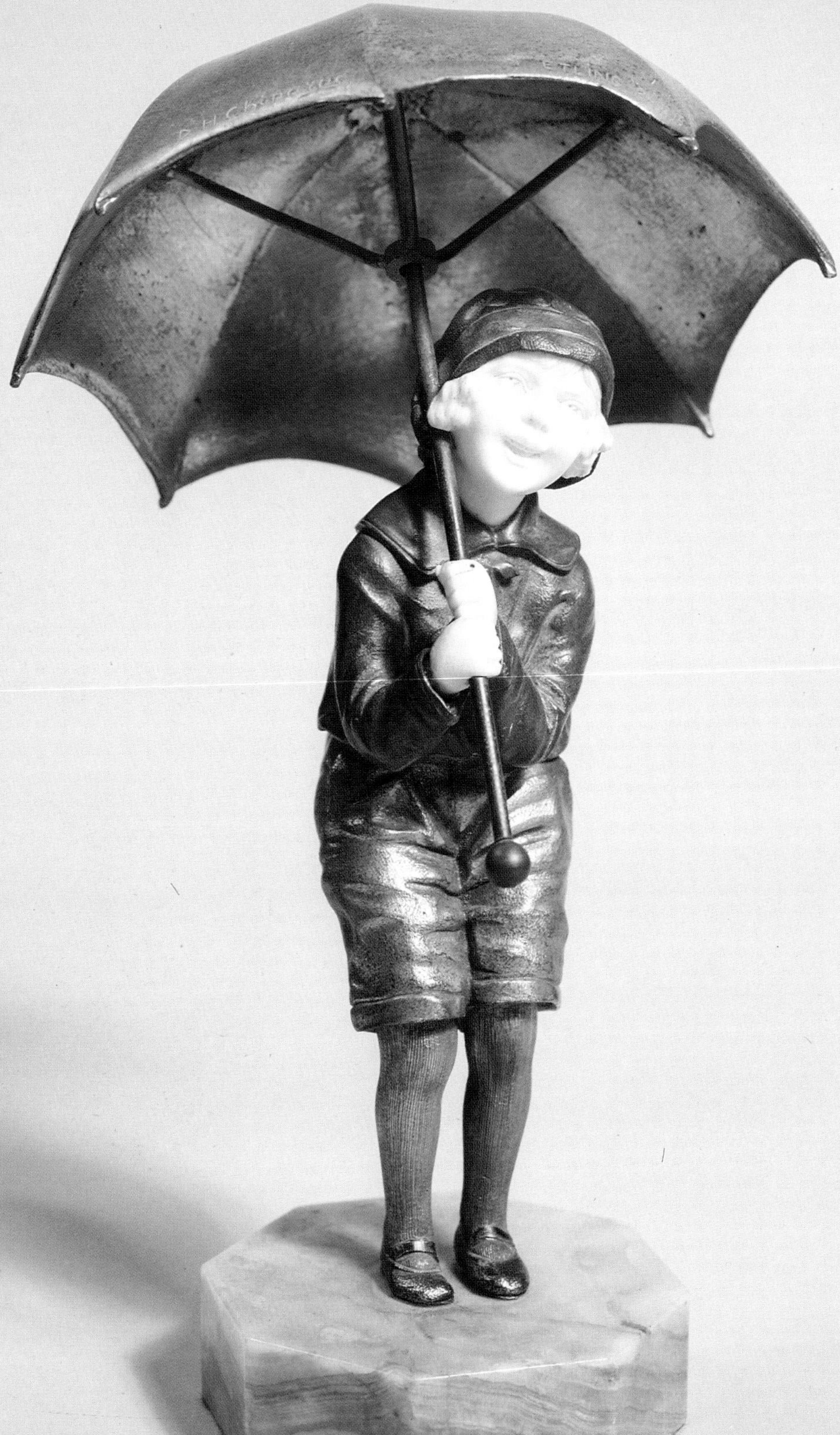

Left: D.H. Chiparus
Child with Umbrella
25cm: 9¾in.

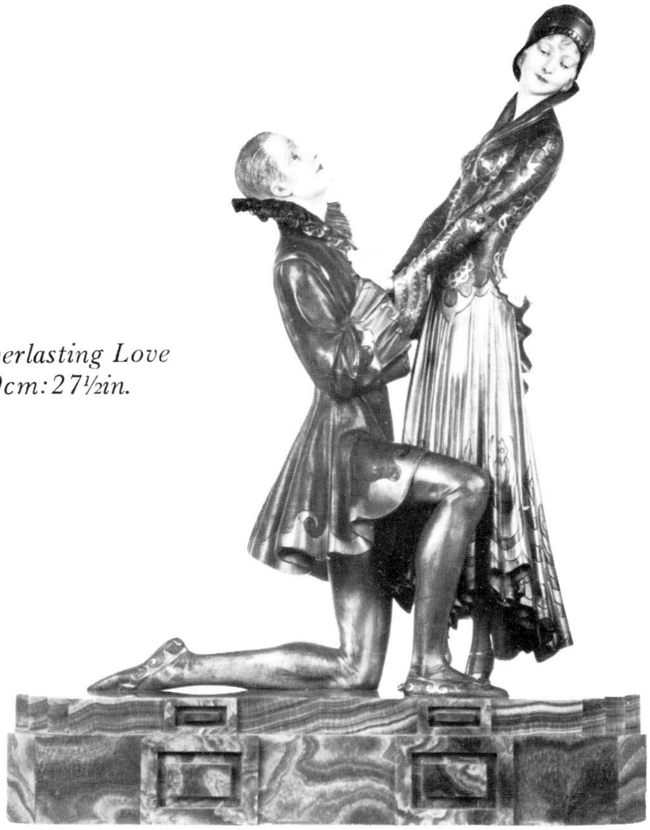

Everlasting Love
70cm: 27½in.

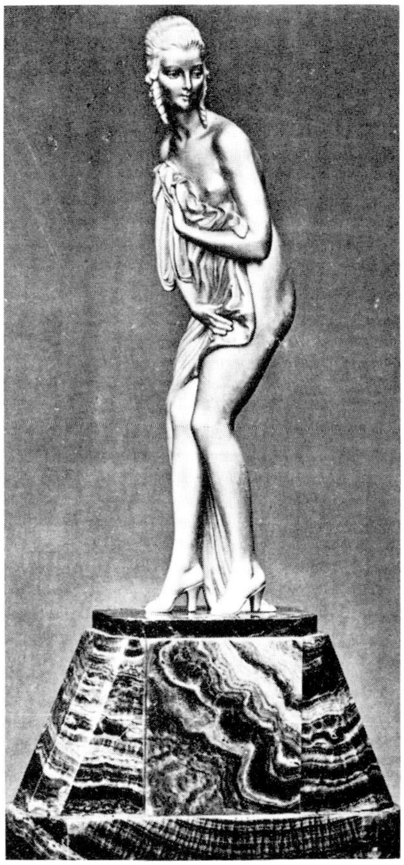

Ninon, 46cm: 18in.

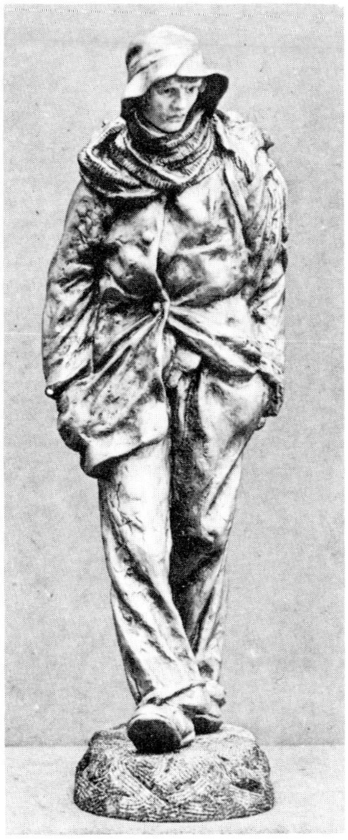

Rag-and-Bone Man
40cm: 15¾in.

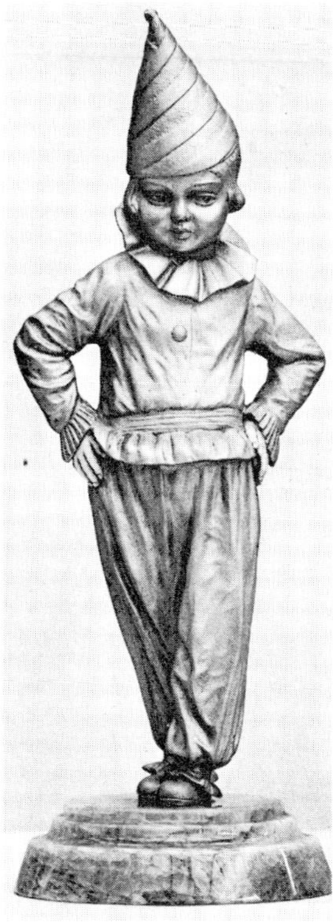

Fancy Dress Ball
25cm: 10in.

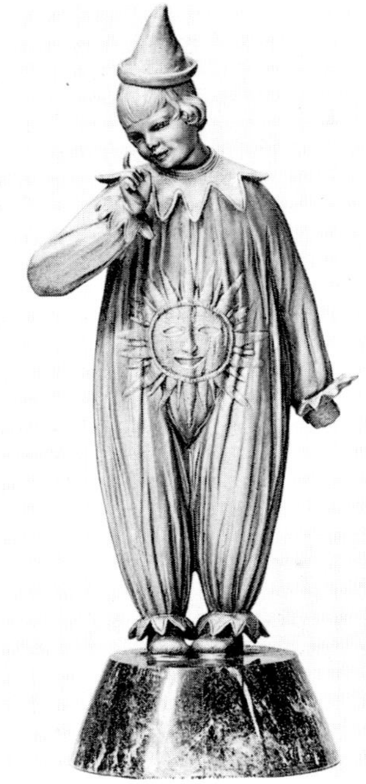

Clown
29cm: 11½in.

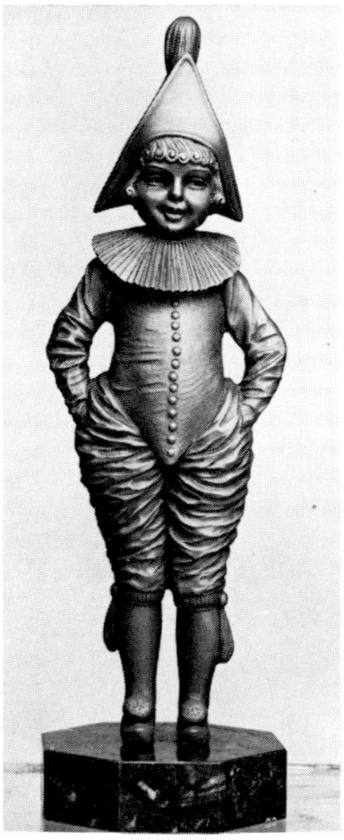

Punch
25cm: 10in.

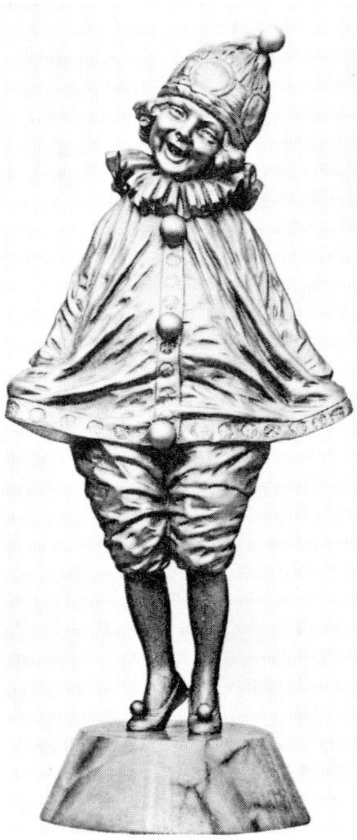

Little Clown
22cm: 8½in.

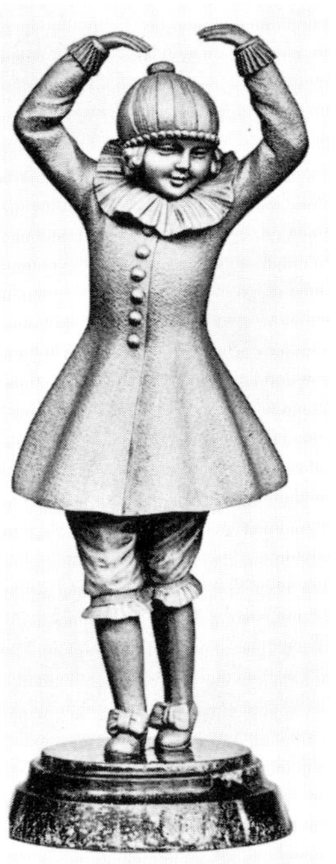

Fancy Dress
25cm: 10in.

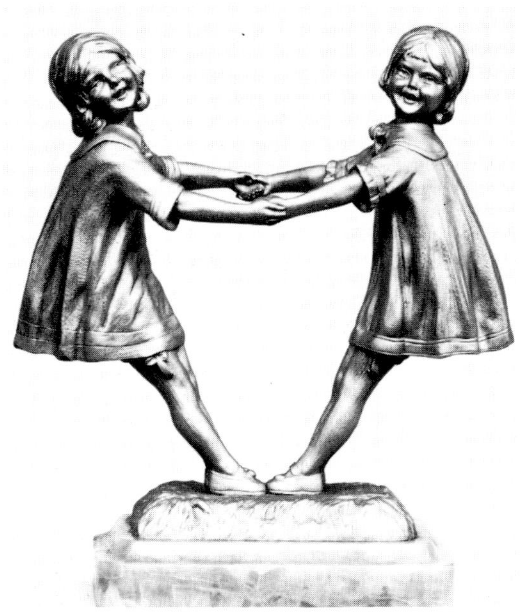

The Two Little Maidens
18cm: 7in.

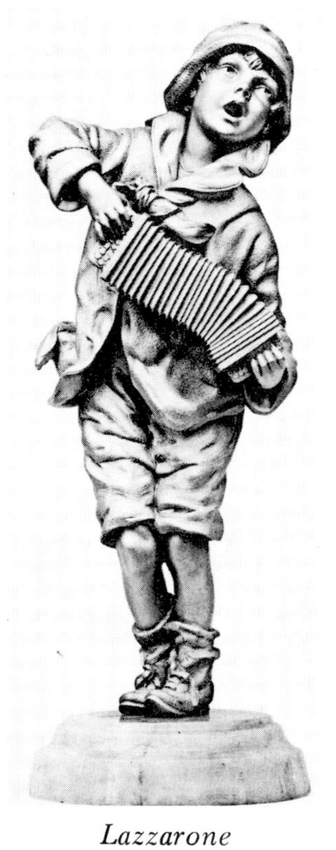

Lazzarone
24cm: 9½in.

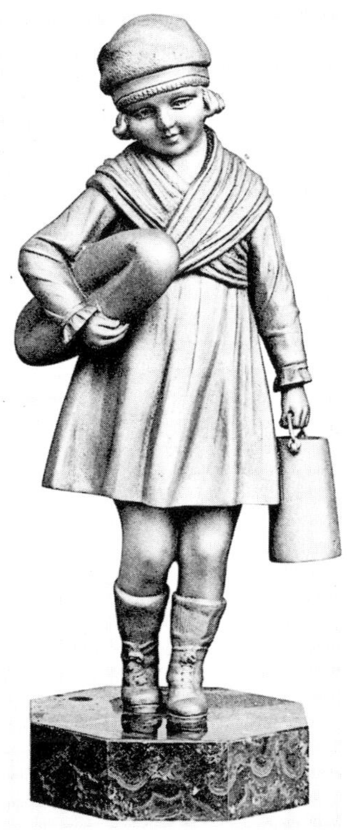

Errands
23cm: 9in.

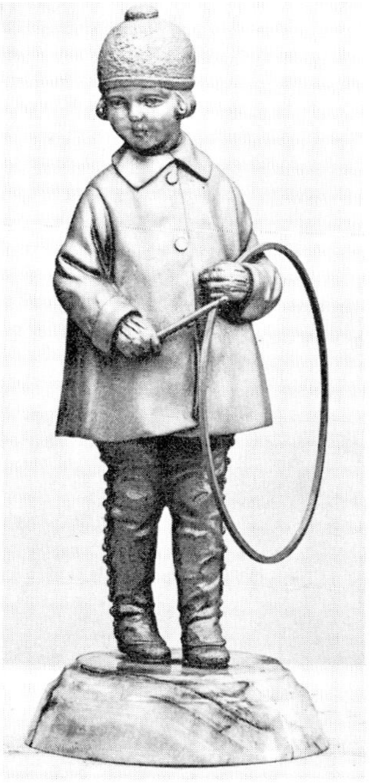

Walking
25cm: 10in.

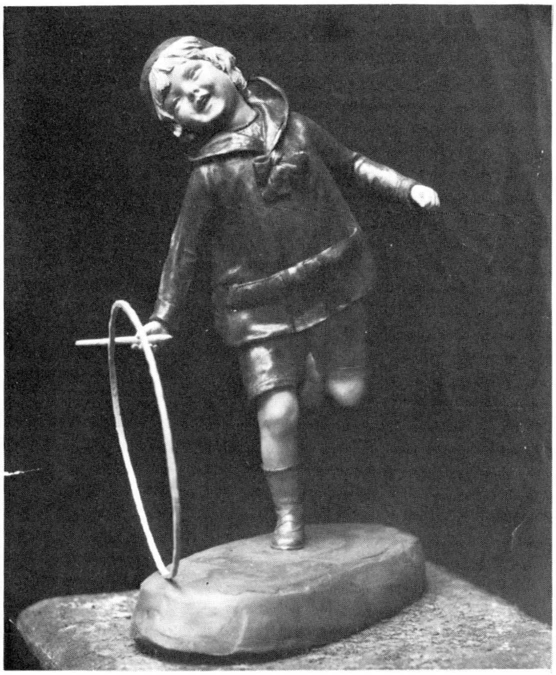

Boy with Hoop, 18cm: 7in.

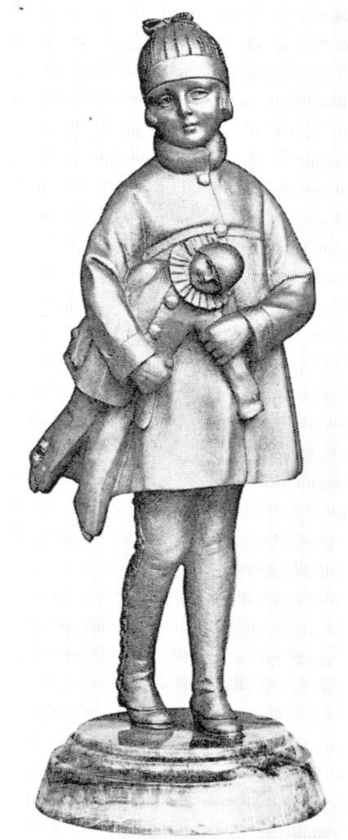

My Puppet
25cm: 9¾in.

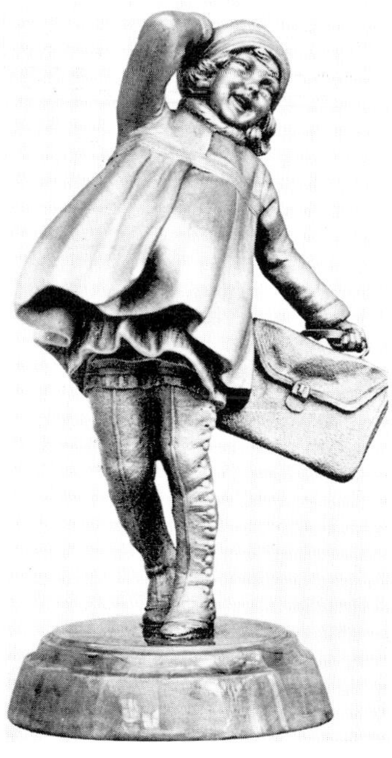

The School Girl
19cm: 7½in.

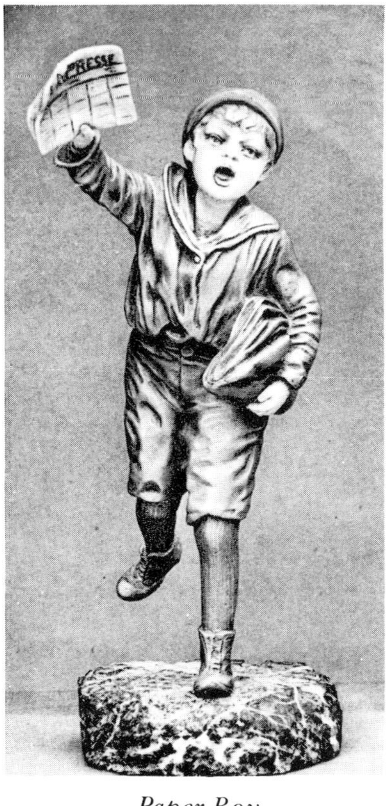

Paper Boy
25cm: 10in.

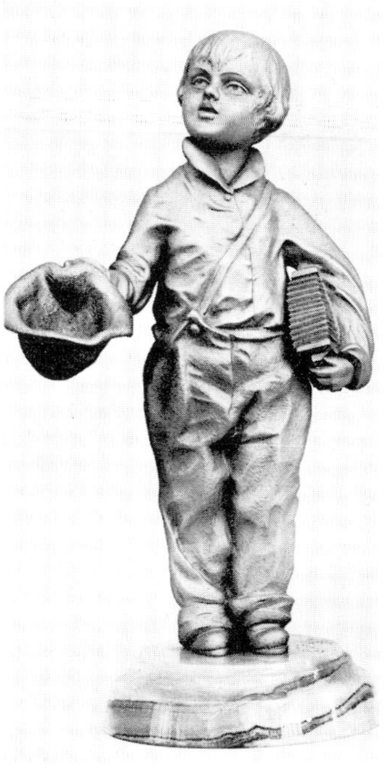

Little Beggar
18cm: 7¼in.

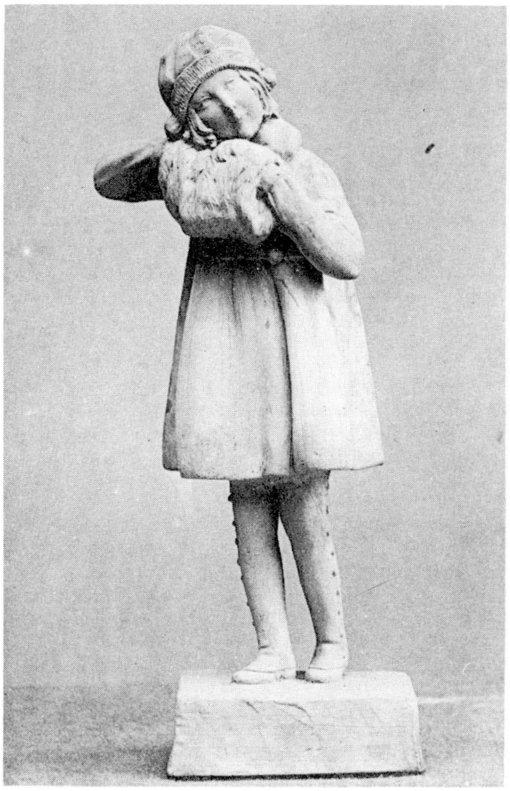

Little Chilly One, 23cm:9in.

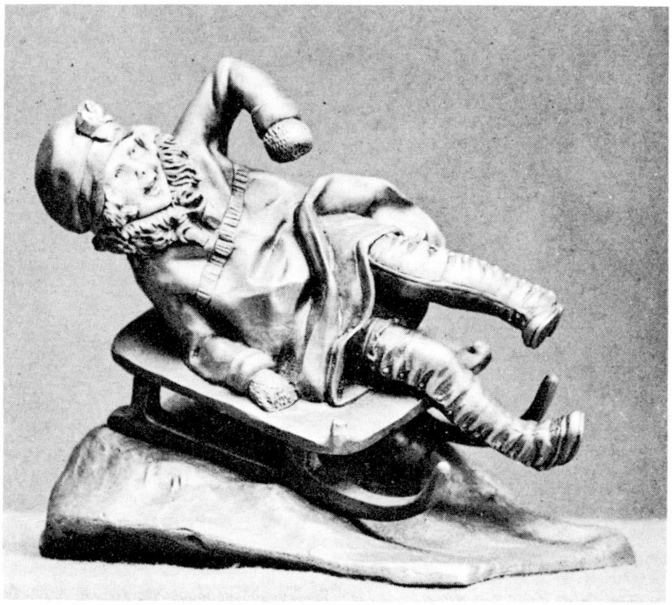

Swiss Toboggan, 15cm:6in.

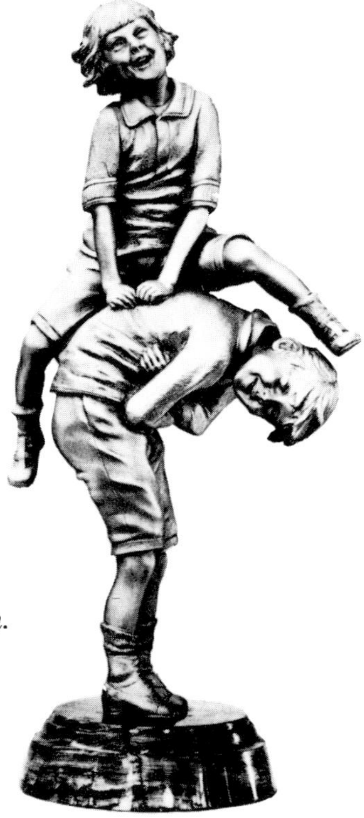

Leap Frog
26cm:10¼in.

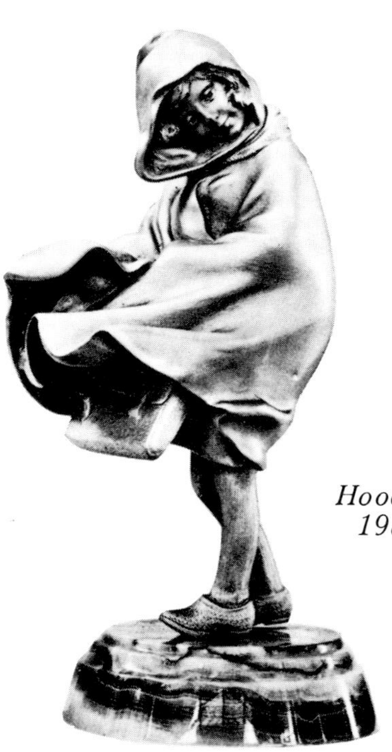

Hooded Cloak
19cm:7½in.

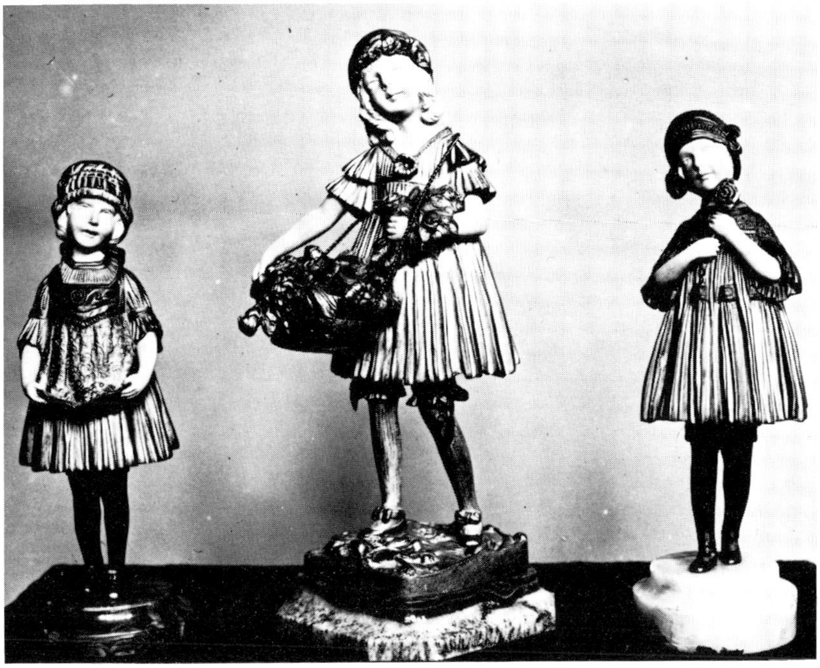

Cherries
22cm: 8½in.

Flower Gatherer
28cm: 11in.

The Rose
23cm: 9in.

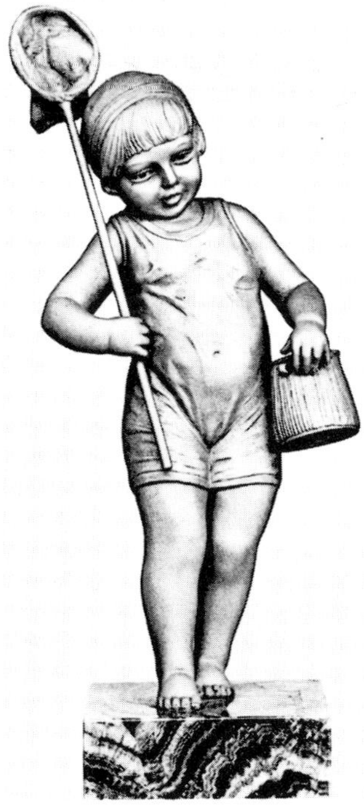

Fishing for Shrimps
24cm: 9½in.

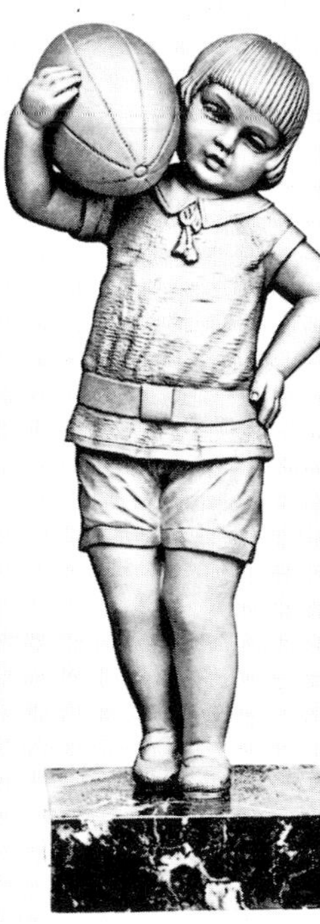

Rugby Man
22cm: 8¾in.

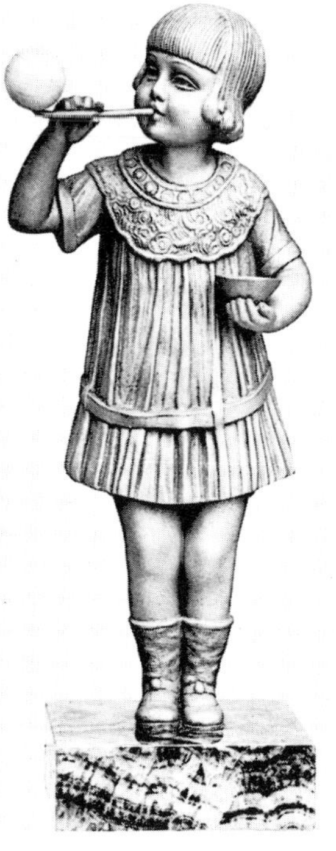

Bubble Blower
23cm: 9in.

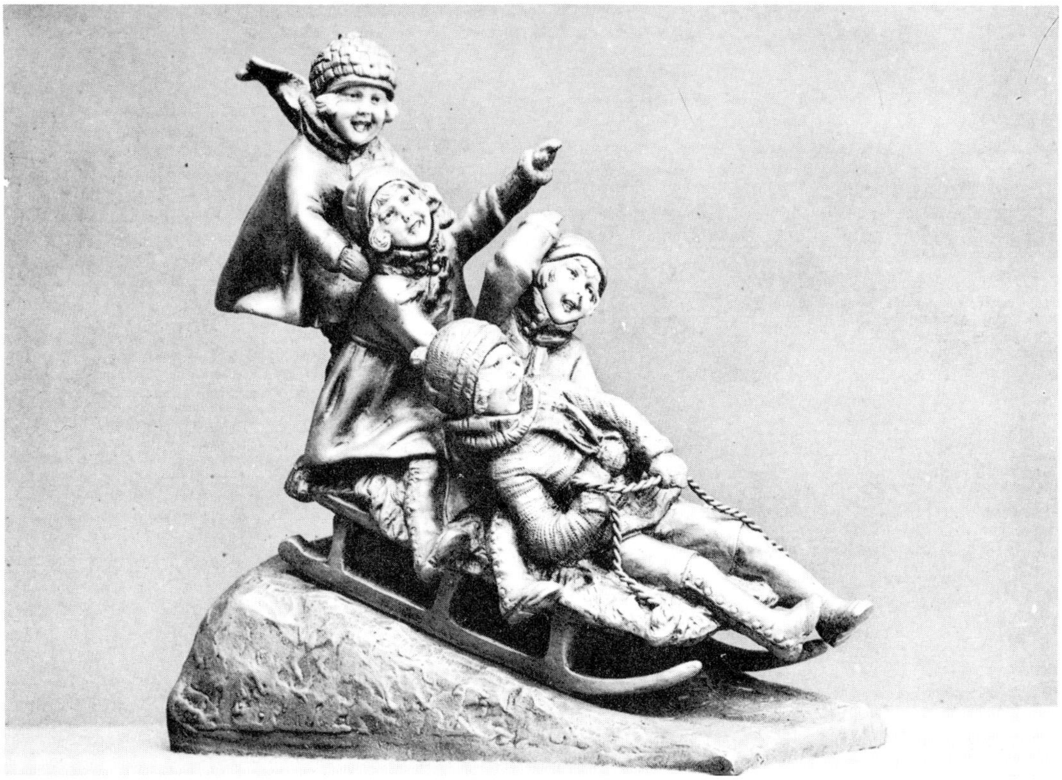

Toboggan, 25cm: 10in.

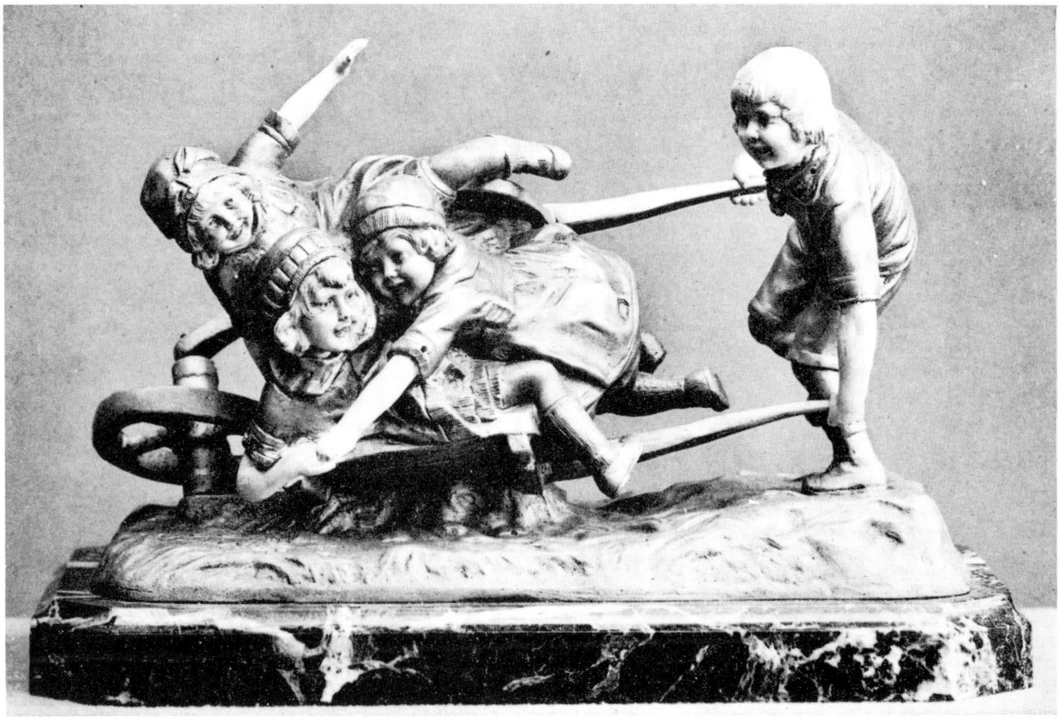

Wheelbarrow, 19cm: 7½in.

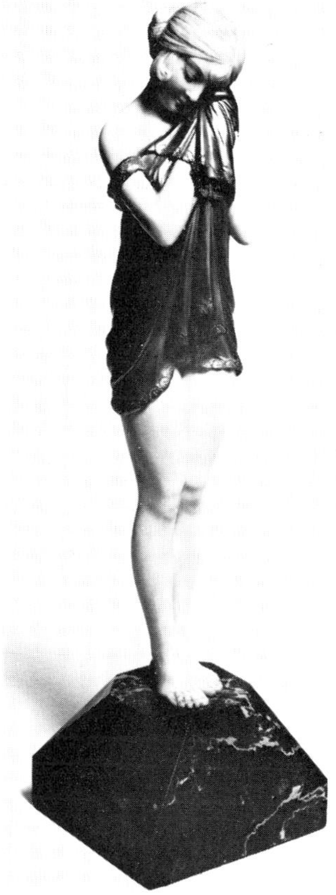

The Little Sad One
31cm:12in.
17cm:6¾in.

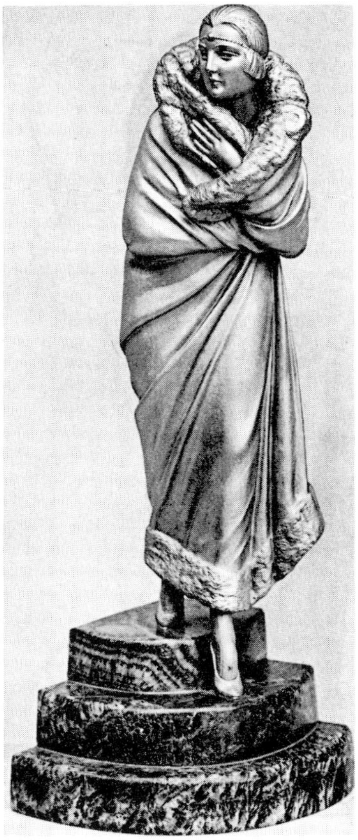

Leaving the Opera
36cm:14in.

Innocence
38cm:15in.
25cm:10in.
20cm:8in.
13cm:5in.

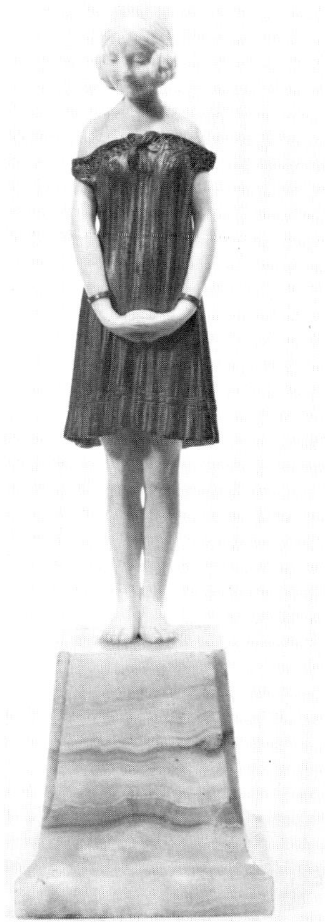

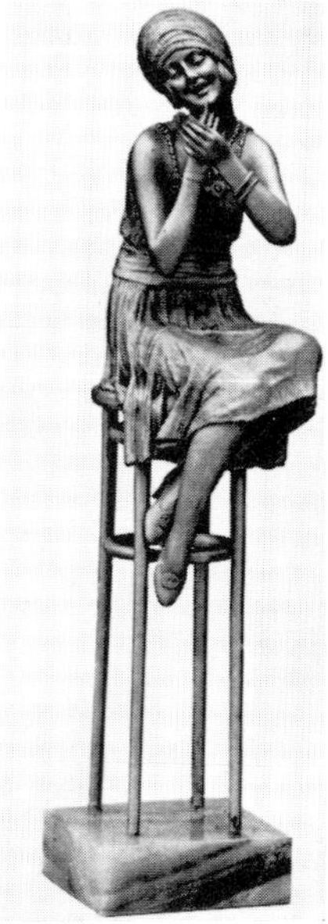

A Little Rouge
39cm:15¼in.

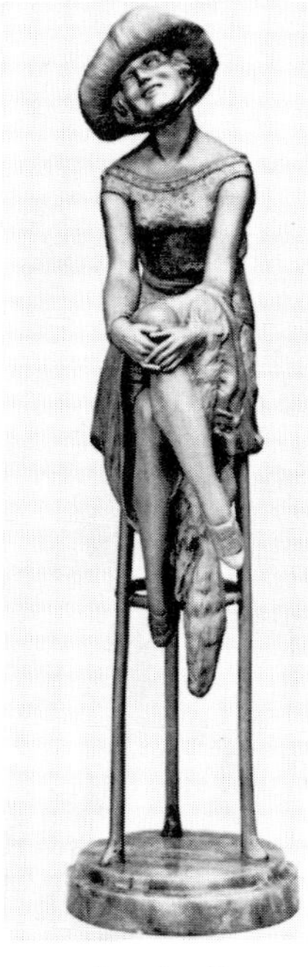

At the Bar
43cm:17in.

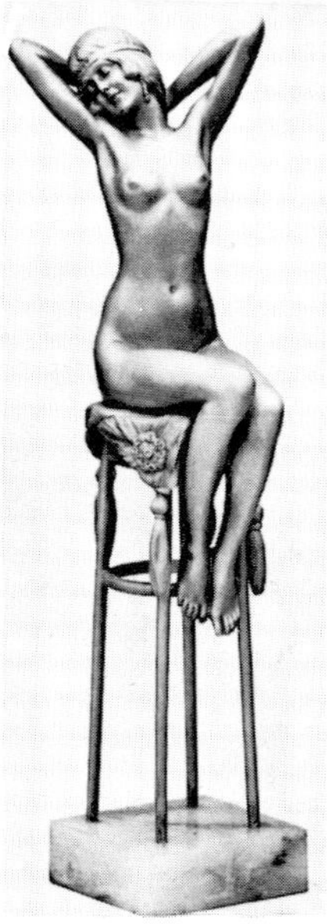

Awakening
39cm:15¼in.

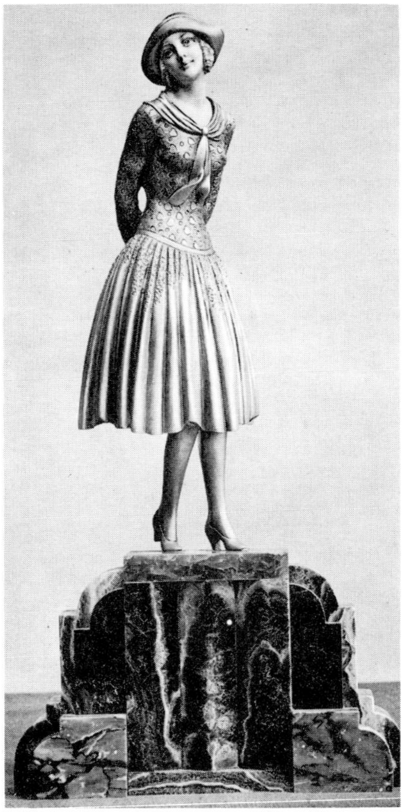

Simplicity
53cm:21in.
34cm:13½in.

The figures in the colour plate right are all by D.H. Chiparus. **Above:** *Friends Forever, 64cm:25¼in.; 43cm:17in.; 29cm:11½in.* **Below left:** *A Dancer, 58cm:23in.; 33cm:13in.* **Below right:** *Starlight, 58cm:23in.; 33cm:13in.*

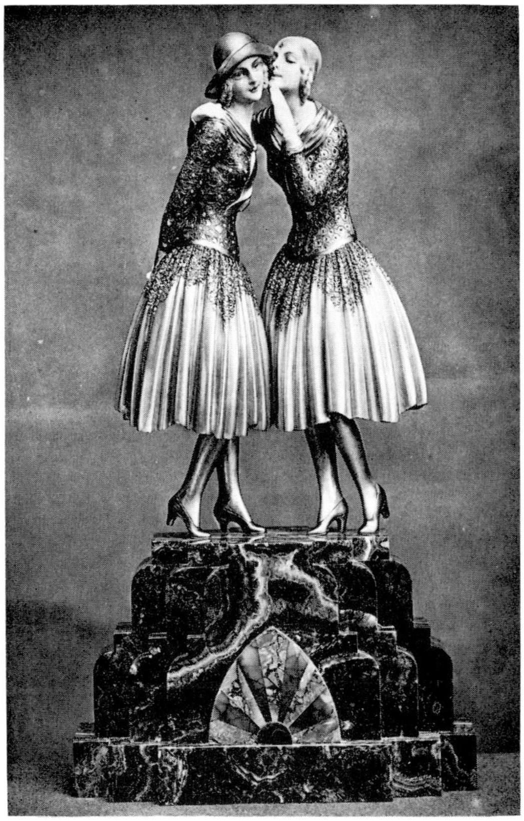

The Secret
56cm:22in.
38cm:15in.

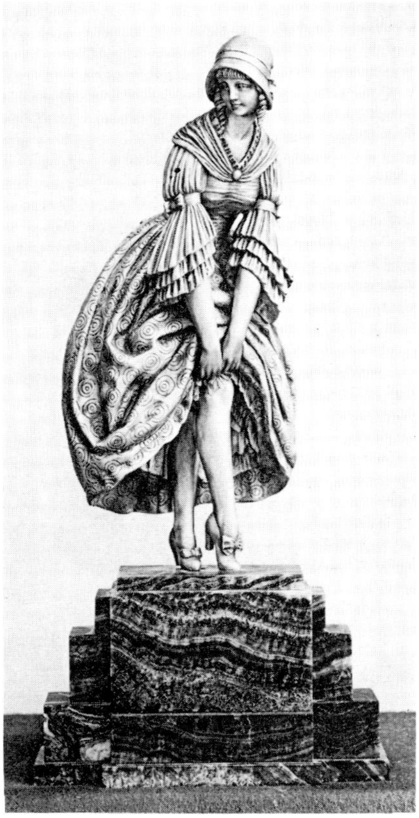

A Slight Accident
40cm:15¾in.
32cm:12½in.

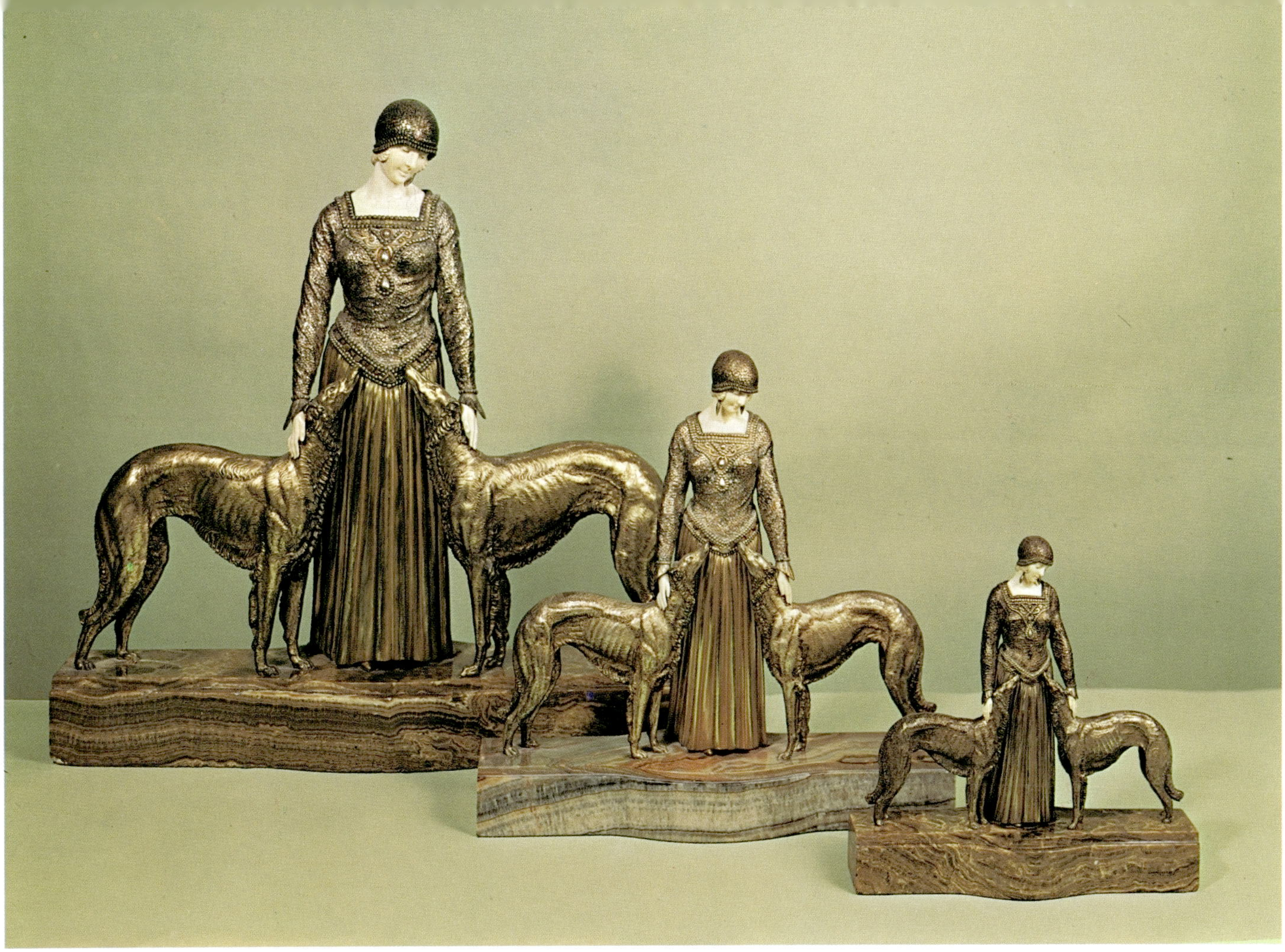

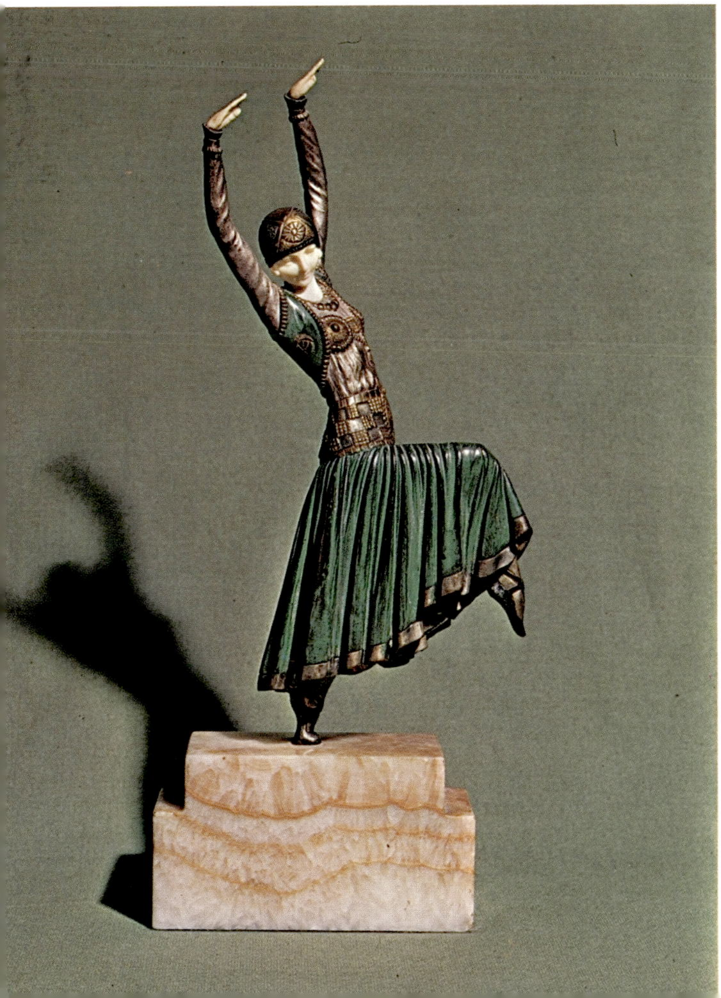

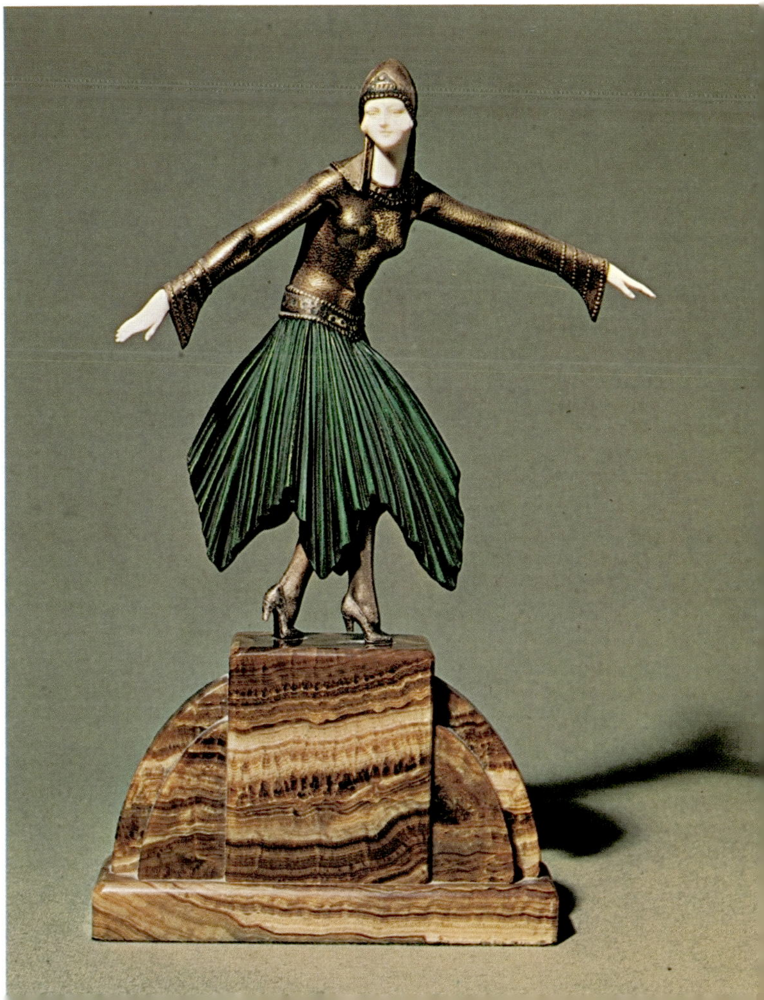

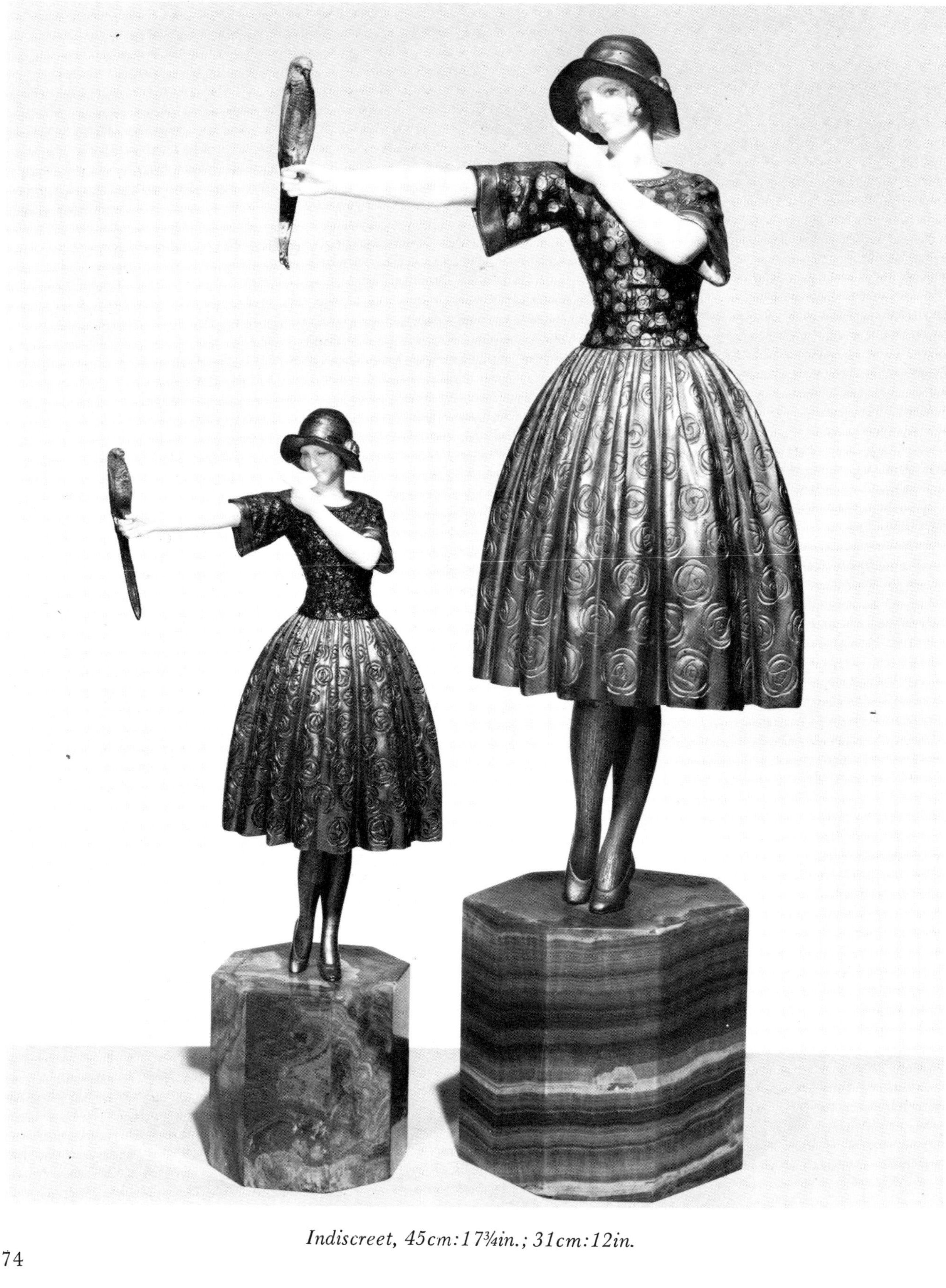

Indiscreet, 45cm:17¾in.; 31cm:12in.

The Squall
31cm:12½in.
19cm:7½in.

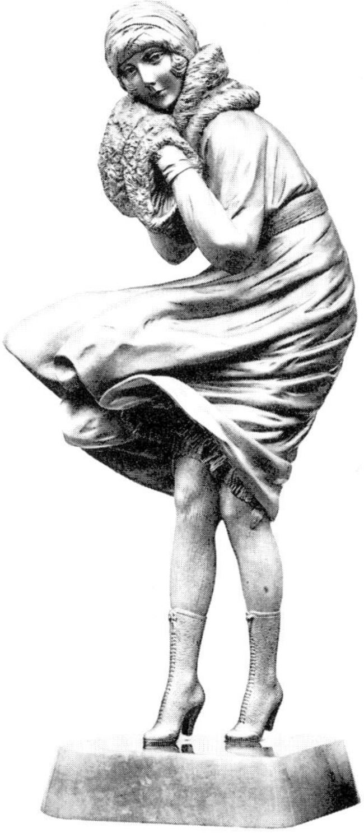

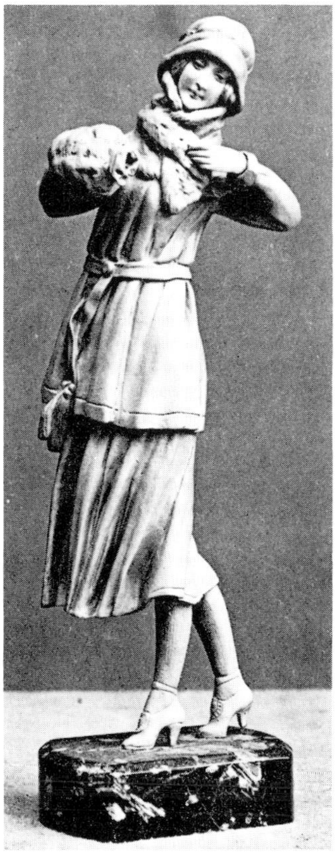

Winter
32cm:12½in.

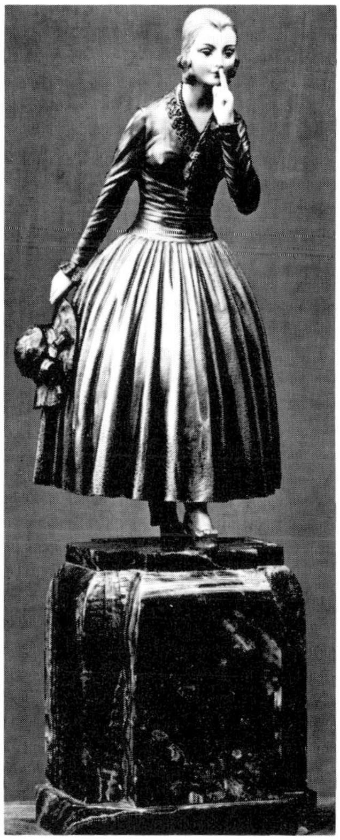

Hush
38cm:15in.

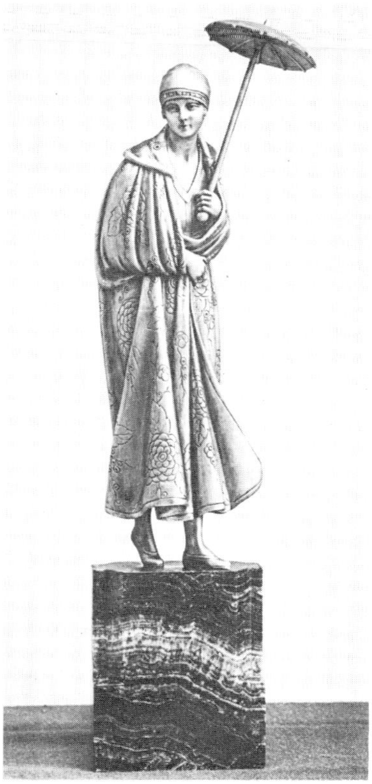

On the Beach
46cm:18in.

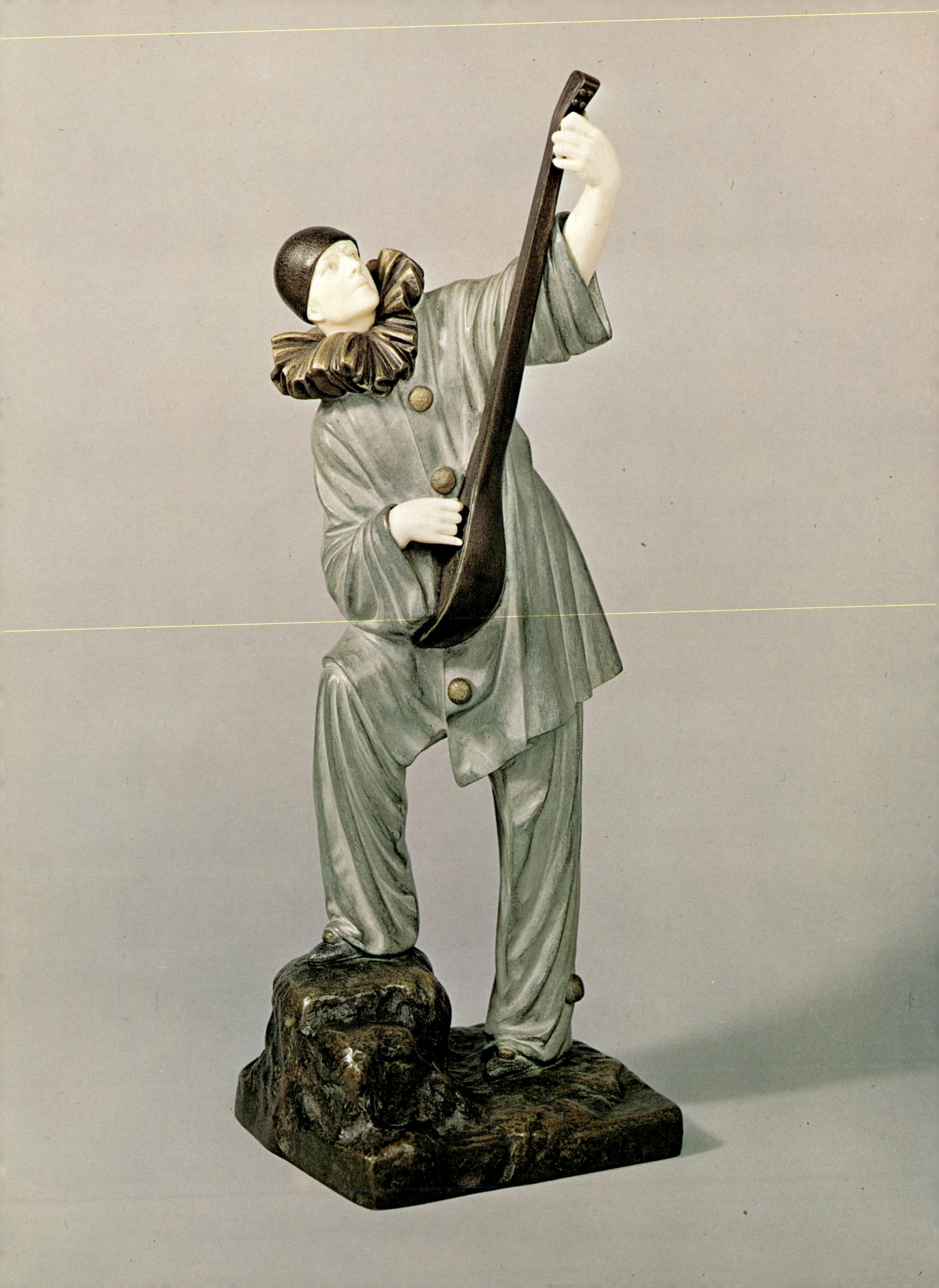

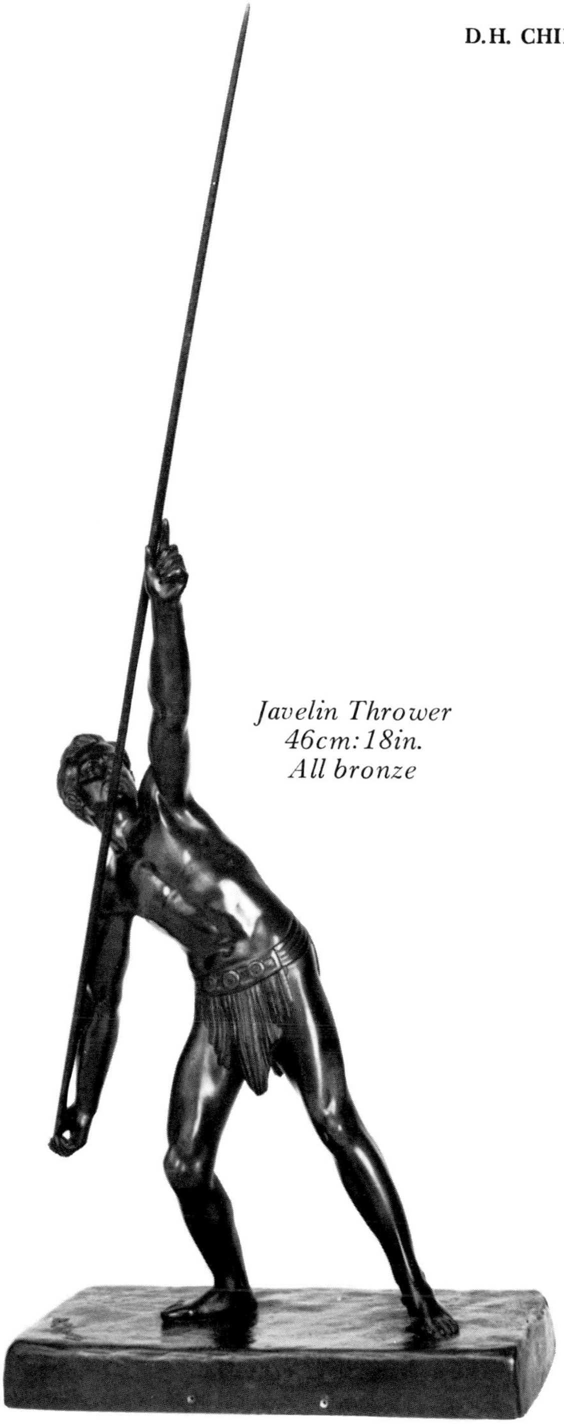

Javelin Thrower
46cm:18in.
All bronze

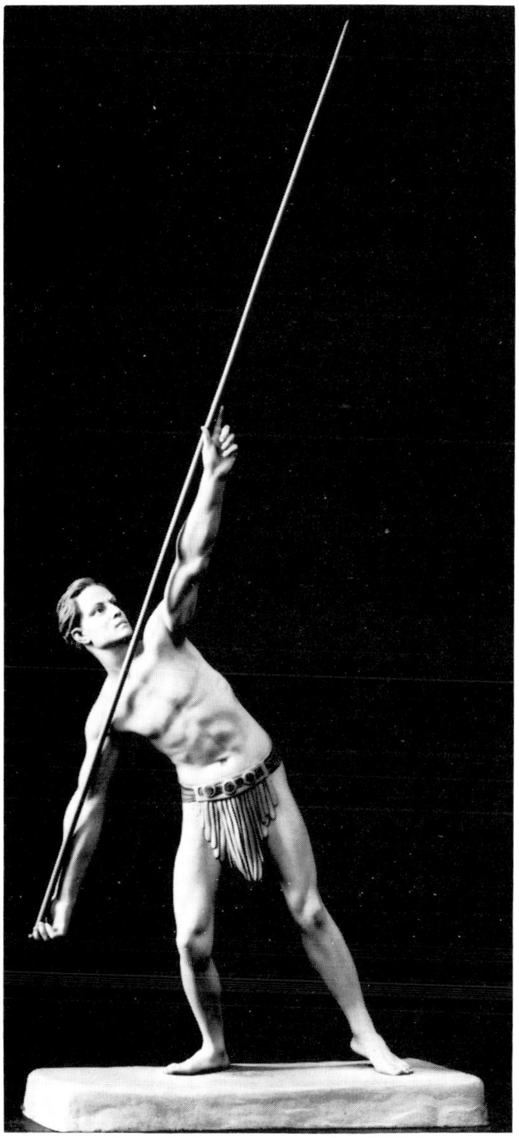

Javelin Thrower
100cm:39½in.
70cm:27½in.
50cm:19½in.
Bronze and ivory

Left: D.H. Chiparus. Pierrot,
40cm:15¾in.; 29cm:11½in.

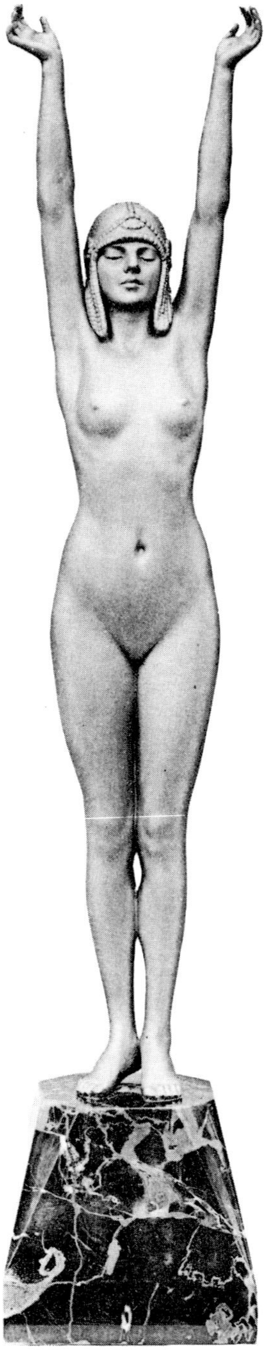

Invocation
48cm:18¾in.
24cm:9¼in.

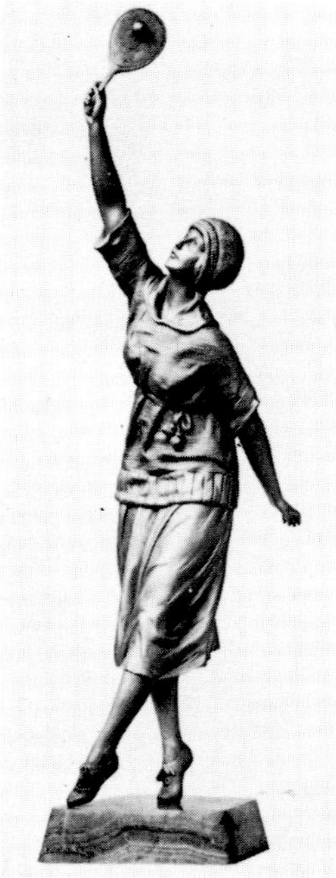

Tennis Player
43cm:17in.

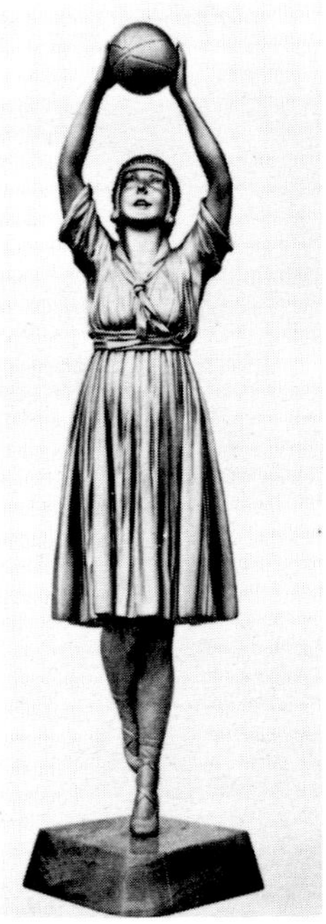

Ball Game
40cm:15¾in.

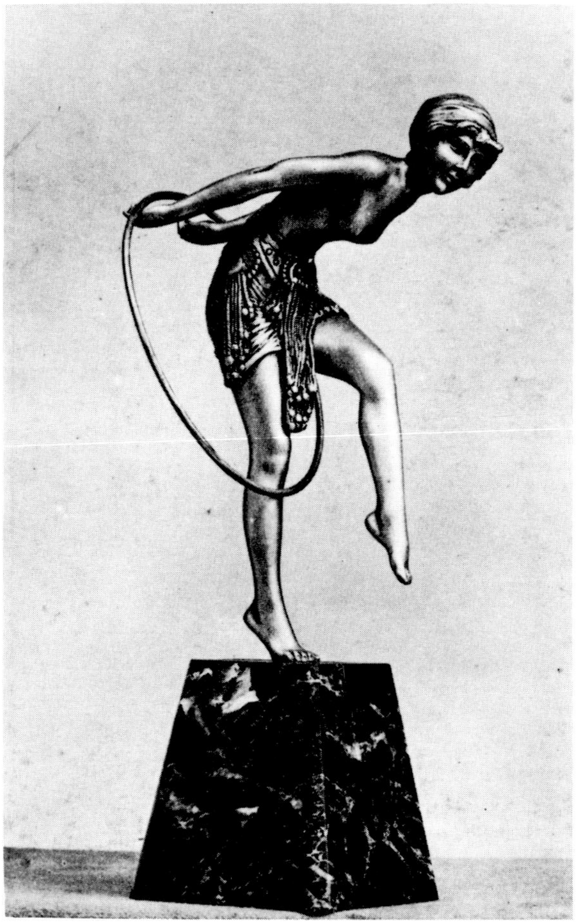

Young Girl, 27cm:10¾in.

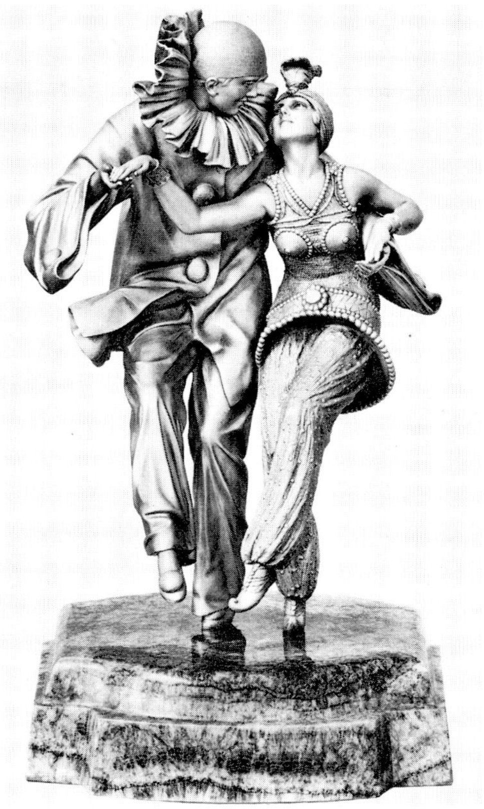

Fancy Dress
49cm:19¼in.
33cm:13in.

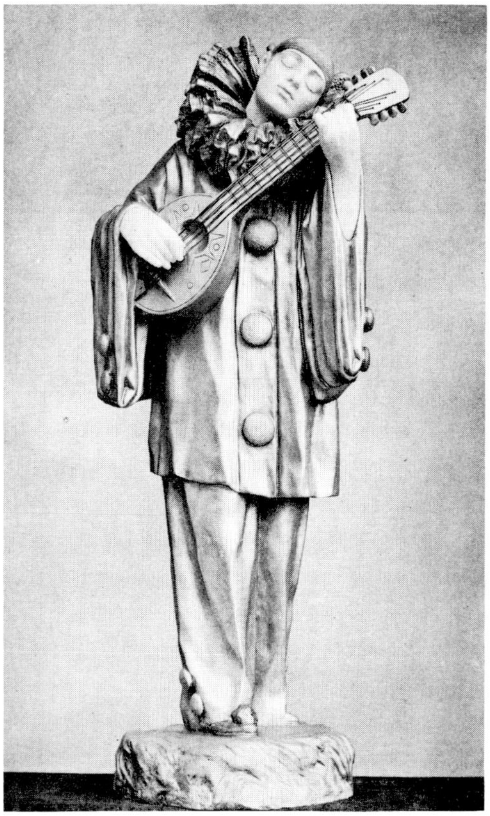

The Clown's Dream
78cm:30½in.

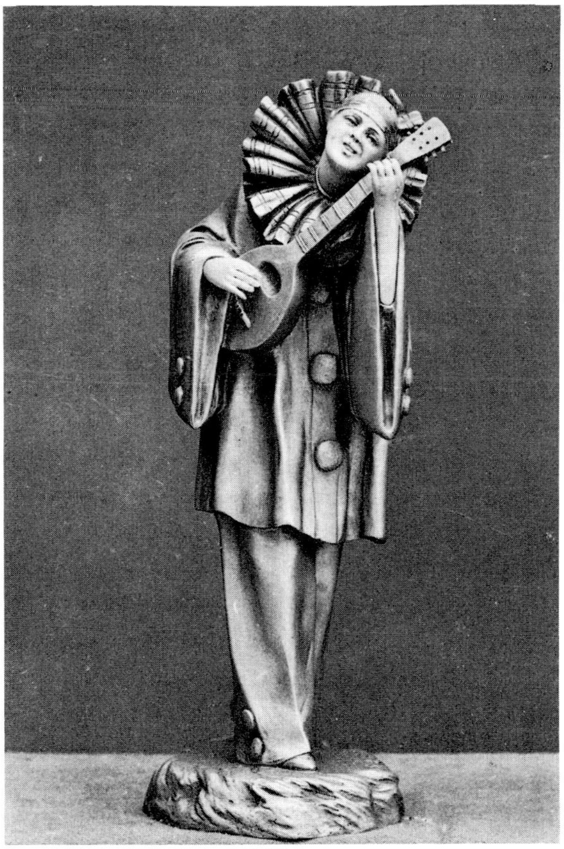

Clown
33cm:13in.

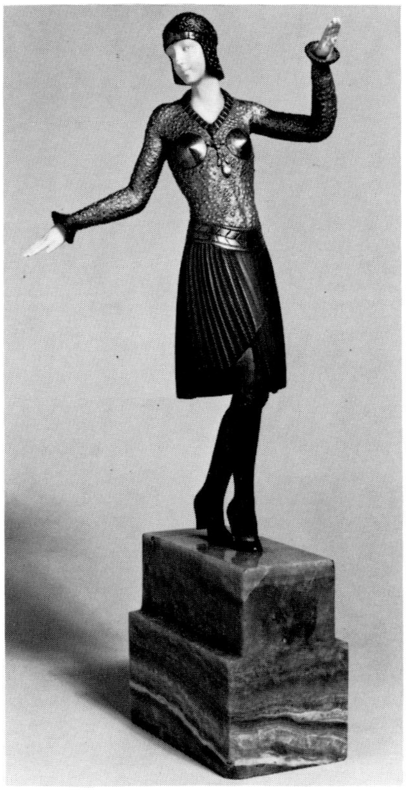

Egyptian Style Dancer
34cm:13½in.

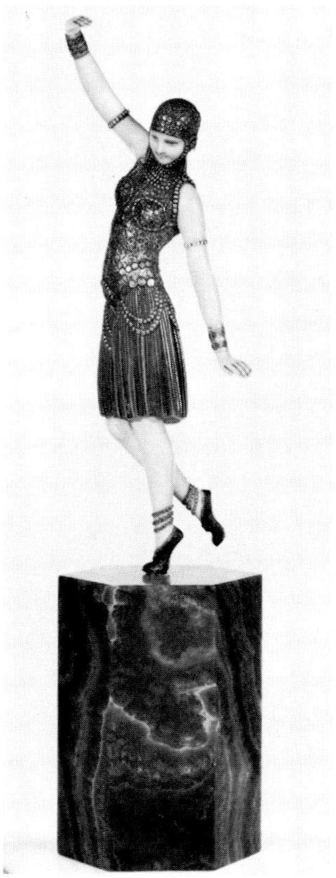

Dancer of Lebanon
37cm:14½in.

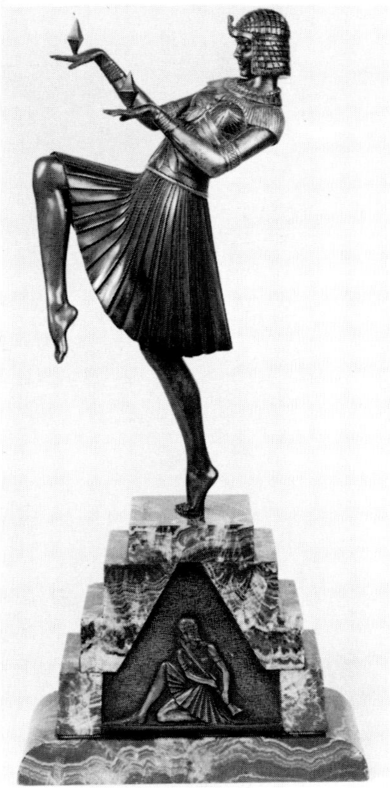

Nubian Dancer
39cm:15½in.

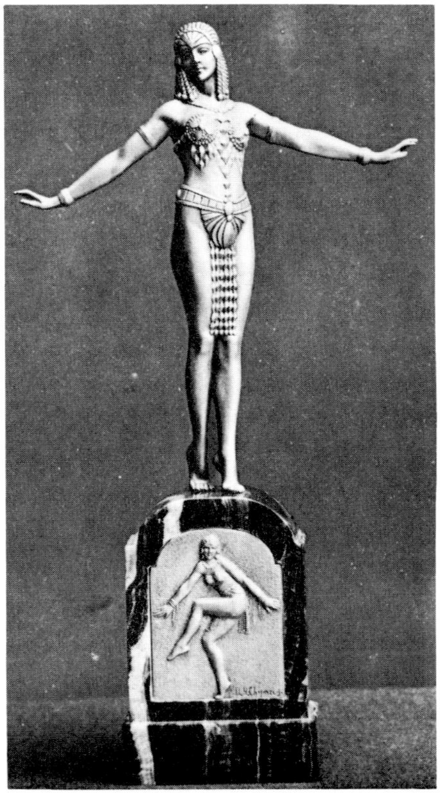

Syrian Dancer
34cm:13½in.

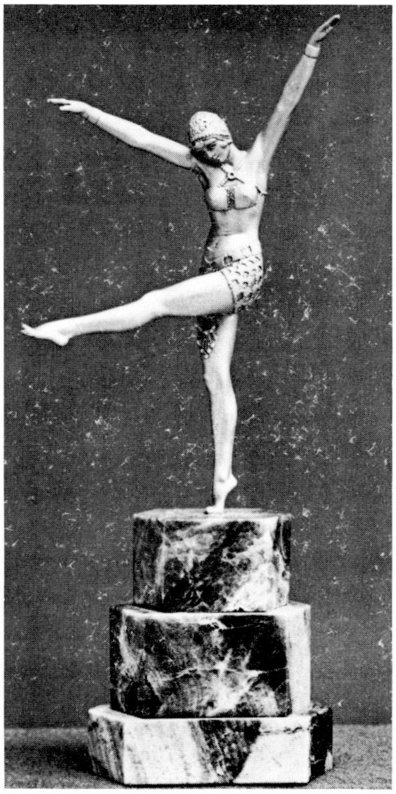

Dancer of Olynthus
37cm:14½in.

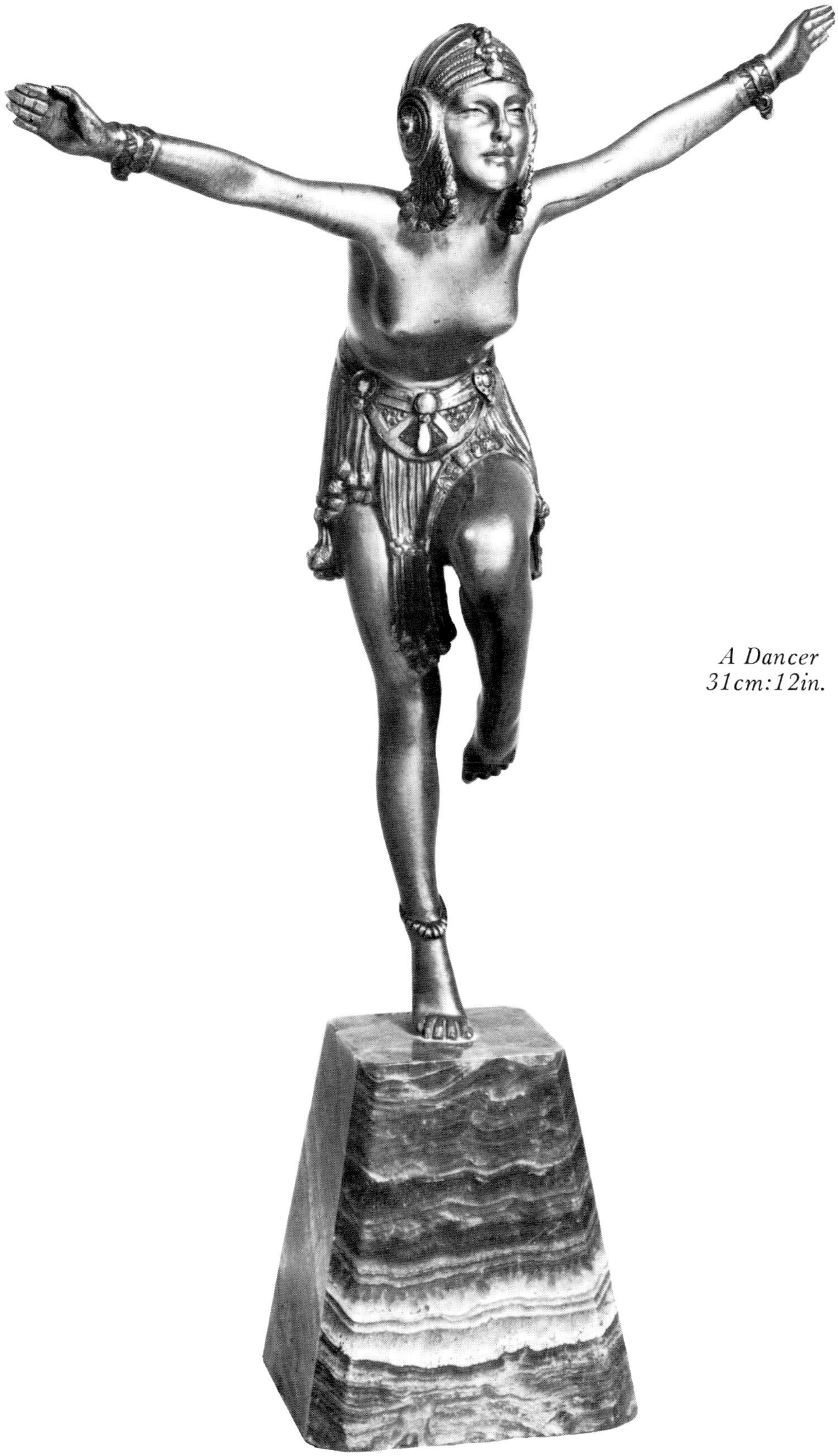

A Dancer
31cm:12in.

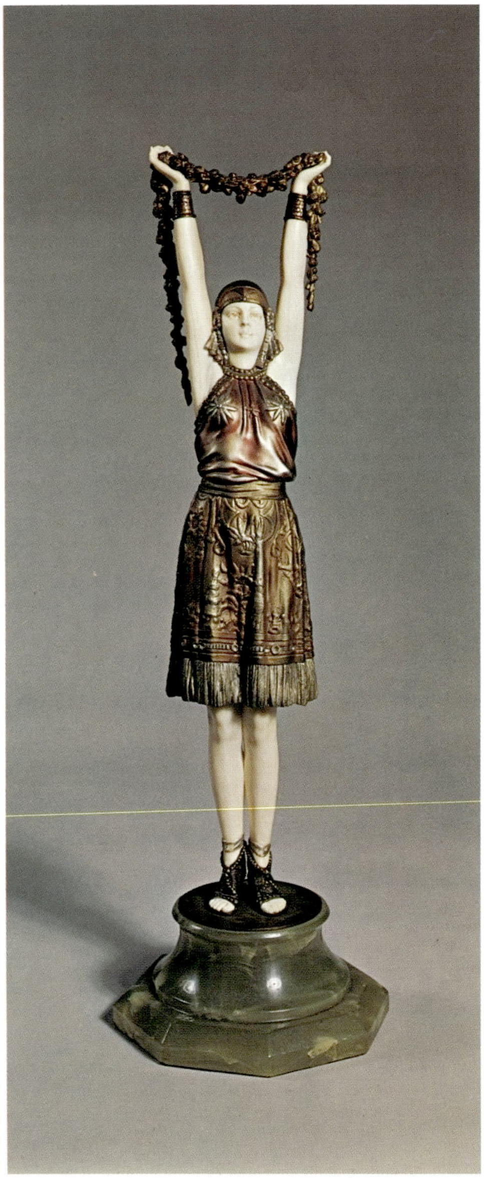

First Flowers
42cm: 16½in.

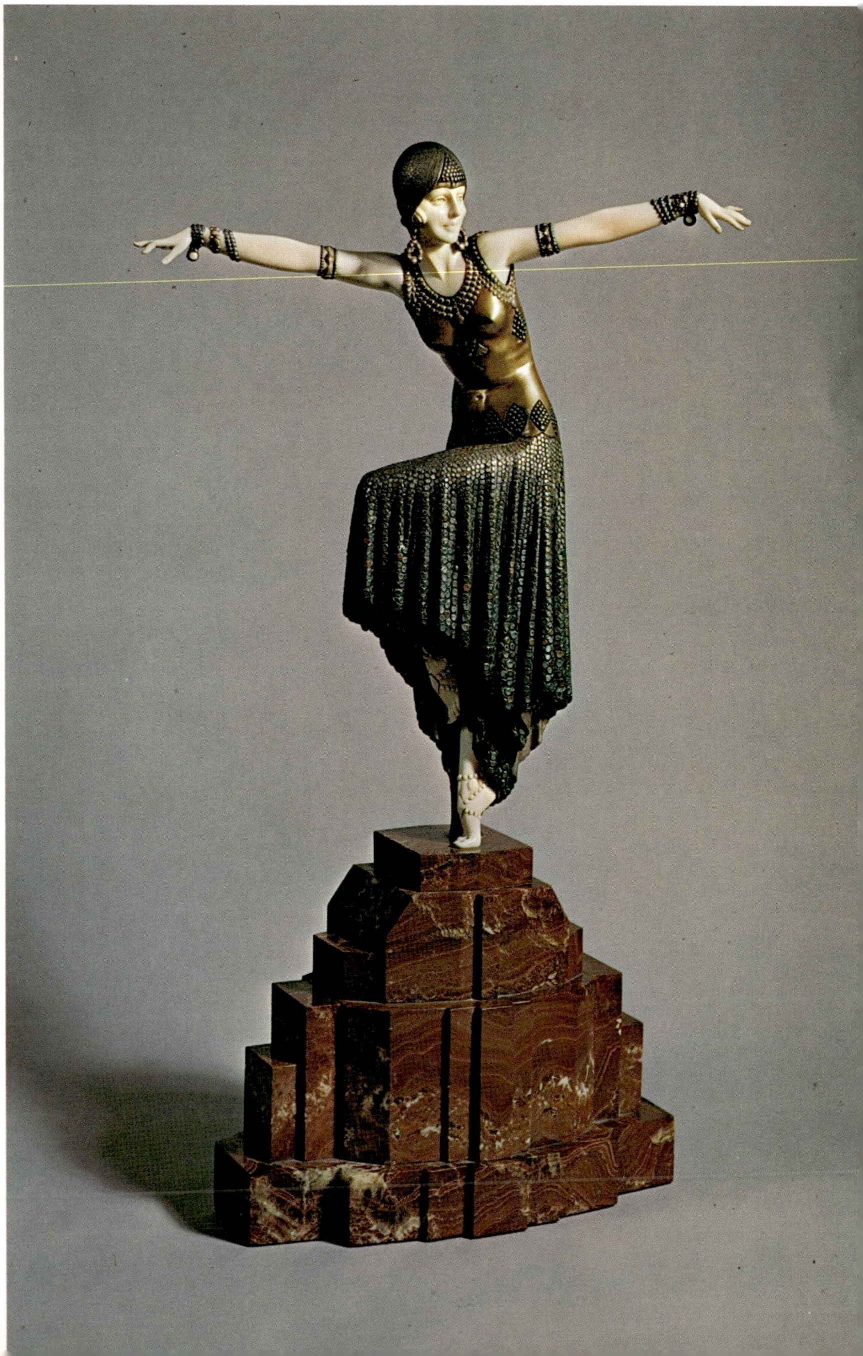

A Dancer
60cm: 23½in.
42cm: 16½in.

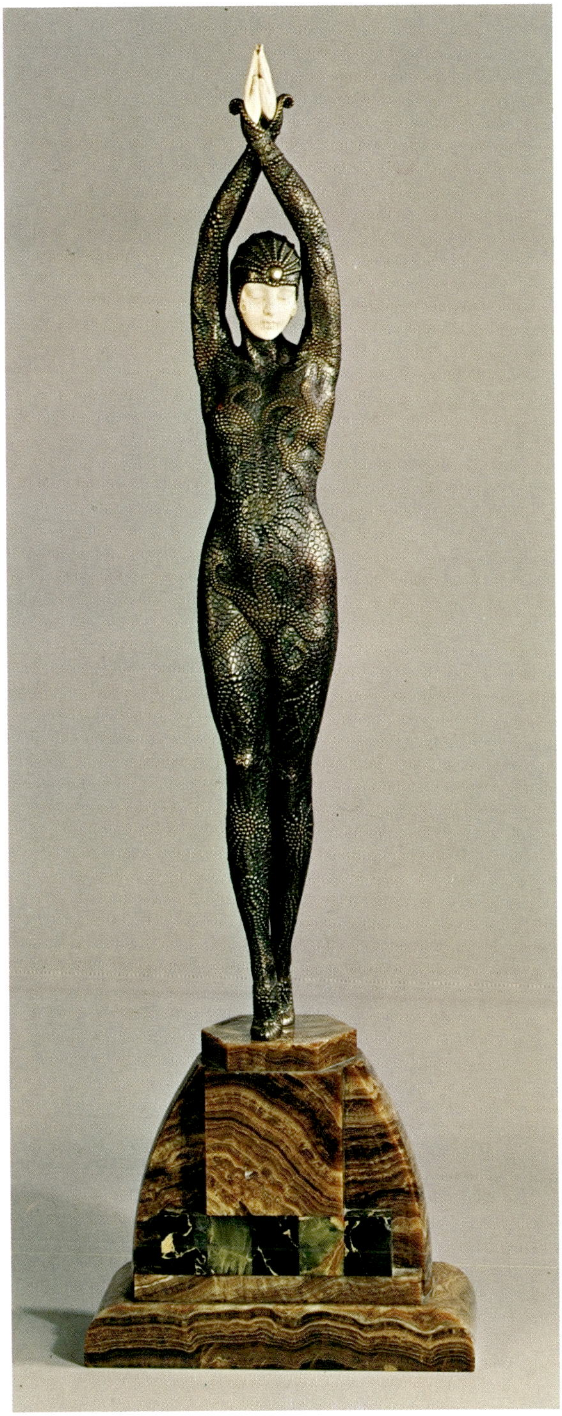

Starfish
70cm: 27½in.
39cm: 15¼in.

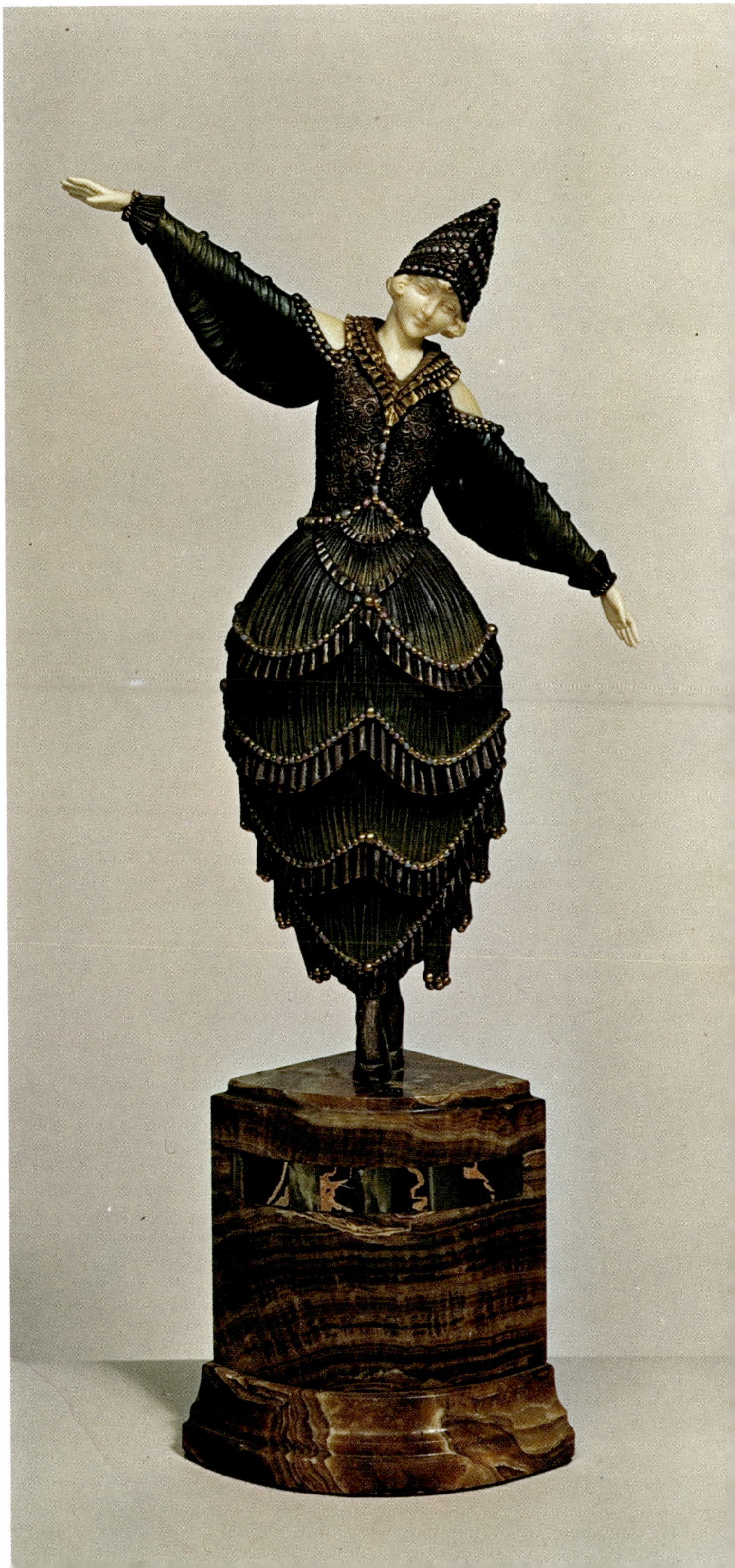

Carnival
43cm: 17in.

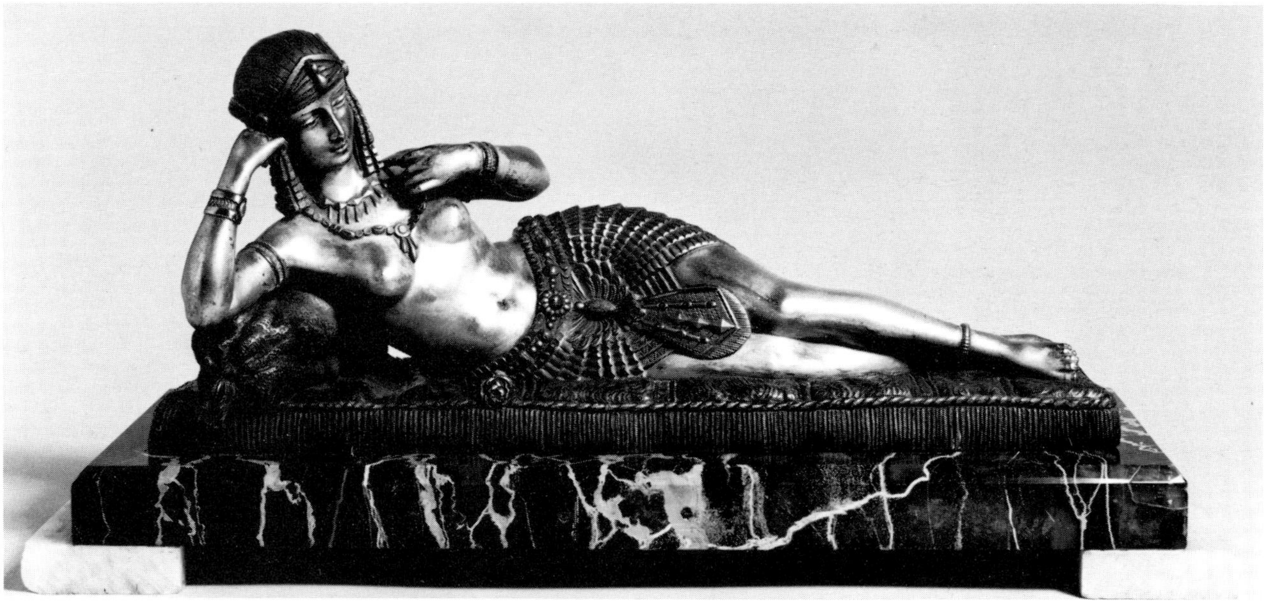

Cleopatra, 20cm:8in.

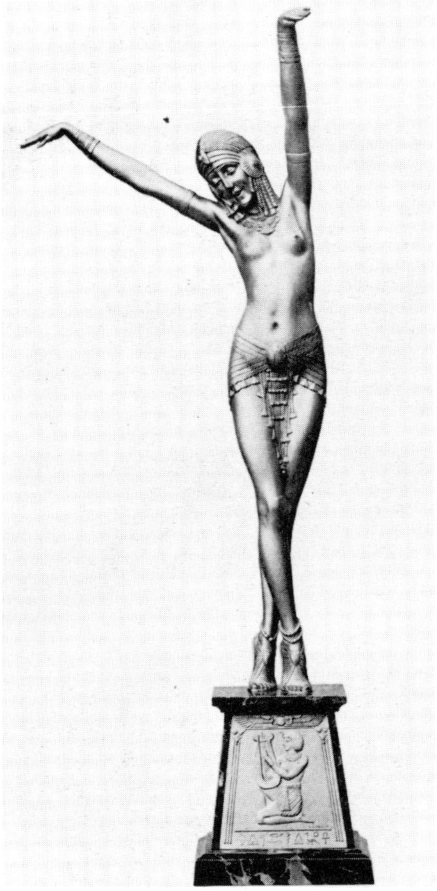

Egyptian Dancer
73cm:28¾in.
54cm:21¼in.
30cm:12in.

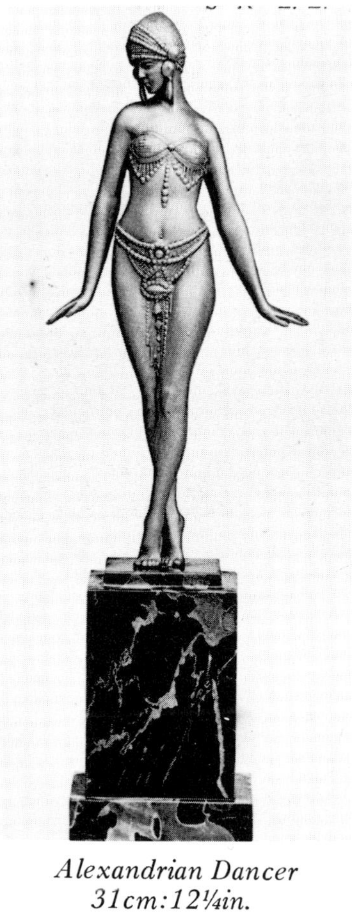

Alexandrian Dancer
31cm:12¼in.

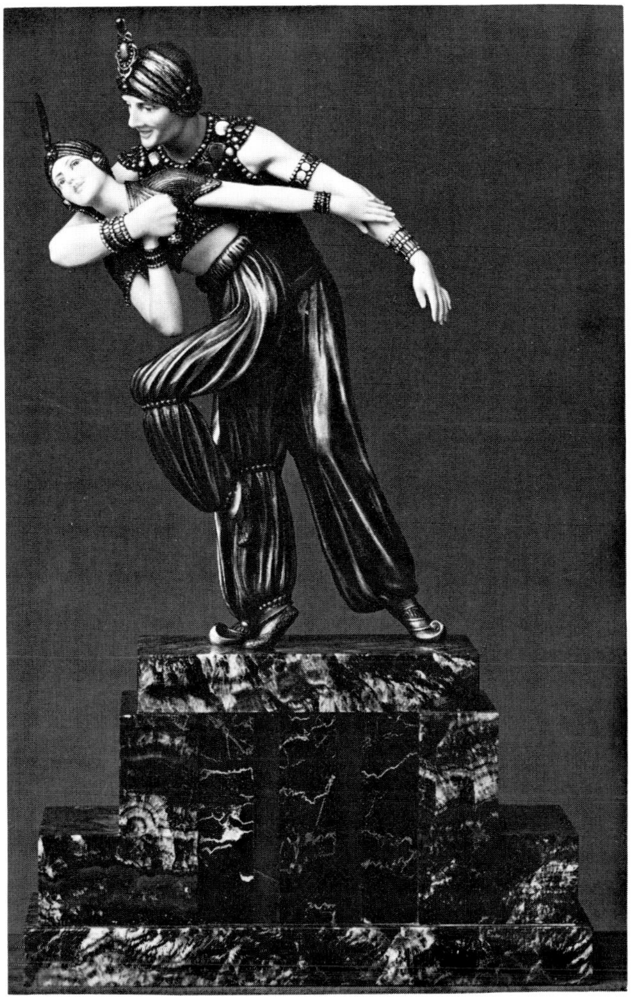

Persian Dance, 51cm:20in.

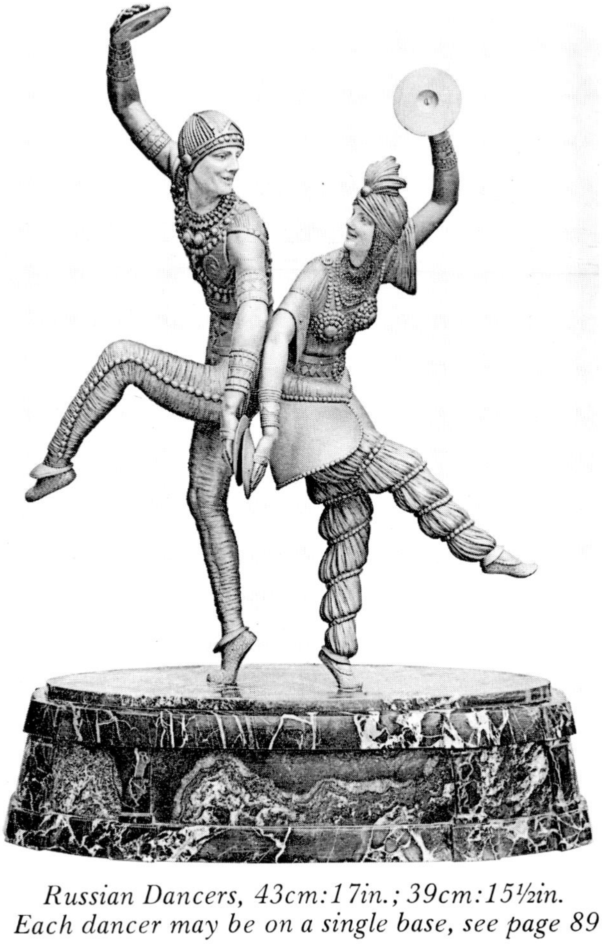

Russian Dancers, 43cm:17in.; 39cm:15½in.
Each dancer may be on a single base, *see page 89*

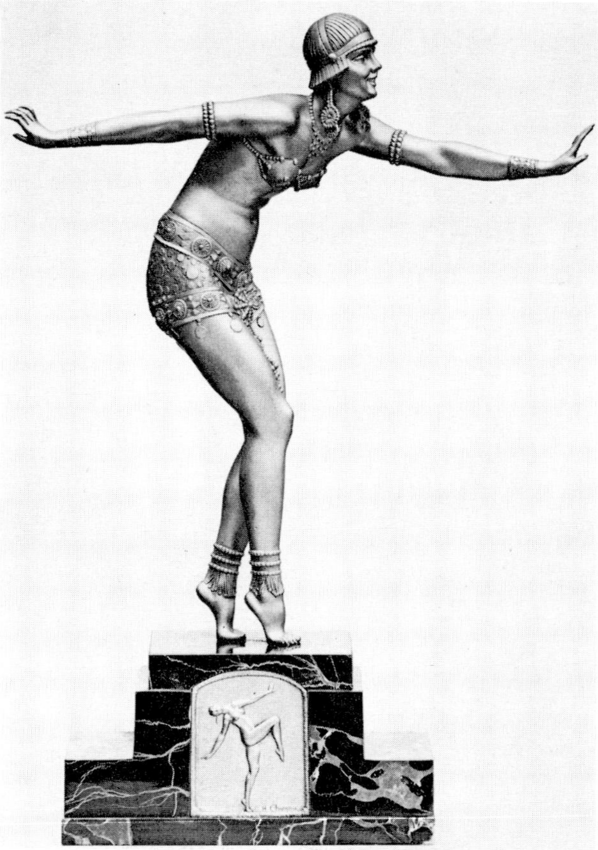

Phœnician Dancer
55cm:21½in.

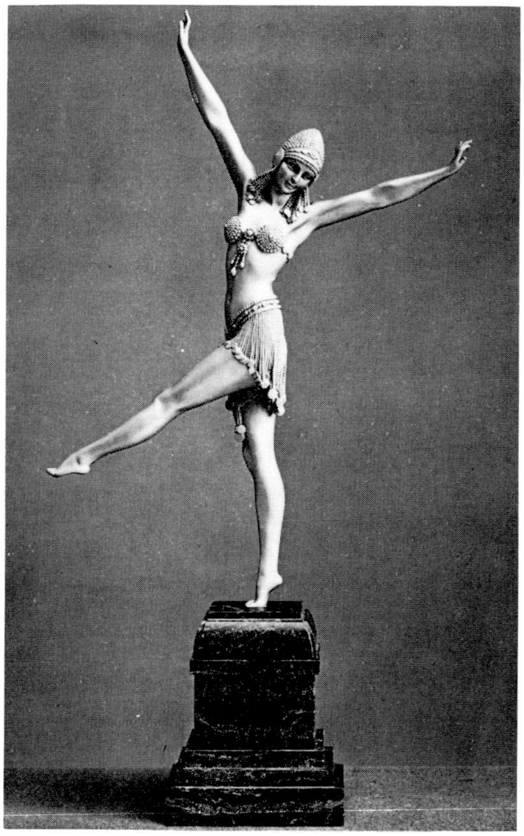

Dancer of Palmyra
67cm:26¼in.
44cm:17¼in.
33cm:13in.

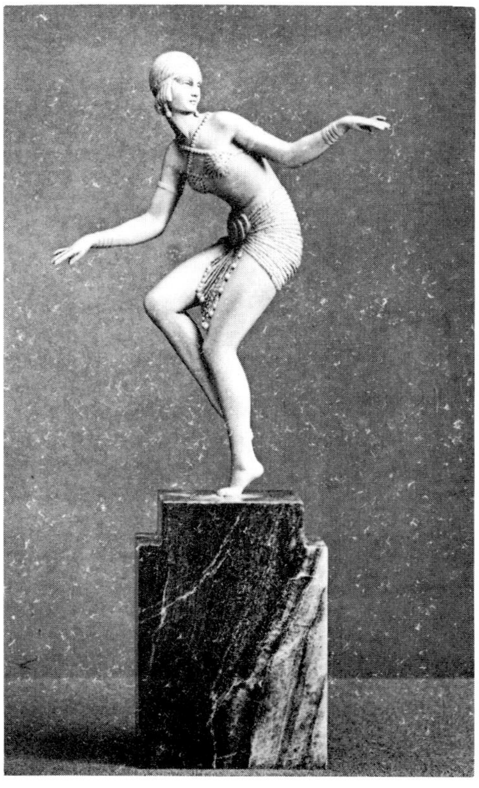

Delhi Dancer, 36cm:14in.

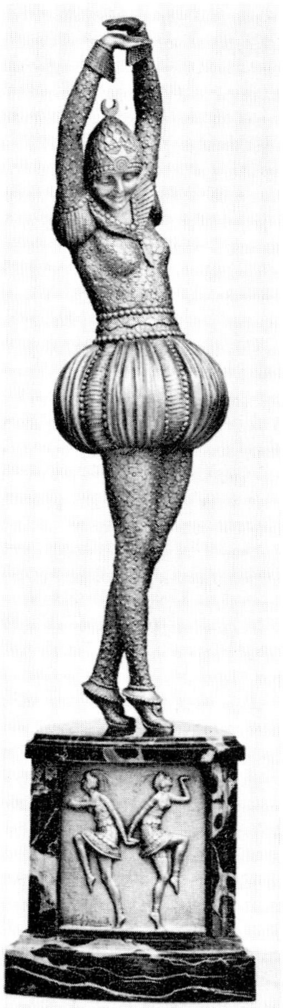

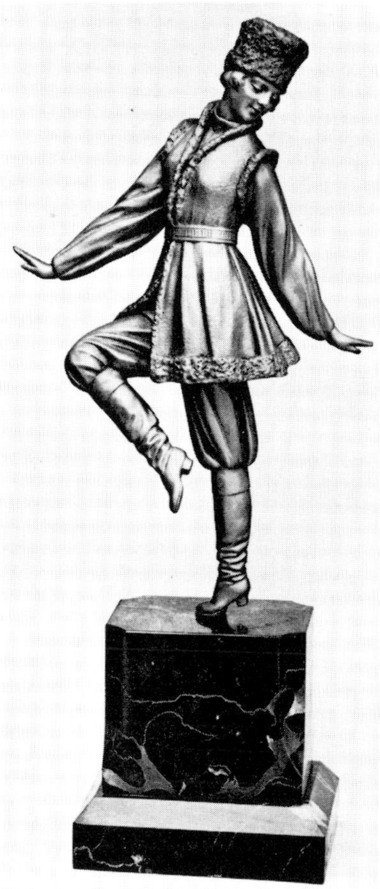

Russian Peasant Dancer
41cm:16in.; 26cm:10¼in.

Bayadère
52cm:20½in.

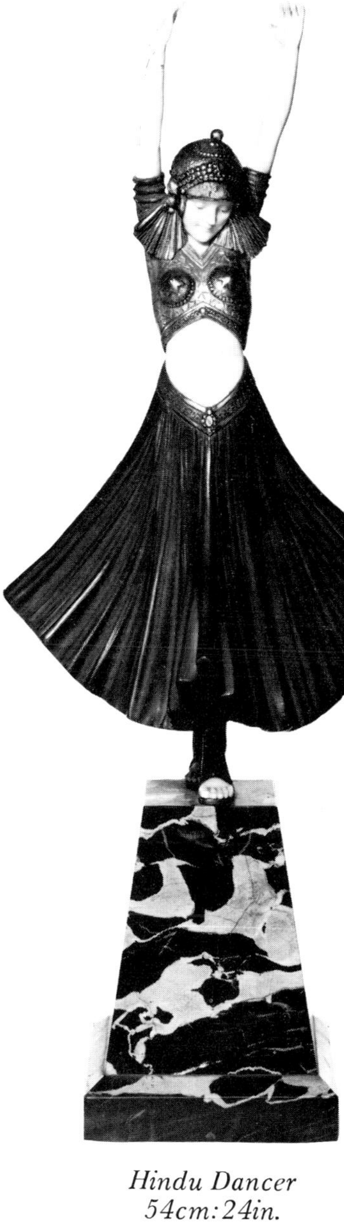

Hindu Dancer
54cm:24in.
38cm:15in.

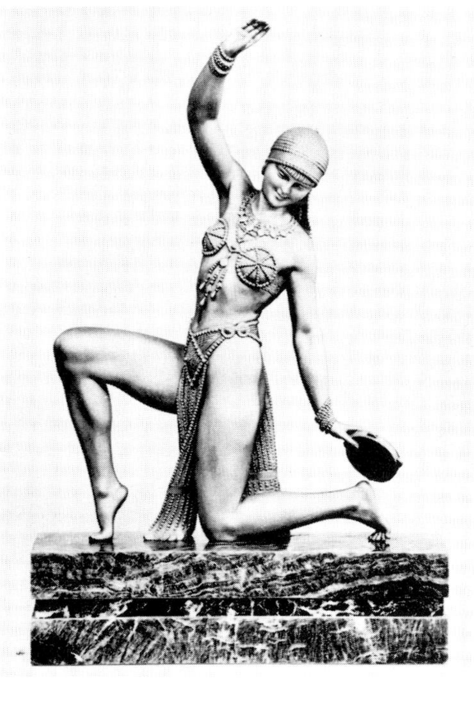

Kashmiri
Dancer
57cm:22½in.

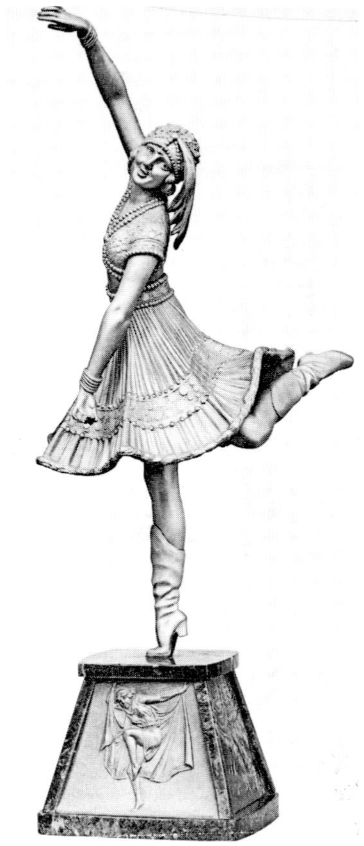

Cossack Dancer
55cm:21¾in.

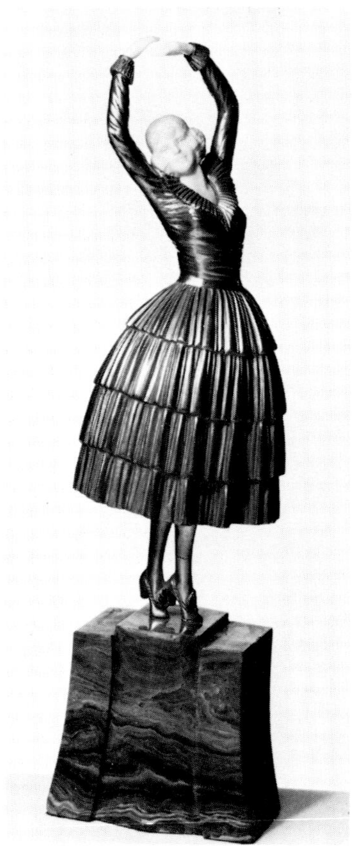

Ballet Dancer
34cm:13¼in.

Right: D.H. Chiparus. Russian Dancers taken from Scheherazade, *depicting Nijinsky with Ida Rubinstein. 43cm:17in.; 39cm:15½in.* *See also page 85.*

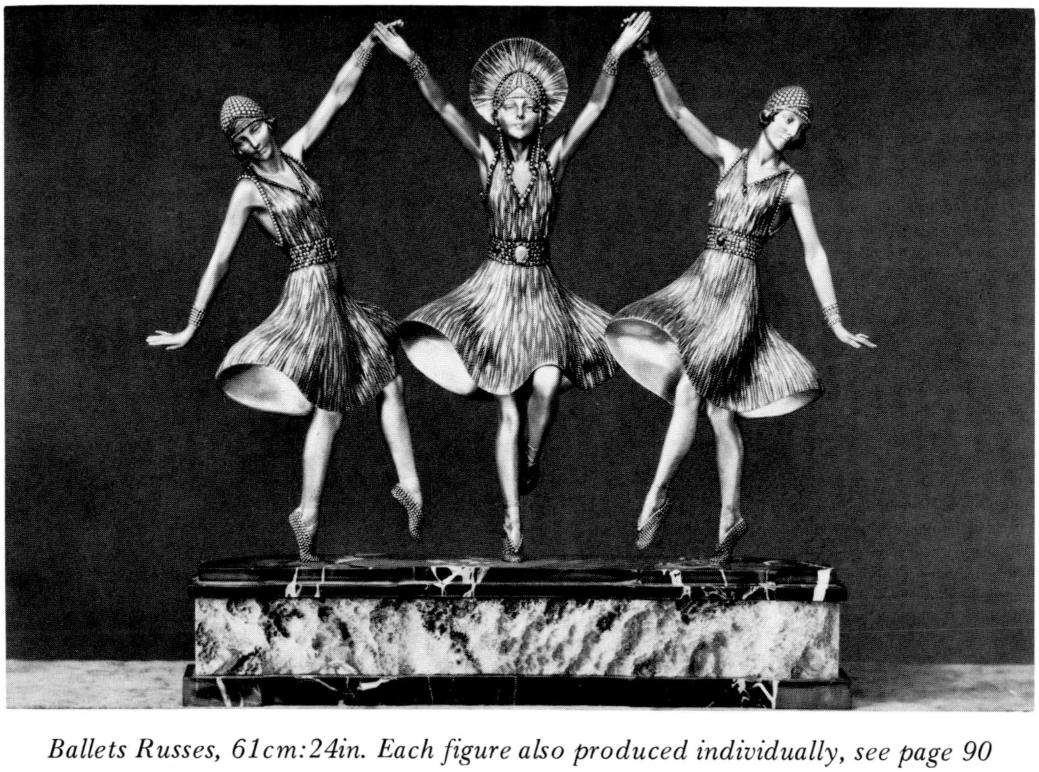

Ballets Russes, 61cm:24in. Each figure also produced individually, *see page 90*

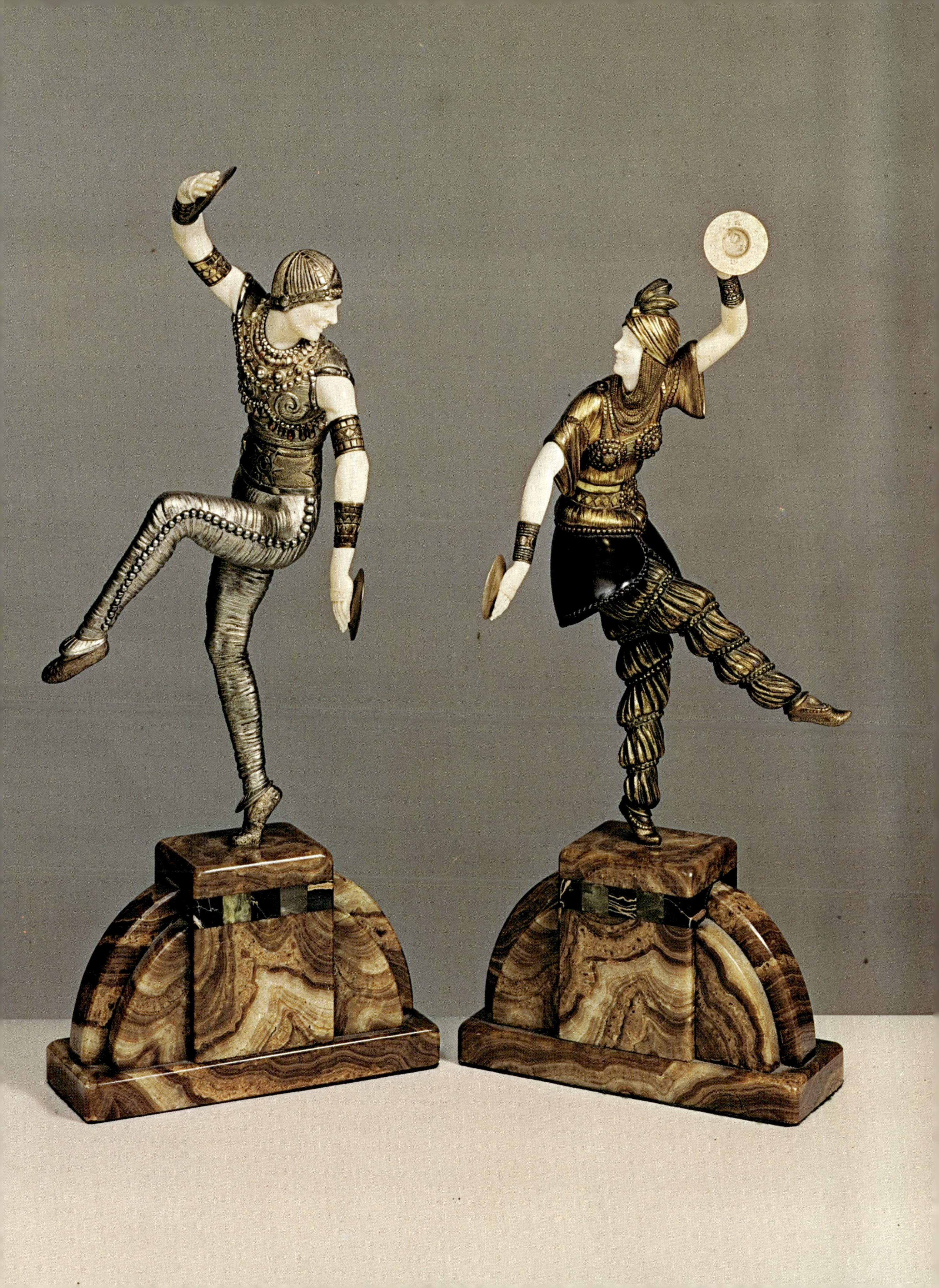

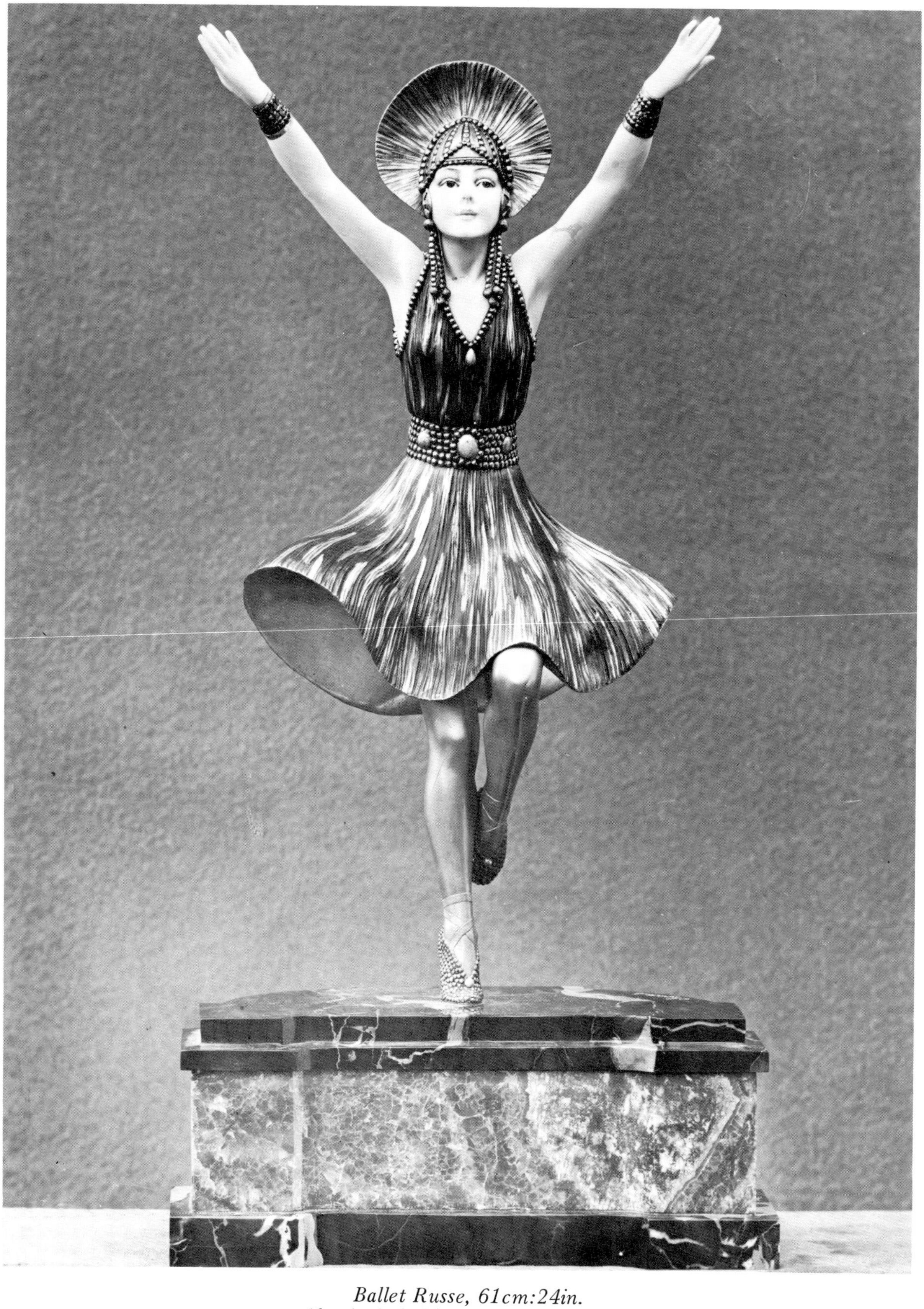

Ballet Russe, 61cm:24in.
Also included in a group, see page 88

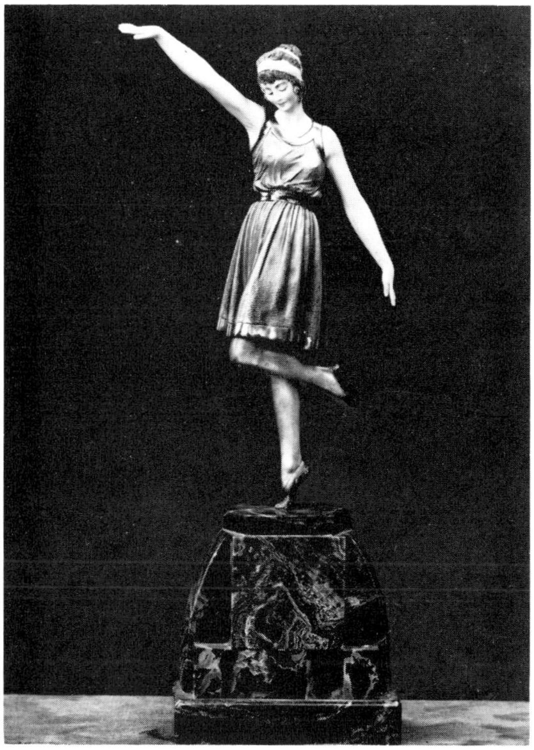

Old Style Dance, 42cm:16½in.

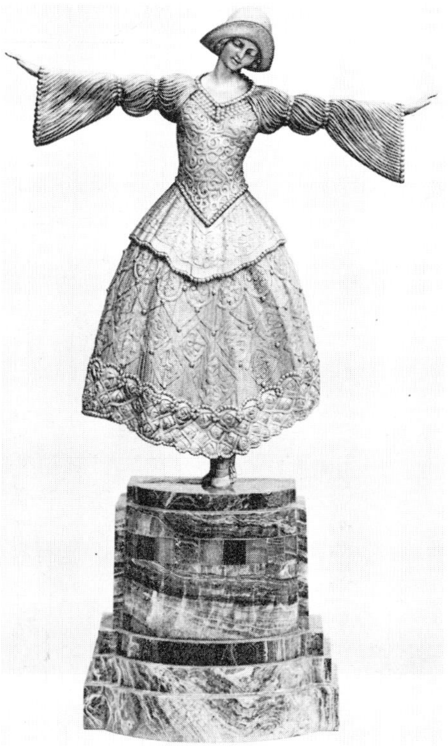

The Nimble Dancer
47cm:18½in.

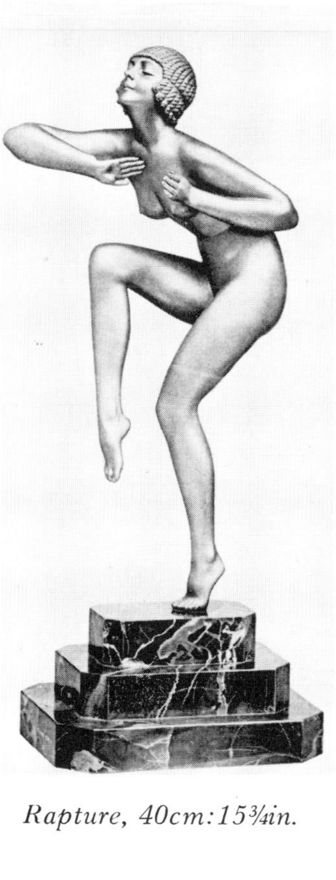

Rapture, 40cm:15¾in.

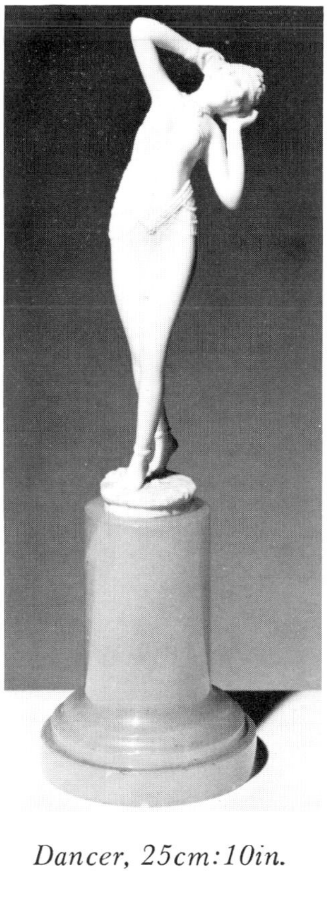

Dancer, 25cm:10in.

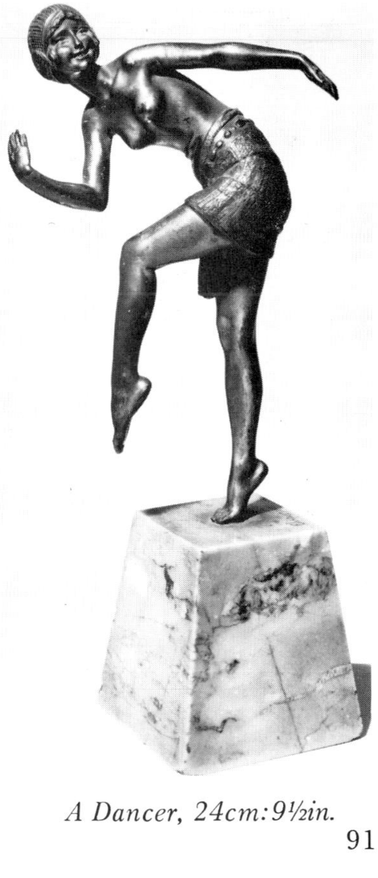

A Dancer, 24cm:9½in.

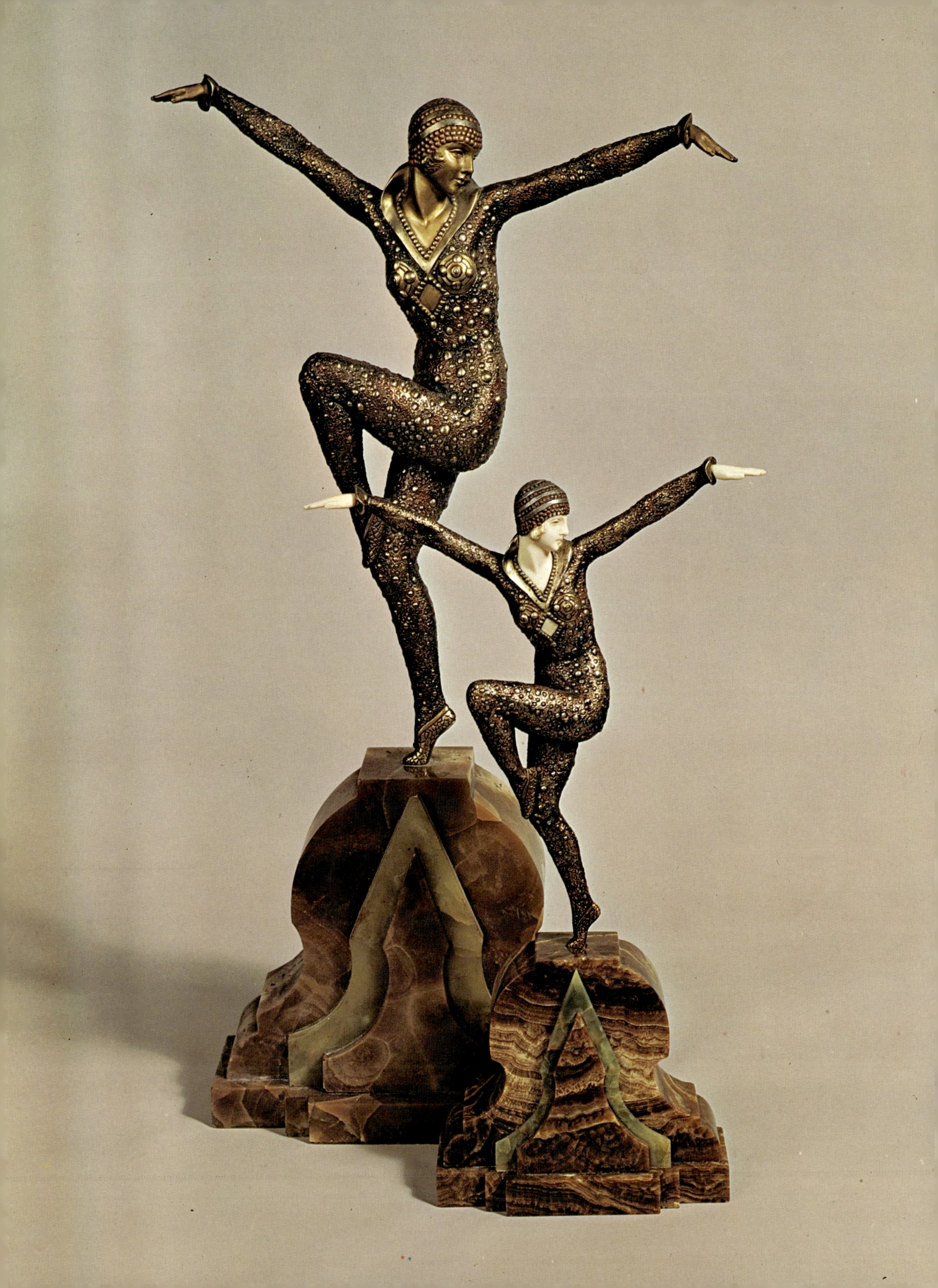

Left: D.H. Chiparus
Dancer of Kapurthala
55cm:21¾in.; 30cm:12in.

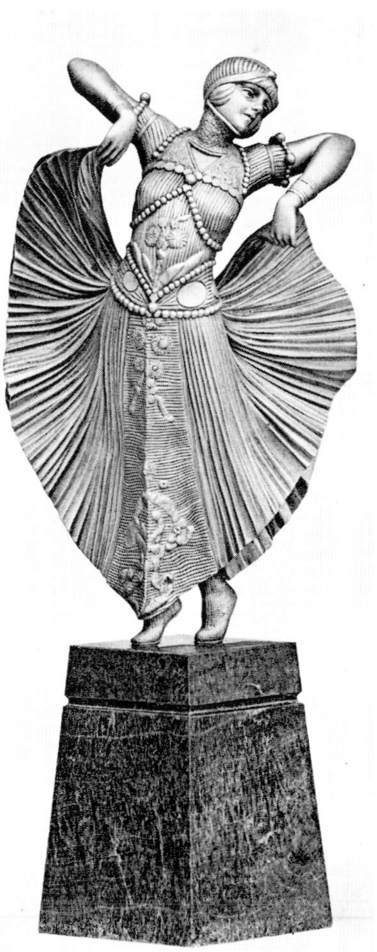

Butterfly Dance, 48cm:19in.

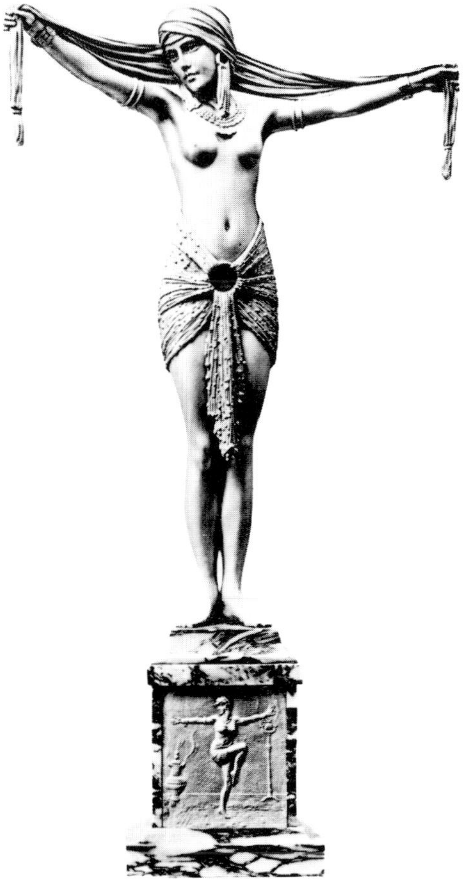

Scarf Dancer
67cm:26¼in.

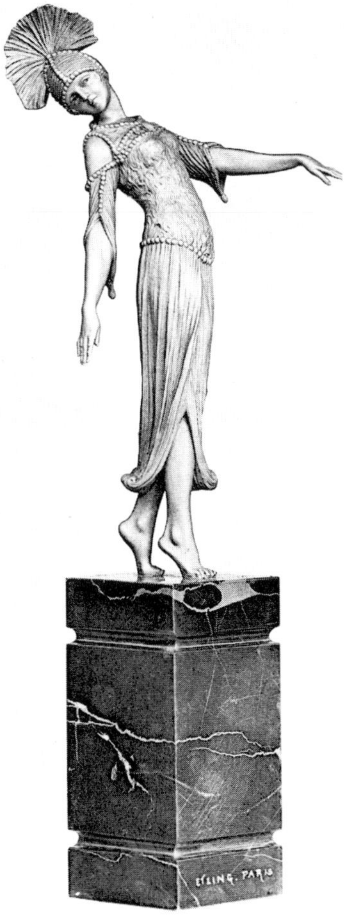

Revue Dancer, 35cm:13¾in.

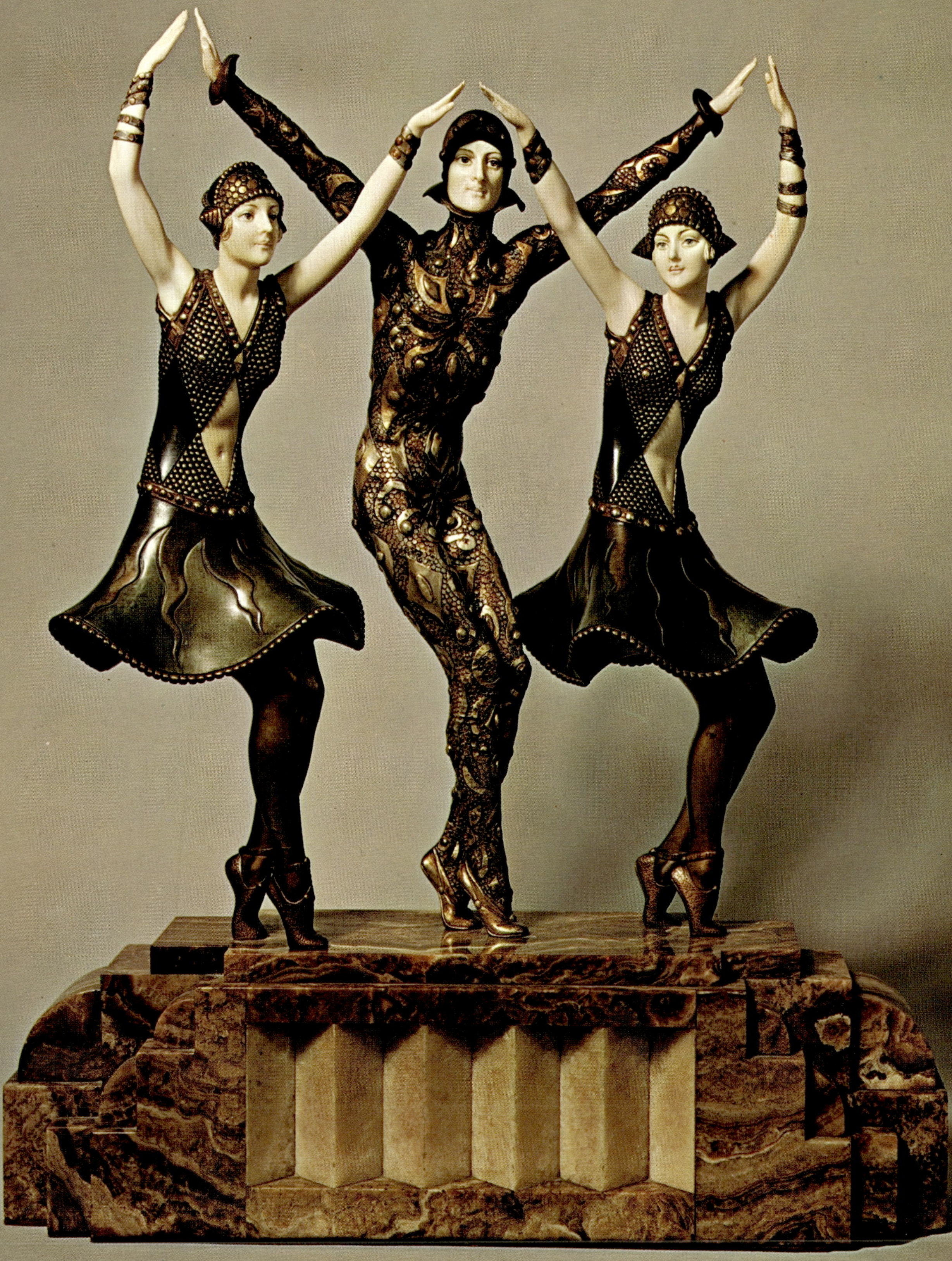

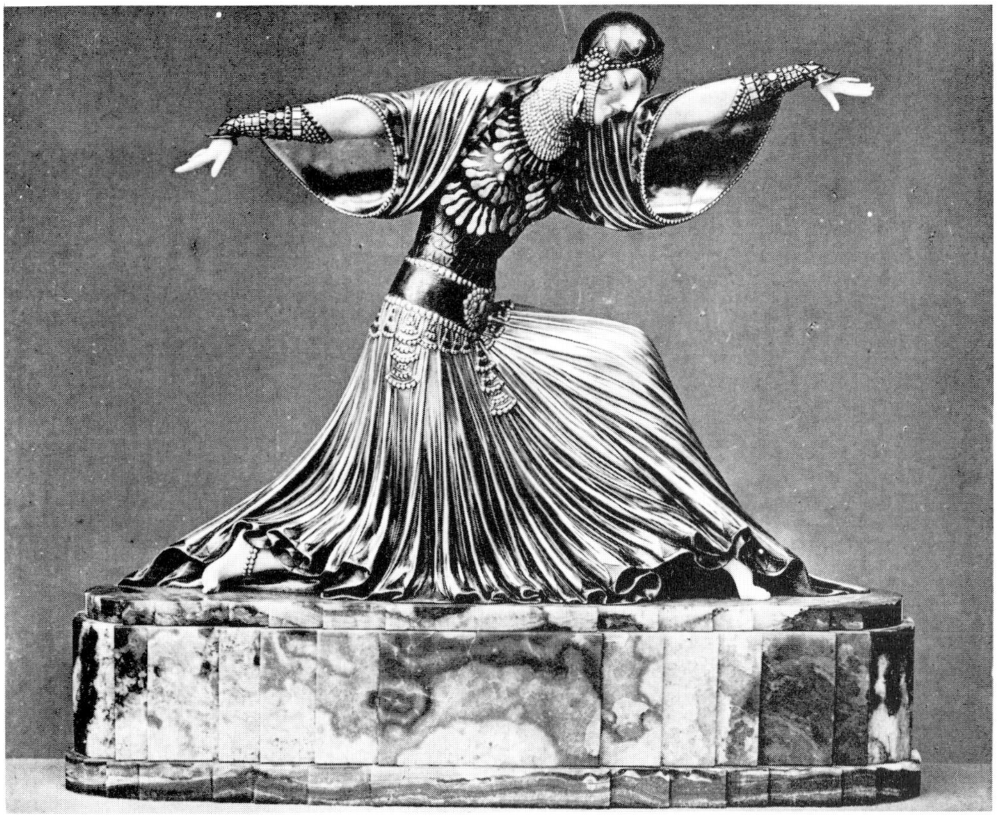

Thaïs, 56cm: 22in.

Kamorna, 52cm: 20½in.

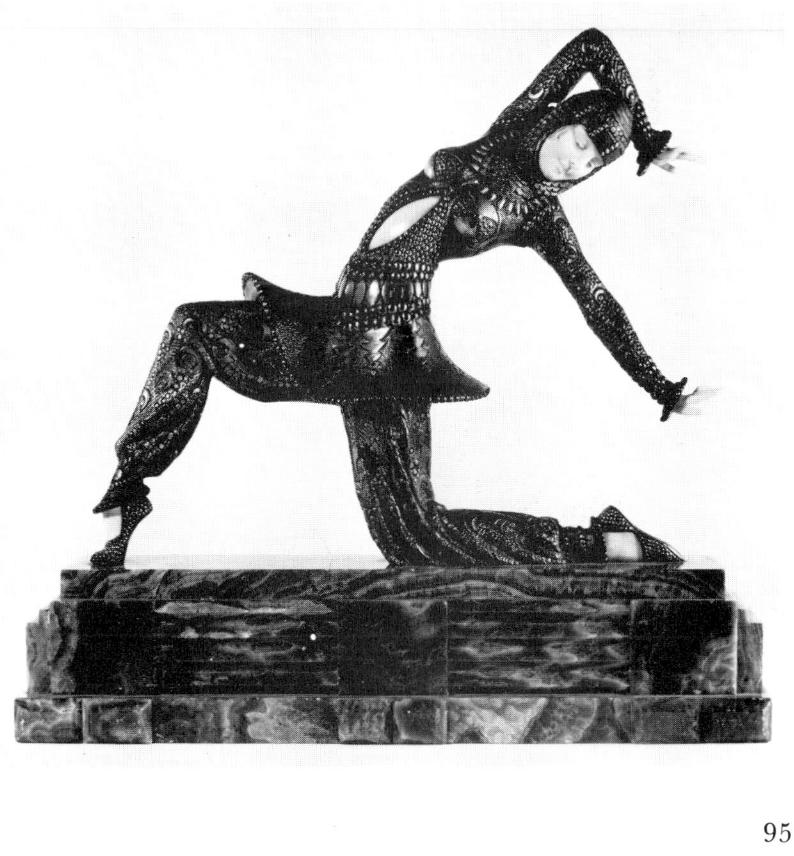

Left: *D.H. Chiparus. Finale, 63cm: 24¾in.; 42cm: 16½in.; 23cm: 9in. Figures may be mounted individually, when the centre is known as Astra (see page 97) and the left-hand figure as Star (see page 98).*

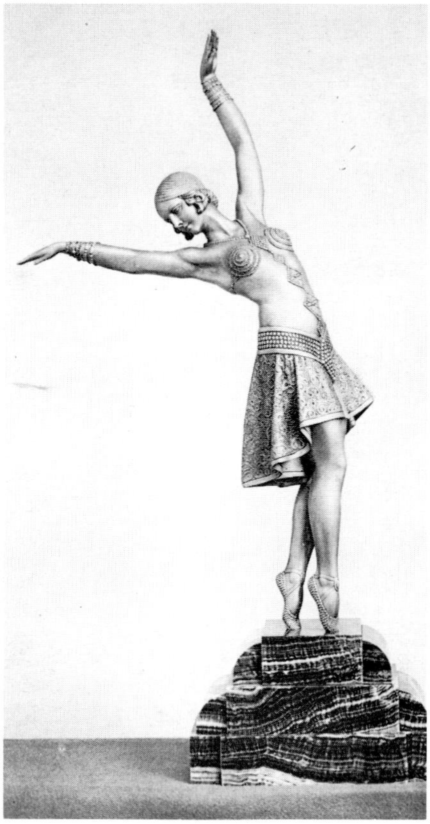

Vedette
80cm:31½in.
57cm:22½in.
37cm:14½in.

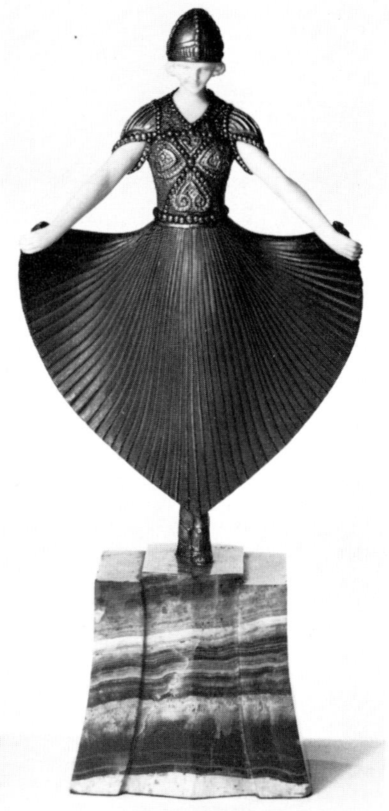

Actress
45cm:17¾in.
31cm:12in.

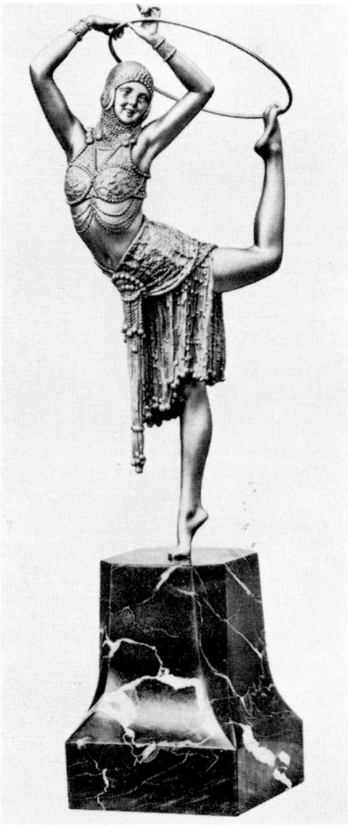

Dancer with Ring
47cm:18½in.

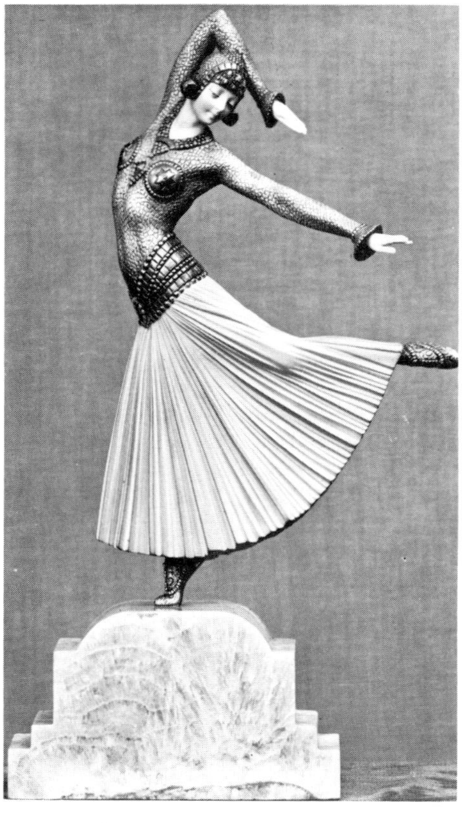

Ayouta
47cm:18½in.
29cm:11½in.

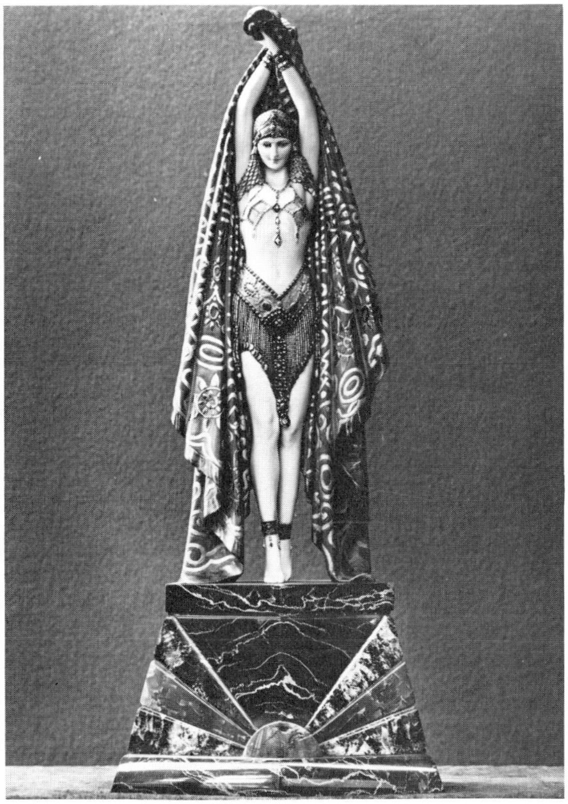

Antinea, 67cm:26½in.

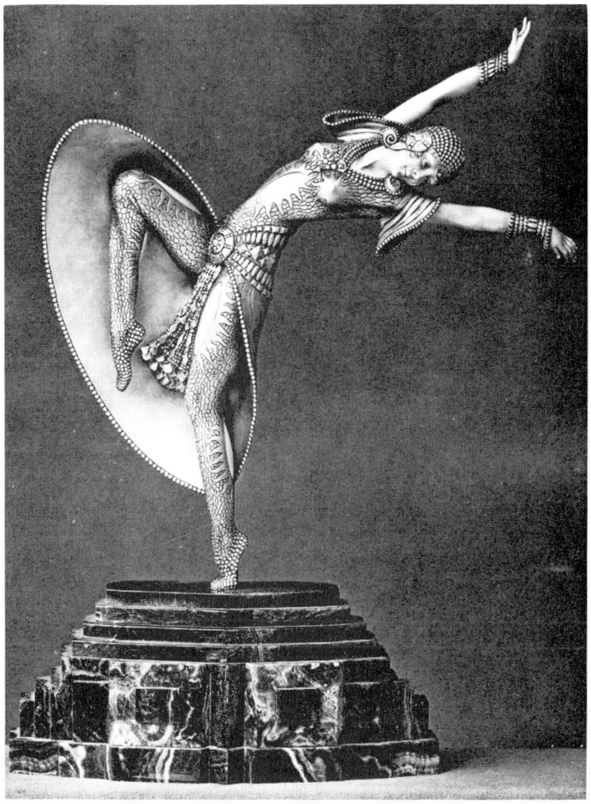

Alméria, 67cm:26½in.; 43cm:17in.

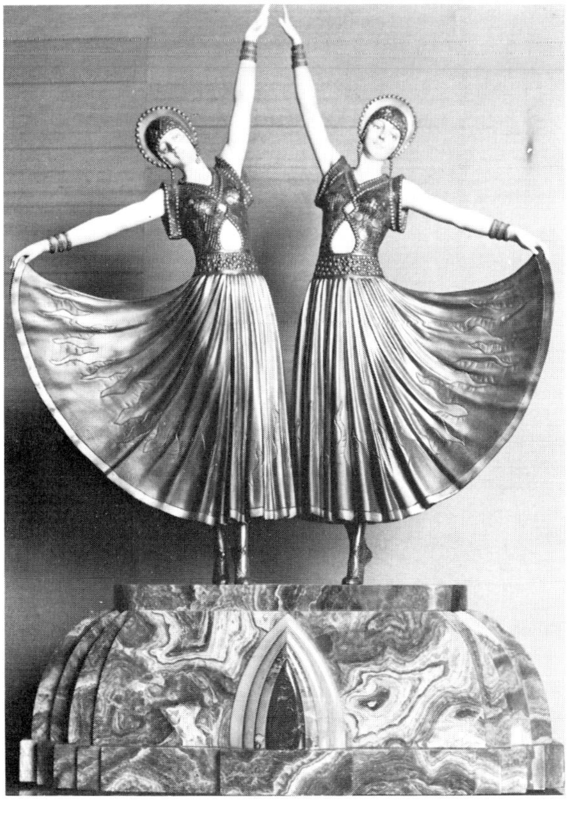

The Sisters
74cm:29in.
45cm:17½in.

Astra
43cm:17in.
See also page 94

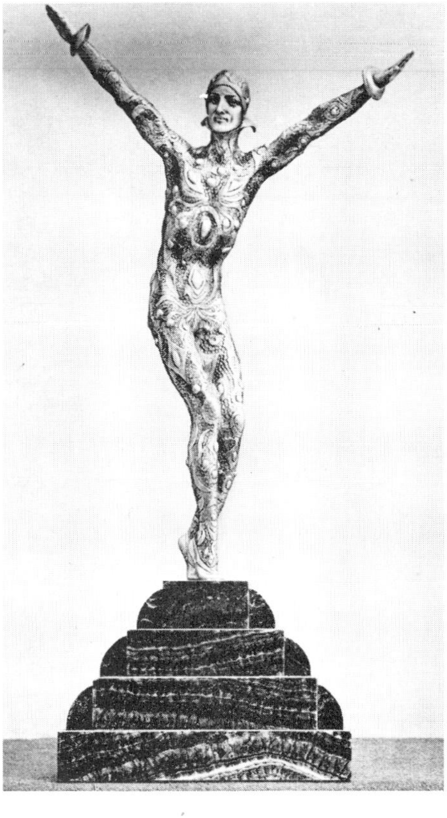

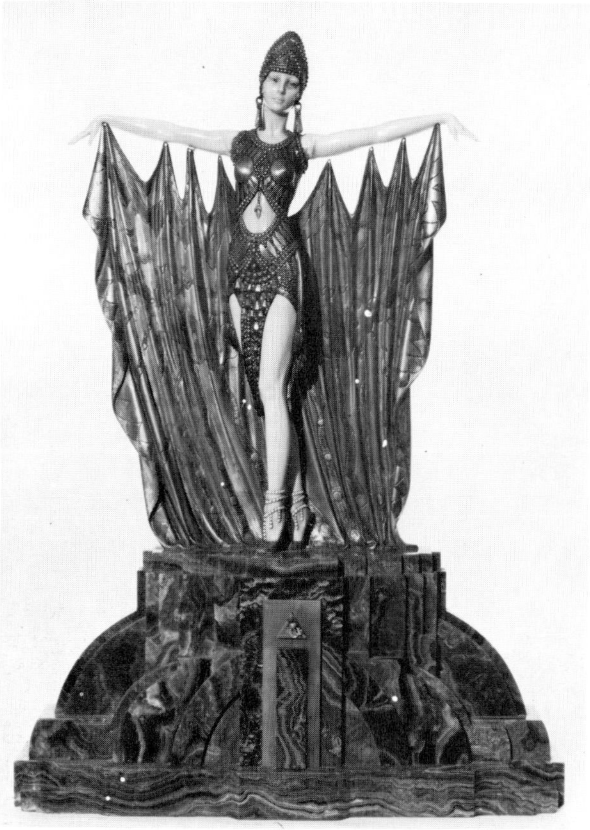

Semiramis, 66cm:21½in.

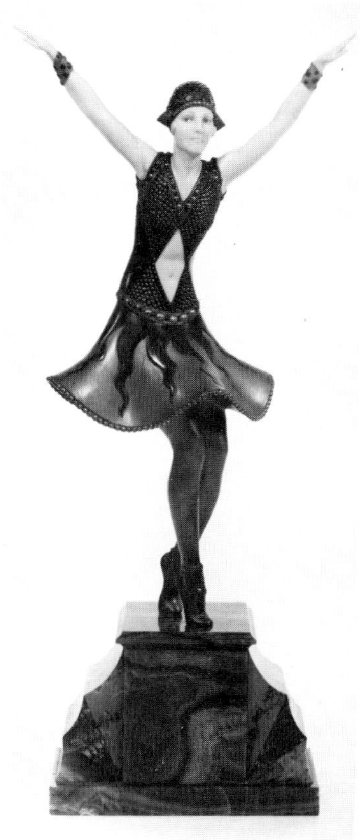

Star, 56cm:22¼in.
See also page 94

Right:
Orilla
62cm:24½in.
38cm:15in.
28cm:11in.

Far right:
Hungarian Dancer
50cm:19½in.
37cm:14in.

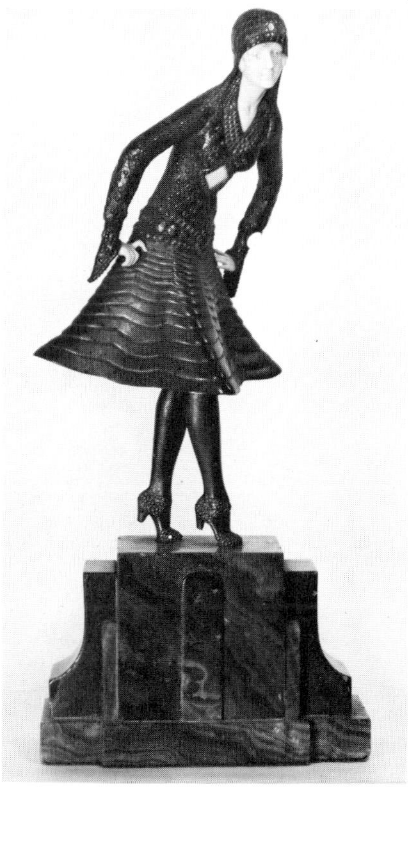

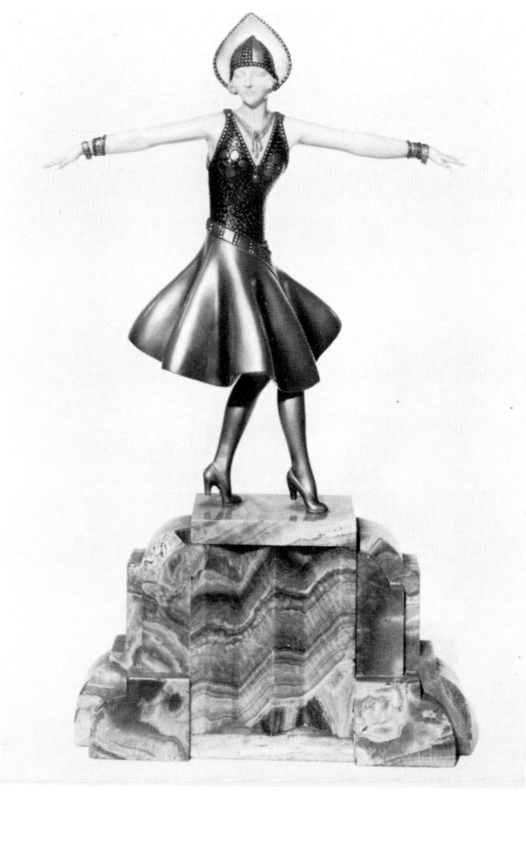

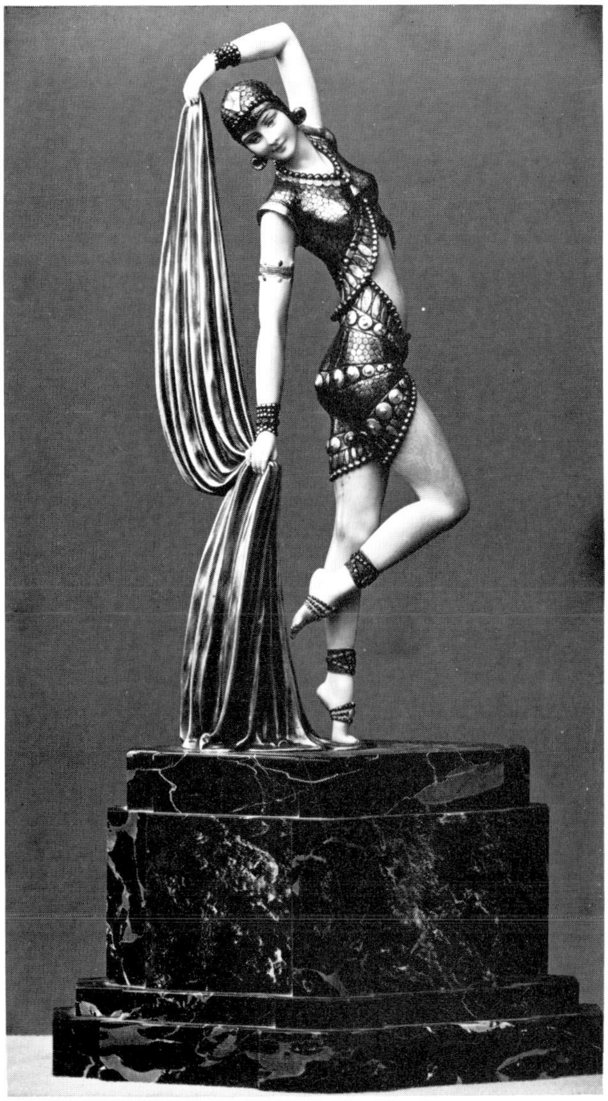

Yambo
61cm:24in.

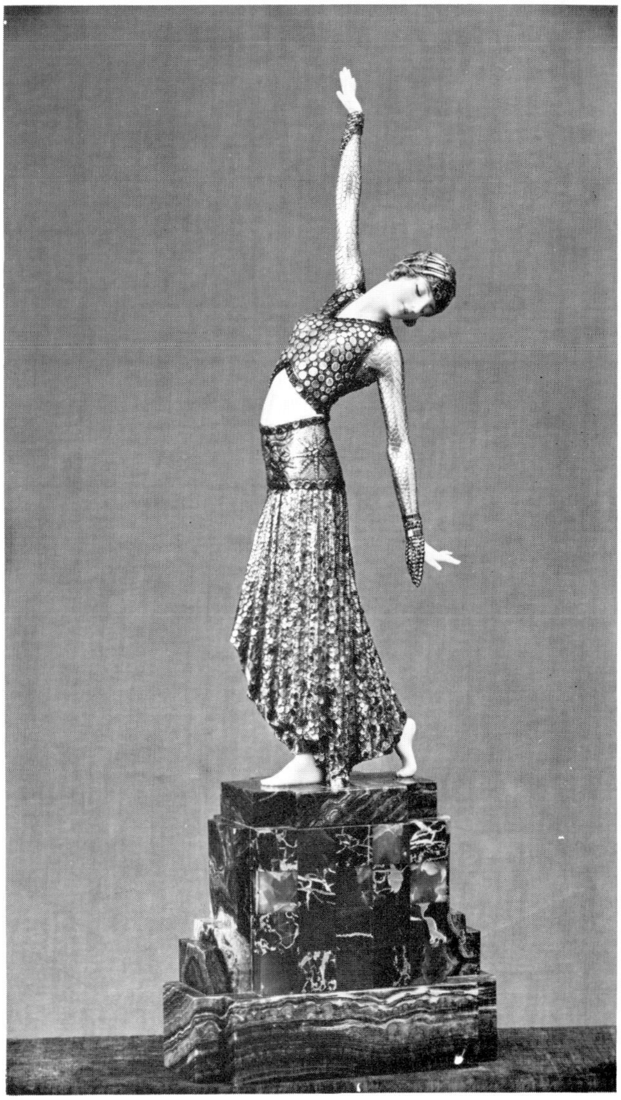

Footsteps
58cm:23in.
38cm:15in.

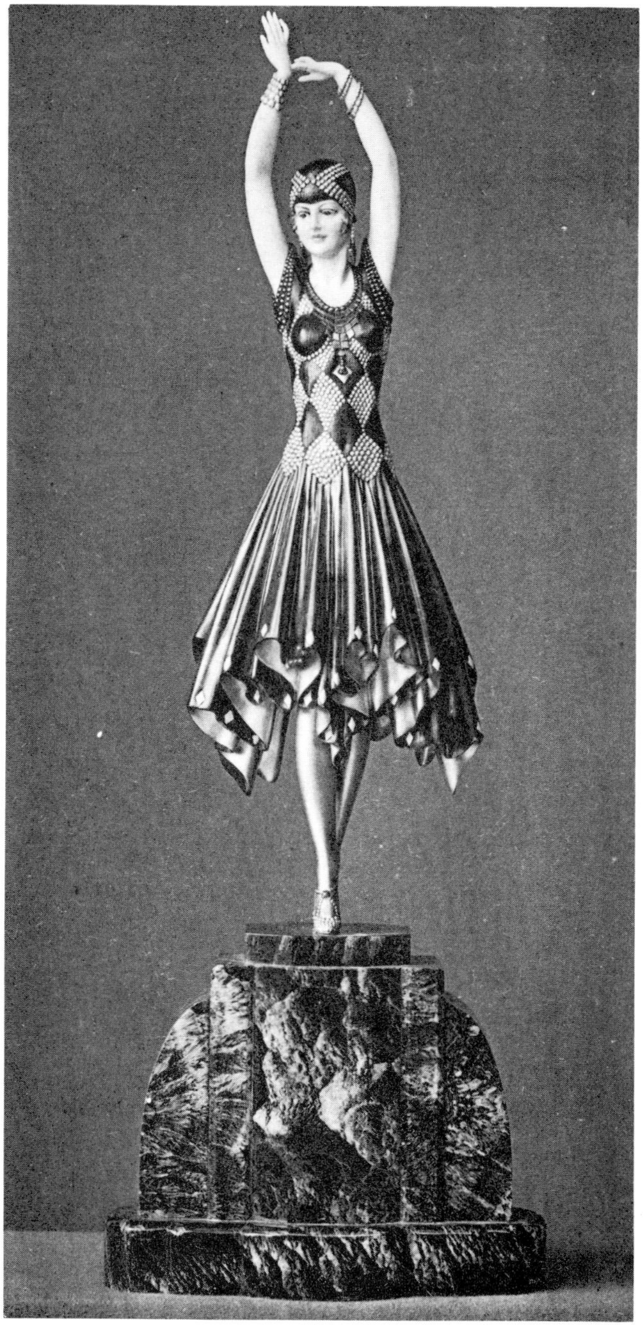

Miss Kita, 69cm:27in.

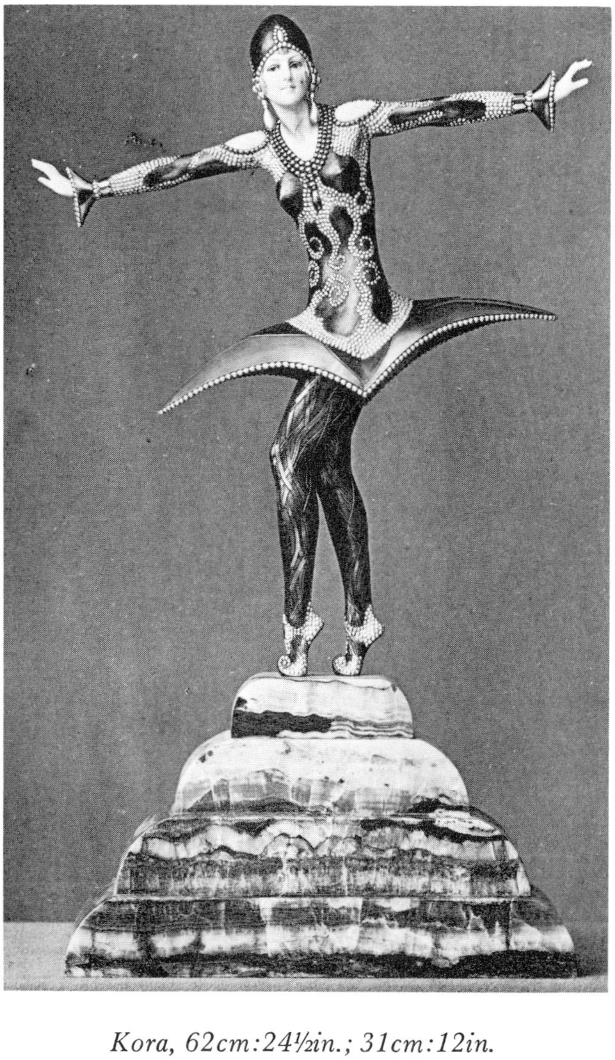

Kora, 62cm:24½in.; 31cm:12in.

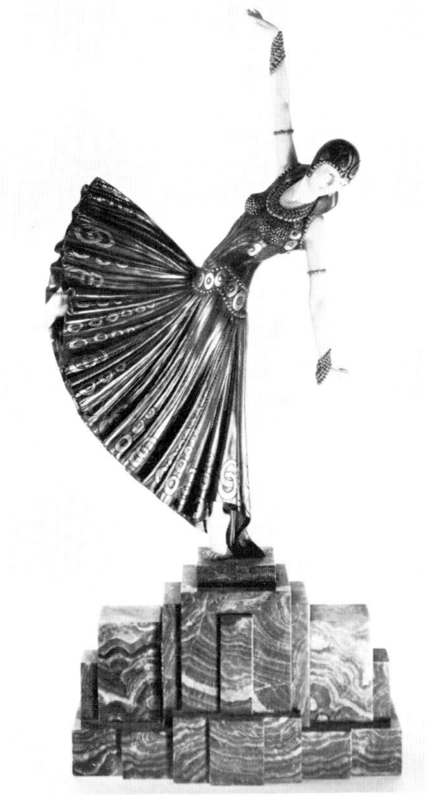

Testris
68cm:26¾in.

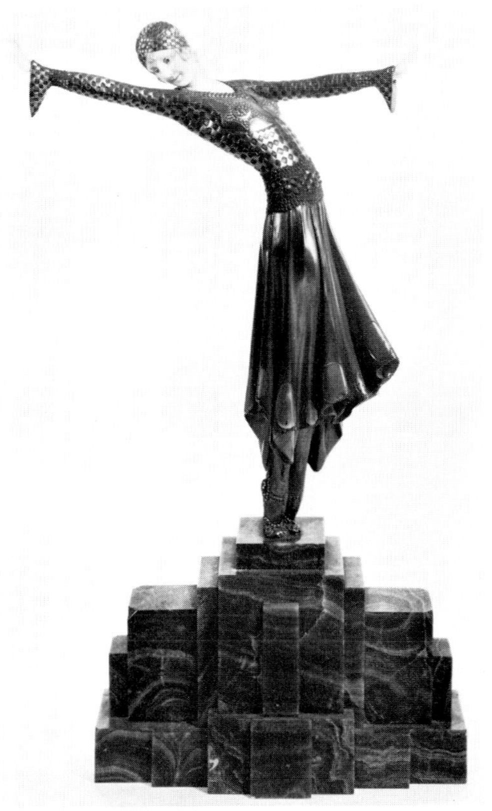

A Dancer, 39cm:15½in.

Miro
57cm:22½in.
38cm:15in.

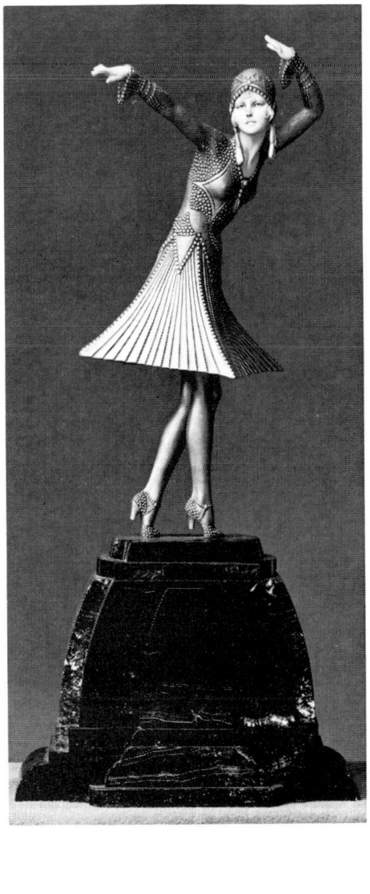

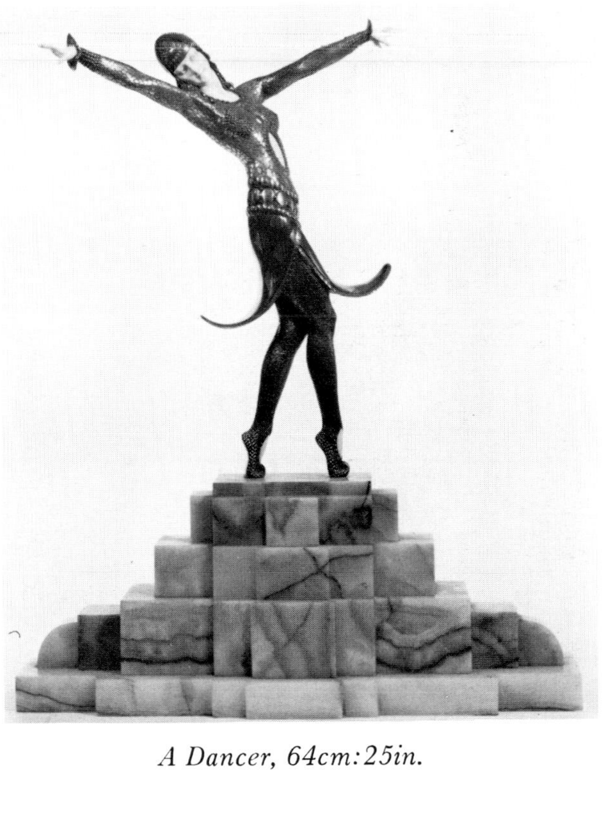

A Dancer, 64cm:25in.

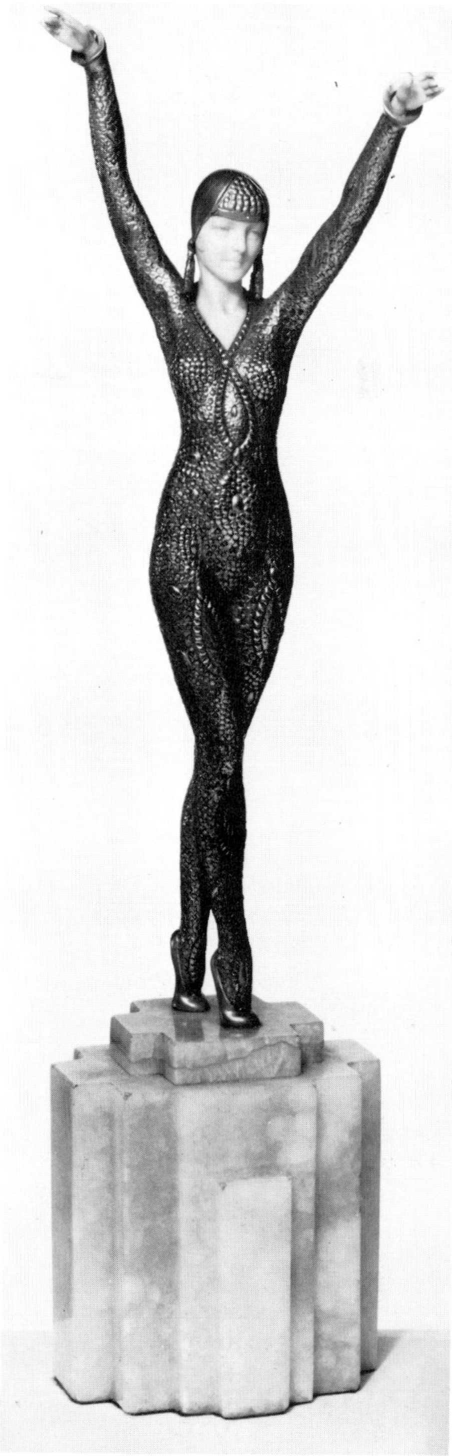

Dourga, 63cm:24¾in.; 29cm:11½in.

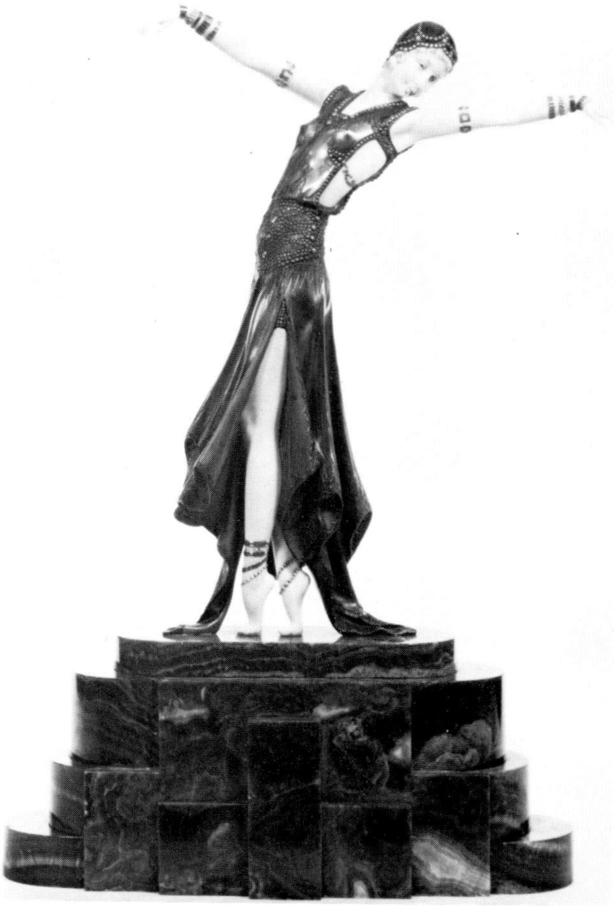

A Dancer, 52cm:20½in.

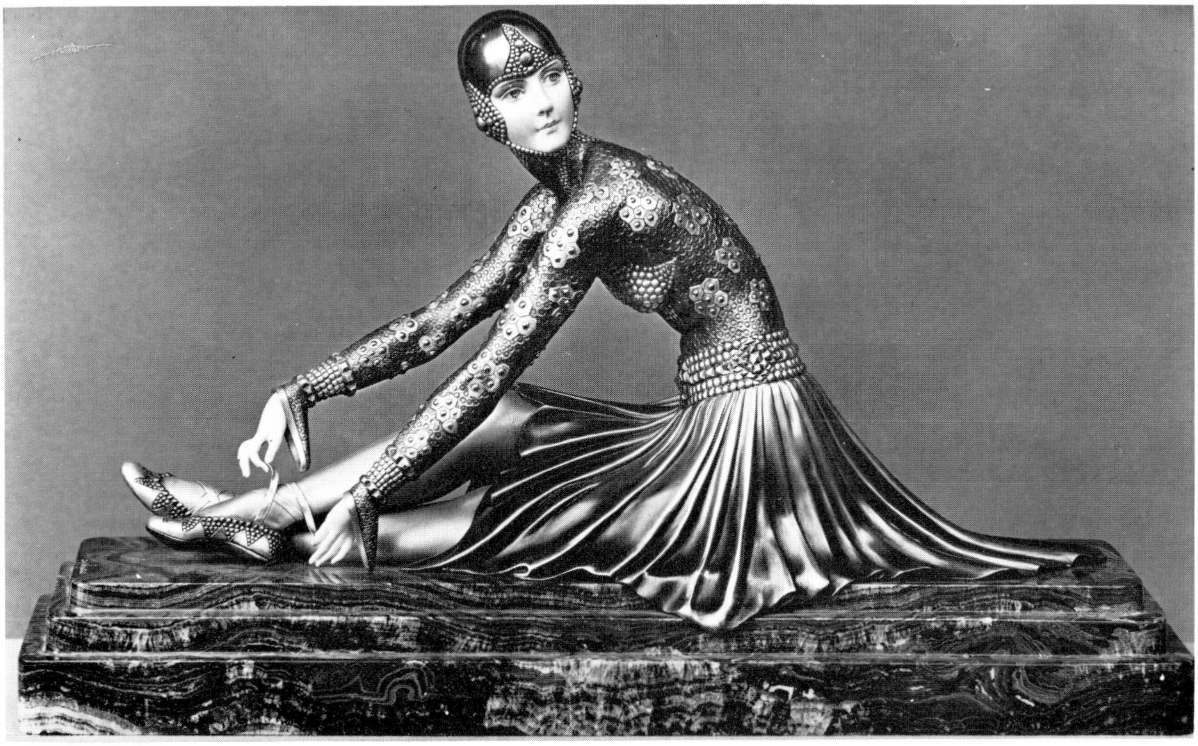

Tanara, 38cm:15in.; 25cm:10in.; 19cm:7½in.

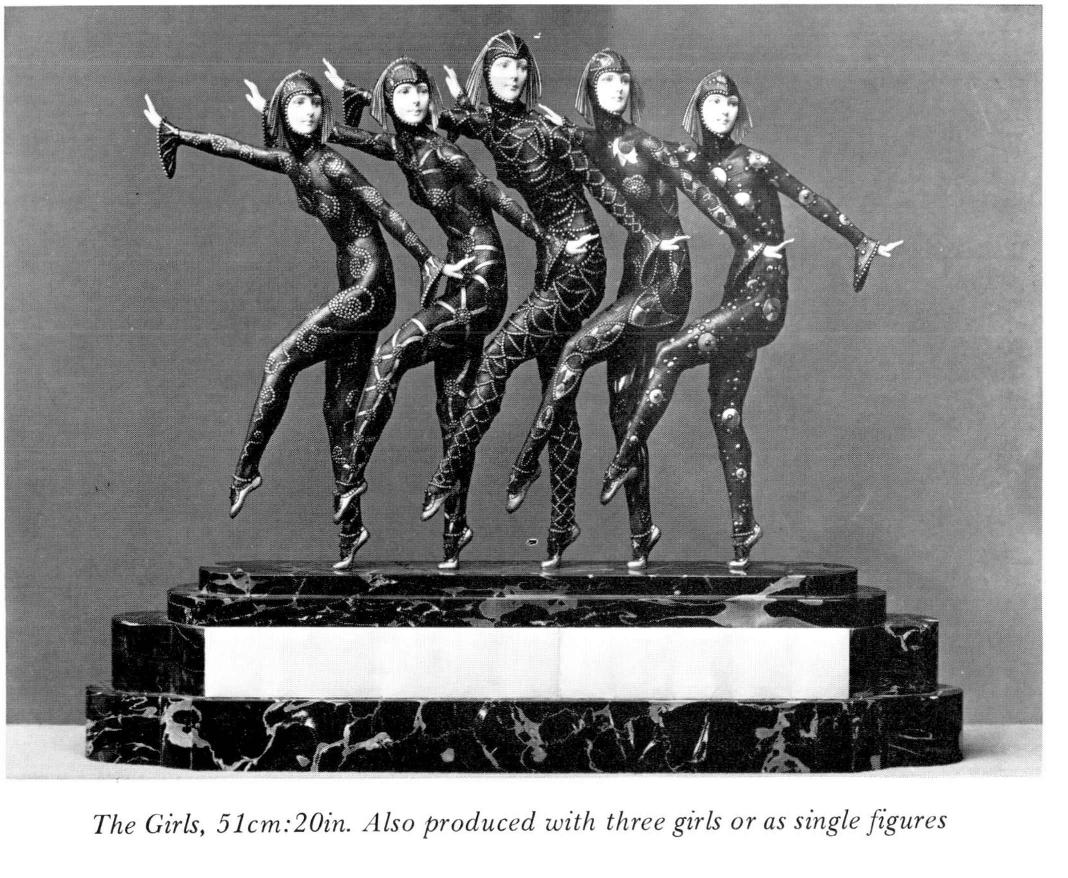

The Girls, 51cm:20in. Also produced with three girls or as single figures

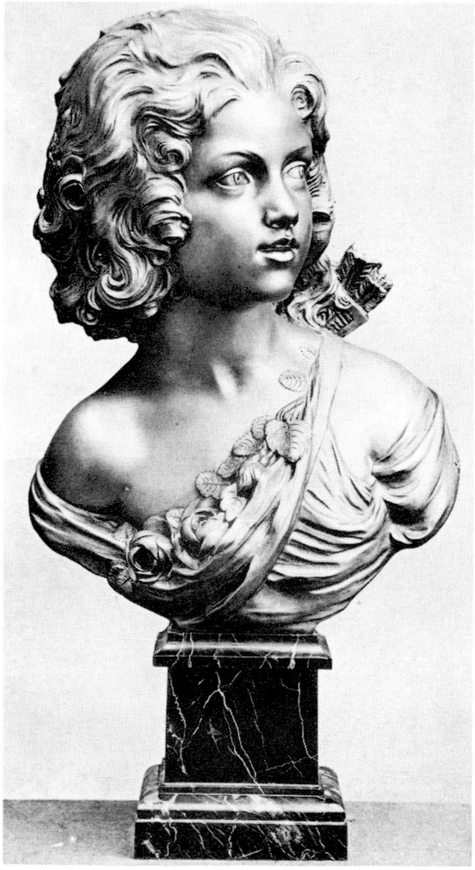

Triumphant Love
(bust)
59cm: 23¼in.
40cm: 15¾in.
20cm: 8in.
Exhibited 1921

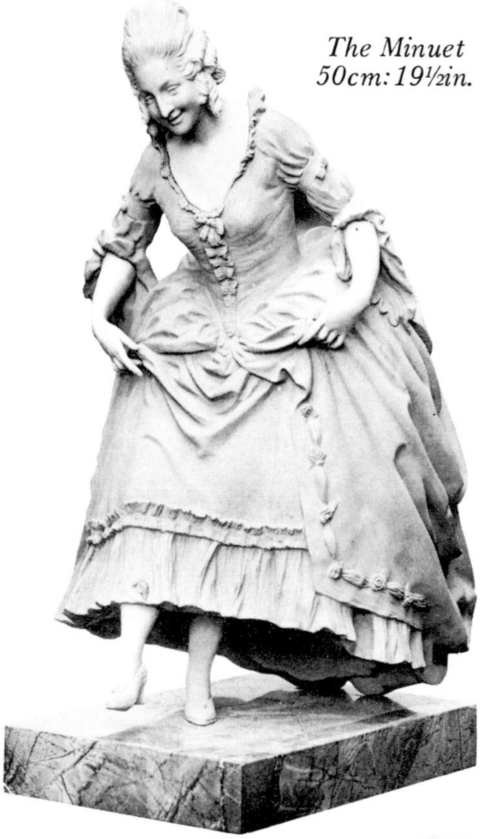

The Minuet
50cm: 19½in.

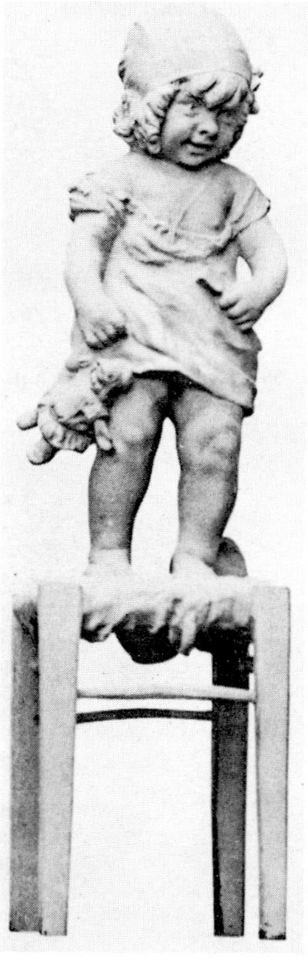

Nénette
32cm: 12½in.
22cm: 8½in.

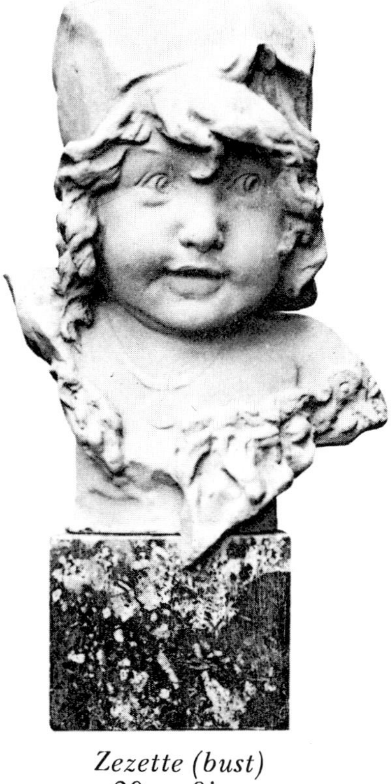

Zezette (bust)
20cm: 8in.

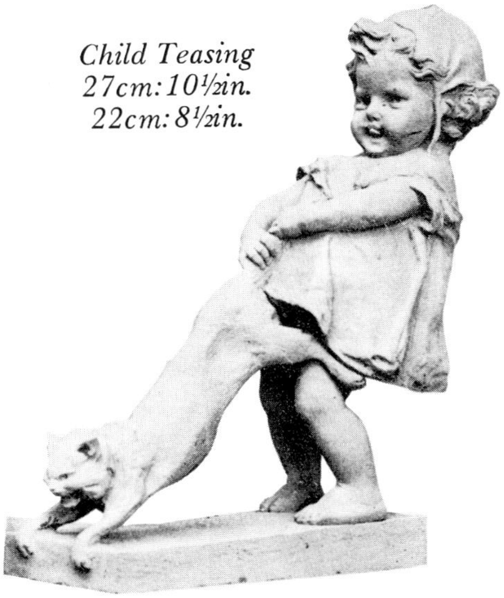

Child Teasing
27cm:10½in.
22cm:8½in.

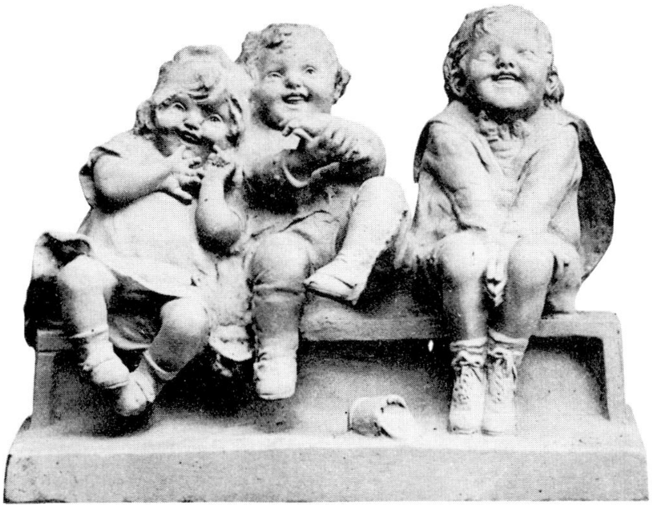

Children Watching Punch and Judy Show
20cm:8in.; 12cm:4¾in.

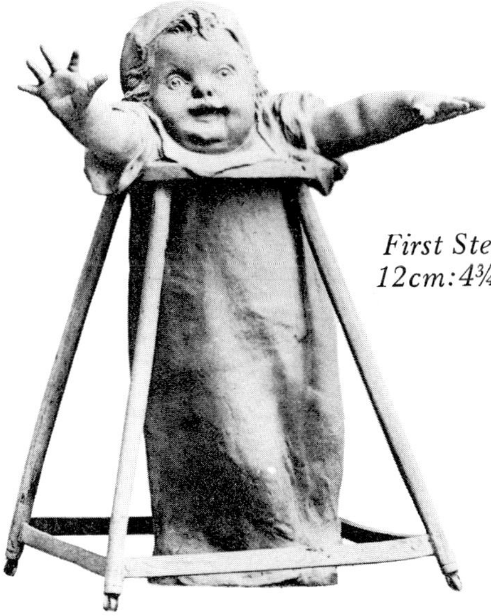

First Steps
12cm:4¾in.

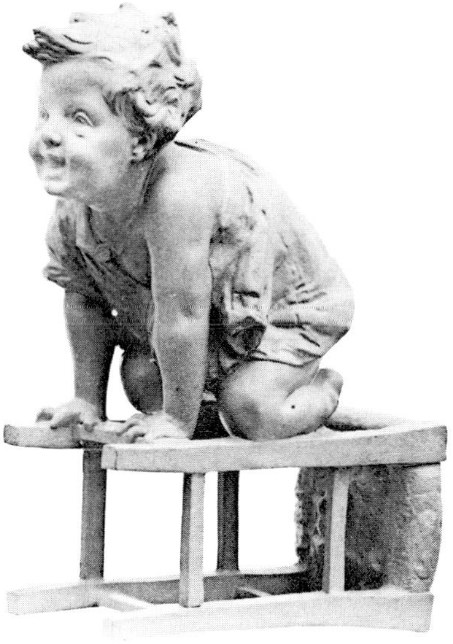

The Acrobat, 23cm:9in.; 15cm:6in.

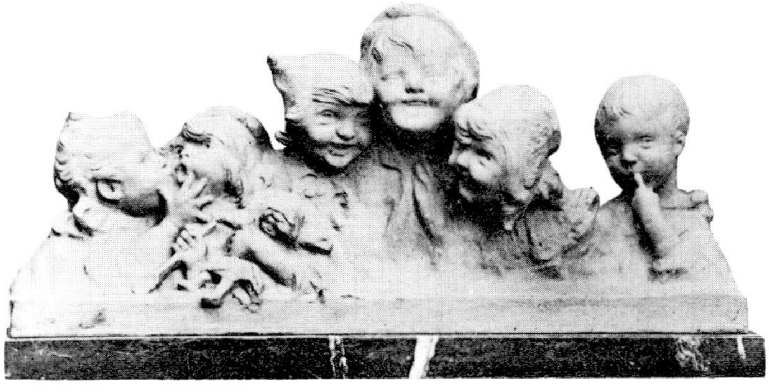

Murmur, 15cm:6in.

GEO. CLERC

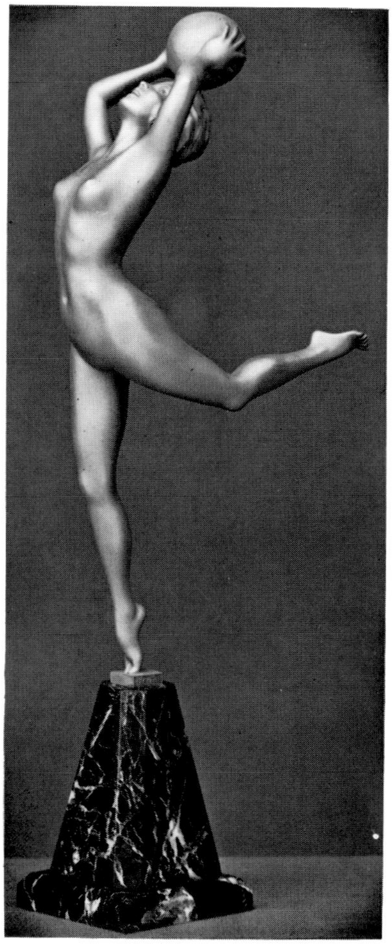

Sport, 51cm:20in.

CL. J.R. COLINET

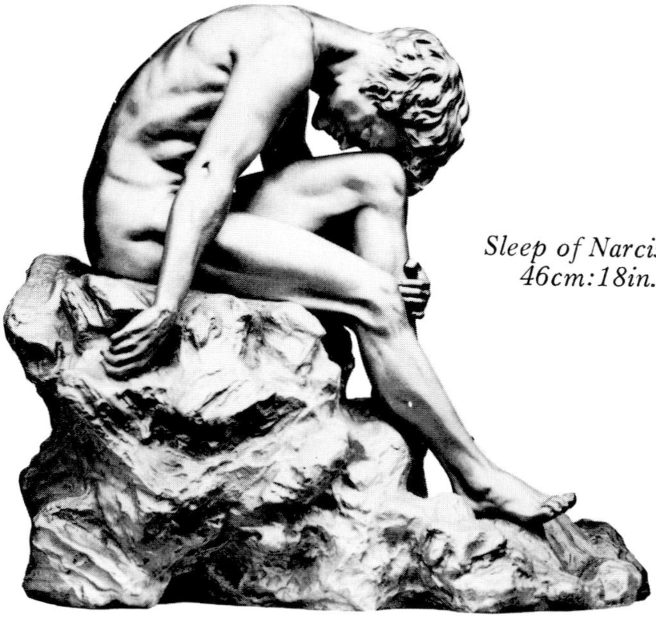

Sleep of Narcissus
46cm:18in.

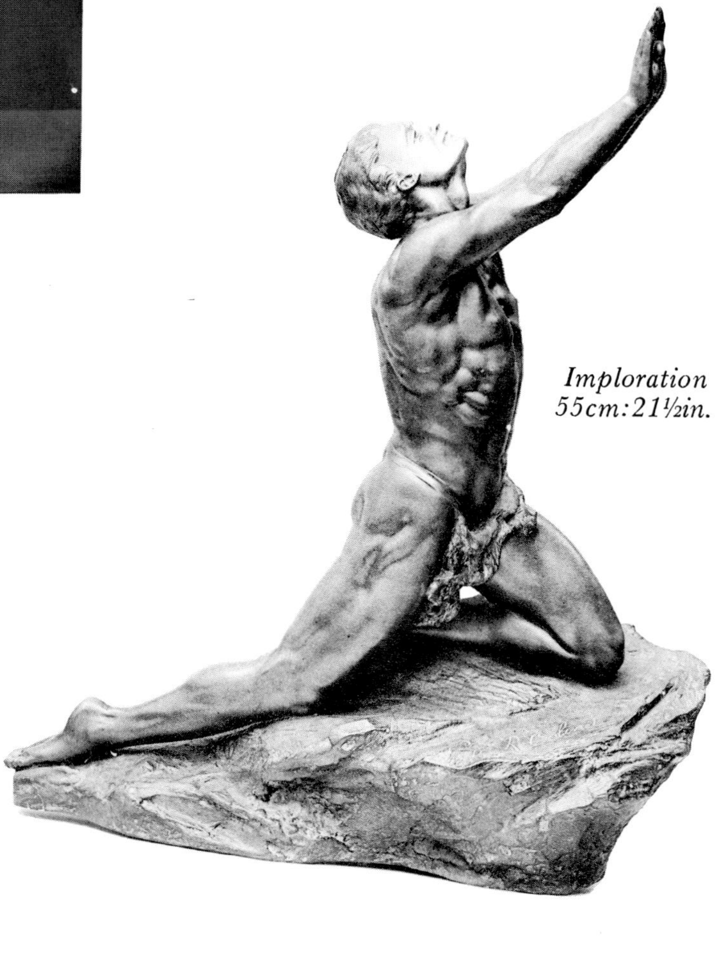

Imploration
55cm:21½in.

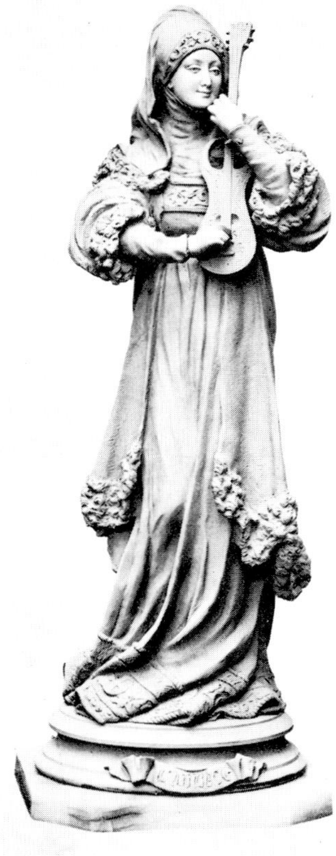

Morning Serenade
57cm:22½in.

Joan of Arc
58cm:23in.

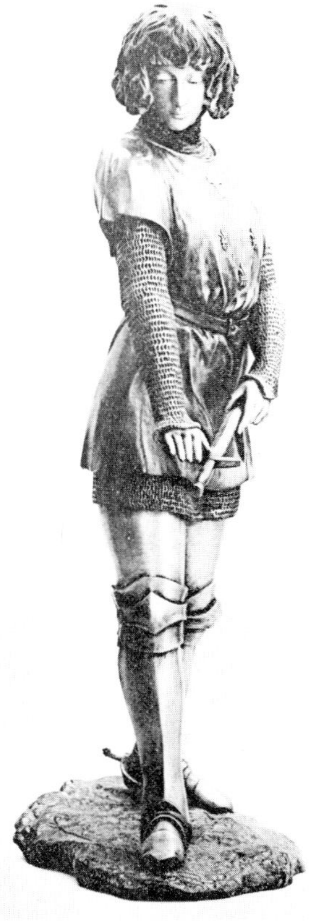

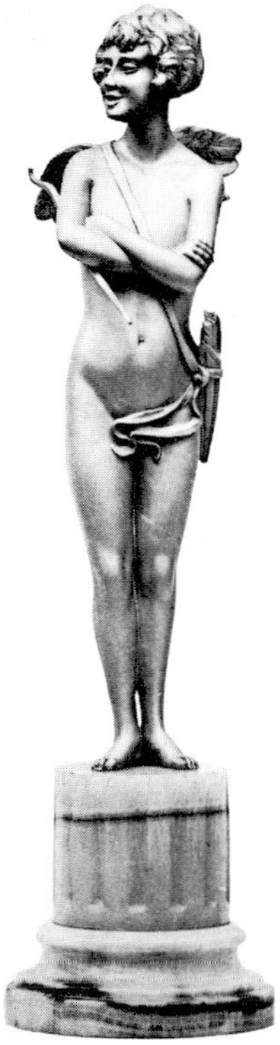

Cupid
40cm:15¾in.

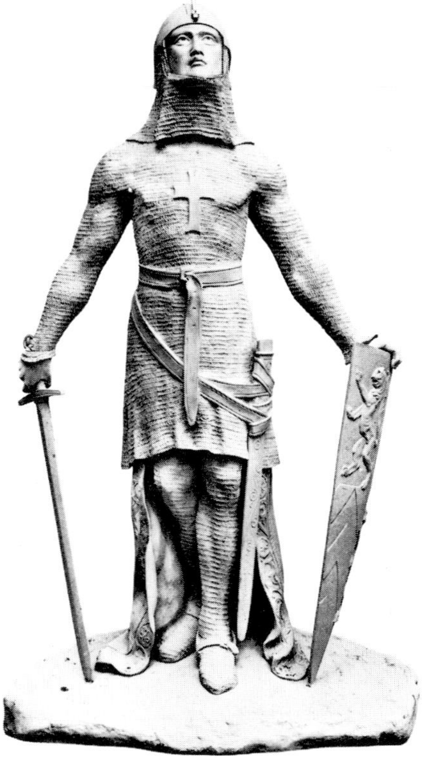

The Crusader, 65cm:25½in.
Bronze and ivory

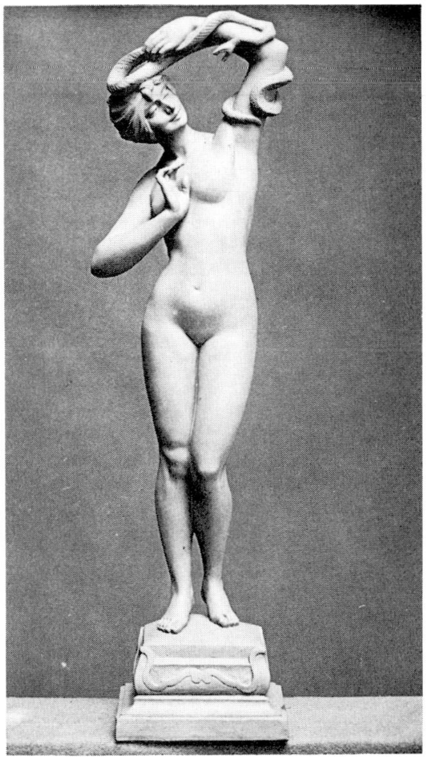

Naked Snake Charmer
64cm:25¼in.; 25cm:10in.

CL. J.R. COLINET

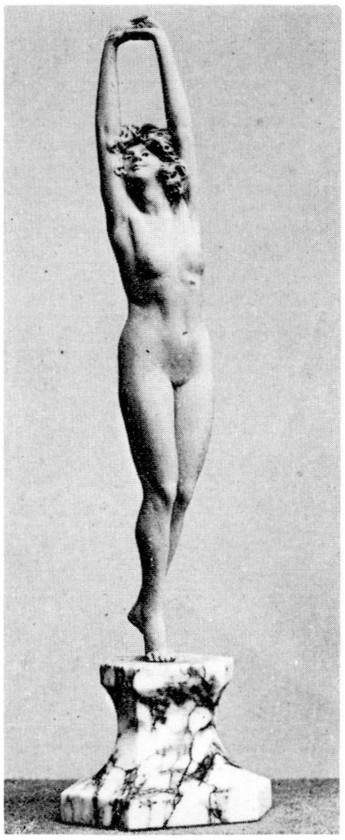

Dawn
26cm: 10¼in.

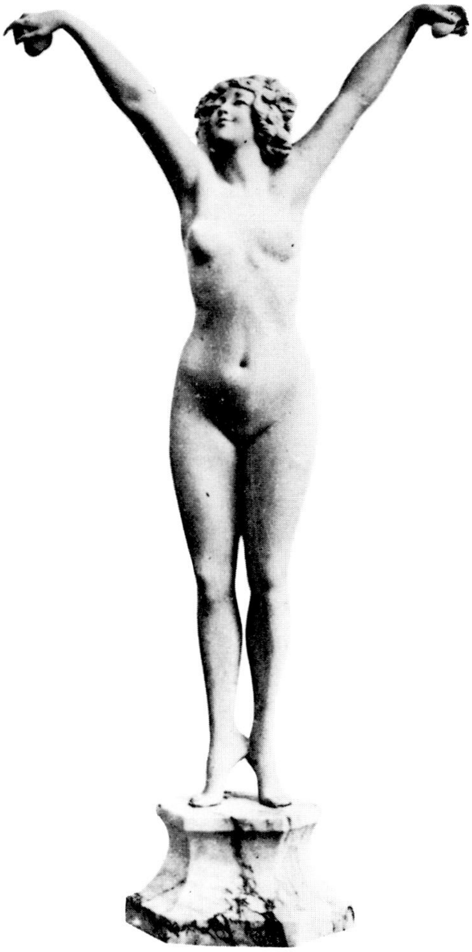

Andalusian
76cm: 30in.
51cm: 20in.
42cm: 16½in.
33cm: 13in.
25cm: 10in.
20cm: 7¾in.

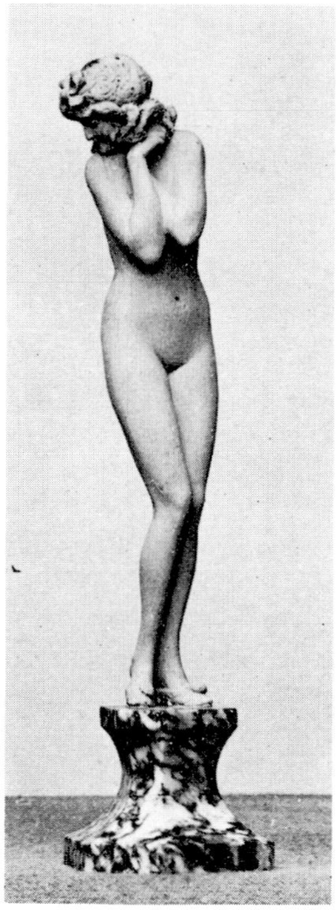

Darling
23cm: 9in.

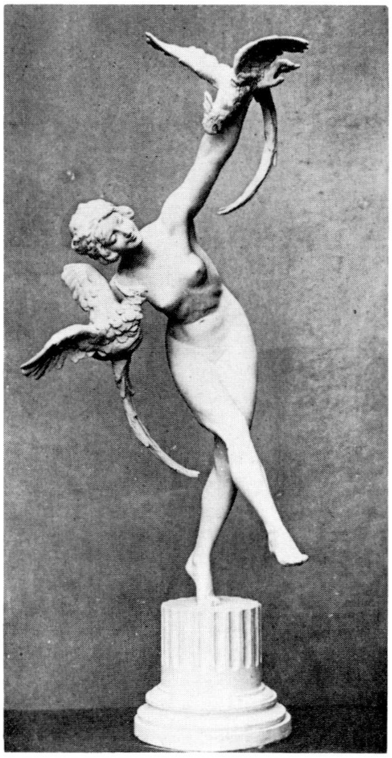

Beside the Missouri
51cm: 20in.
36cm: 14in.

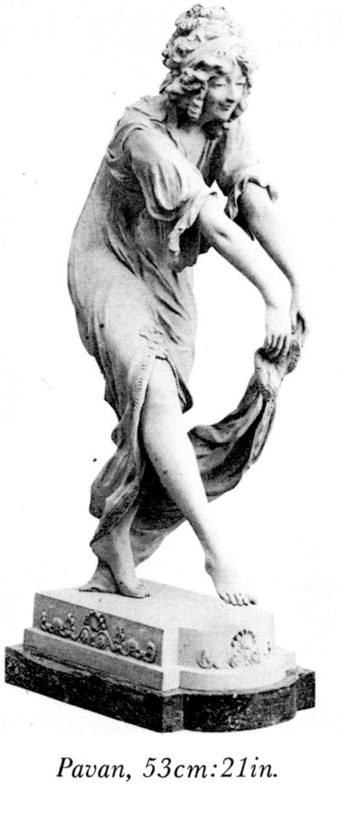

Pavan, 53cm: 21in.

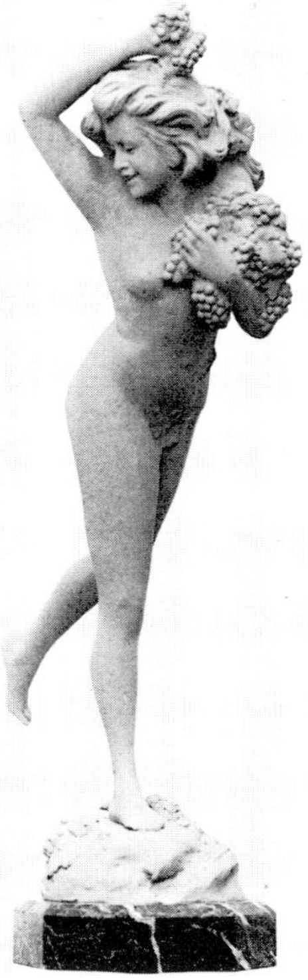

Priestess of Bacchus
42cm:16½in.

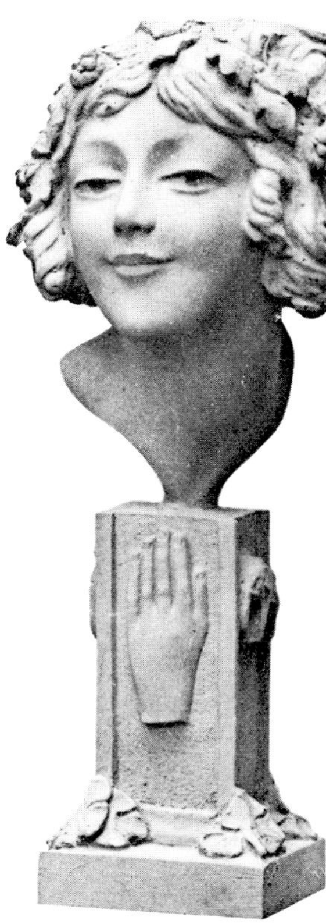

Fetish
18cm:7in.

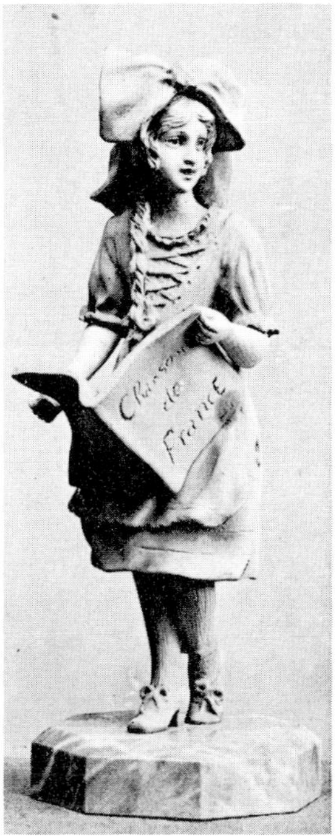

Song of France
22cm:8½in.
Bronze and ivory

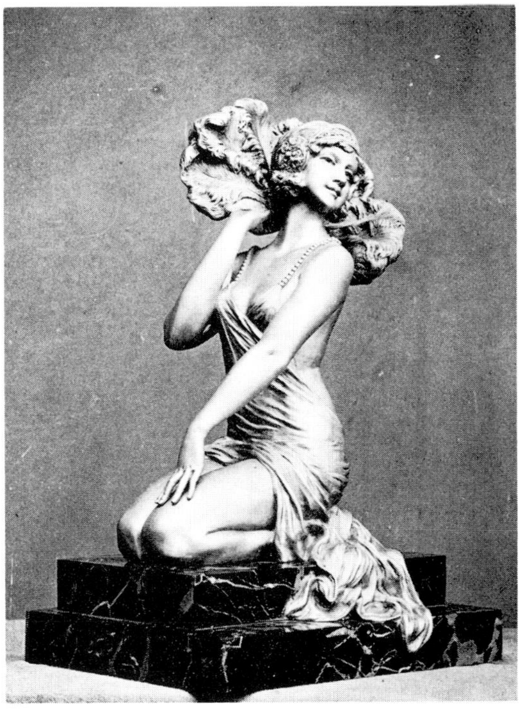

Modern Venus (1921), 45cm:17¾in.

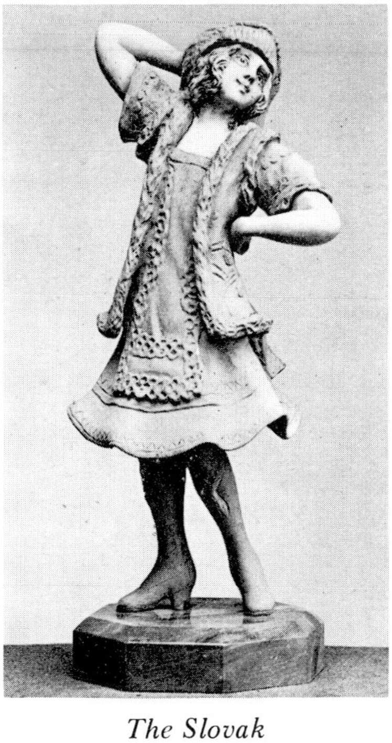

The Slovak
21cm:8¼in.
Bronze and ivory

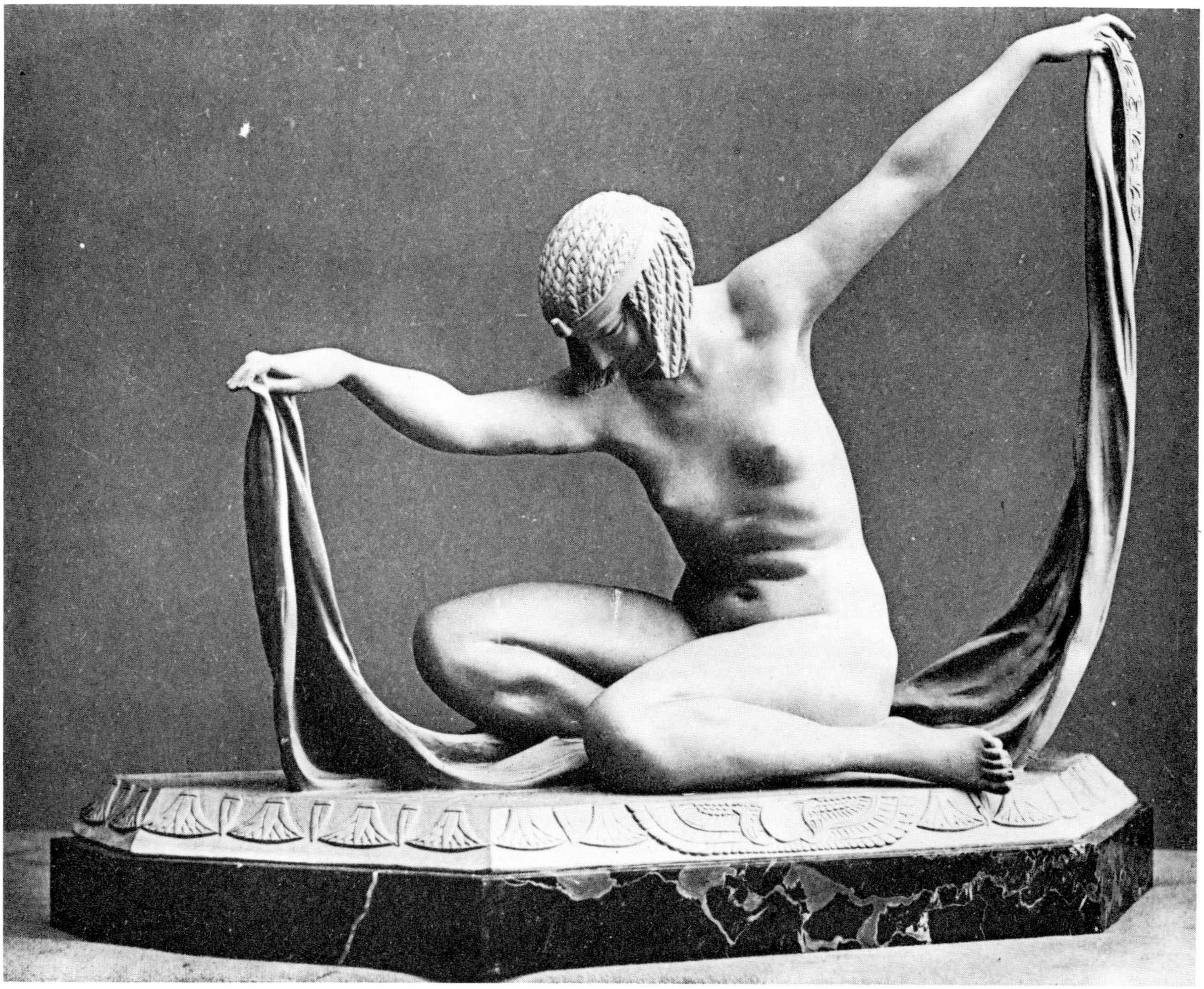

Isis, 42cm:16½in.

Right. Above: *Towards the Unknown (Valkyrie), by Cl. J.R. Colinet, 75cm:29½in.; 32cm:12½in.* Below left: *Russian Dancer by Joé Descomps, 48cm:19in.; 29cm:11½in.* Below right: *Dancer by Gerdago, 36cm:14in.*

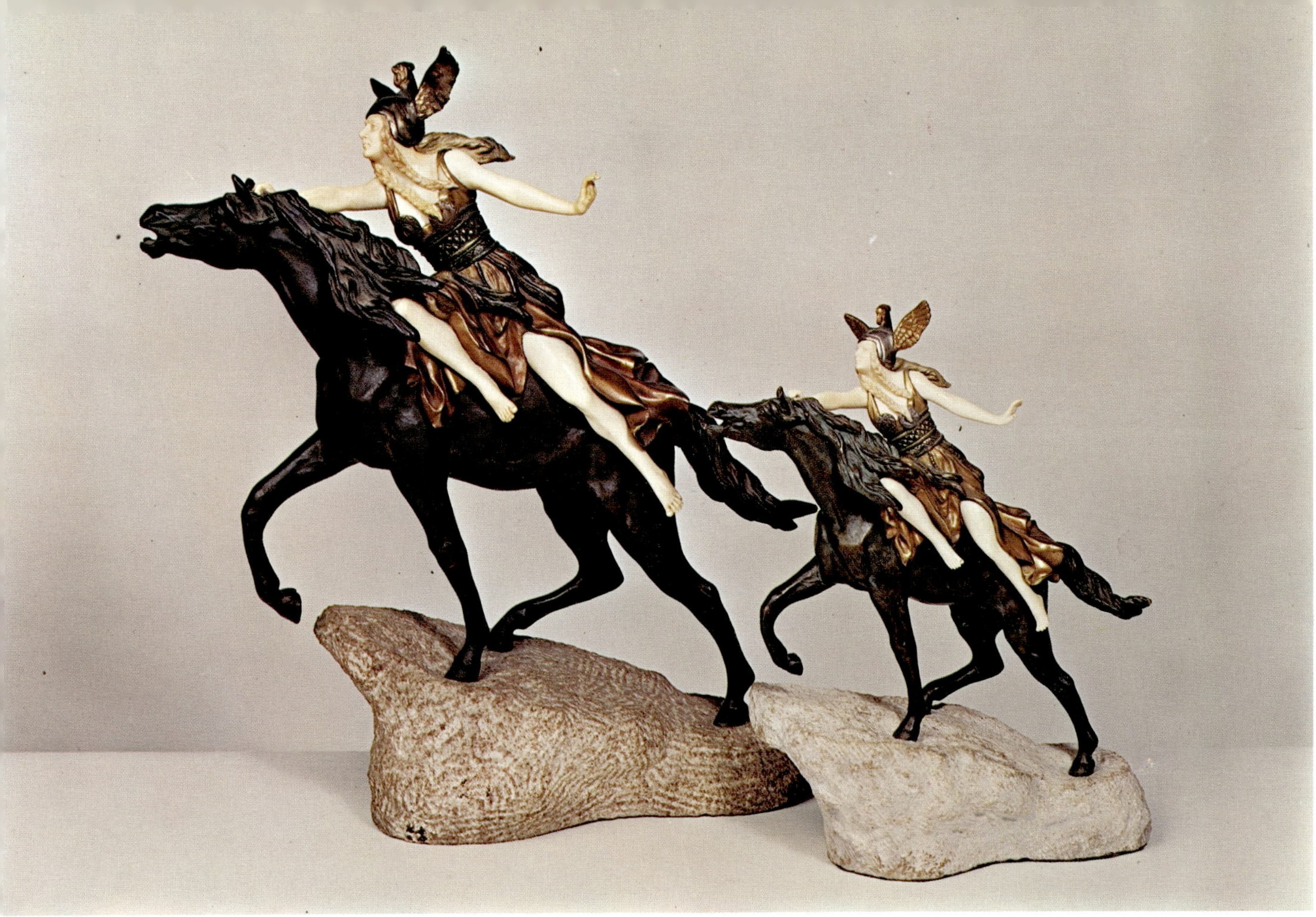

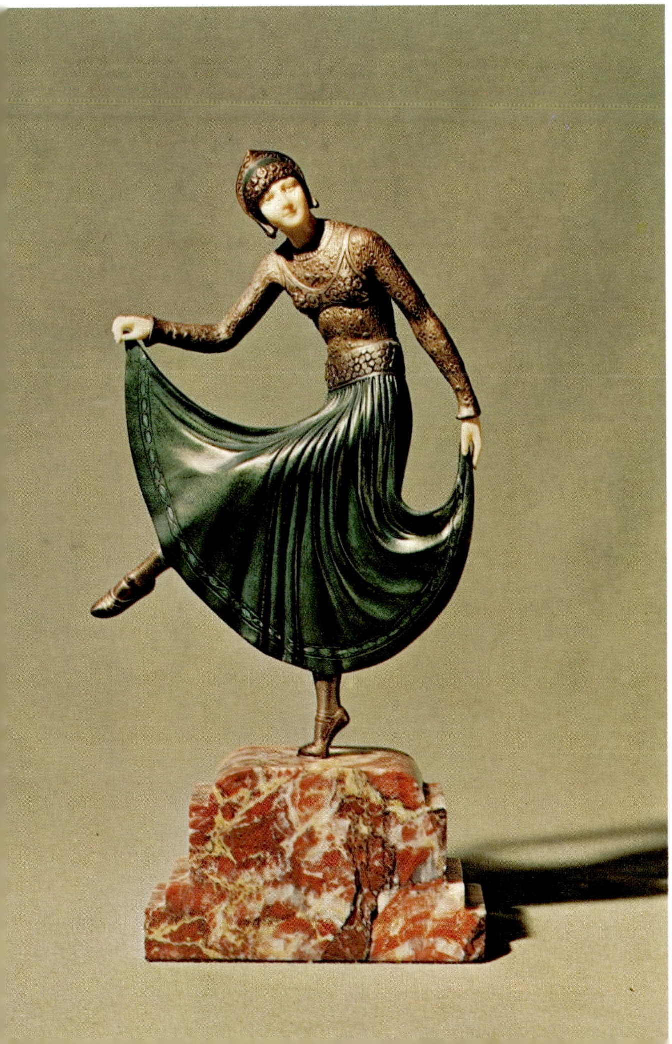

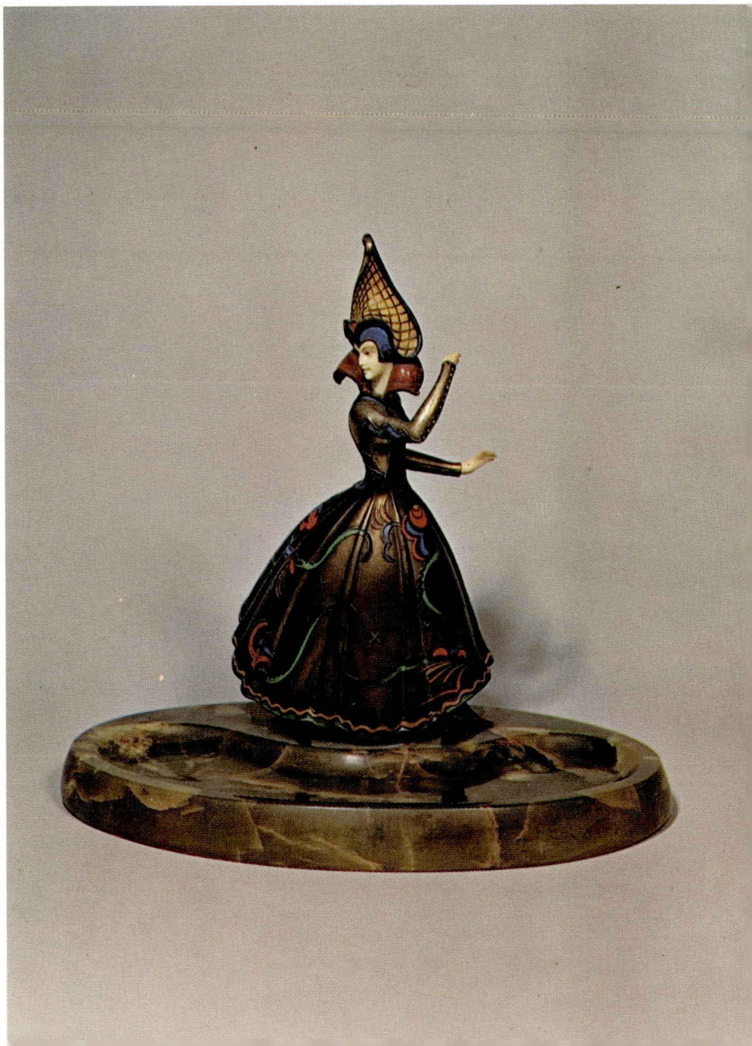

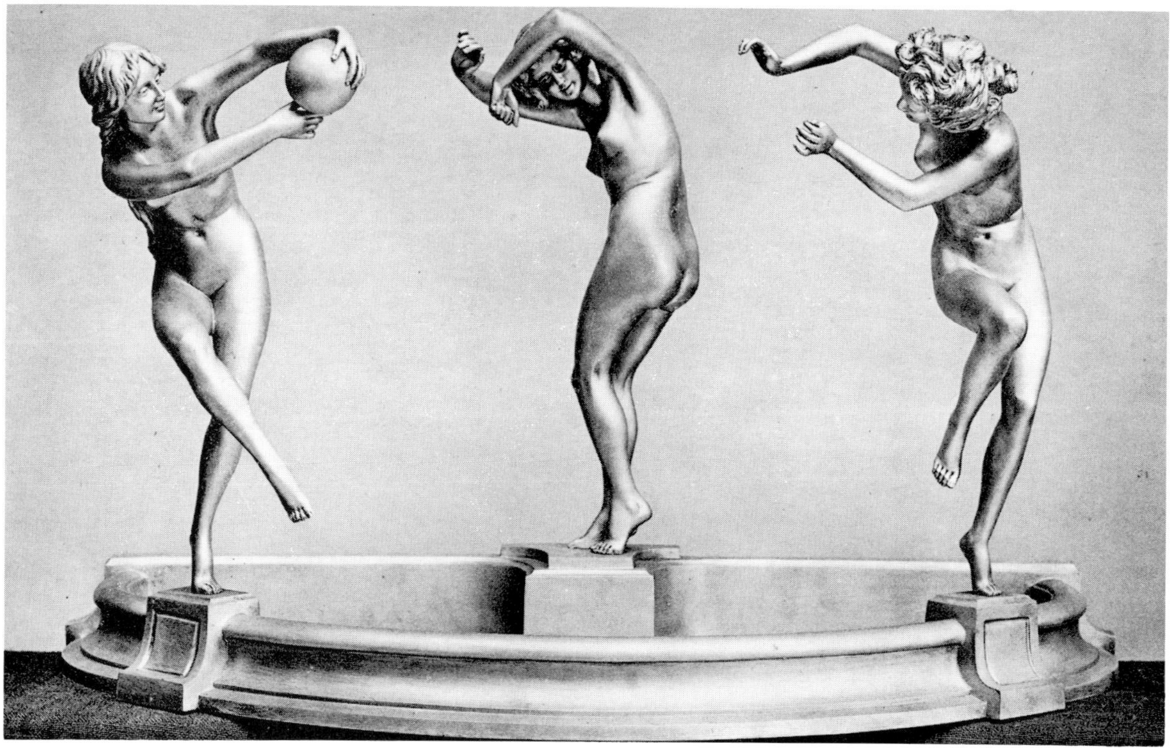

The Balloon Players, 40cm:15¾in.

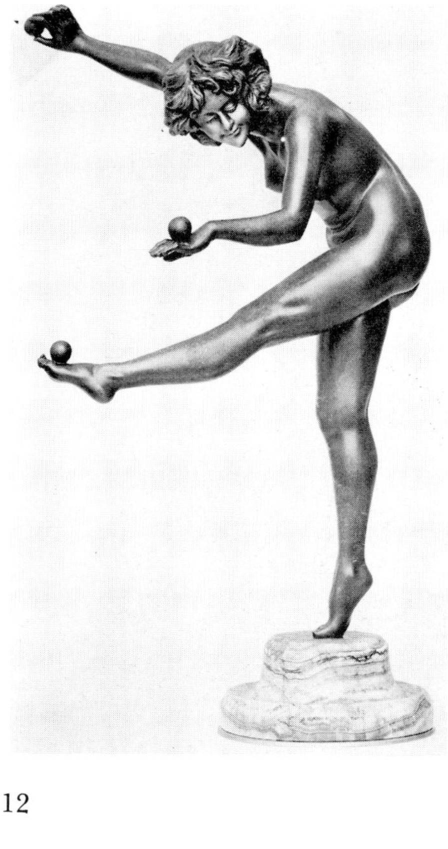

Juggler
60cm:23½in.
37cm:14½in.
25cm:10in.
18cm:7in.

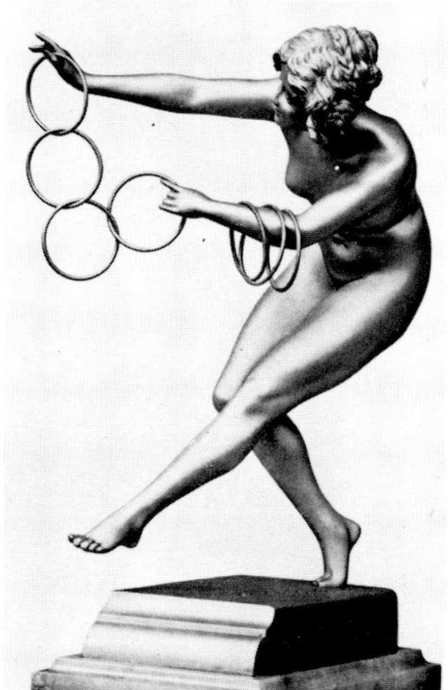

The Magic Links
31cm:12in.; 25cm:10in.
20cm:8in.

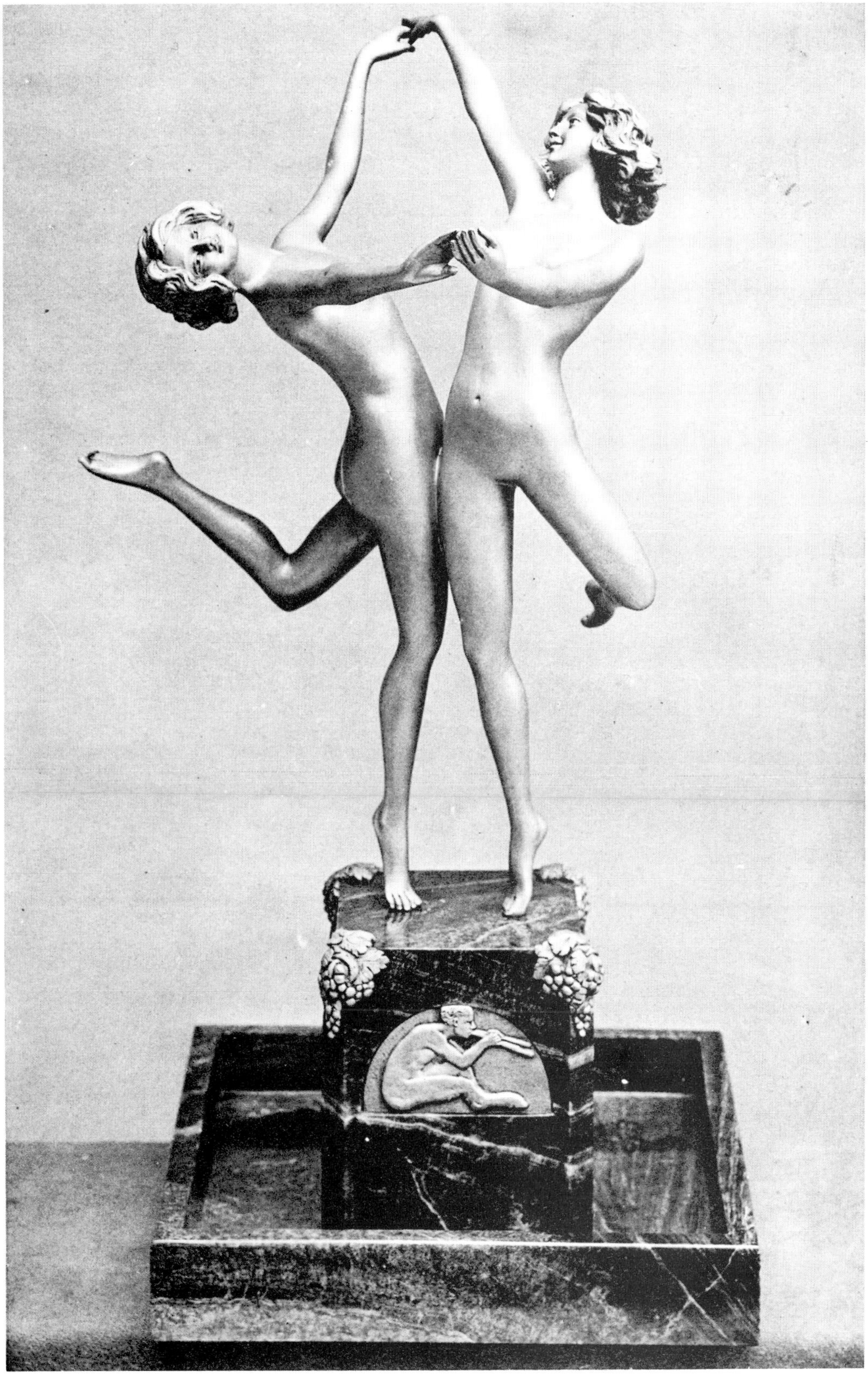

Country Dance (1925), 53cm:21in.

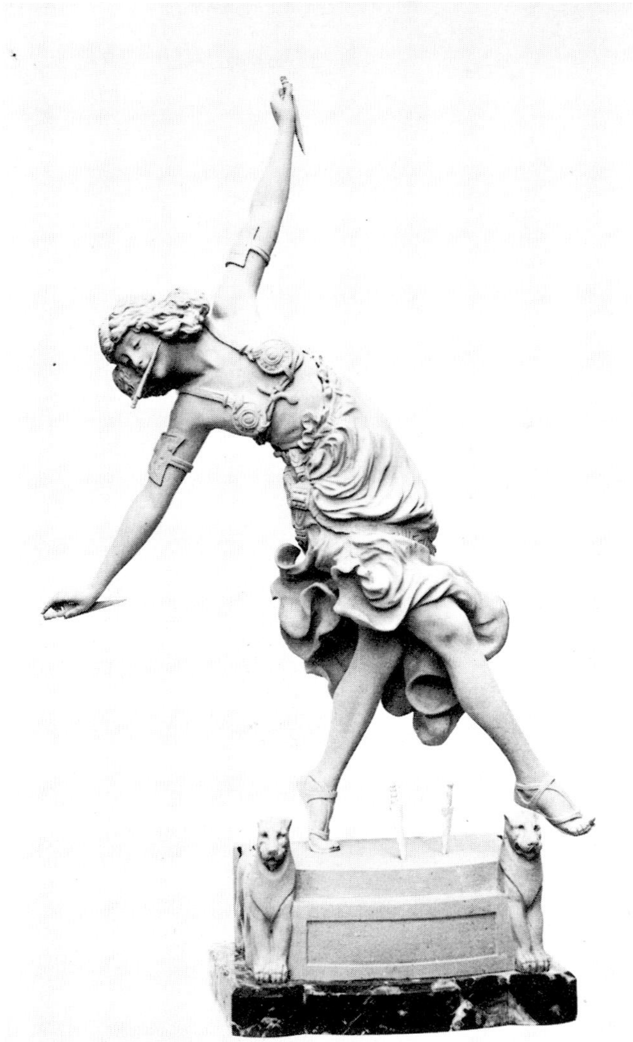

Dance of the Daggers, 49cm:19½in.

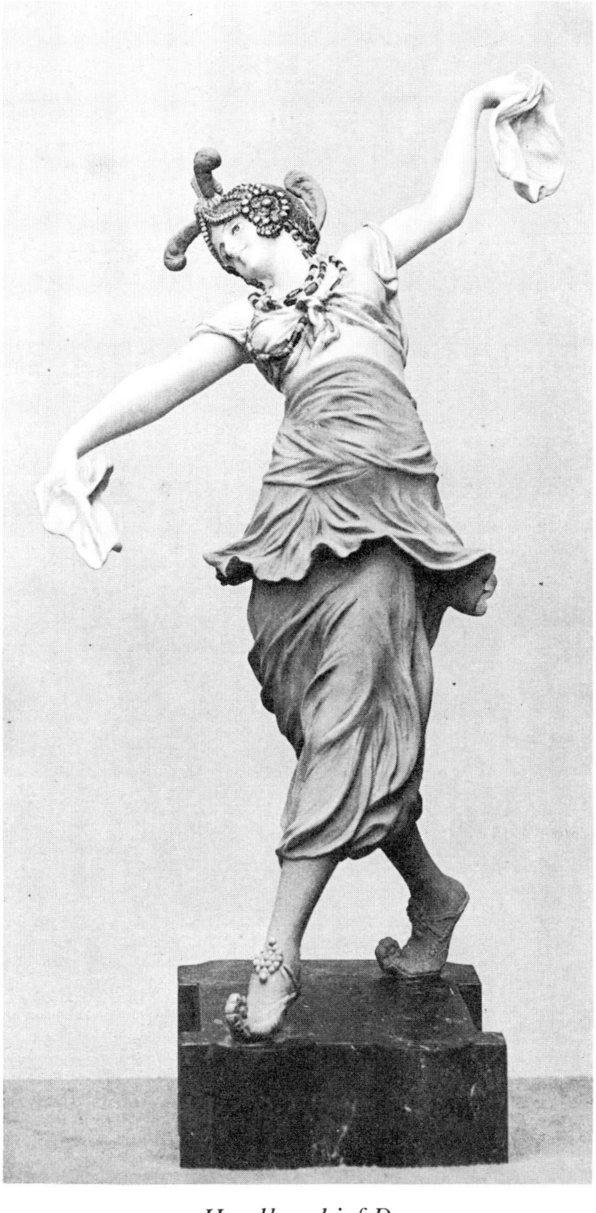

Handkerchief Dance
44cm:15¾in.; 30cm:11¾in.
Bronze and ivory

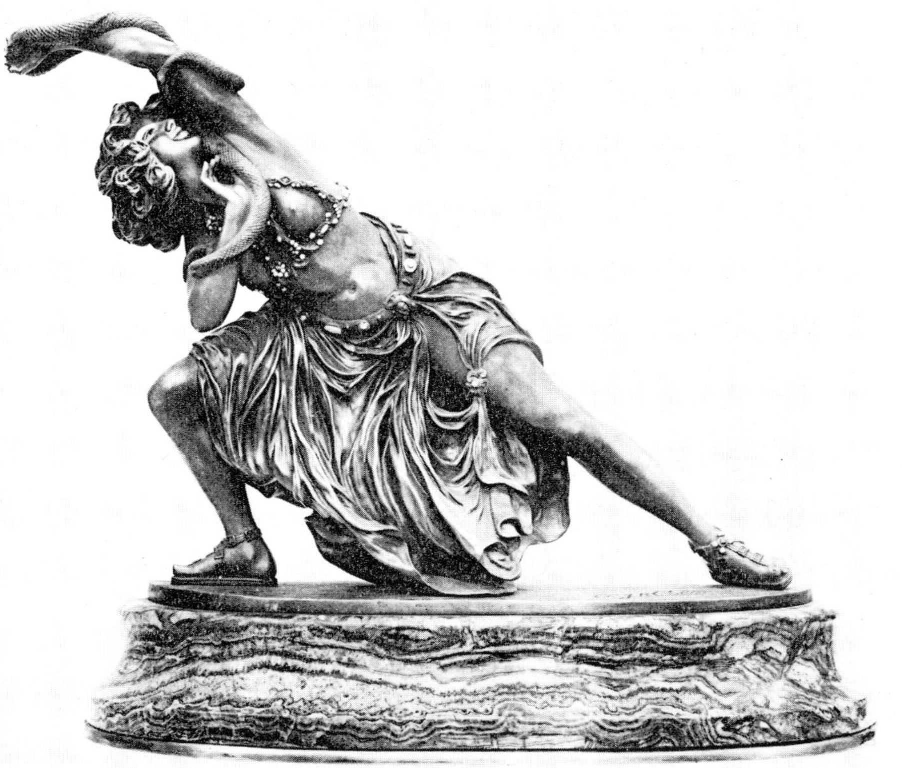

Dance of Carthage, 55cm:21½in.; 28cm:11in. Bronze and ivory

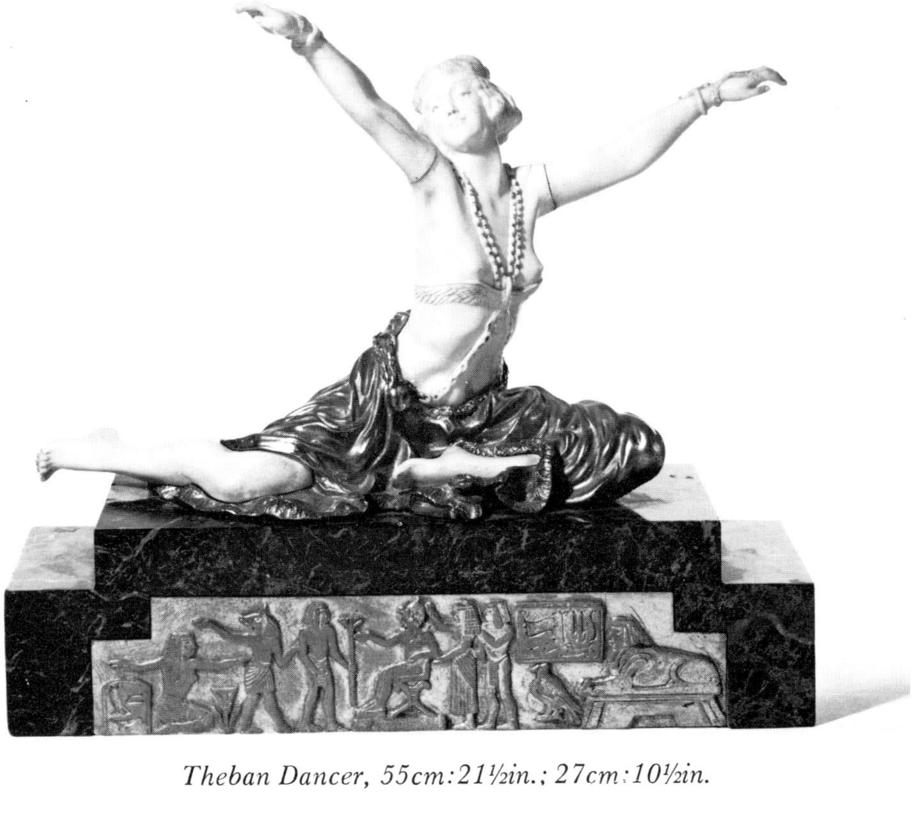

Theban Dancer, 55cm:21½in.; 27cm:10½in.

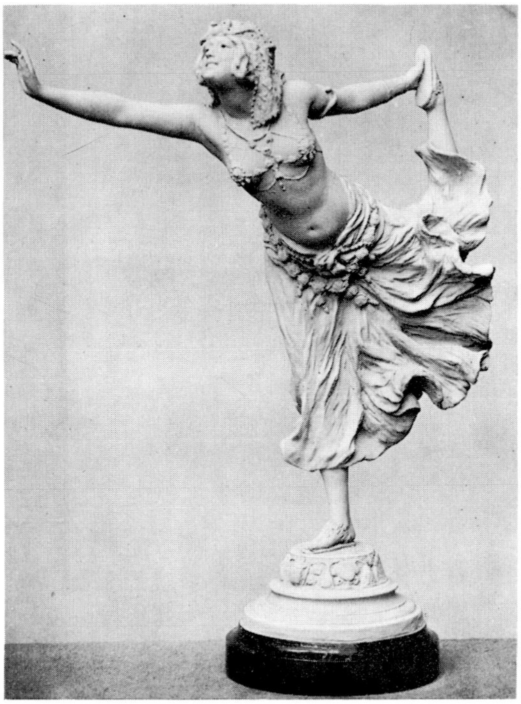

Egyptian Dancer, 44cm:17½in.; 30cm:11¾in.

Crimean Dancer
50cm:19½in.
31cm:12in.

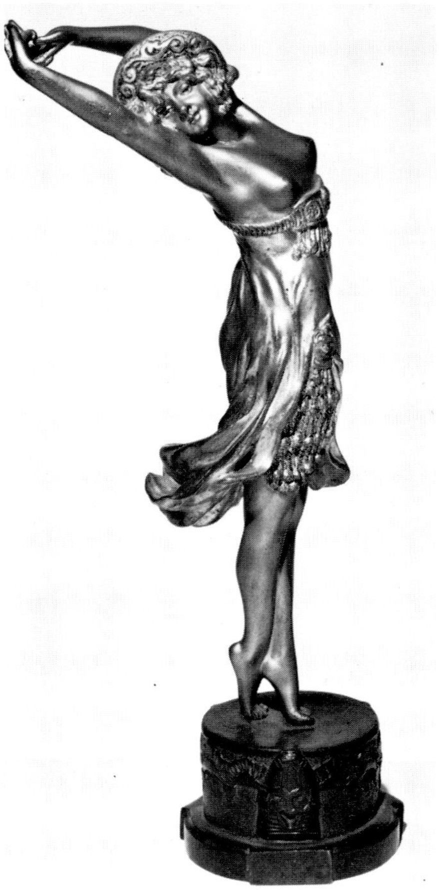

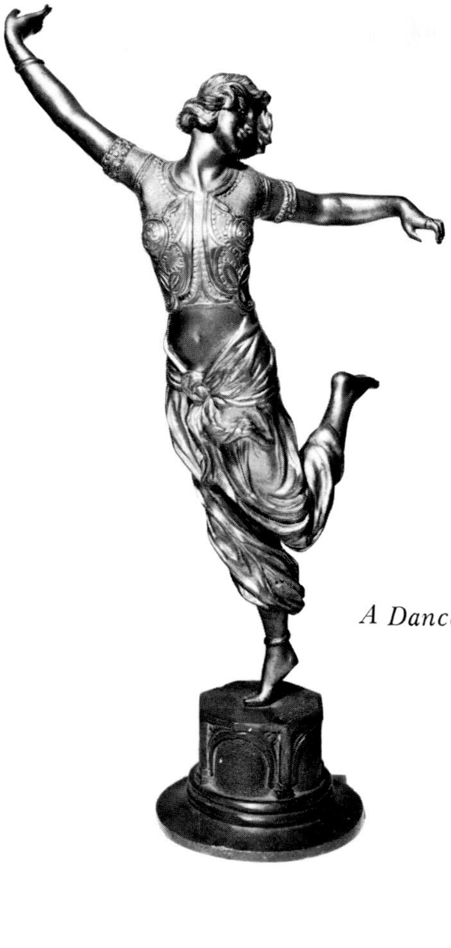

A Dancer, 31cm:12in.

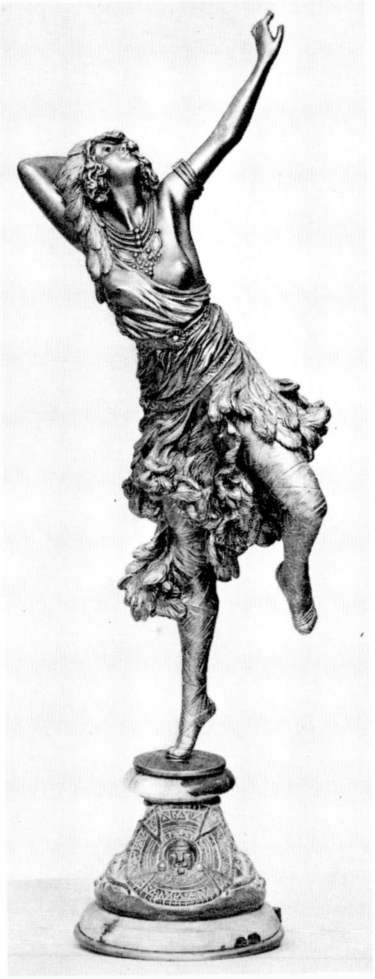

Sun Dancer, 51cm:20in.

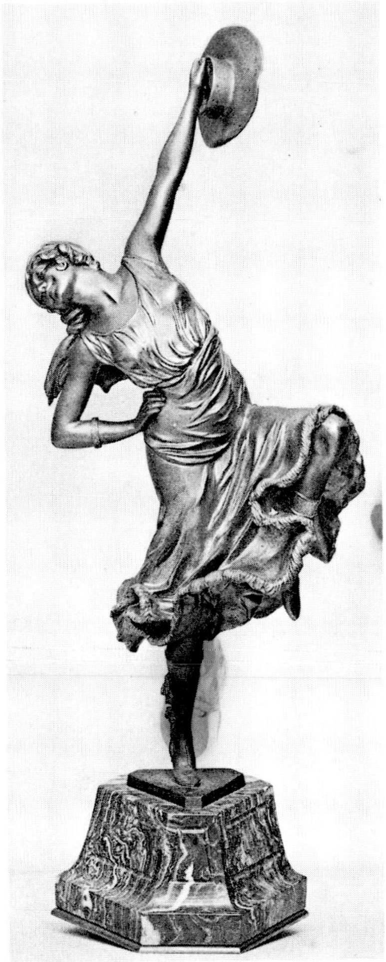

Mexican Dancer
50cm:20in.
33cm:13¼in.

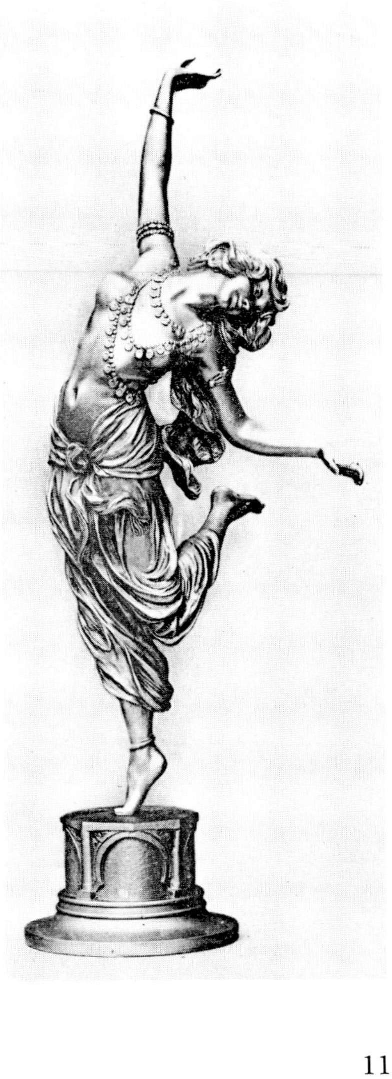

Oriental Dancer
50cm:19½in.
31cm:12in.

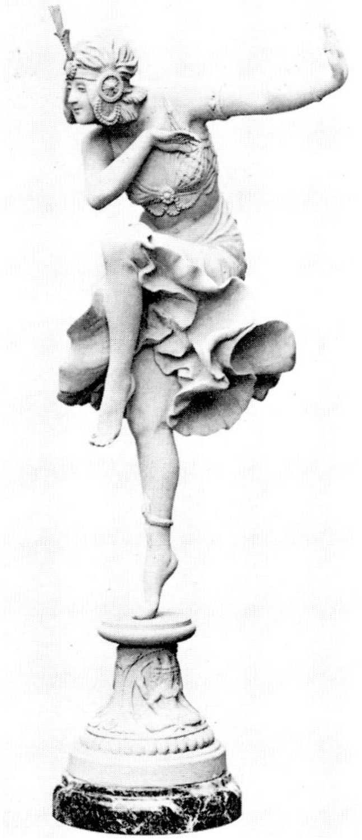

Hindu Dancer
45cm: 17½in.; 36cm: 14in.

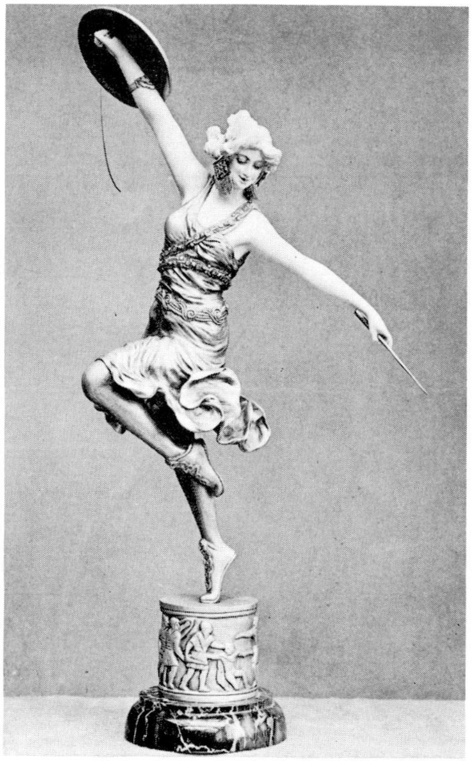

Roman Dancer, 50cm: 19¾in.

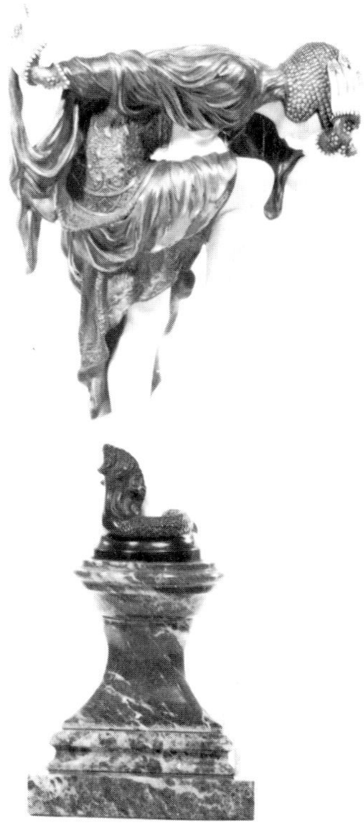

Ankara Dancer
64cm: 25in.; 44cm: 17¼in.

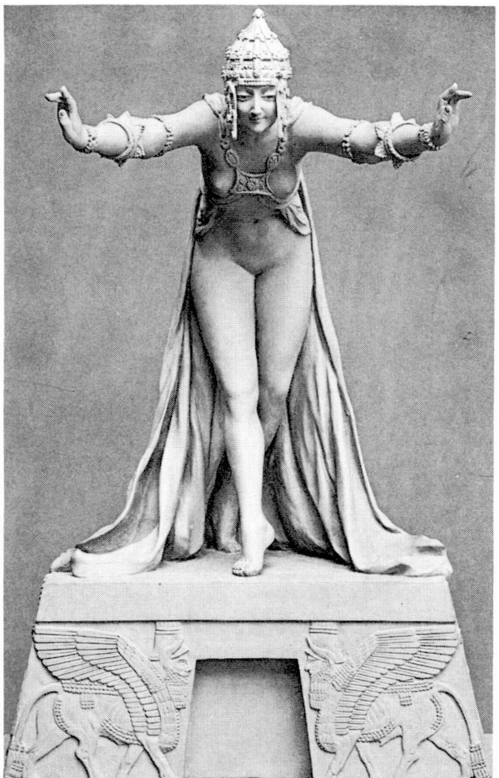

The Assyrian Dancer
66cm: 26in.

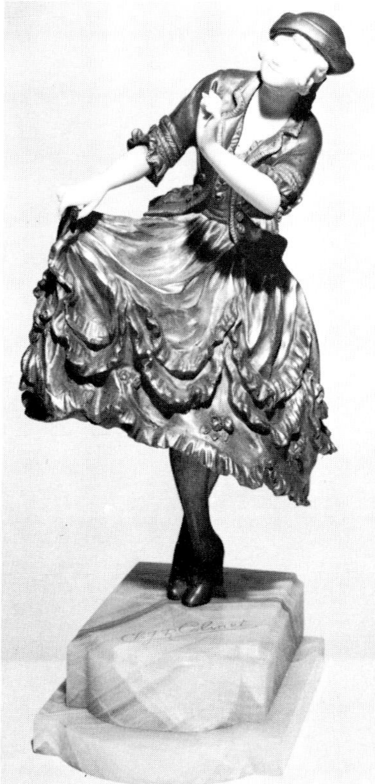

Pierrette
37cm: 14½in.

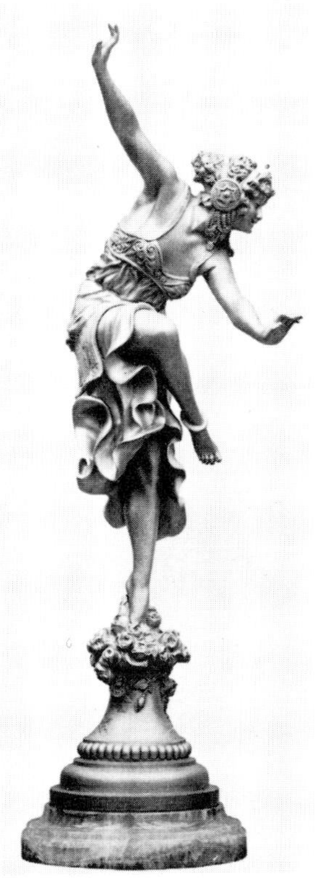

Corinthian Dancer
47cm:18½in.
35cm:13¾in.
25cm:10in.

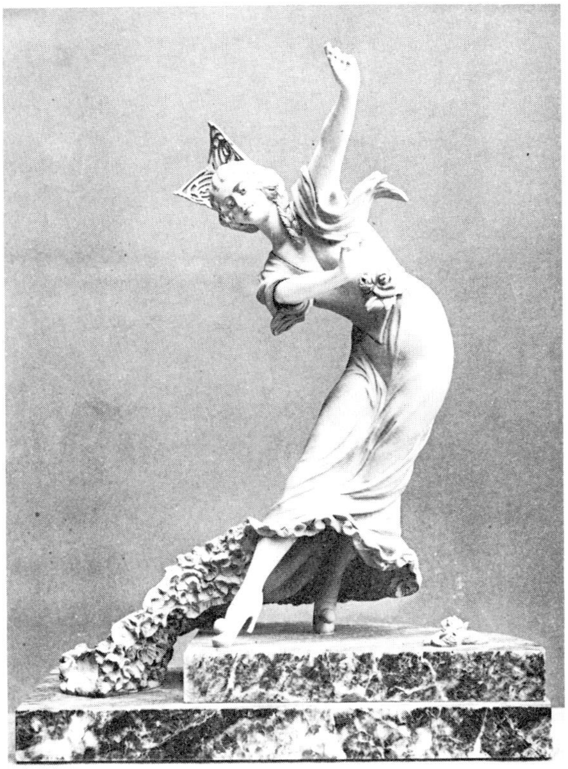

Manola, 44cm:17½in.

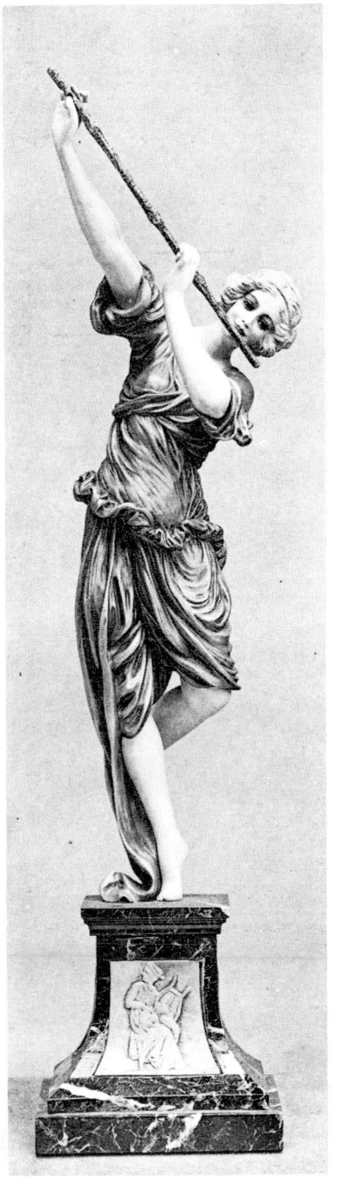

The Flute Player
45cm:17¾in.

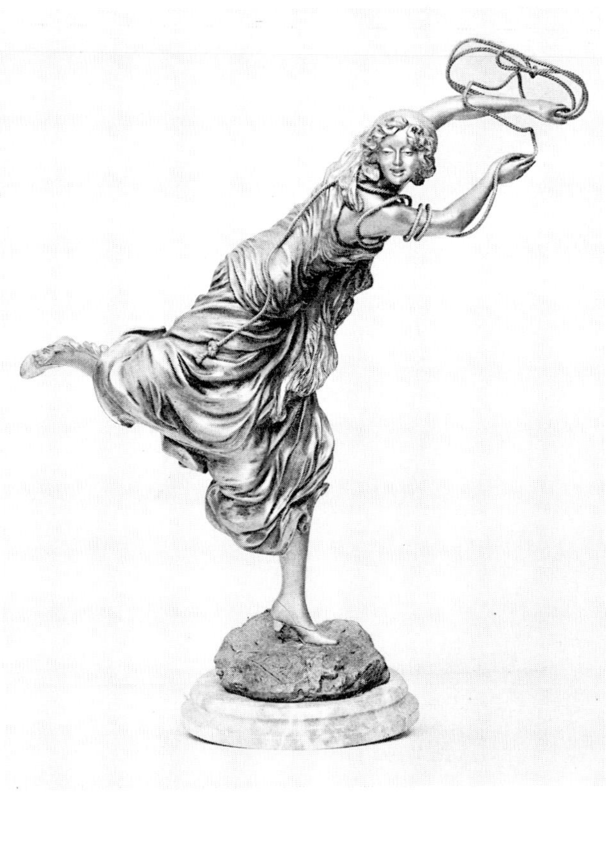

The Lasso Thrower
45cm:17¾in.

A. COLOMBIER

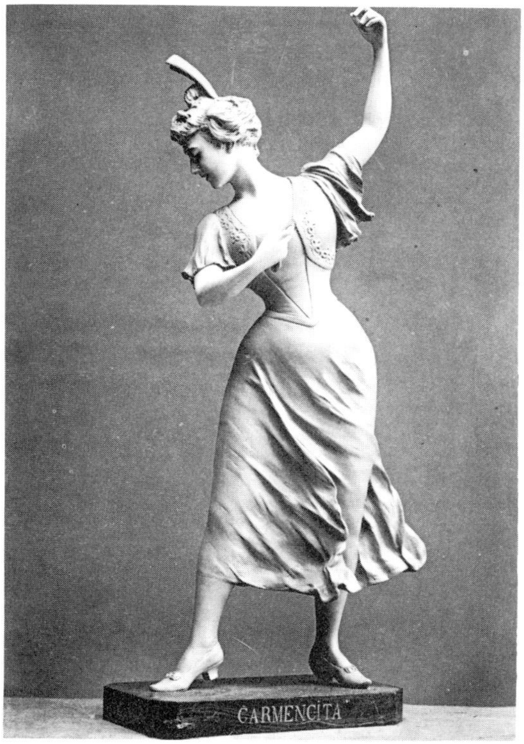

Carmencita, 57cm:22½in.
46cm:18in.; 25cm:10in.

J. COSTA

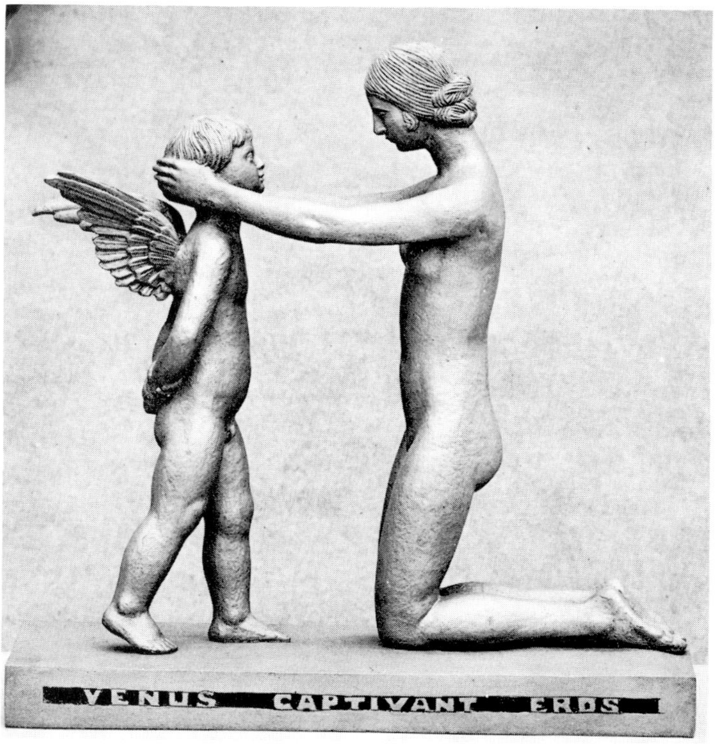

Venus Capturing Eros, 39cm:15½in.
Grand Prix at the
International Exhibition of Decorative Arts

MAURICE CONSTANT

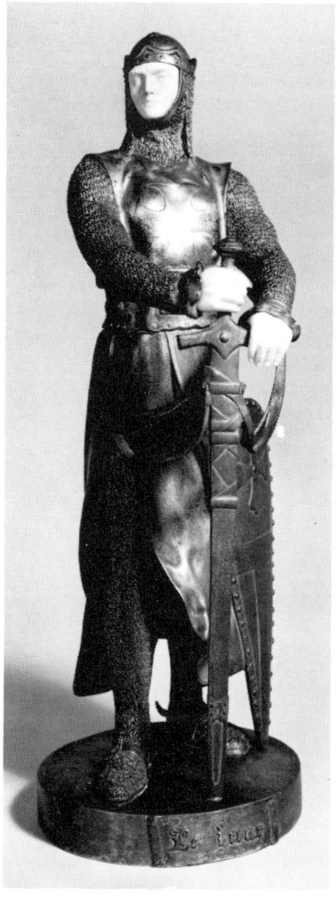

The Crusader
58cm:23in.
38cm:15in.

F.H. COUTHEILLAS

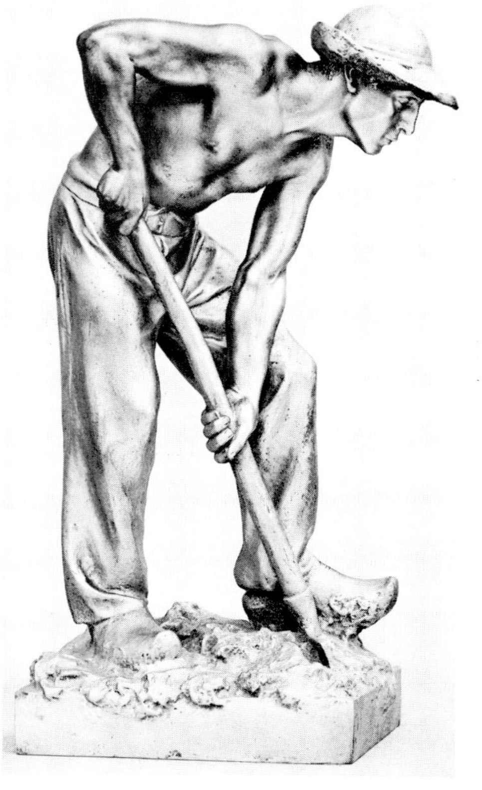

The Earth
56cm:22in.

PAUL D'AIRE

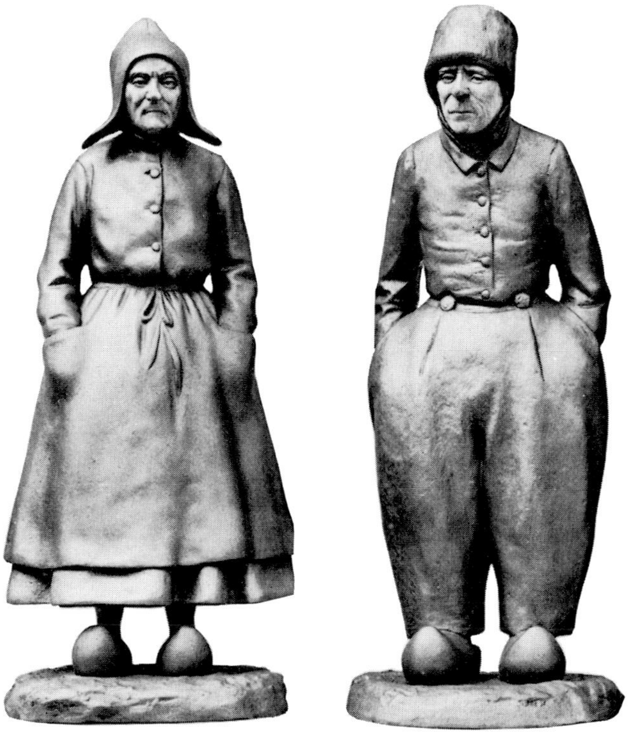

Dutch Fisher Folk, 31cm:12in.; 22cm:8½in.

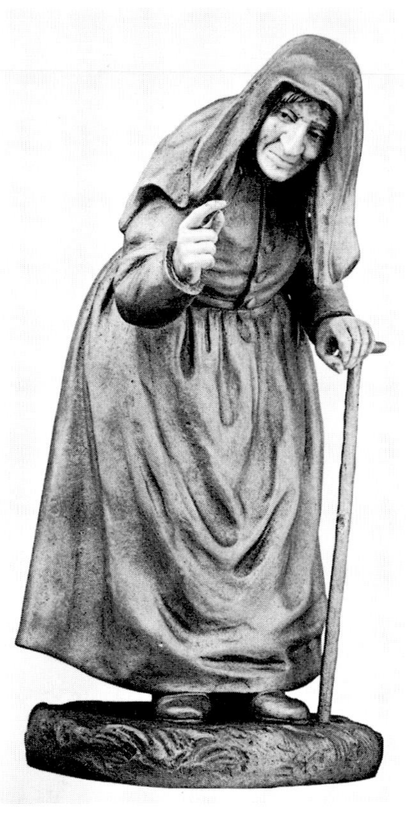

Witch
22cm:8½in.
15cm:6in.

DAKON

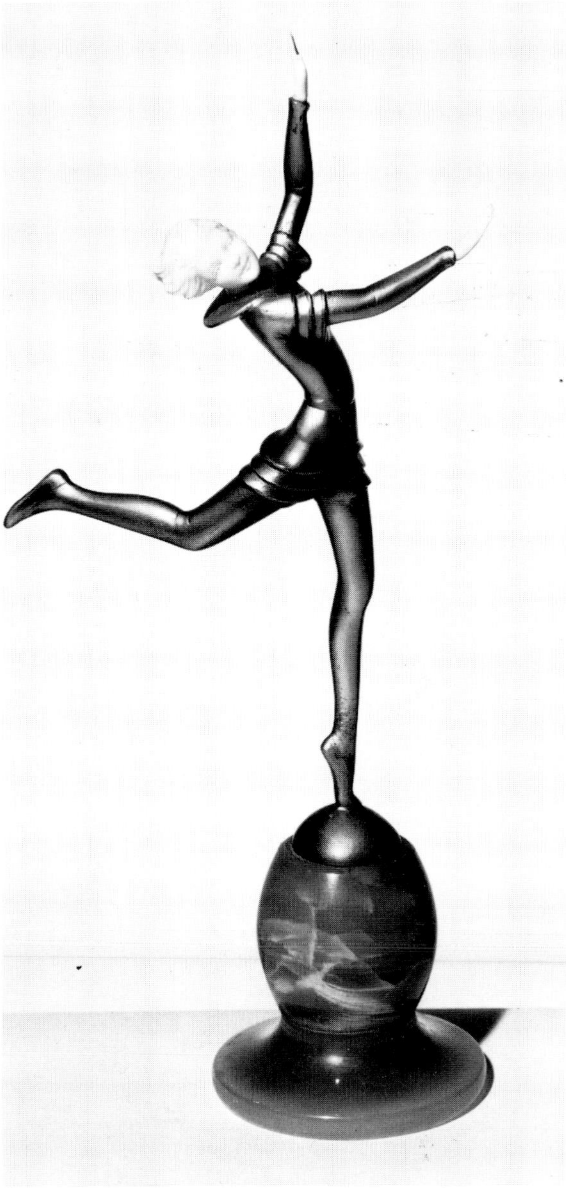

Dancer, 20cm:8in.

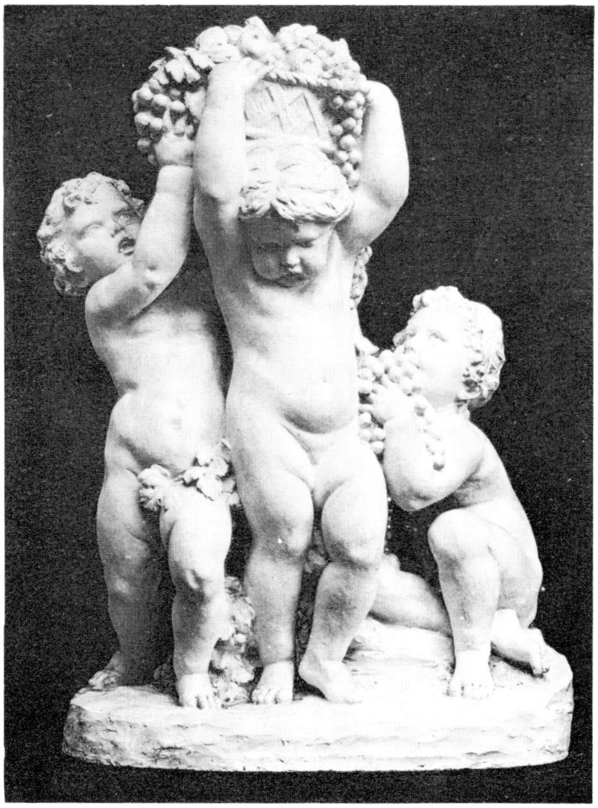

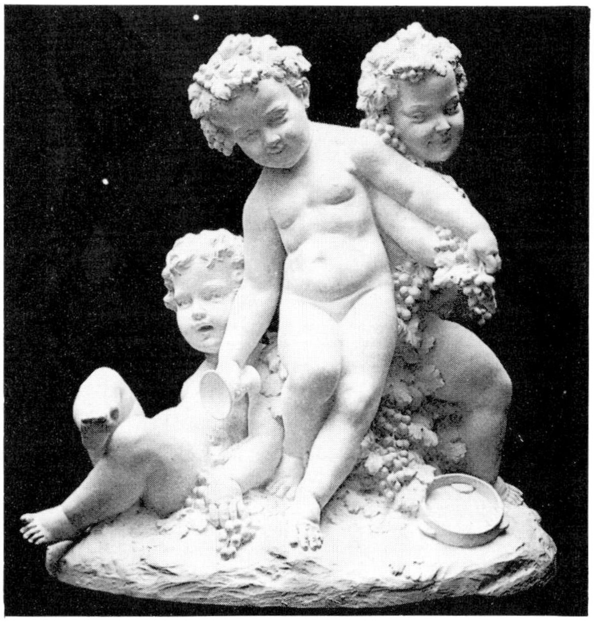

Above: Bacchanal, 50cm:19½in.

Left: Autumn, 70cm:27½in.

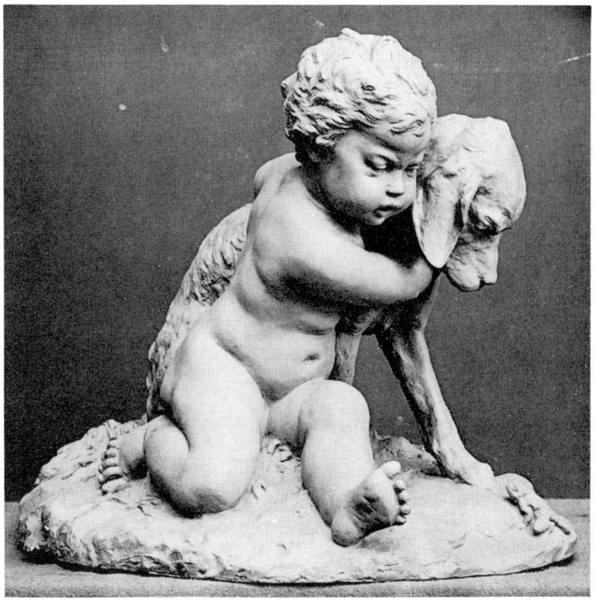

Above: Old Friend, 40cm:15¾in.

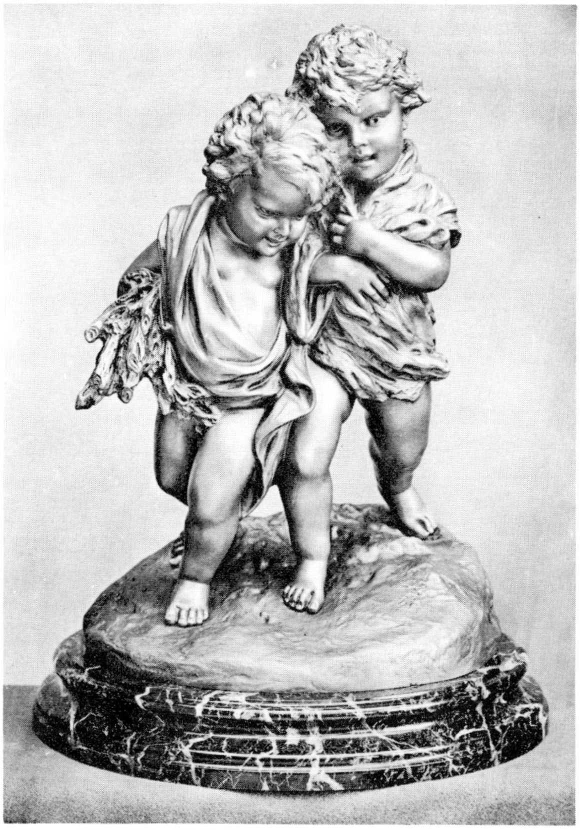

Right: Near Shelter, 40cm:15¾in.
Exhibited 1924 in Paris

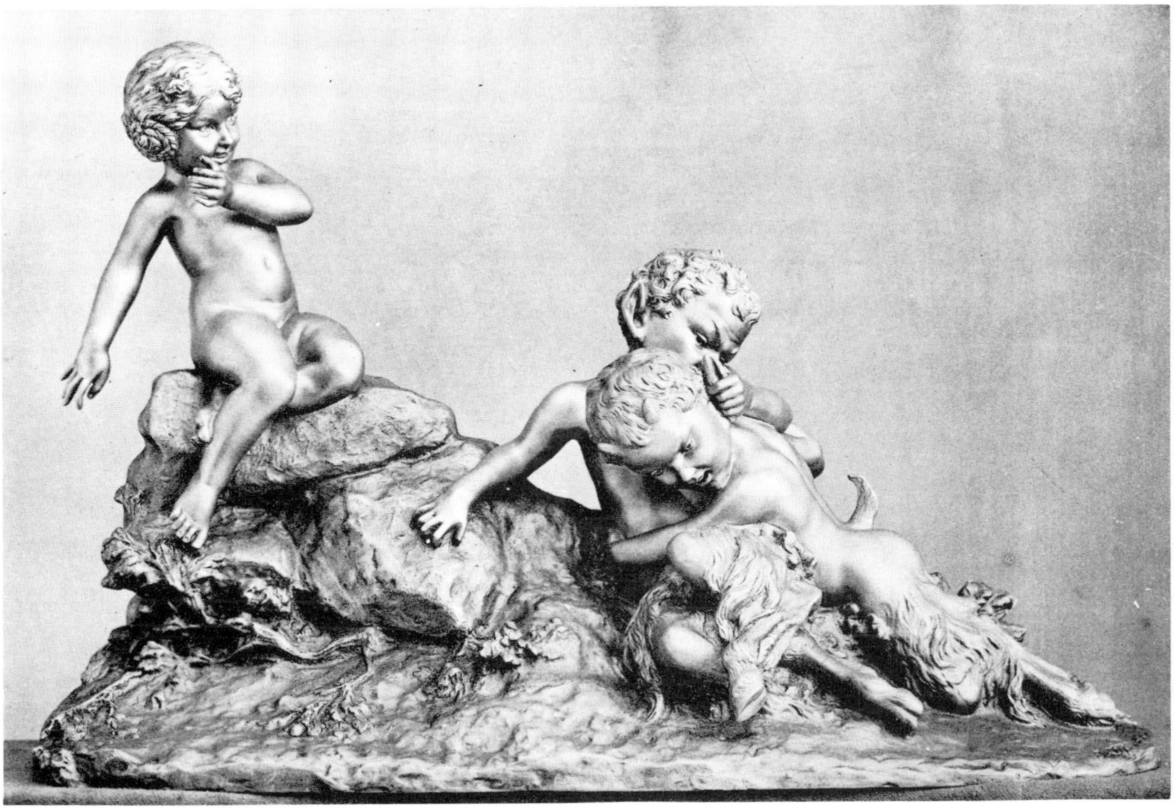

Rivalry, 41cm:16in.

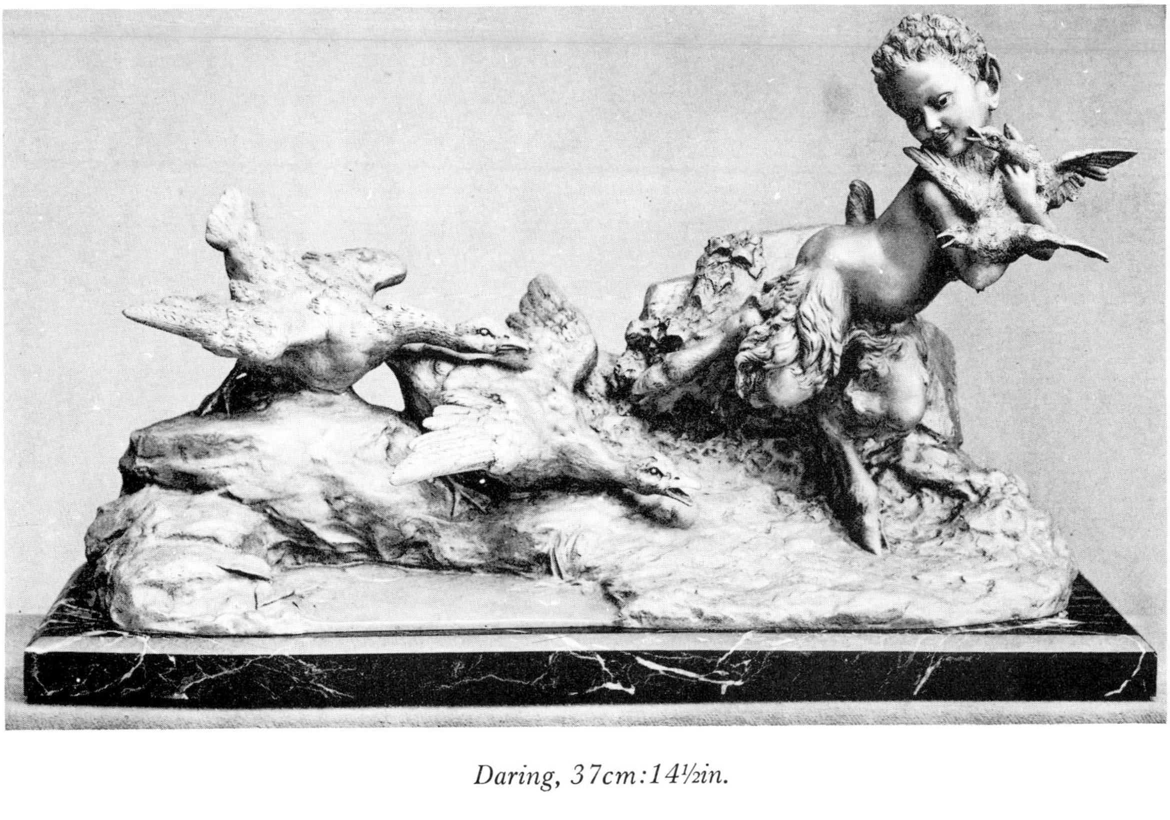

Daring, 37cm:14½in.

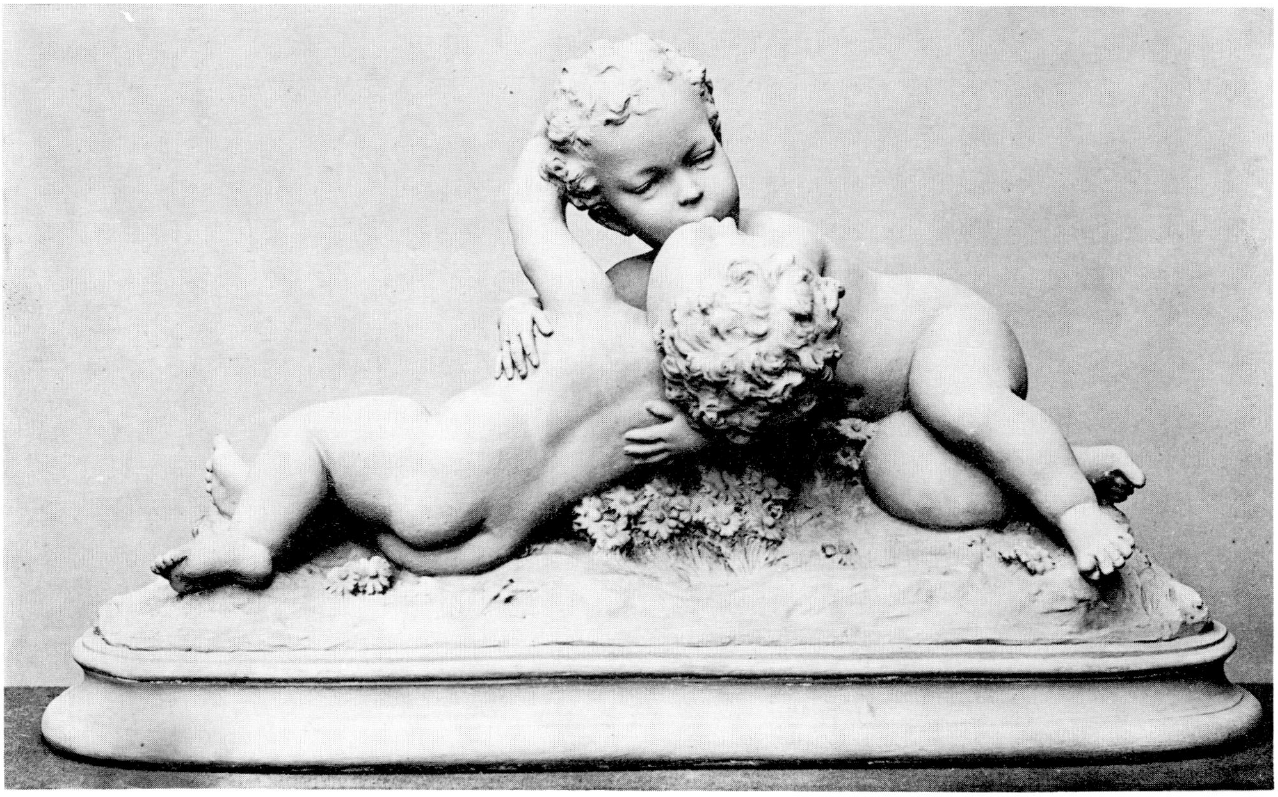

The Kiss, 38cm:15in.

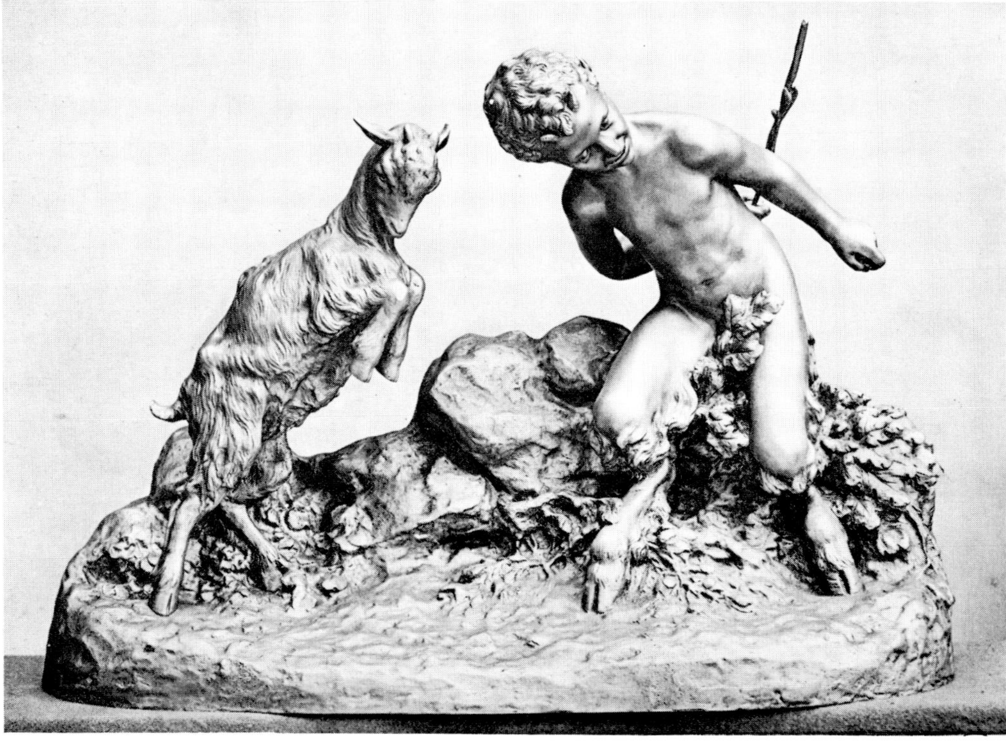

Young Faun Playing, 42cm:16½in.

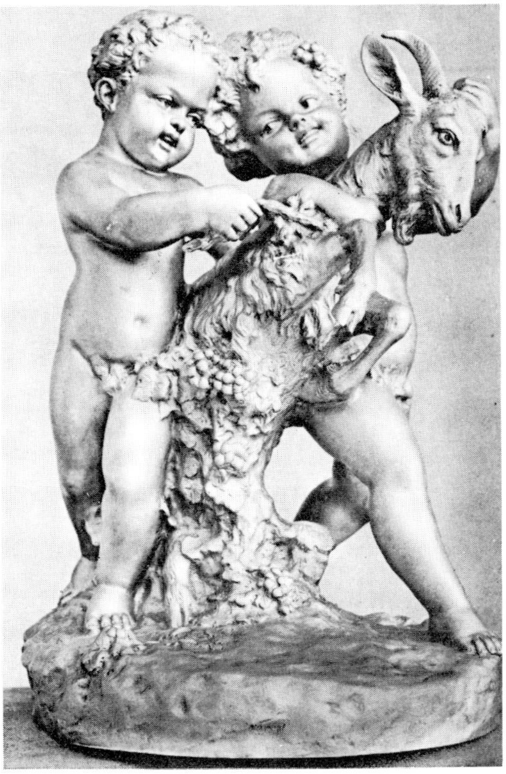

Rural Delight, 38cm:15in.

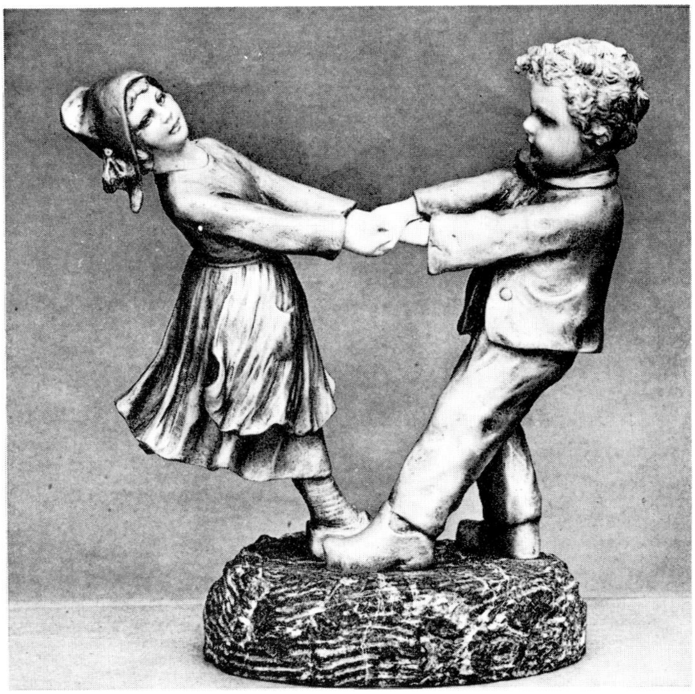

Dutch Dance, 20cm:8in.

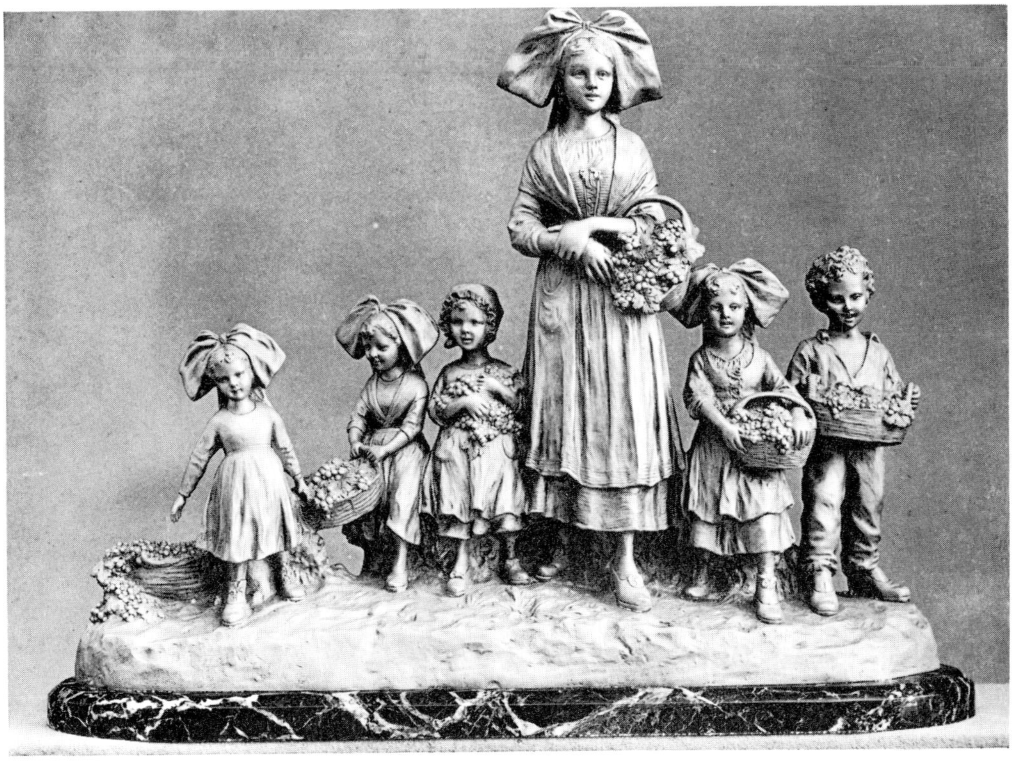

Wine Festival, 48cm:19in.

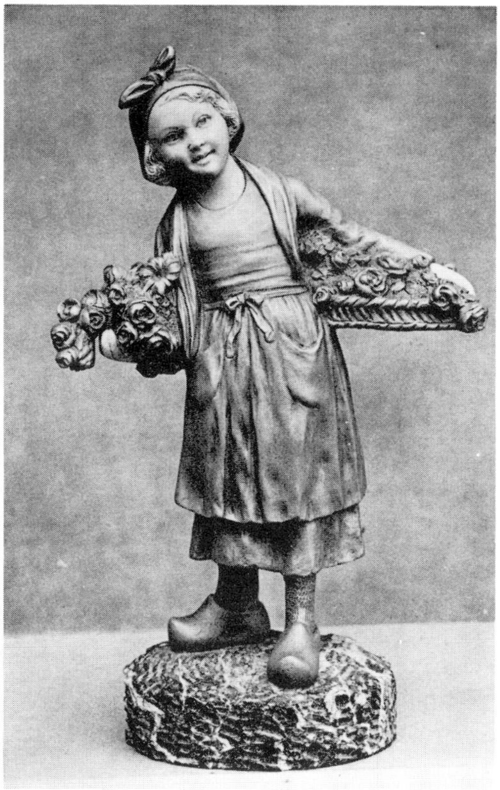

Little Flower Seller
25cm: 9¾in.

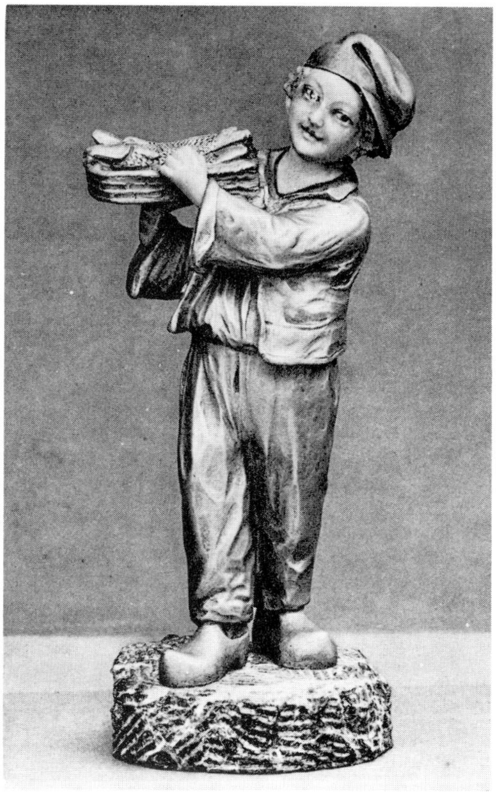

Little Fisherman
23cm: 9in.

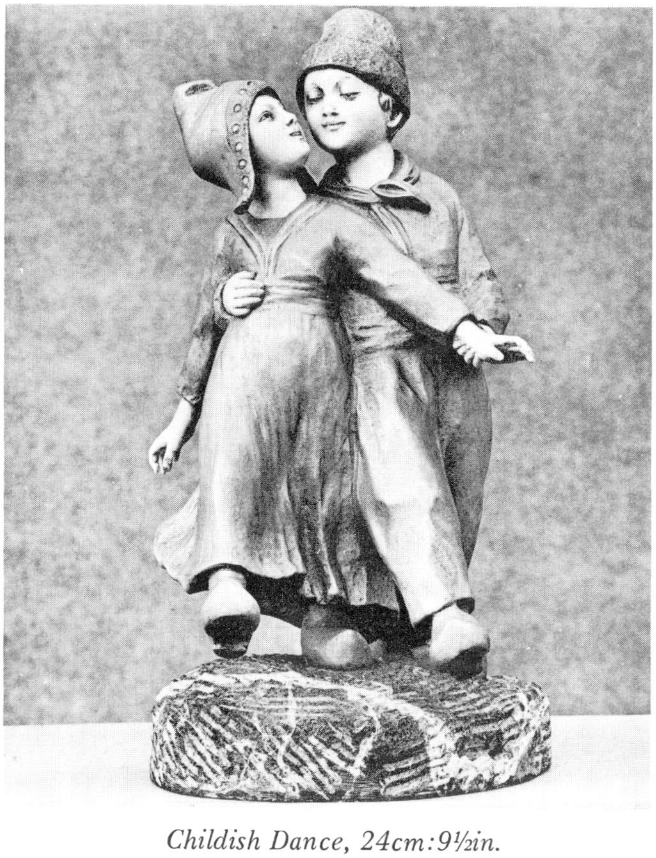

Childish Dance, 24cm: 9½in.

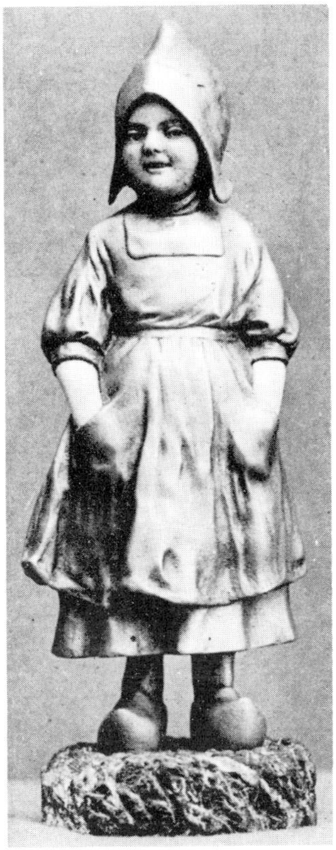

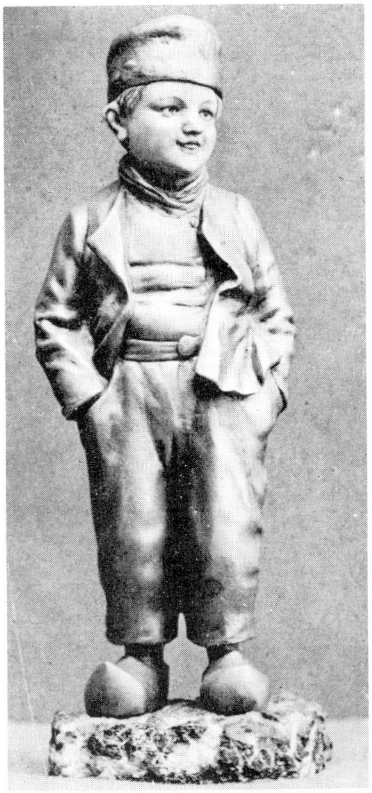

Dutch Children, 24cm:9½in.

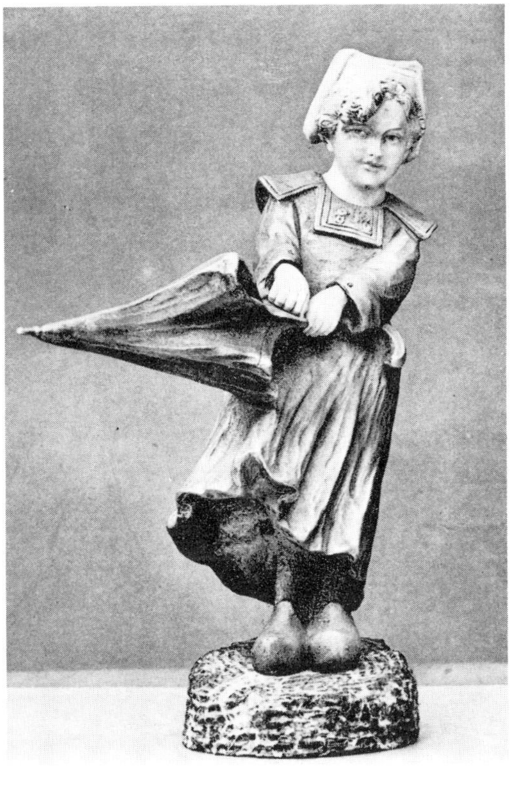

Gust of Wind, 21cm:8¼in.

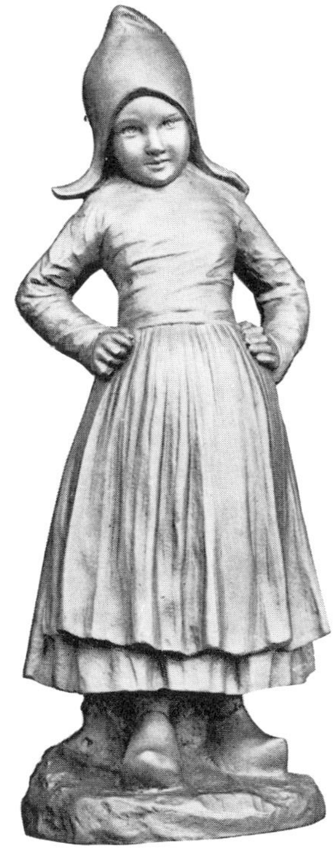

Dutch Girl, 24cm:9½in.

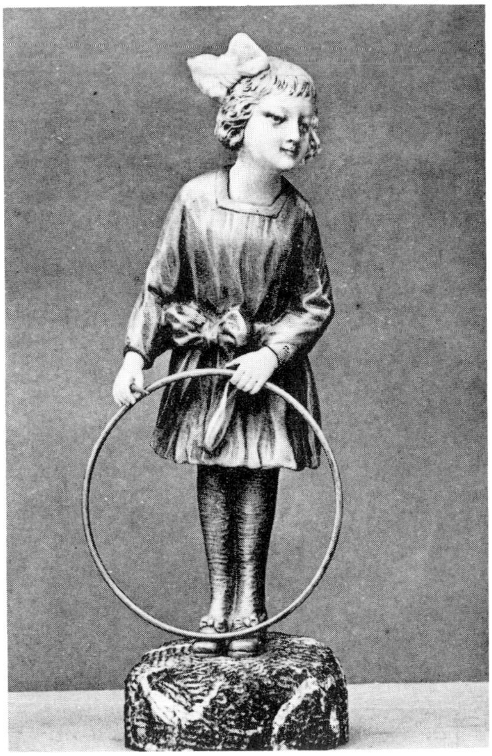

Young Girl with Hoop, 22cm:8½in.

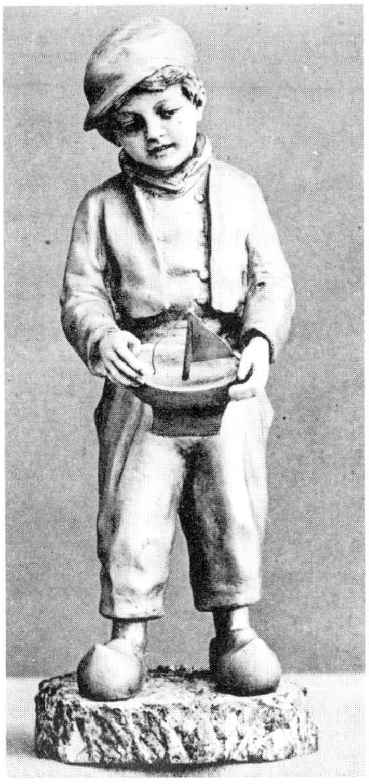

Future Admiral, 25cm:9¾in.

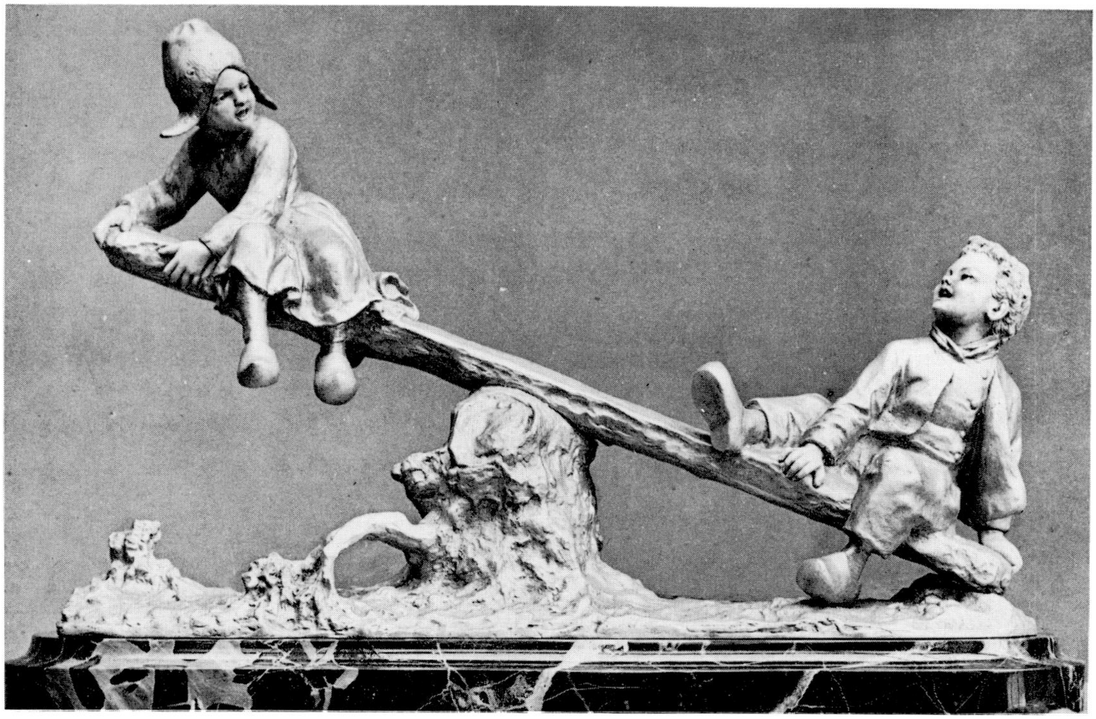

See-Saw, 31cm:12¼in.

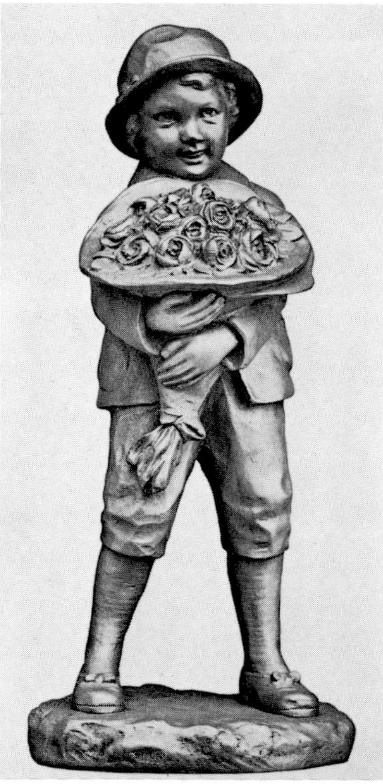

Fete Day, 23cm:9in.

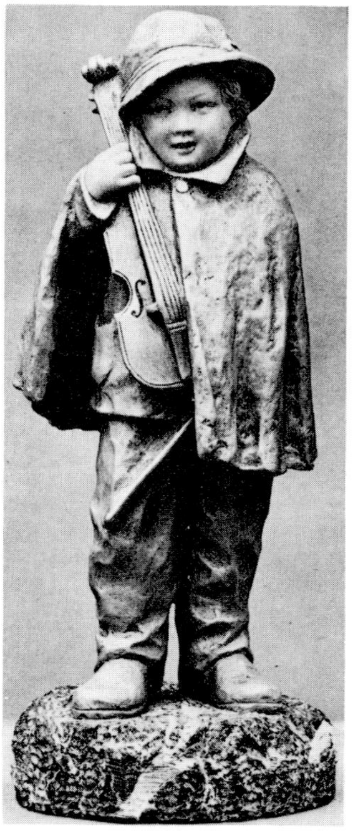

Little Violinist, 22cm:8½in.

S. DEBRY

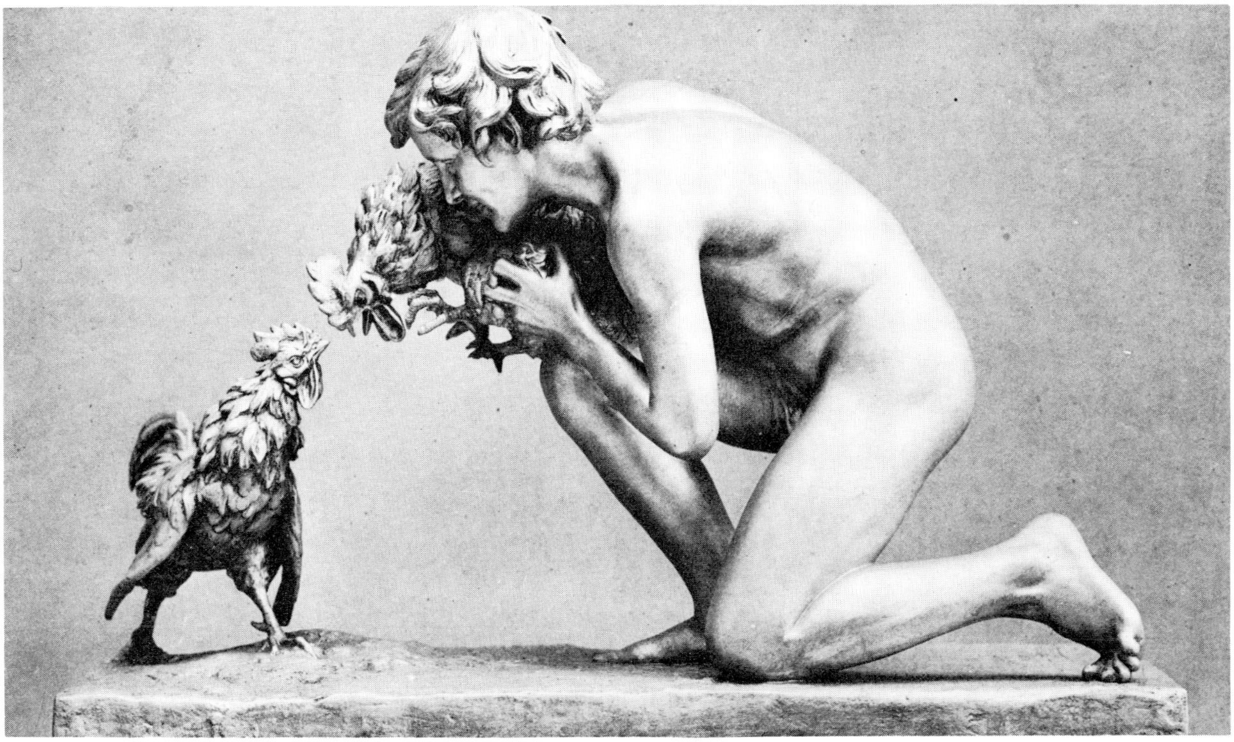

Cock Fight, 42cm:16½in.

M. DEBUT

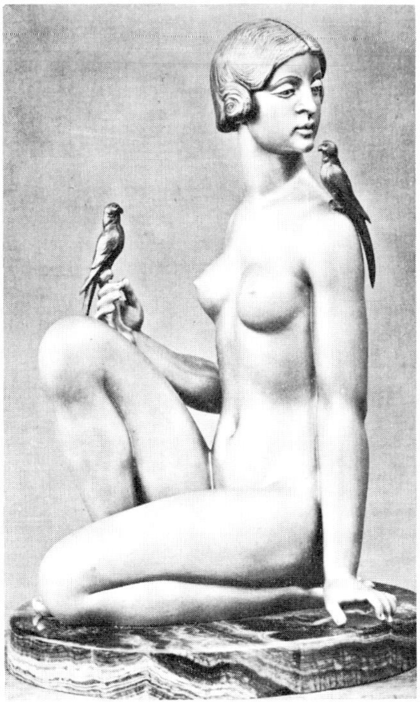

Parakeets, 46cm:18in.

DELAGRANGE

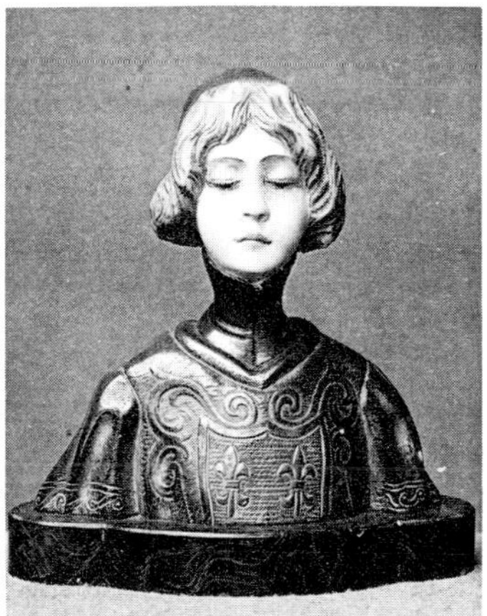

Prayer Book
16cm:6½in.
11cm:4½in.
7cm:2¾in.

Templar
74cm:29in.
47cm:18½in.
32cm:12½in.

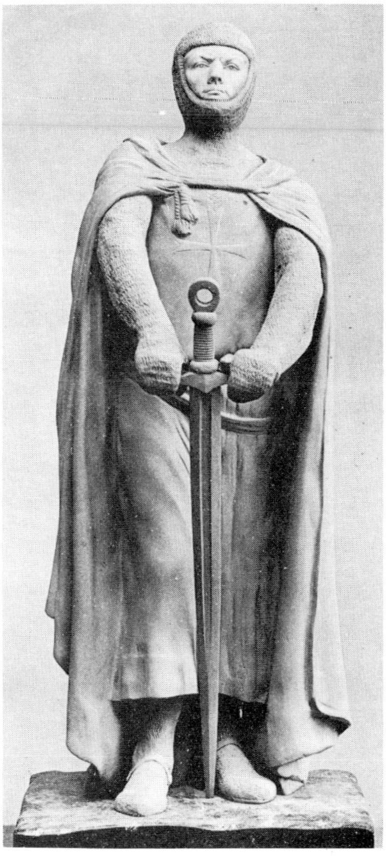

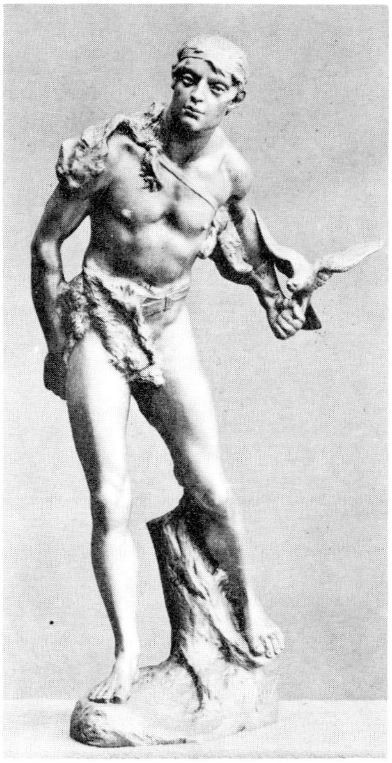

Falconer, 42cm:16½in.

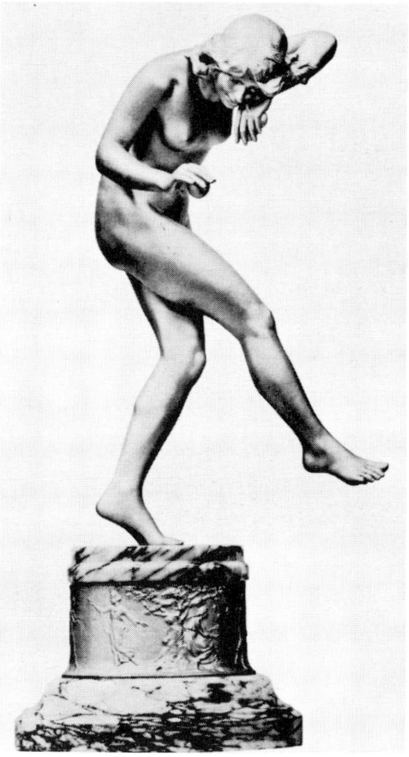

Dance of the Apple, 63cm:24¾in.

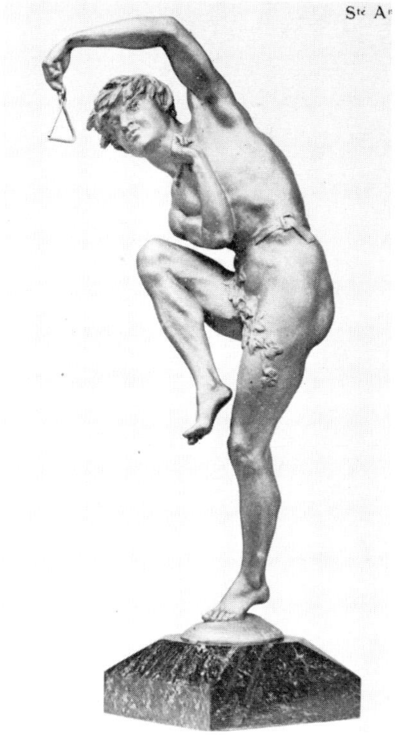

Faun with Triangle, 44cm:17¼in.

JOÉ DESCOMPS

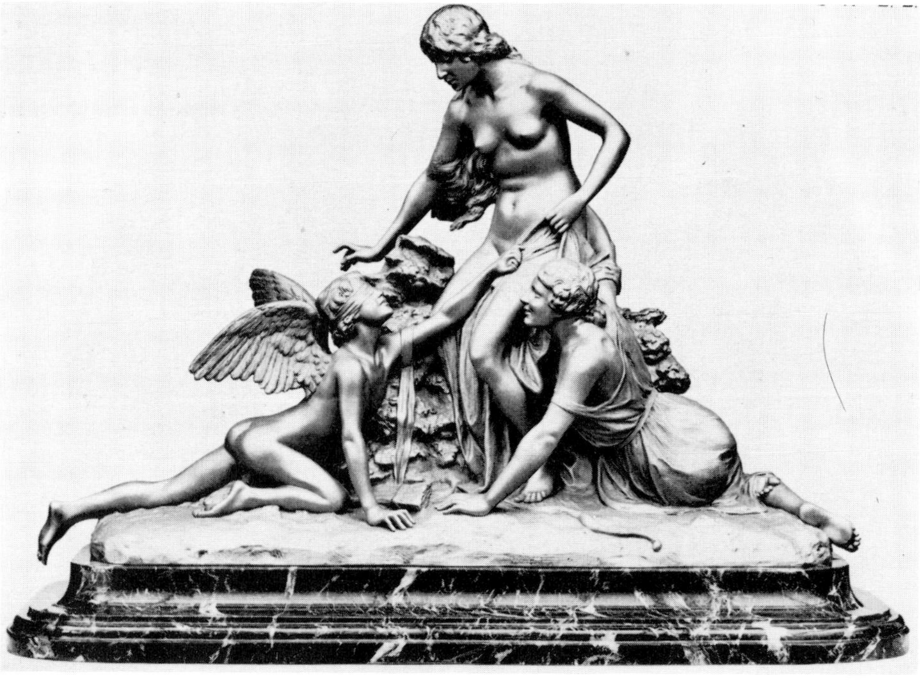

Blind Man's Buff
52cm:20½in.

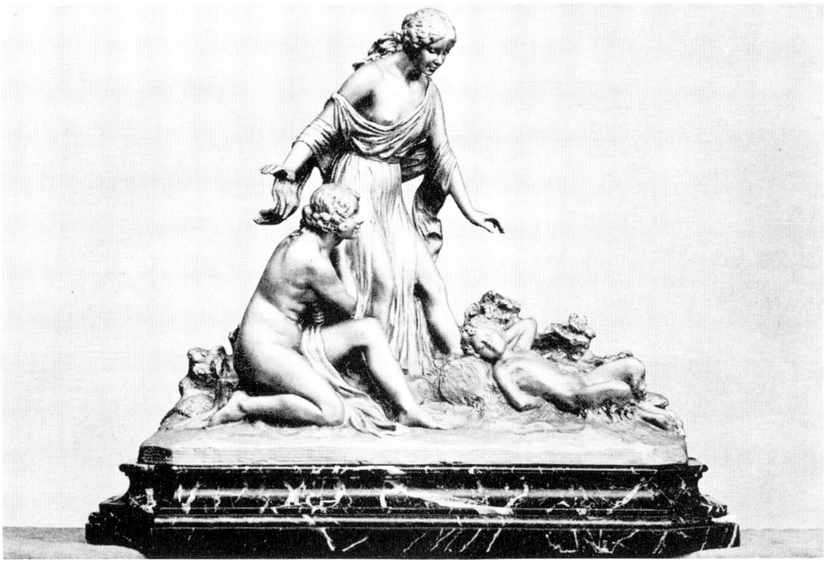

Surprise Meeting, 54cm:21¼in.

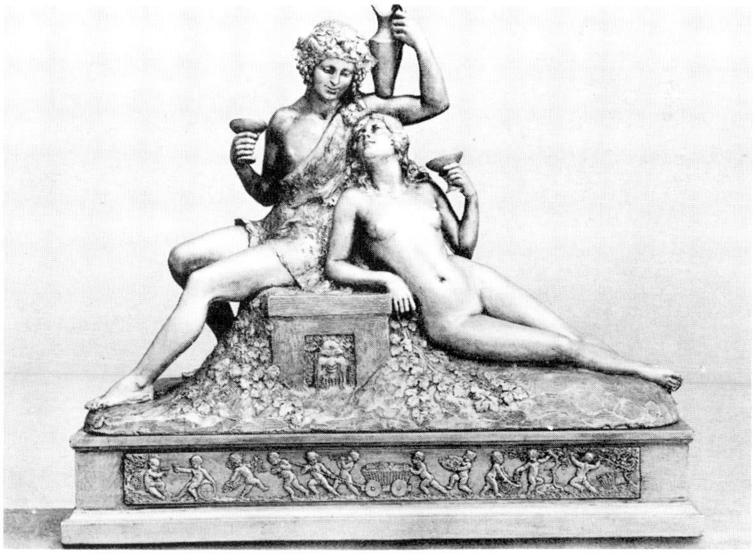

Bacchus and Ivresse, 55cm:21½in.

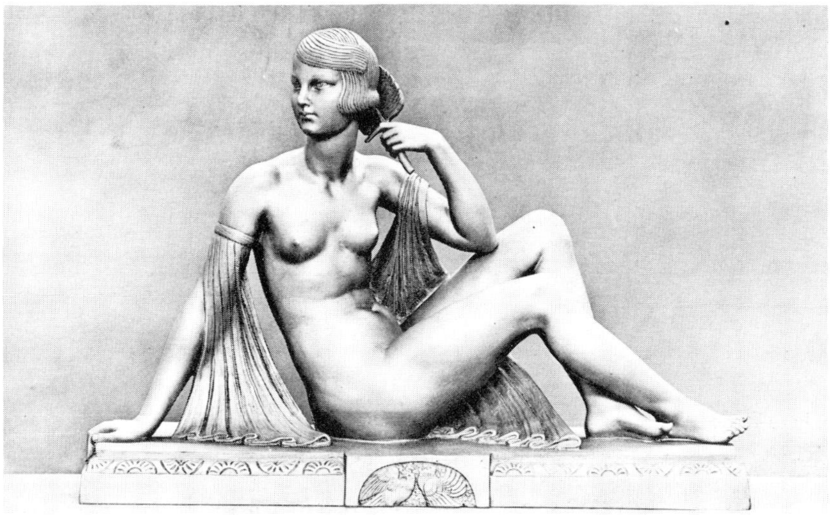

Meditation, 44cm:17¼in.

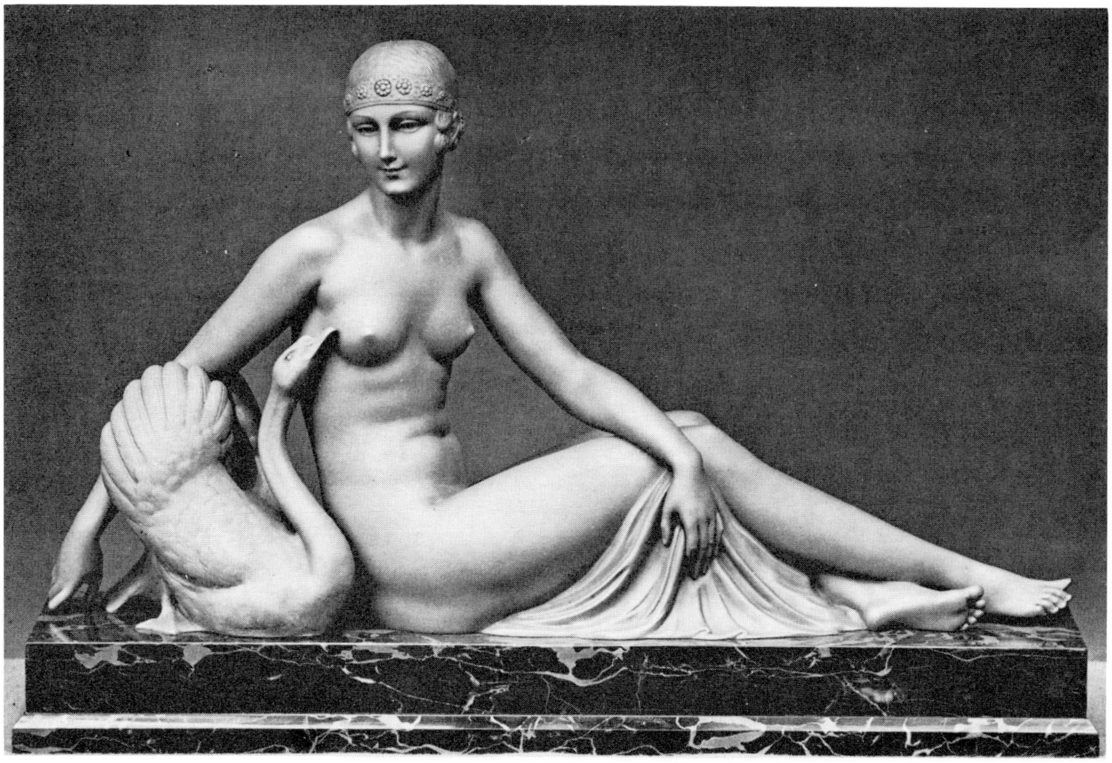

Girl with Swan, 40cm:15in.

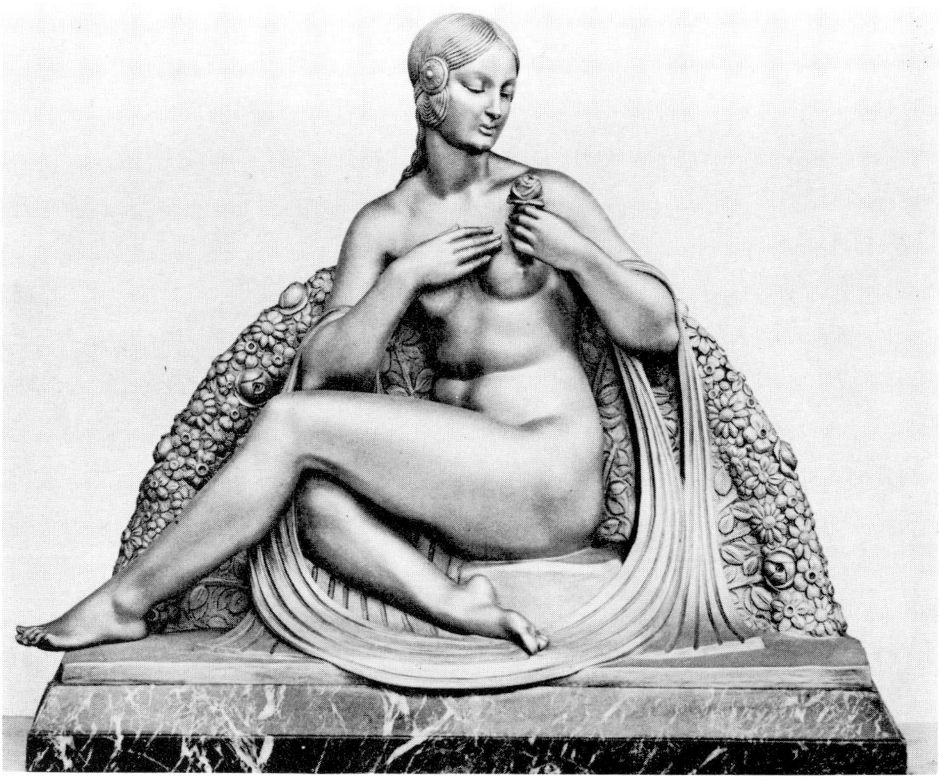

Scent of the Rose, 45cm:17¾in.

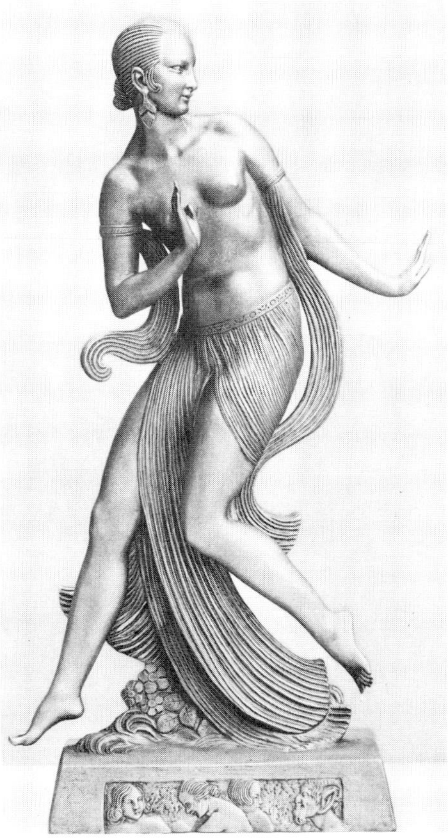

Nymph, 49cm:19¼in.

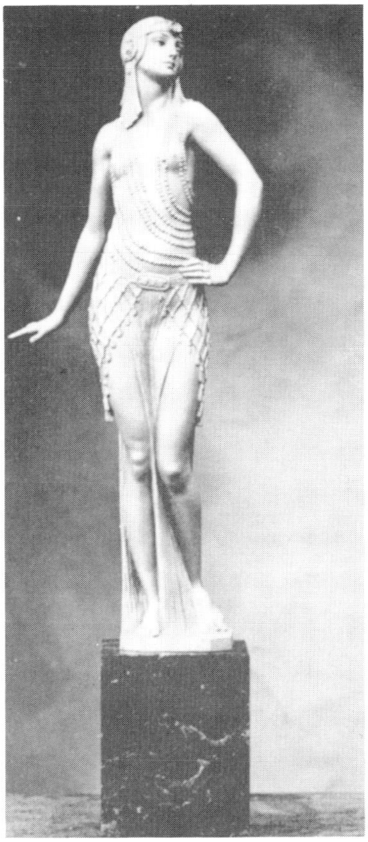

Regal, 44cm:17¼in.
25cm:10in.; 22cm:8½in.
Original cost about £18 in 1936

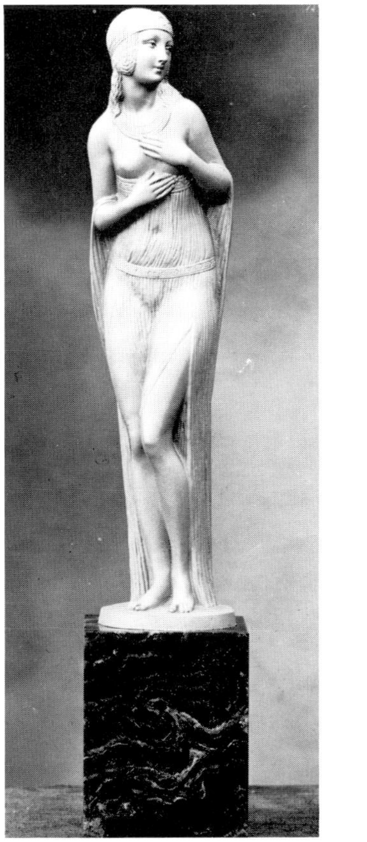

Enchanted
39cm:15½in.; 22cm:8½in.

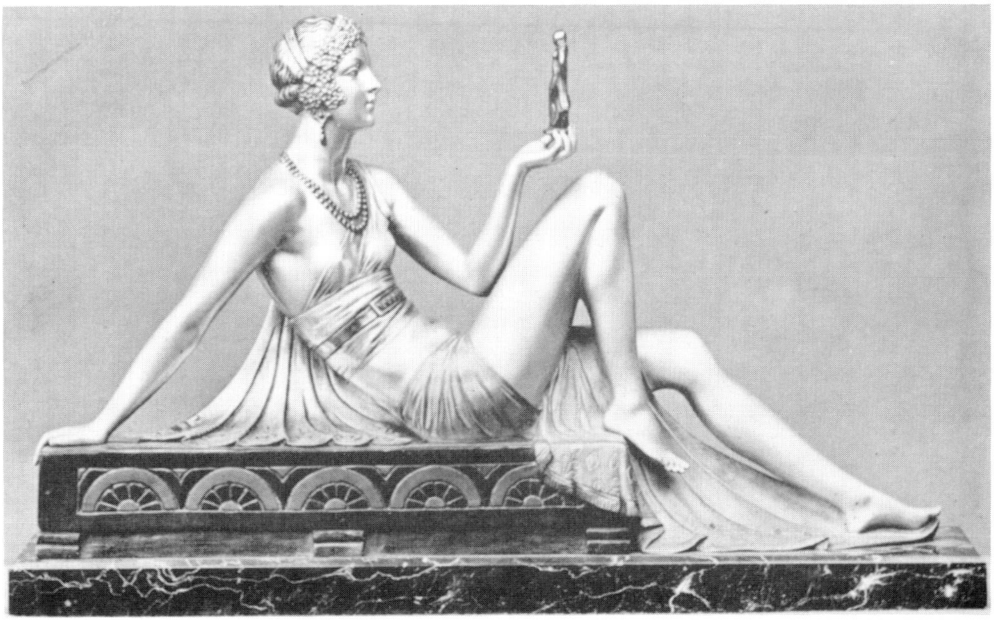

Comparison
34cm:13½in.

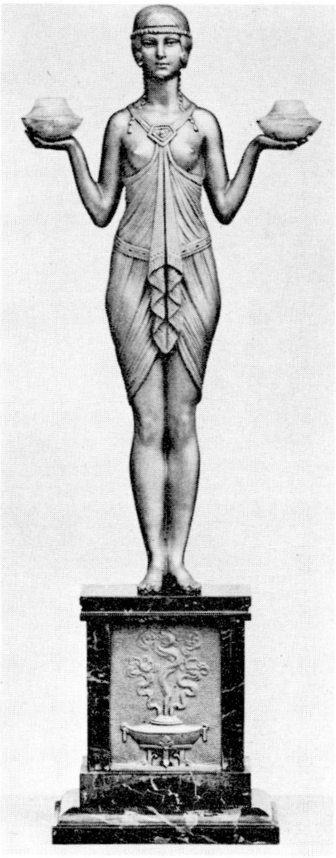

Young Slave, 50cm:19¾in.

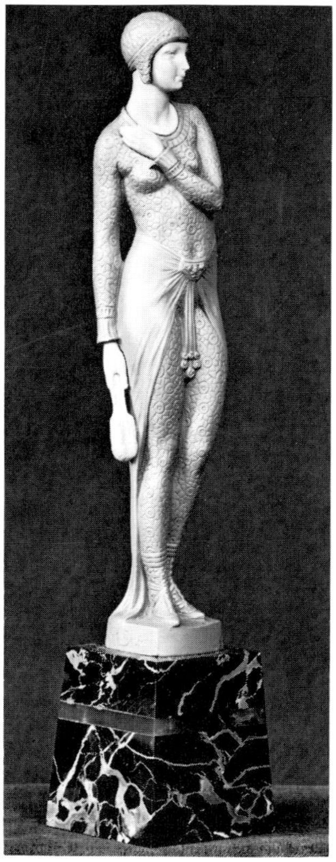

Beauty of Paris
25cm:10in.; 20cm:8in.

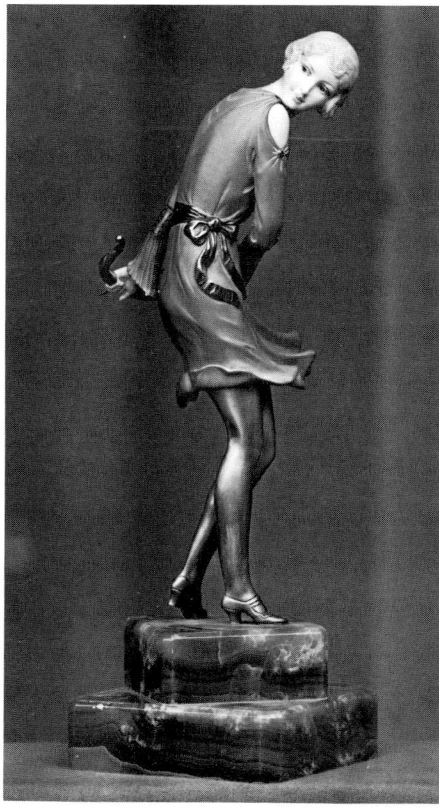

First Arrows, 43cm:17in.

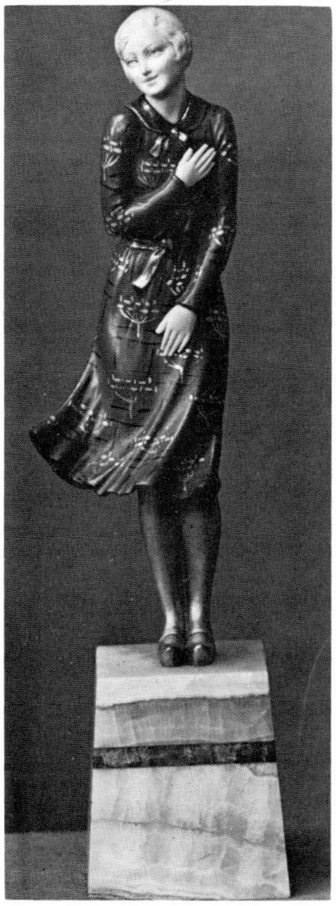

Chilly, 34cm:13½in.

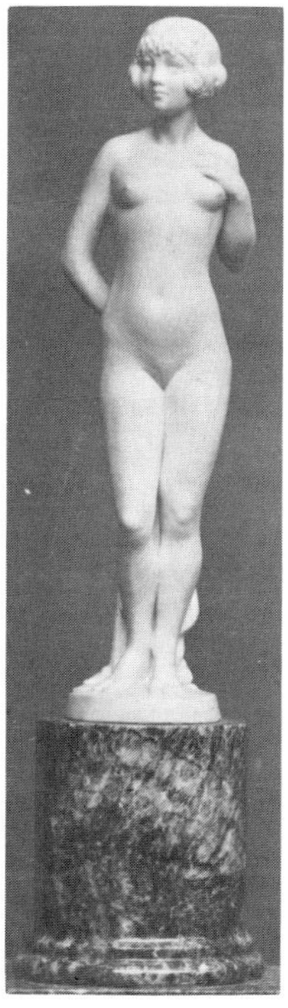

Chloe
16cm:6¼in.; 11cm:4½in.

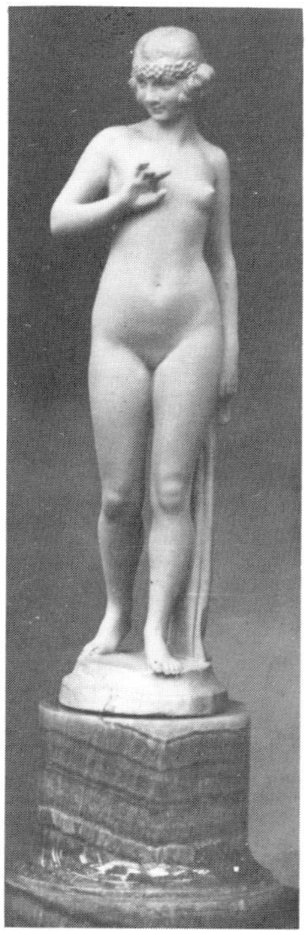

Candid, 22cm:8½in.

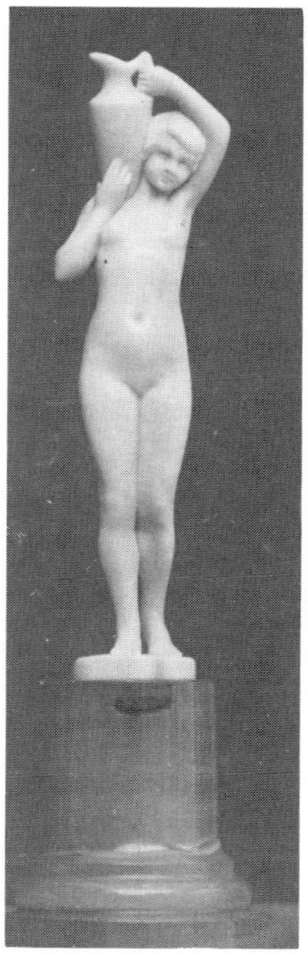

Water Carrier
22cm:8½in.
16cm:6¼in.

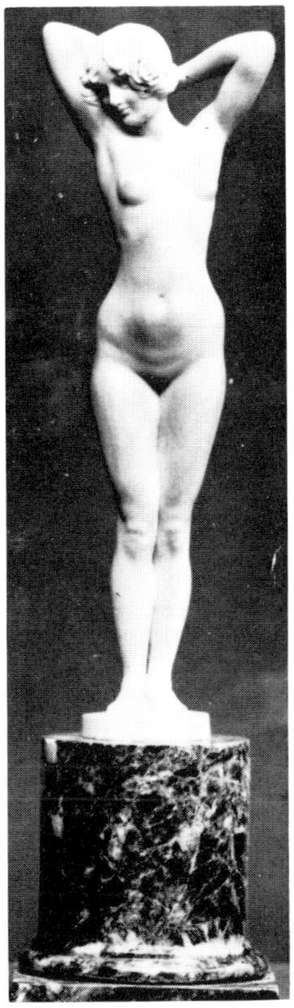

Nude, 16cm:6¼in.

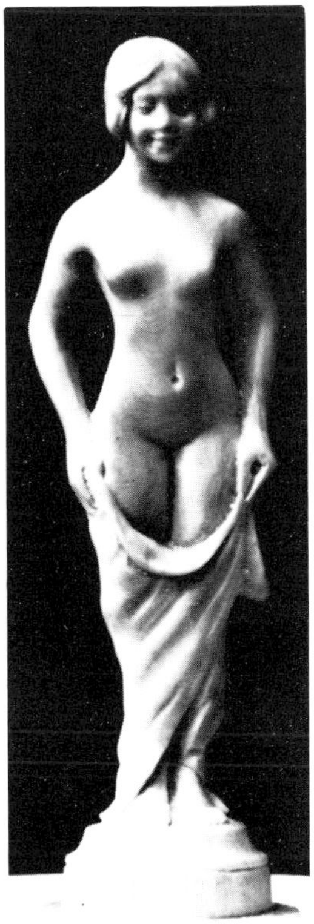

The Falling Shift
11cm:4¼in.

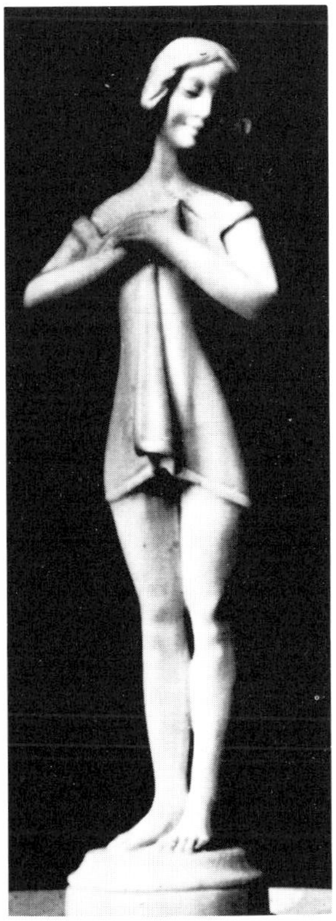

In a Chemise
11cm:4¼in.

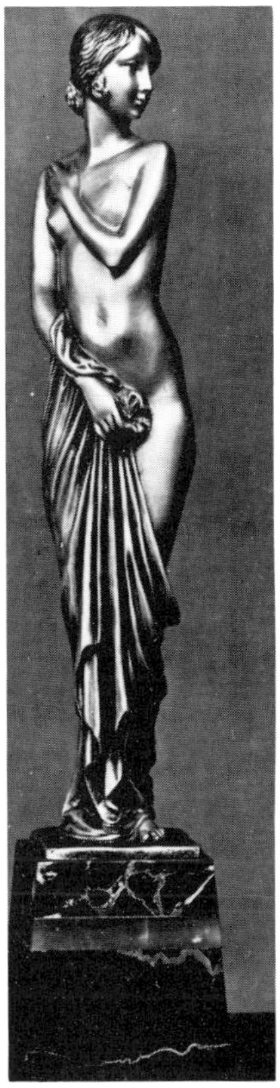

Cool
25cm:10in.
20cm:8in.

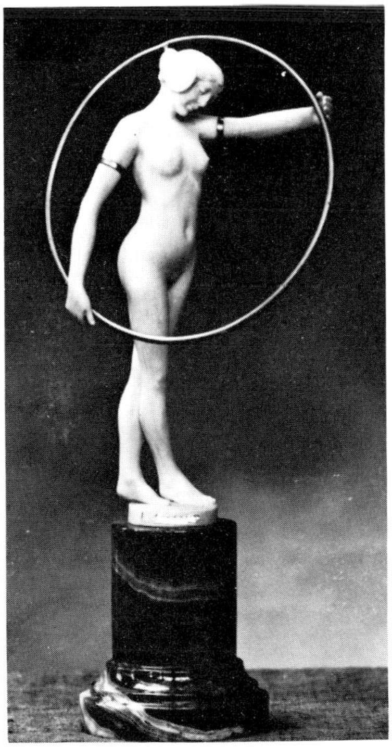

Dancer with Ring, 21cm:8¼in.

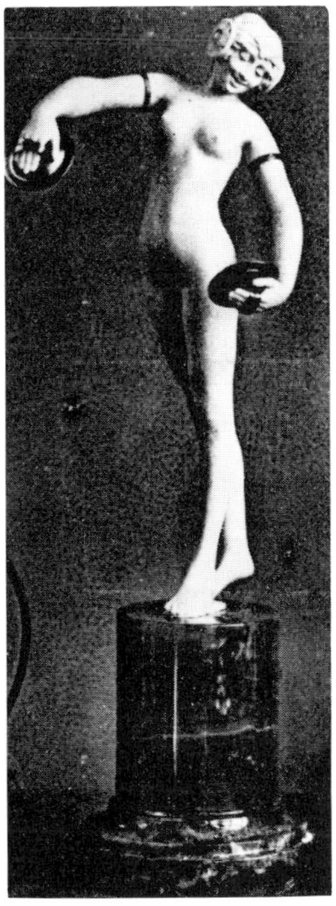

Cymbals Dancer
21cm:8¼in.

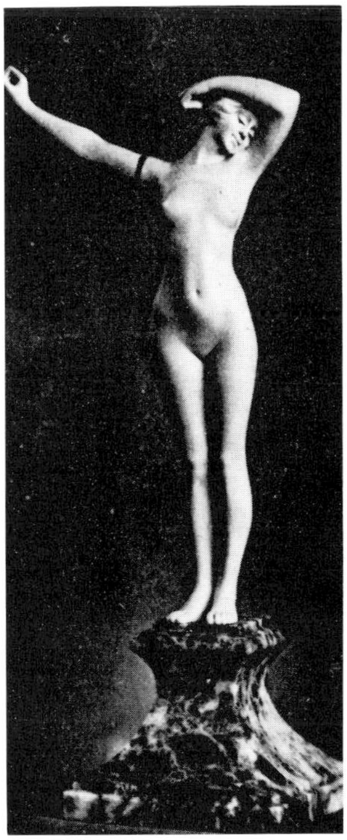

Dawn
20cm:7¾in.
13cm:5¼in.

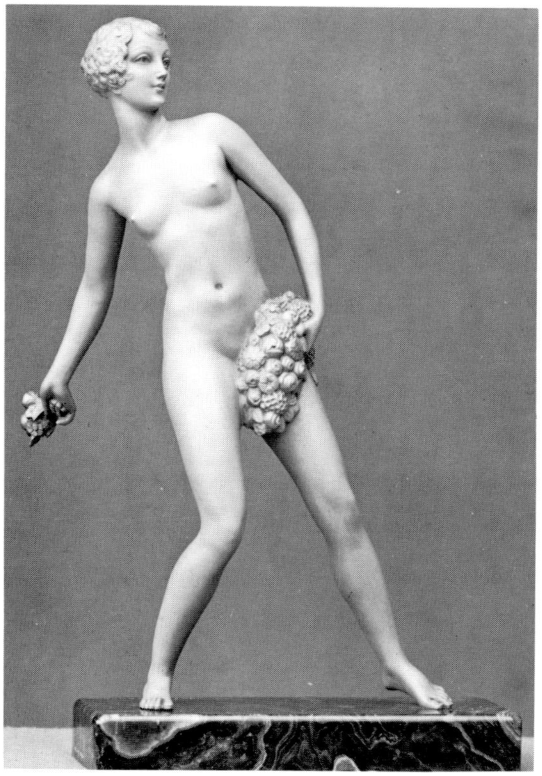

Battle of Flowers, 34cm:13½in.

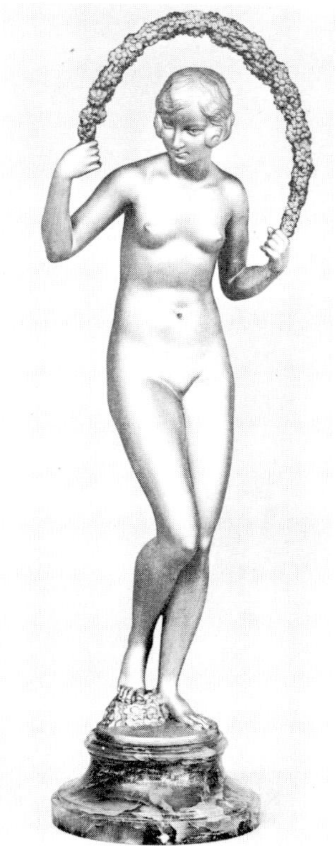

Girl with Garland
51cm:20in.; 28cm:11in.
Exhibited 1925 Arts Décoratifs

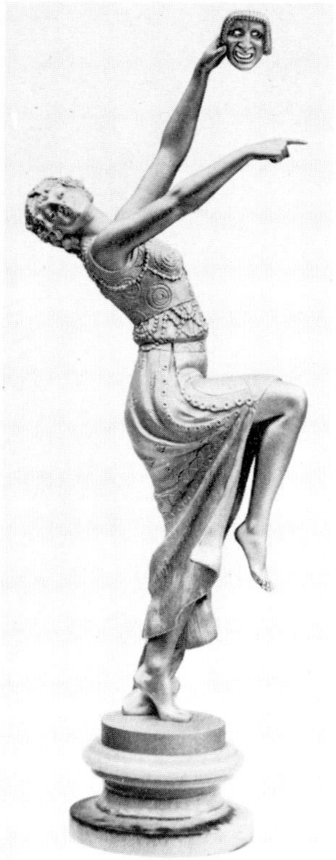

Mask Dance, 65cm:25½in.
45cm:17¾in.; 32cm:12½in.

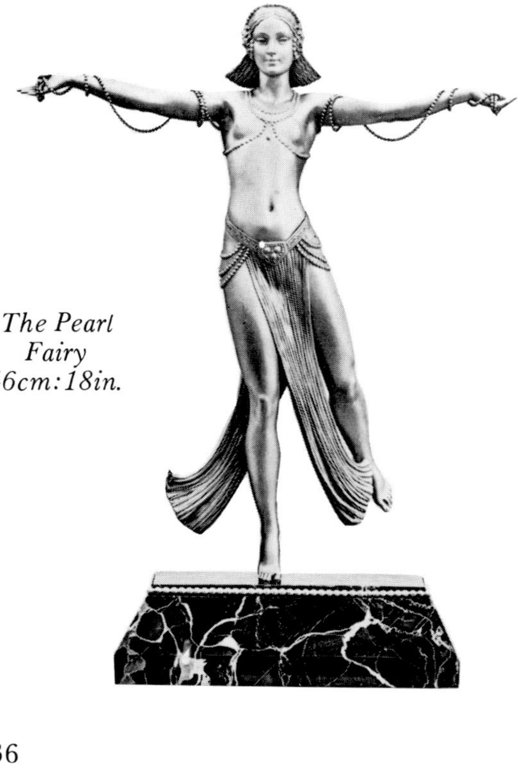

The Pearl
Fairy
46cm:18in.

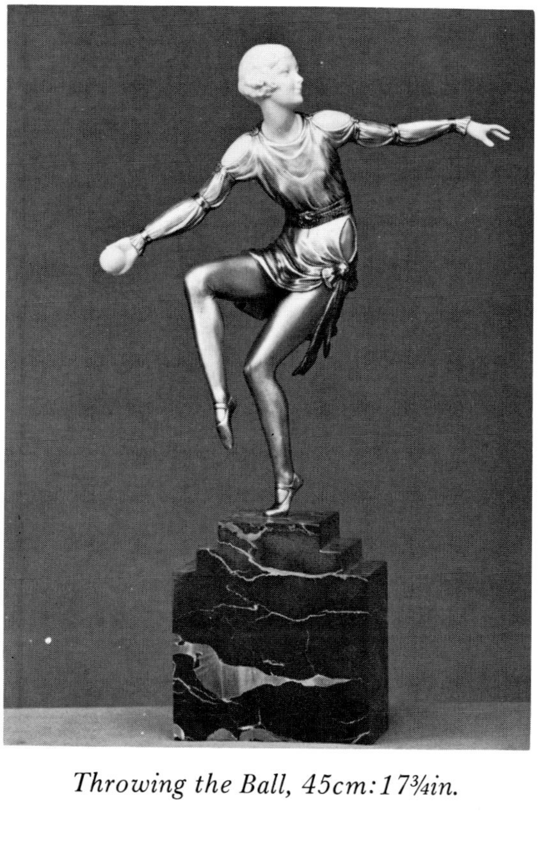

Throwing the Ball, 45cm:17¾in.

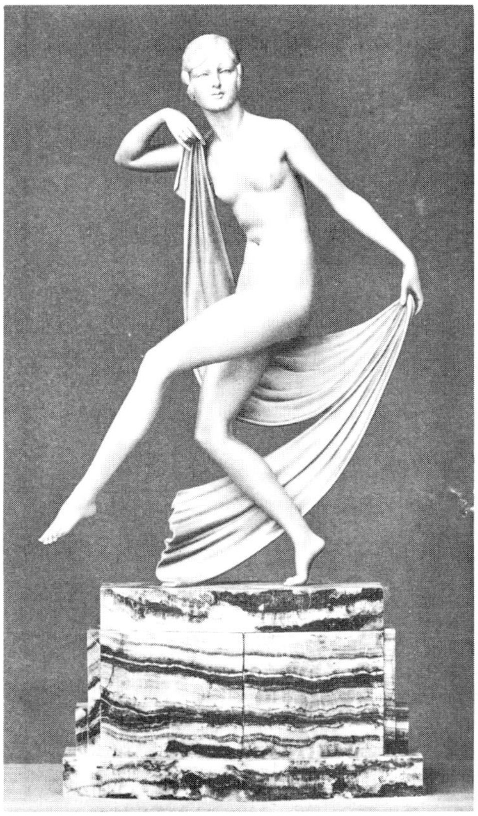

Modern Dancer
70cm: 27½in.

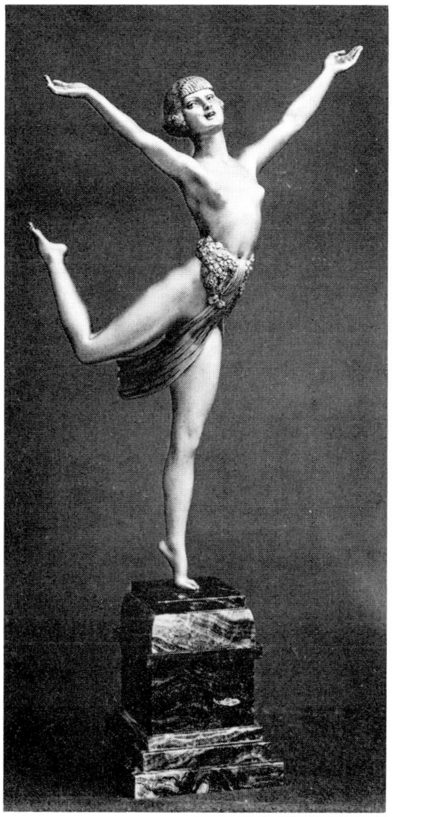

Spring Song
47cm: 18½in.

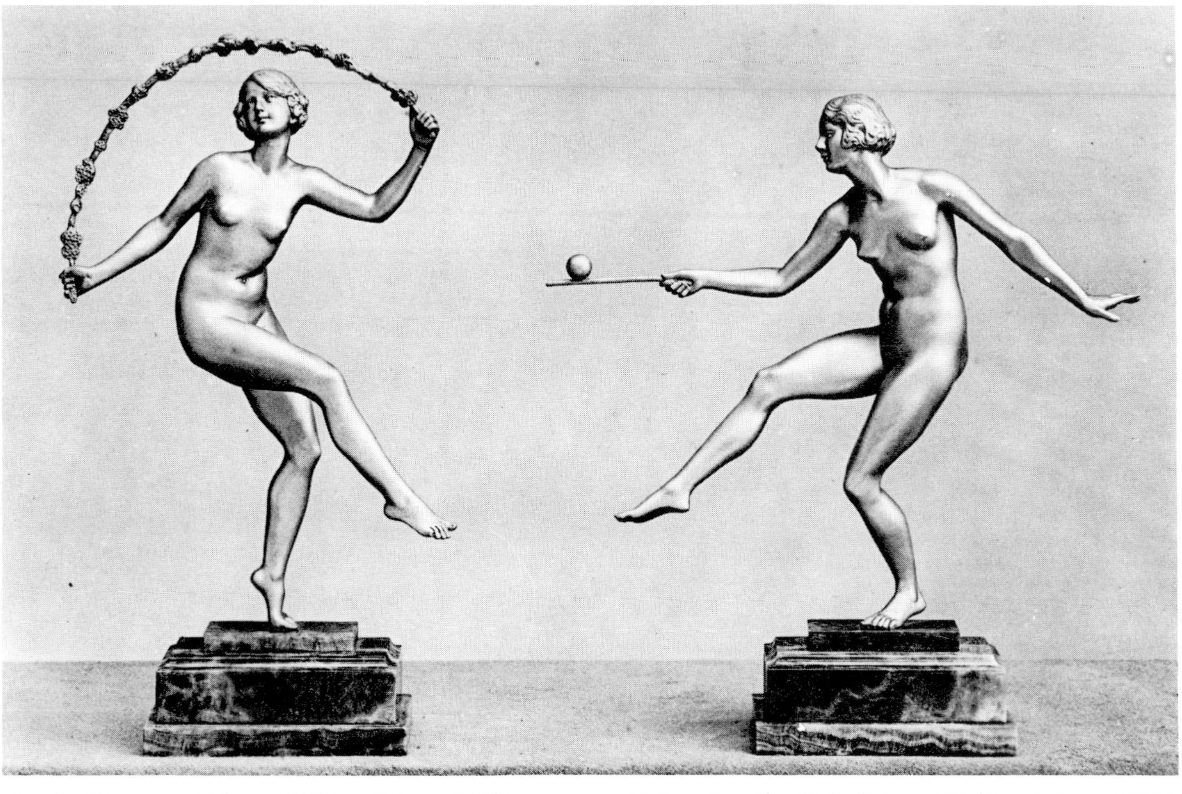

Apple Blossom, 34cm: 13¼in.; 26cm: 10¼in. *Balancing the Ball, 34cm: 13¼in.; 26cm: 10¼in.*

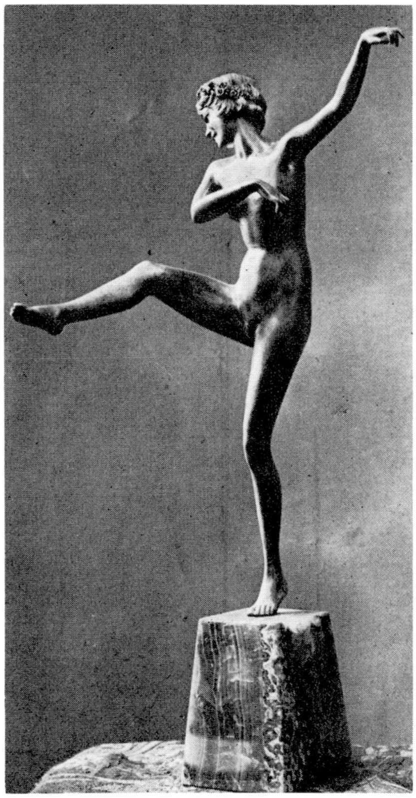

Joy
33cm: 13in.

Rythme
(nude)
28cm: 11in.

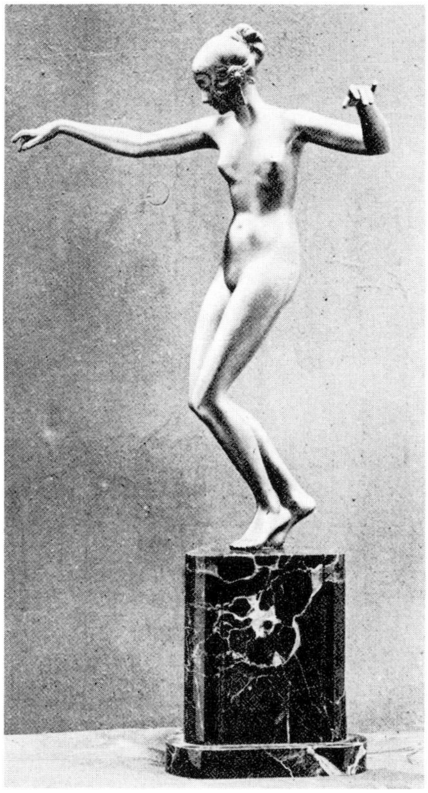

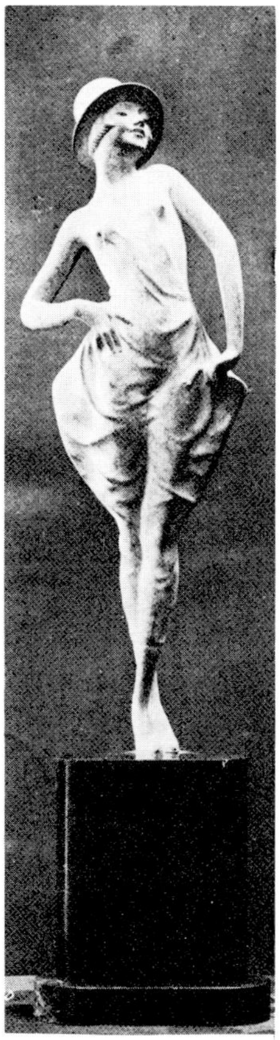

Pride
(draped)
43cm: 17in.

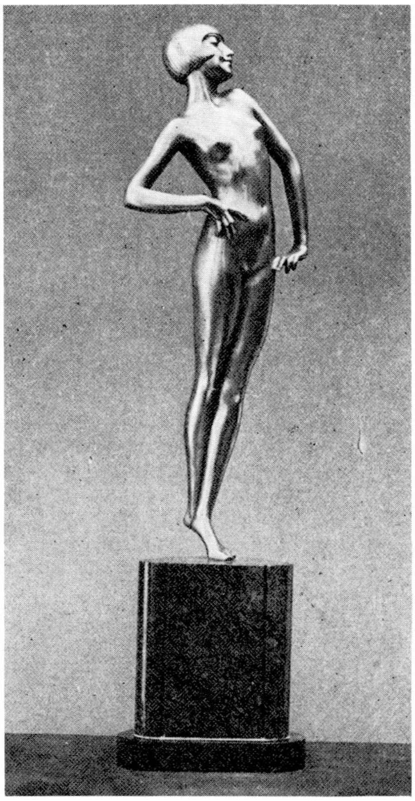

Pride
(nude)
46cm: 18in.

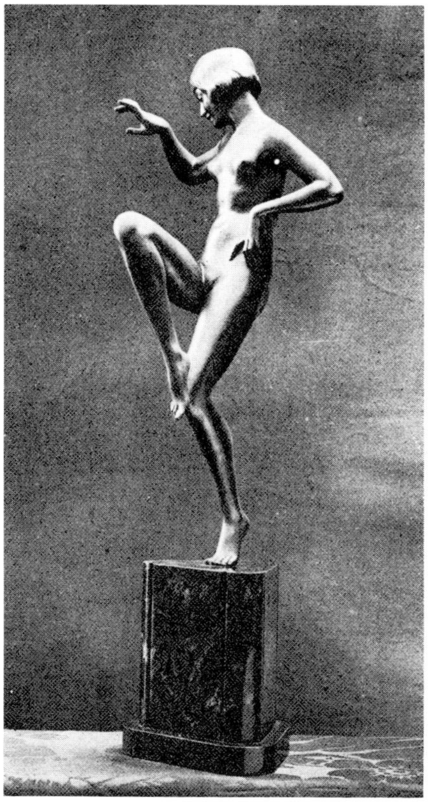

A Dance Step
37cm: 14in.

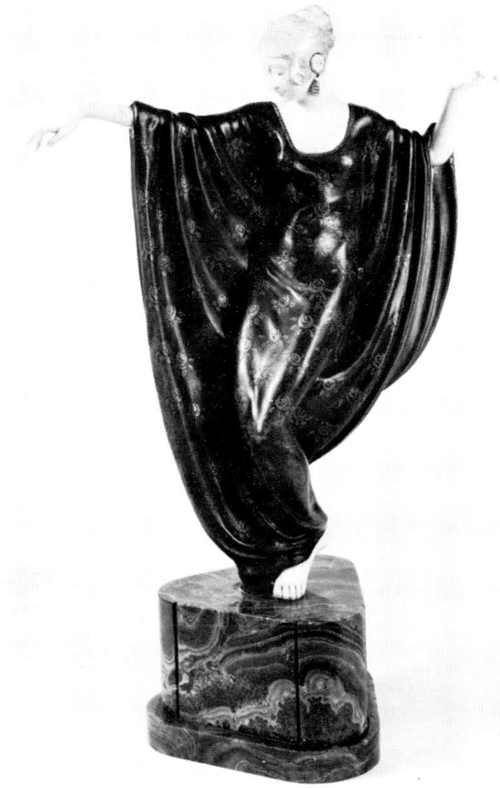

Rythme (draped), 27cm:10¾in.

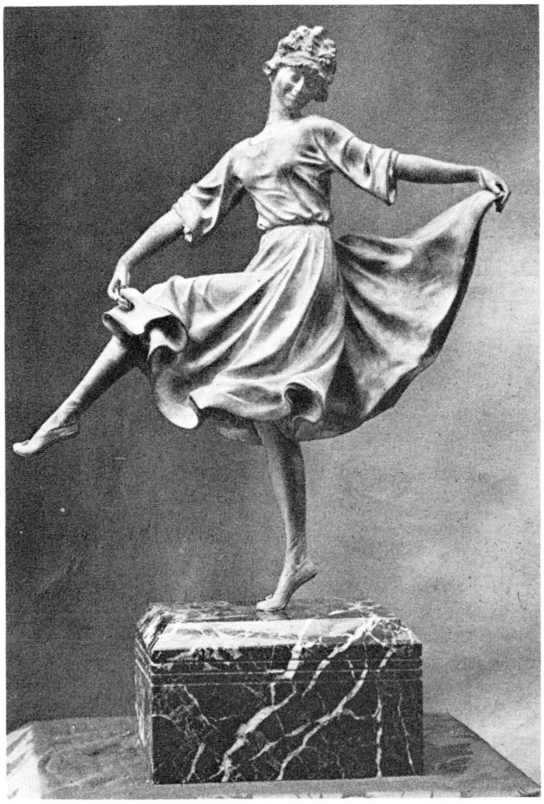

Country Dance, 45cm:17½in.

E. DROUOT

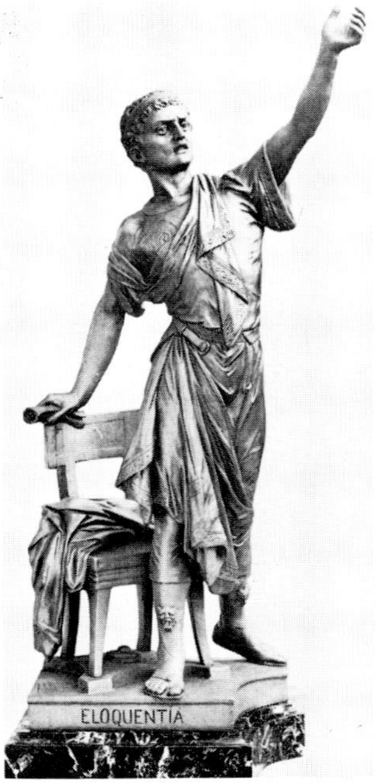

Oratory, 70cm:27½in.

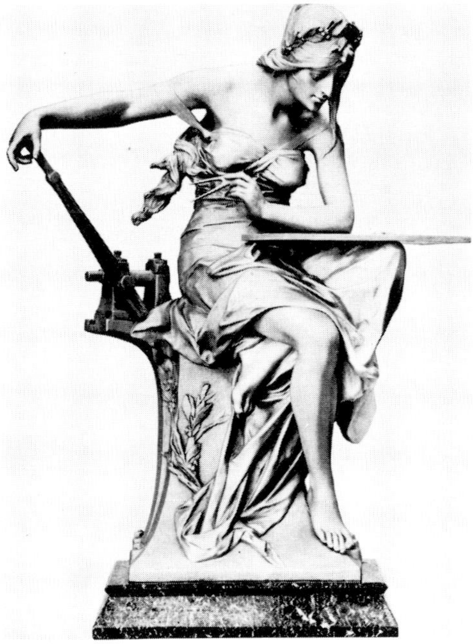

Industry, 60cm:23½in.

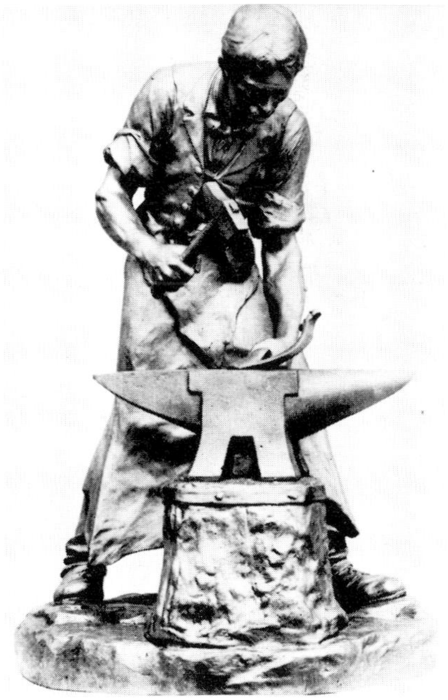

The Worker
53cm:21in.; 43cm:17in.
33cm:13in.; 24cm:9½in.

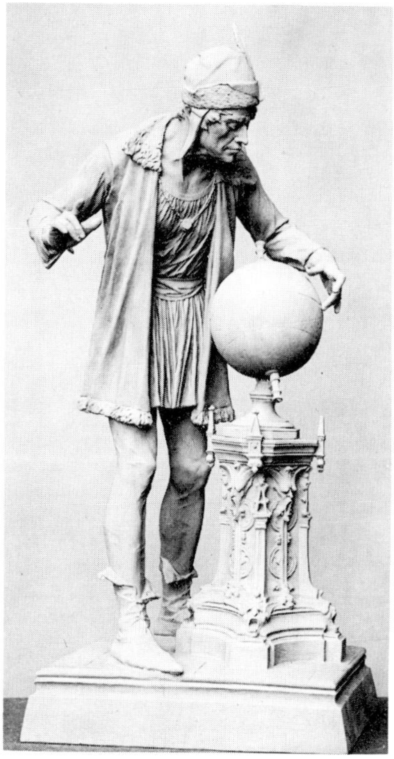

The Astrologer. 70cm:27½in.

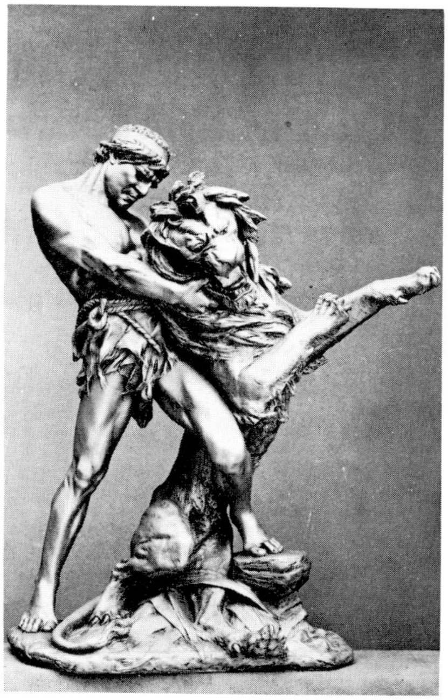

Hercules, 69cm:27in.
Exhibited 1923 in the
Salon des Artistes Français

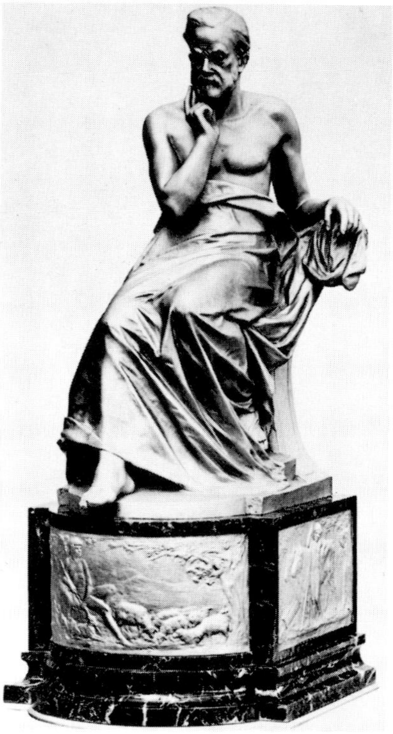

Pasteur
64cm:25in.; 47cm:18½in.
31cm:12¼in.

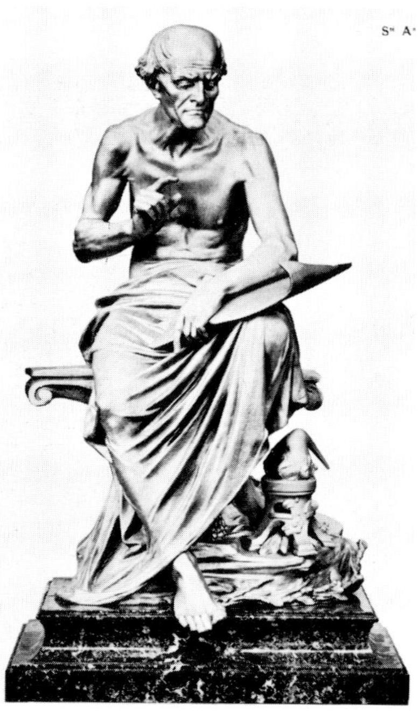

Science
64cm:25in.; 45cm:17¾in.
31cm:12¼in.; 20cm:8in.

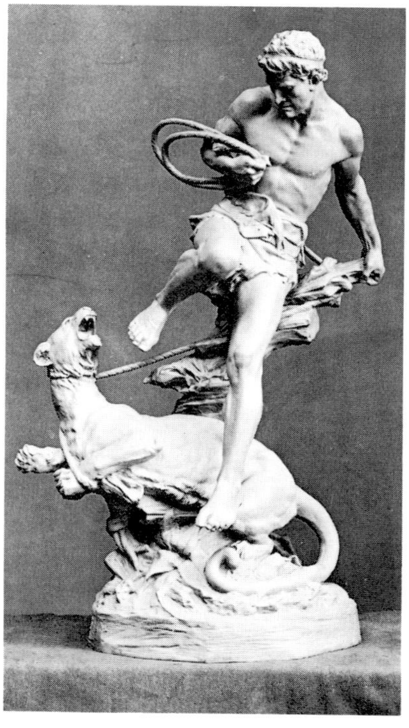

Capture, 87cm:34¼in.

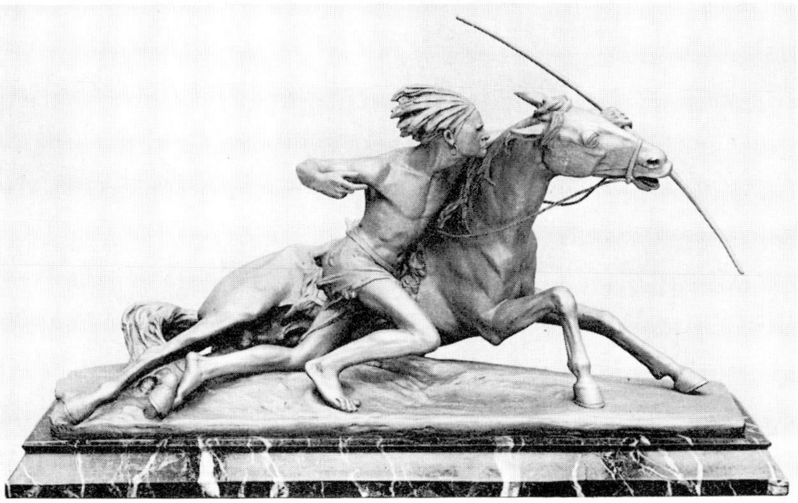

Alert, various heights

On the Track of Deer
53cm:21in.

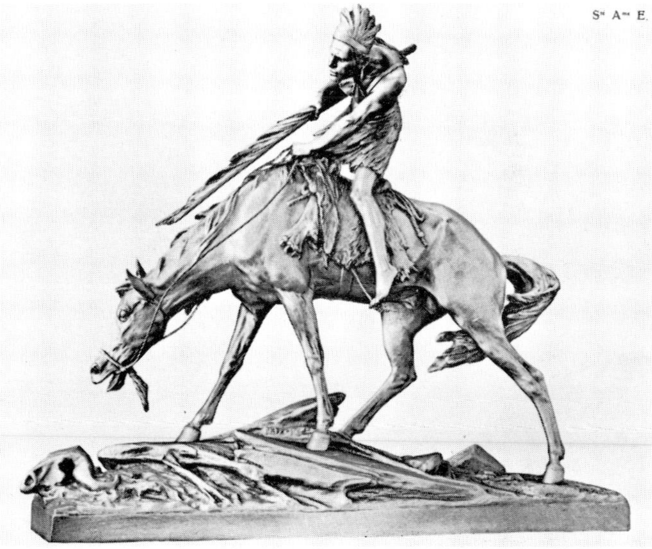

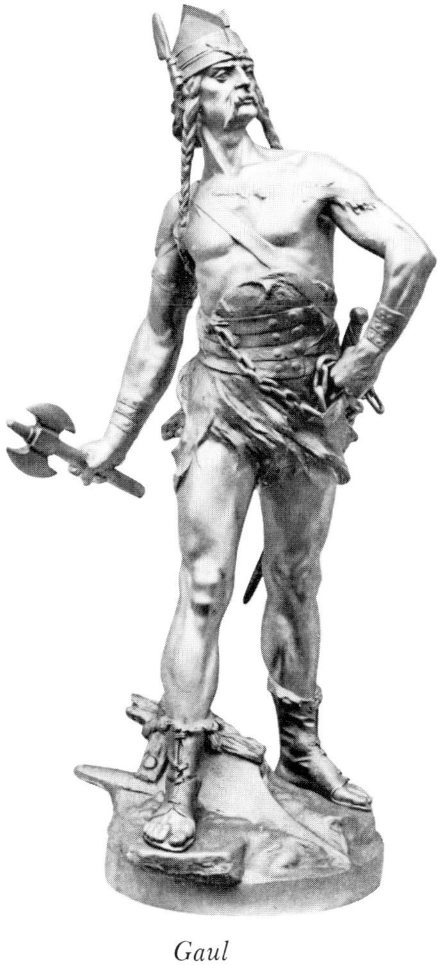

Gaul
82cm:32¼in.; 61cm:24in..
41cm:16in.

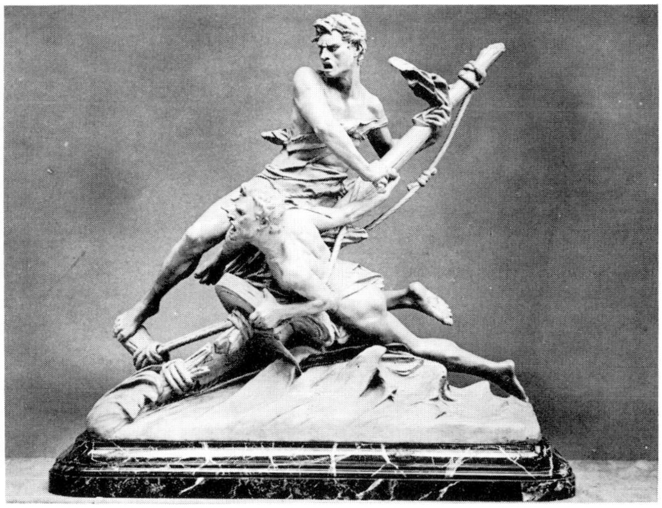

Shipwrecked, 73cm:28¾in.
Also in another size

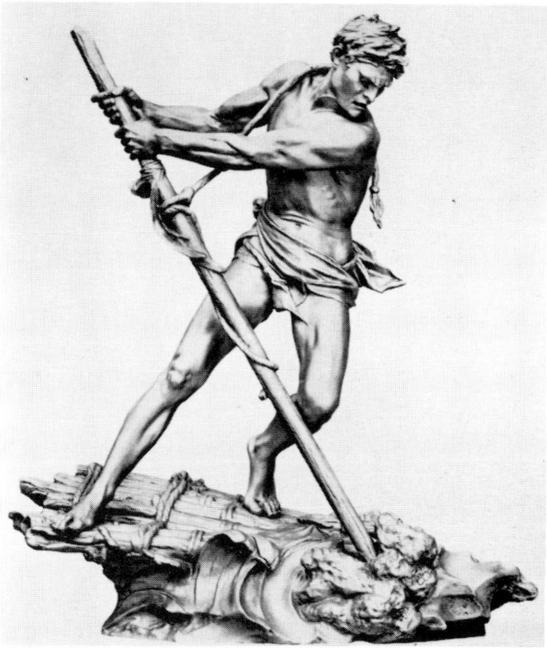

Man and the Elements
75cm: 29½in.
47cm: 18½in.

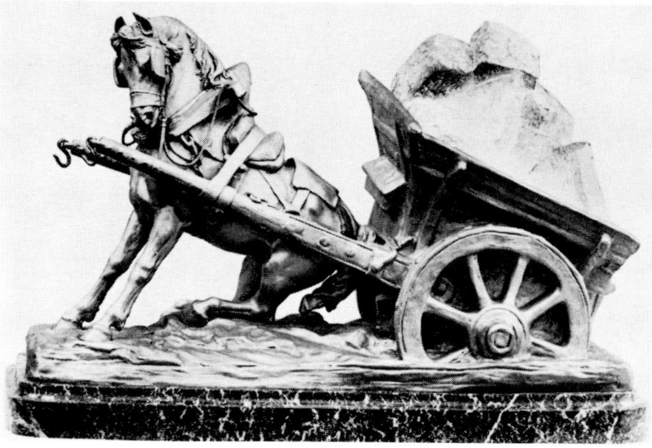

Mud Bound Cart, 43cm: 17in.

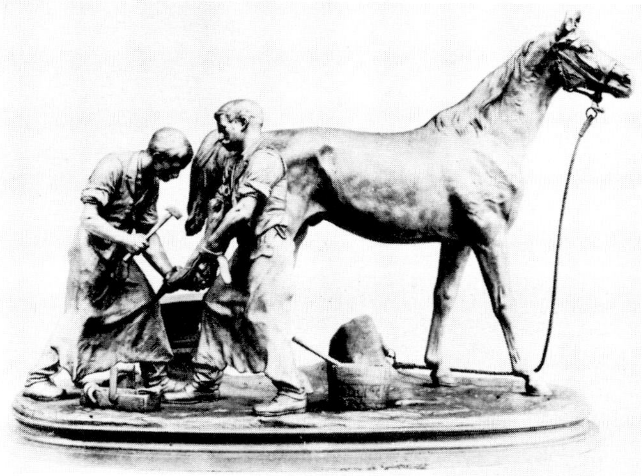

Farrier
80cm: 31½in.; 66cm: 26in.
50cm: 19¼in.; 35cm: 13¾in.

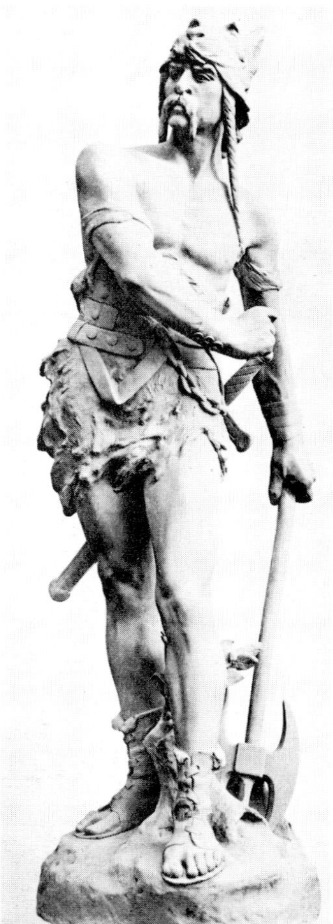

Gaul
77cm: 30¼in.
58cm: 22¾in.
44cm: 17¼in.

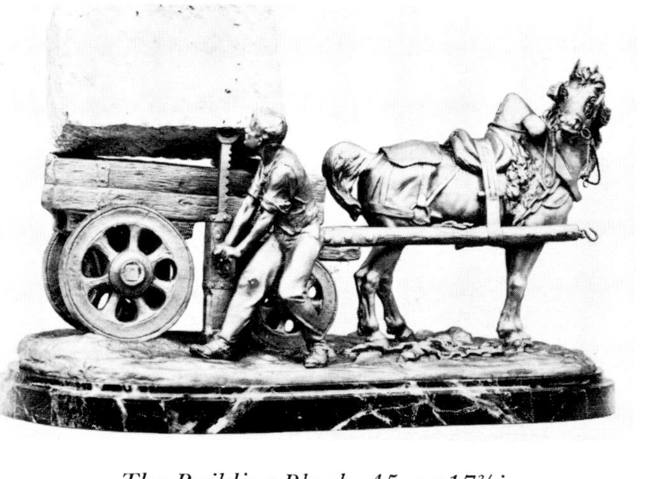

The Building Block, 45cm: 17¾in.

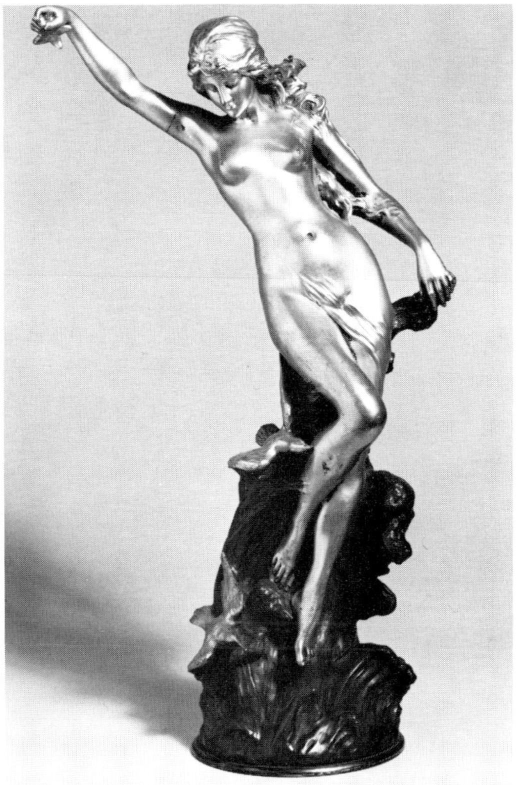

A Sea Nymph, 41cm:16in.

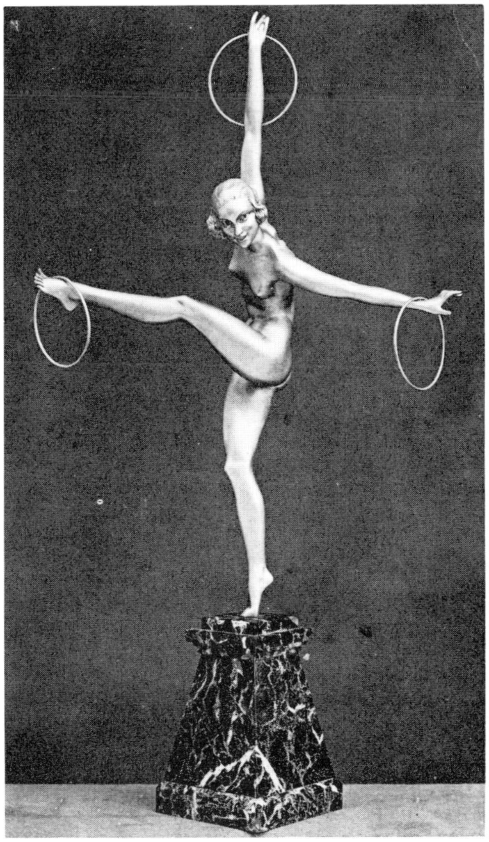

DUVERNET

Dancer of the Rings
67cm:26¼in.
50cm:19½in.
34cm:13½in.

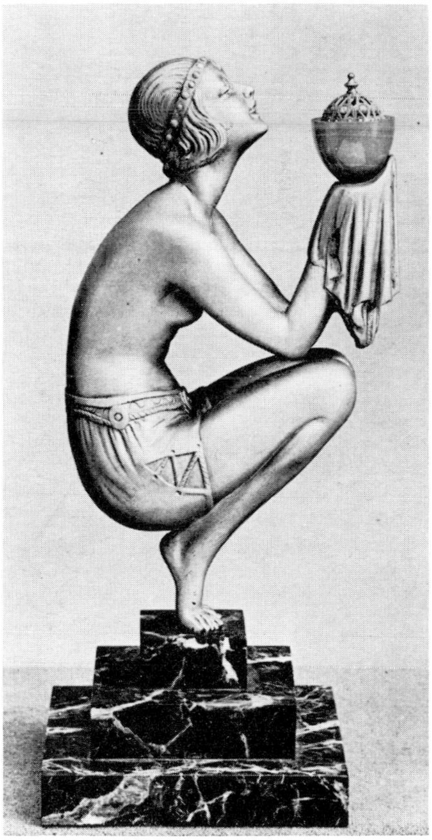

Oblivion
31cm:12¼in.

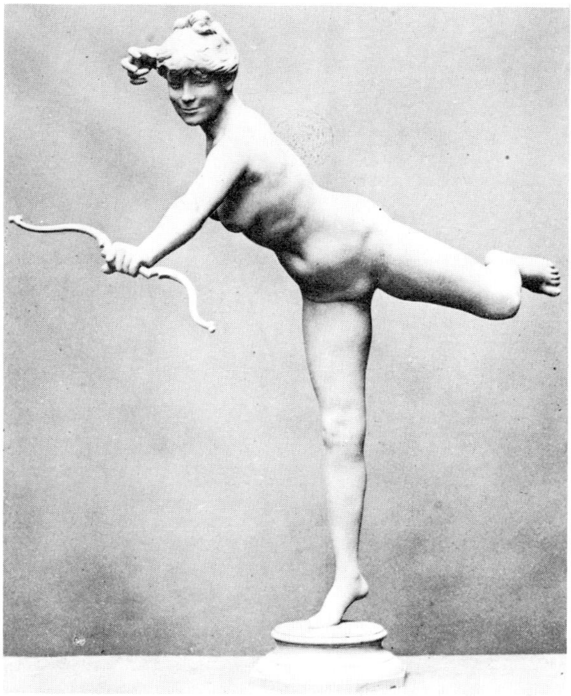

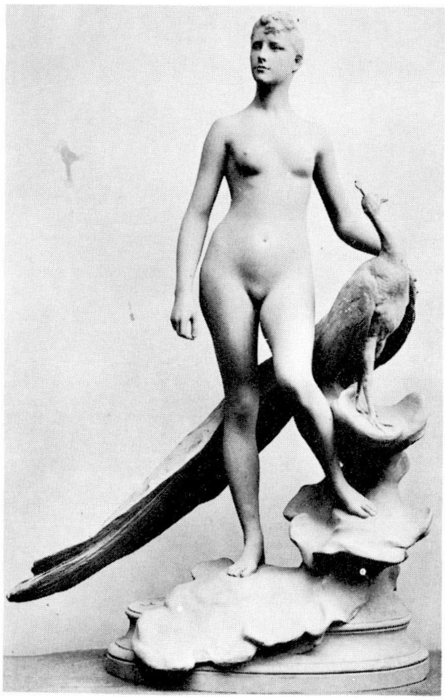

Woman with Peacock
75cm:29½in.
52cm:20½in.

Huntress, 57cm:22½in.; 43cm:17in.

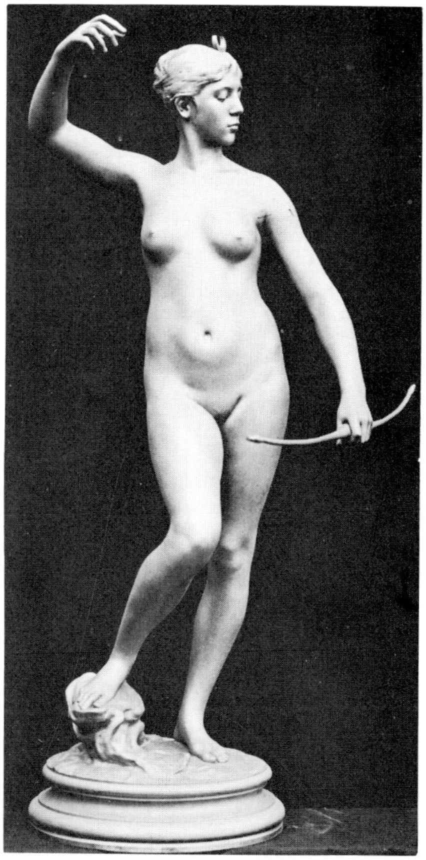

Diana
103cm:40½in.
77cm:30¼in.
46cm:18in.
13cm:5in.

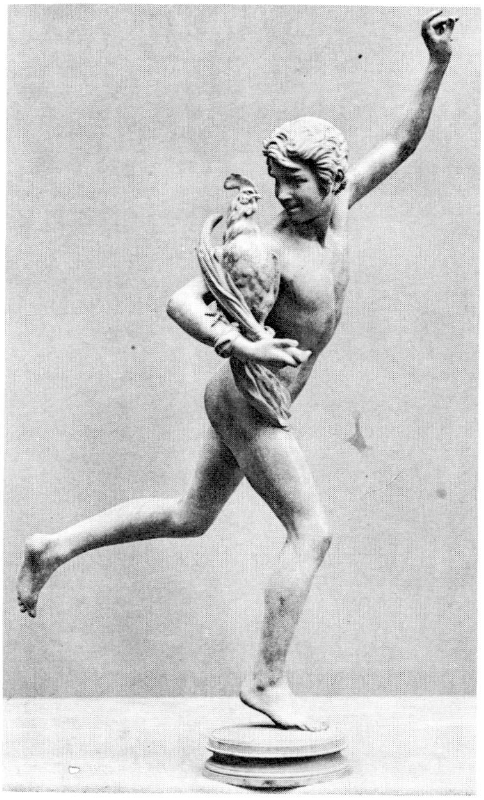

Winner of the Cock Fight
87cm:34½in.; 62cm:24½in.
34cm:13¼in.

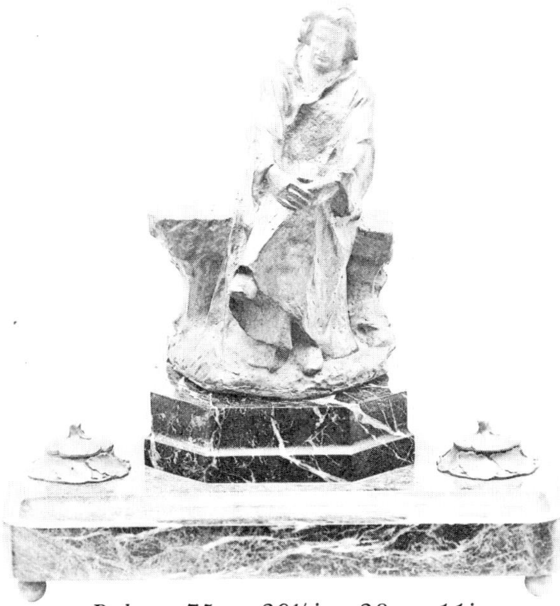

Balzac, 75cm:29½in.; 28cm:11in.
(Inkstand 11cm:4½in.)

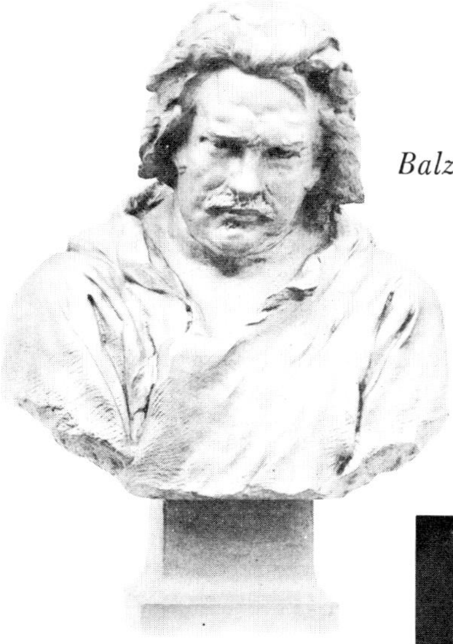

Balzac, 54cm:21¼in.

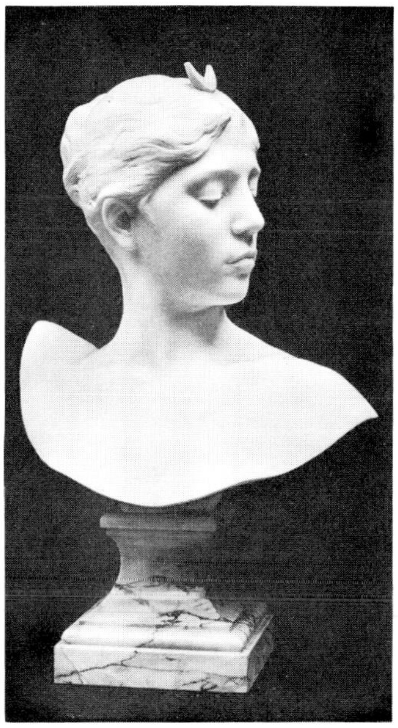

Diana
59cm:23¼in.; 34cm:13¼in.
25cm:9¾in.; 15cm:6in.
10cm:4in.

FANROSE

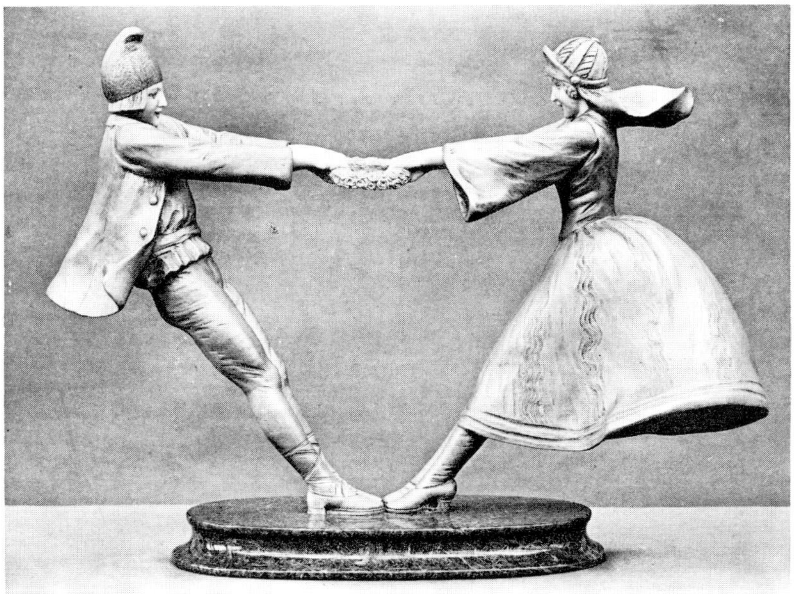

Garland Dance, 26cm:10¼in.

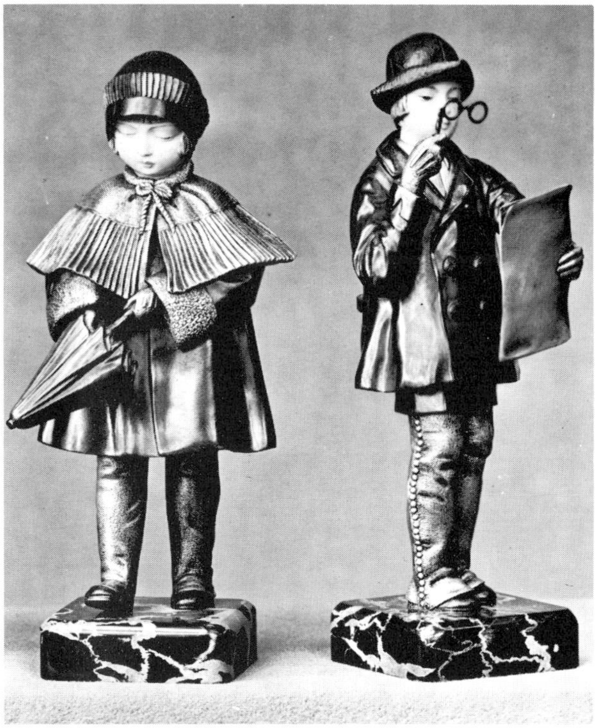

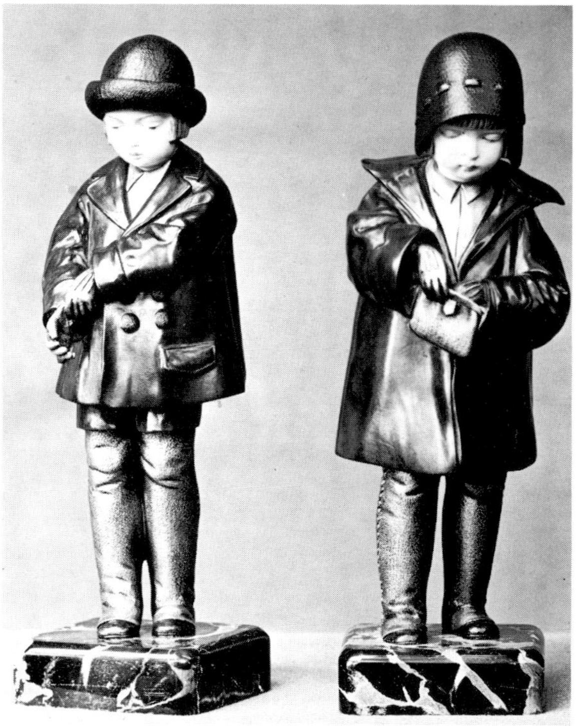

Going Out in the Rain 20cm: 8in.

Late News 20cm: 8in.

Young Man of the World 20cm: 8in.

Off to Market 20cm: 8in.

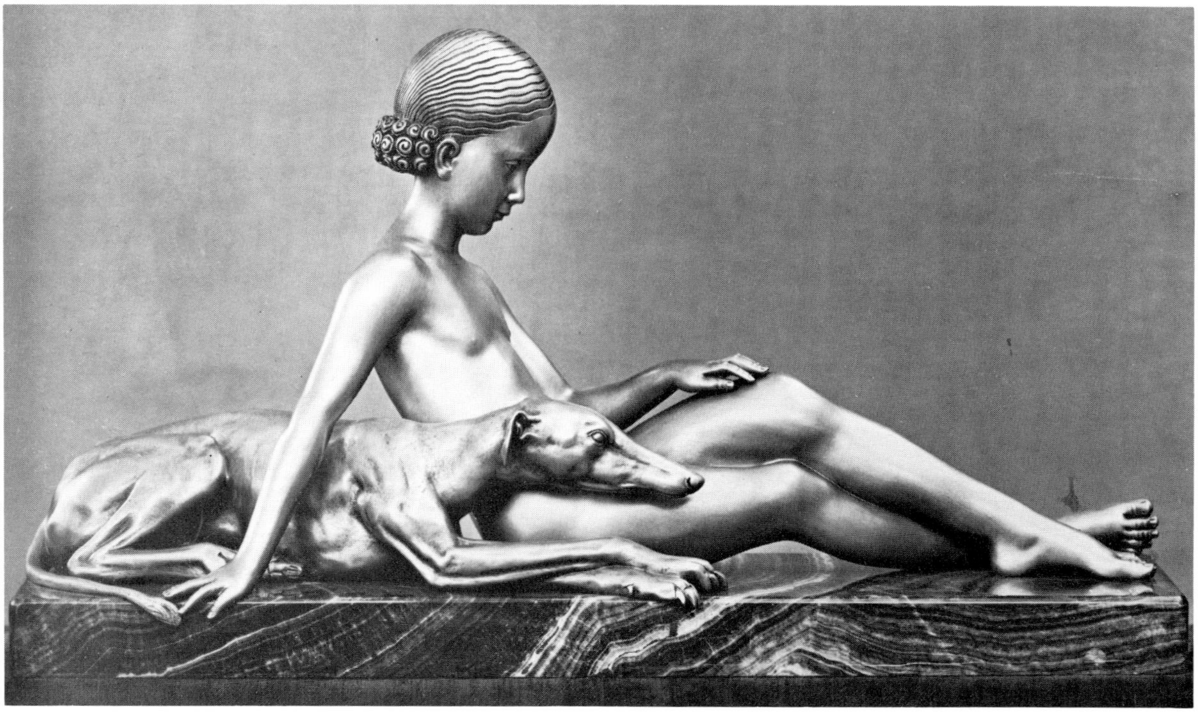

Girl and Dog, 23cm: 9in.

FAYRAL

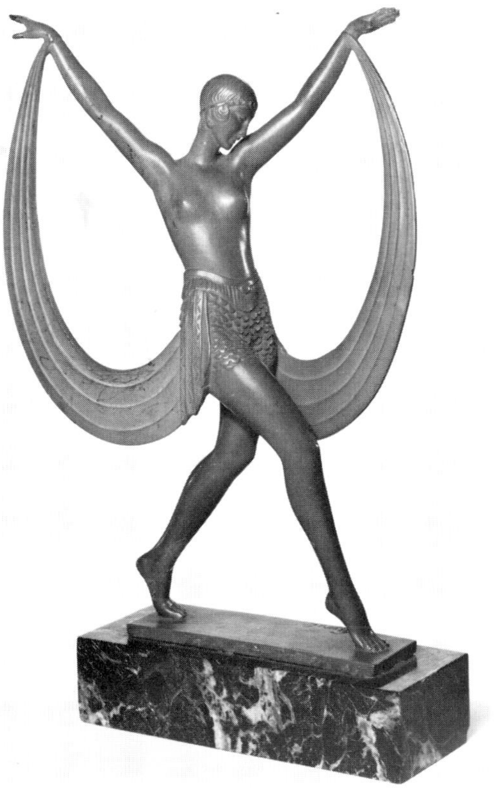

Dancer, 41cm:16¼in.

G. FLAMAND

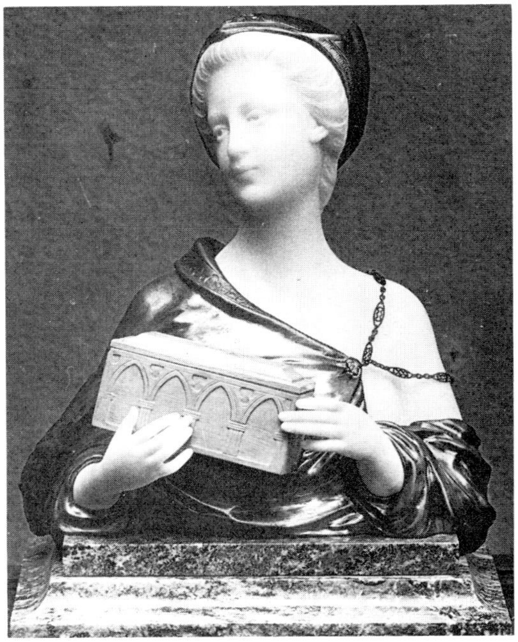

Bust of Woman with Box, 28cm:11in.

FELLI

Battle of Flowers
80cm:31½in.
64cm:25in.
50cm:19½in.

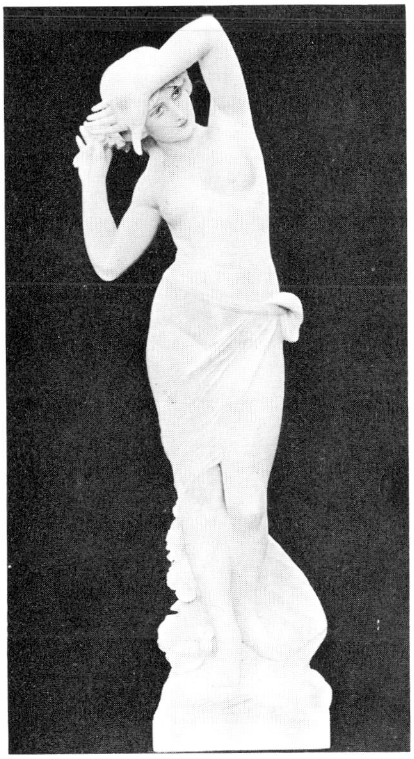

L. FONTINELLE

A Dancer
38cm:14¾in.

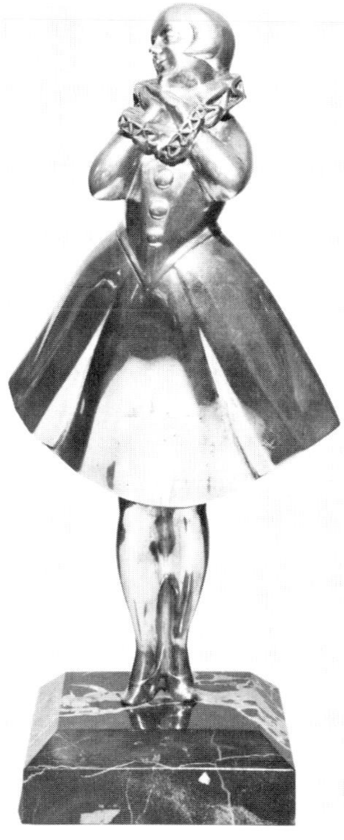

FOURNIER

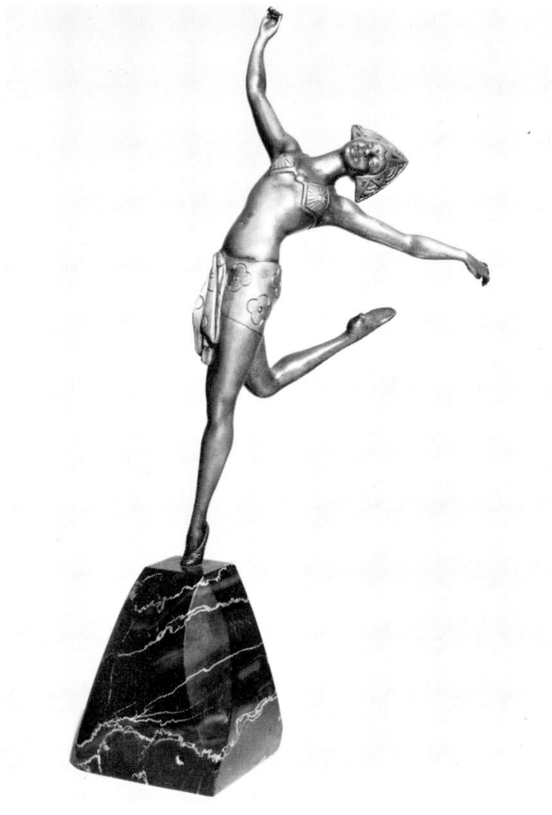

A Dancer, 43cm:17in.

HENRY FUGERE

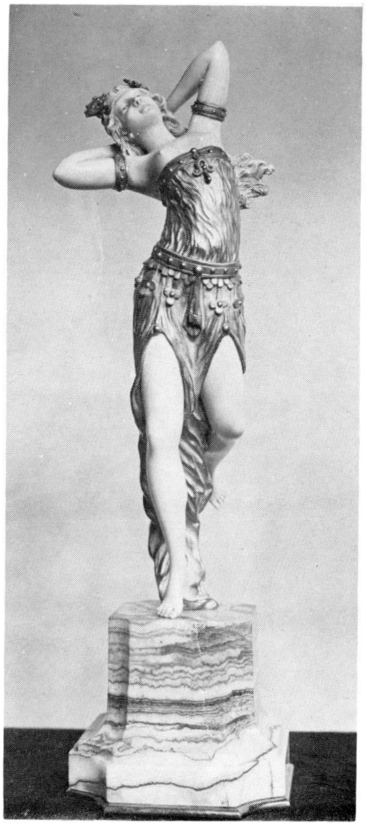

Salome
41cm:16in.

FRANCISQUE

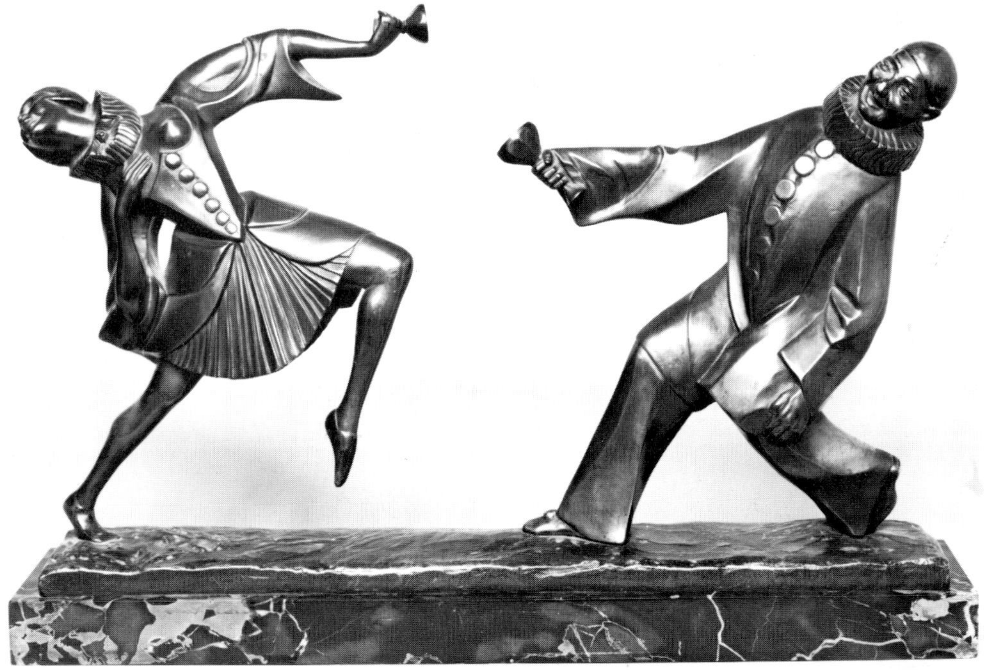

Two Dancers, 41cm:16in.

J. GALLO

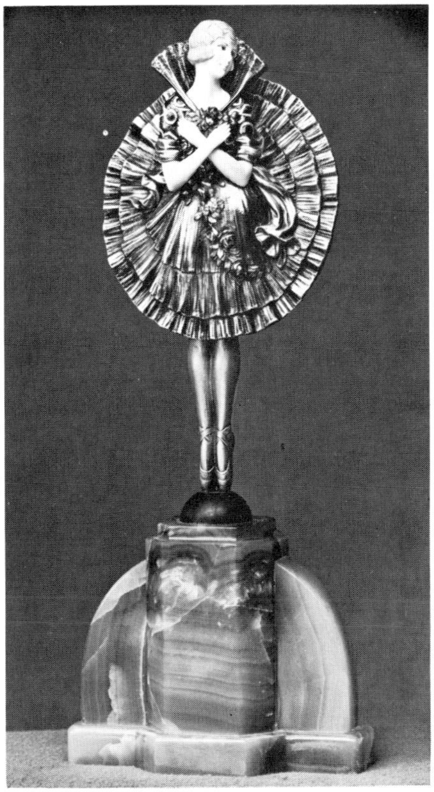

Parisian Dancer, 41cm:16¼in.

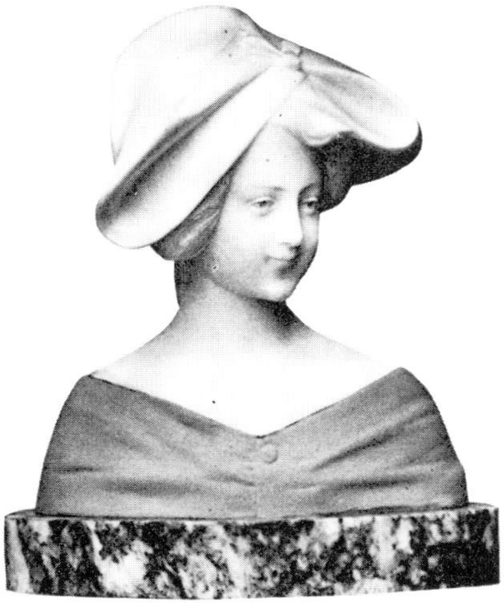

Wilhelmine, 20cm: 7¾in.

A. GENNAIS

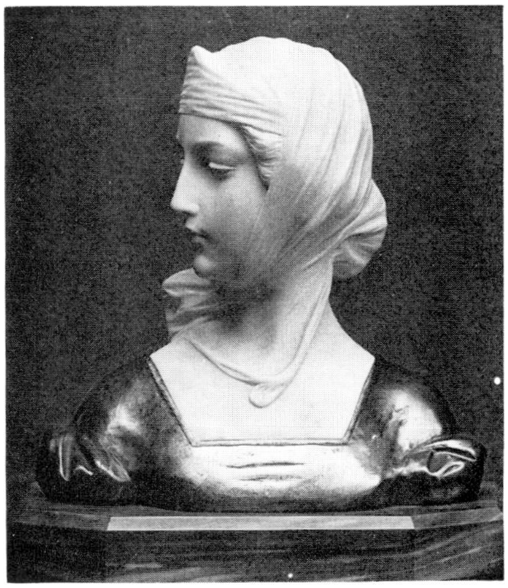

Beatrice, 31cm:12¼in.

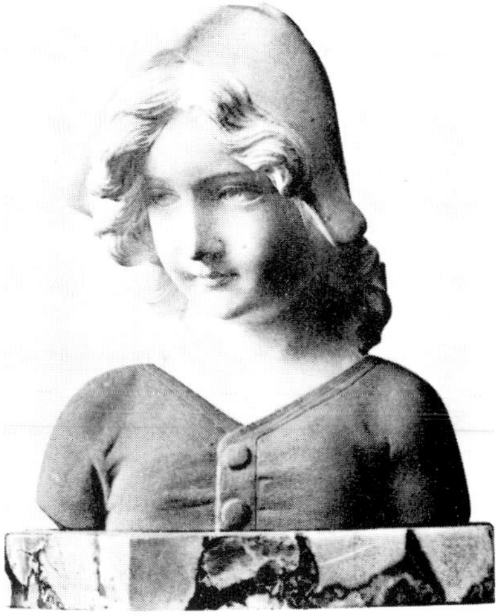

Country Girl, 15cm:6in.

A. GENNARELLI

Pilot
57cm:22½in.

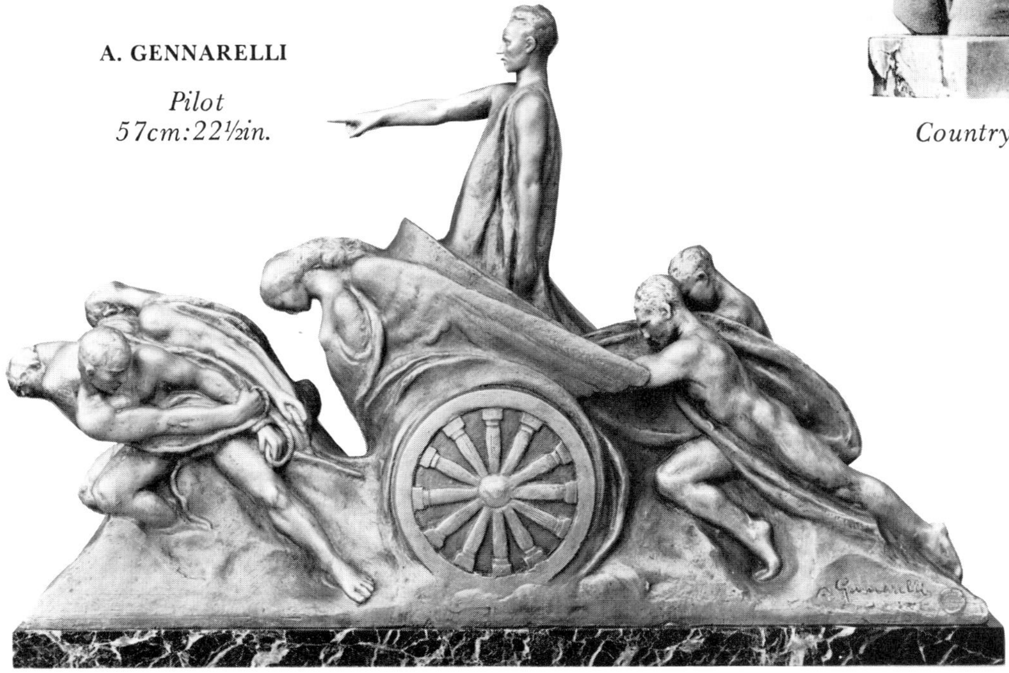

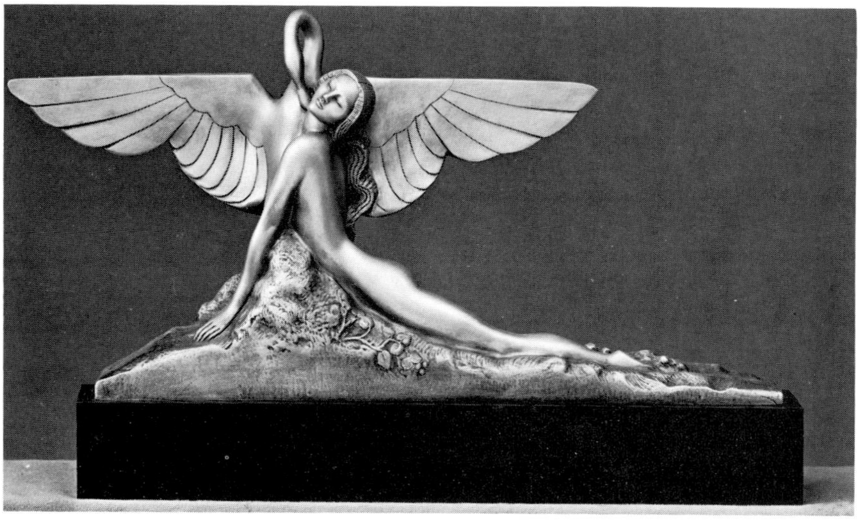

Leda
36cm:14in.

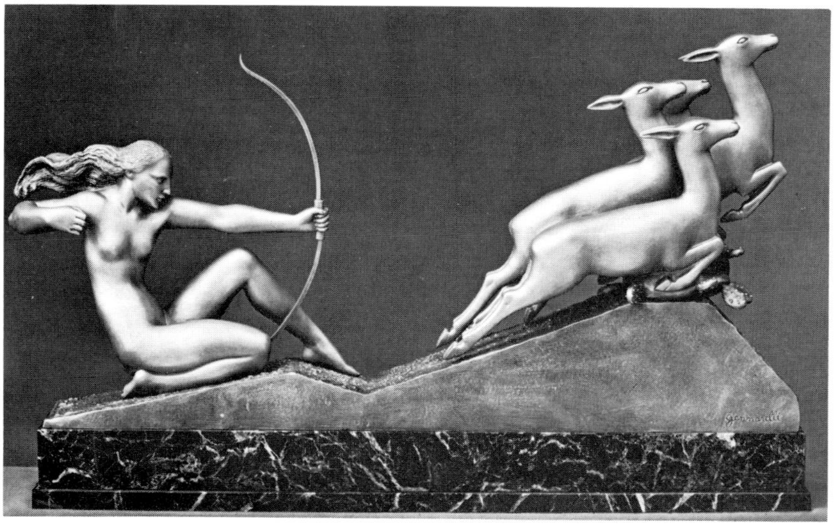

The Chase, 48cm:19in.

Towards Destiny
35cm:14in.; 24cm:9½in.

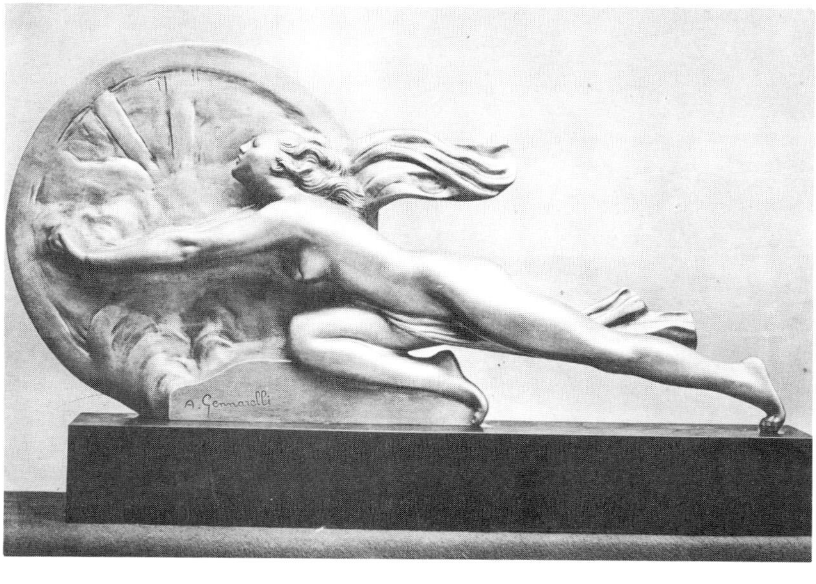

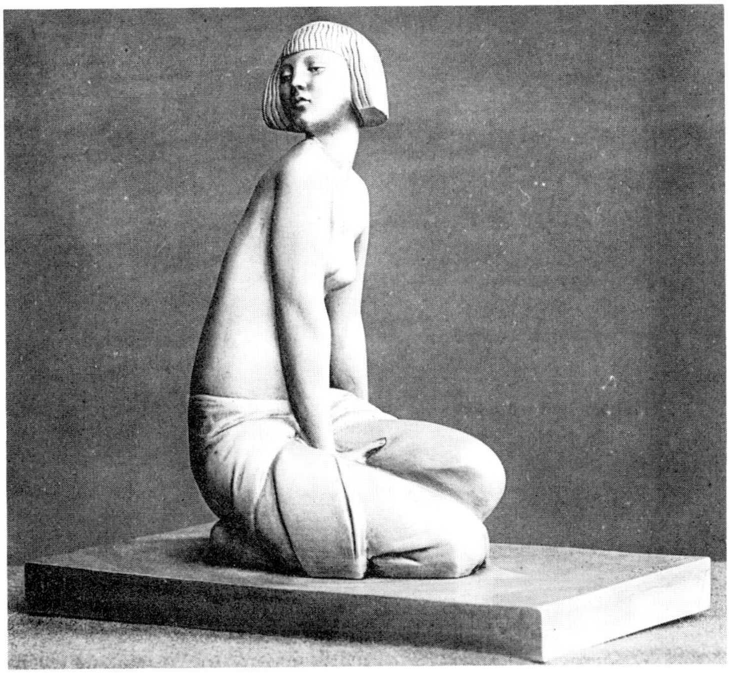

Aspasie, 21cm: 8¼in.

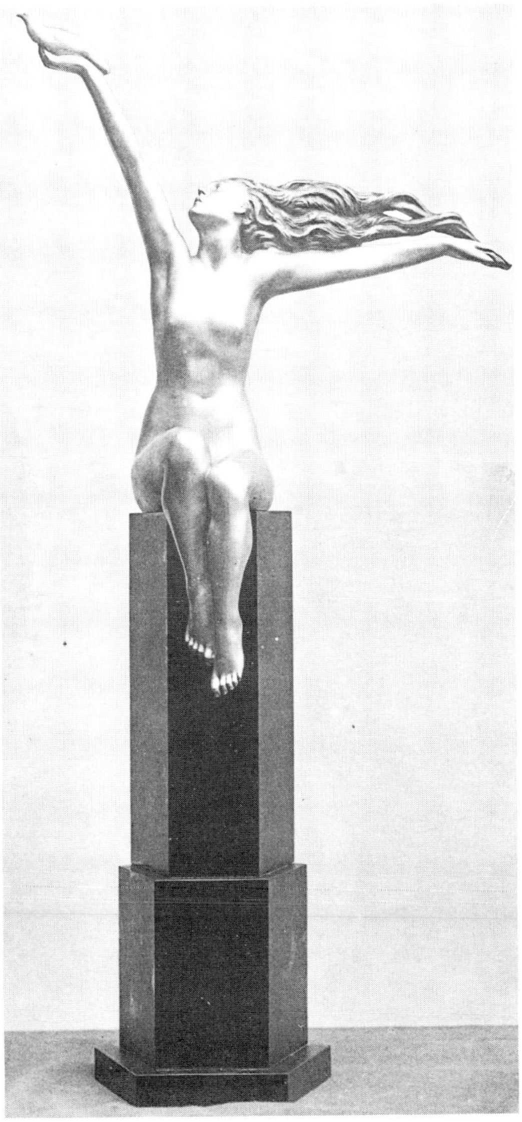

The Carrier Pigeon
86cm: 33¾in.; 57cm: 22½in.
36cm: 14¾in.

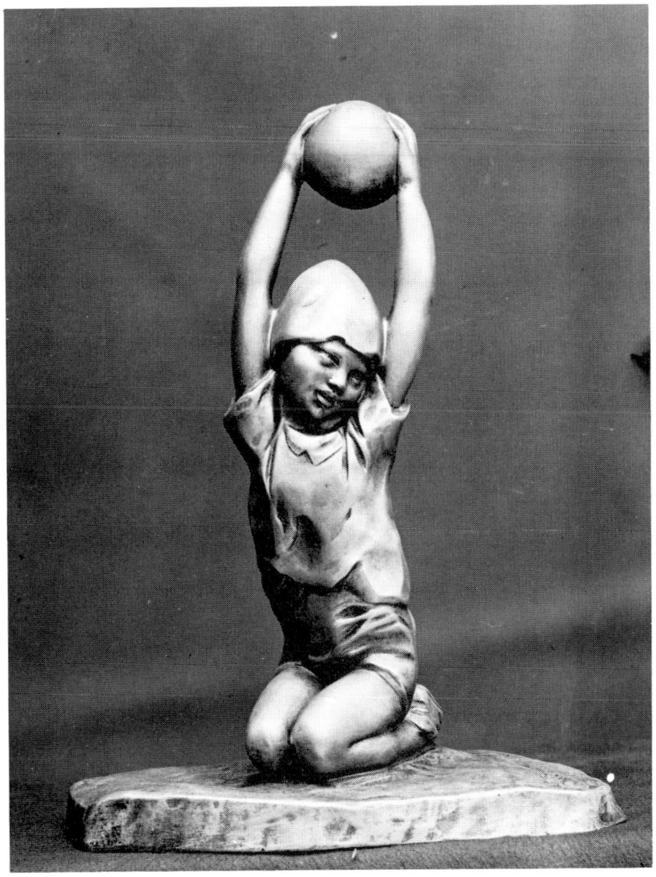

Child with Ball, 28cm: 11in.

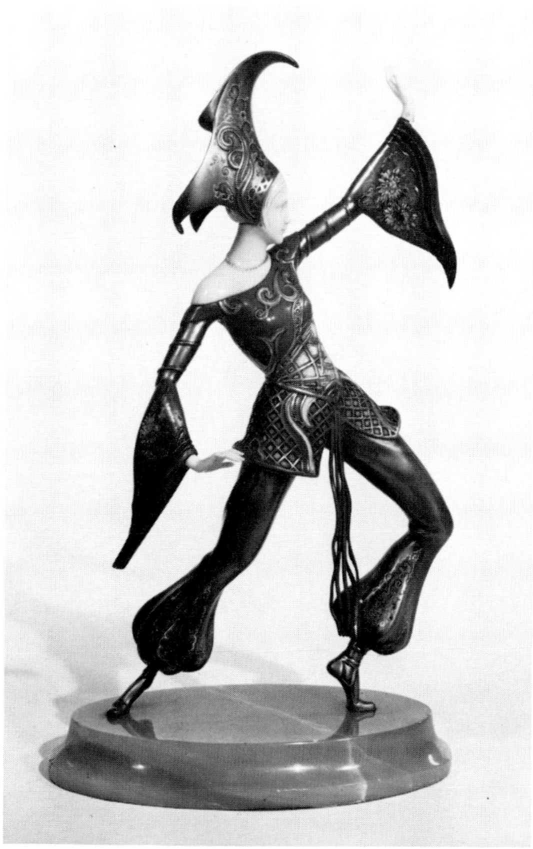

A. Dancer, 36cm:14in.

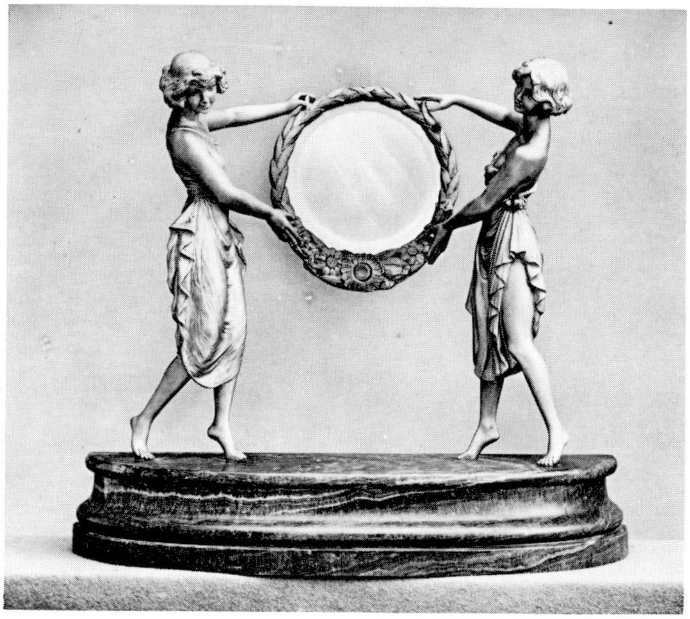

Girls and Mirror (1925), 47cm:18½in.

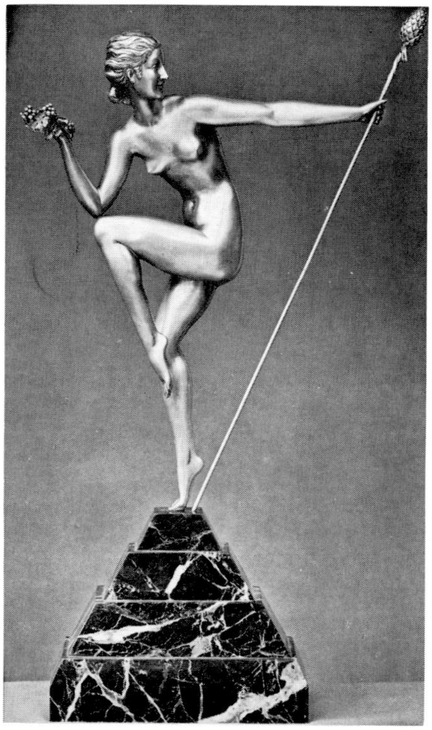

Song of Autumn, 62cm:24½in.

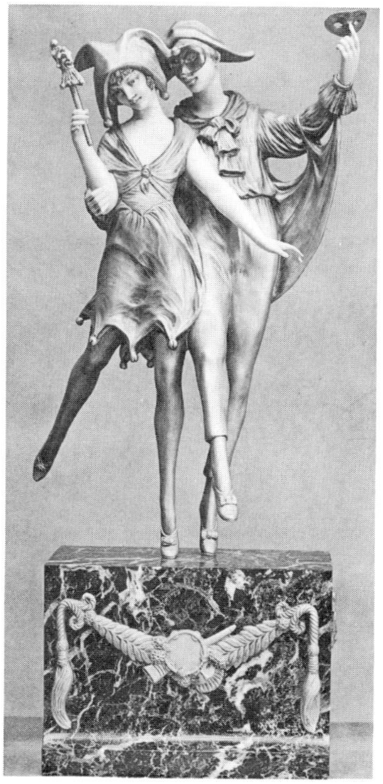

Seduction, 56cm:22in.

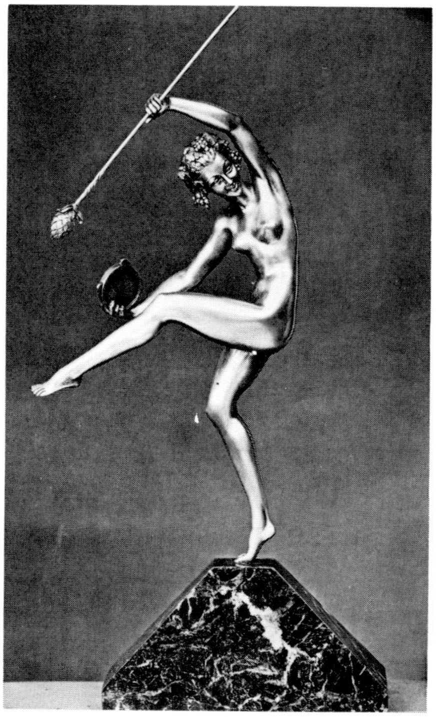

Bacchant with Thyrse, 60cm:23½in.

A. GODARD

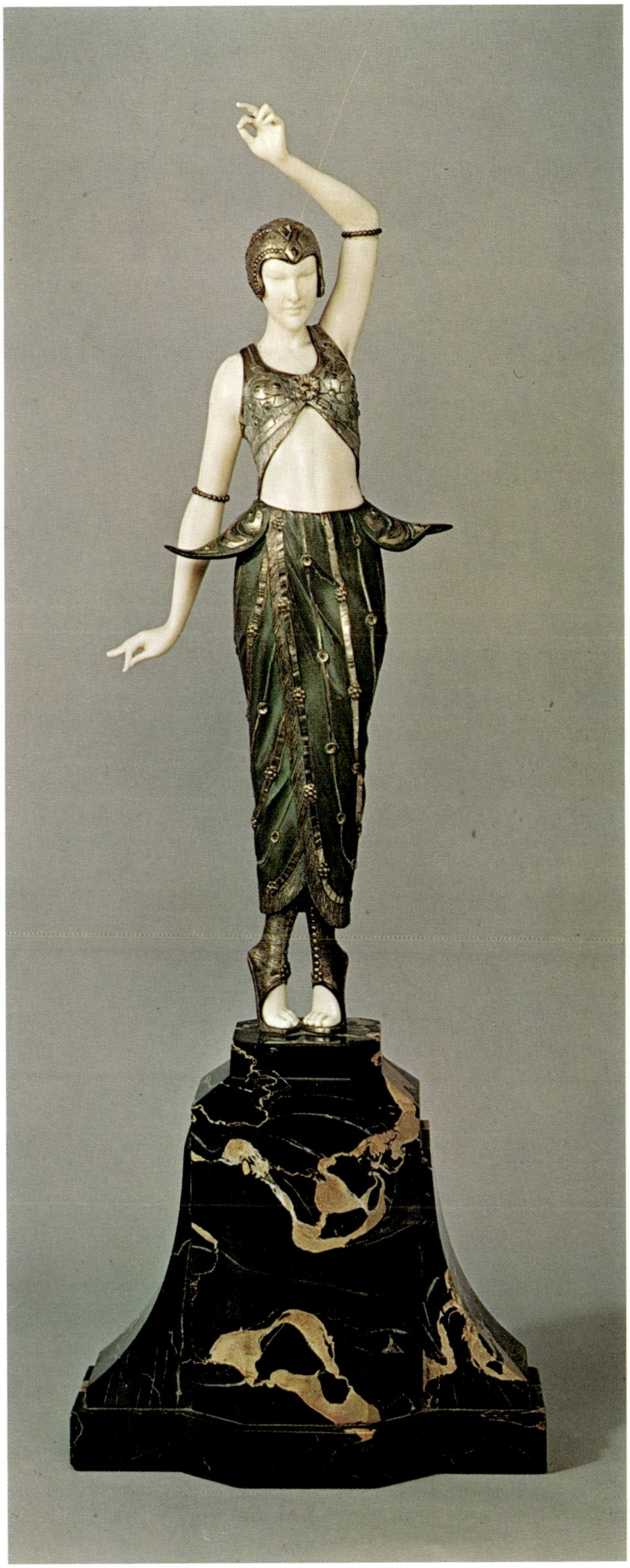

Dance of the Indies
50cm: 19¾in.

R. MARQUET

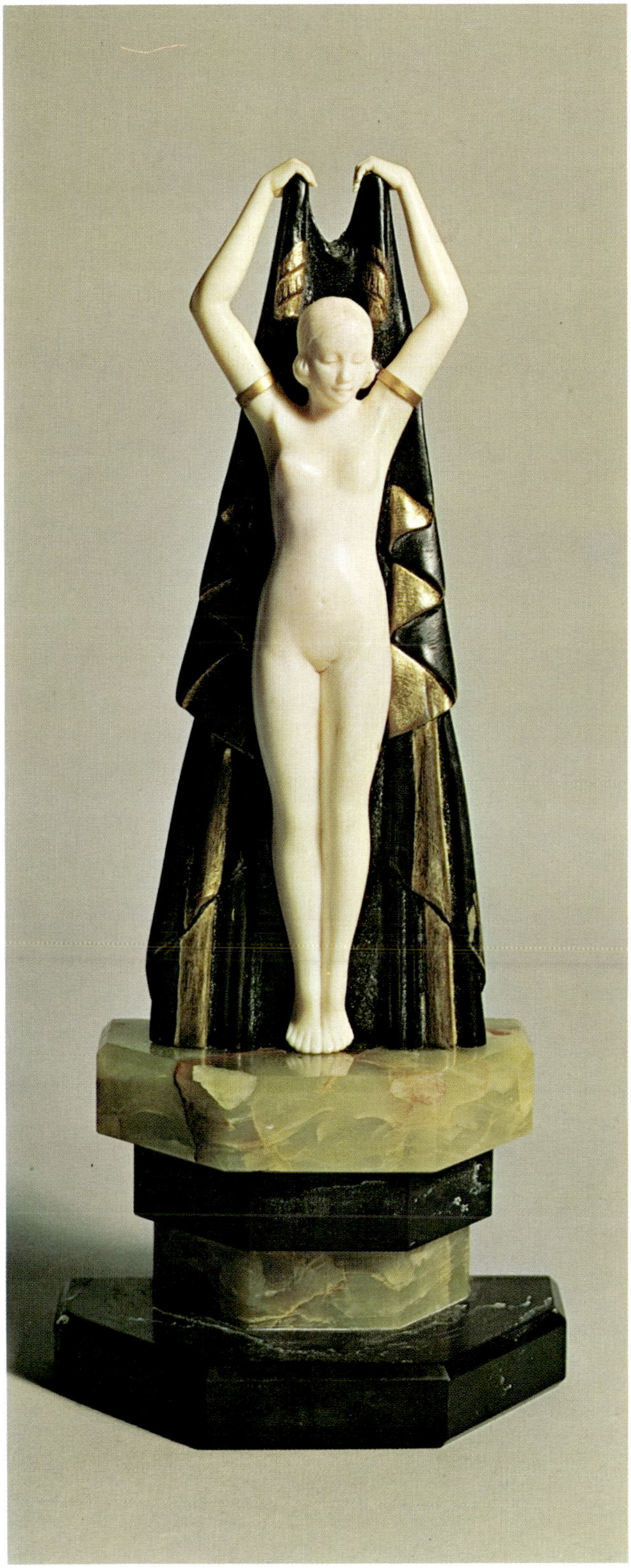

Ivory nude with bronze cloak
25cm: 10in.

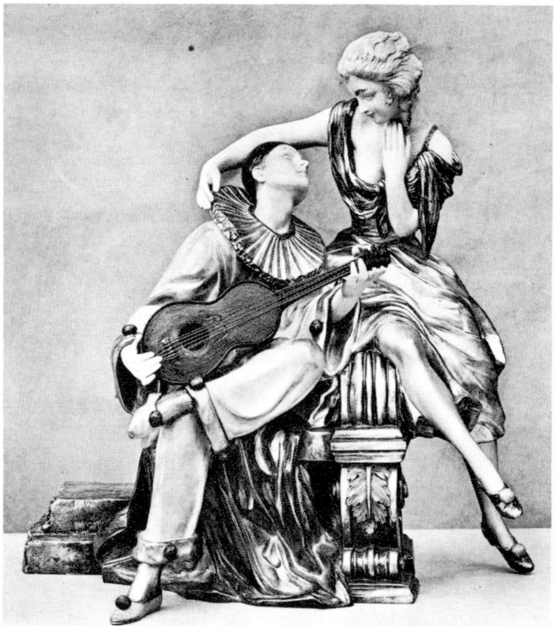

Romance, 39cm: 15¼in.

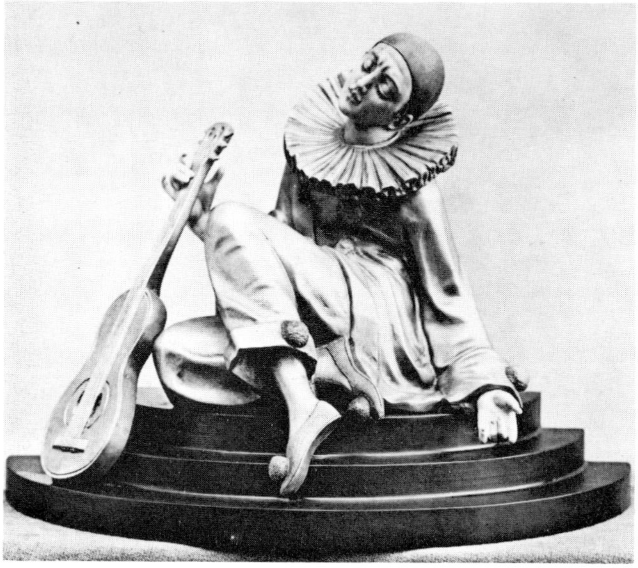

Sleep of the Pierrot, 48cm: 19in.
Exhibited Decoratif Arts, 1925

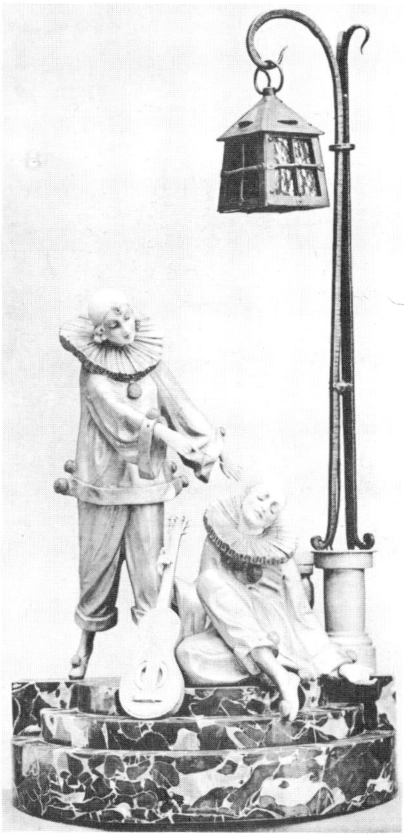

Awakening of the Pierrot
68cm: 26¾in., wired as a lamp

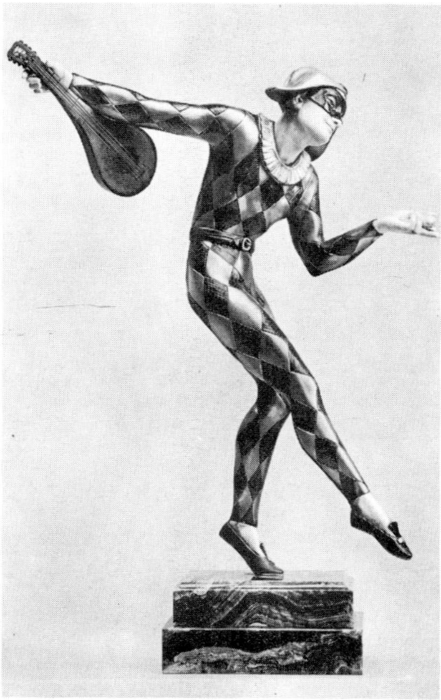

Harlequinade with Rose
45cm: 17¾in.

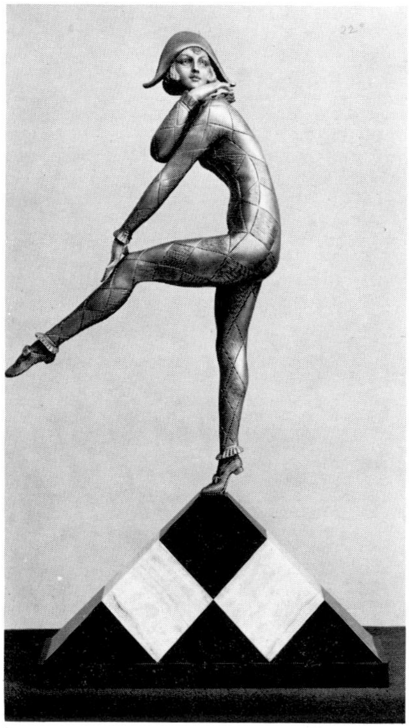

Dance of the Harlequinade
55cm: 21½in.; 37cm: 14½in.

A. GILBERT

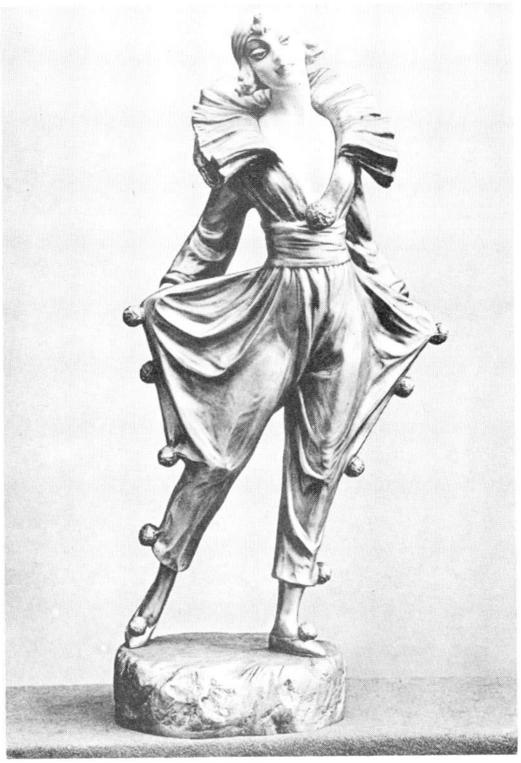

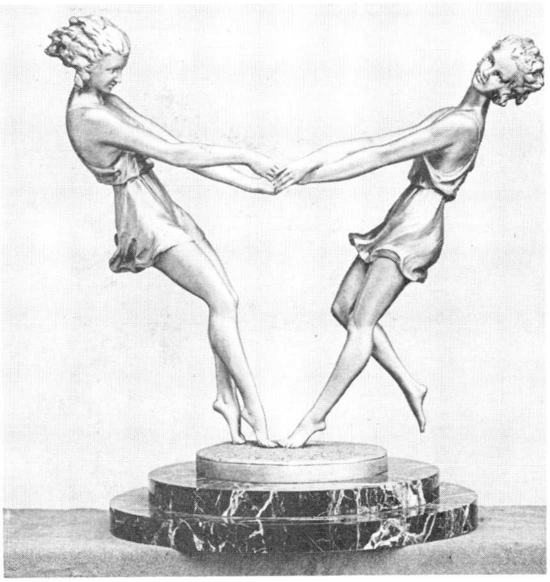

Whirling, 40cm: 15¾in.; 28cm: 11in.

On Parade, 58cm: 22¾in.
33cm: 13in.; 22cm: 8½in.

A. GODARD

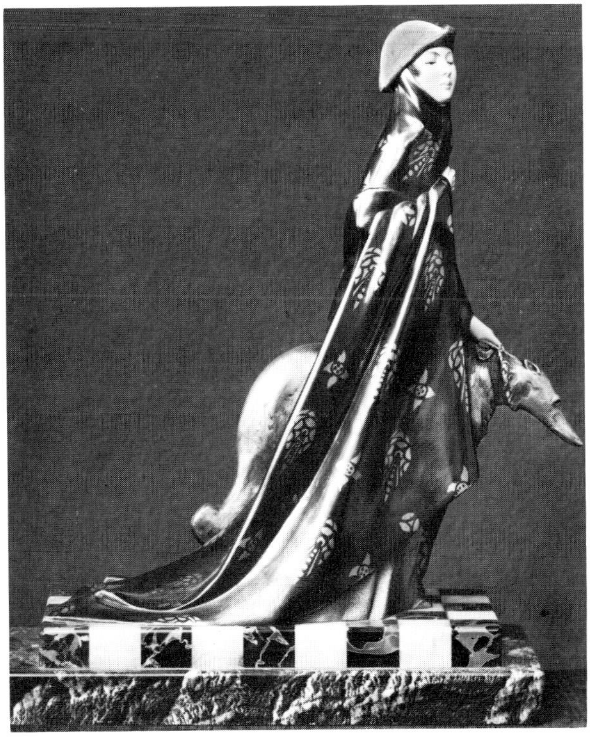

Venetian, 40cm: 15¾in.; 25cm: 10in.

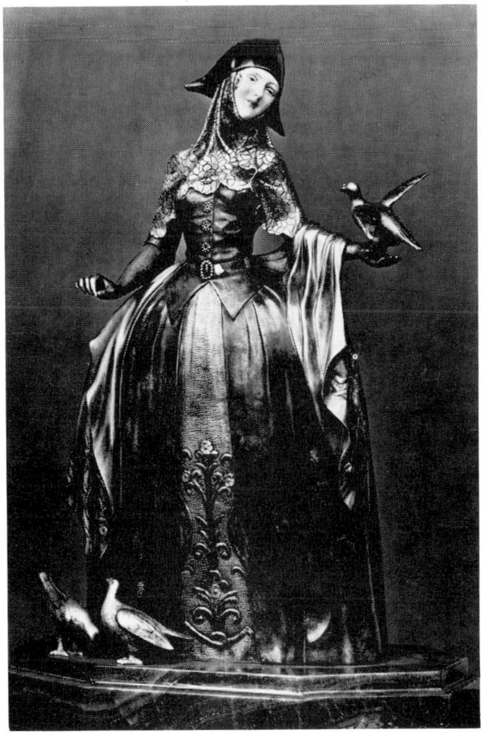

St. Mark's Square, 40cm: 15¾in.

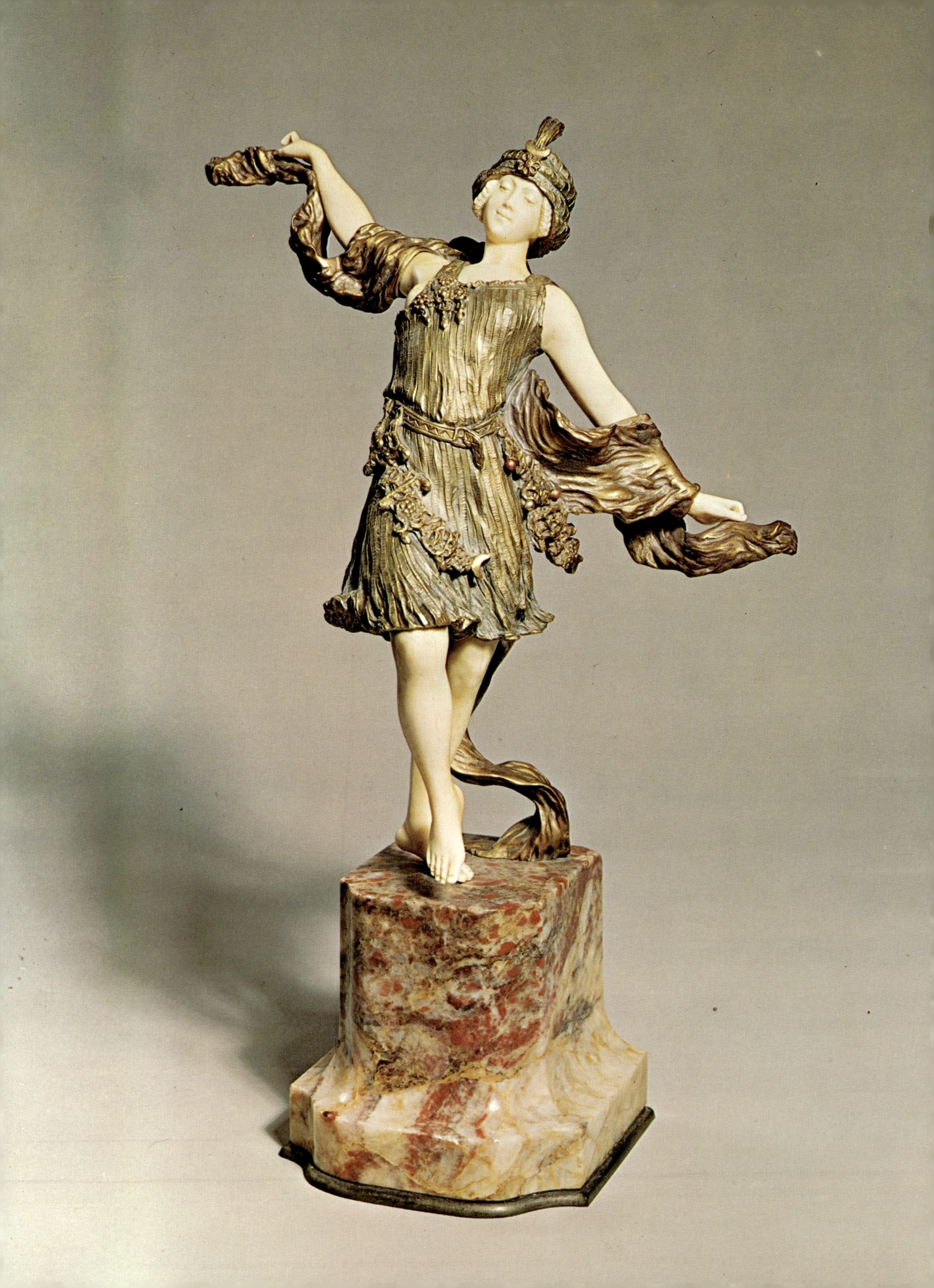

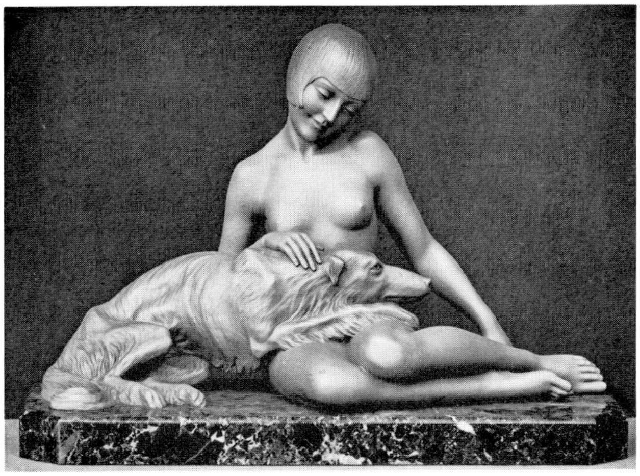

The Pet Dog, 40cm:15¾in.

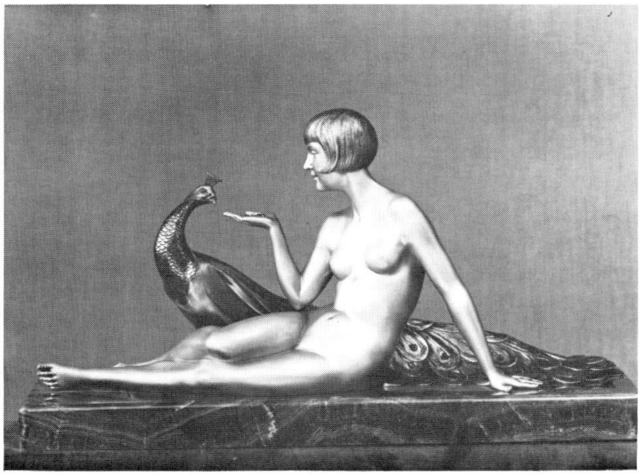

Girl with Peacock, 31cm:12¼in.

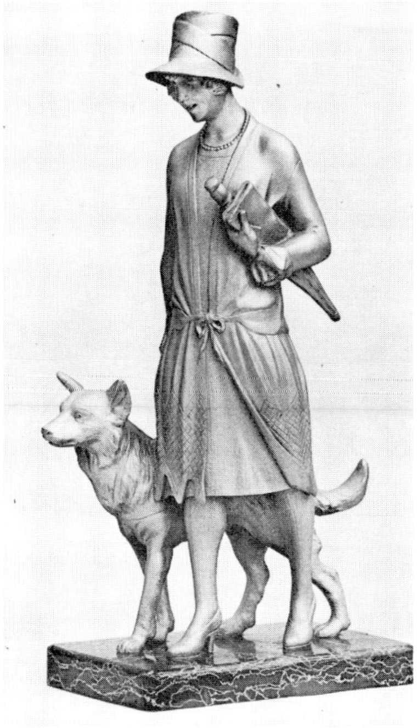

Morning Walk
31cm:12¼in.

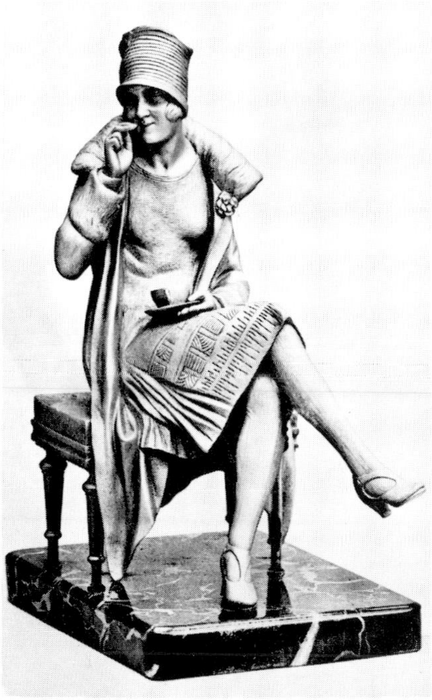

Visiting, 27cm:10½in.

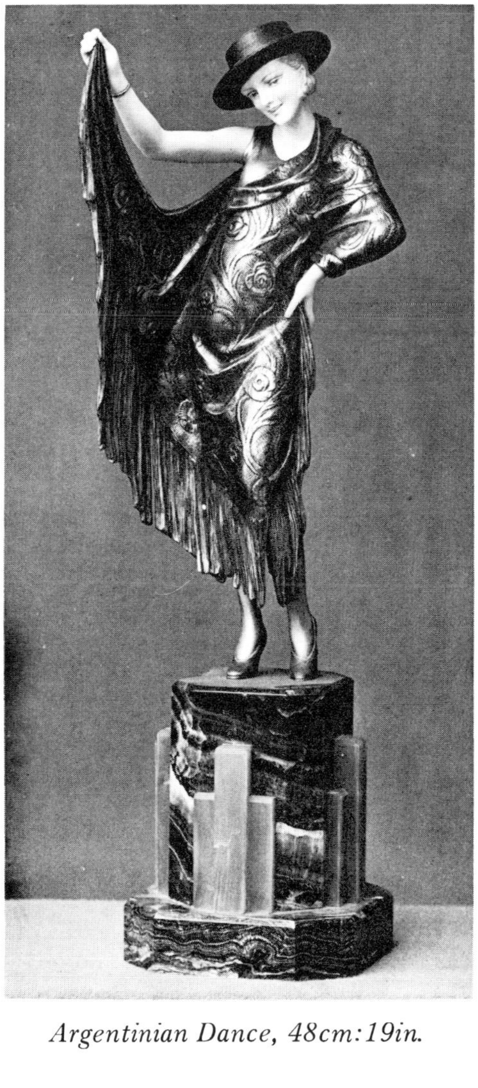

Argentinian Dance, 48cm:19in.

Left: Kernalan
Indian Dancer
37cm:14½in.

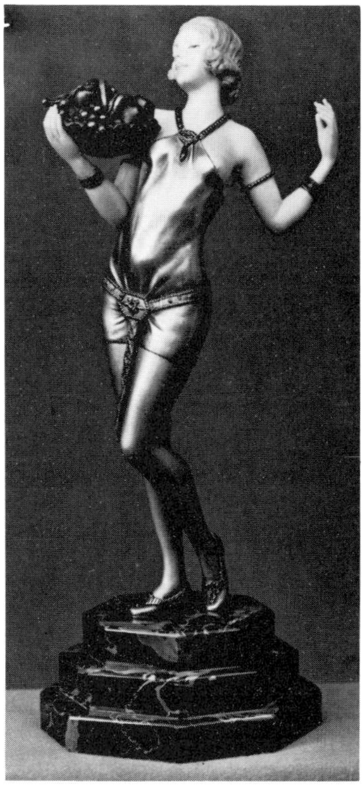

Beautiful Slave, 39cm: 15½in.

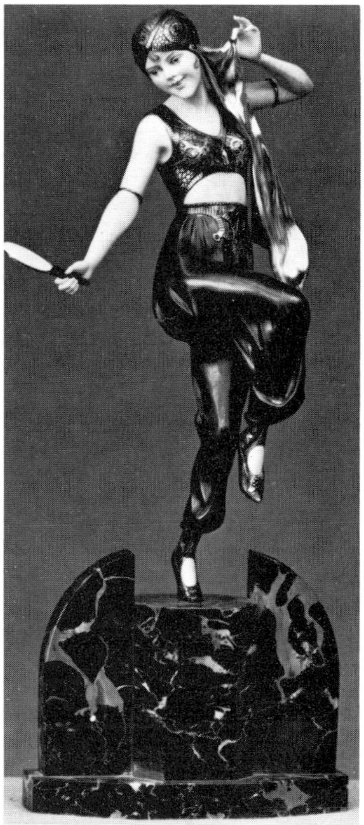

Favourite, 50cm: 19¾in.

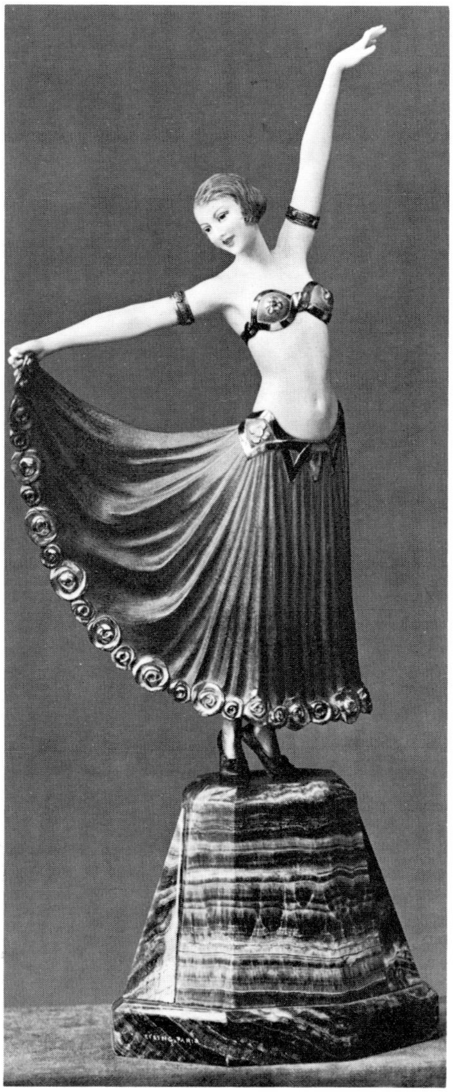

Syrian Dancer, 48cm: 19in.

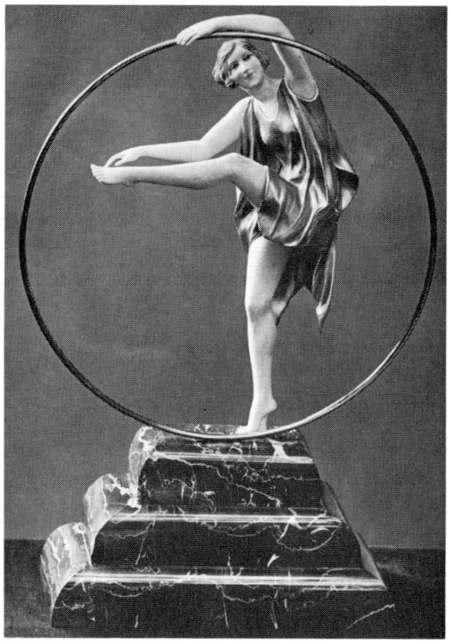

Georgian Dancer, 44cm: 17½in.

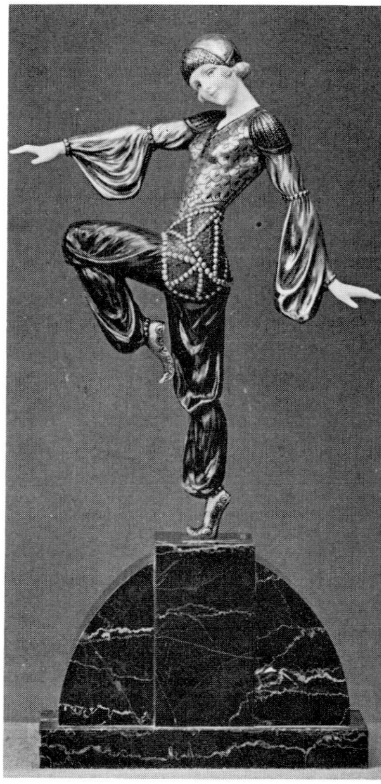

Charm of the Orient
49cm: 19¼in.

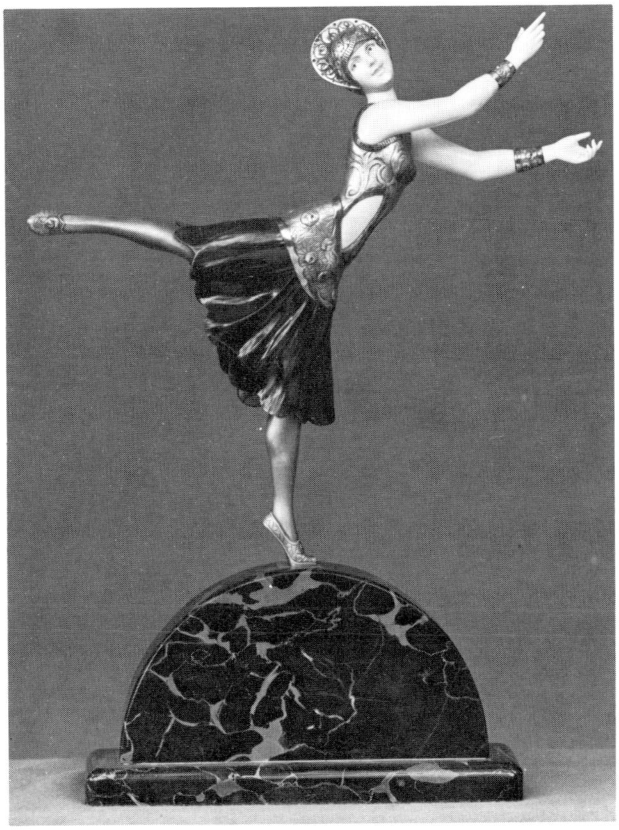

Aicha, 46cm:18in.

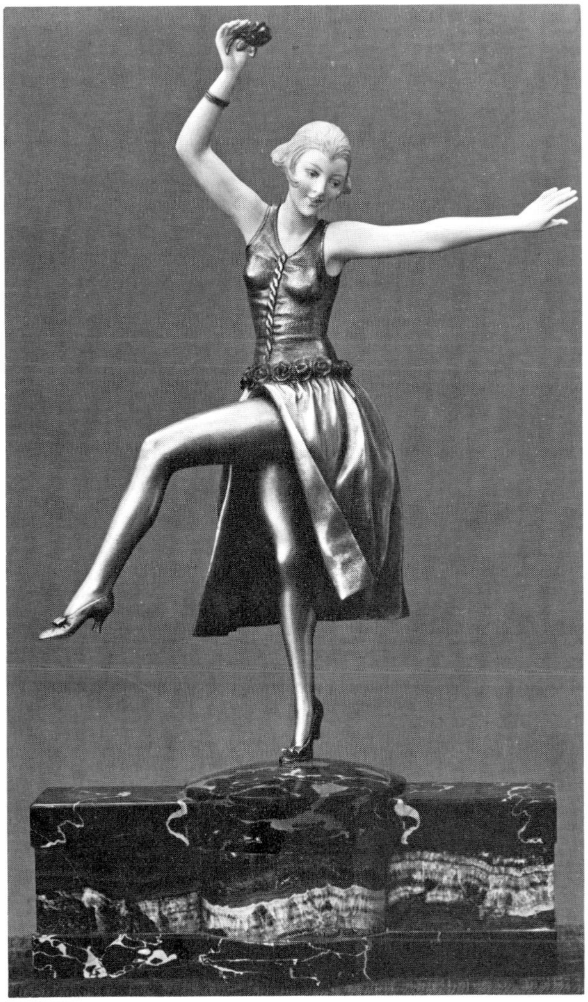

Dance of the Rose, 46cm:18in.

Bubble Dance
51cm:20in.
36cm:14in.
Figure posed at the Folies-Bergère, Paris, in 1930 by Georgia Graves, who was trained by Ernest Belcher of Los Angeles

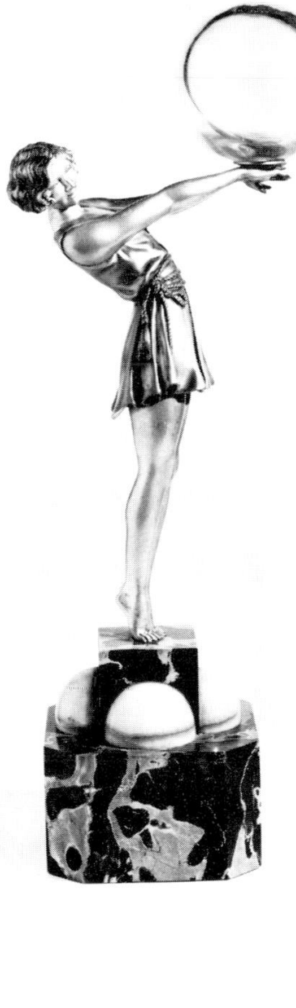

GOMERTE

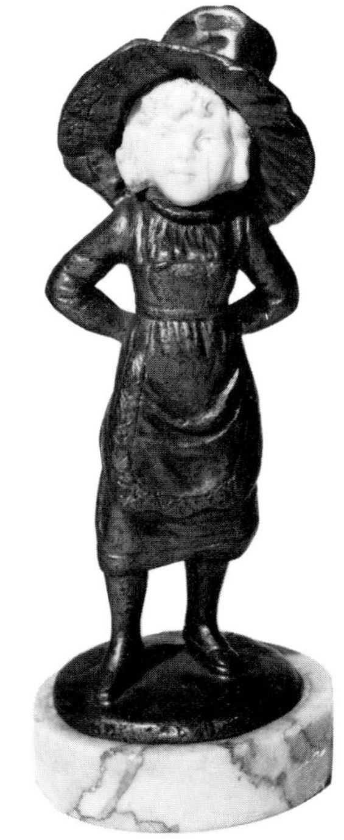

A Child, 16cm:6¼in.

G. GORI

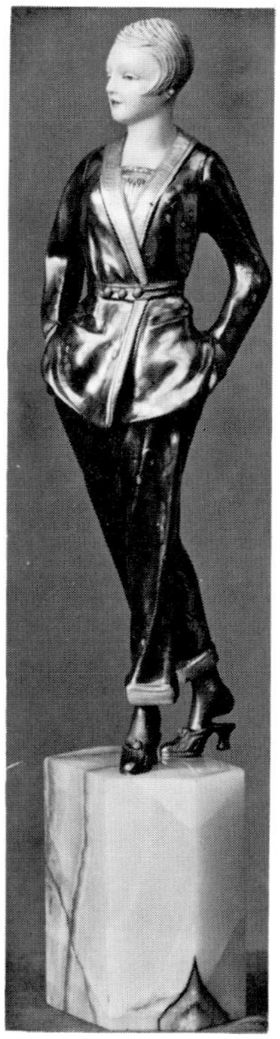

Pyjamas
32cm:12½in.

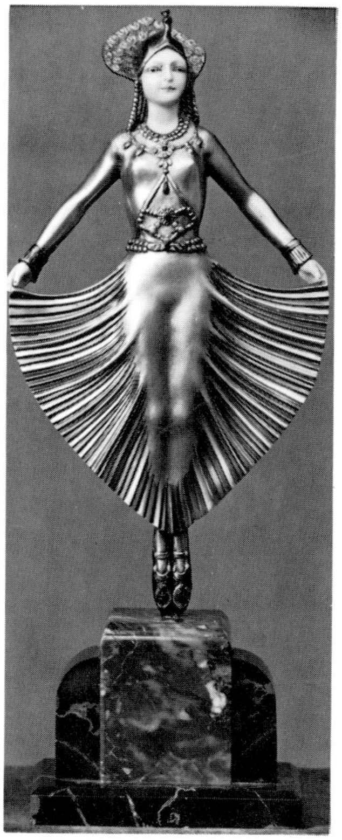

Egyptian Dancer
34cm:13½in.

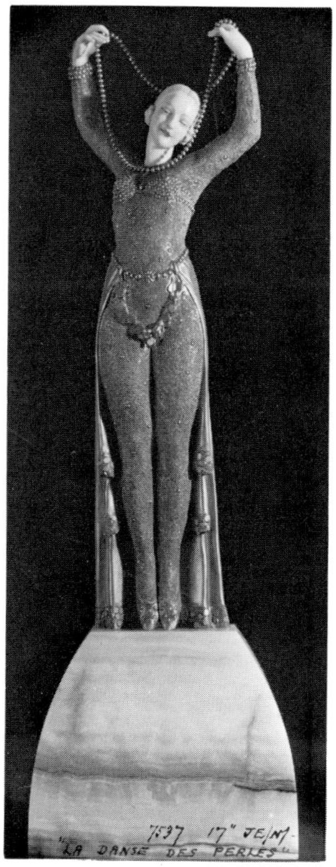

Dance of Pearls
43cm:17in.

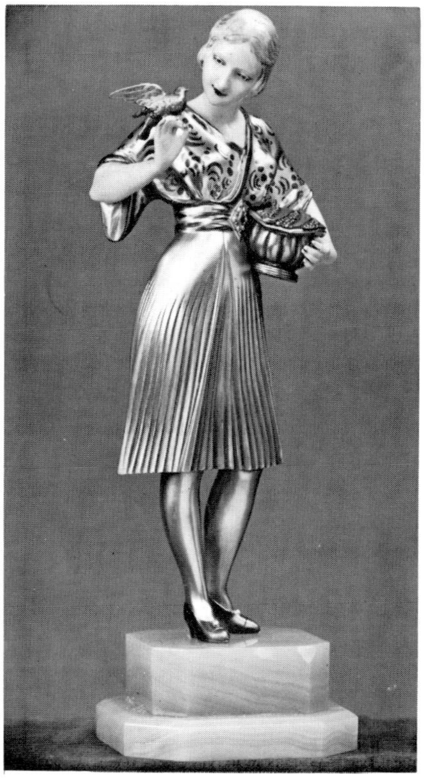

The Charmer, 38cm:15in.

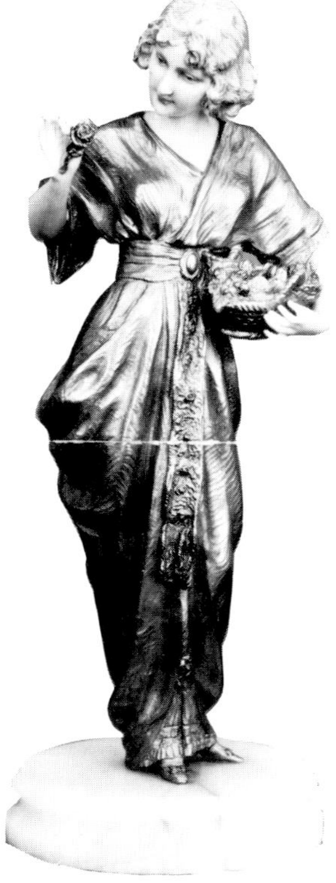

Flower Girl, 35cm:13¾in.

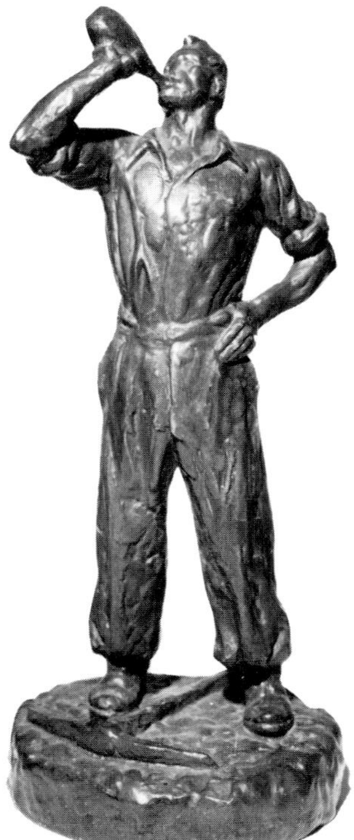

A Workman, 30cm:11¾in.

G. GORI

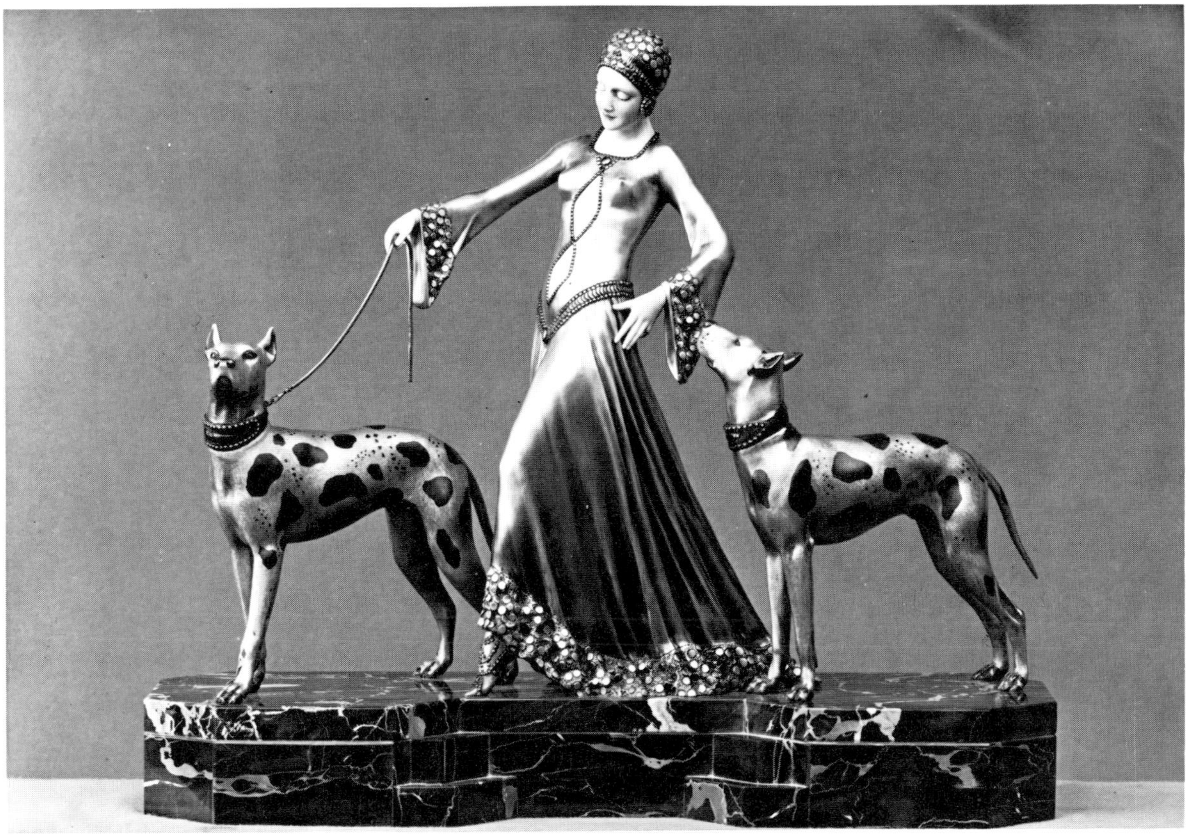

The Guardians, 56cm:22in.

A. GORY

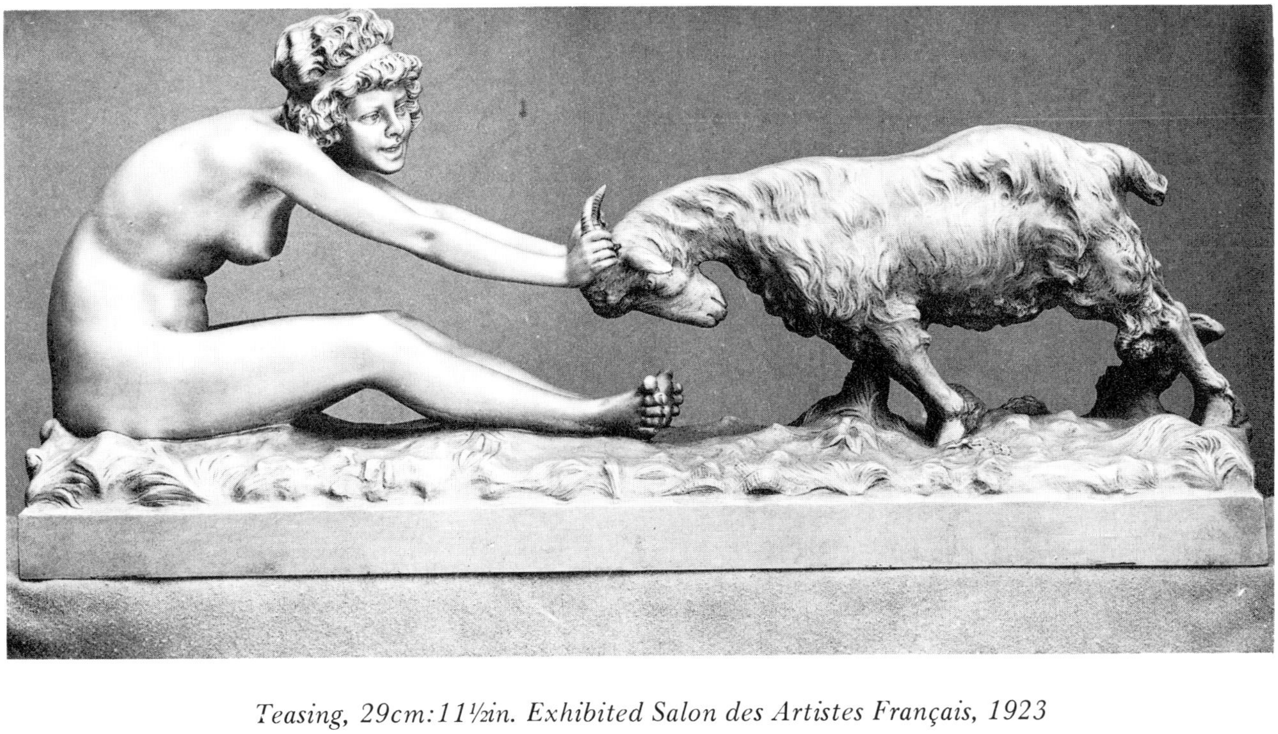

Teasing, 29cm:11½in. Exhibited Salon des Artistes Français, 1923

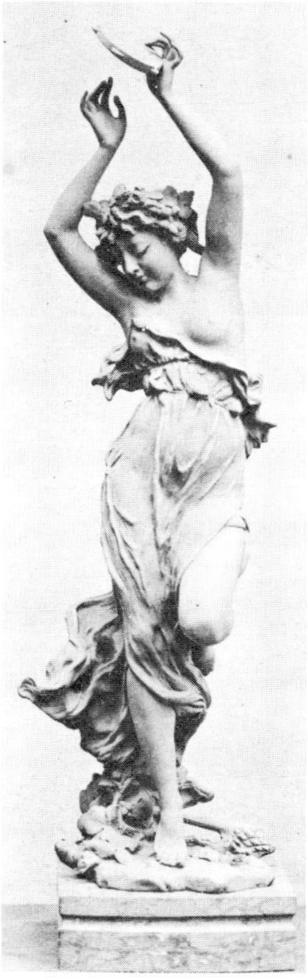

Bacchante with Tambourine
72cm:28¼in.
50cm:19¾in.

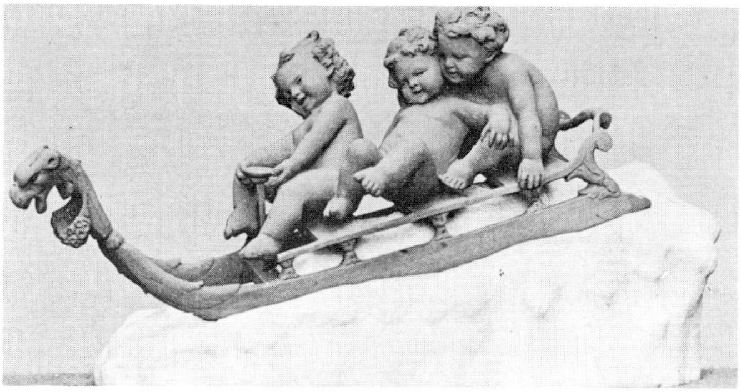

Bobsleigh, 20cm:8in.

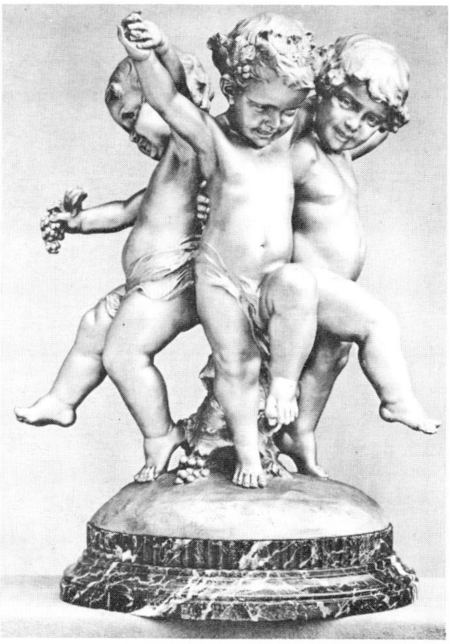

The Dance, 57cm:22½in.

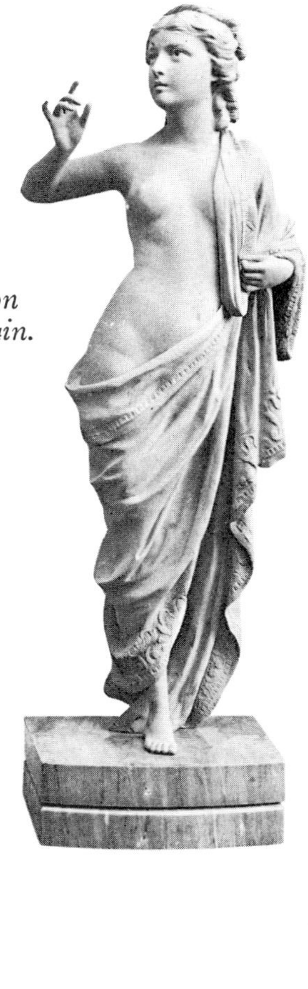

Inspiration
59cm:23¼in.

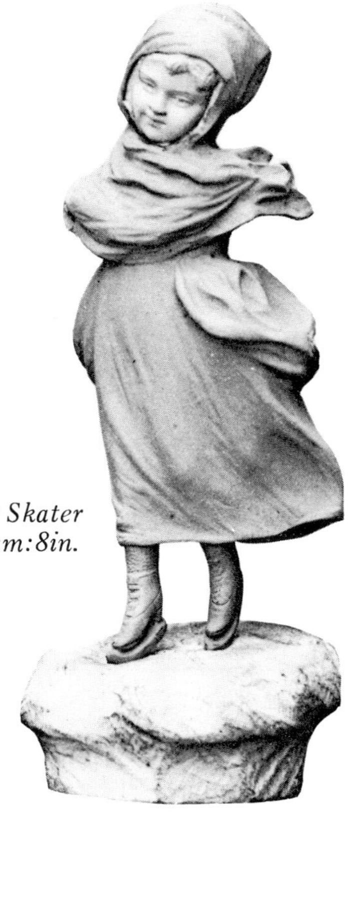

The Skater
20cm:8in.

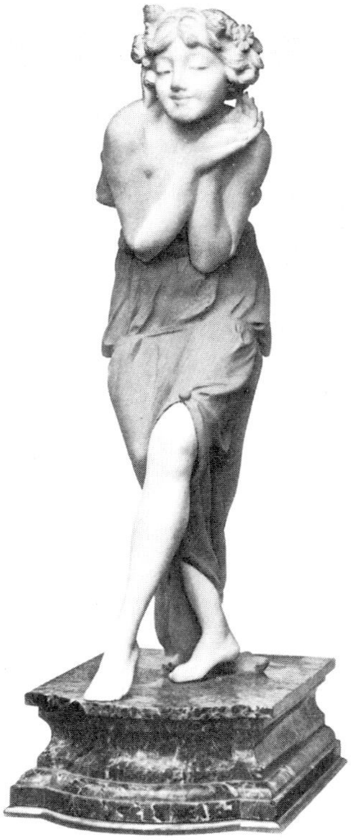

Curious, 50cm:19½in.

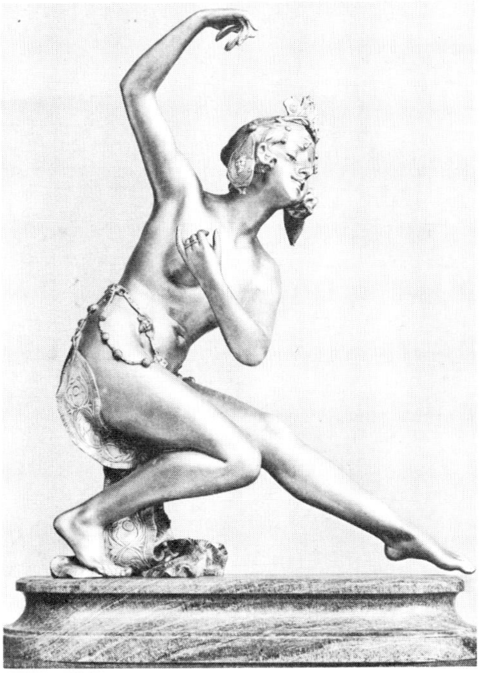

Dance with Castanets, 69cm:27¼in.

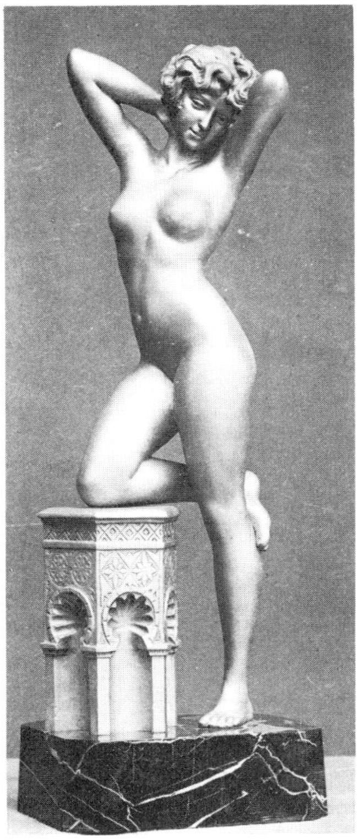

Awaking, 52cm:20½in.

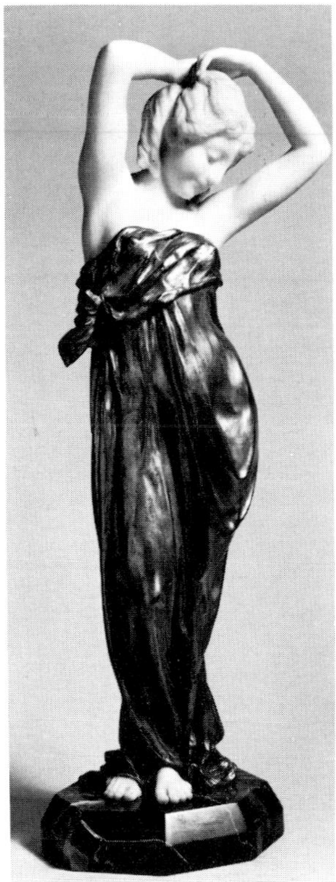

Dressing, 60cm:23½in.

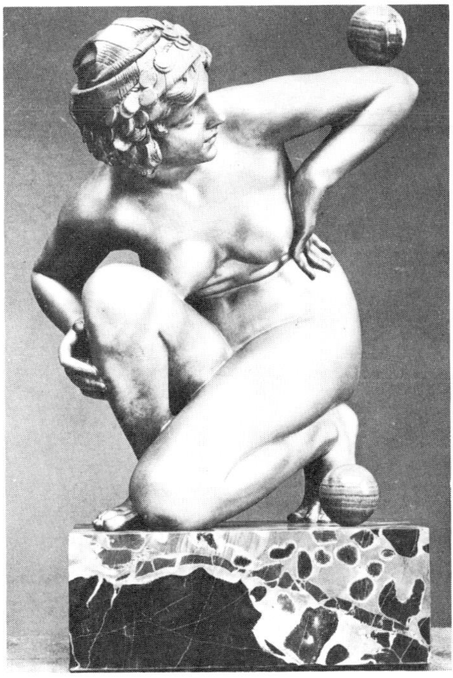

Girl with Ball, 47cm:18½in.

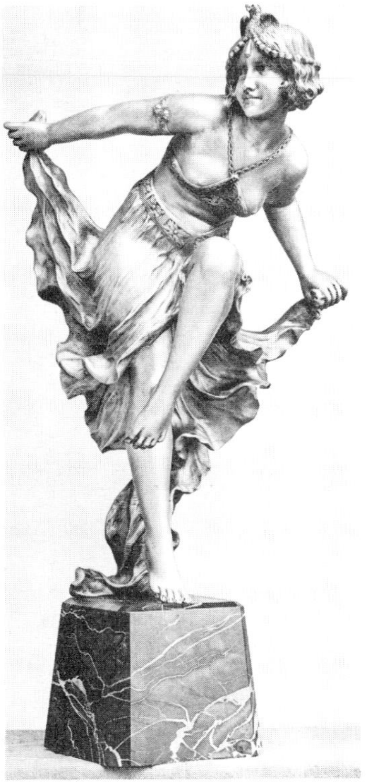

Dancer, 66cm:26in.

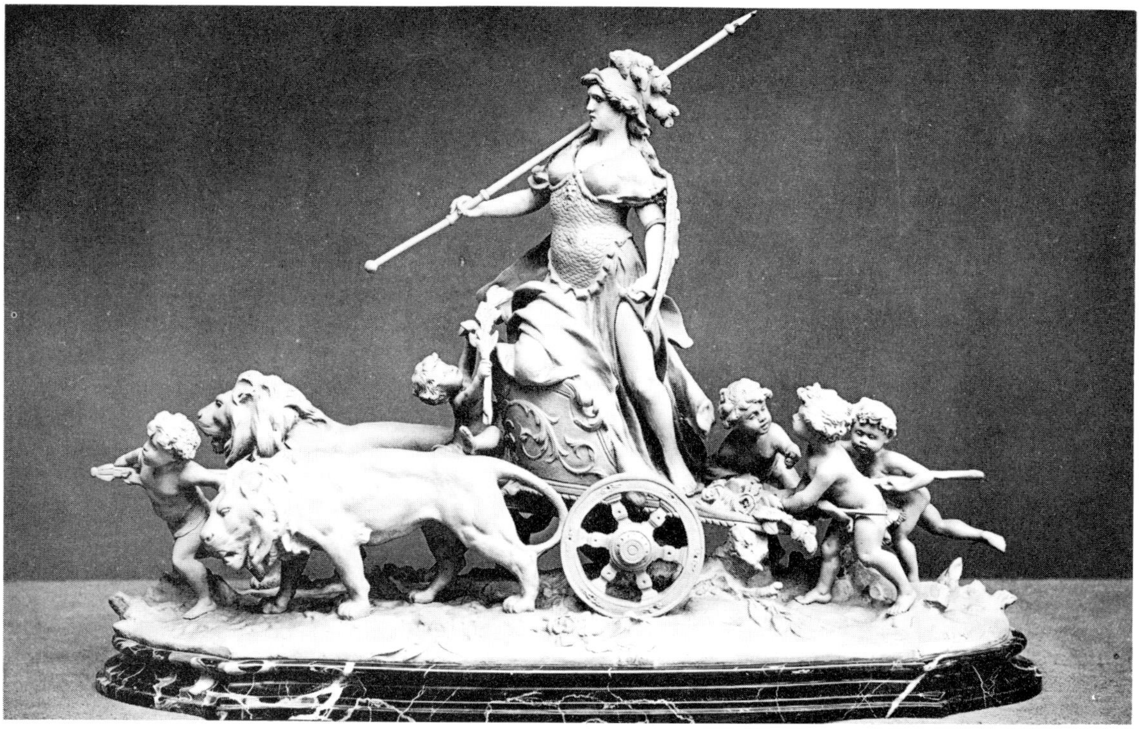

Chariot, 42cm: 16½in.

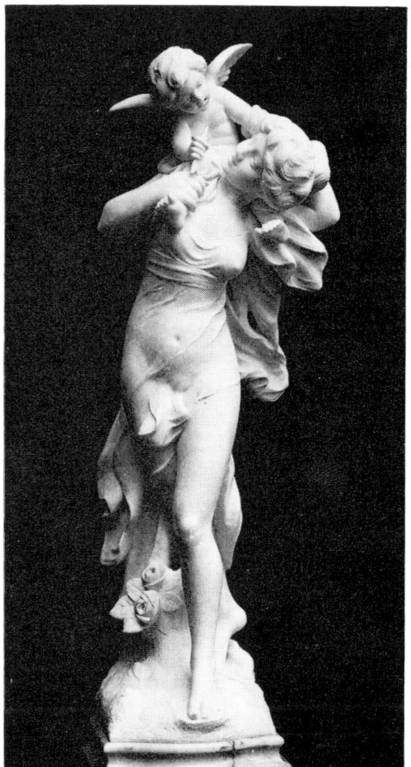

Captive
90cm: 35½in.; 65cm: 25½in.

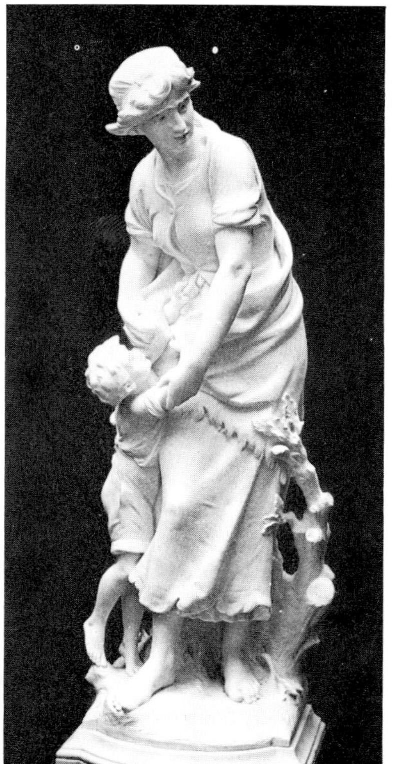

Protection, 83cm: 32½in.

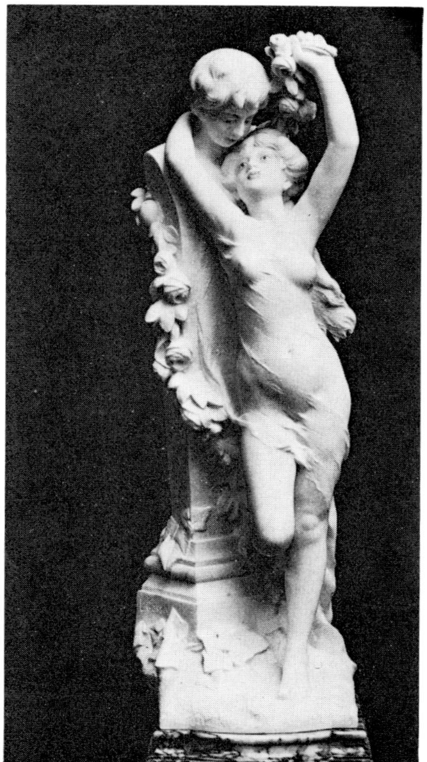

Ode of Love
80cm: 31½in.; 65cm: 25½in.

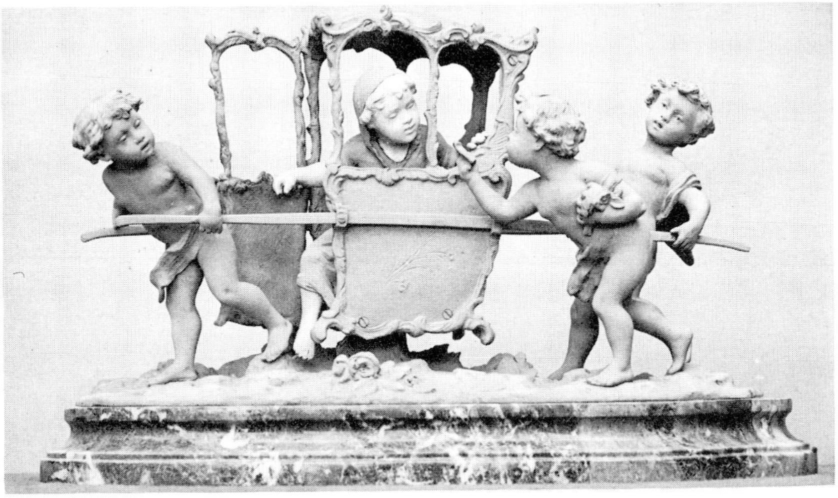

Sedan Chair, 26cm:10¼in.

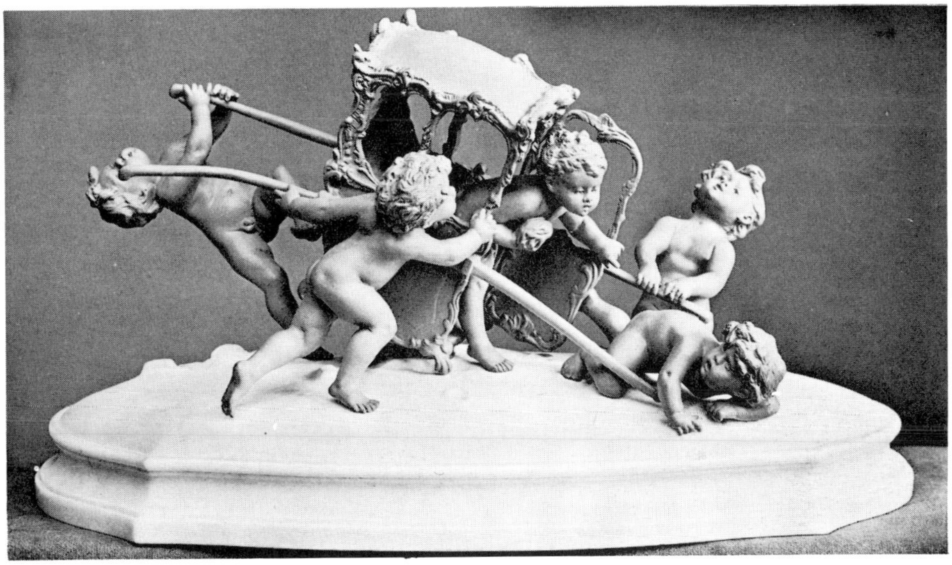

Accident of the Sedan Chair 27cm:10½in.

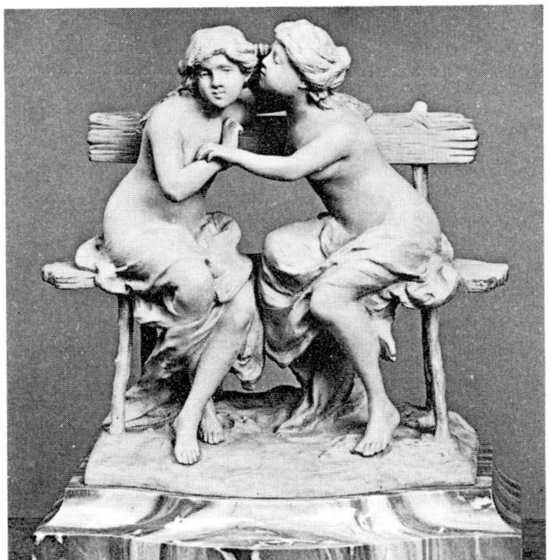

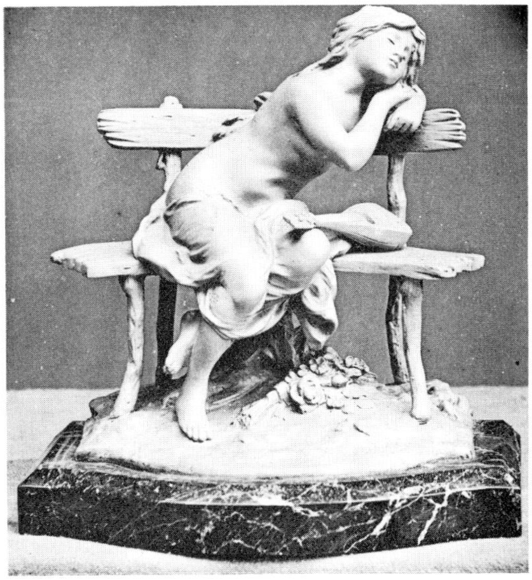

Left: Confidence 25cm:10in.

Right: Resting Grasshopper 22cm:8¾in.

GENEVIÈVE GRANGER

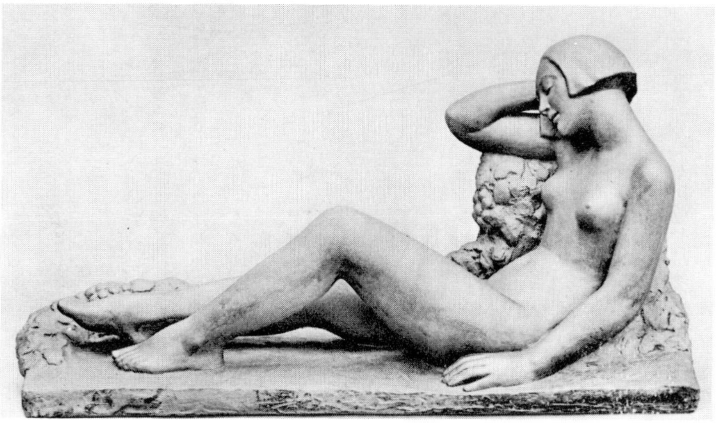

Sleeping Beauty, 38cm:15in.
Exhibited Decoratif Arts, 1925

GREBER

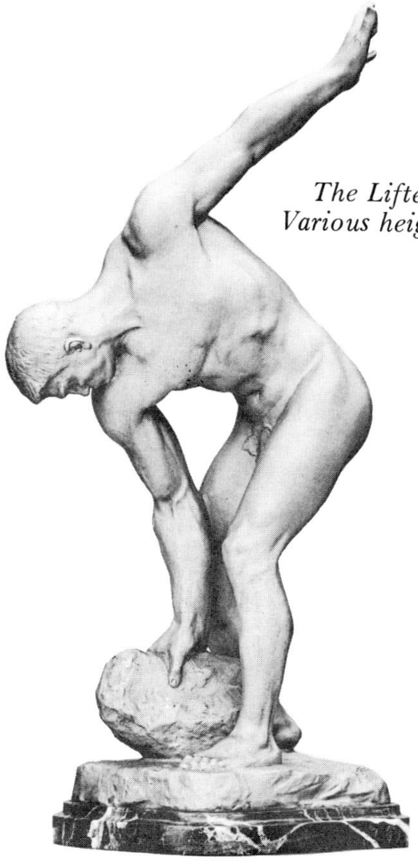

The Lifter
Various heights

GRÉGOIRE

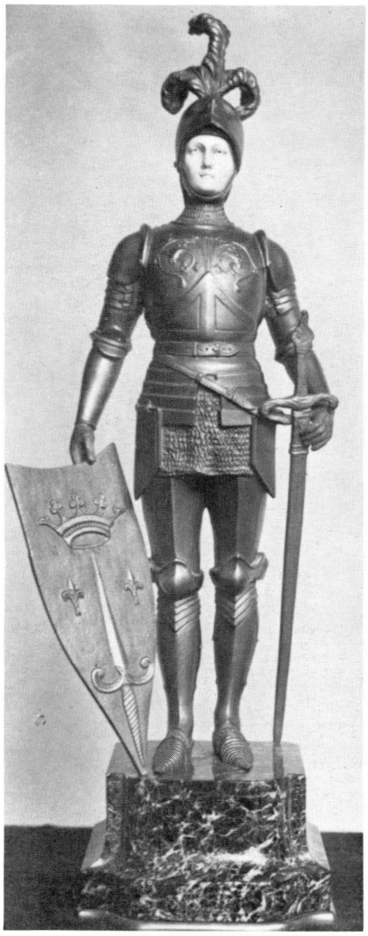

Knight, 46cm:18in.

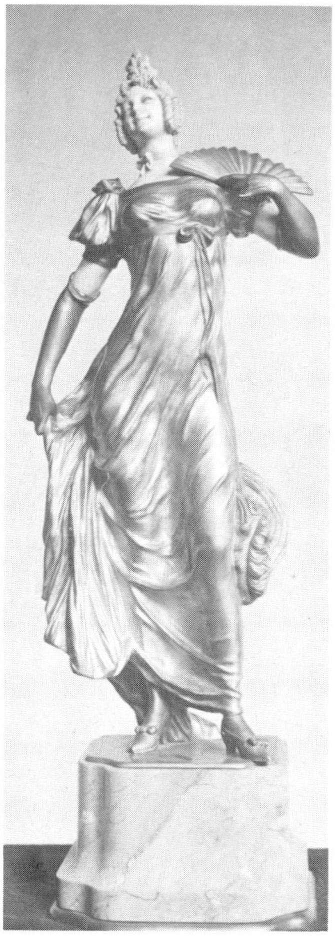

Exquisite, 51cm:20in.

A. GREVIN

Winged Figure
with Muff
31cm:12in.

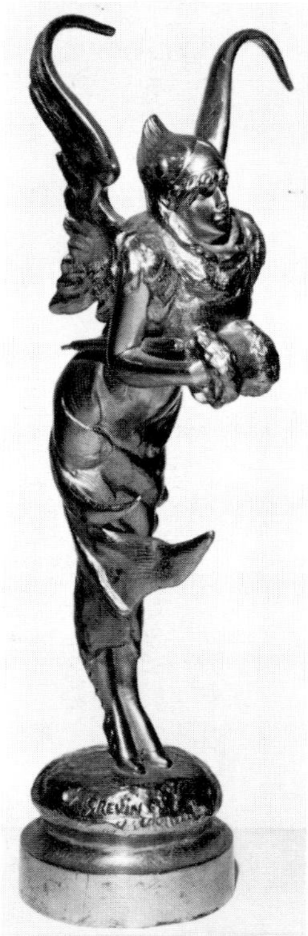

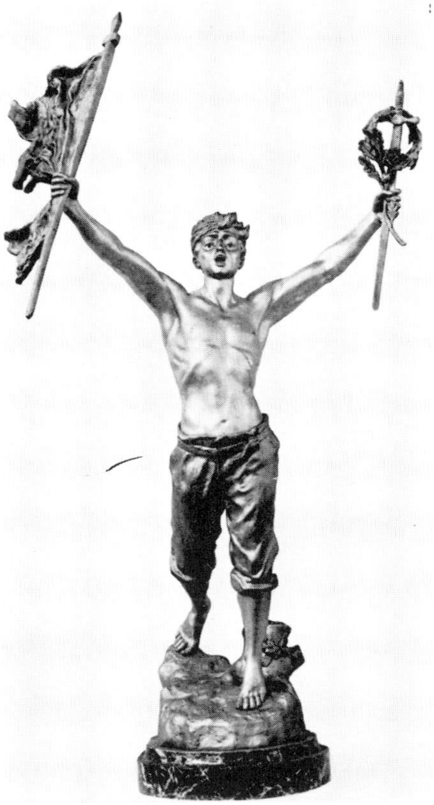

Cry of Victory
85cm:33½in.
55cm:21½in.

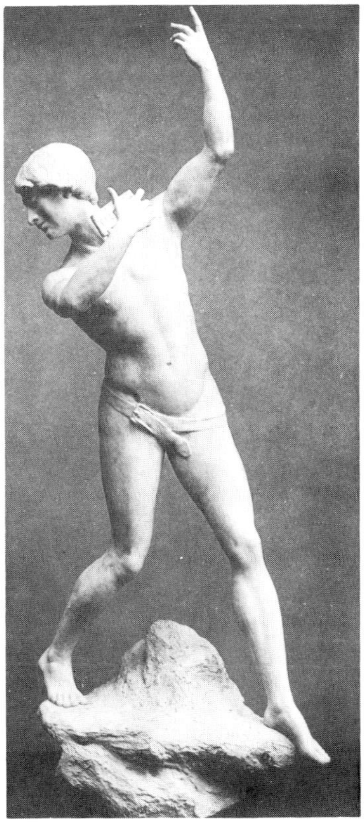

Happy Youth
96cm:37¾in.
64cm:25in.
42cm:16½in.

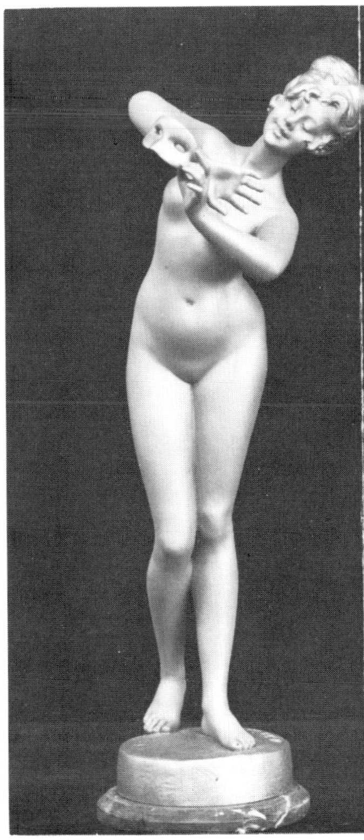

The Velvet Mask
31cm:12in.

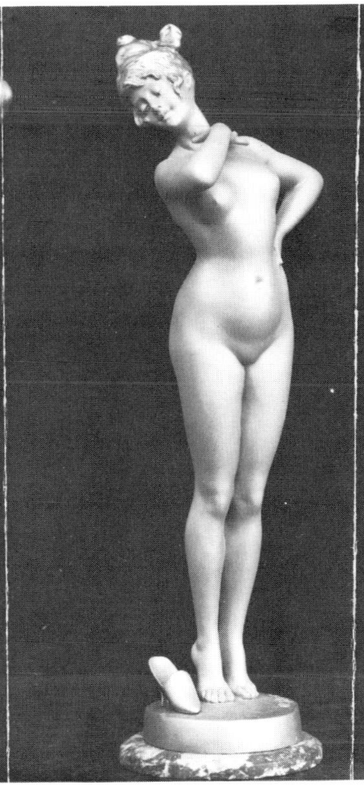

The Pose
32cm:12½in.

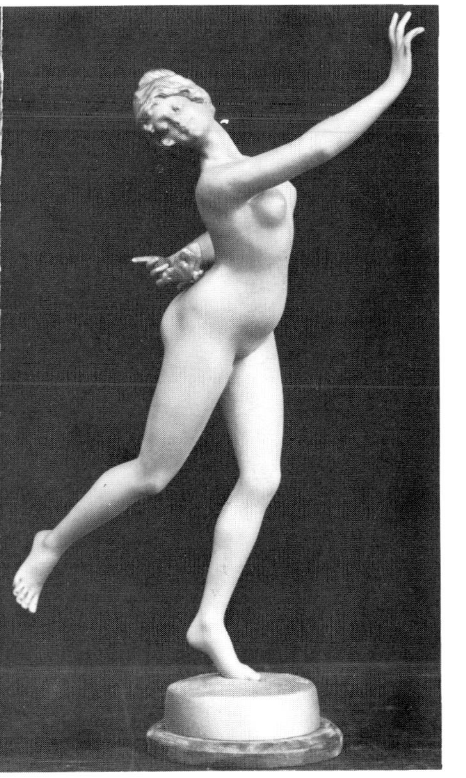

Surprise
32cm:12½in.

H. GRÜN

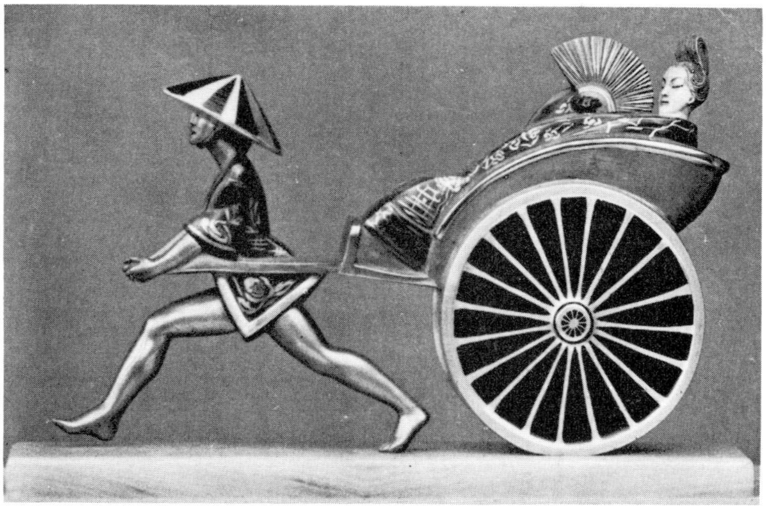

Rickshaw, 23cm:9in.

RAYMONDE GUERBE

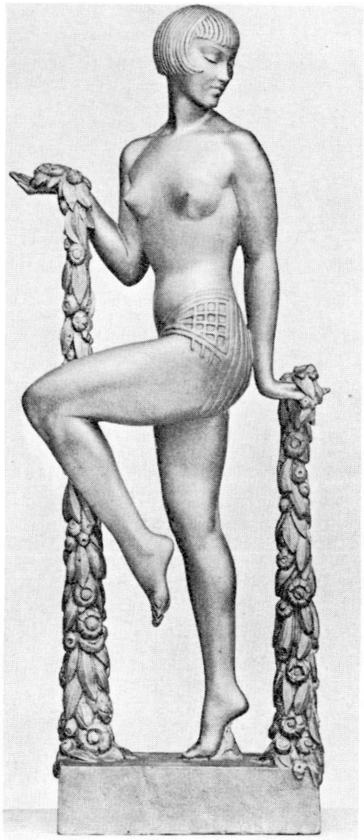

Flower Dance
40cm:15¾in.

A. GUERVAL

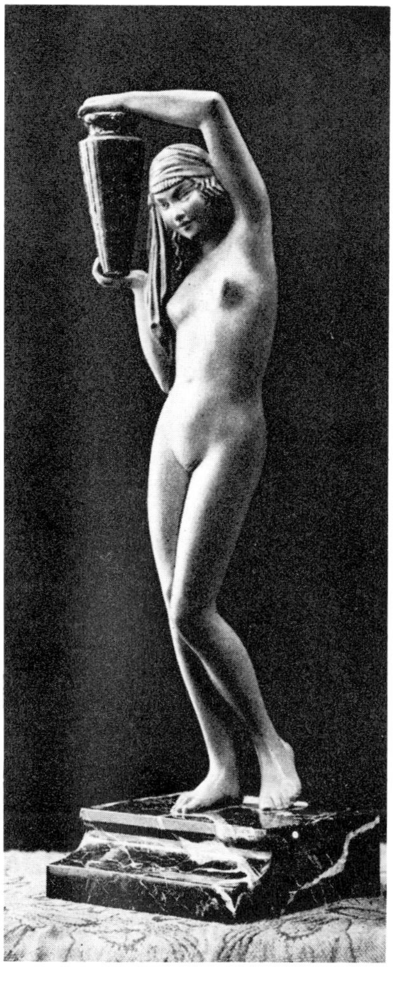

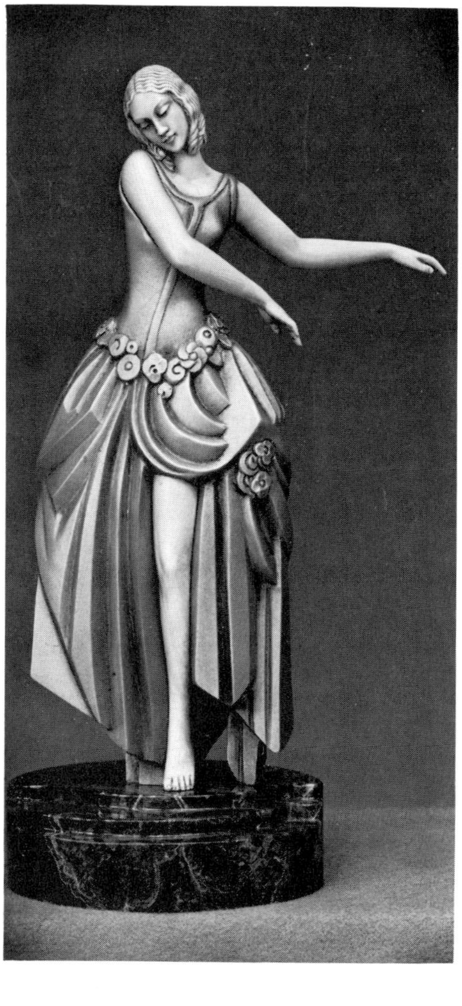

Left:
The Minuet, 26cm:10¼in.

Far left: Chrysis
34cm:13¼in.

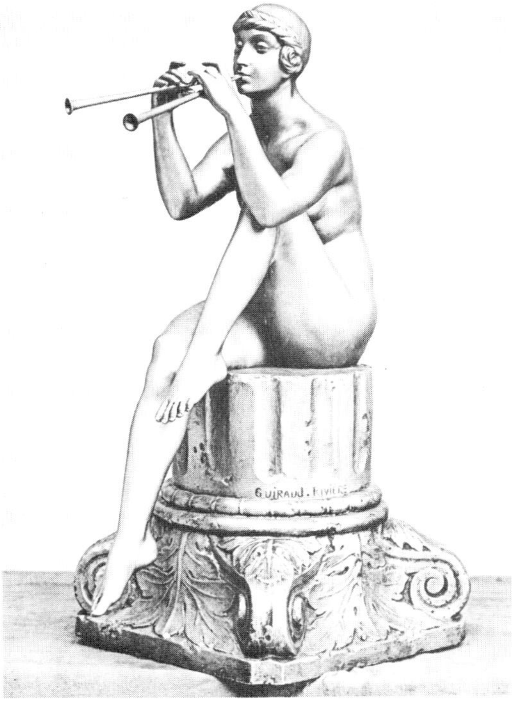

The Piper, 60cm: 23½in.
Exhibited Salon des Humoristes Français, 1923

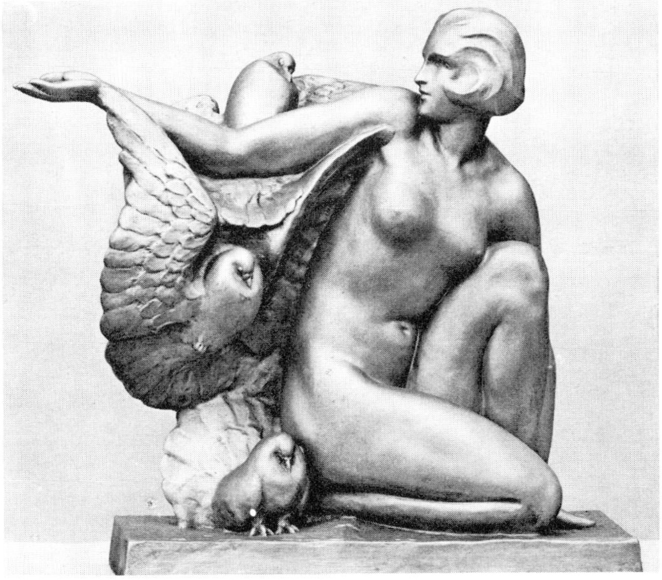

Girl with Pigeons, 50cm: 19¾in.; 33cm: 13in.

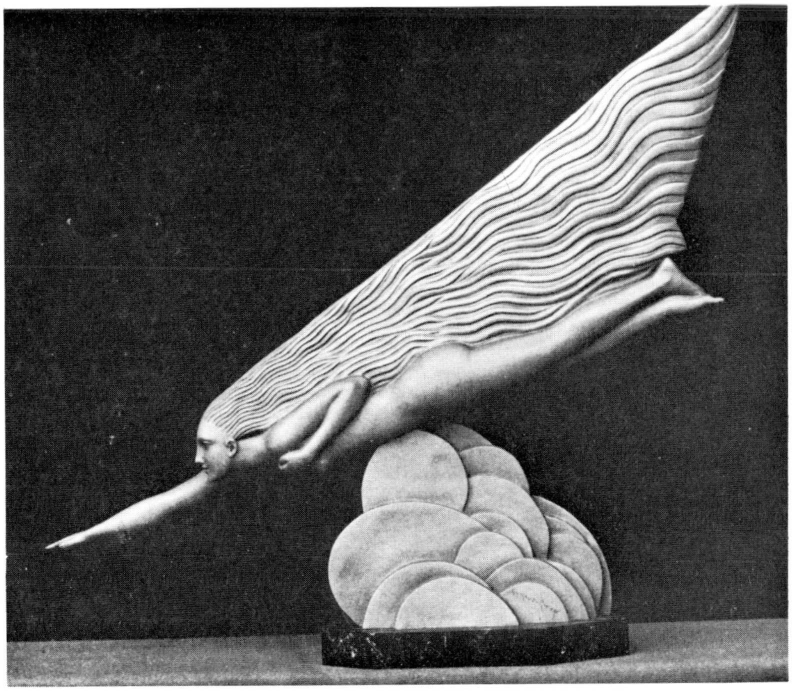

The Comet, 52cm: 20½in.

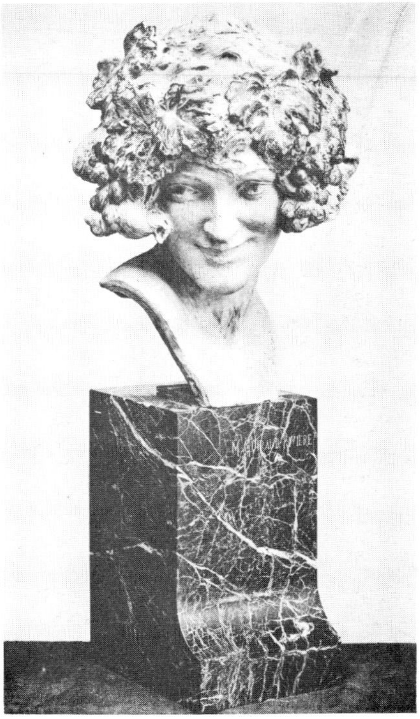

Head of Bacchante, 62cm: 24½in.
Exhibited Salon des
Humoristes Français, 1923

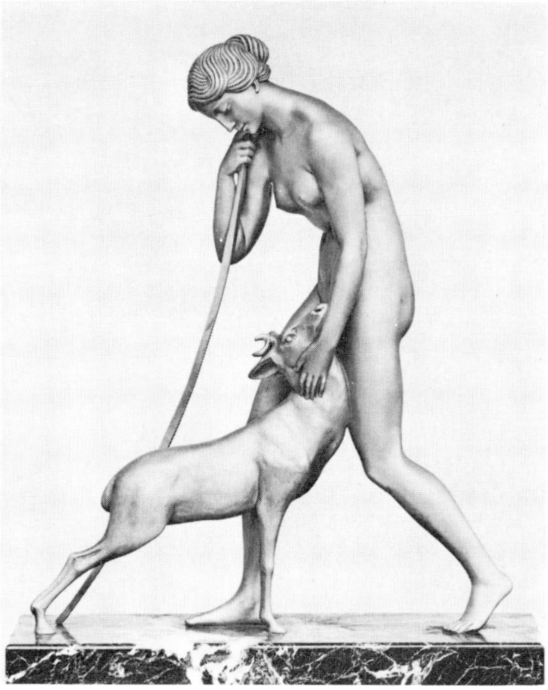

Girl with Hind, 47cm:18½in.

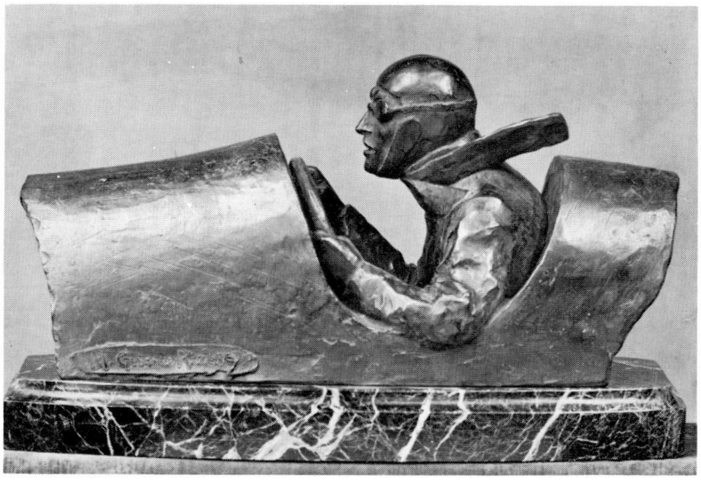

Racing Motorist, 28cm:11in.

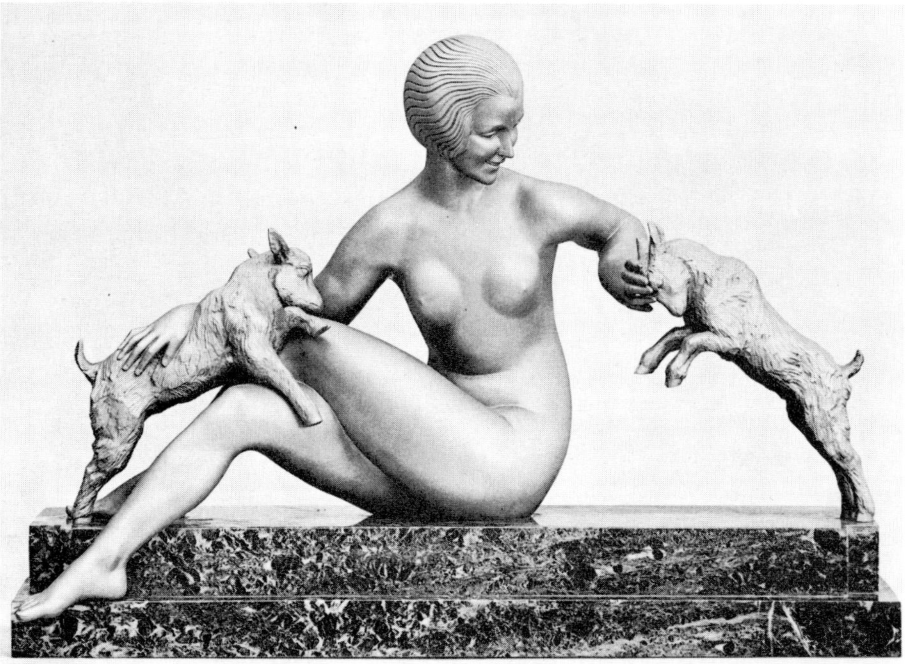

Girl with Two Goats, various heights

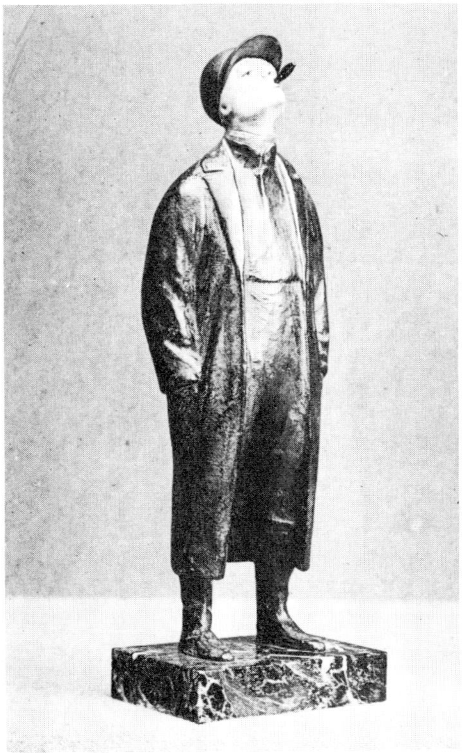

The Winner, 25cm:10in.

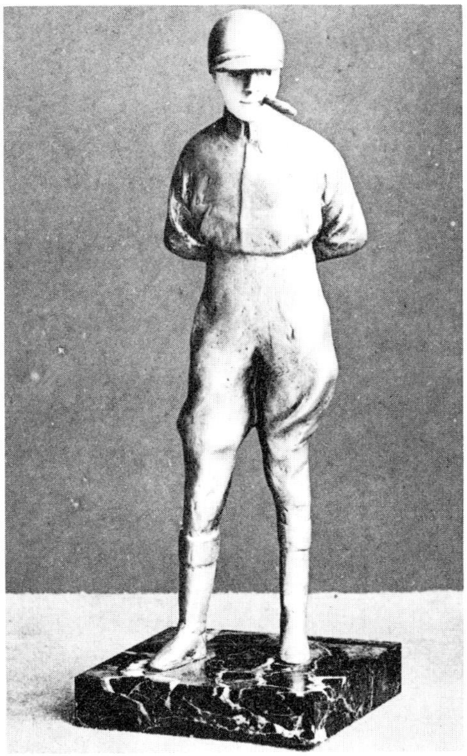

The Loser, 25cm:10in.

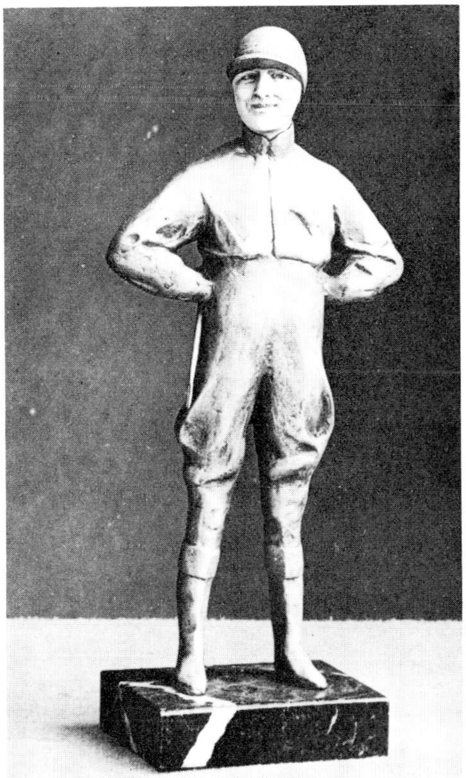

Before the Race, 25cm:10in.

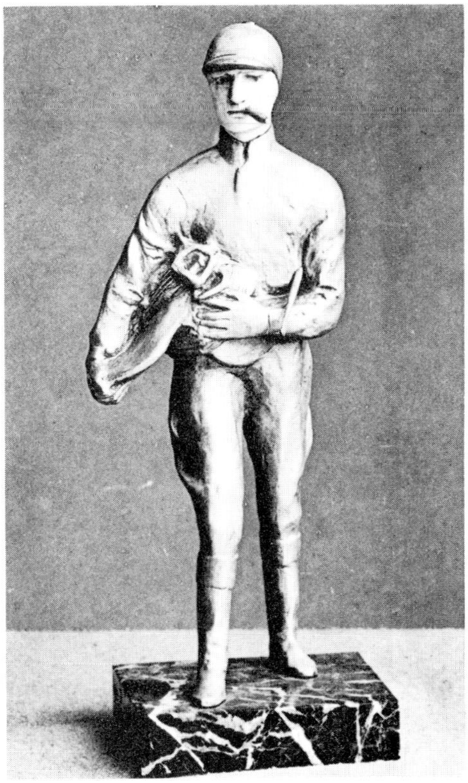

The Weigh-in, 25cm:10in.

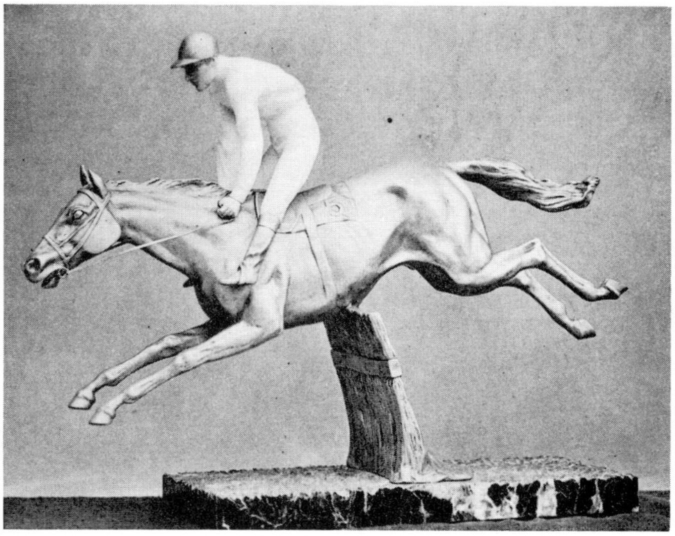

Jockey Jumping the Hedge, 40cm:15¾in

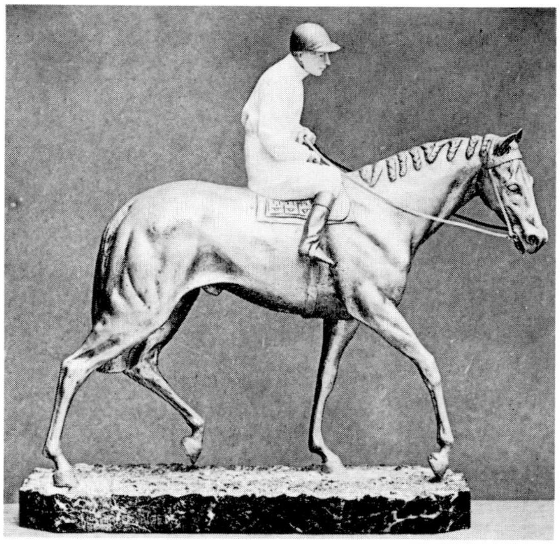

Returning to the Saddling Room
40cm:15¾in.

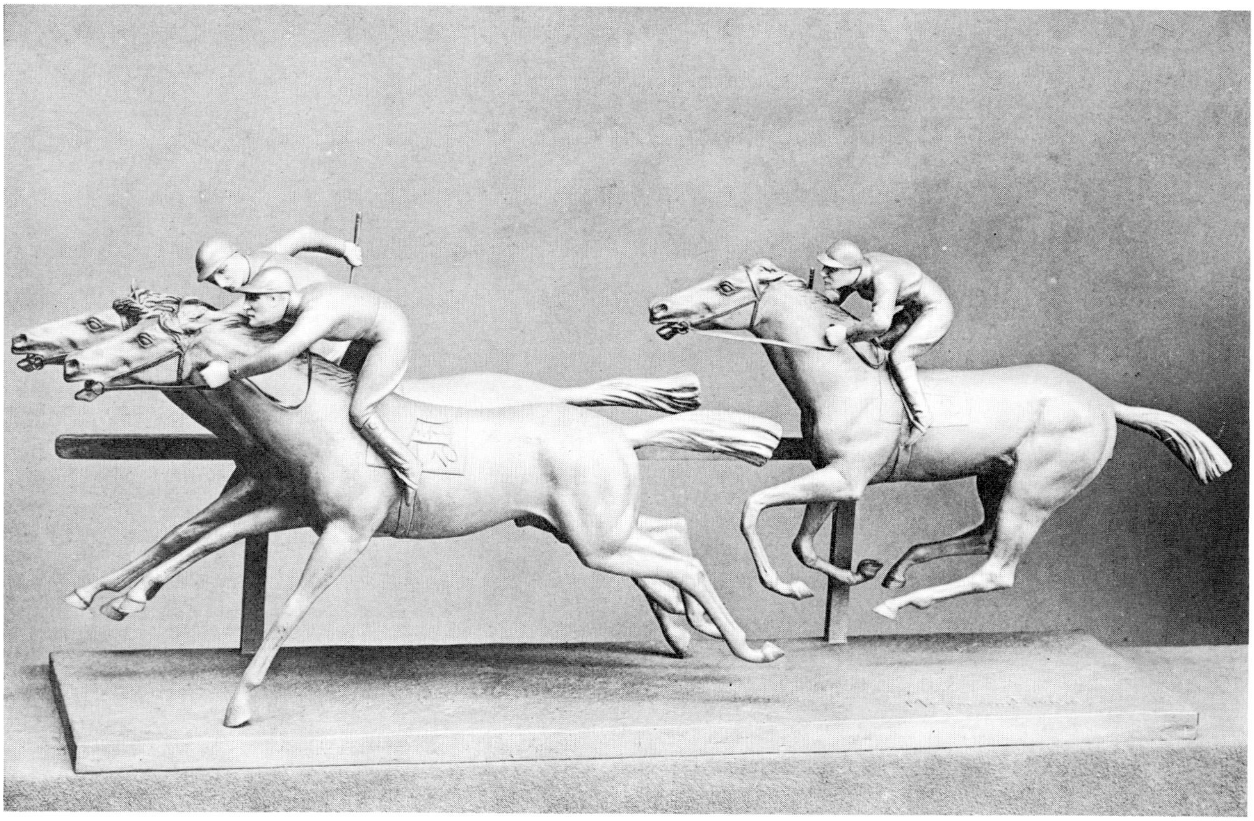

End of the Race, 31cm:12in.
Three versions, one as illustrated, one with two jockeys and one with a single jockey

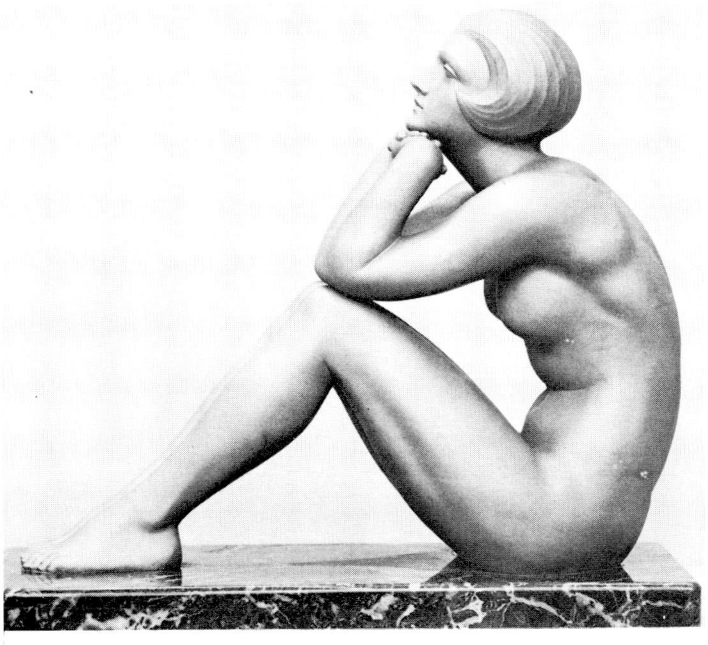

Thoughts, 36cm:14in.

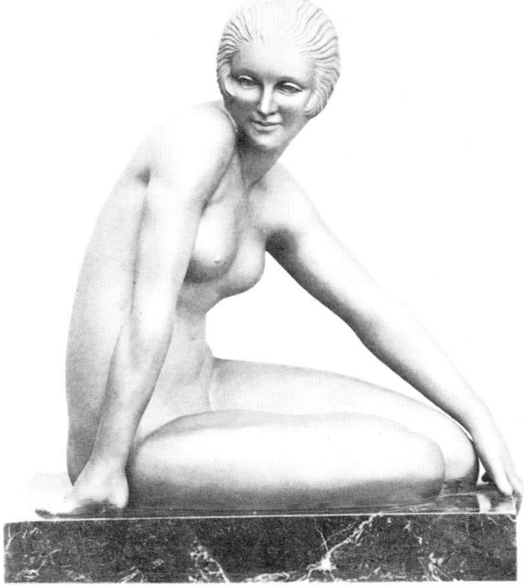

Fœmina, 42cm:16½in.

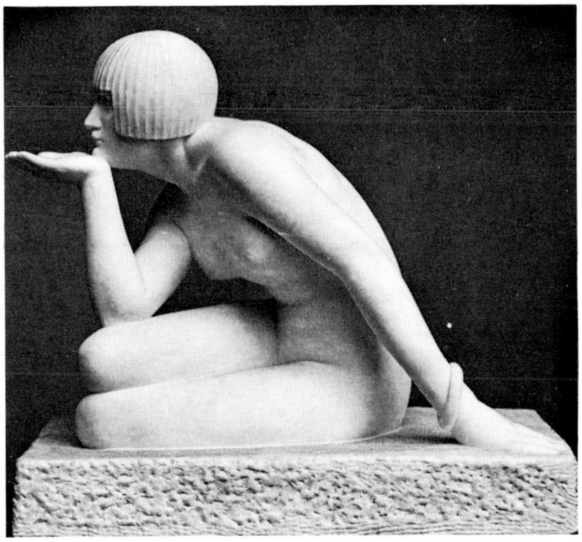

Enigma, 38cm:15in.; 19cm:7½in.
Exhibited at the International Art Exhibition, Paris, 1925

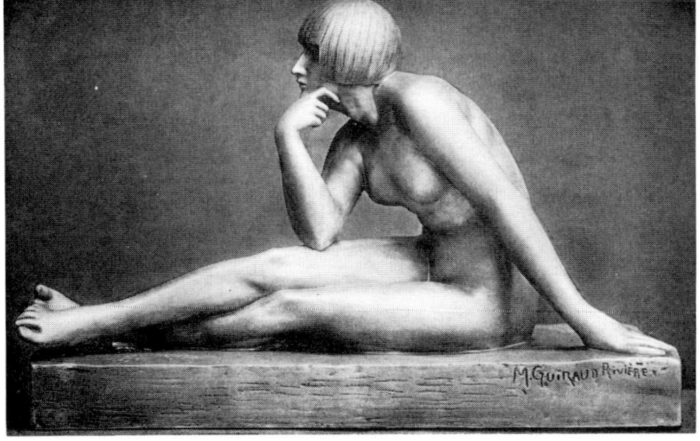

Antinéa, 37cm:14½in.; 14cm:5½in.

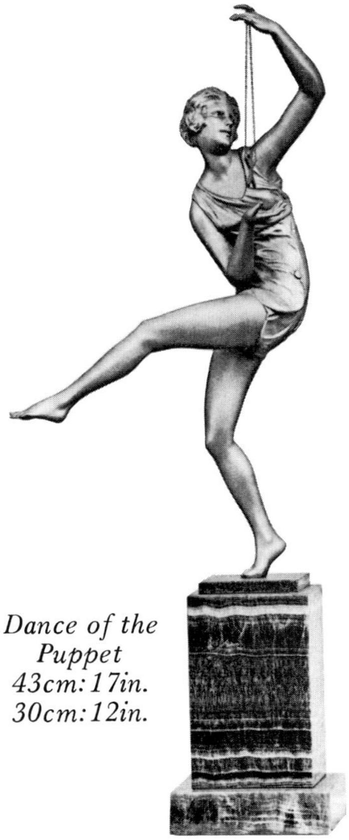

Dance of the Puppet
43cm:17in.
30cm:12in.

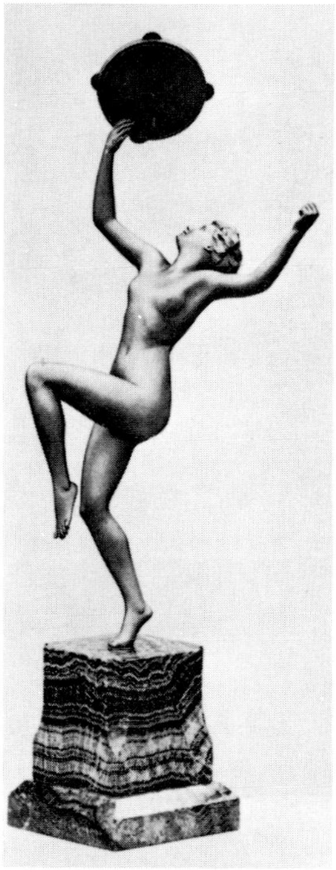

Tambourine Dance
56cm:22in.

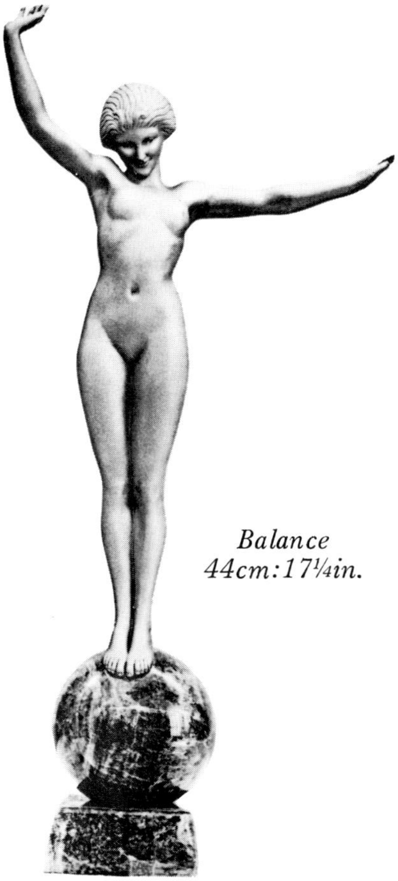

Balance
44cm:17¼in.

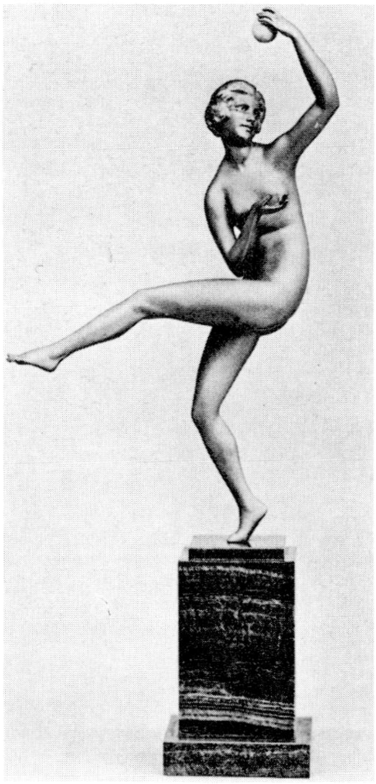

Dancer with Ball
47cm:18½in.

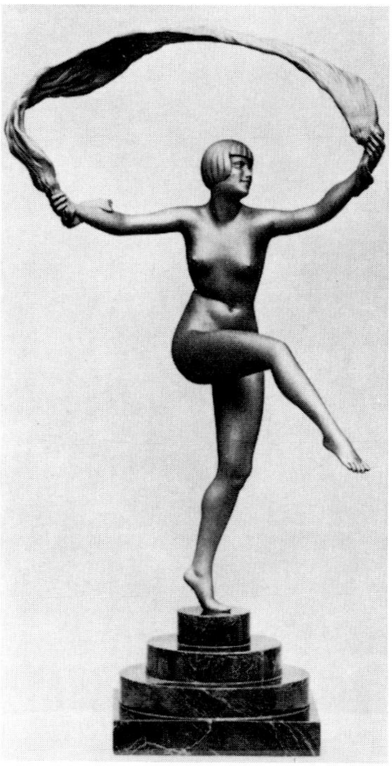

The Swirling Scarf
50cm:19¾in.

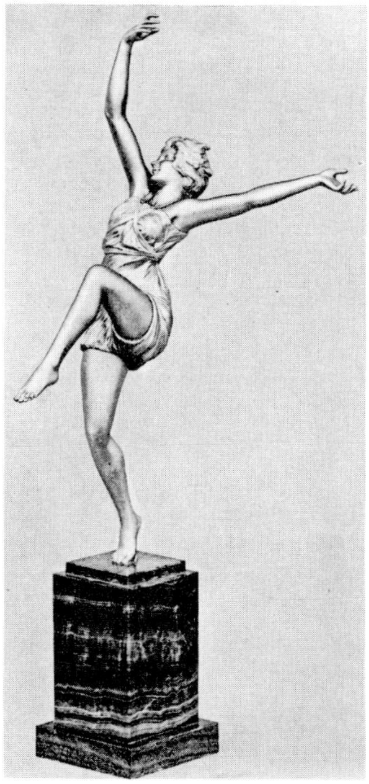

Bacchanale, 45cm:17½in.

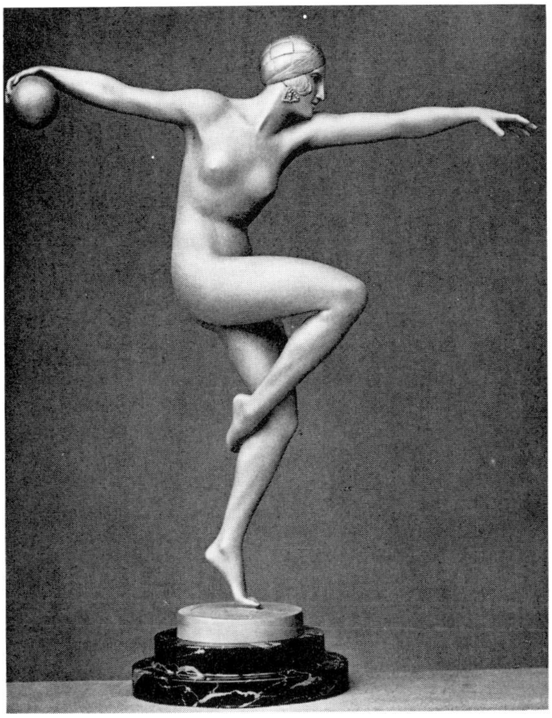

Ball Player, 65cm:23in.

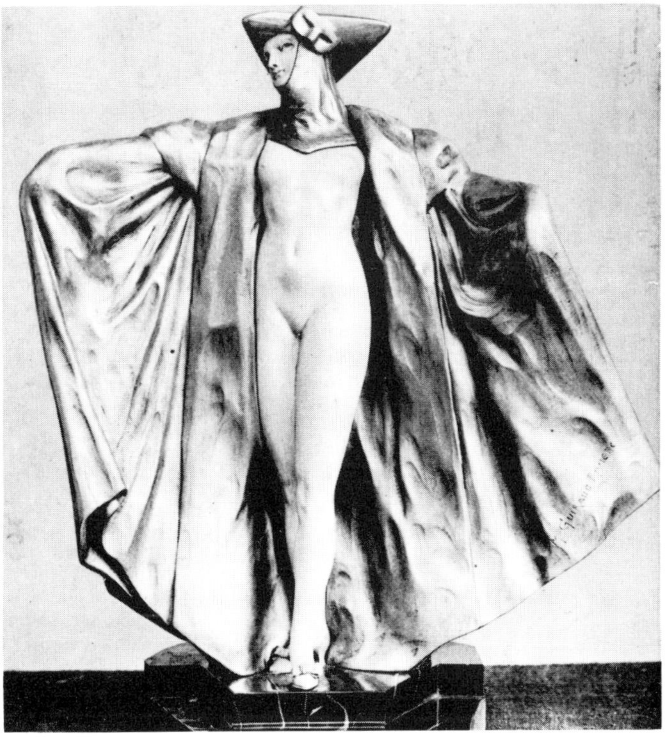

Venetian, 31cm:12¼in.

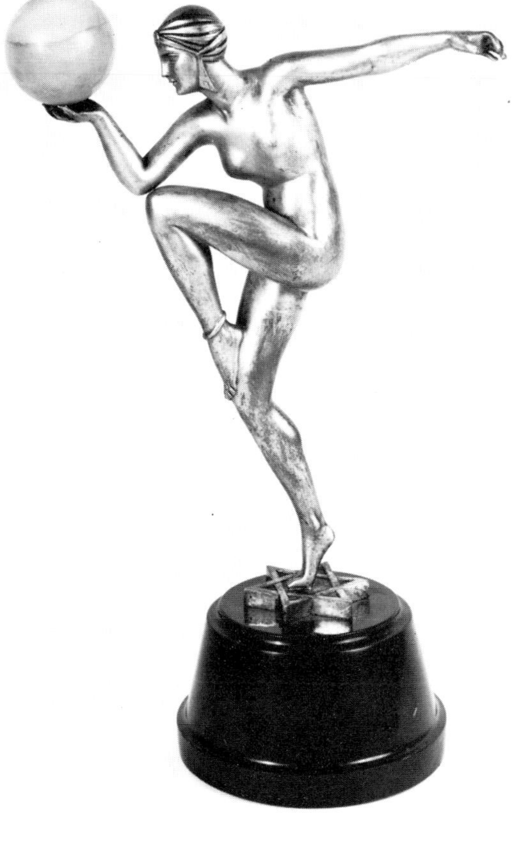

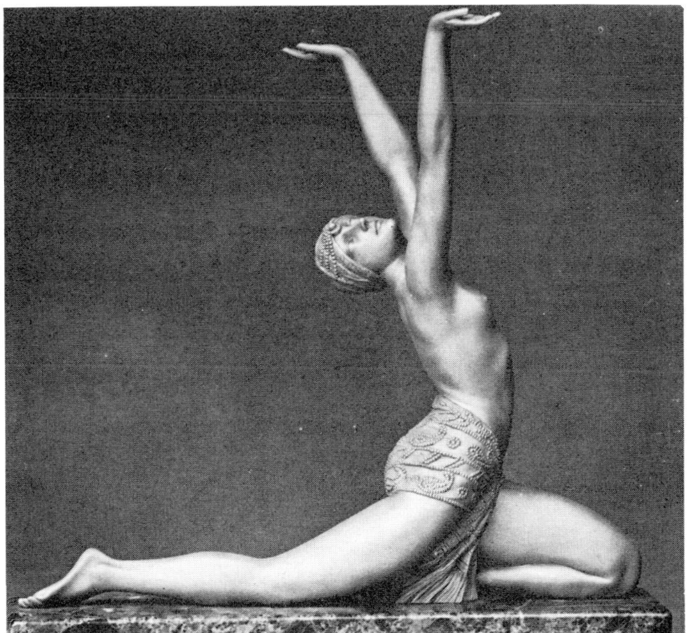

Imploration, 53cm:21in.

Stella, 60cm:23½in.; 31cm:12in.

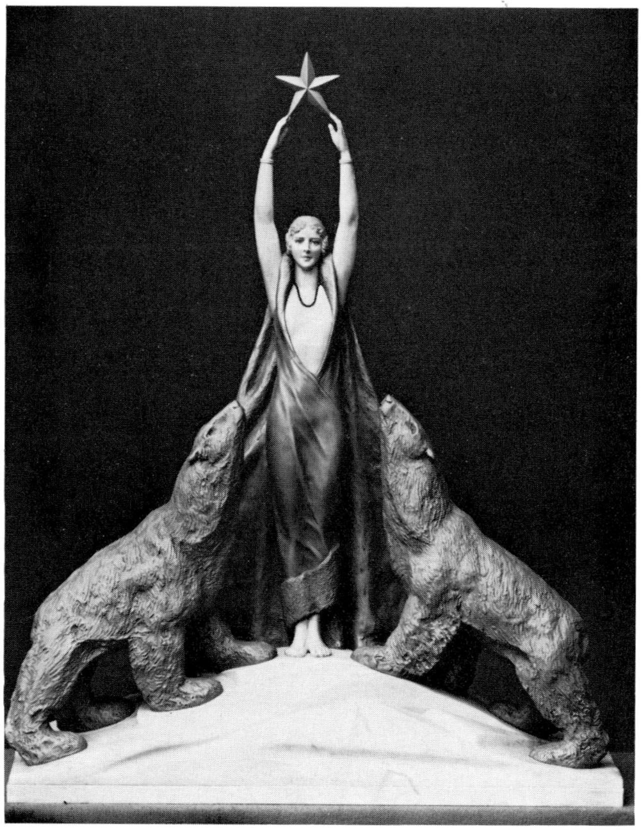

Nordica, 78cm:30¾in.

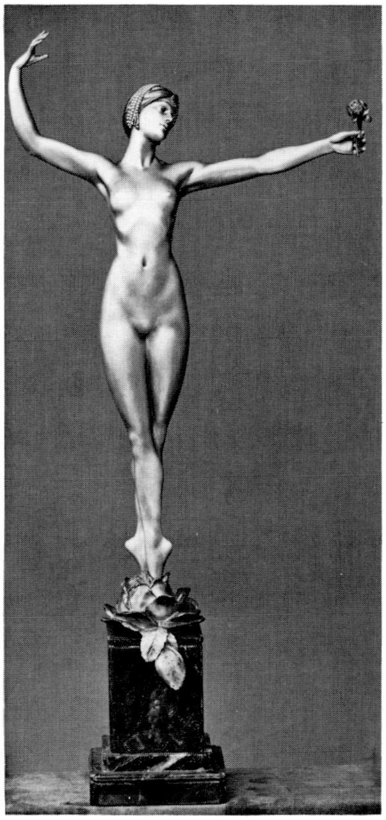

Rose of Baghdad, 81cm:32in.

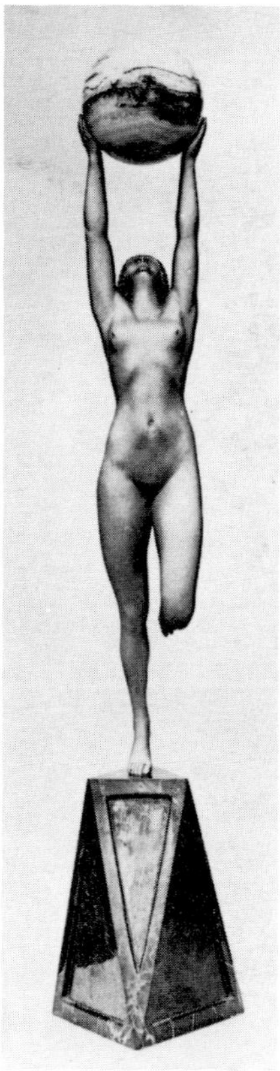

Girl with Ball. 60cm:23½in.

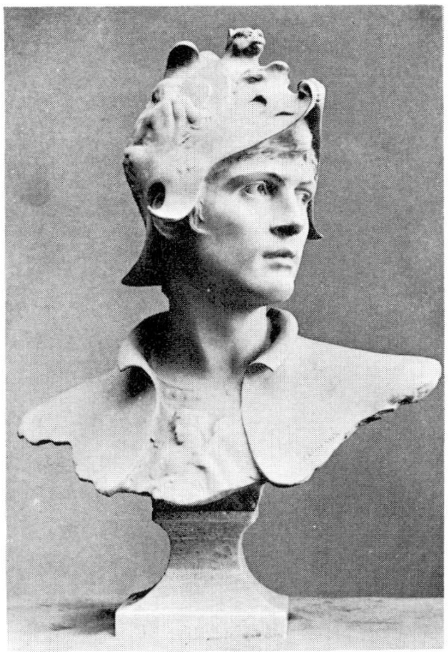

Roman Warrior
67cm:26½in.
39cm:15½in.
21cm:8¼in.

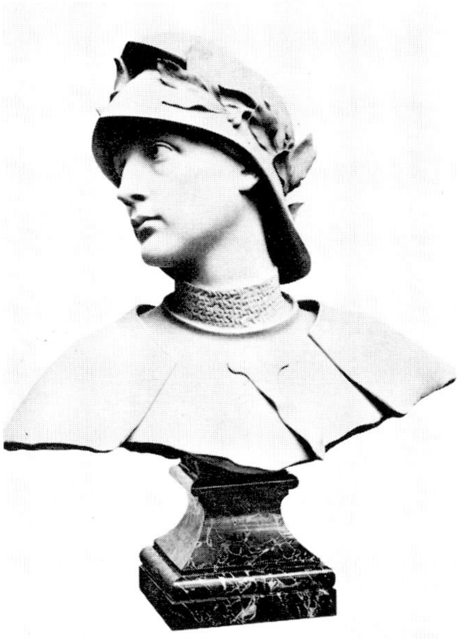

The Helmet
65cm:25½in.

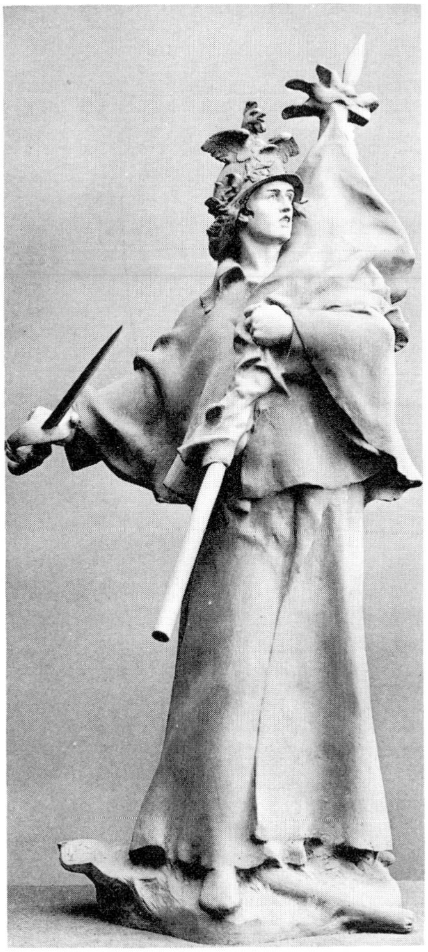

Defence of the Flag
70cm:27½in.

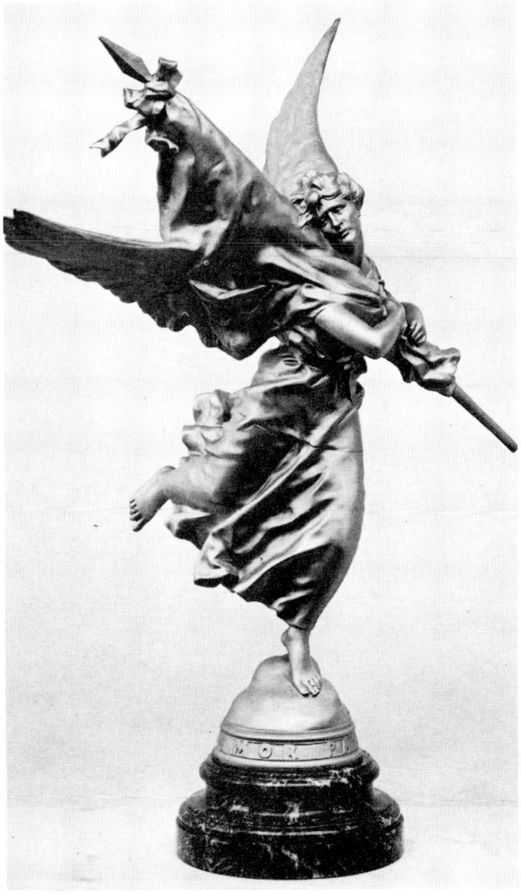

Love of the Flag
98cm:38½in.; 50cm:19½in.
Exhibited 1911

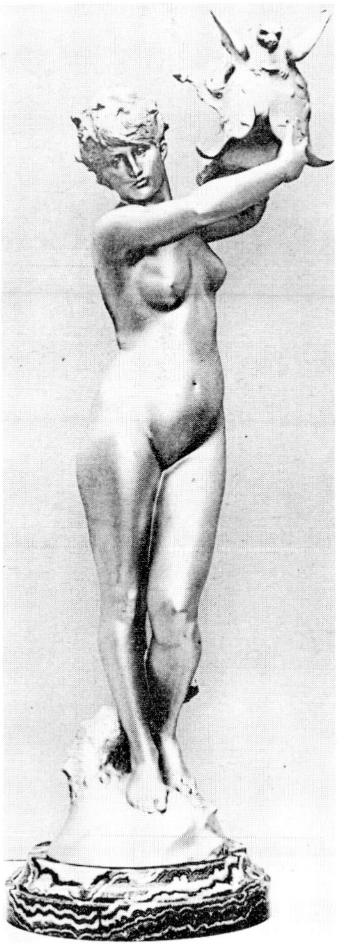

Nereid
60cm:23½in.; 35cm:13¾in.

HAUCHECORNE

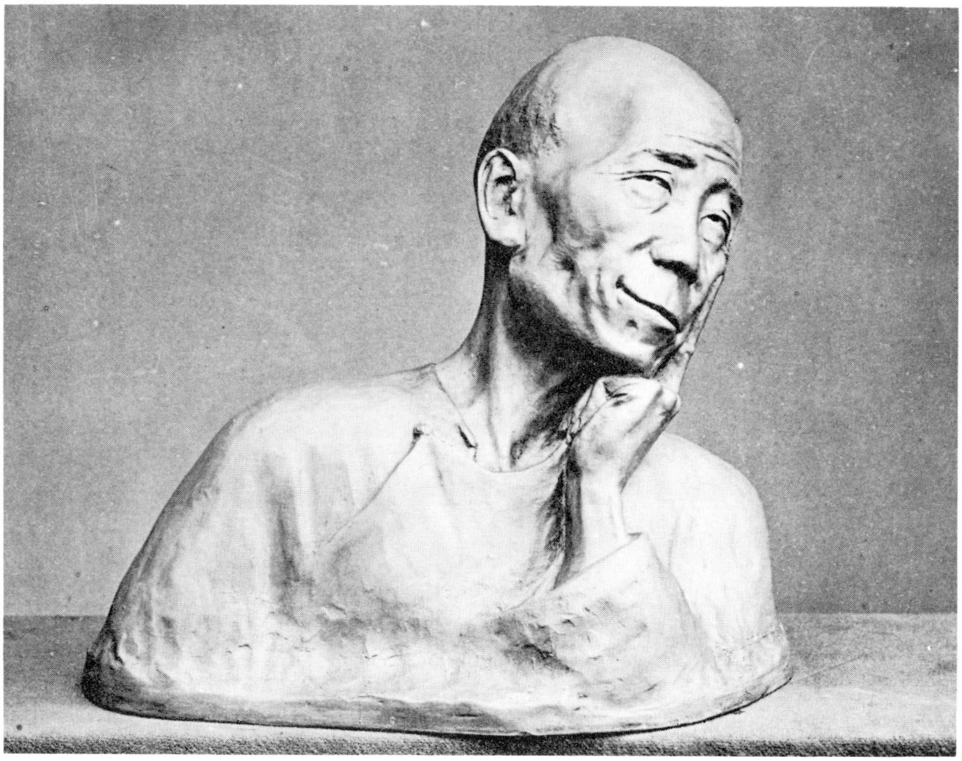

Contemplation of the Future
27cm: 10½in.

Exhibited at the Salon des Artistes Français, 1925

HUFSMAN

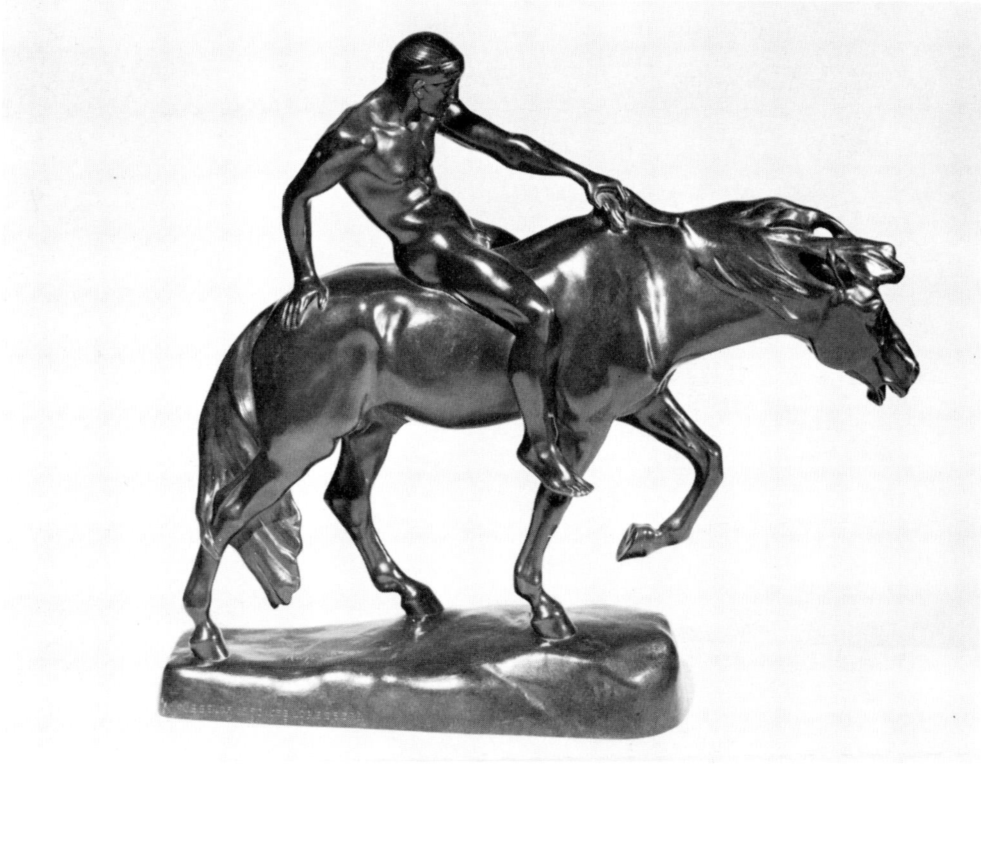

Horse Rider
34cm: 13½in.

Flute Player 59cm: 23¼in.

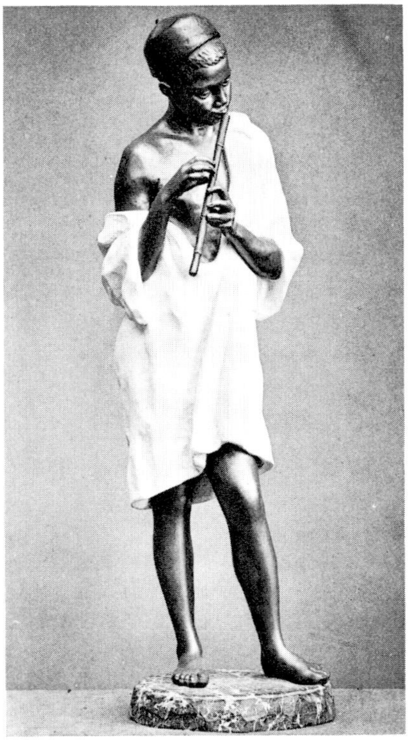

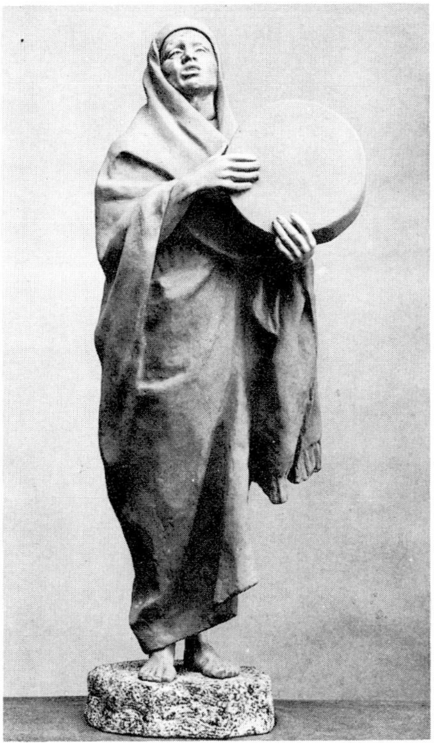

Arab with Tambourine 60cm: 23½in.

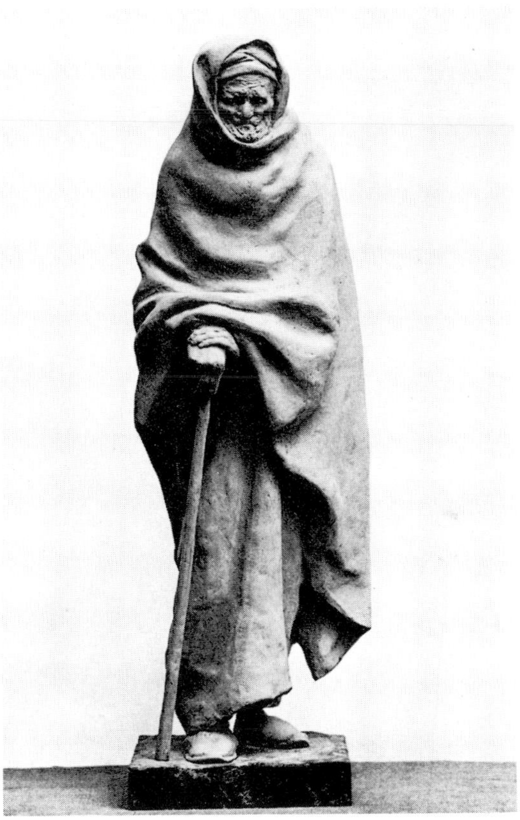

Arab, 45cm: 17¾in.

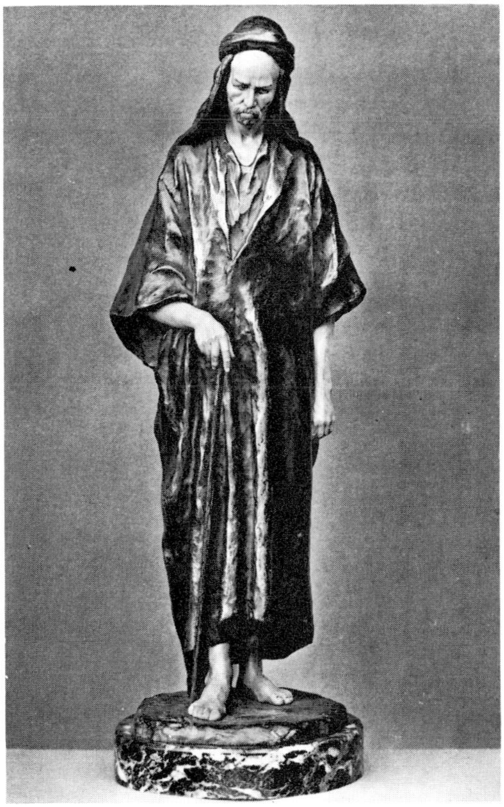

Alone, 63cm: 24¾in.

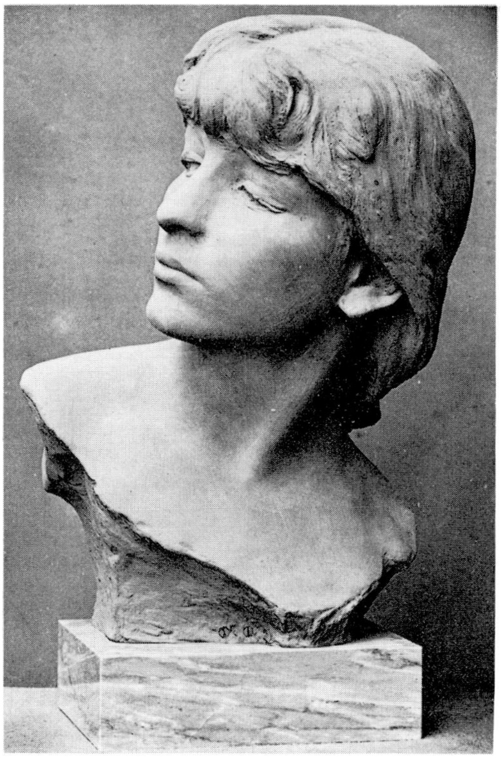

Scorn
37cm:14½in.
17cm:6¾in.

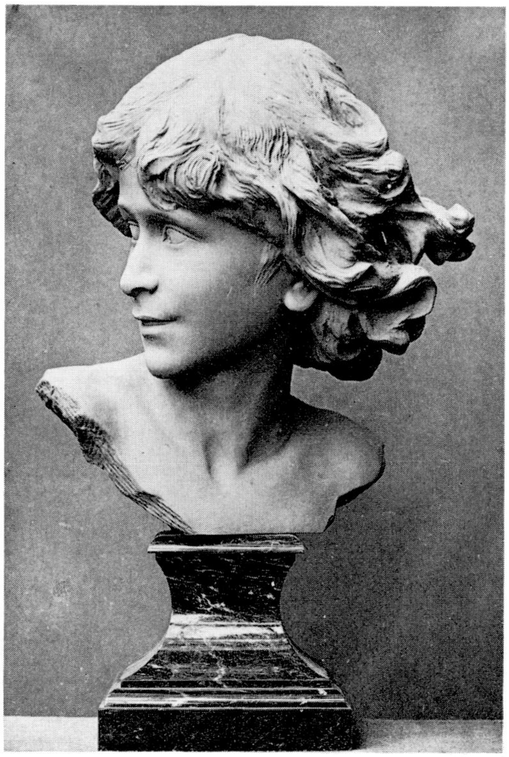

Fun
52cm:20½in.
32cm:12½in.
21cm:8¼in.
15cm:6in.

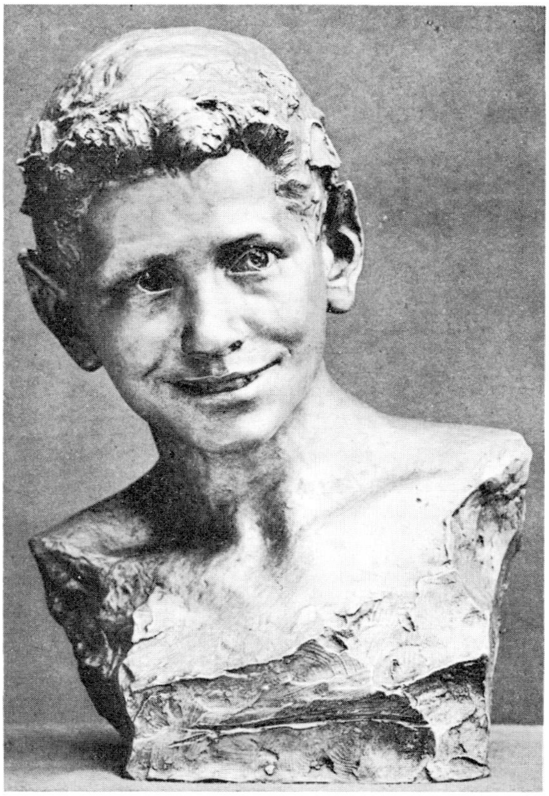

Bust of Pan, 36cm:14in.

Right. **Above:** *Two Girls, signed by Laurent Hely, 53cm:21in.* **Below:** *Three Figures by R. Lor, 23cm:9in.*

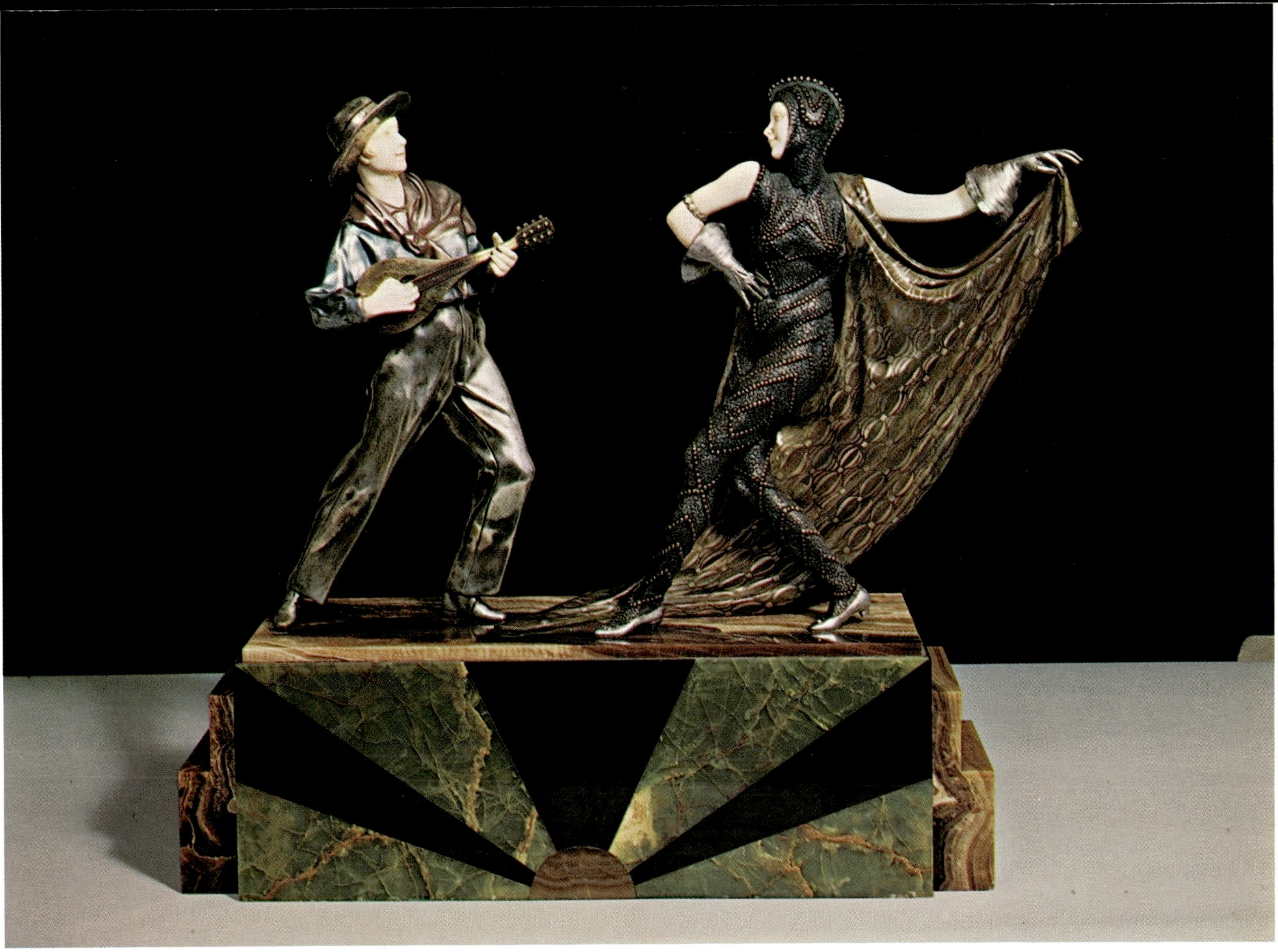

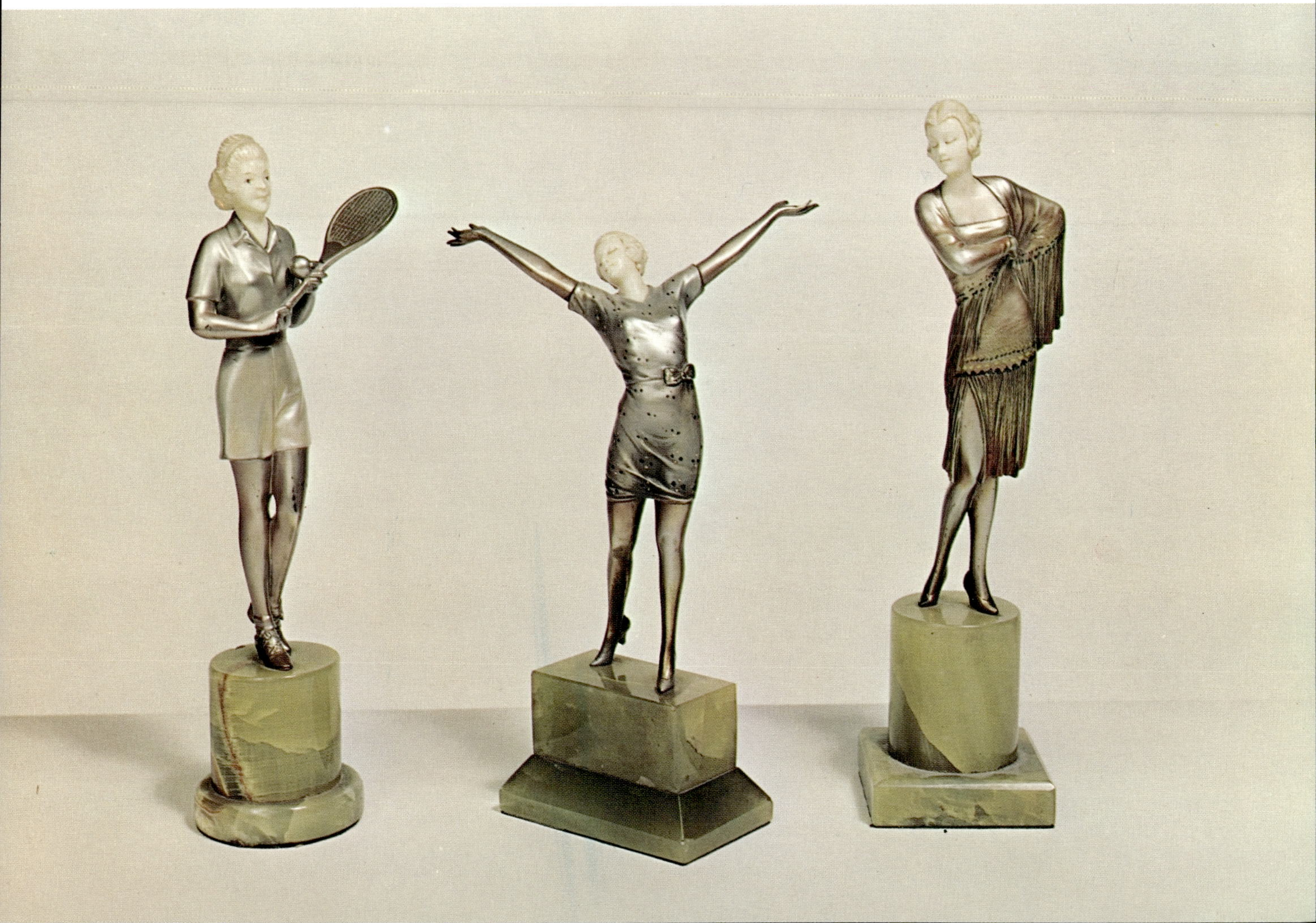

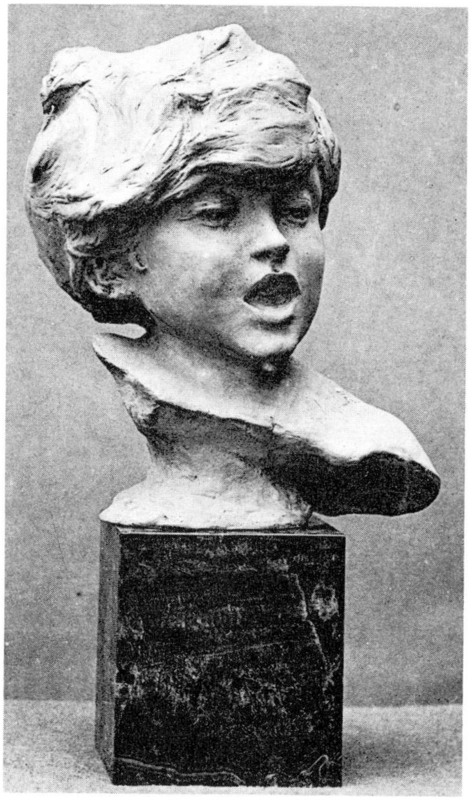

Vagabond
28cm:11in.

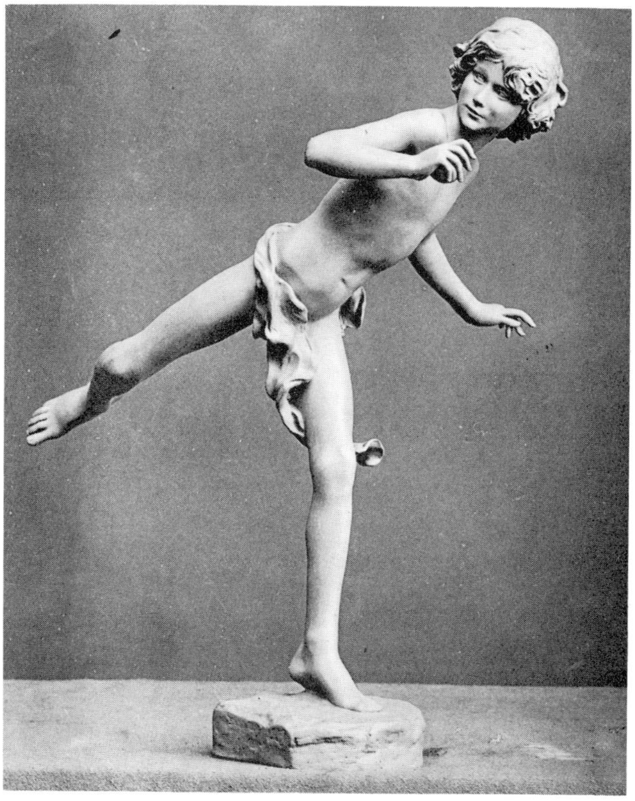

Fun, 80cm:31½in.
55cm:21½in.; 32cm:12½in.

JOREL

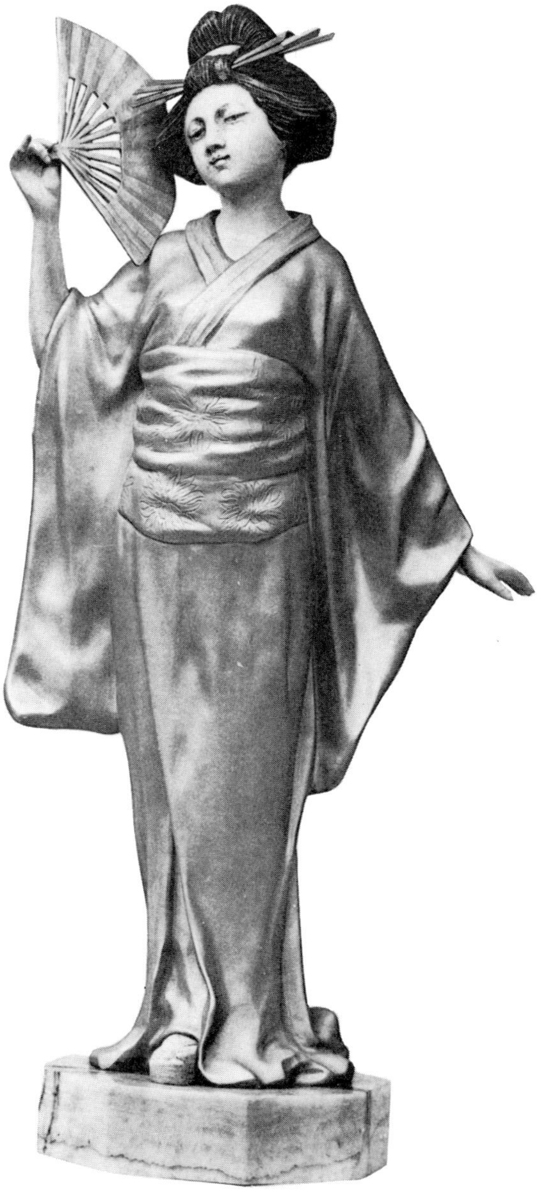

Madam Chrysanthemum
42cm:16½in.

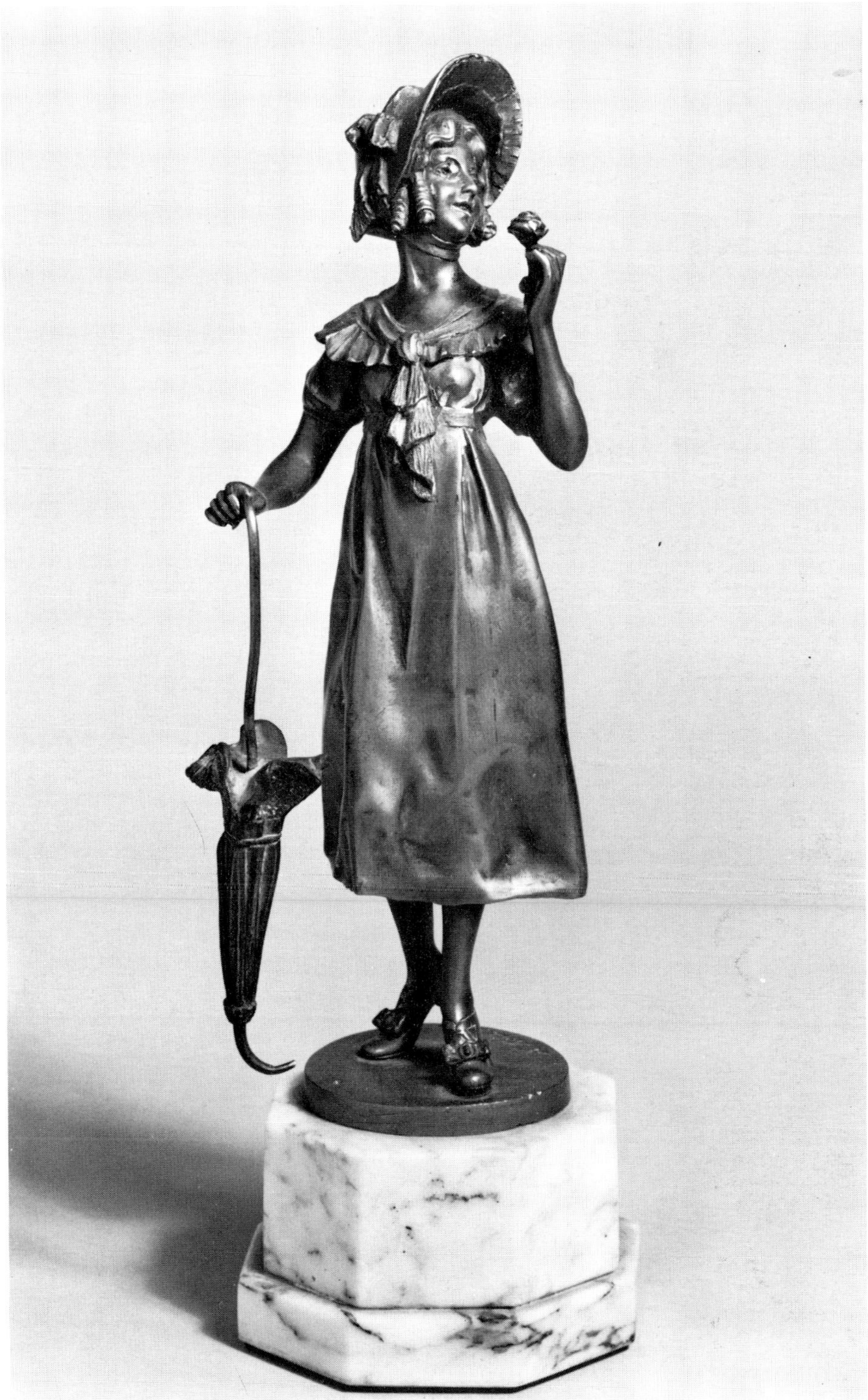

A Victorian Lady, 29cm:11½in.

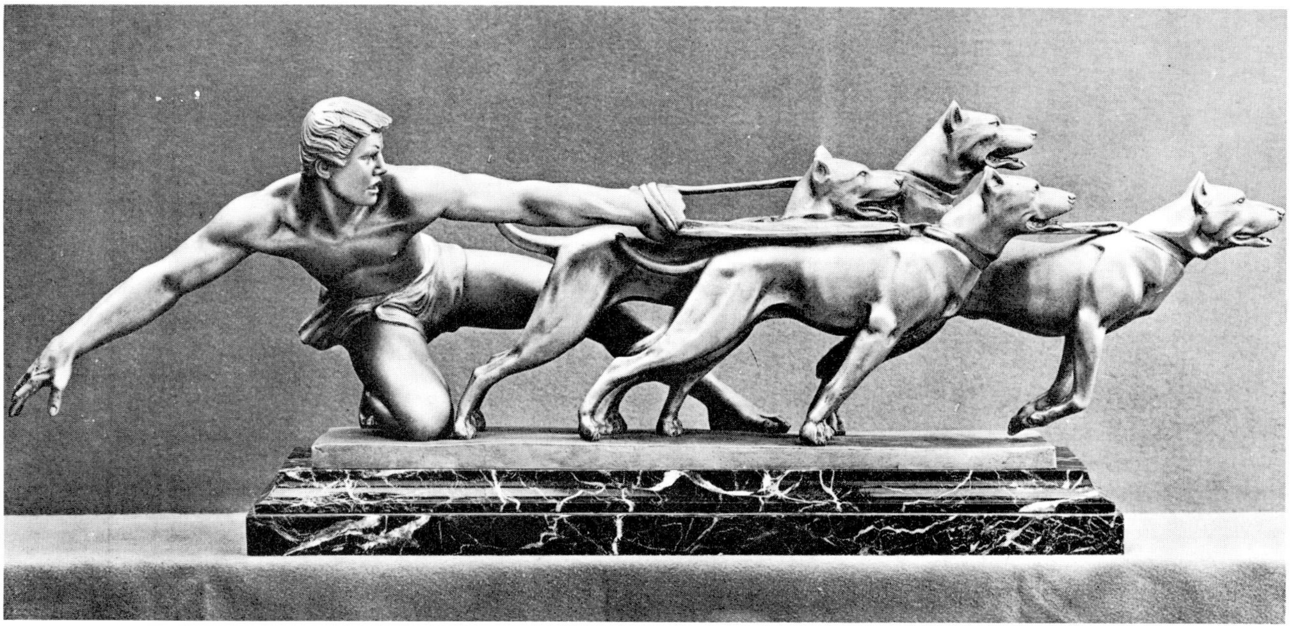

The Release, 35cm:13¾in.

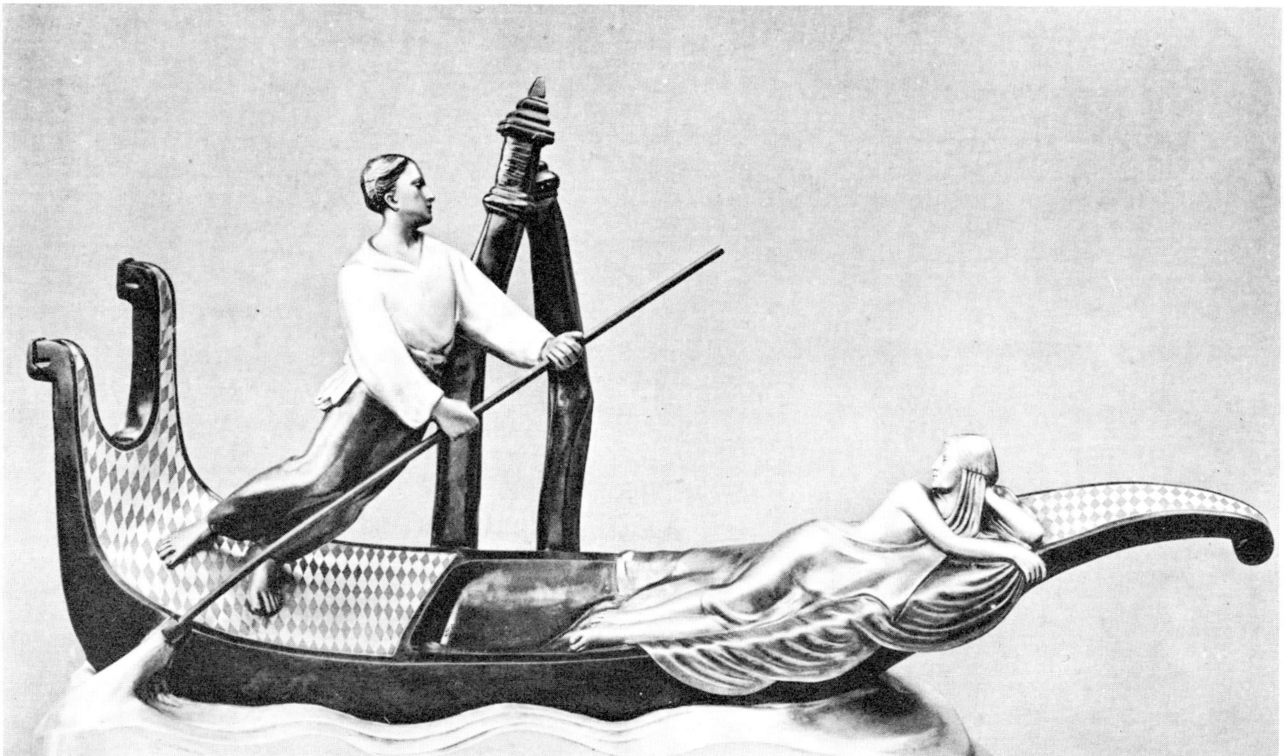

Venice, 50cm:19½in.

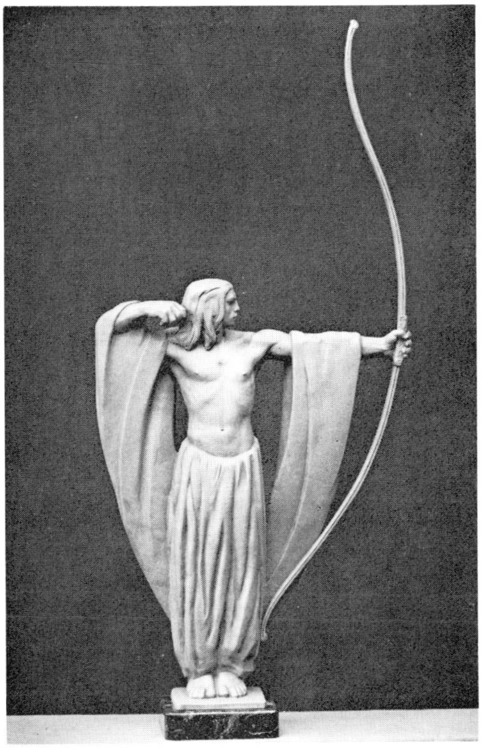

The Archer, 75cm: 29½in.

Genie and the Lamp 44cm: 17¼in.

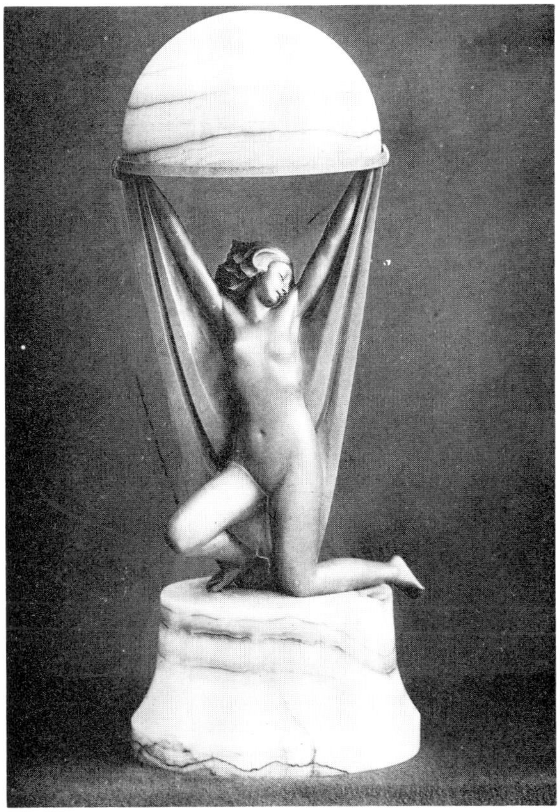

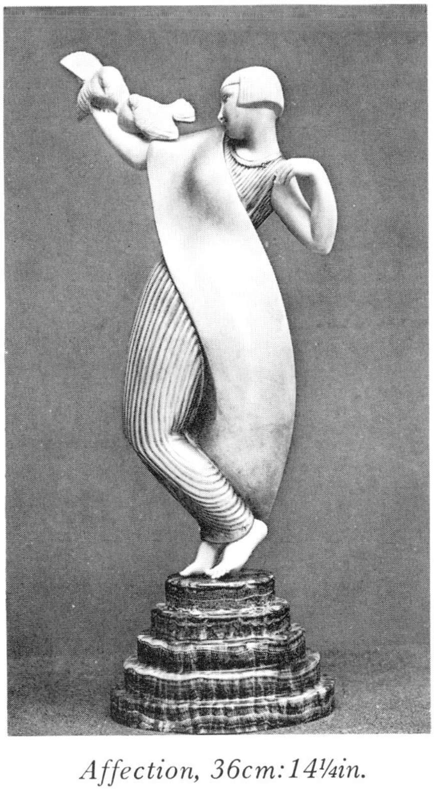

Affection, 36cm: 14¼in.

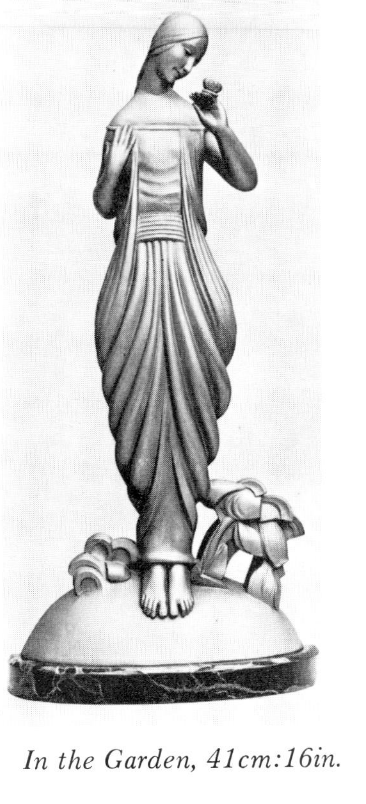

In the Garden, 41cm: 16in.

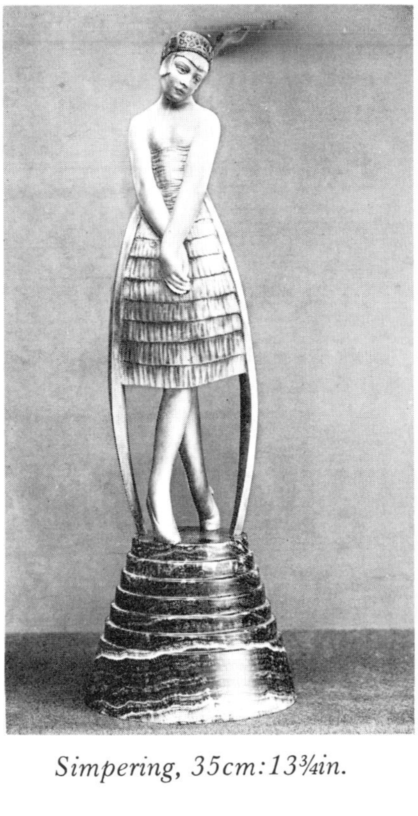

Simpering, 35cm: 13¾in.

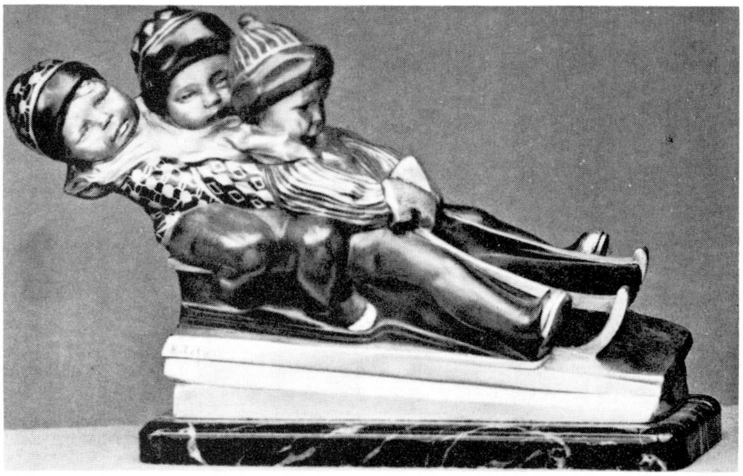

Winter Sport, 18cm: 7in.

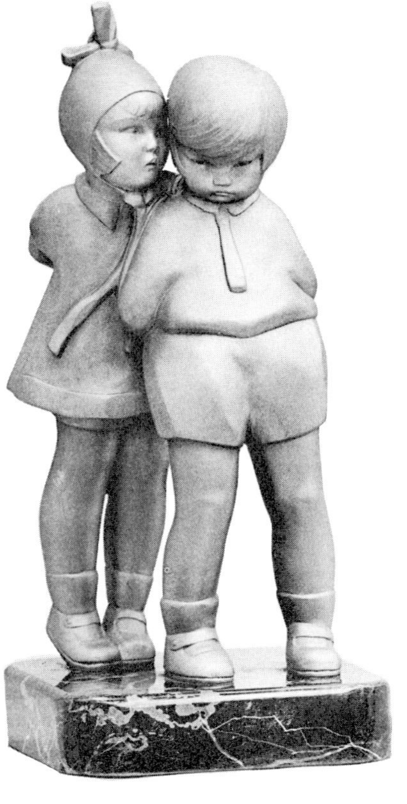

Childish Secrets, 27cm: 10¾in.

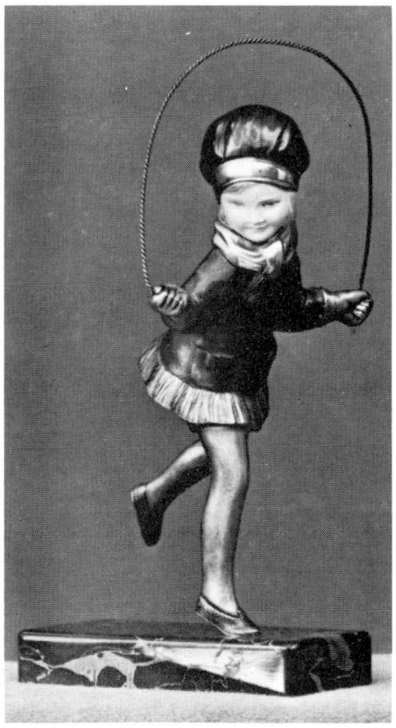

Recreation, 22cm: 8¾in.

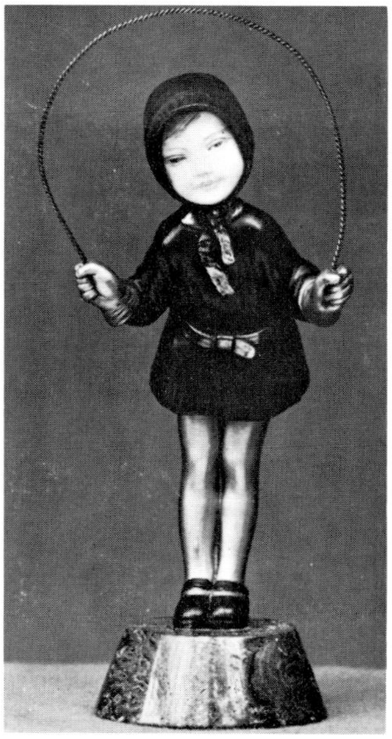

Watch Me! 22cm: 8½in.

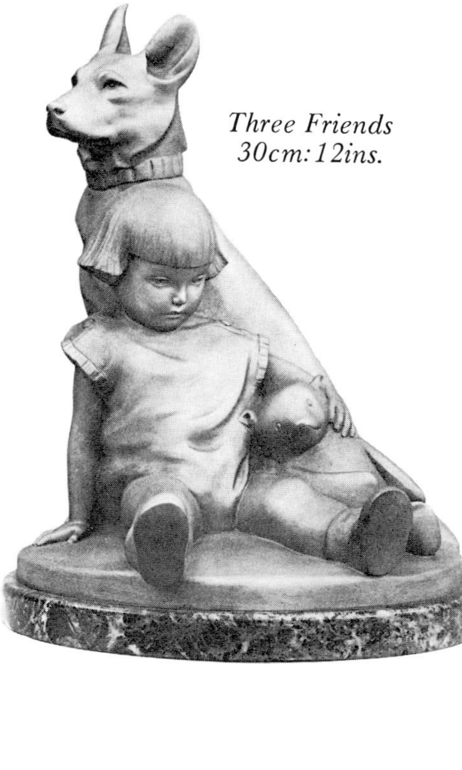

Three Friends 30cm: 12ins.

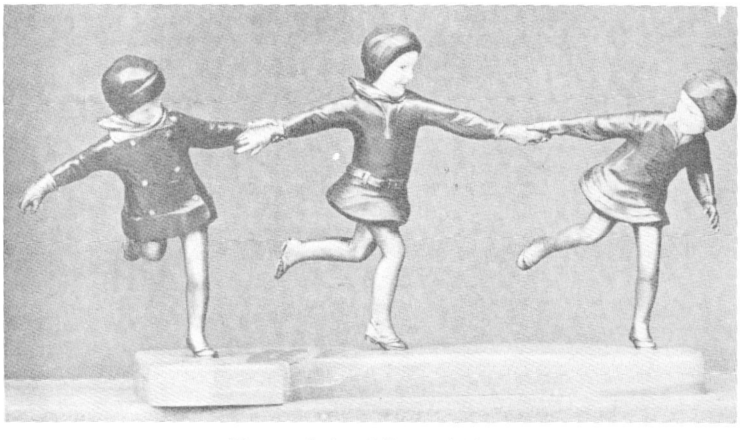

Farandole, 25cm: 10in.

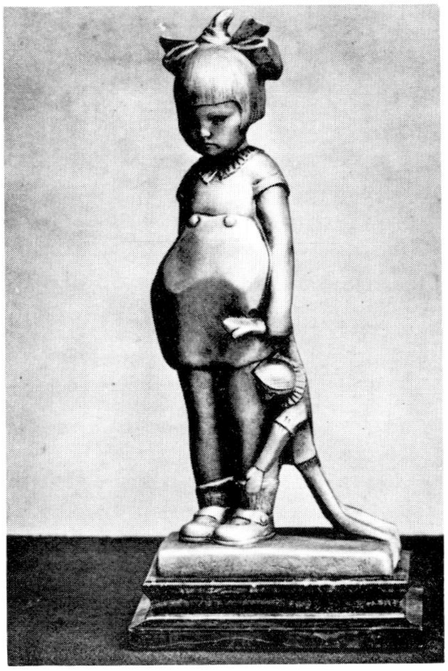

Puppet, 27cm:10¼in.

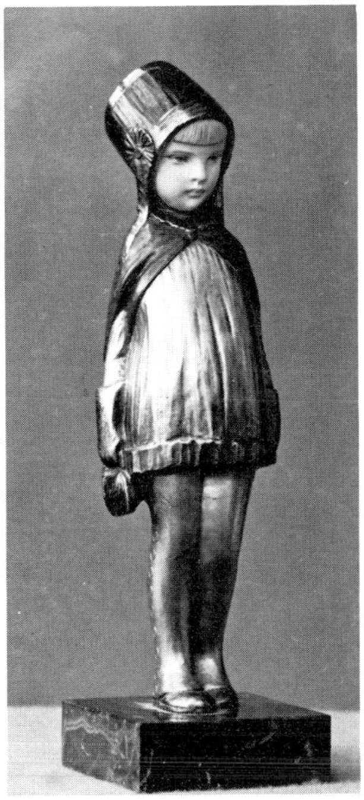

Off to the Champs Elysées 21cm:8¼in.

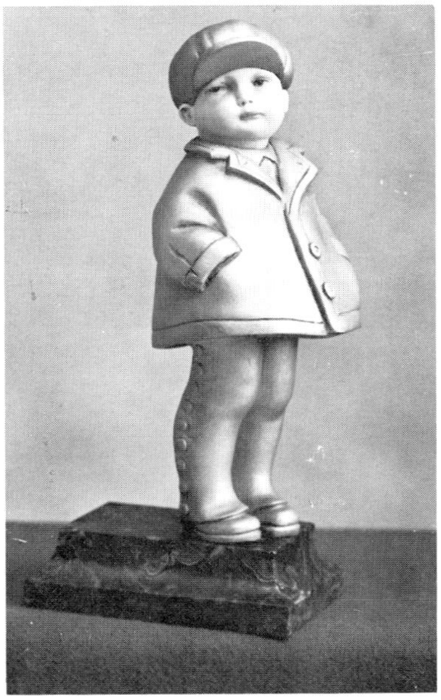

Freddy, 23cm:9in.

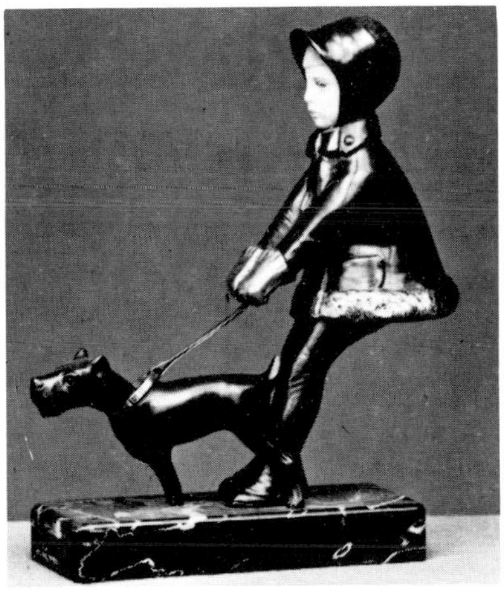

Disobedient, 19cm:7½in.

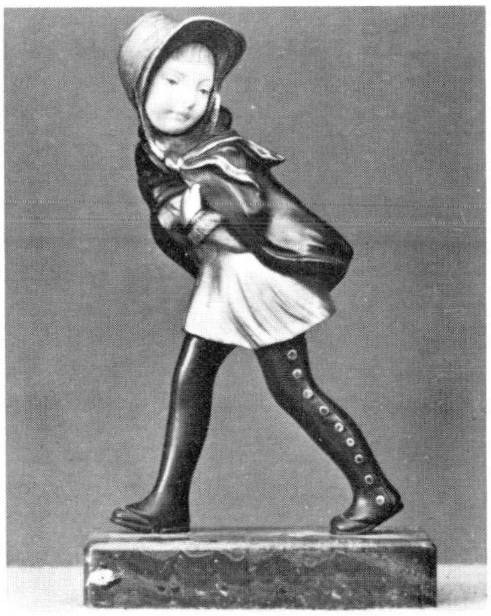

To the Park, 20cm:8in.

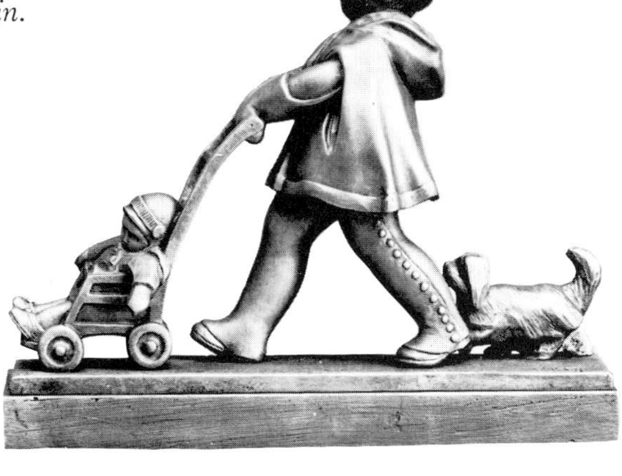

Promenade, 25cm:10in.

KERNALAN

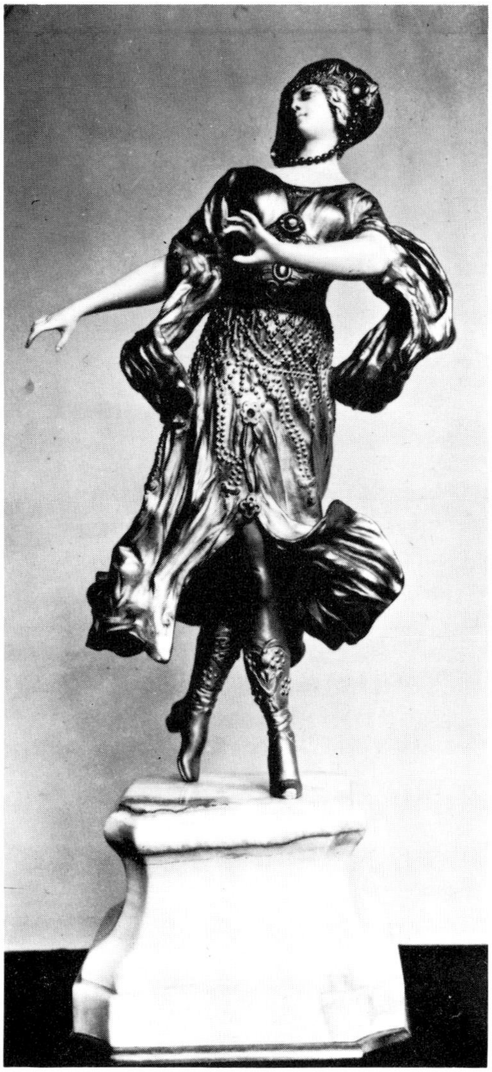

Russian Dancer, 42cm:16½in.

S. KINSBURGER

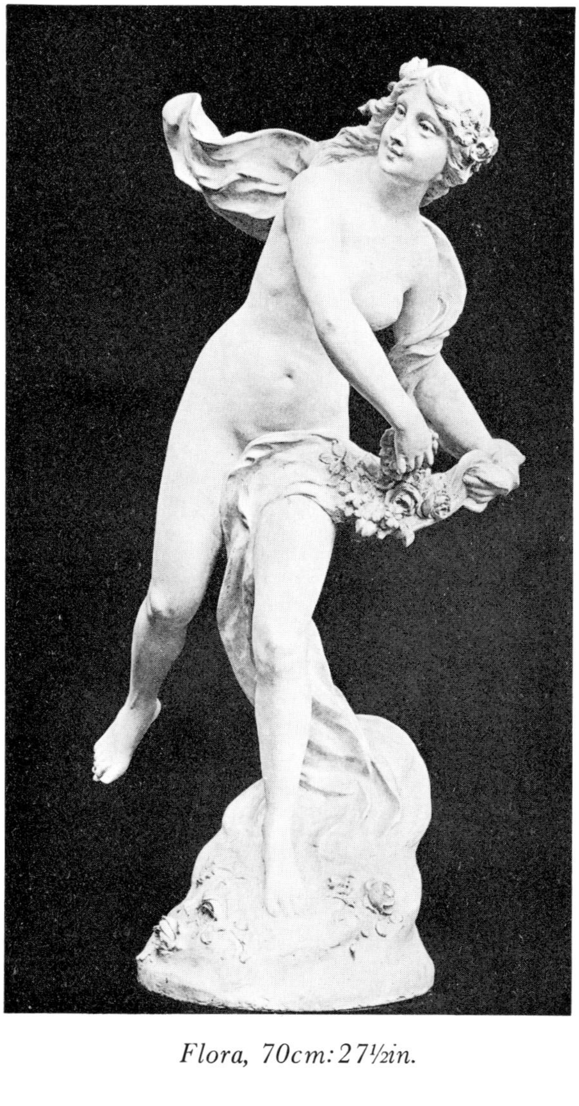

Flora, 70cm:27½in.

LAMBEAUX

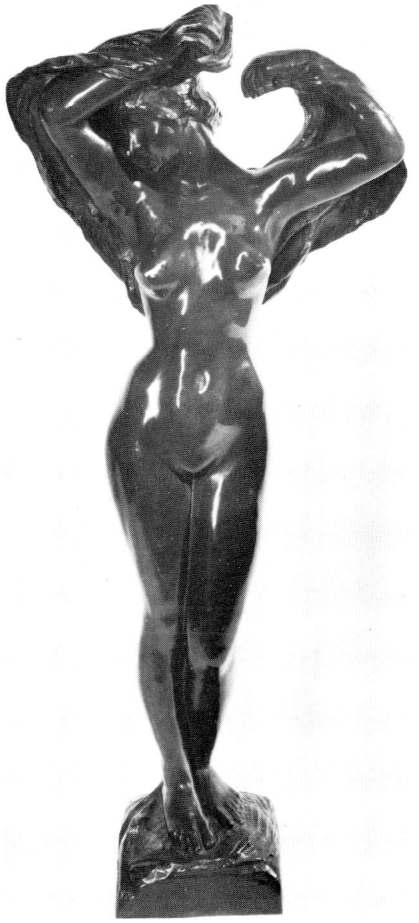

A Nude, 102cm:40in.

EMILE LAPORTE

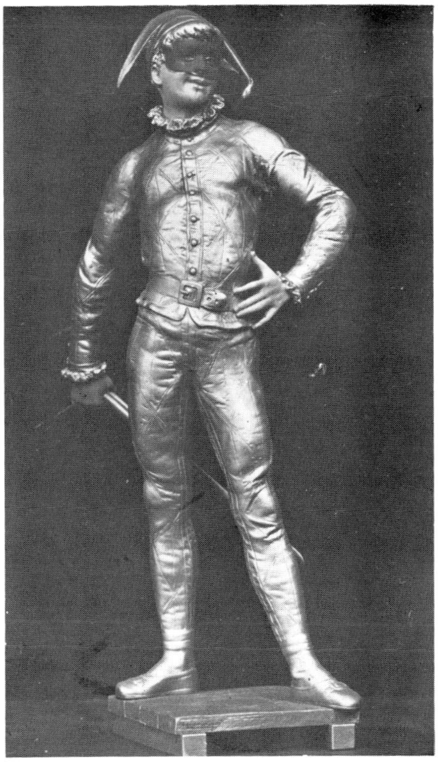

Harlequin, 33cm:13in.

PIERRE LAUREL

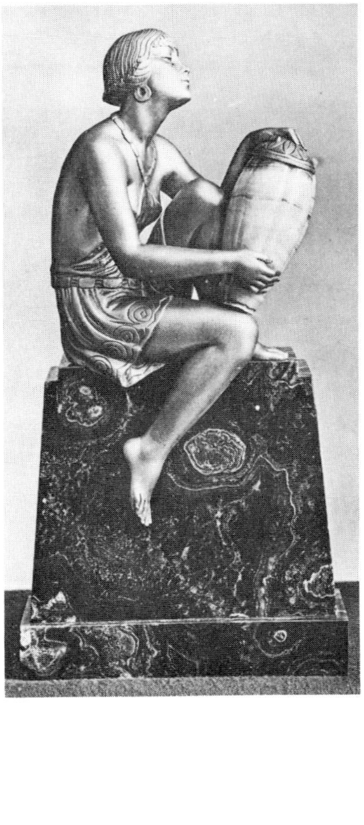

The Perfect Moment 35cm:13¾in. The vase is mounted as an electric light

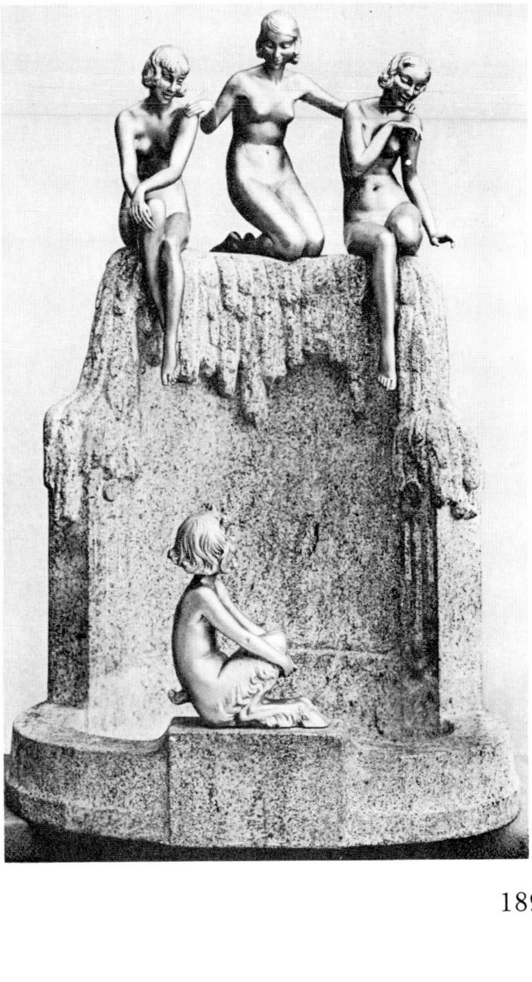

Covetousness 61cm:24in.

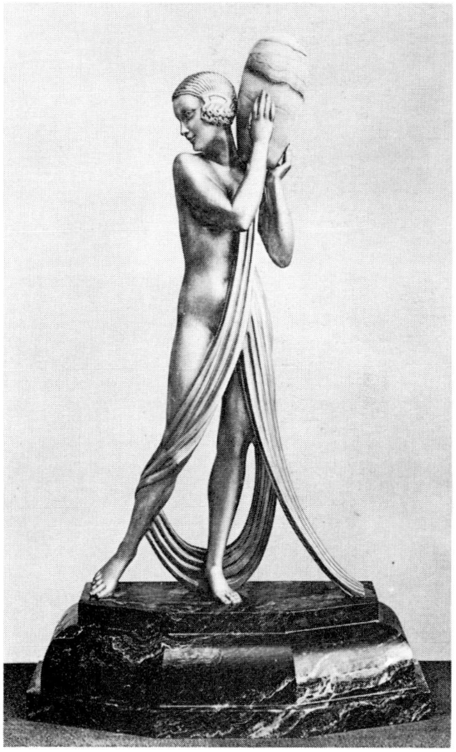

Veil Dance, 49cm: 19¼in.

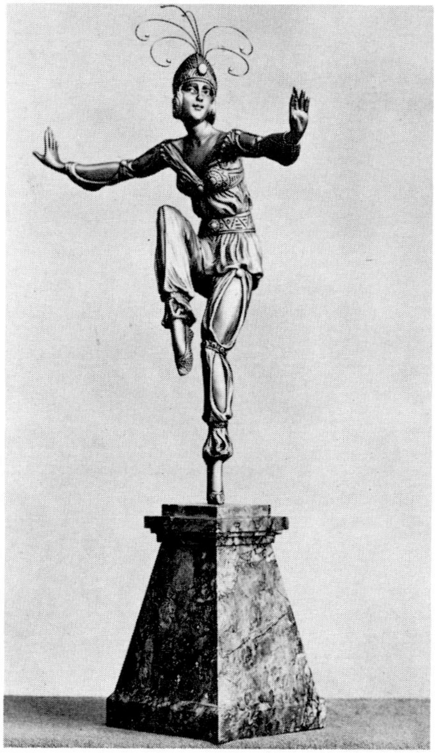

Scheherazade, 55cm: 21½in.

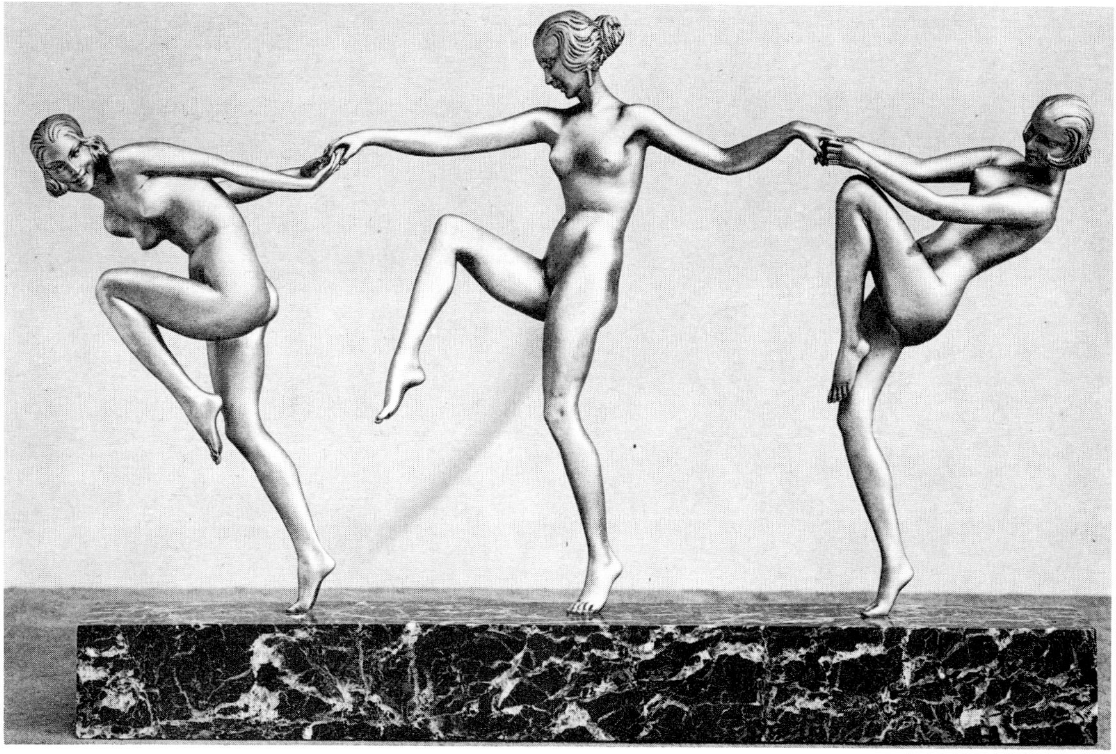

Farandole, 40cm: 15¾in.

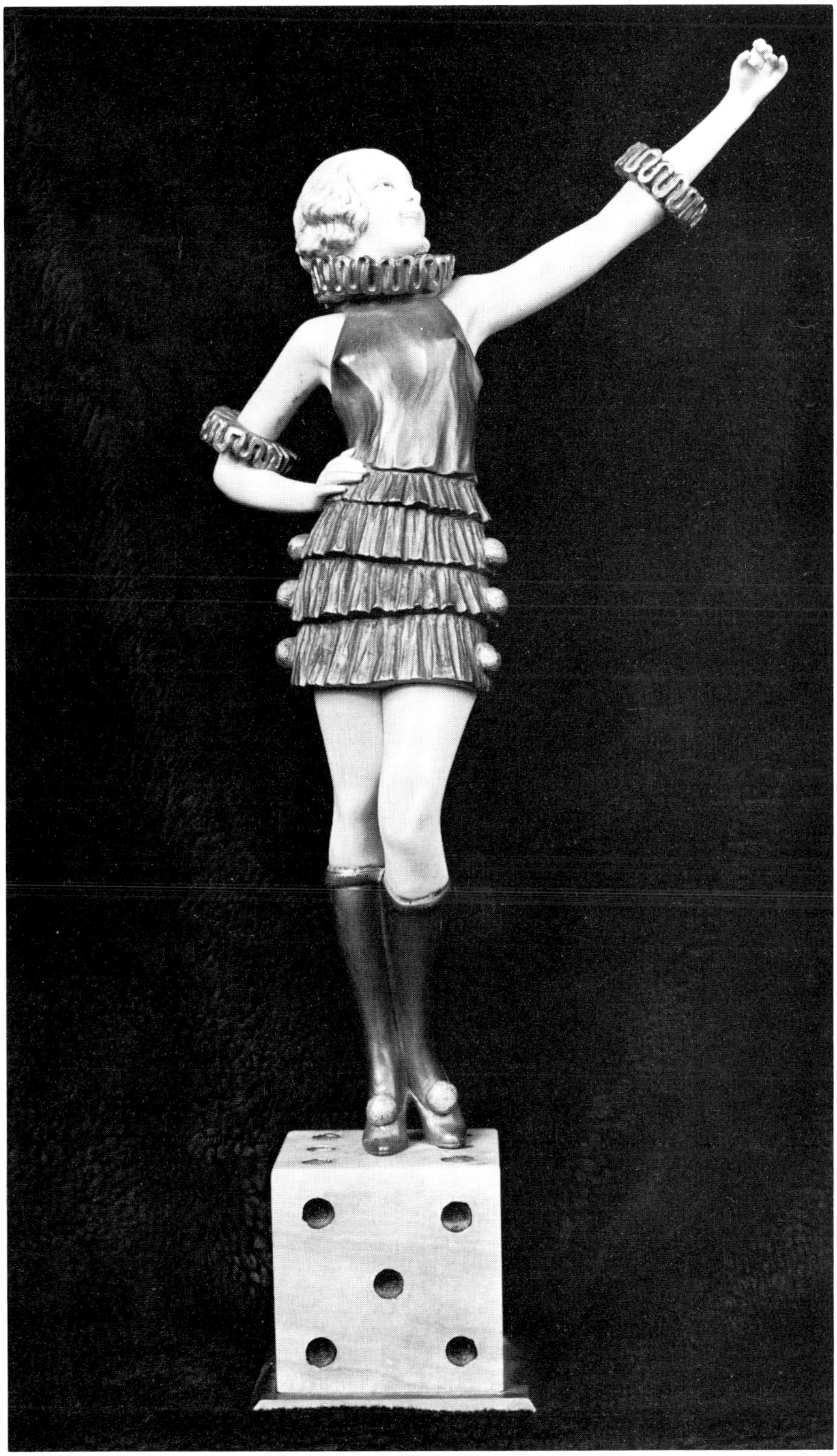

Girl on Dice, 42cm: 16½in.

PIERRE LAUREL

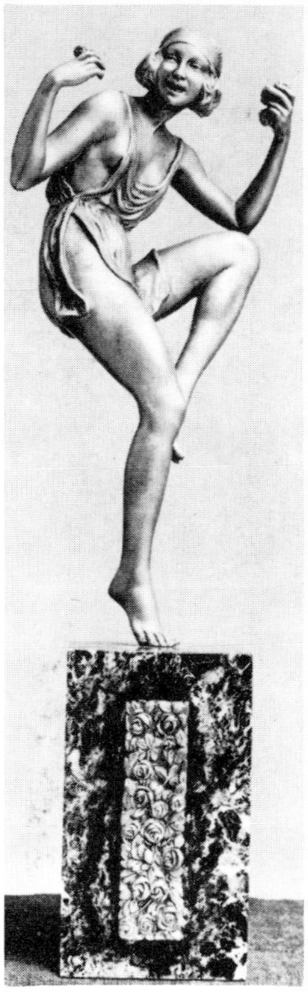

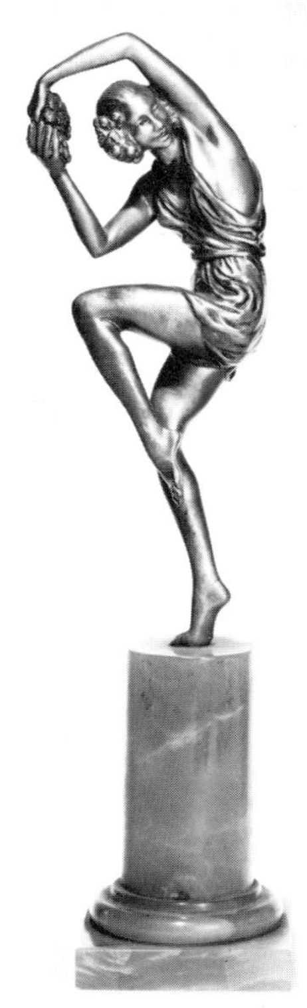

Spring Dance
50cm: 19½in.
34cm: 13½in.

Autumn Dance
51cm: 20in.
34cm: 13½in.

PIERRE LE FAGUAYS

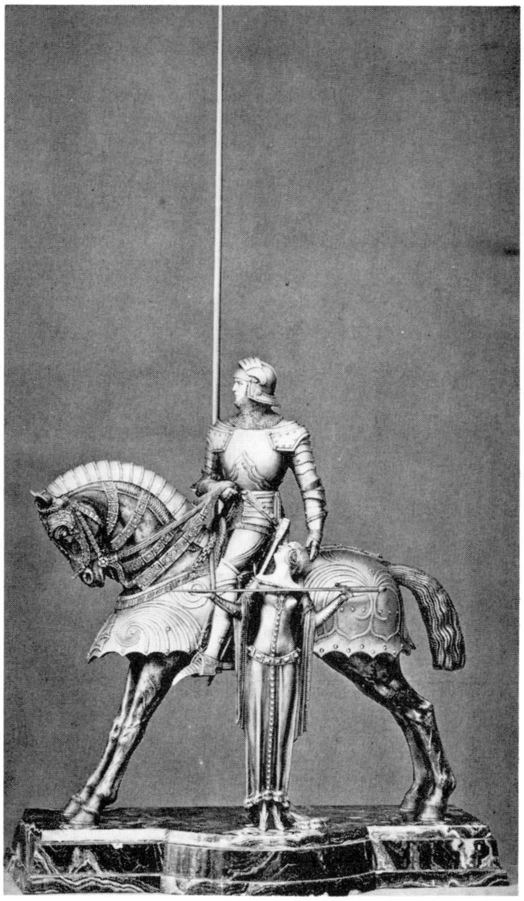

Leaving for the Crusade
56cm: 22in.

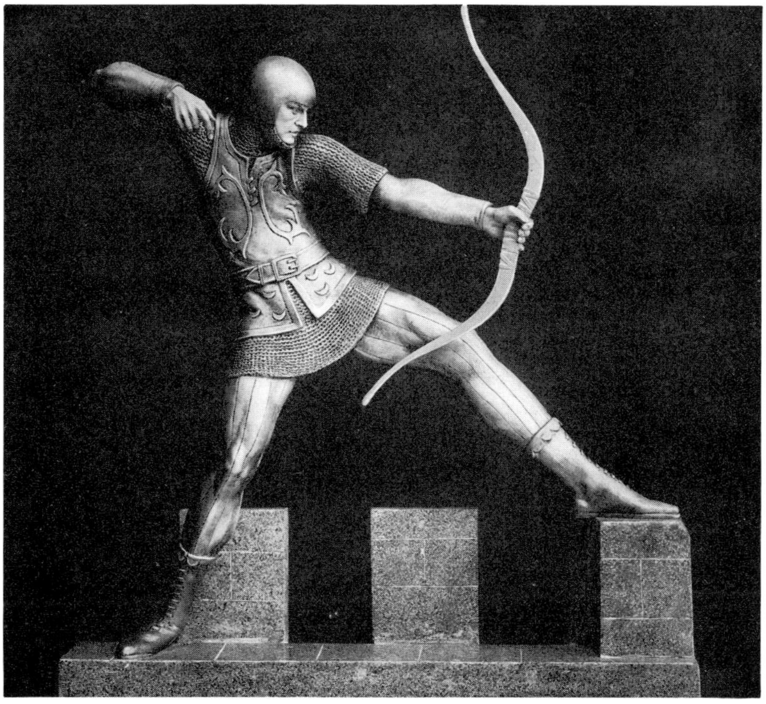

Signal Man, 64cm: 25in.; 43cm: 17in.

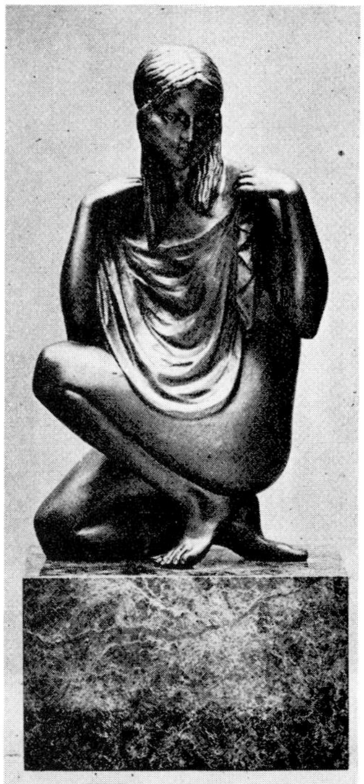

Modesty, 31cm: 12in.

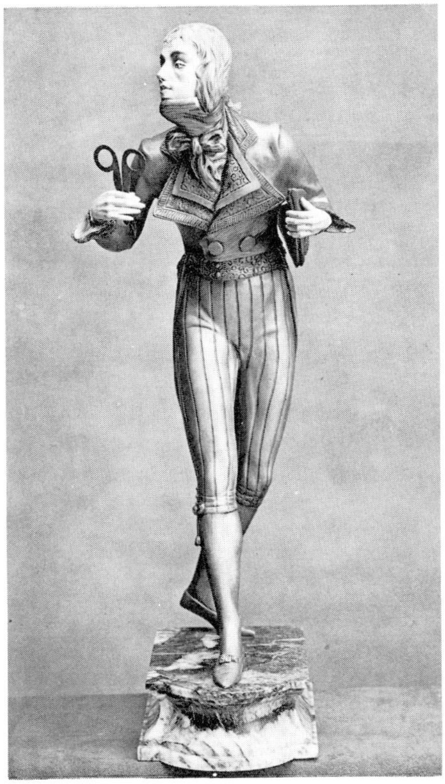

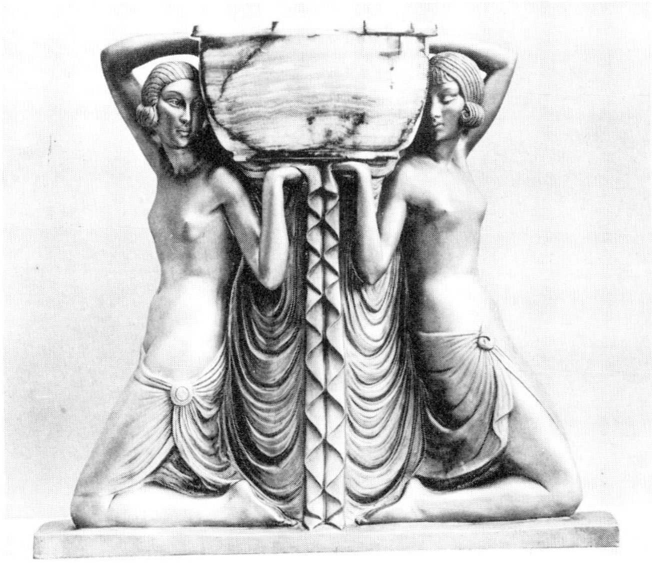

Women with Jardinière, 41cm:16in.

Dandy, 63cm:24¾in.
46cm:18in.; 31cm:12¼in.

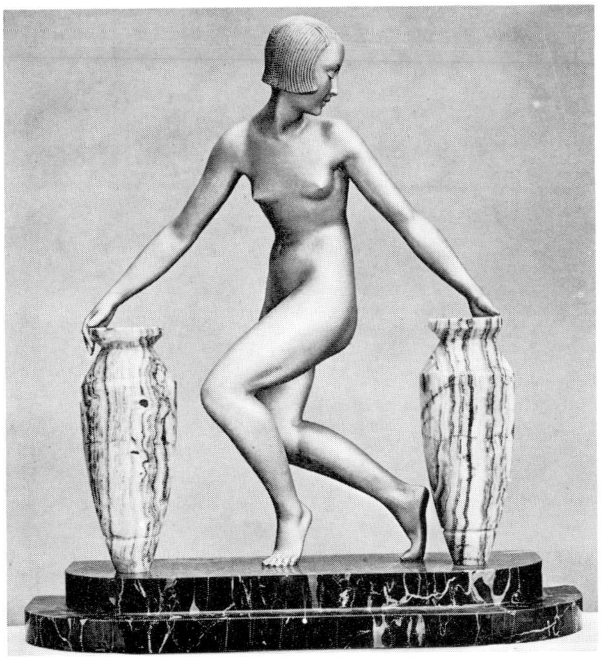

Lady with Vases, 57cm:22½in.

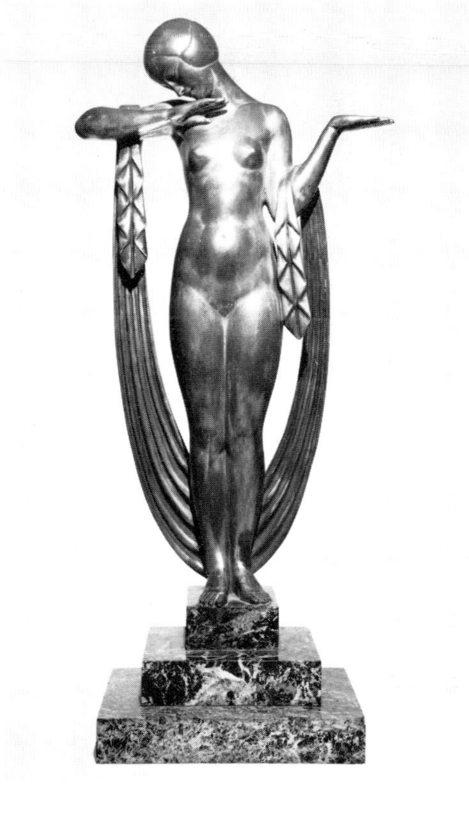

Young Girl with Scarf, 71cm:28in.

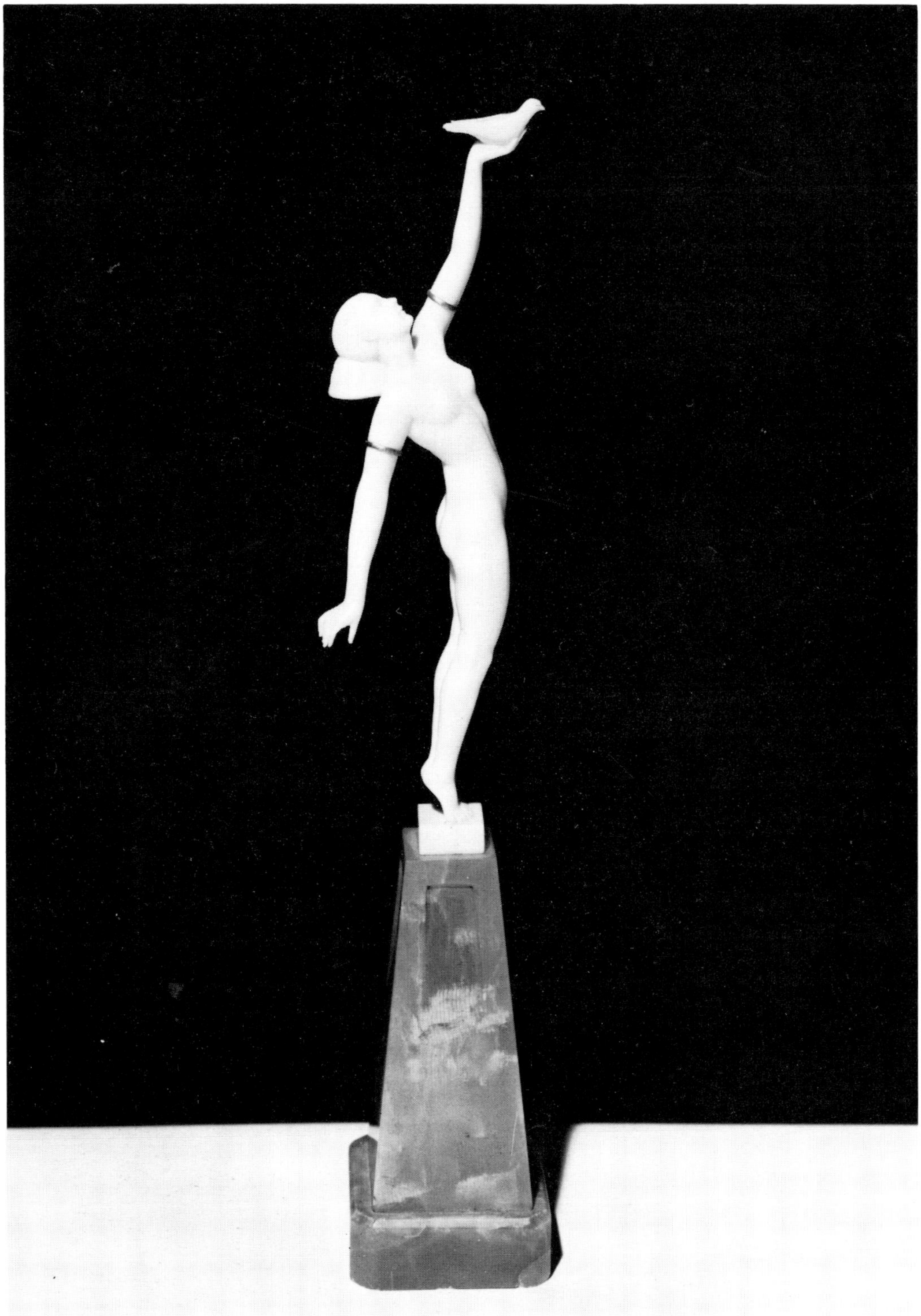

Message of Love, 76cm: 30½in.
47cm: 18½in.; 26cm: 10¼in.

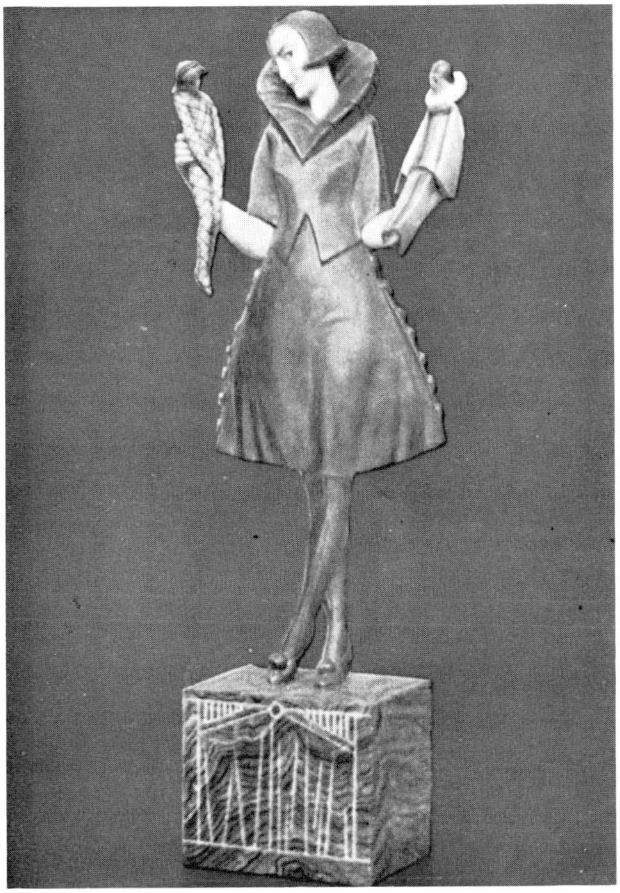

Girl with Puppets, 50cm: 19½in.

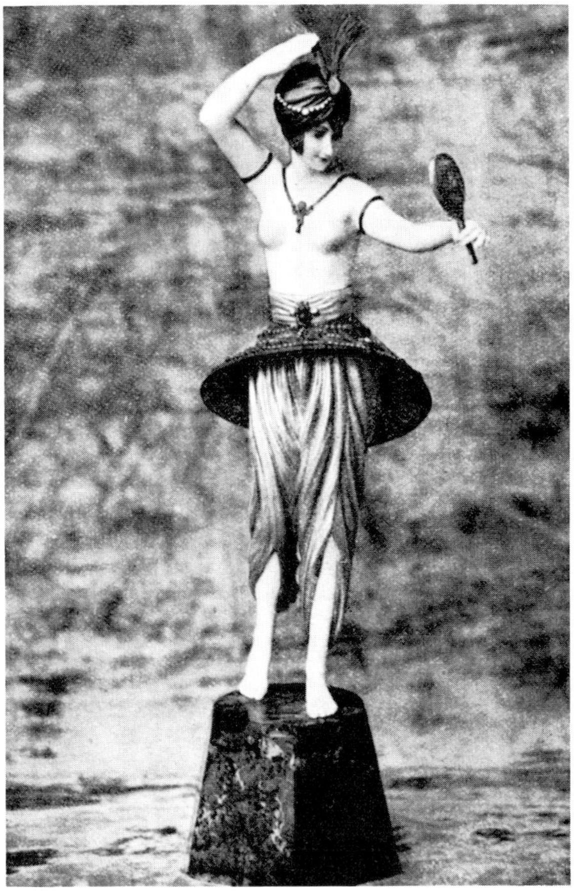

Minaret, 49cm: 19¼in.

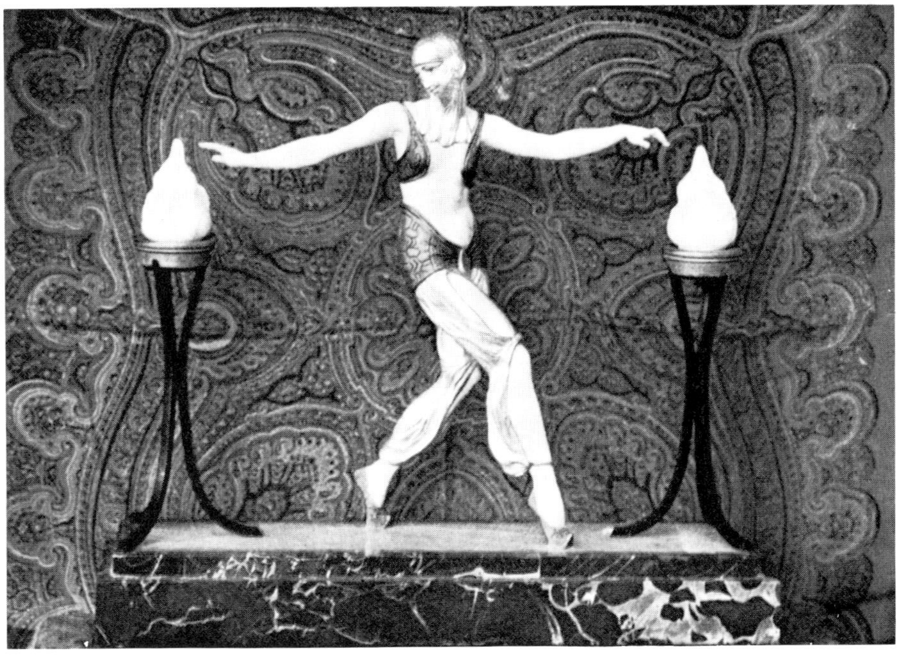

Harem Girl, various heights

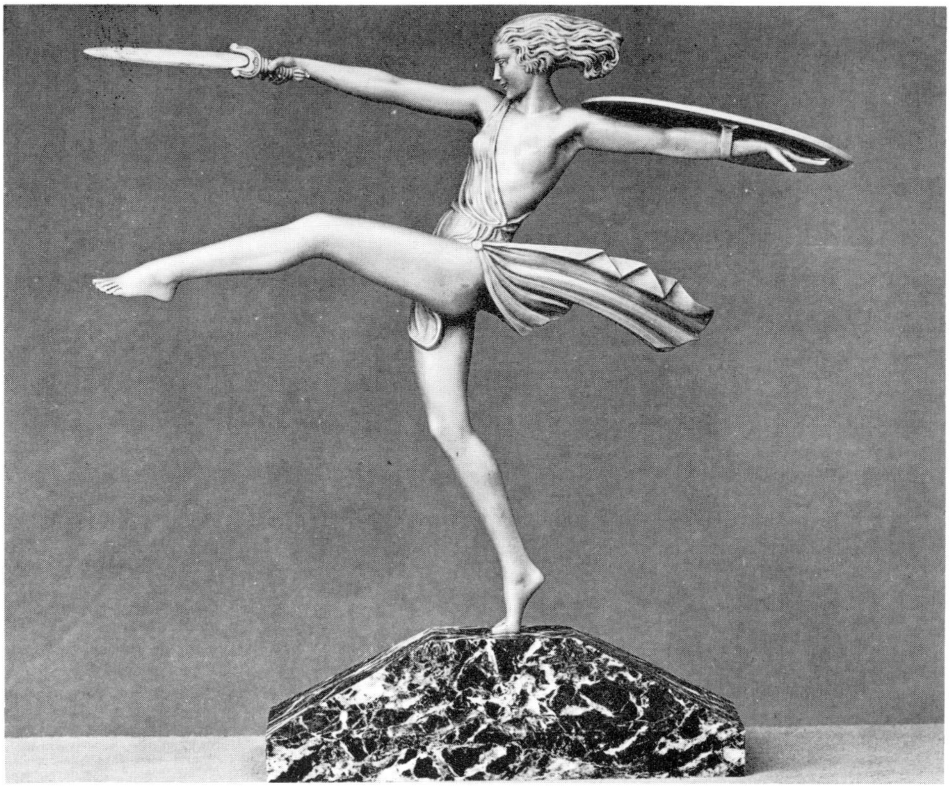

Female Warrior
43cm:17in.
29cm:11¼in.

Dancer with Thyrsus
56cm:22in.; 28cm:11in.
19cm:7½in.

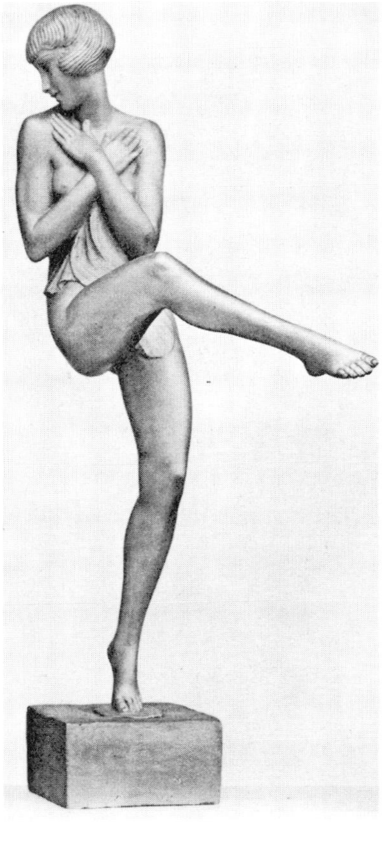

Shy
45cm:17¾in.

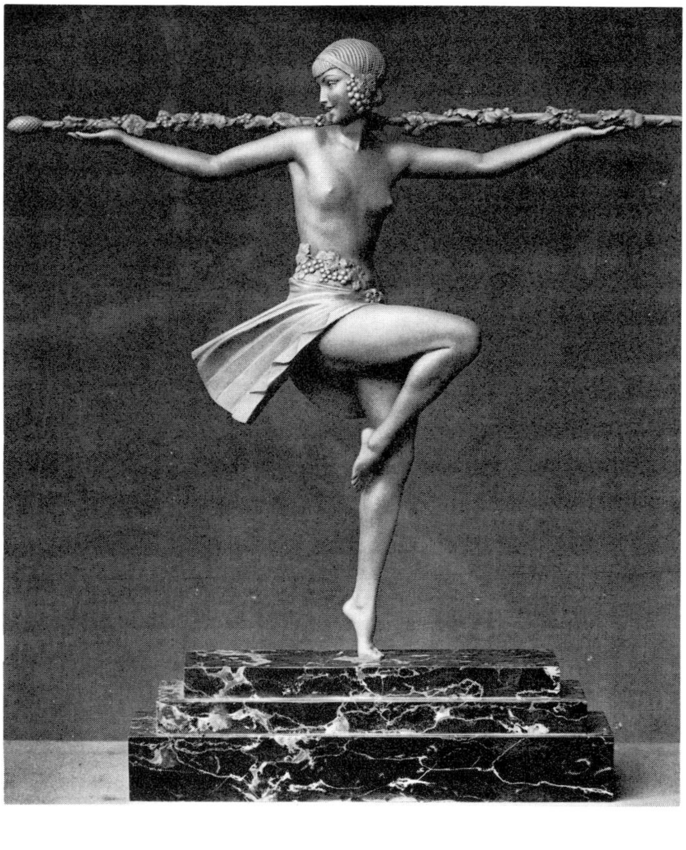

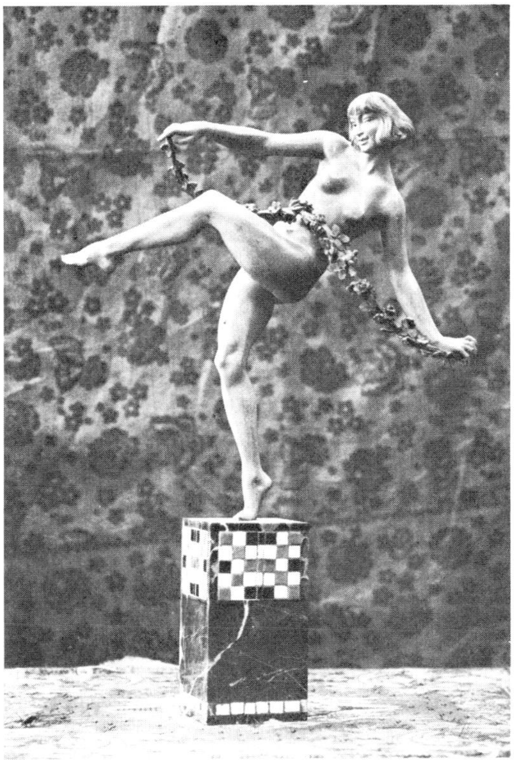

Dancer with Roses, 51cm: 20in.; 36cm: 14in.

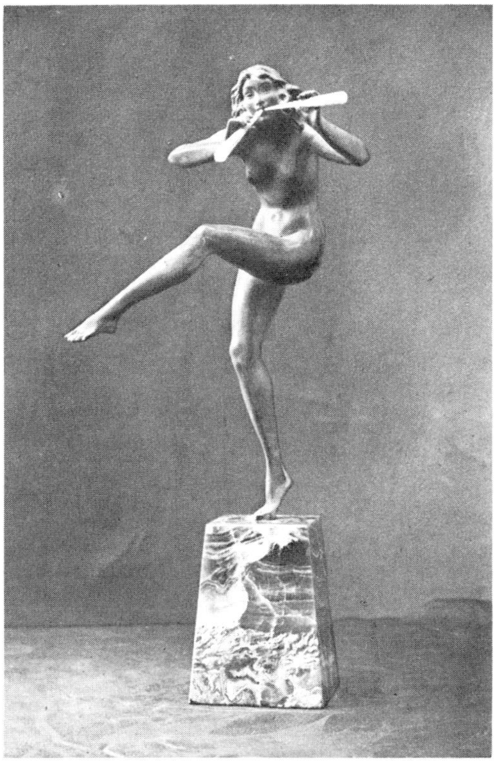

Dancer with Pipes, 32cm: 12¾in.

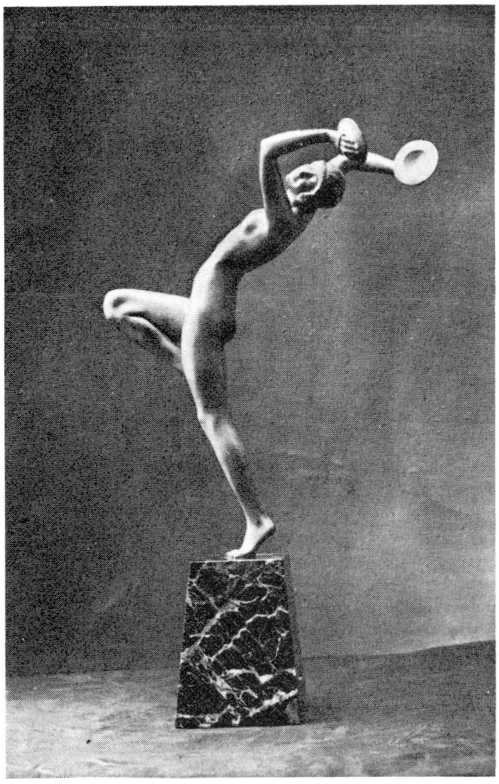

Dancer with Cymbals 25cm: 10in.

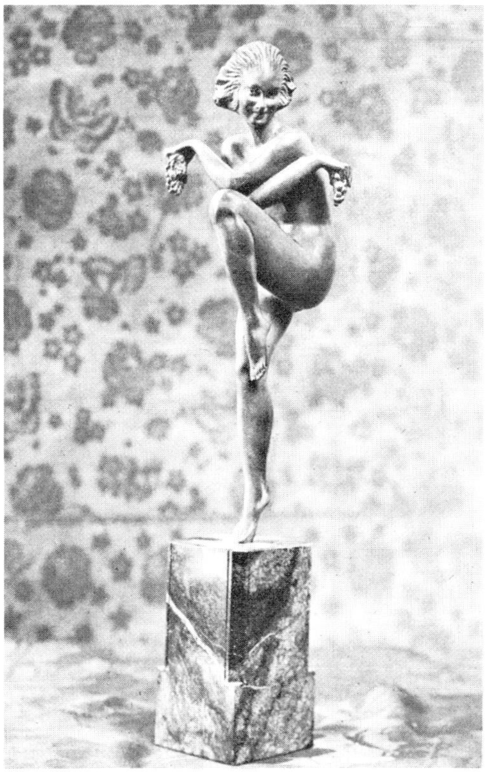

Bacchic Dance 41cm: 16¼in.

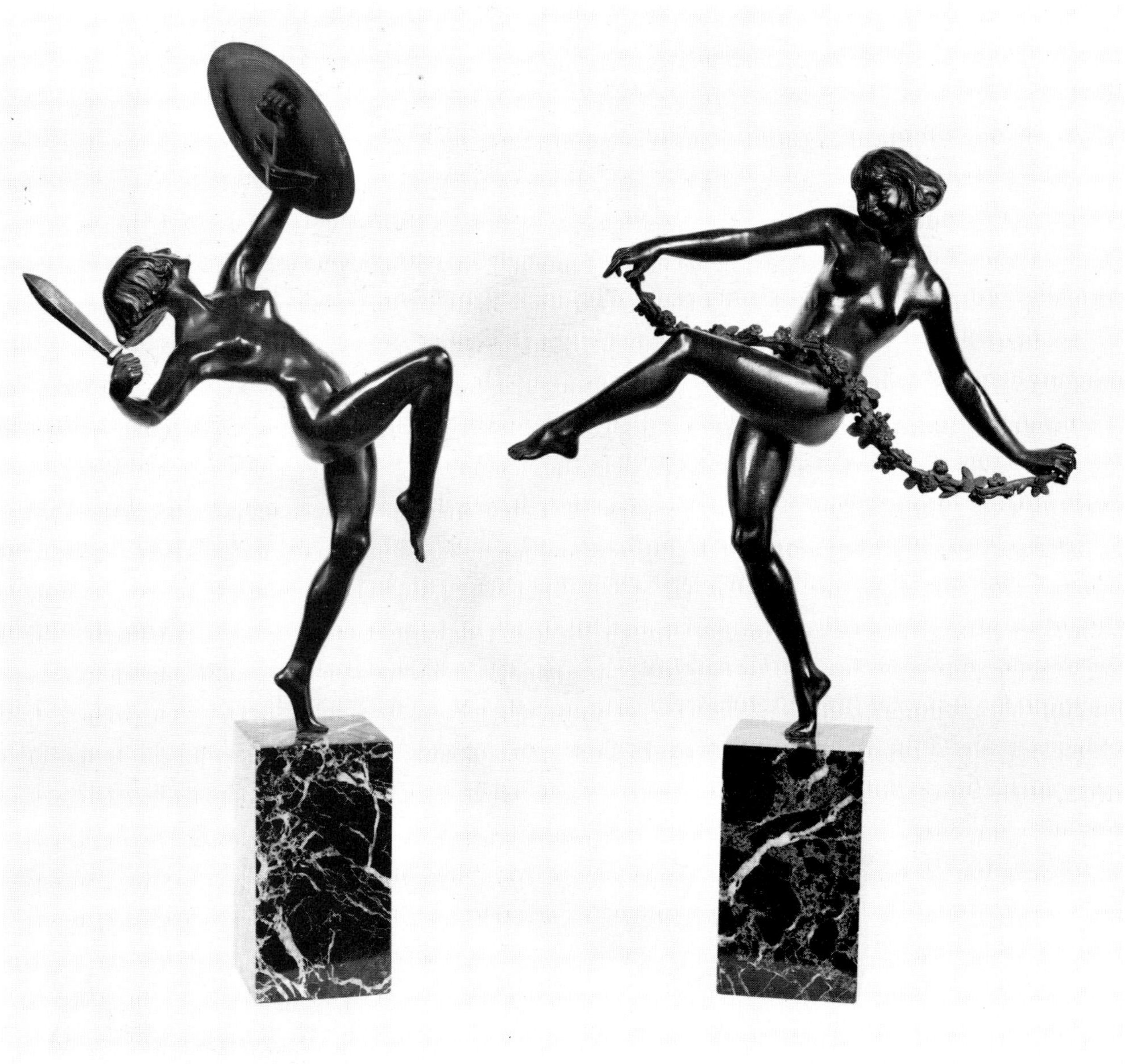

Pair of Dancers, left-hand figure 56cm: 22in.
Right-hand figure 51cm: 20in.

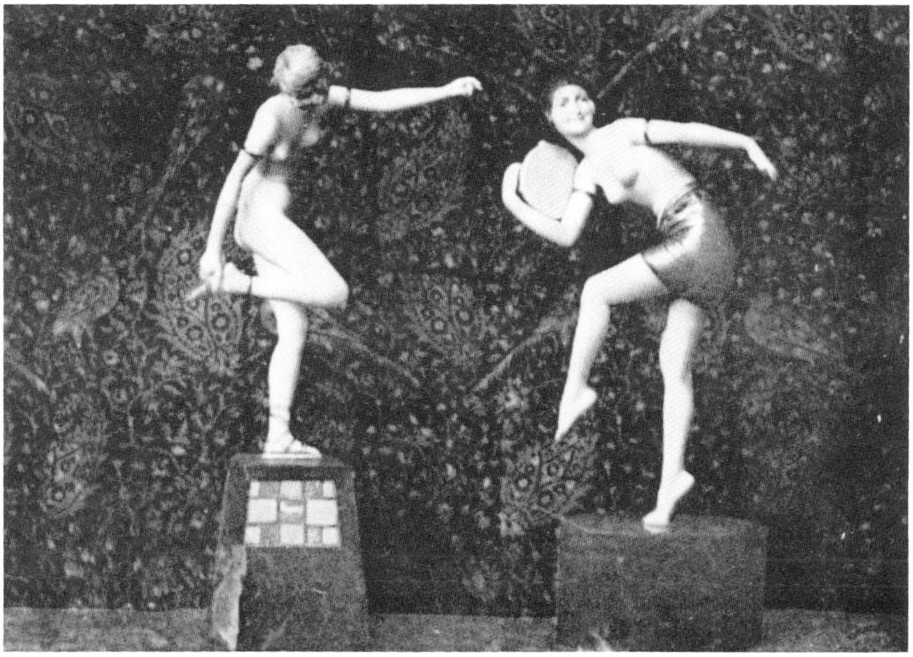

Young Girl with Sandal and Tambourine Dancer, both 25cm:10in.

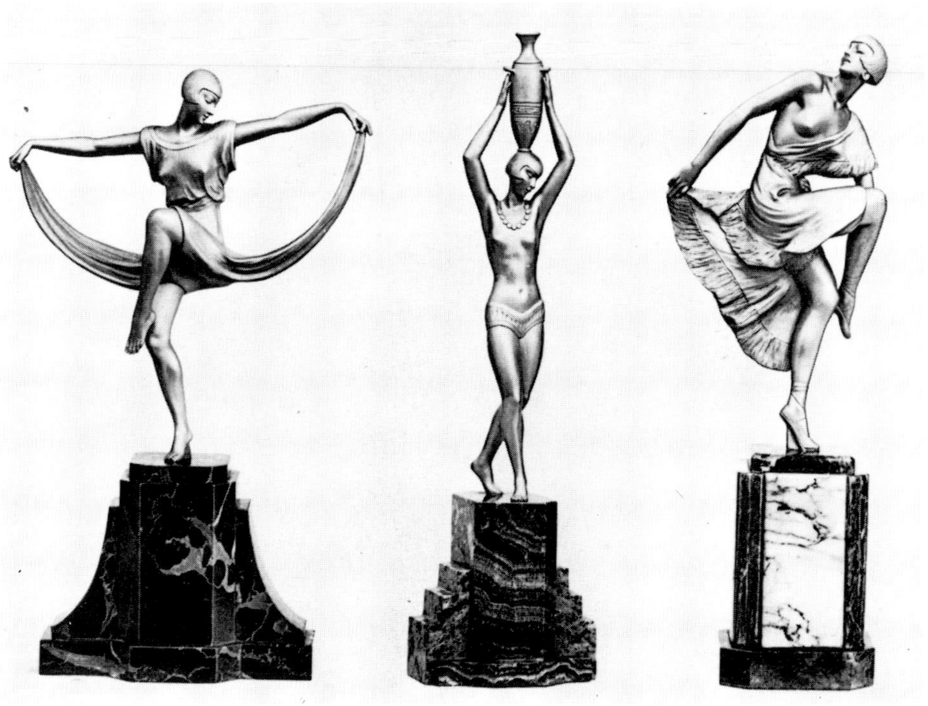

Veil Dancer
31cm:12in.

Oriental
37cm:14½in.

Flamenca
29cm:11½in.

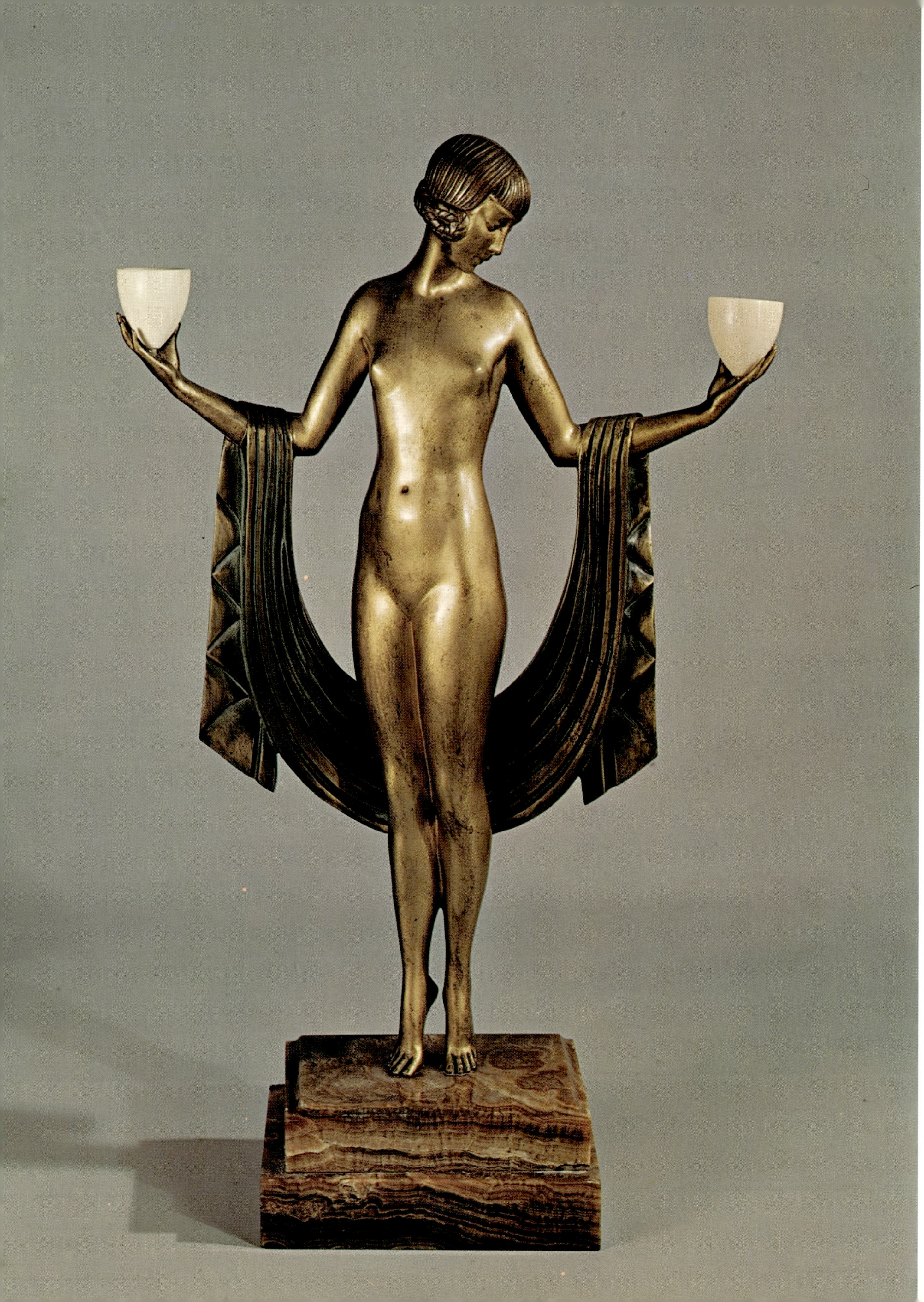

LEMO

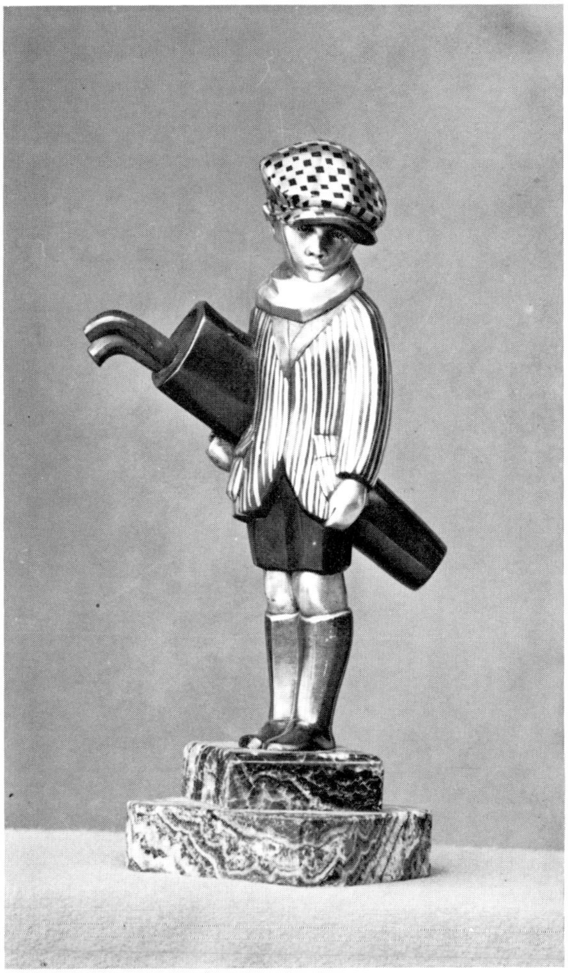

Caddy, 26cm:10¼in.

F. LEMOYNE

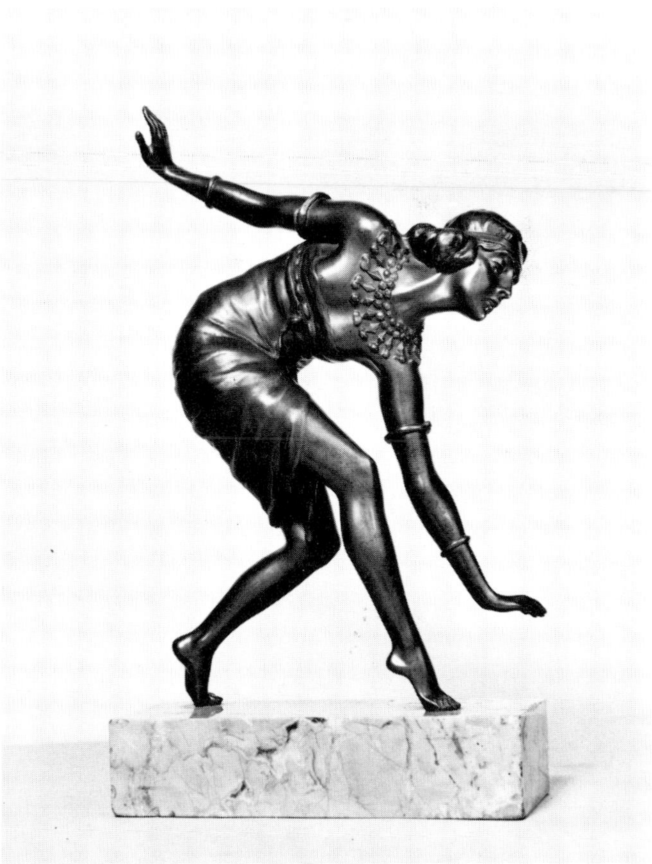

Left: Vestal by Pierre Le Faguays
52cm:20½in.; 36cm:14in.

A Figure, 41cm:16in.

PIERRE LENOIR

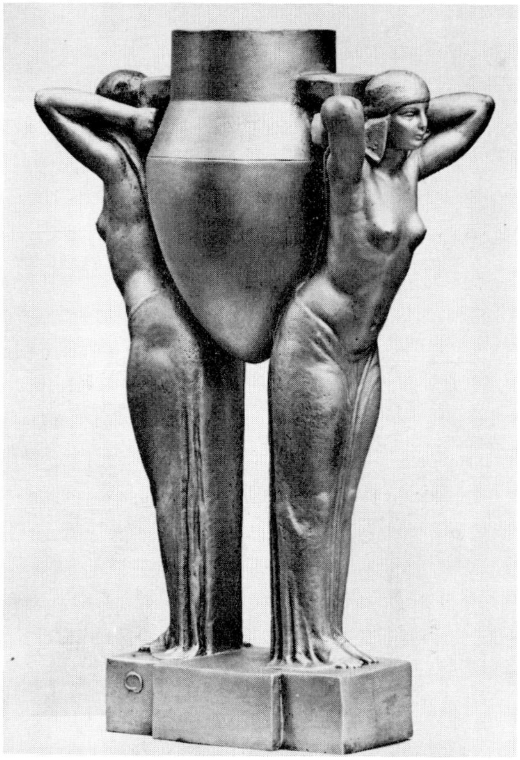

Two Women Carrying a Vase, 62cm:24½in.

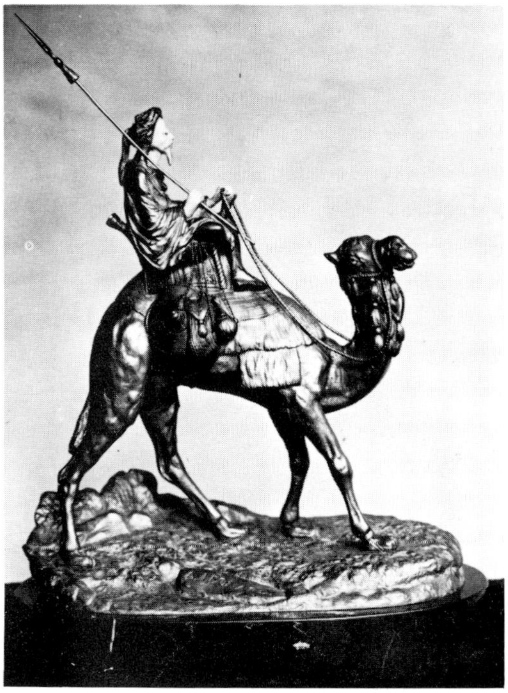

Dromedary, 27cm:10¾in.

AG. LÉONARD

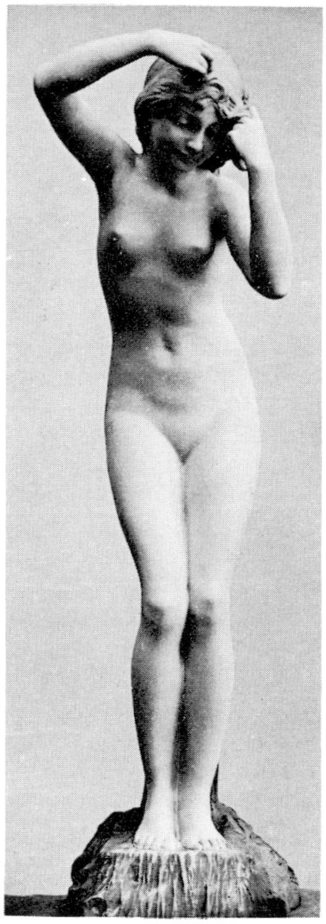

Spring, 62cm:24½in.

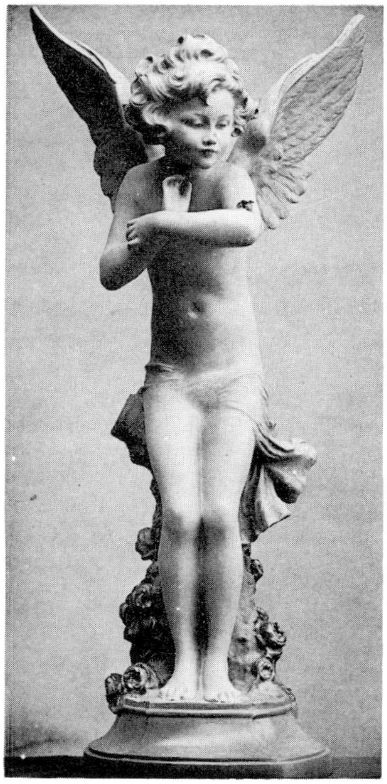

Eros, 60cm:23½in.

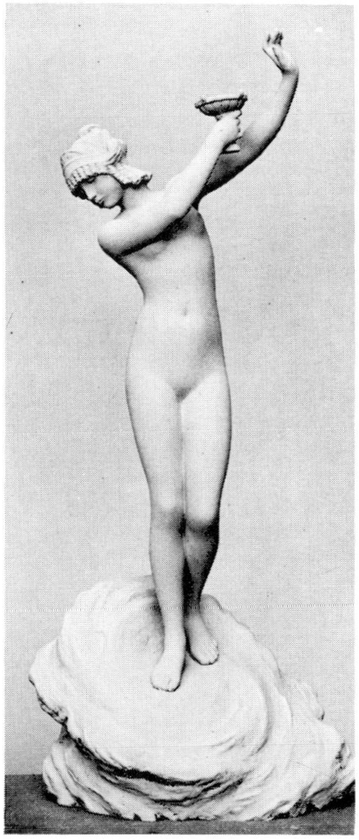

Goddess of Youth
65cm:25½in.
35cm:13¾in.

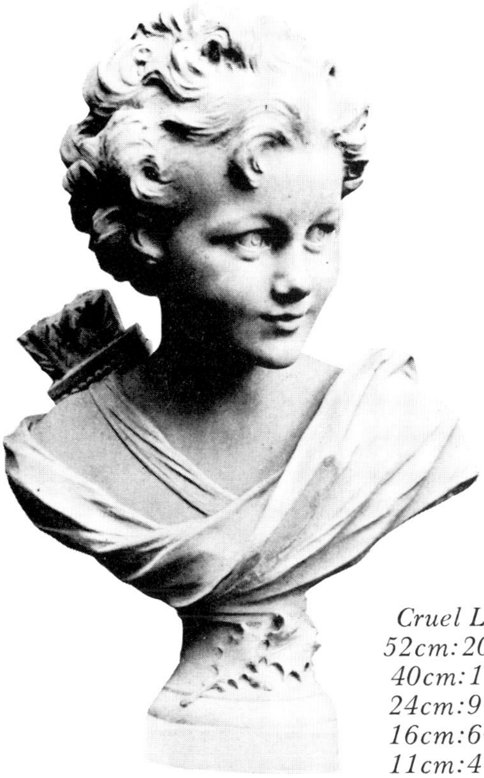

Cruel Love
52cm:20½in.
40cm:16in.
24cm:9½in.
16cm:6¼in.
11cm:4½in.

Rose and Butterfly
60cm:23½in.
44cm:17¼in.
17cm:6¾in.

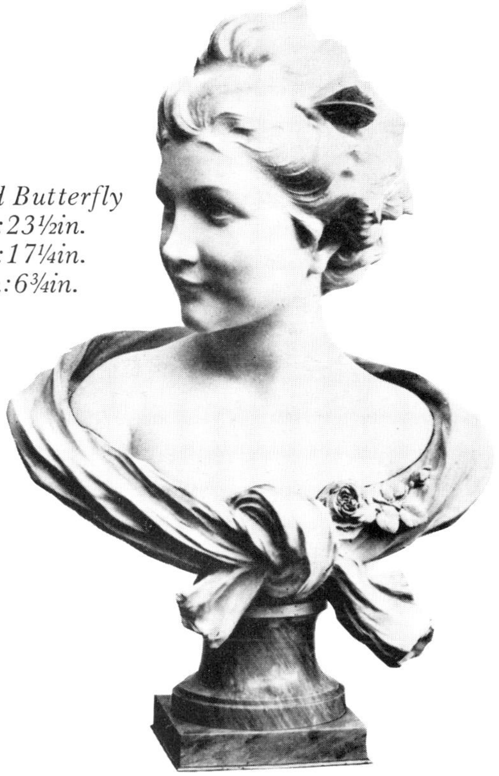

Chilly Love
48cm:19in.

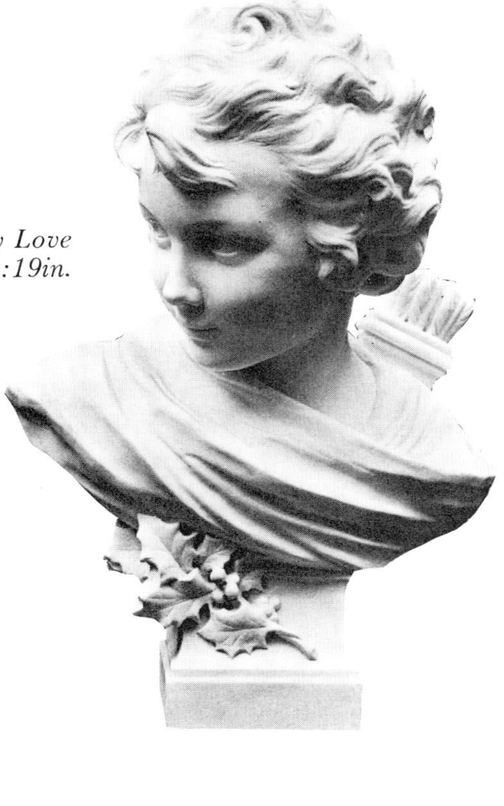

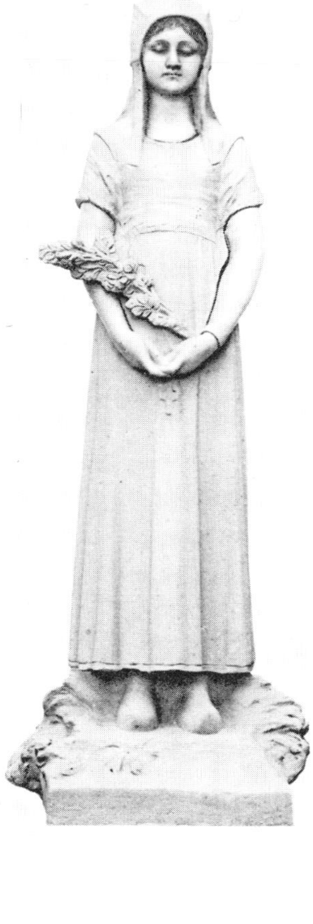

The Palms
44cm:17¼in.

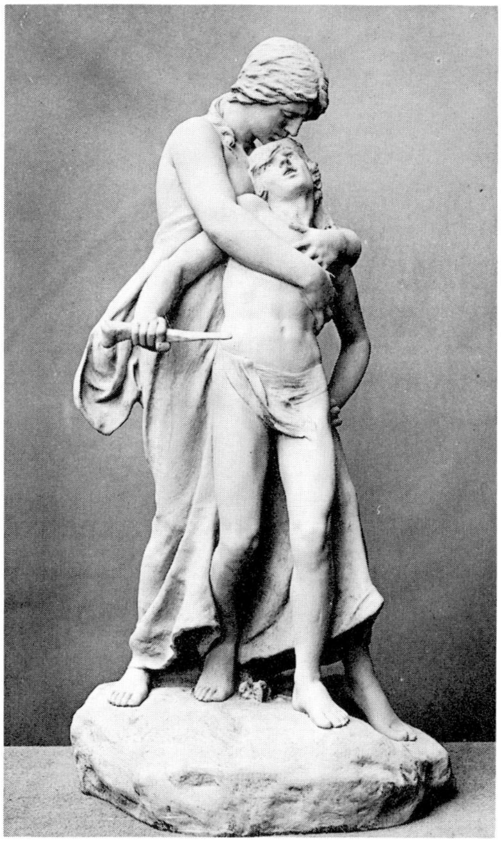

After the Combat
97cm: 38in.
52cm: 20½in.

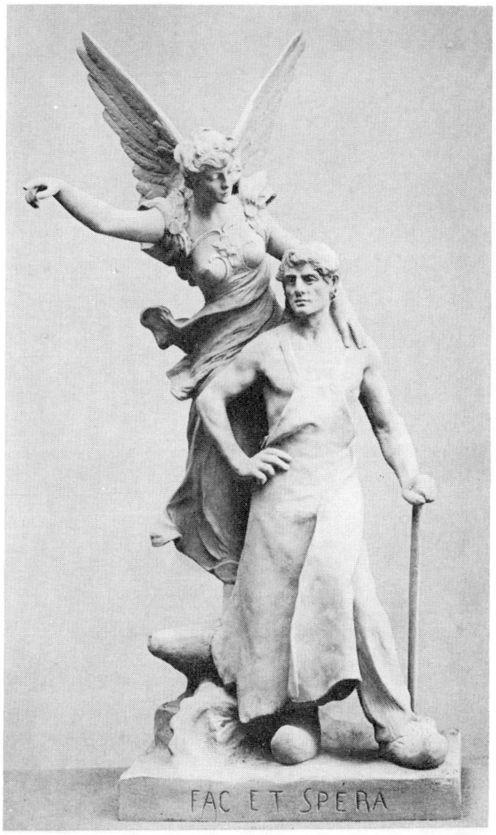

Fac et Spera
85cm: 33½in.
54cm: 21¼in.

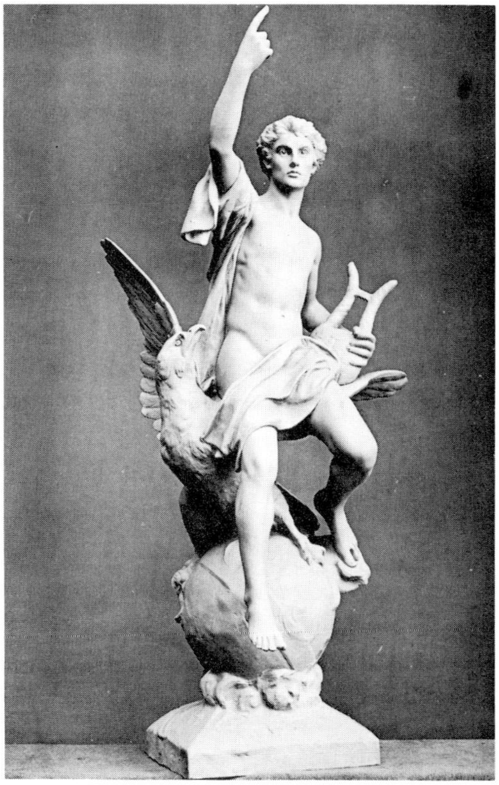

God of Arts, 86cm: 34in.
Another height exists

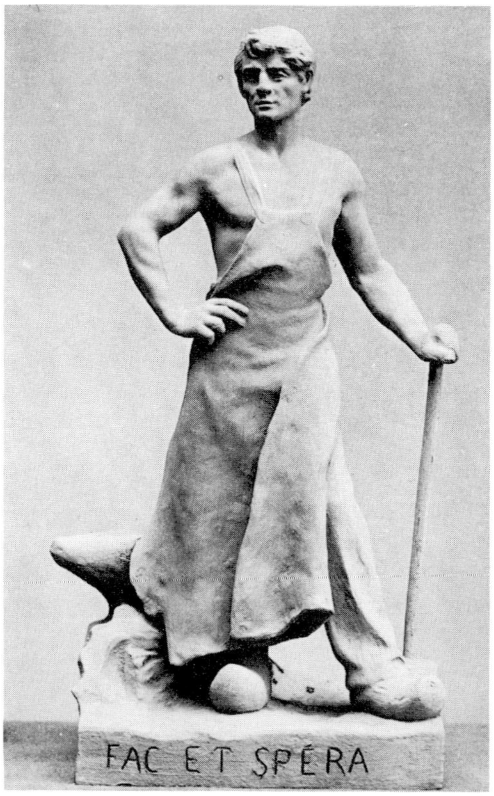

Work
60cm: 23½in.
40cm: 15¾in.

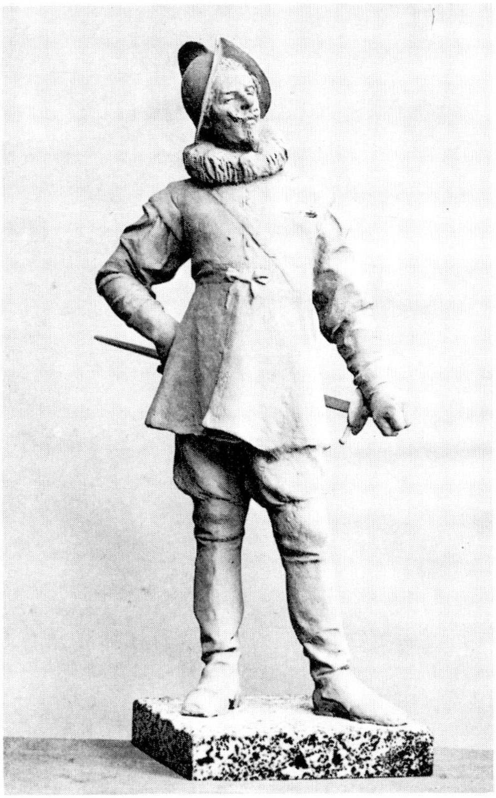

Cyrano
63cm: 24¾in.
43cm: 17in.
31cm: 12in.

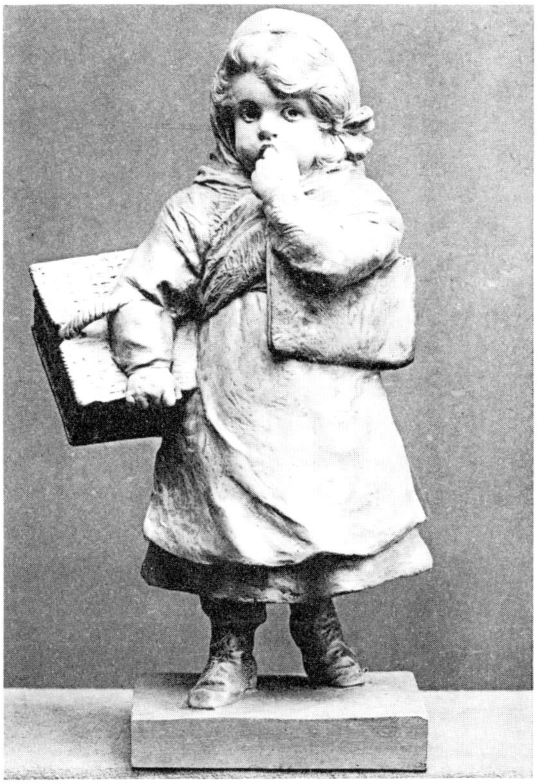

Leaving the Class
30cm: 11¾in.

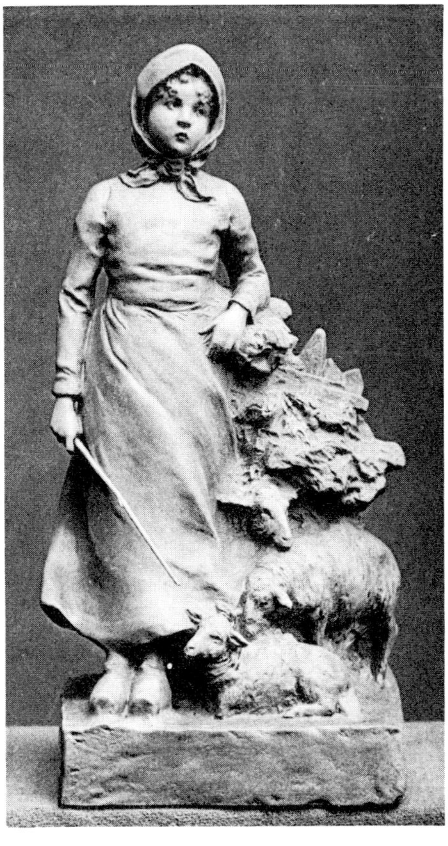

Shepherdess
30cm: 11¾in.

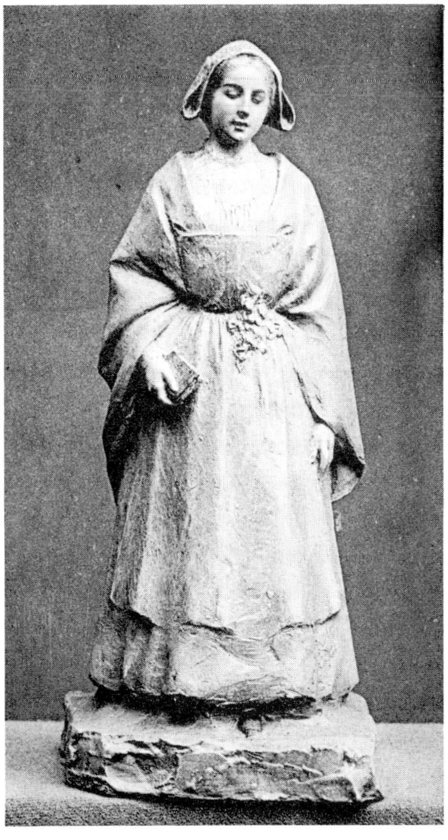

Little Bride
30cm: 11¾in.

H. LEVASSEUR

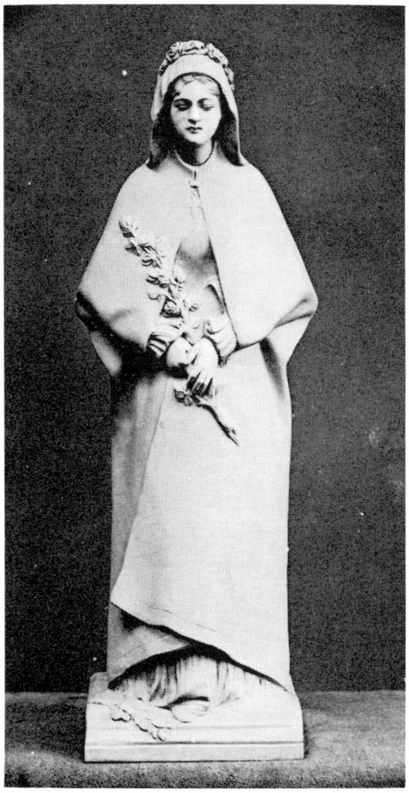

Palm Sunday
34cm:13¾in.

The Torrent
53cm:21in.
Exhibited
in the Salon
des Artistes
Français, 1923

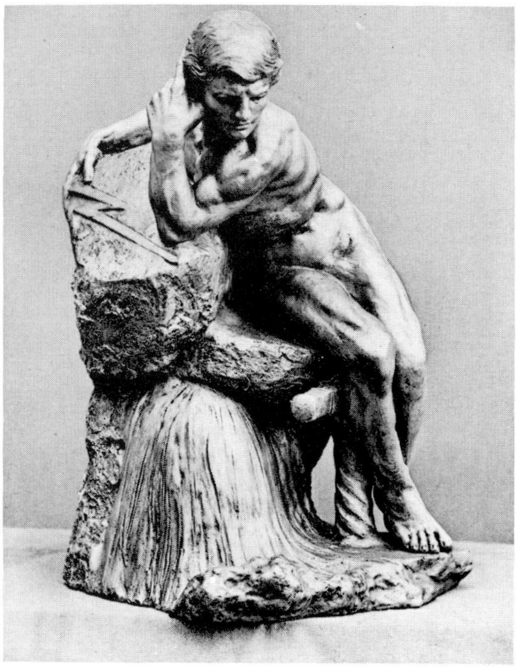

J. LÉVY

Dutch Girl
37cm:14½in.
22cm:8½in.

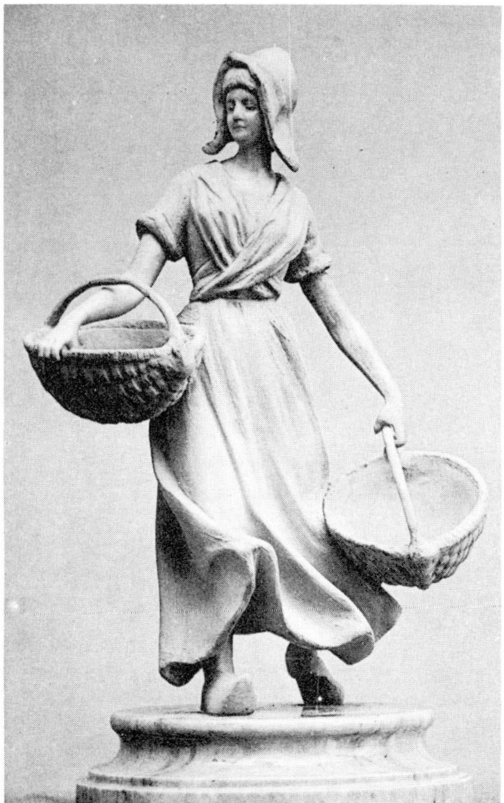

LORENZL

The following are examples of works by LORENZL, who also signed works as LOR and RENZL. All the figures are of similar style and made of bronze or combinations of bronze and ivory. Several appear to be similar in design to works of other artists who may have influenced Lorenzl. Several heights of each example were produced and range from 5-30in. with bases. The figures on pages 208, 210 and 211 depict a selection of dancers.

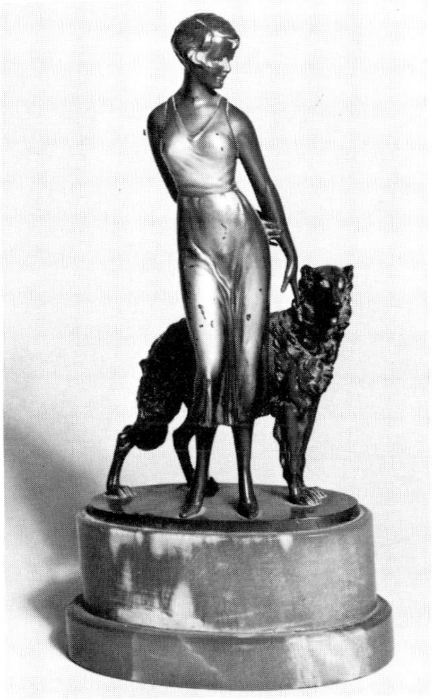
Girl with Dog

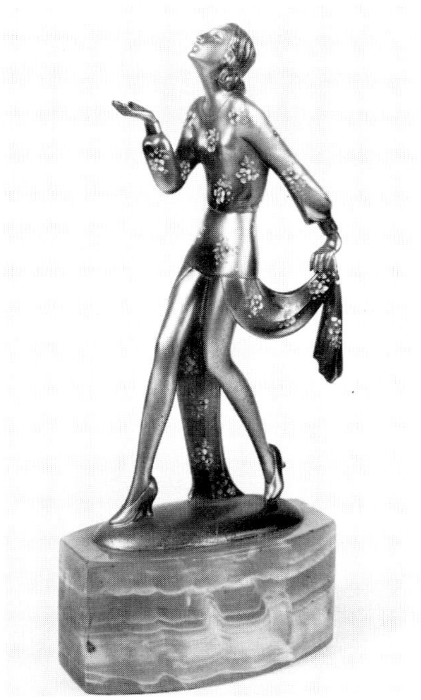
Lady

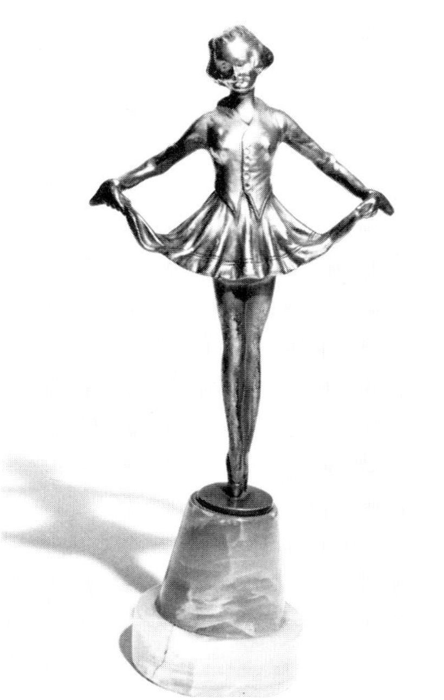
Ballet Dancer

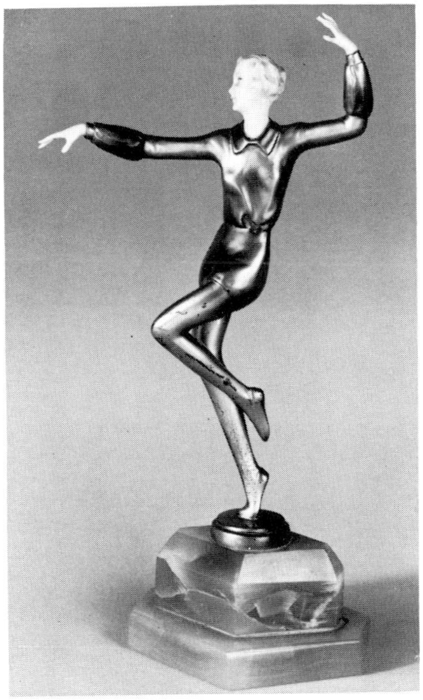
Dancer

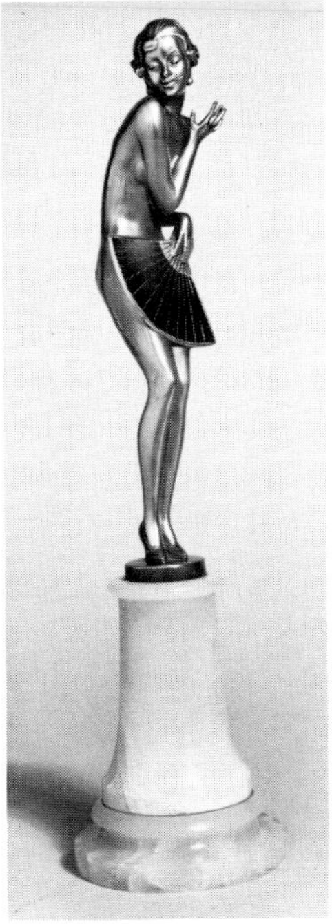
A Fan Dancer

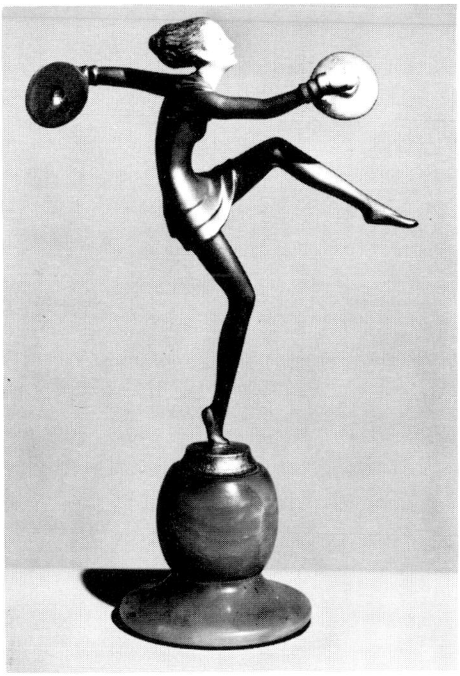
Cymbal Dancer

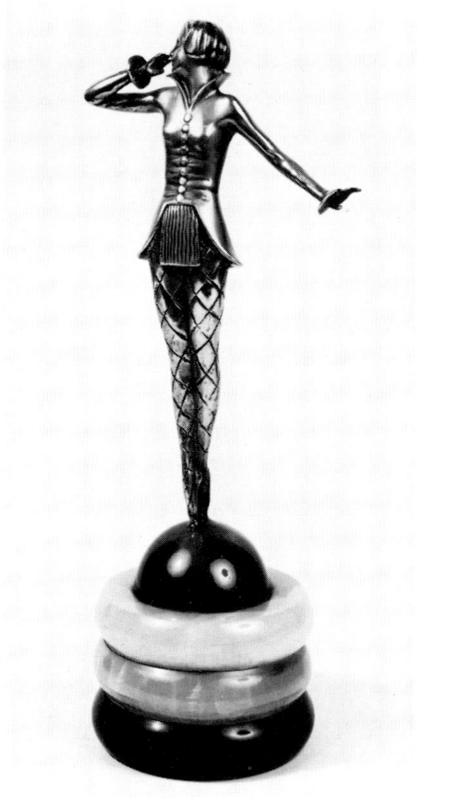

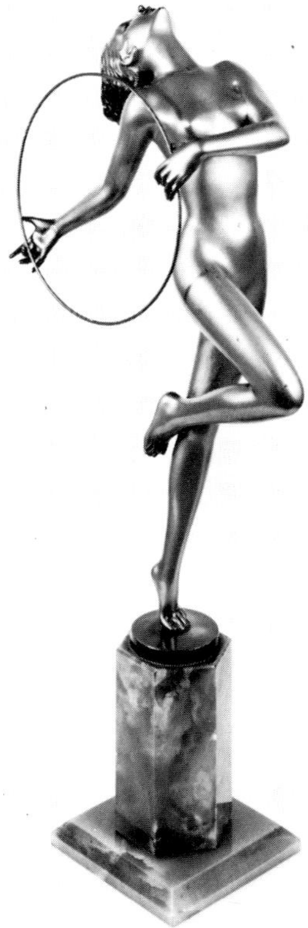

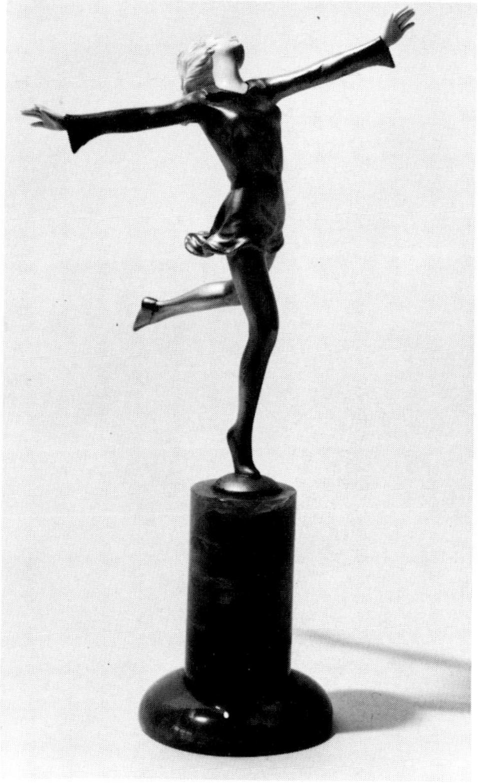

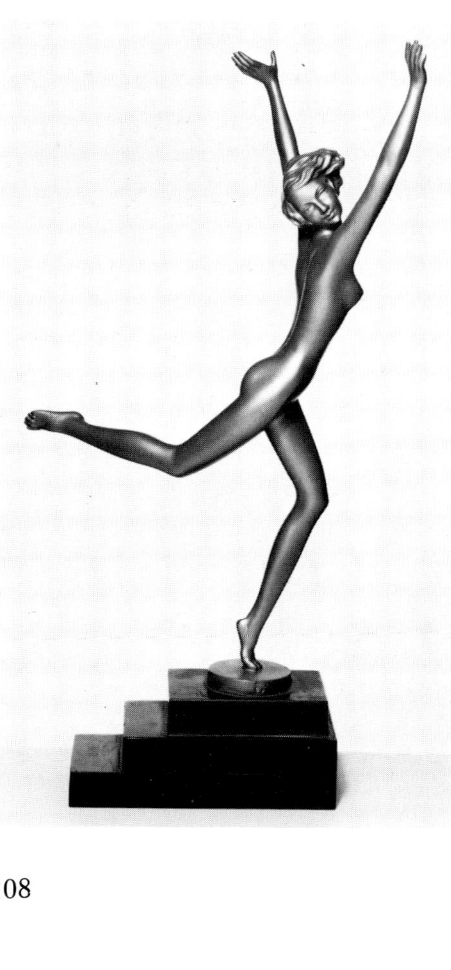

Right: Diana by Lorenzl, 38cm:15in.

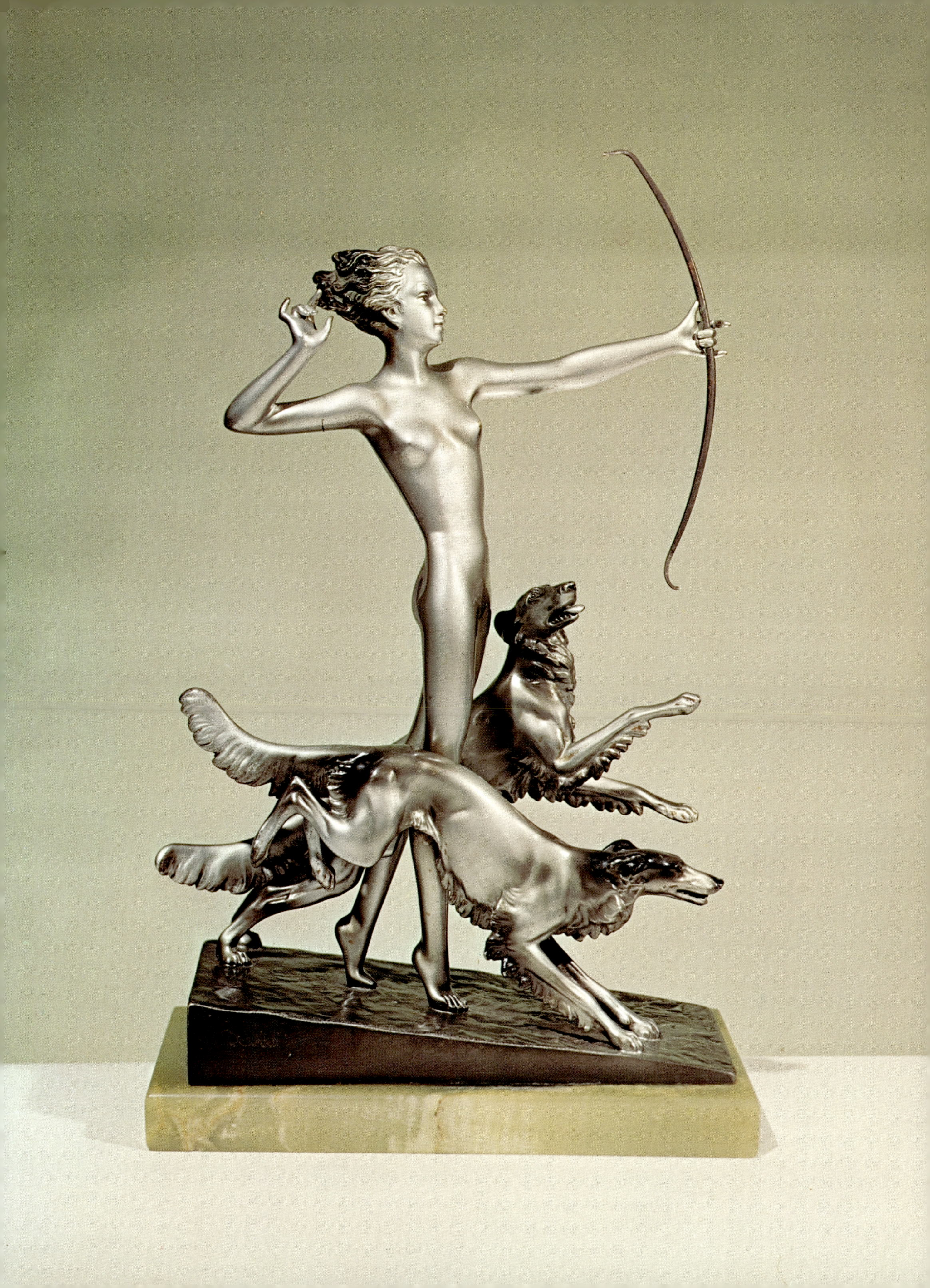

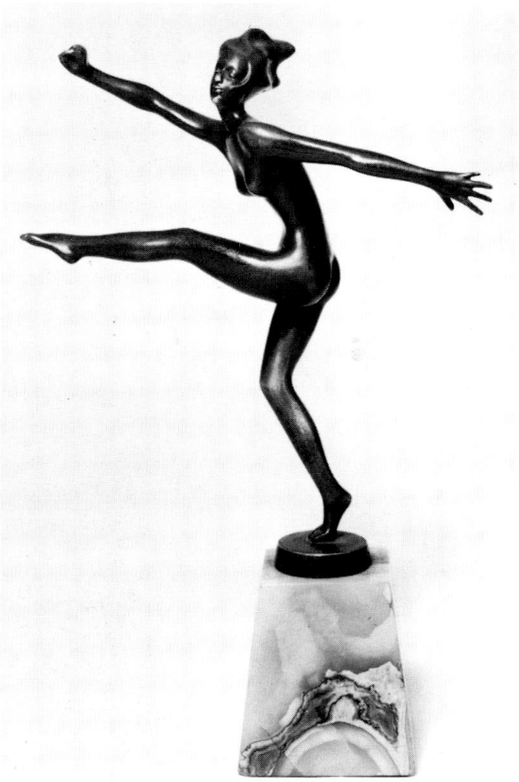

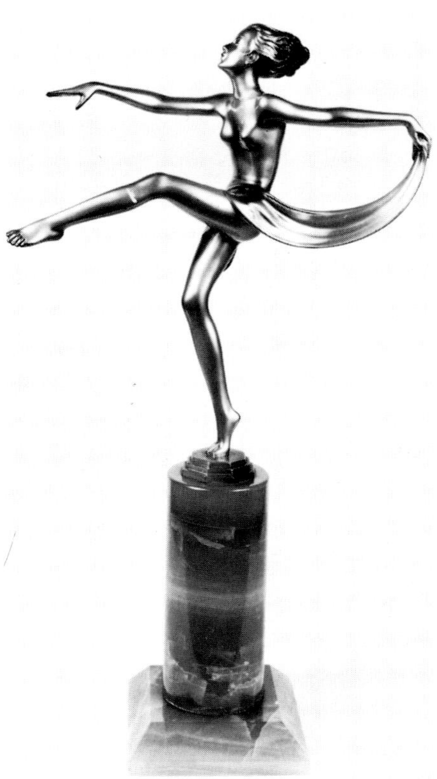

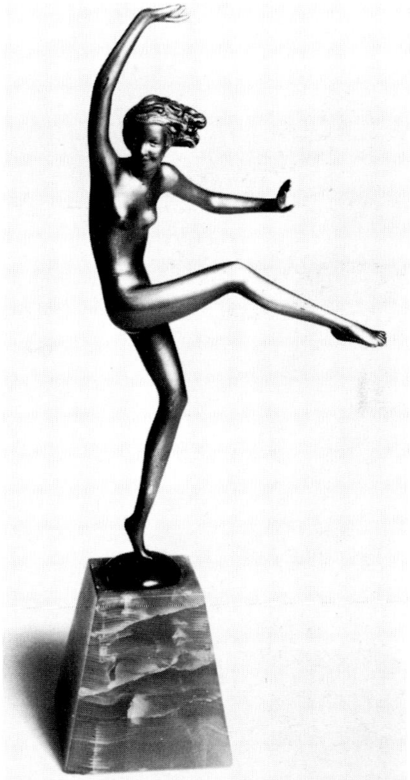

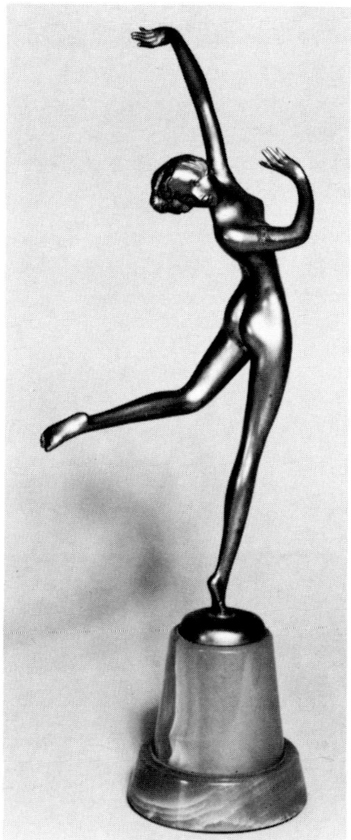

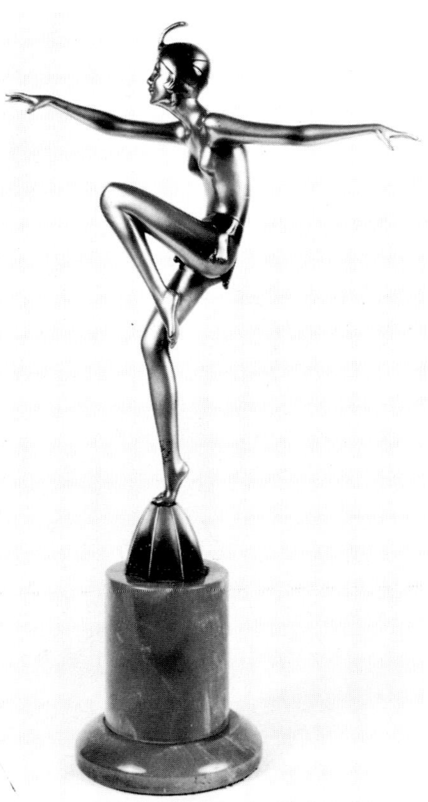

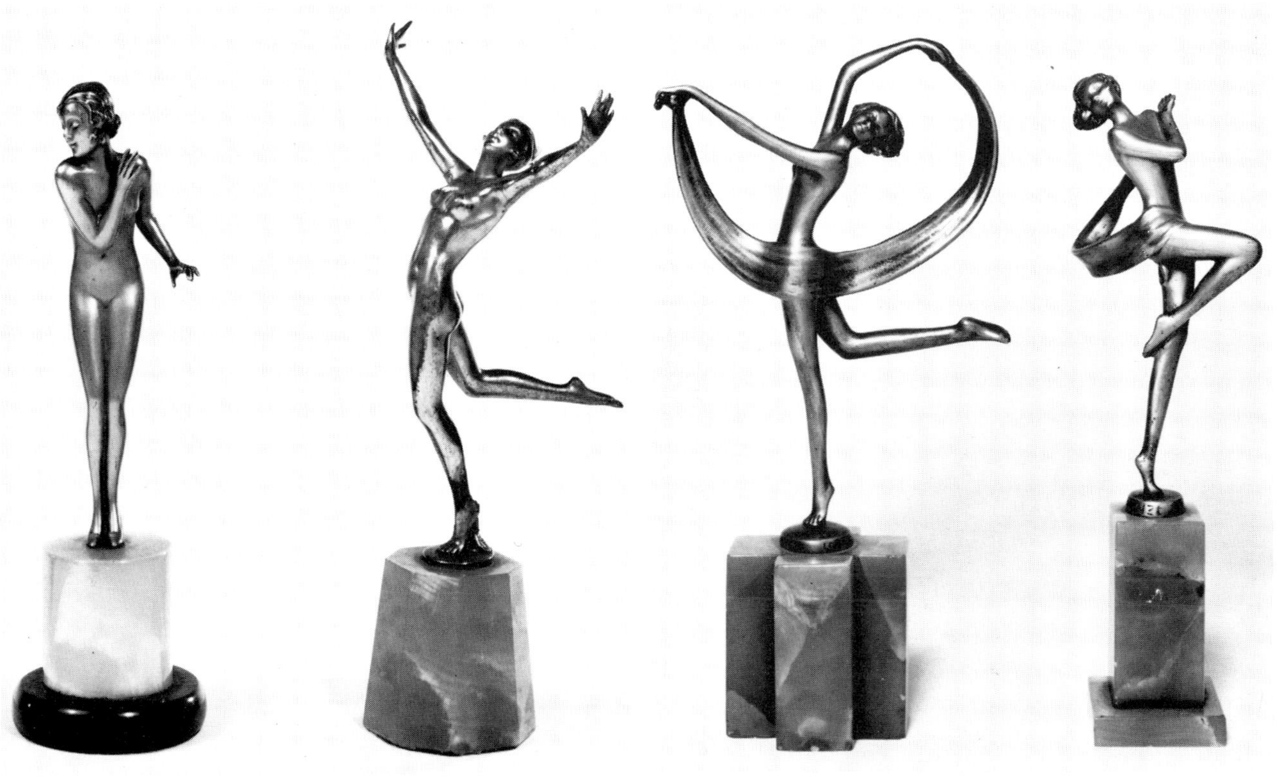

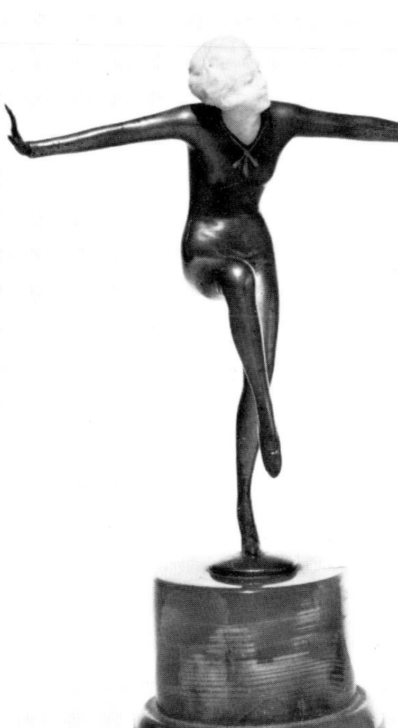

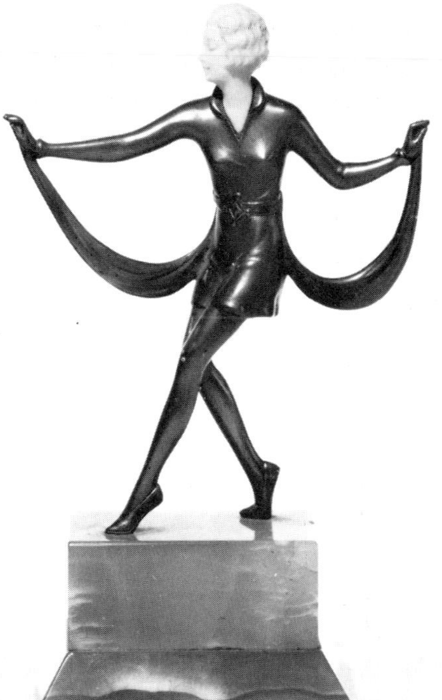

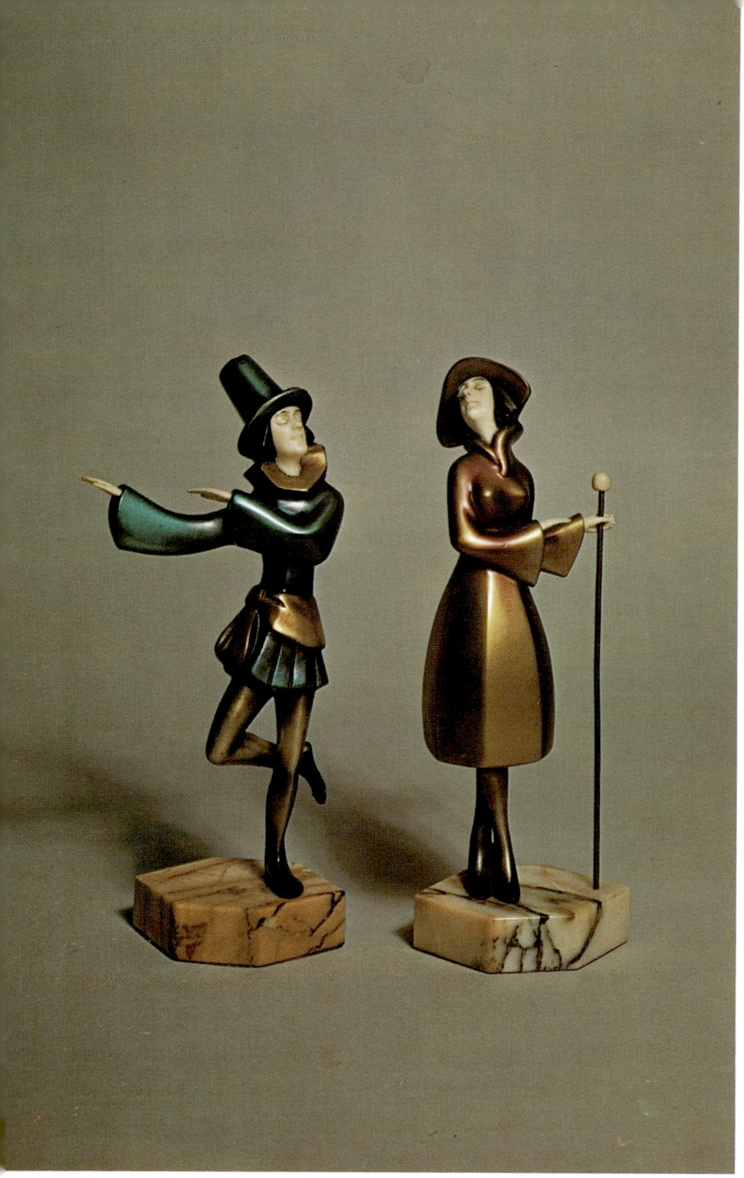

Pair of Figures
18cm: 7¼in.

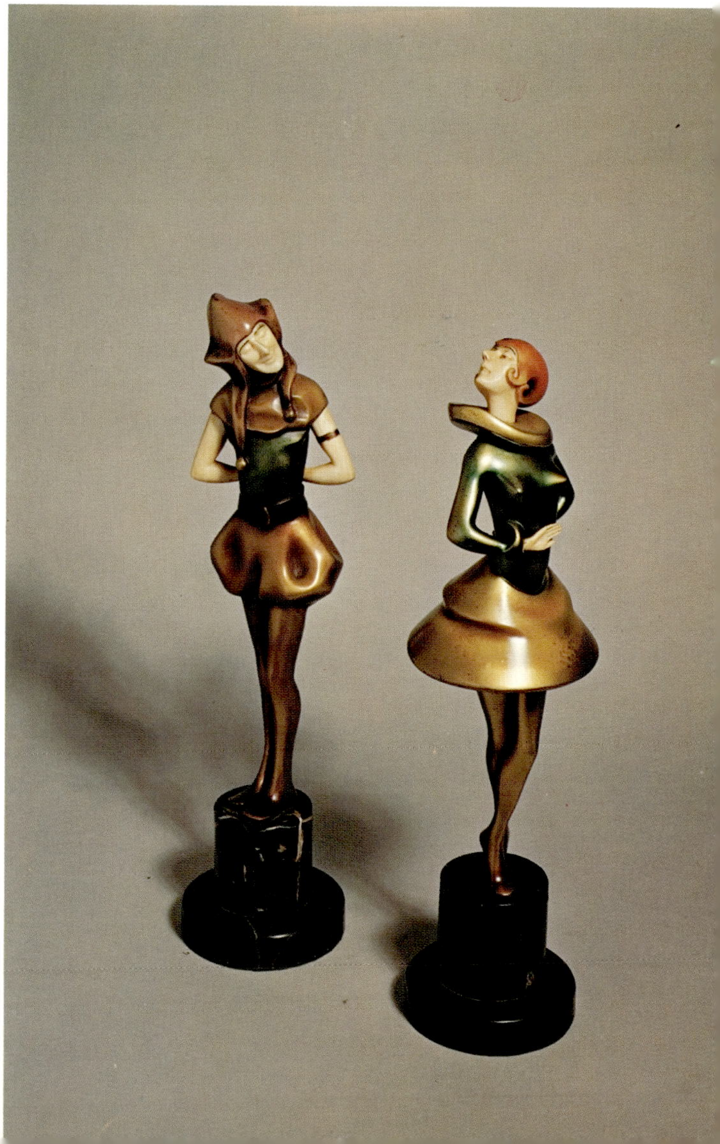

Pair of Figures
38cm: 15in.

LORMIER

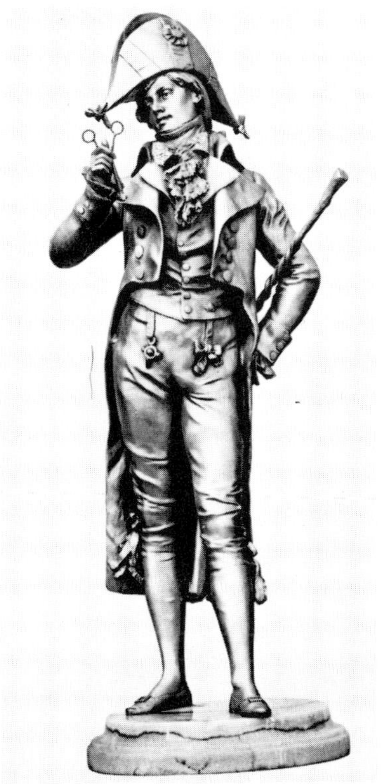

Dandy
71cm:28in.
39cm:15½in.

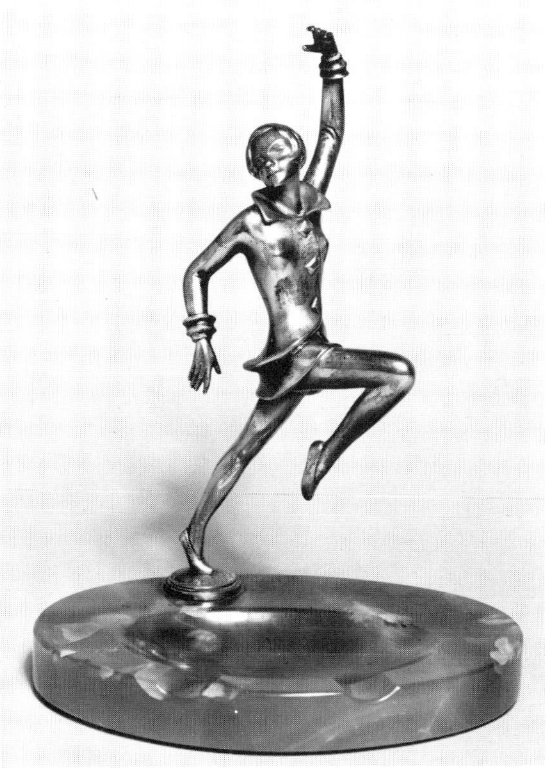

A Dancer
21cm:8¼in.

LUGERTH

Bust, 9cm:3½in.

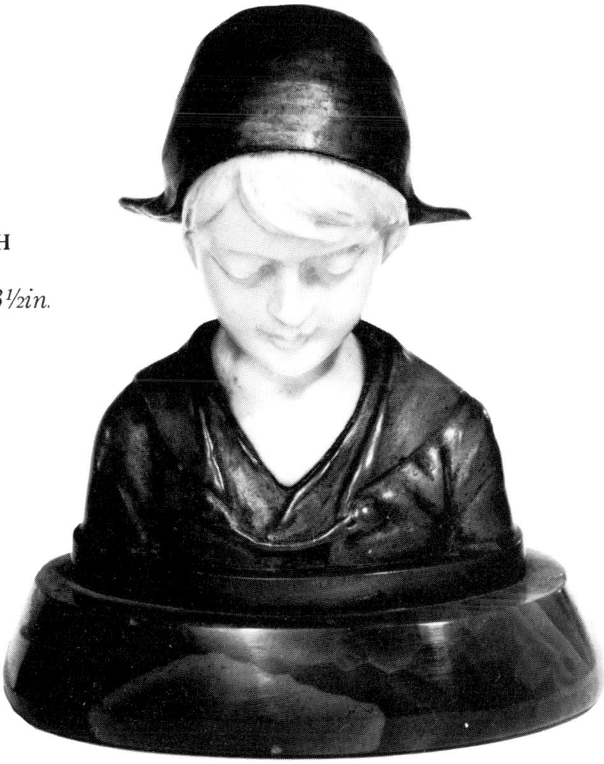

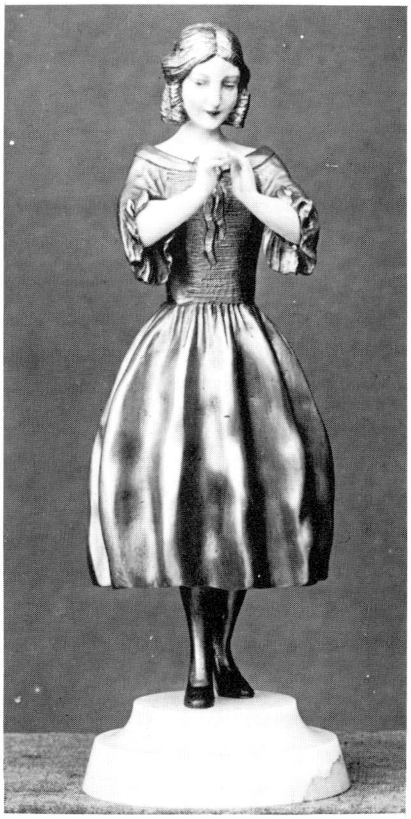

The First Ring, 26cm:10¼in.

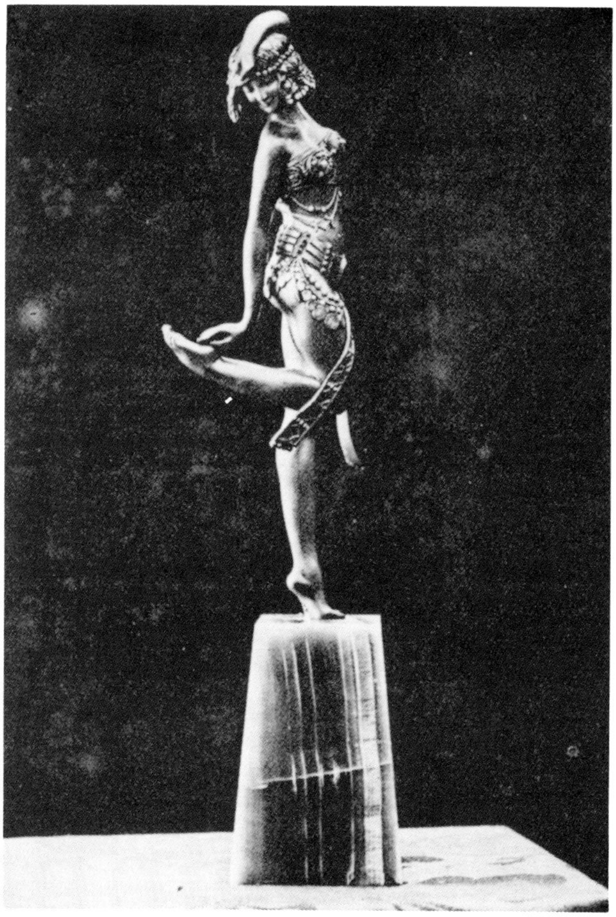

Javanese Dancer, 33cm:13in.

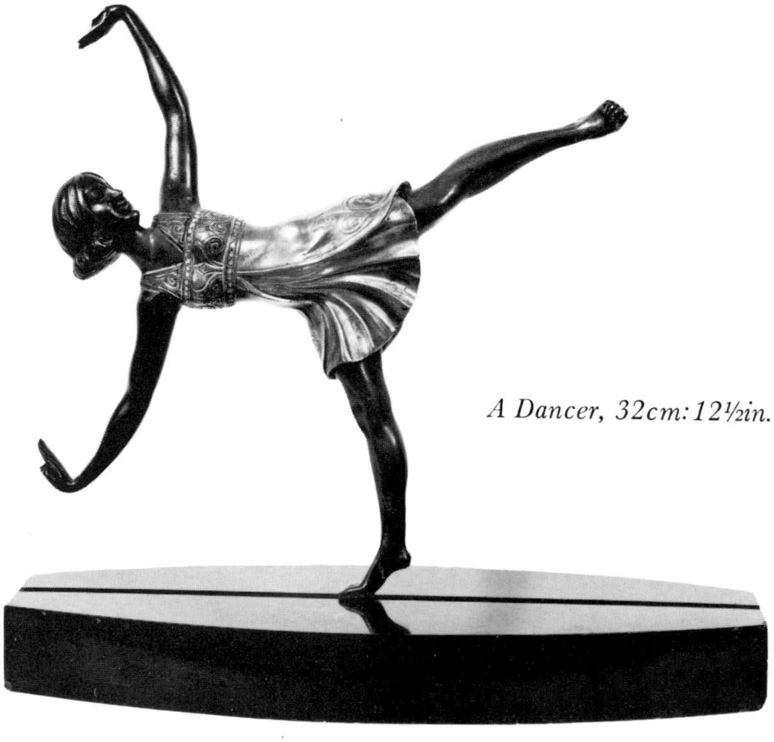

A Dancer, 32cm:12½in.

MADRESSÉ

Courage, 37cm:14½in.; 22cm:8½in.

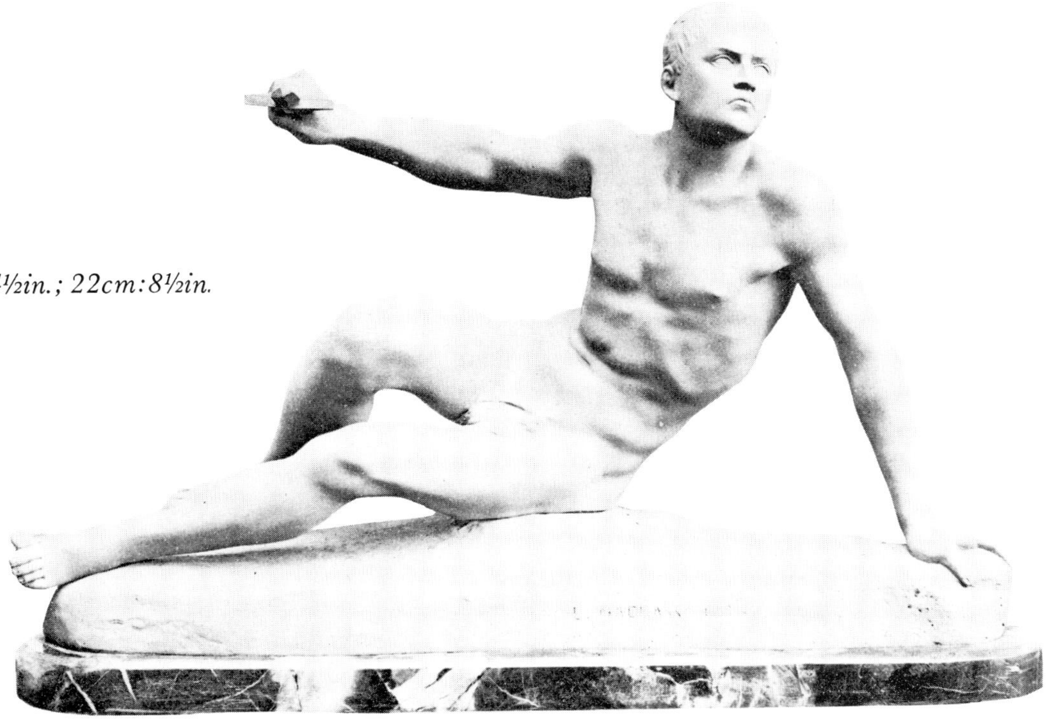

R. MARQUET

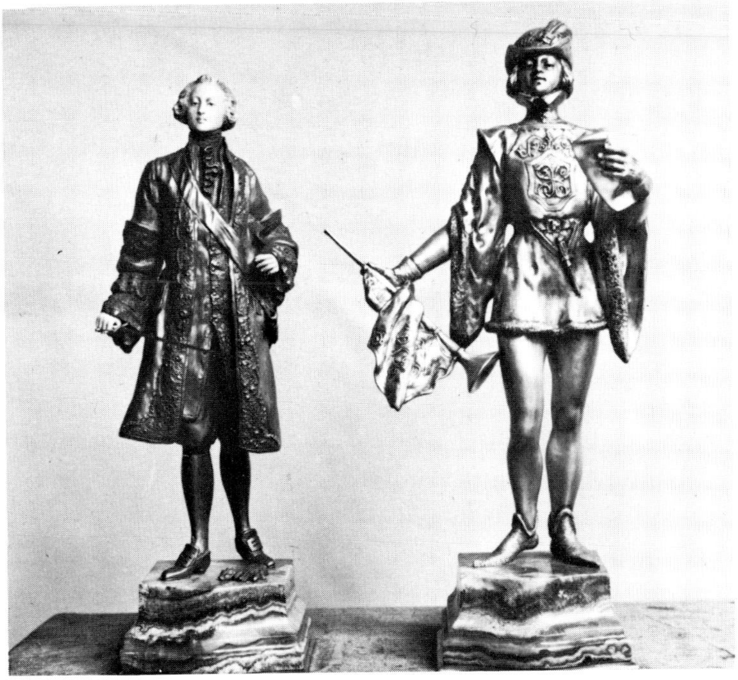

Defiance
30cm:11¾in.

Herald at Arms
32cm:12½in.

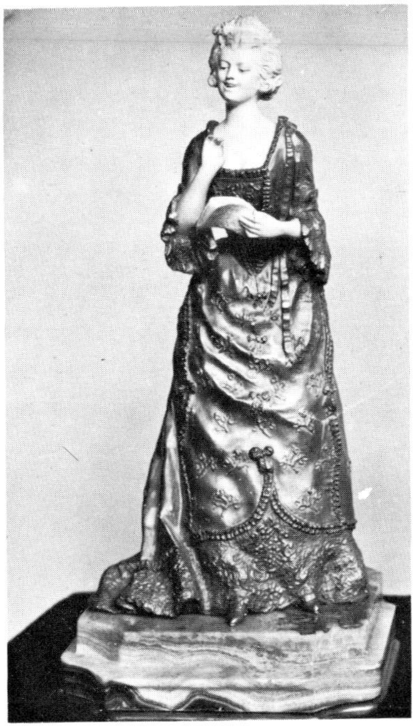

Speaker
31cm:12¼in.

R. MARQUET

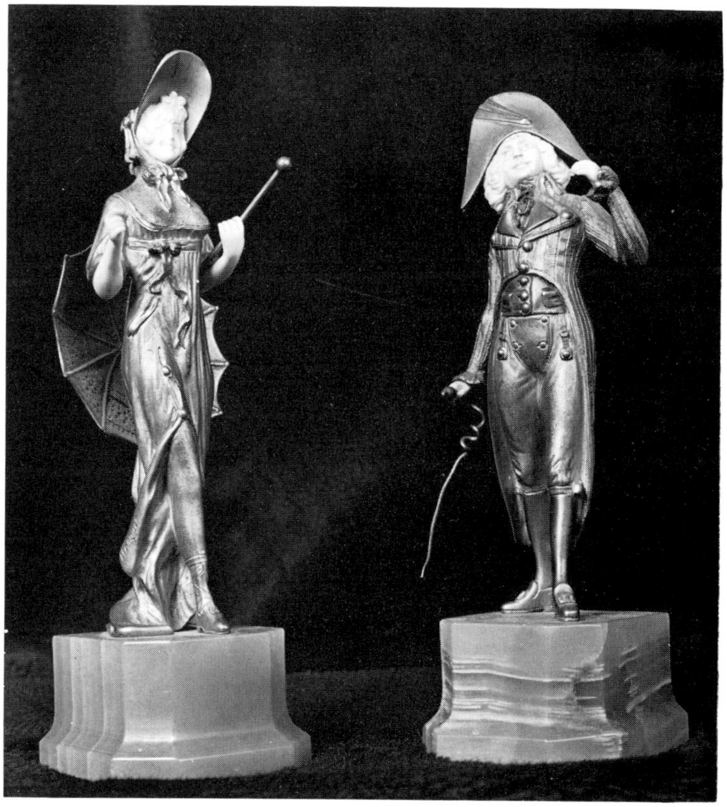

Pair of Figures, 22½cm: 9in.

Draped Piper
58cm: 22¾in.
38cm: 15in.

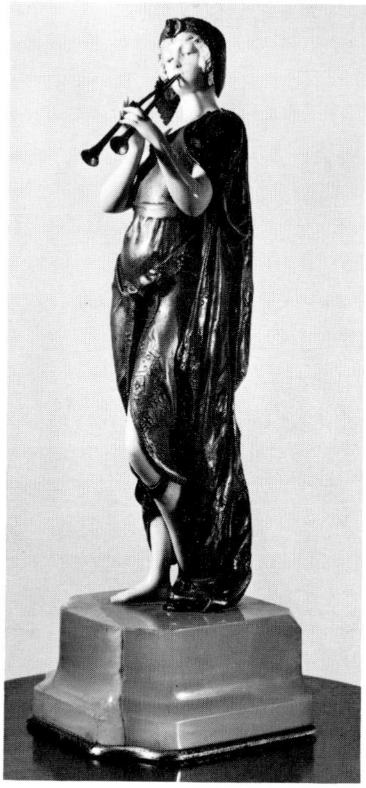

J.E. MASSON

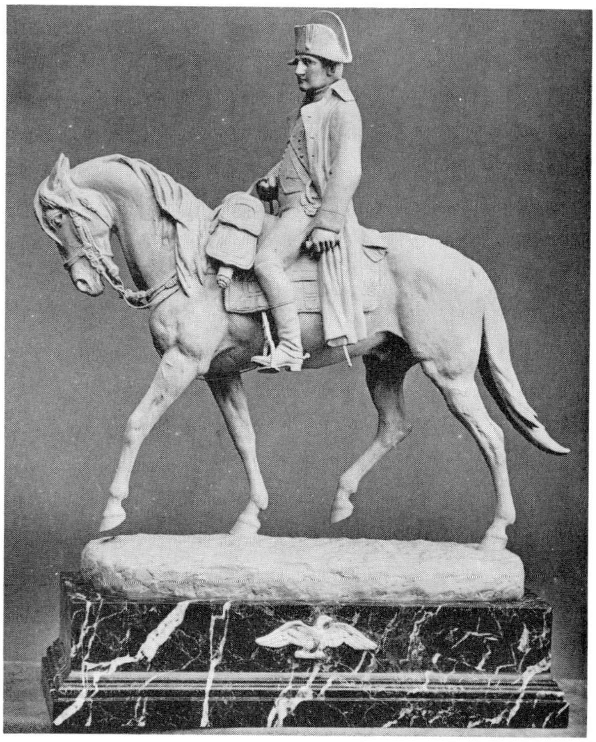

Napoleon, 54cm: 21¼in.

J. MICH

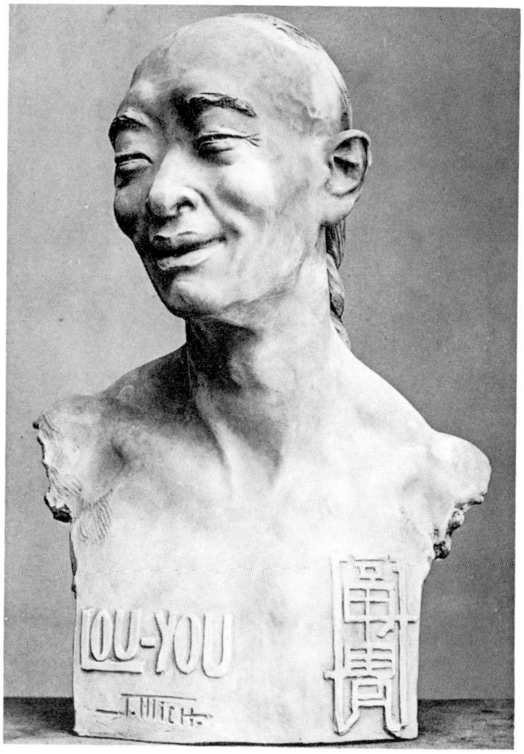

Lou-You, 52cm: 20½in.

C. MIMO

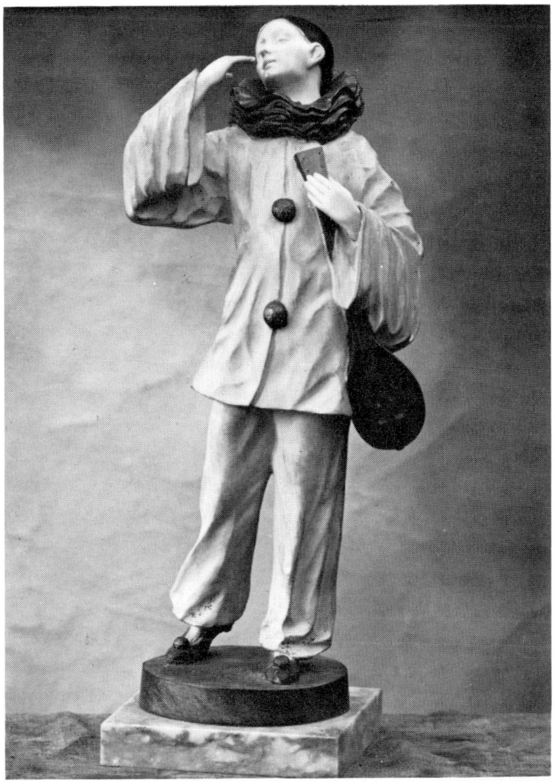

Pierrot, 40cm:15¾in.; 20cm:8in.; 16cm:6¼in.

H. MOLINS

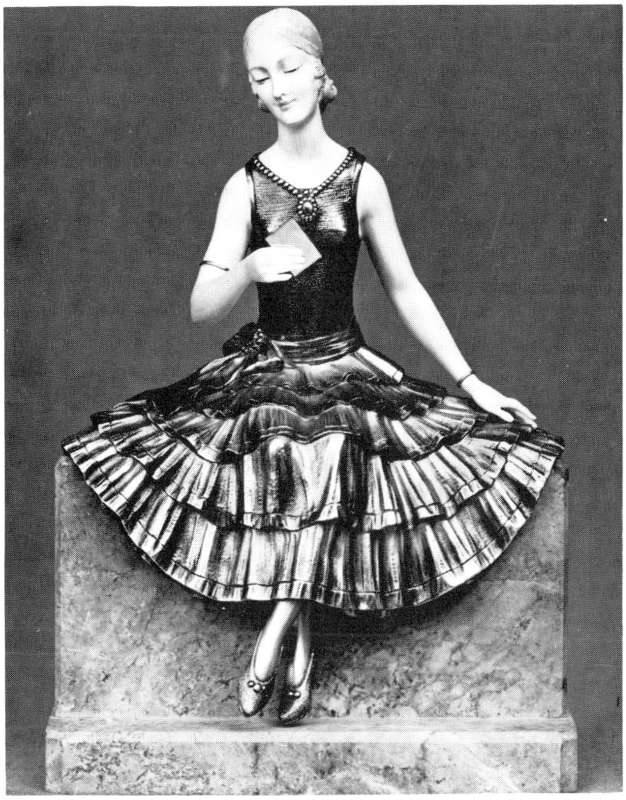

Love Letter, 28cm:11in.

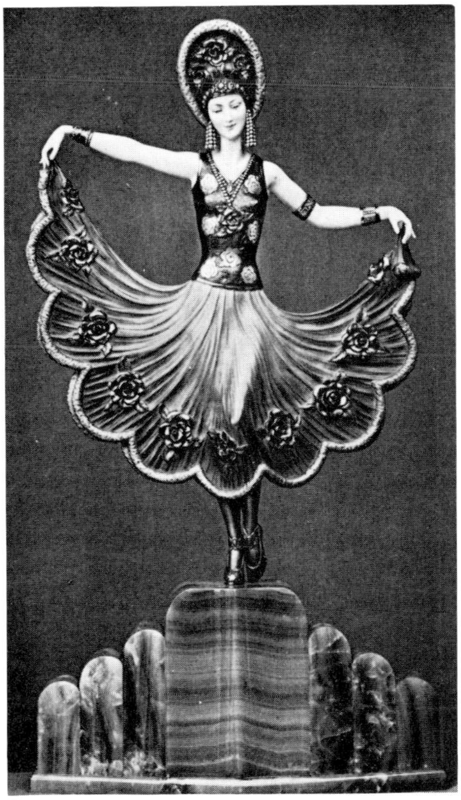

Golden Roses, 67cm:26½in.

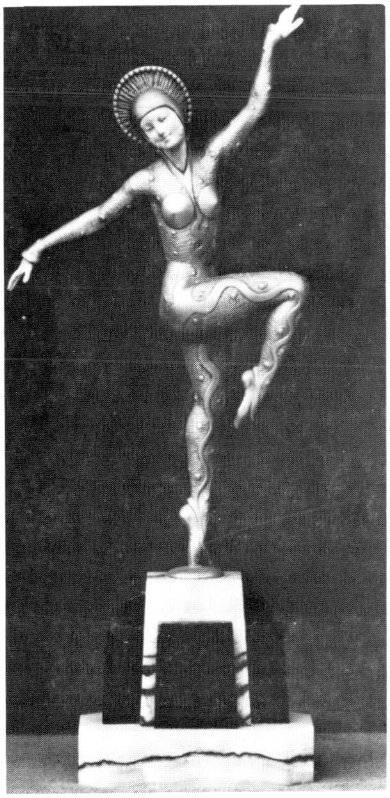

Paris, 40cm:15¾in.

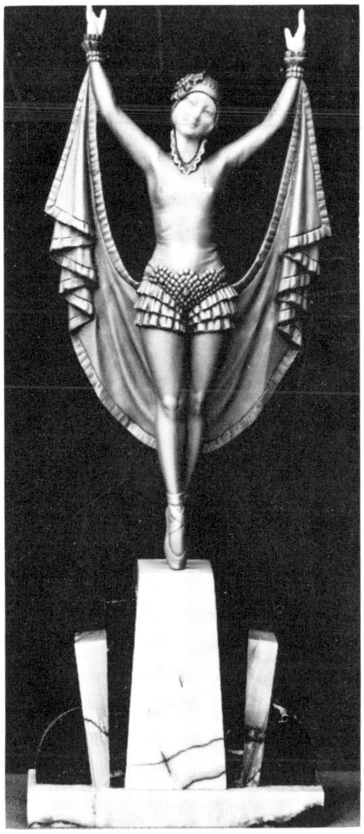

Violet, 41cm:16in.

H. MOLINS

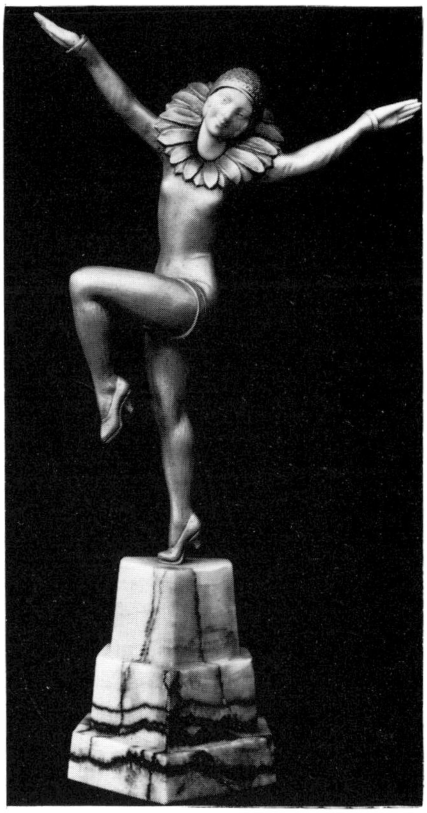

Daisy, 27cm:10½in.

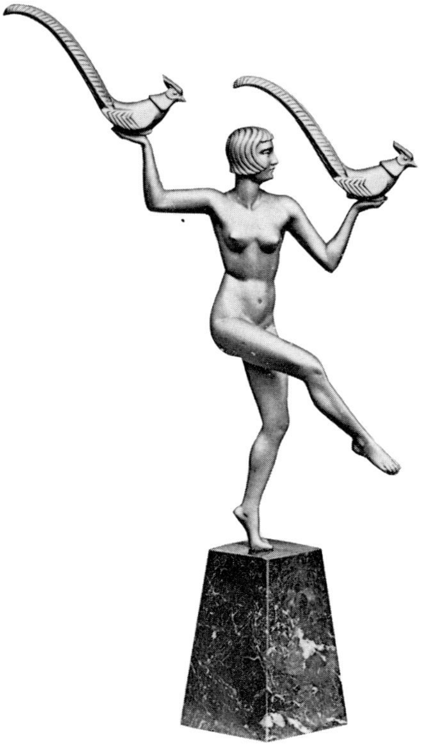

Pheasant dance, 31cm:12in.

H.R. MONCASSIN

Young Bacchant
80cm:31½in.

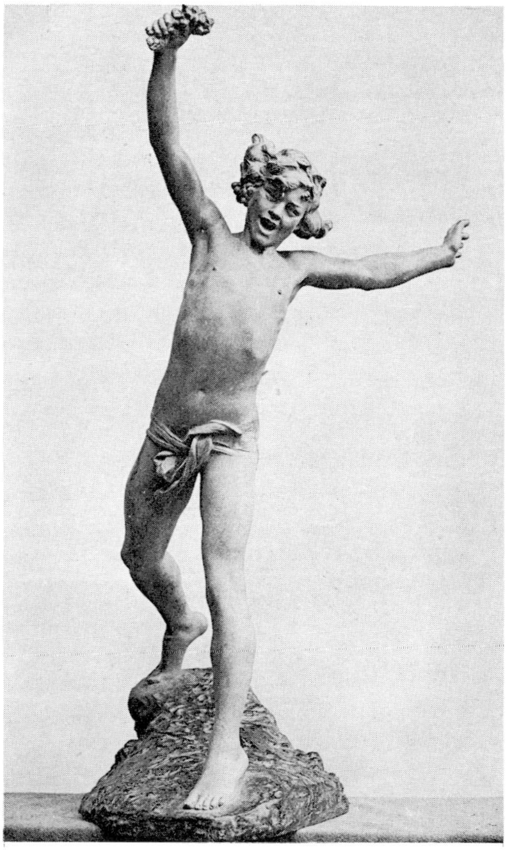

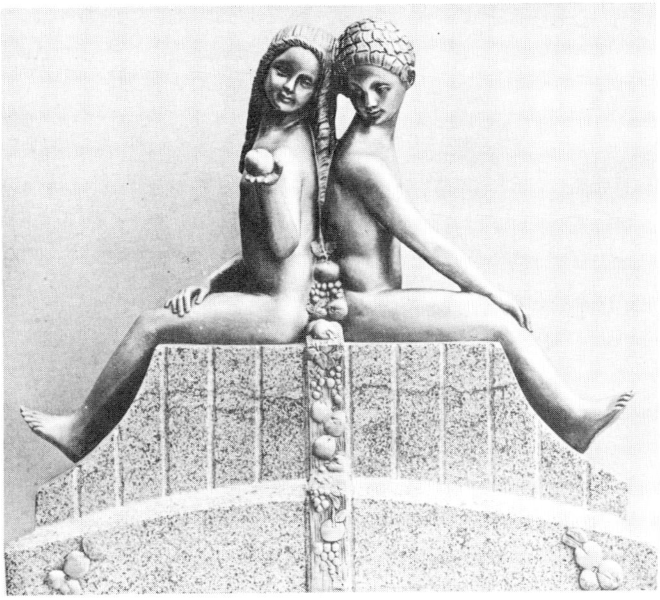

Temptation. 36cm:14¼in.

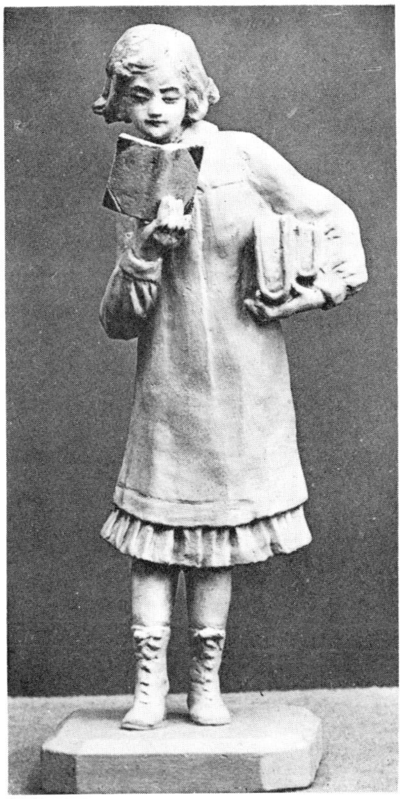

Claudine, 25cm:10in.

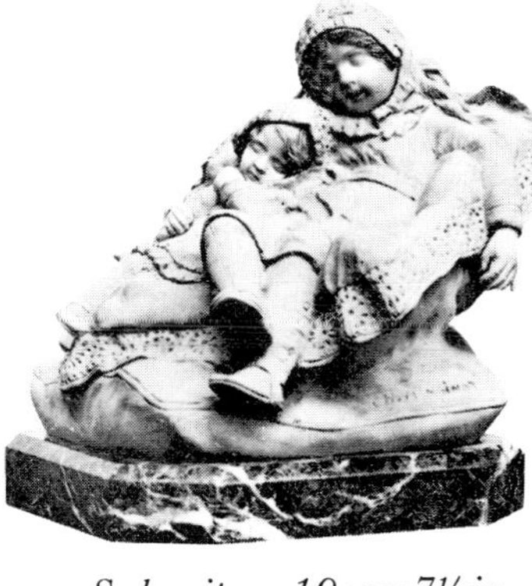

Sybarites, 19cm:7½in.

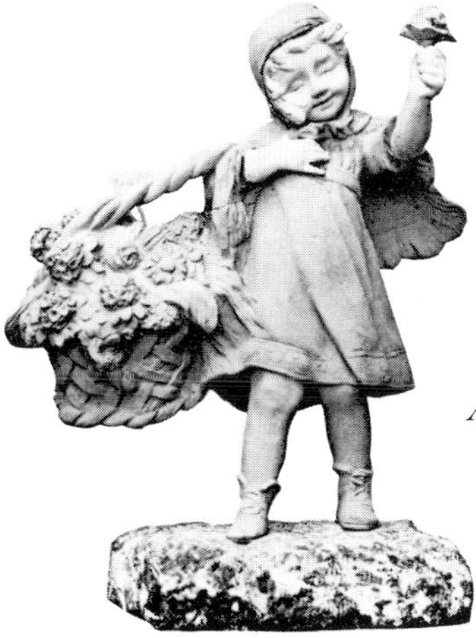

April Flowers 25cm:10in.

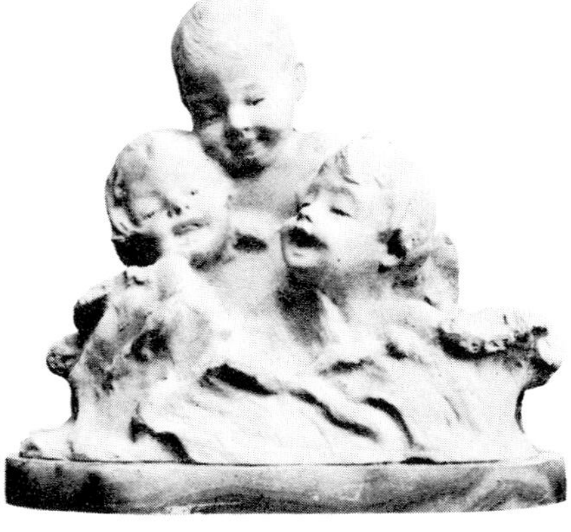

Sea Urchins, 17cm:6½in.

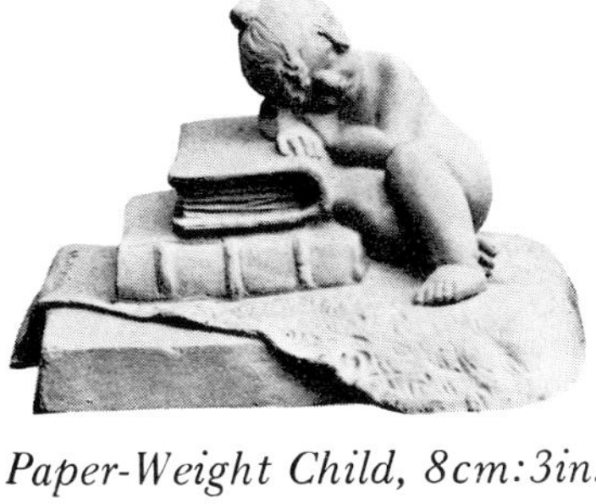

Paper-Weight Child, 8cm:3in.

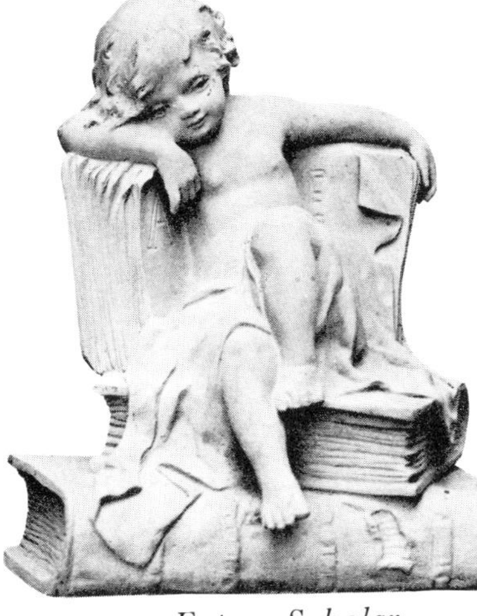

Future Scholar 19cm:7½in.

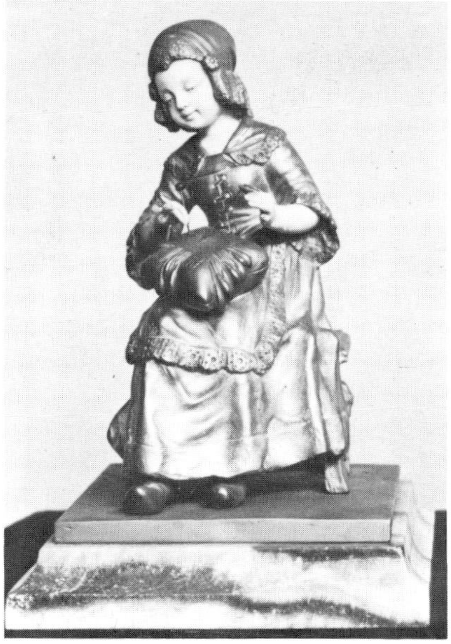

Lace Maker, 21cm:8¼in.

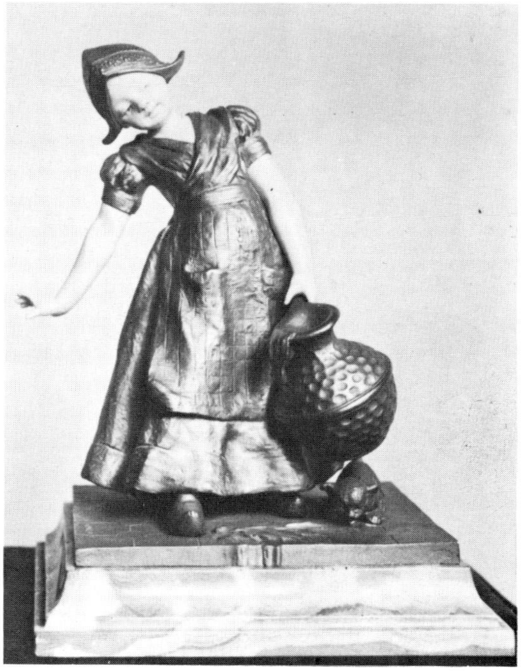

Dutch Milk-Maid, 23cm:9in.

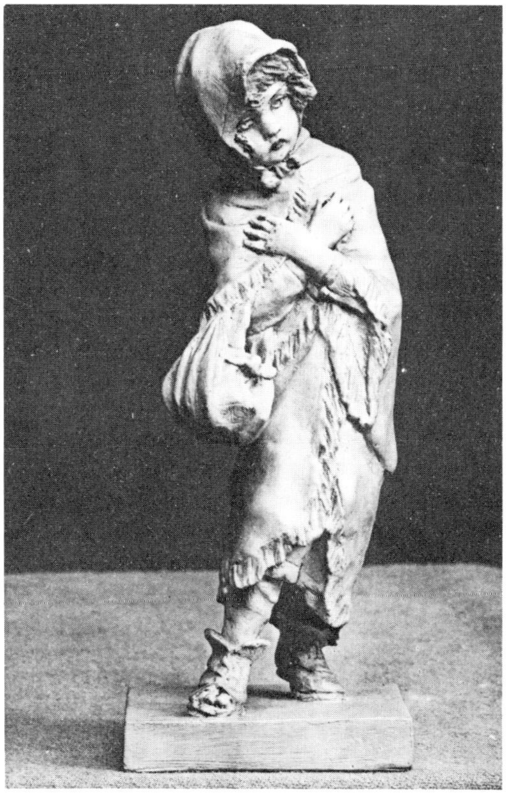

On the Road
25cm: 10in.

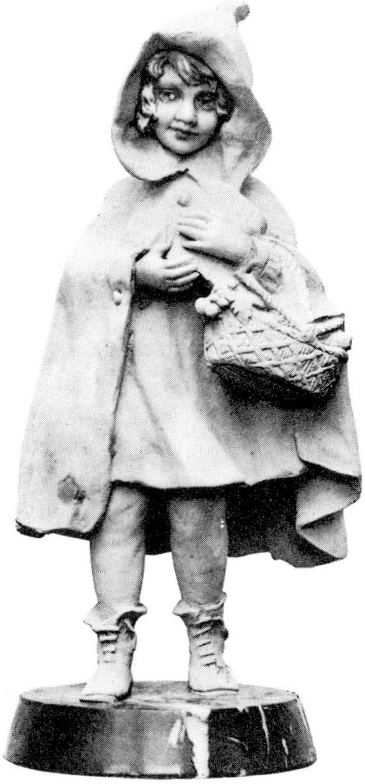

School Girl
25cm:10in.

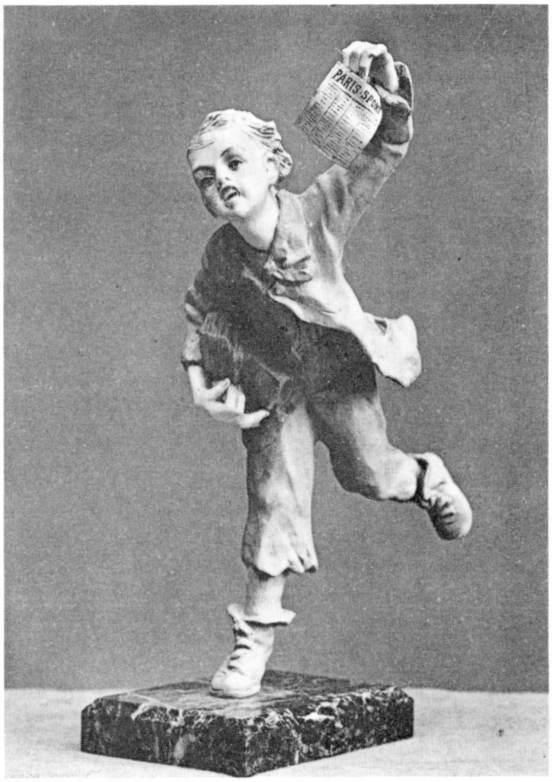

News Boy, 26cm:10¼in.

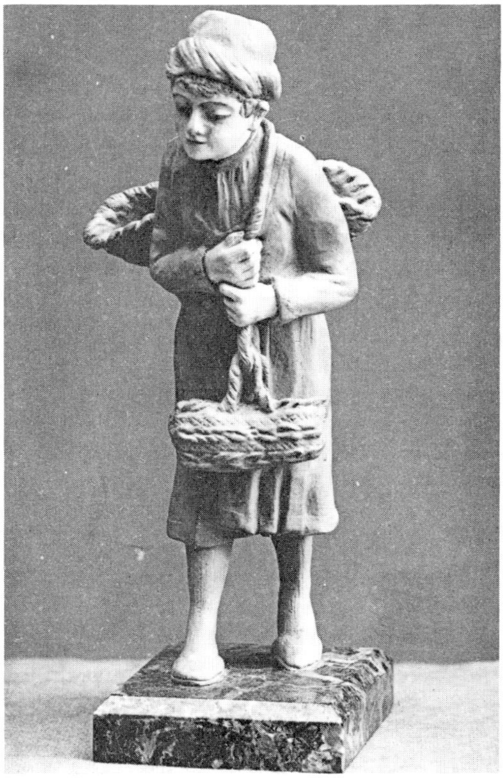

Peanut Seller, 22cm:8¾in.

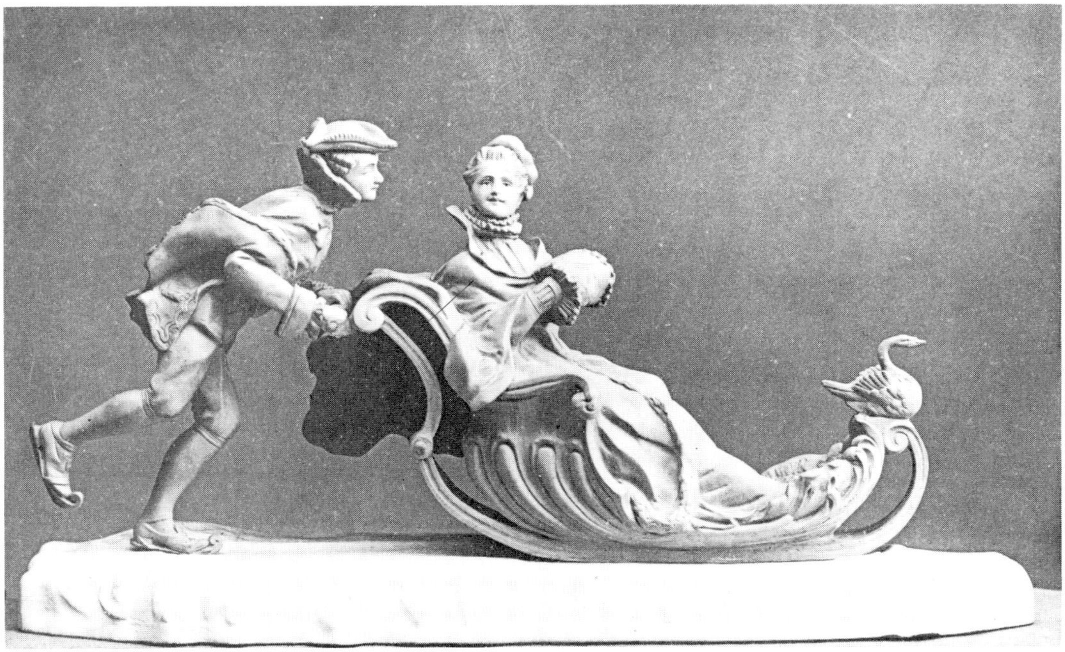

On the Ice, 28cm:11in.

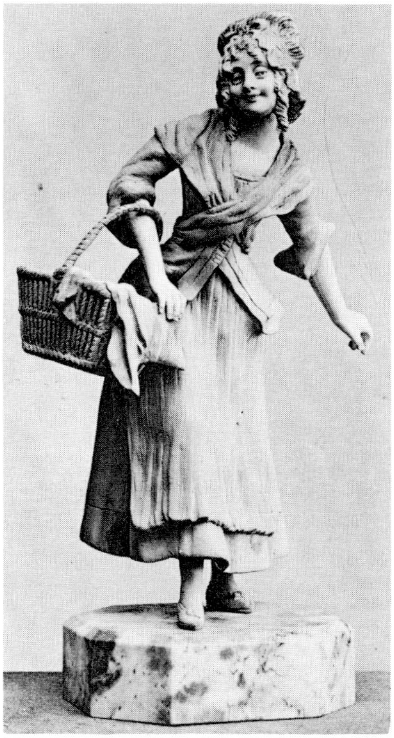

Impudence
38cm:15in.; 23cm:9in.

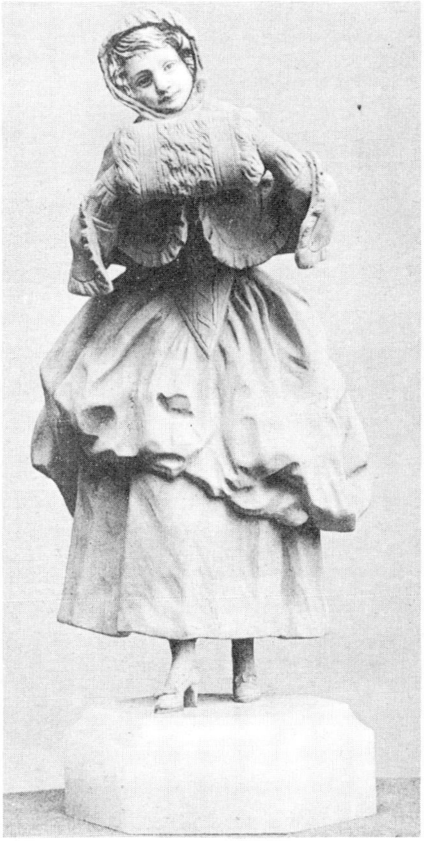

Winter
30cm:11¾in.; 21cm:8¼in.

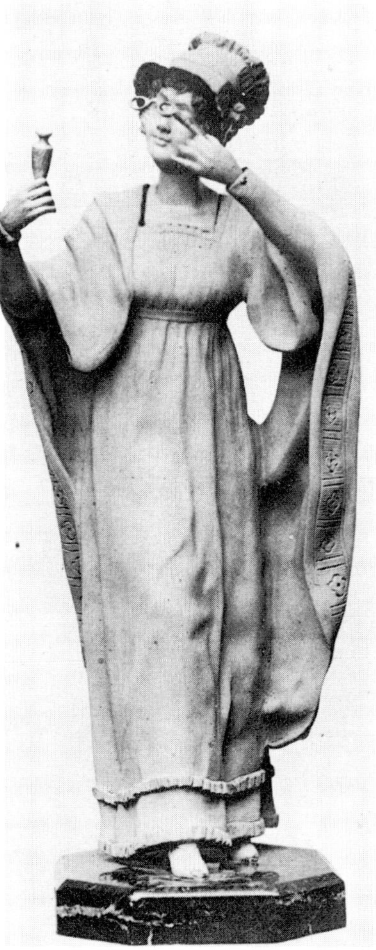

At the Antique Shop
34cm:13½in.

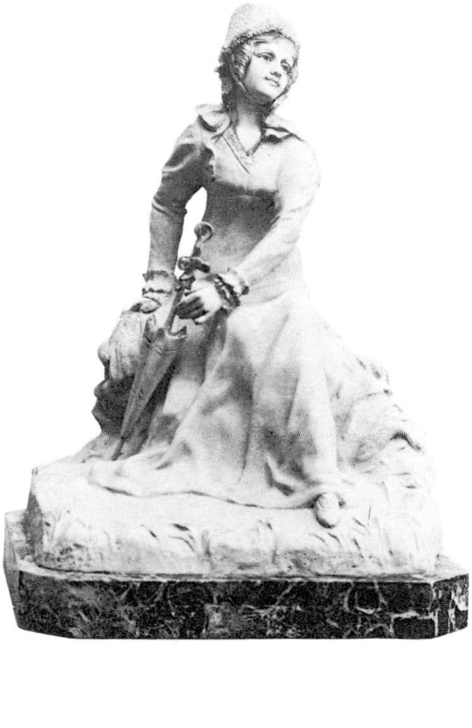

Expectation
23cm:9in.

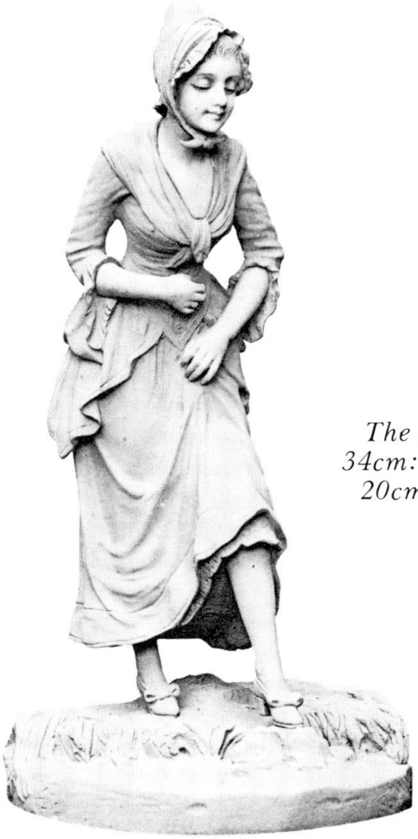

The Ford
34cm:13½in.
20cm:8in.

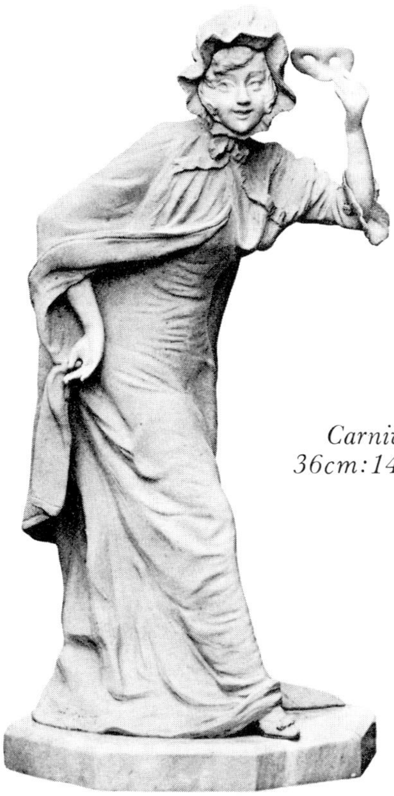

Carnival
36cm:14¼in.

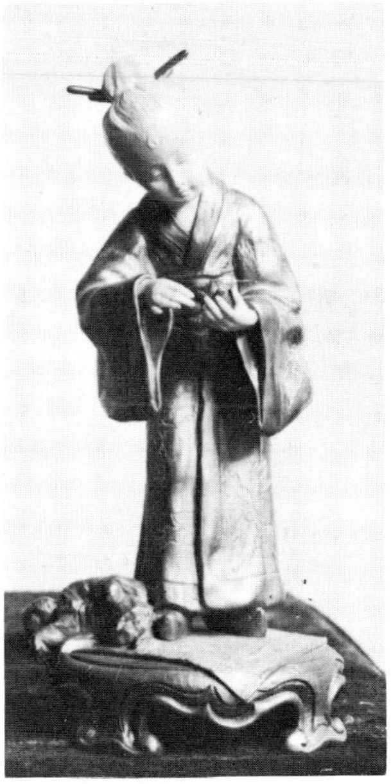

Japanese, 24cm:9½in.

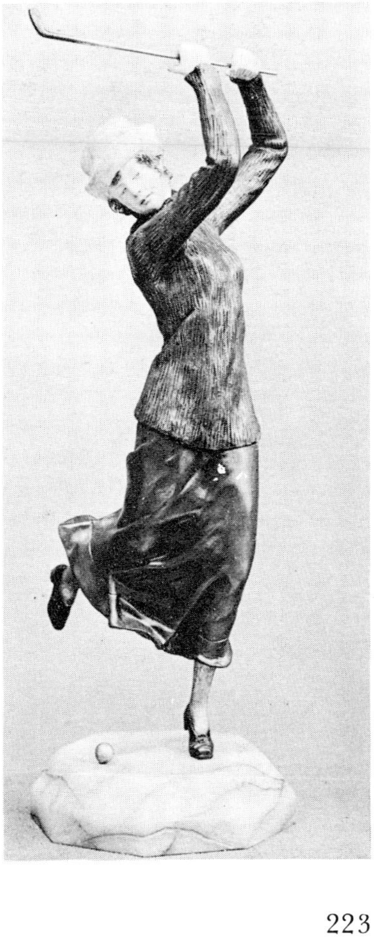

Golfer
45cm:17¾in
25cm:10in.

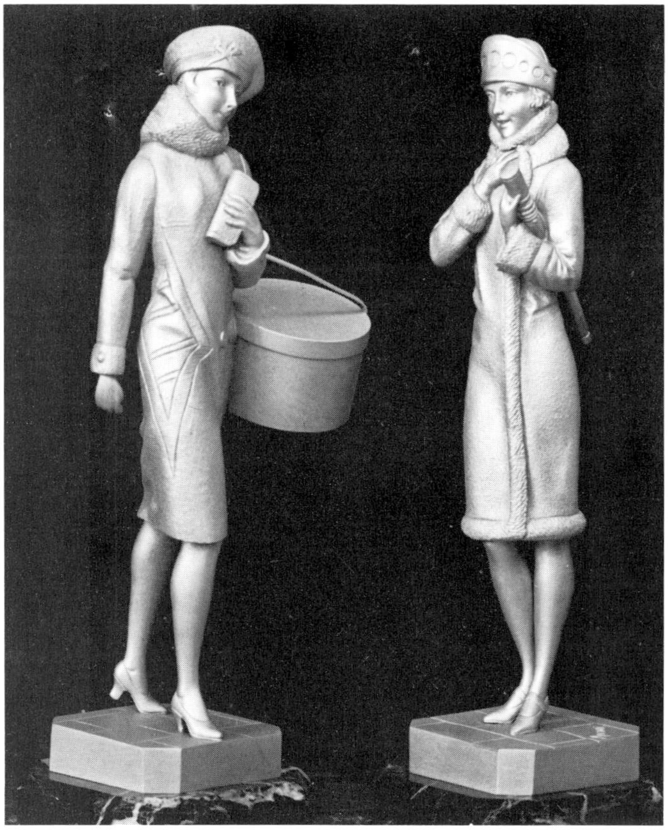

Girl About Town
and
Chilly
(each in two sizes)
26cm:10¼in.
20cm:8in.

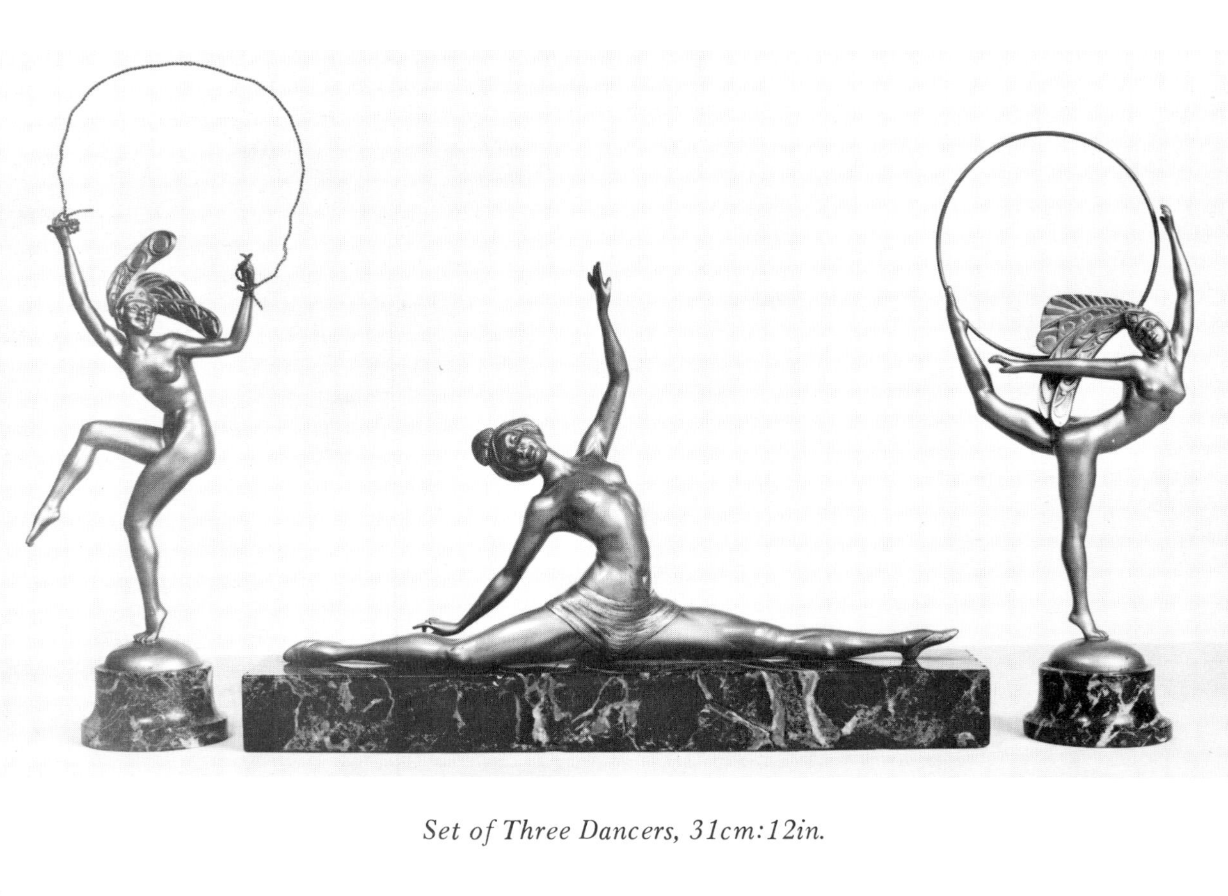

Set of Three Dancers, 31cm:12in.

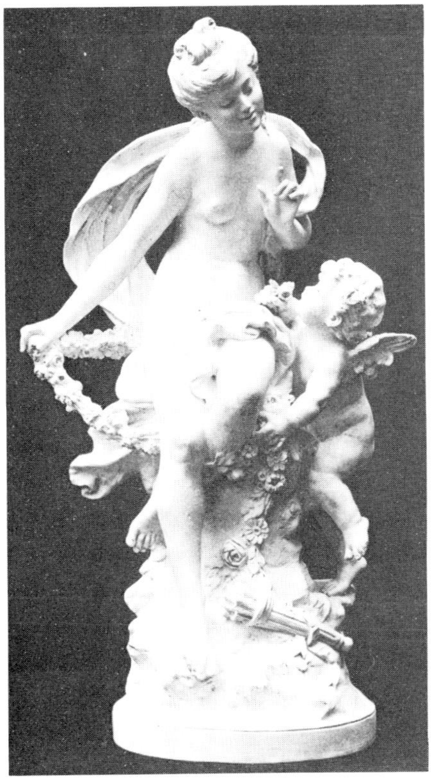

Bond of Love
84cm:33in.
68cm:26¾in.

Big Sister
68cm:26¾in.
57cm:22½in.

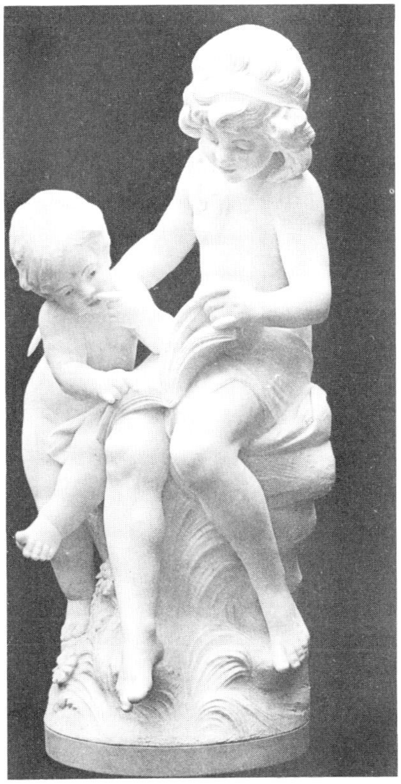

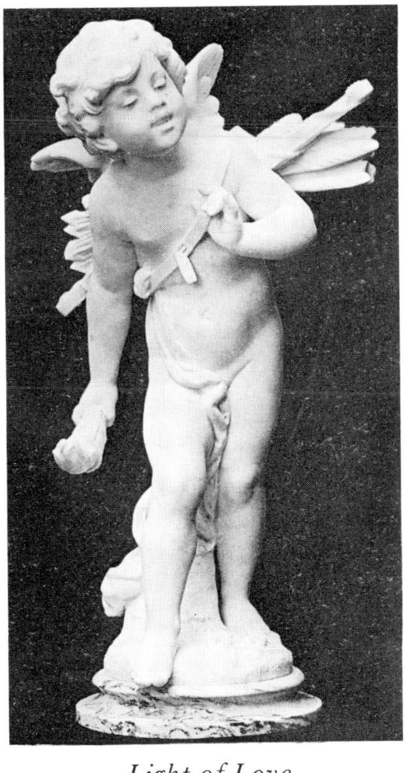

Light of Love
45cm:17¾in.; 25cm:10cm.

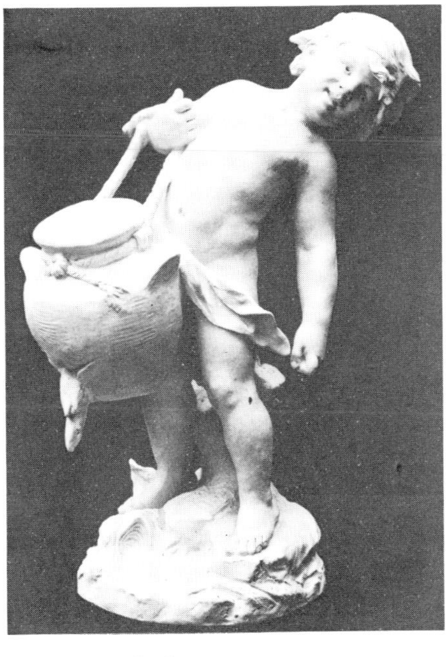

Infant with Pot
60cm:23¾in.
50cm:19¾in.
40cm:15¾in.

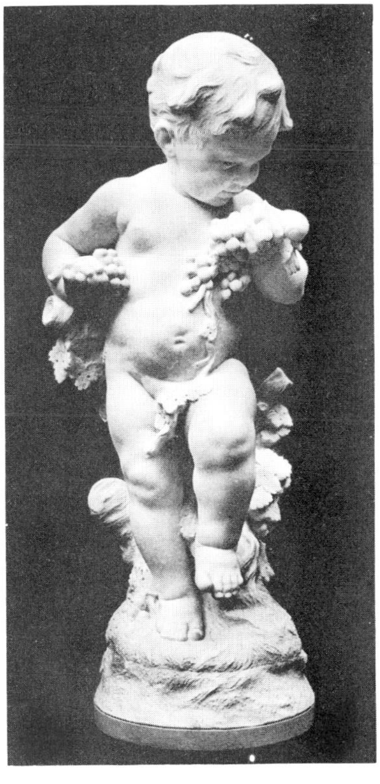

Child in the Vines
60cm:23¾in.; 45cm:17½in.

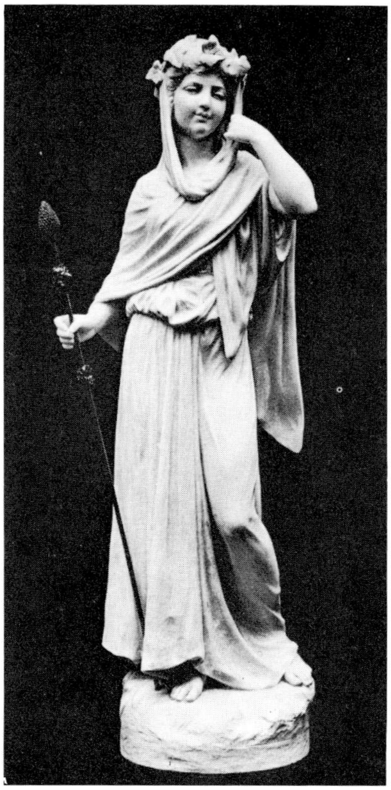

Priestess of Bacchus
75cm: 29½in.
50cm: 19½in.

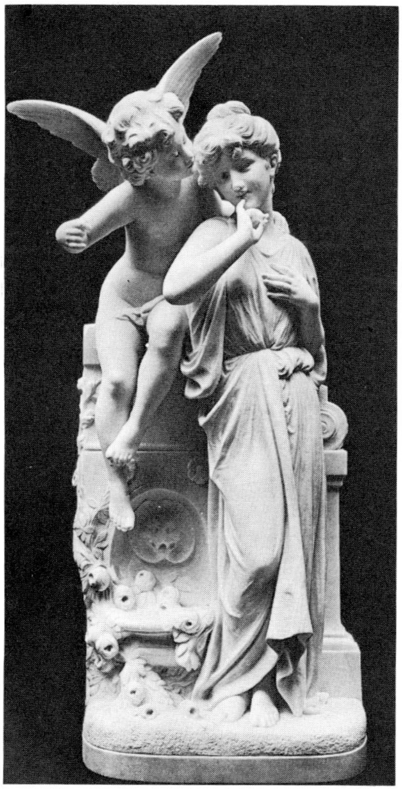

Secret Love
80cm: 31½in.

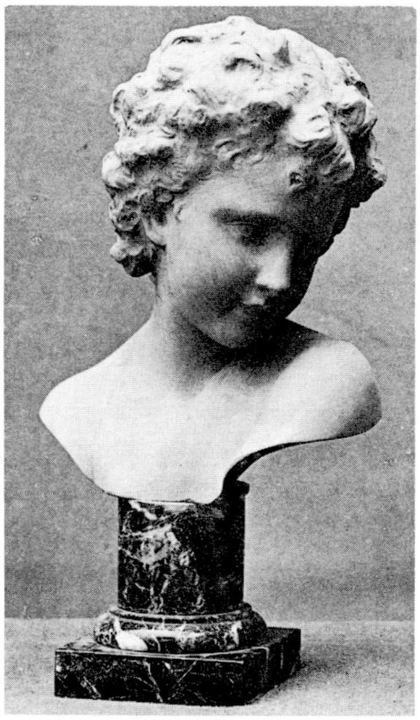

Cupid (bust)
28cm: 11in.
22cm: 8¾in.
15cm: 6in.

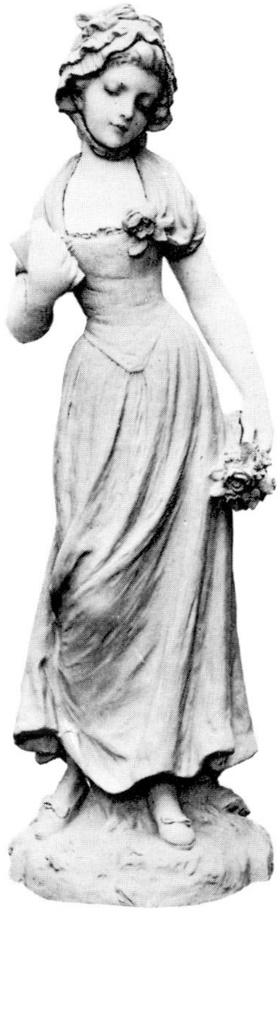

Village Bride
70cm: 27¾in.
38cm: 15in.
24cm: 9½in.

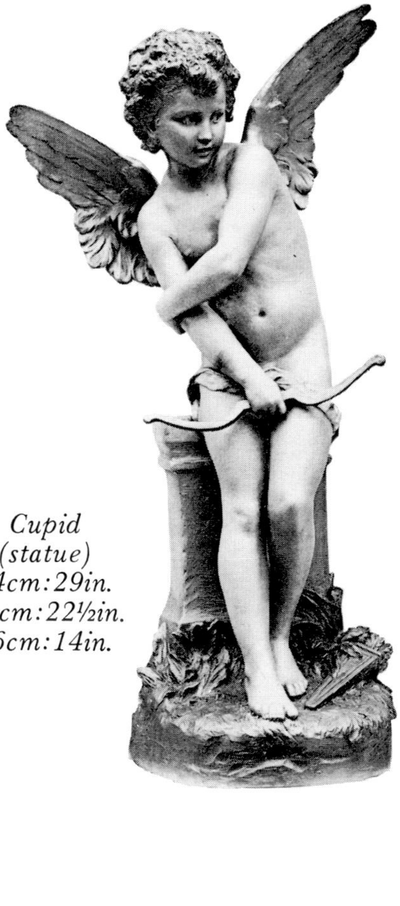

Cupid (statue)
74cm: 29in.
57cm: 22½in.
36cm: 14in.

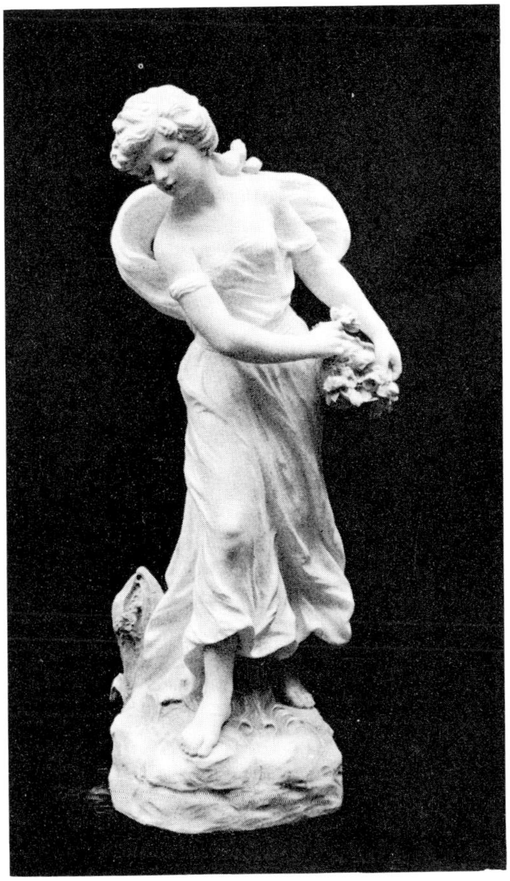

Flower Seller
60cm: 23¾in.

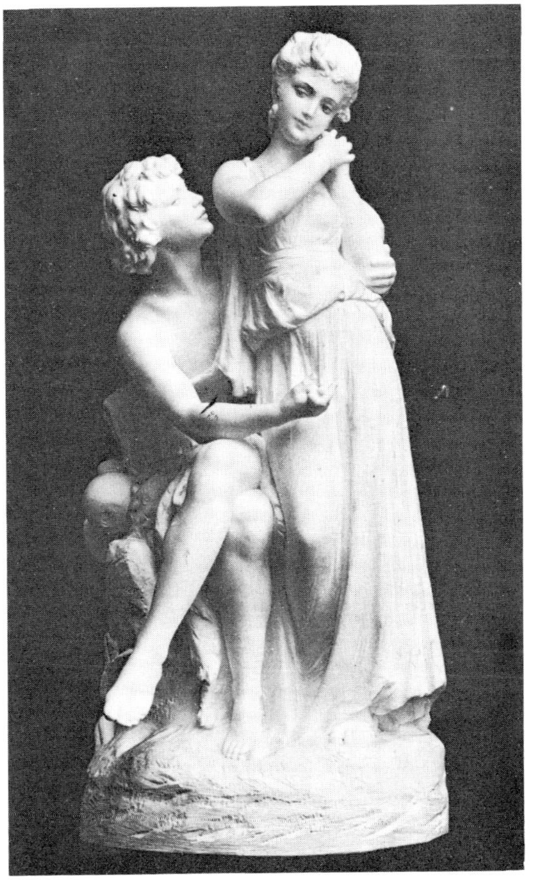

First Love
75cm: 29½in.

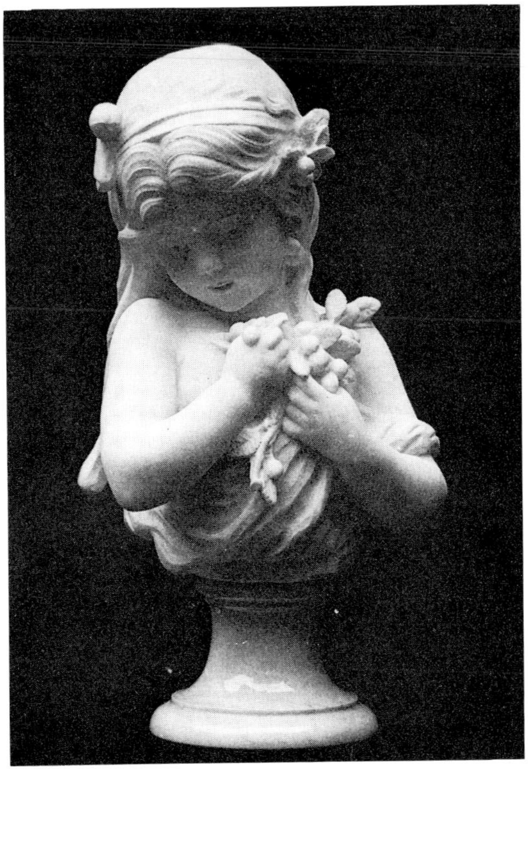

First Cherries
50cm: 19¾in.
40cm: 15¾in.

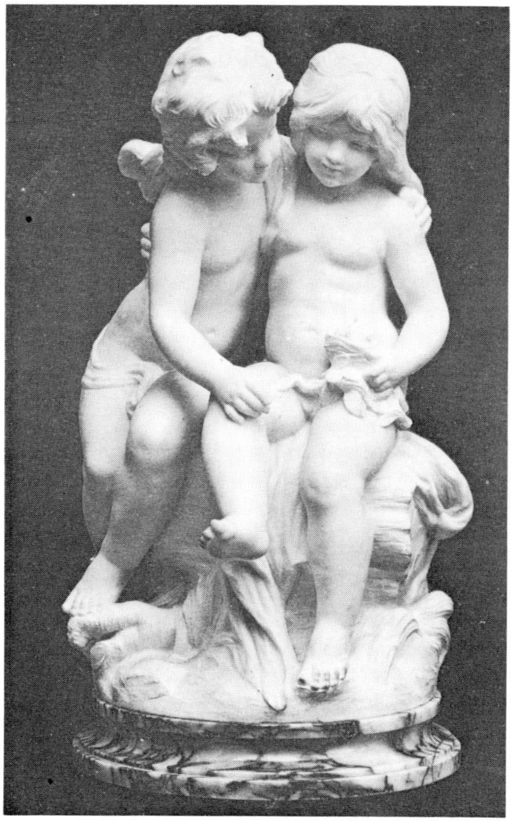

The Nest
65cm:25¾in.
50cm:19¾in.

Little Wanderer
63cm:24¾in.
50cm:19¾in.
42cm:16½in.

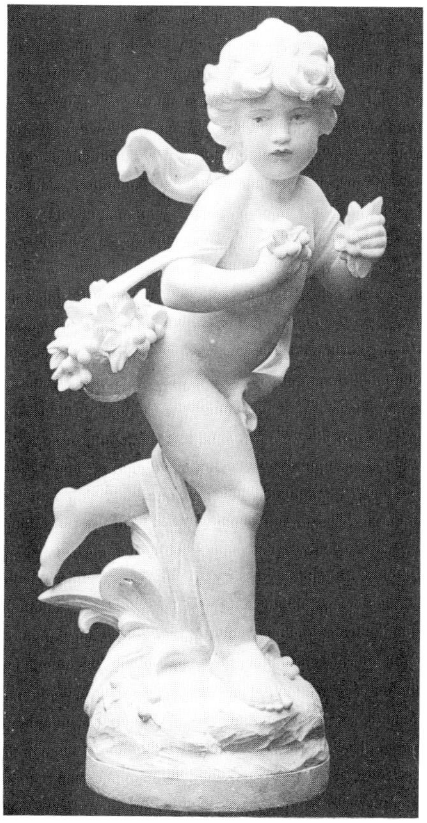

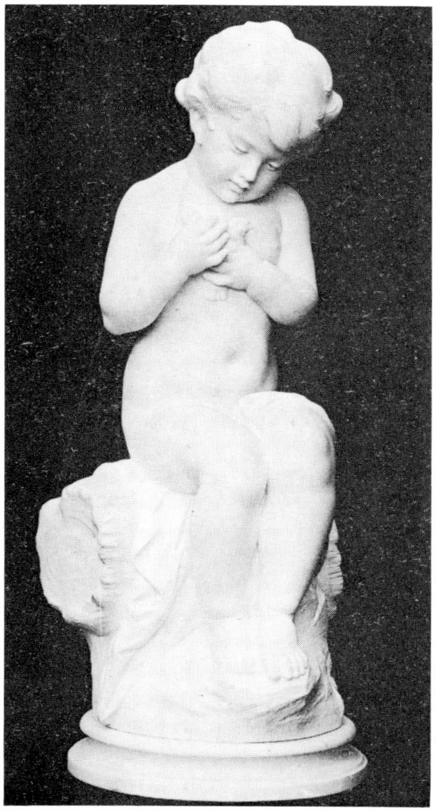

Wounded Bird
59cm:23¼in.
45cm:17¾in.

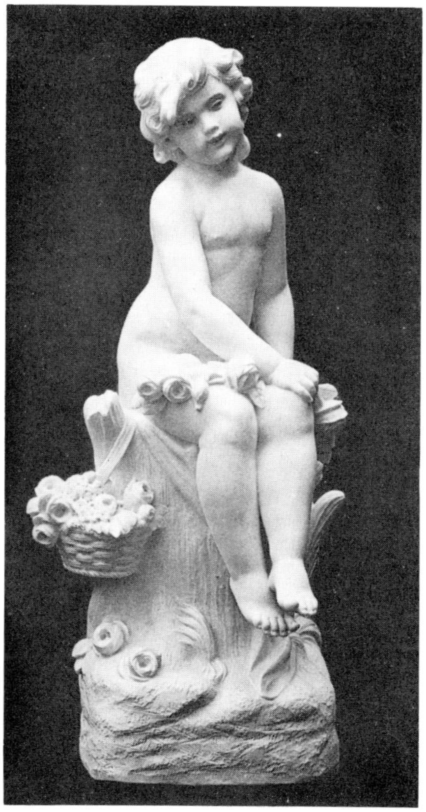

Covetous
60cm:23¾in.
45cm:17¾in.

L.F. MOREAU

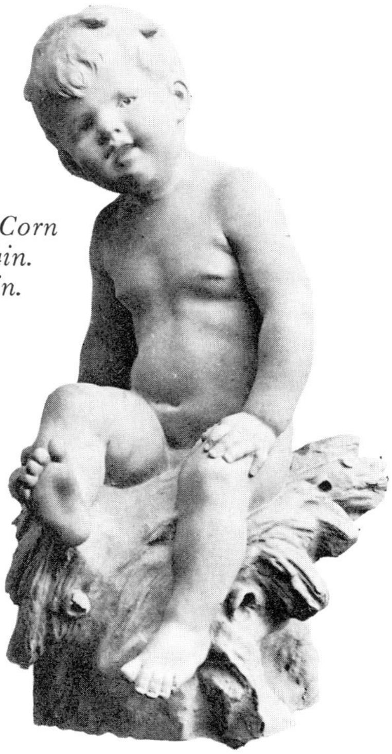

Child in the Corn
44cm:17¼in.
16cm:6¼in.

G.D. MORICE

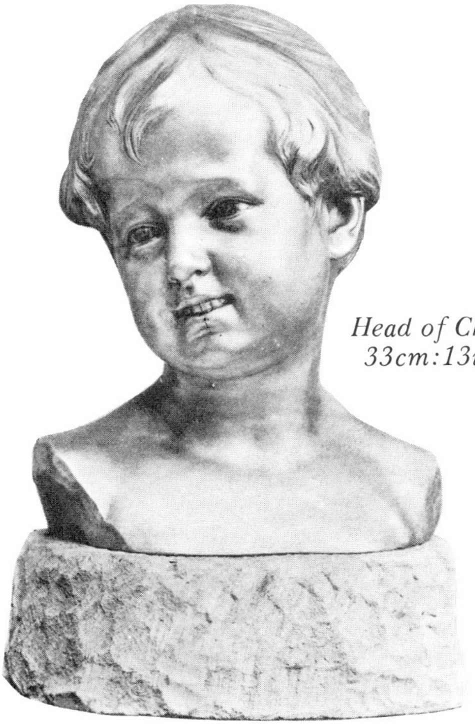

Head of Child
33cm:13in.

MATH. MOREAU

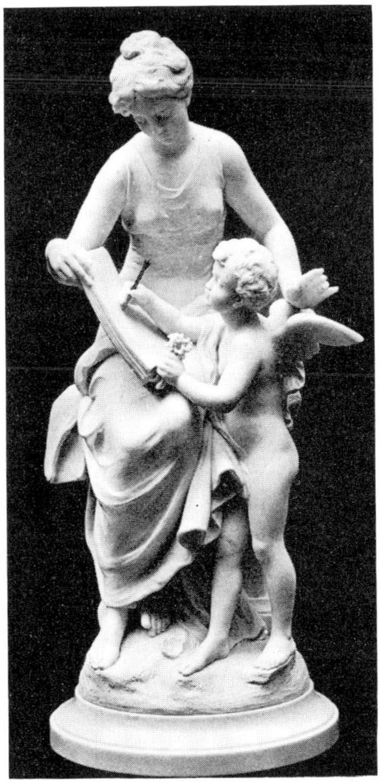

Visit of Love
70cm:27½in.
55cm:21½in.

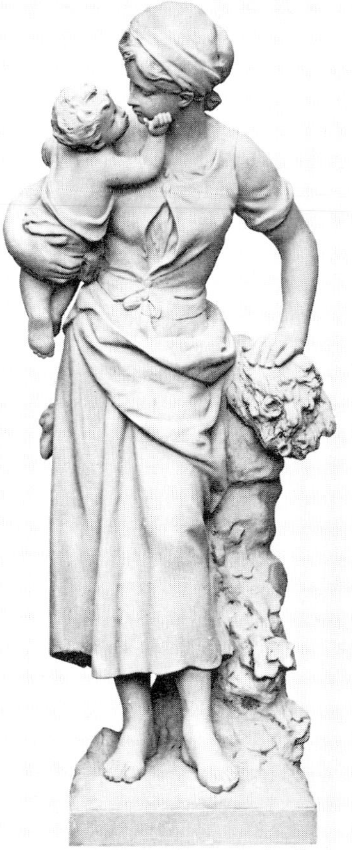

Evening
72cm:28½in.; 48cm:19in.

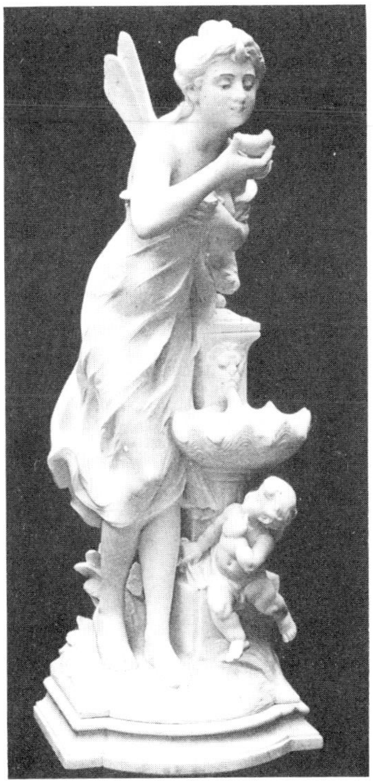

The Spring
73cm:28¾in.
60cm:23¾in.

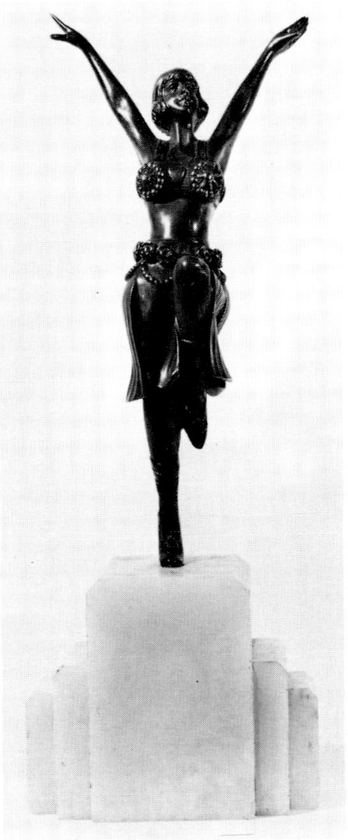

Dancer
37cm: 14½in.

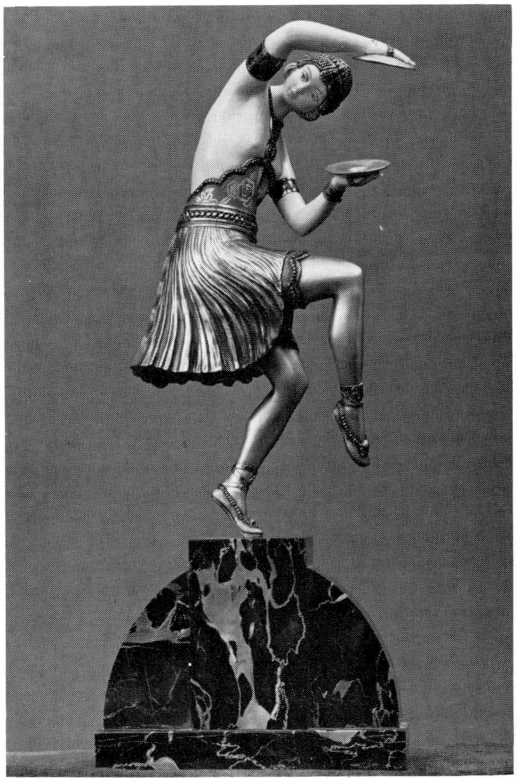

Dance of the Cymbals, 48cm: 19in.

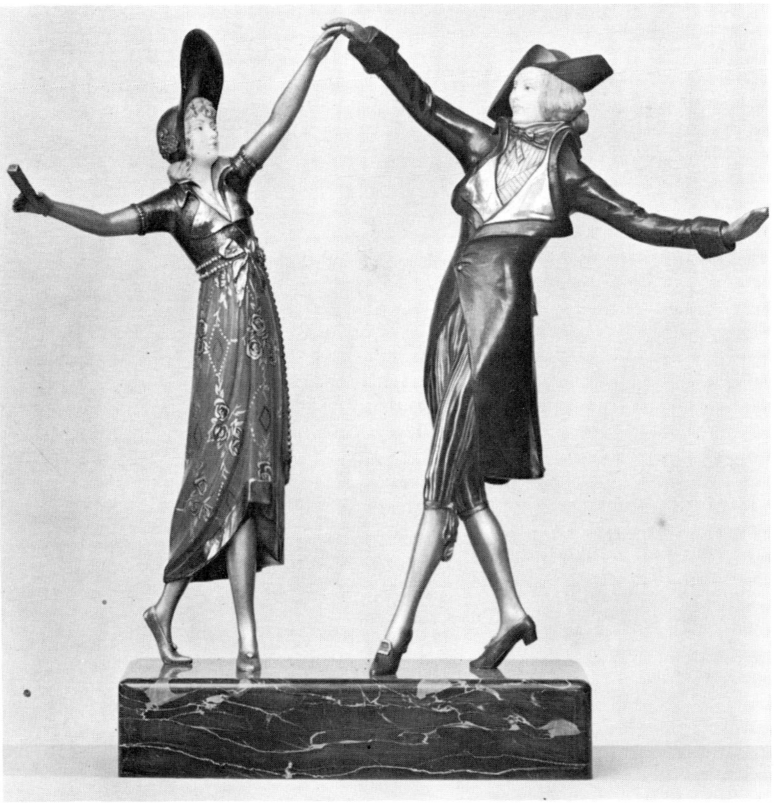

La Pavane
45cm: 17¾in.

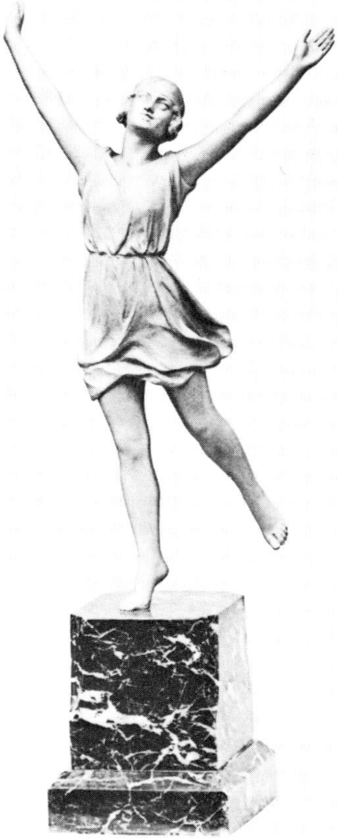

Rhythmic Dance
42cm:16½in.

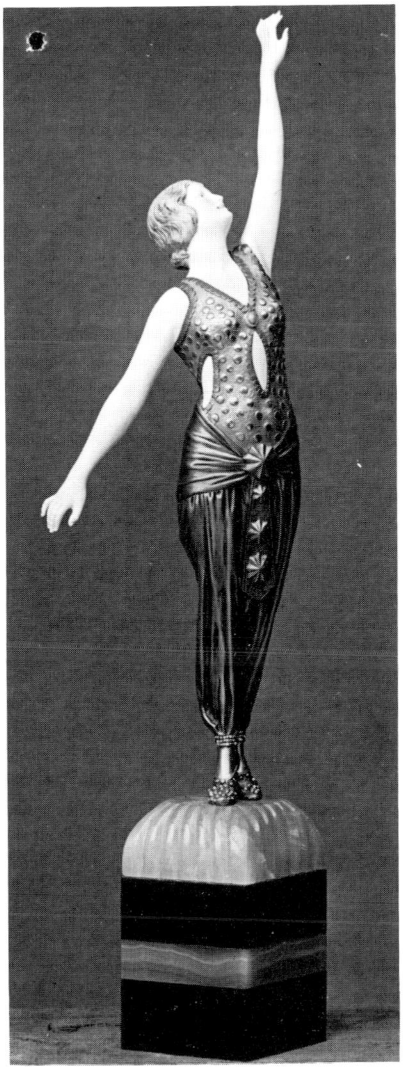

Oriental Dance
50cm:19¾in.

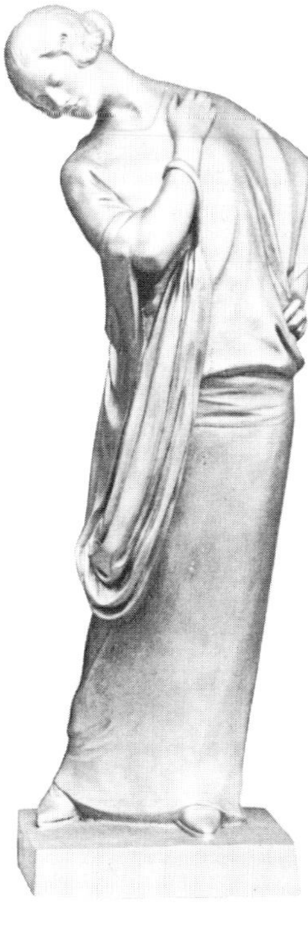

The Glance
34cm:13¼in.

NAMGREB

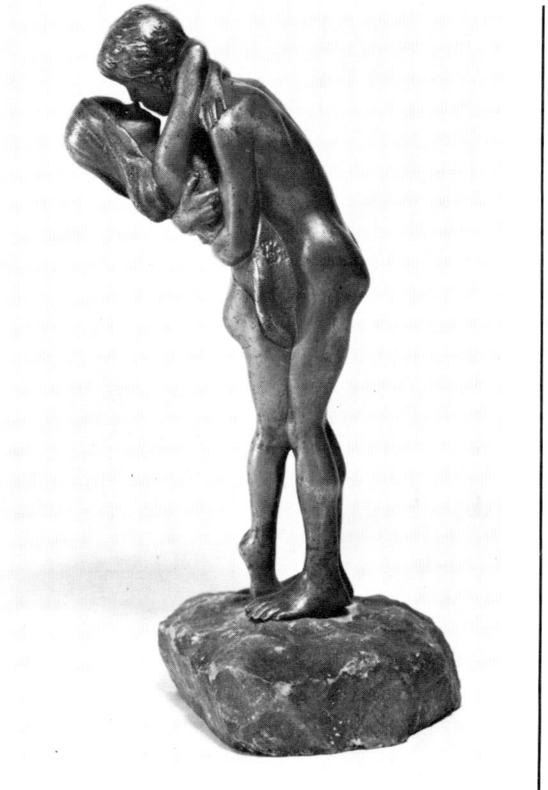

Couple Kissing, 15cm:6in.

R. NANNINI

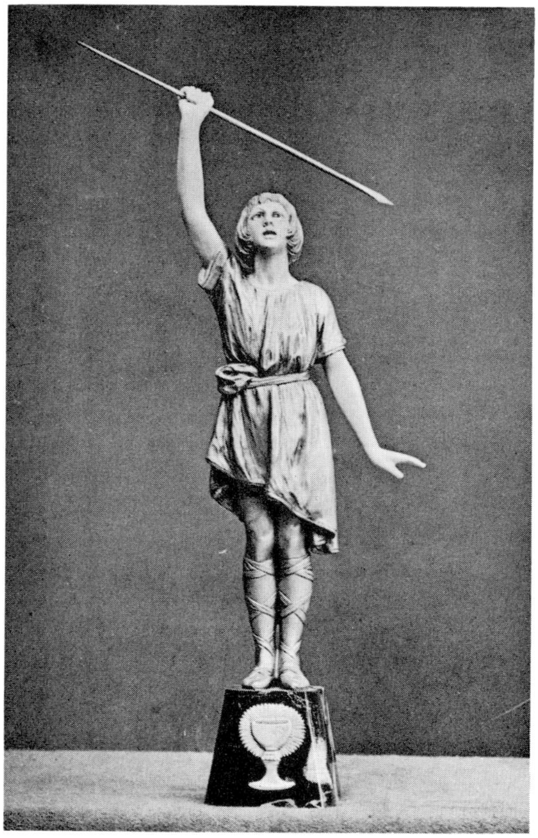

Parsifal
43cm:17in.

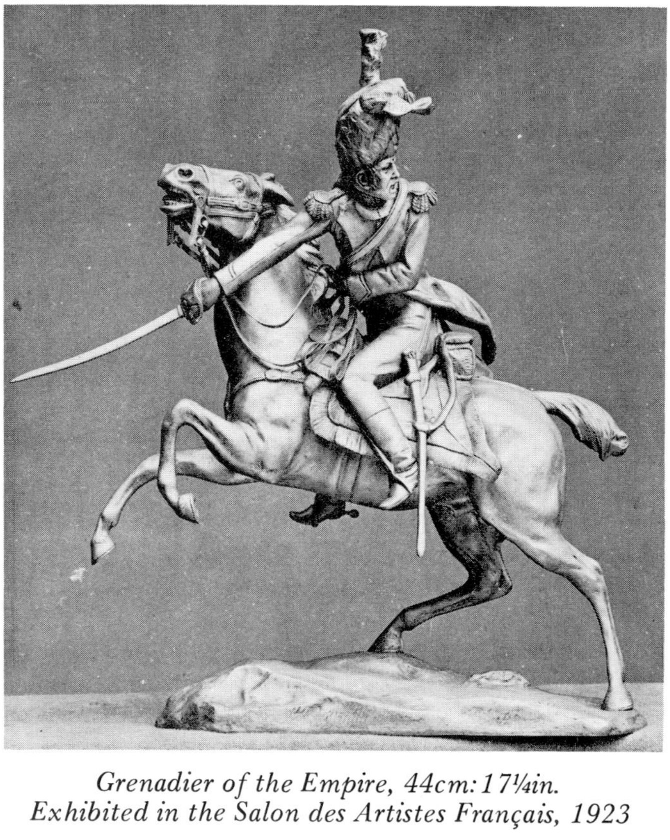

Grenadier of the Empire, 44cm:17¼in.
Exhibited in the Salon des Artistes Français, 1923

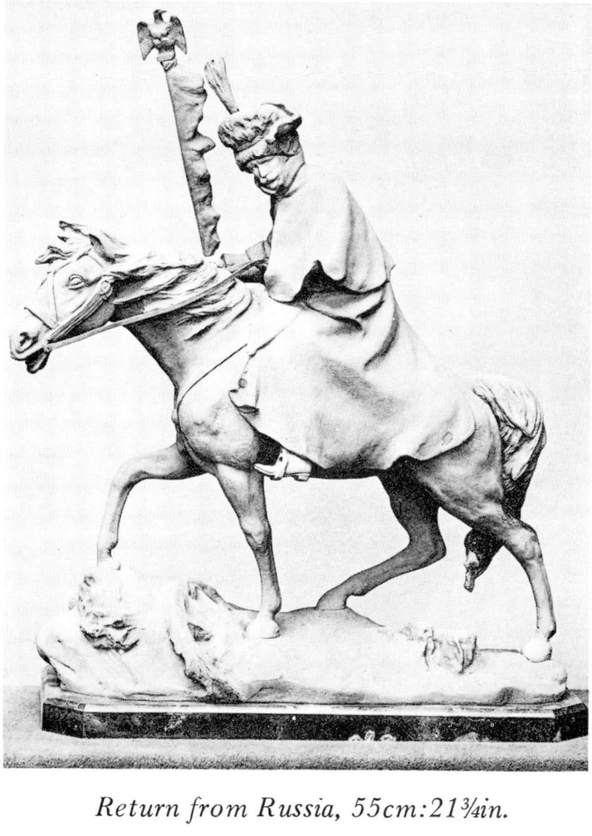

Return from Russia, 55cm:21¾in.

R. NANNINI

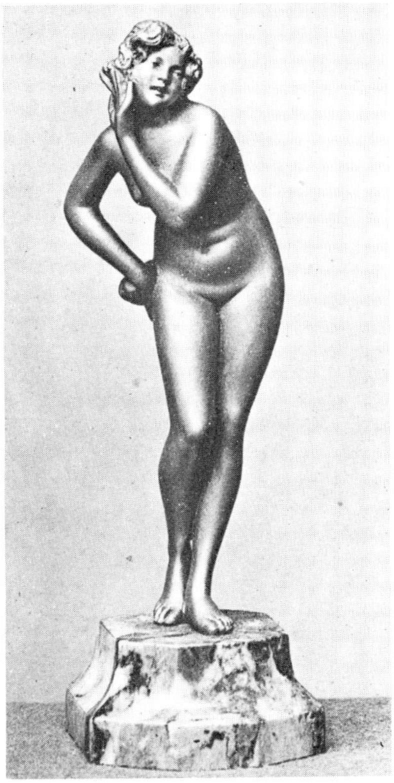

Eve
30cm: 11¾in.; 21cm: 8¼in.

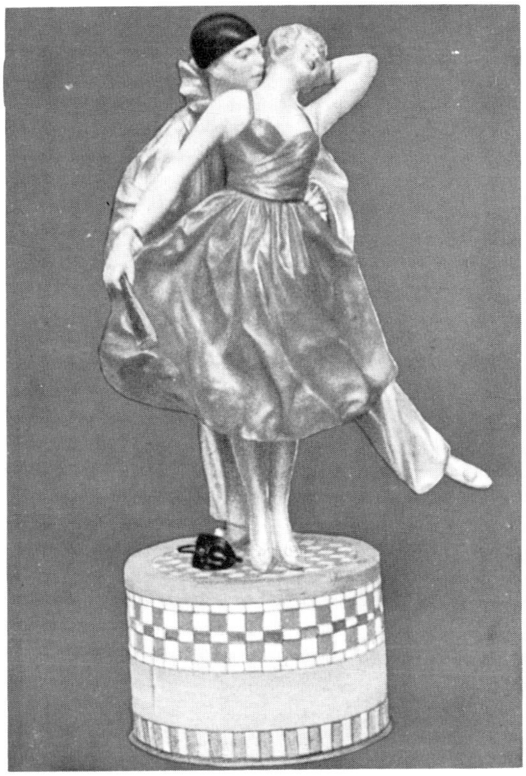

The Vanquished Pierrot
45cm: 17¾in.

TONY NOEL

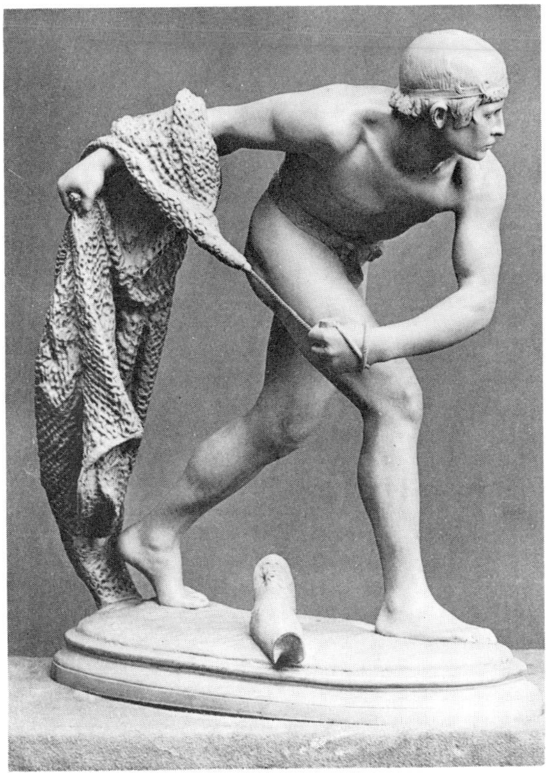

Retiarian
57cm: 22½in.
25cm: 10in.

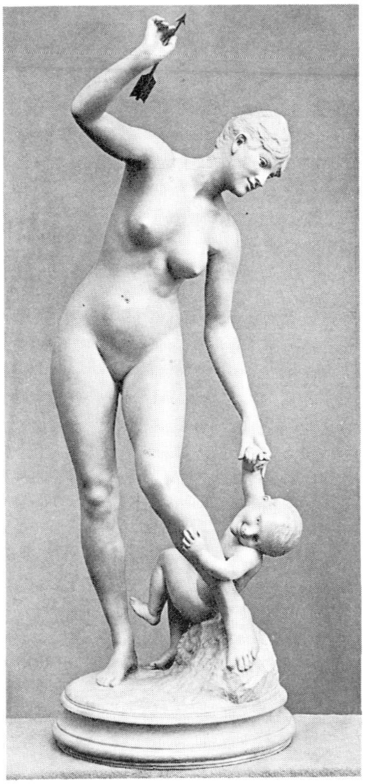

Battle with Cupid
75cm: 29½in.
42cm: 16½in.

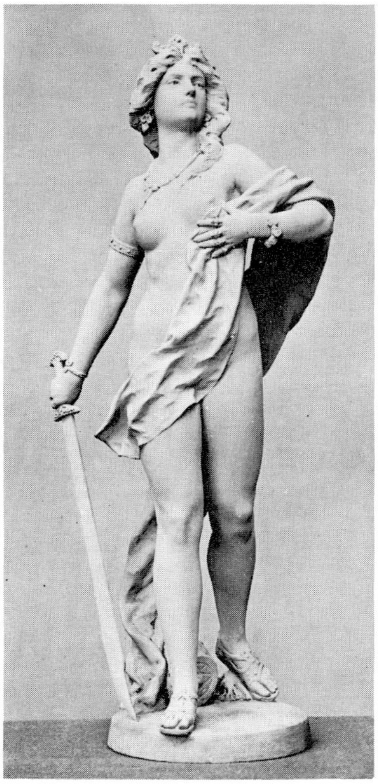

Judith
65cm:25½in.; 31cm:12¼in.

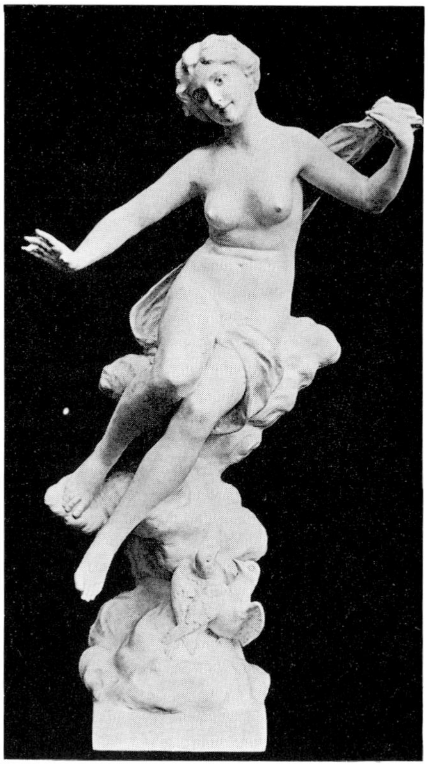

Venus
70cm:27½in.

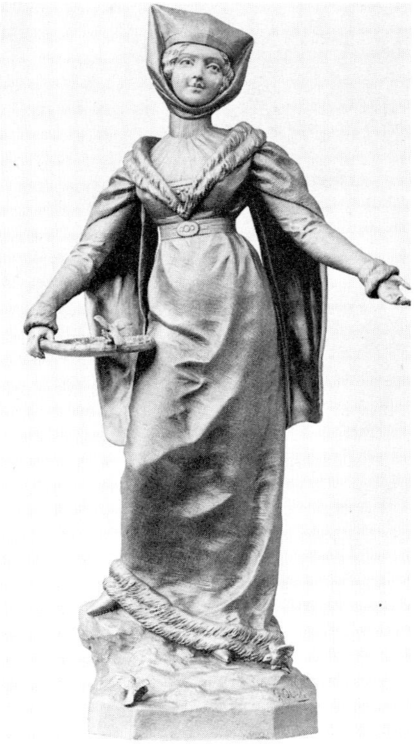

Bird Charmer
44cm:17¼in.

The Beautiful Hat
36cm:14in.

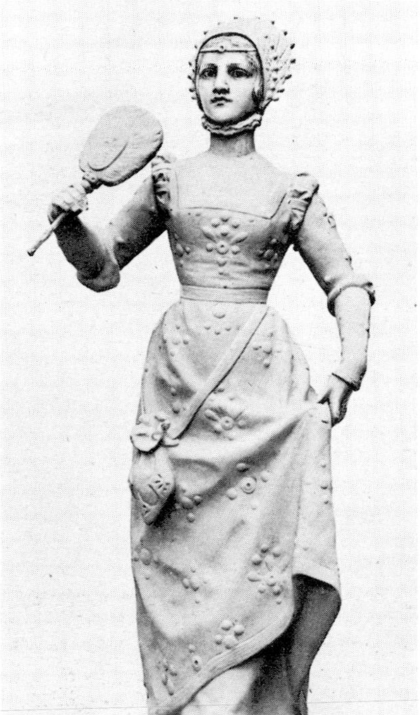

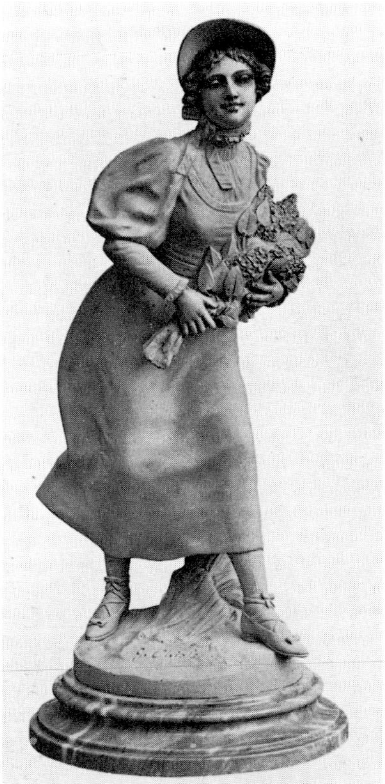

Sweetheart
33cm:13in.

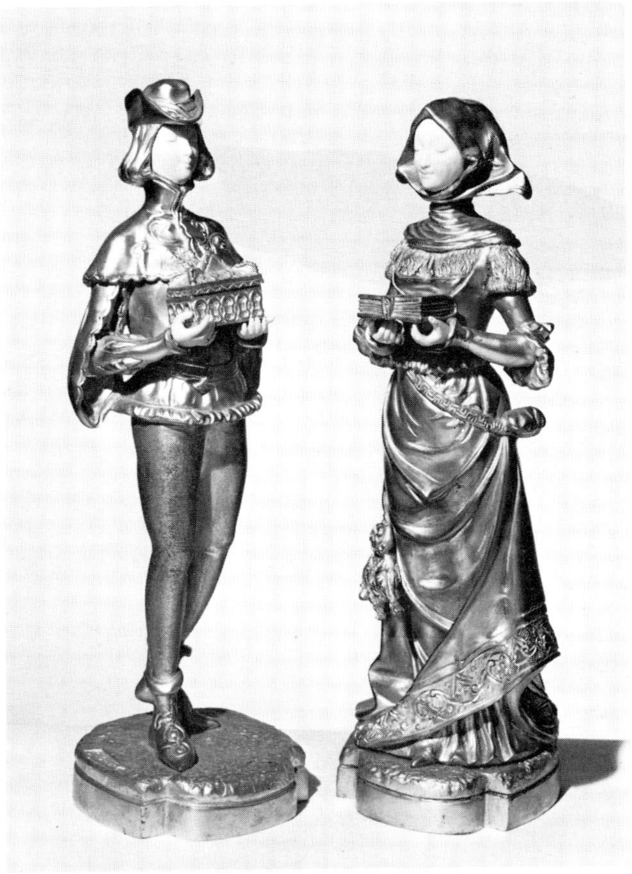

Pair of Figures
37cm: 14¼in.; 33cm: 13in.

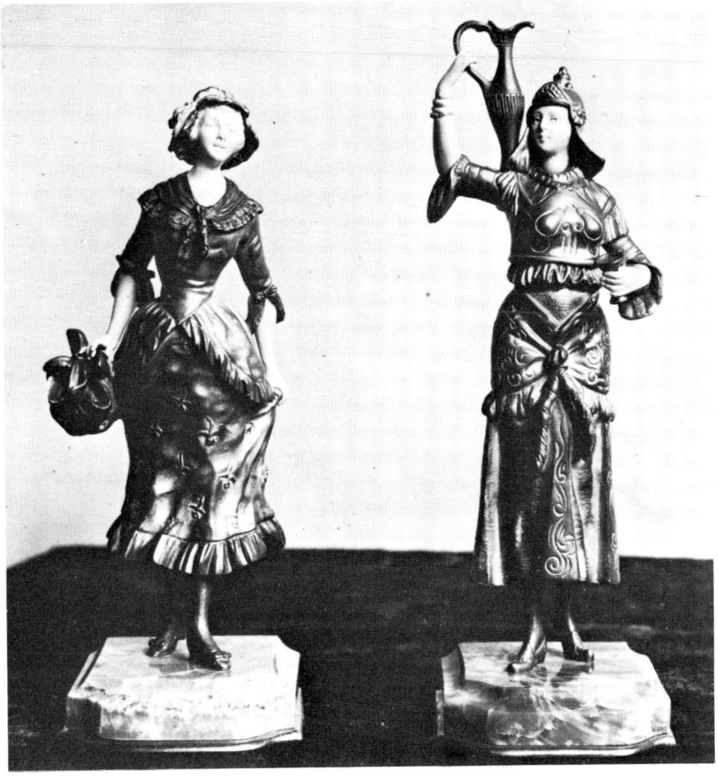

Right: Manon
25cm: 10in.

Far right: Water-Carrier
27cm: 10½in.

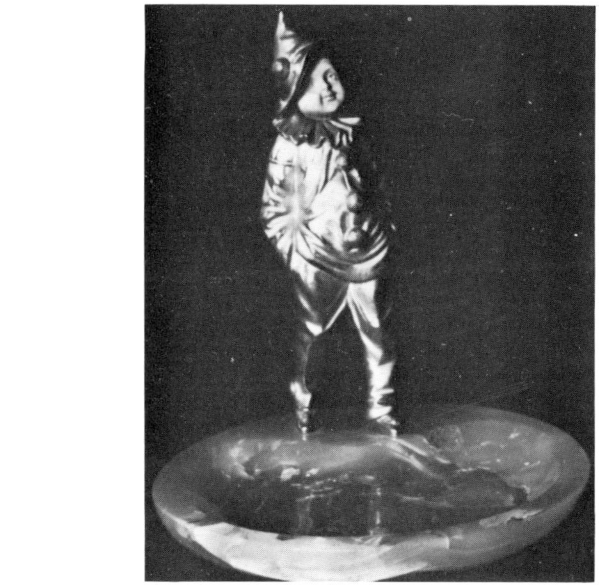

Clown, 17cm:6½in.

Three ashtrays

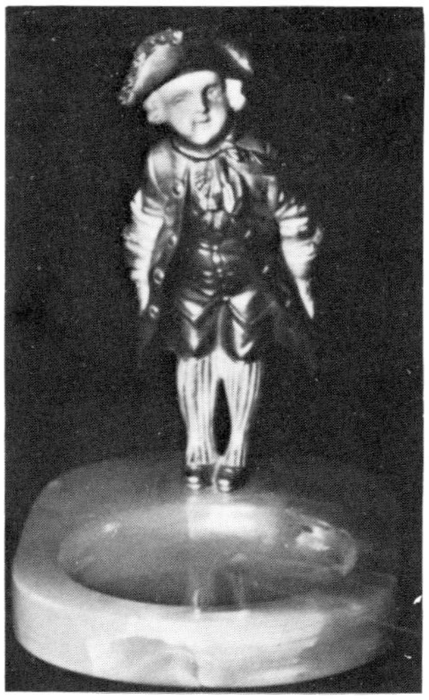

Little Marquis, 15cm:6in.

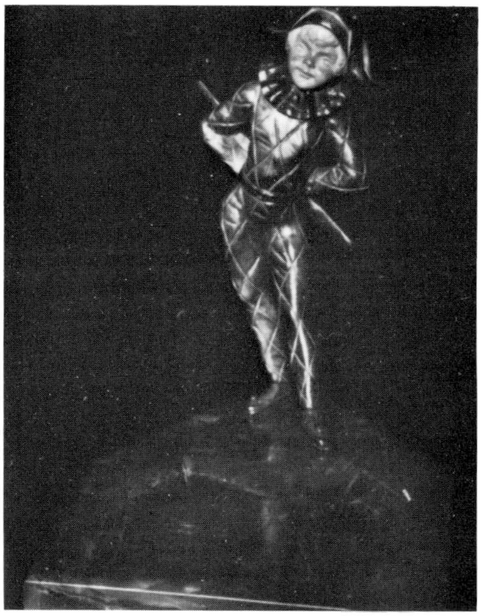

Harlequin, 21cm:8¼in.

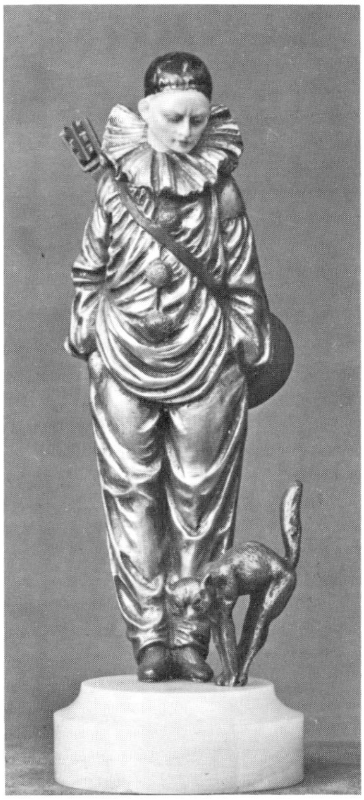

Clown and Cat
24cm:9½in.

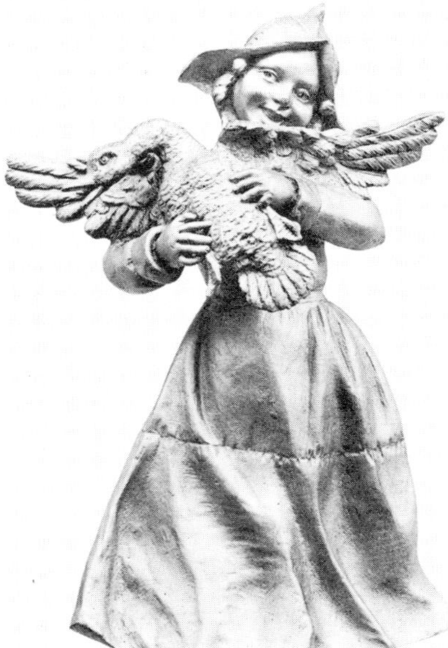

Dutch Farmer
25cm:10in.; 16cm:6¼in.

Right: Columbine and Harlequin by Prof. Otto Poertzel. 35cm:13¾in.

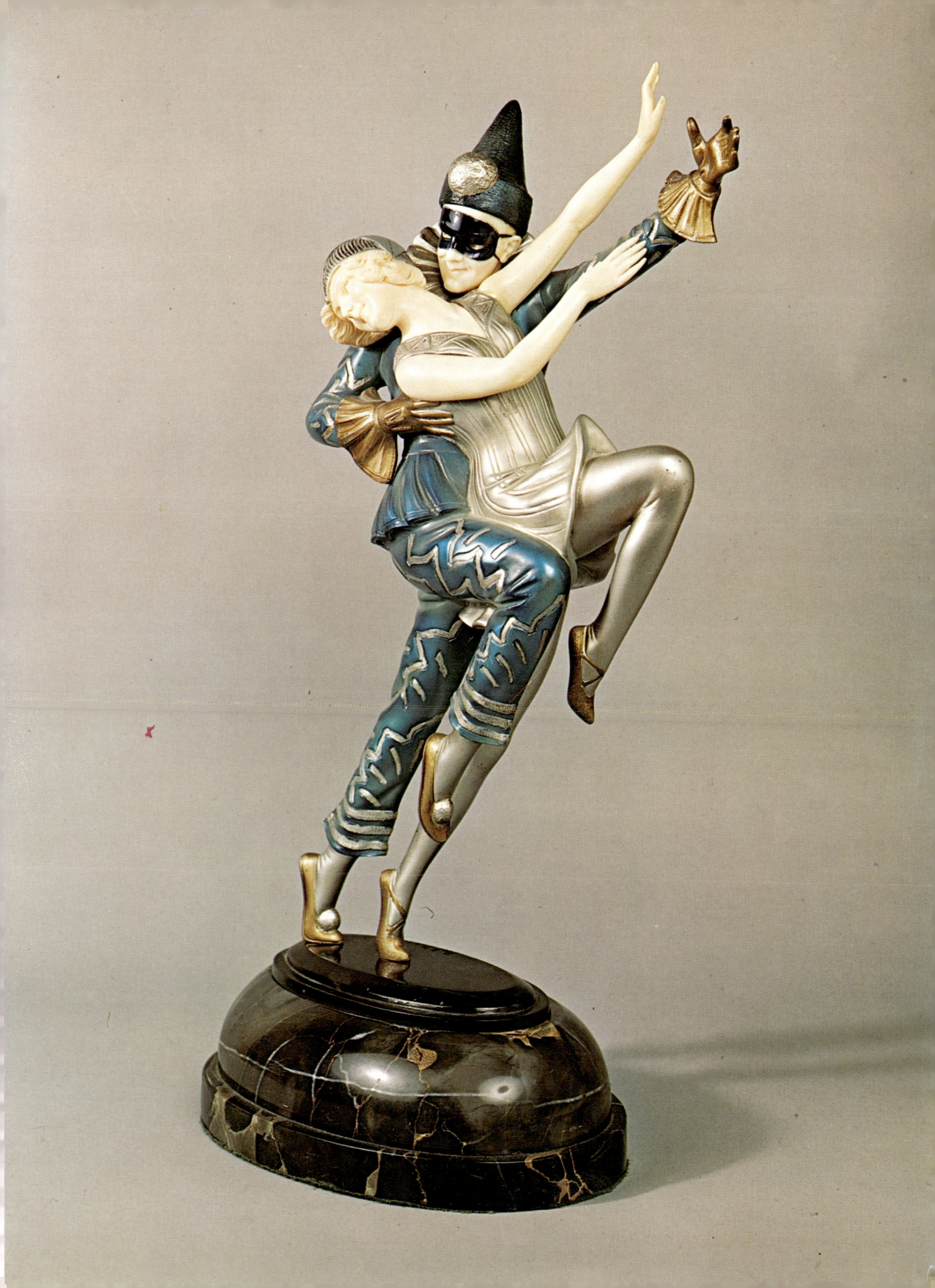

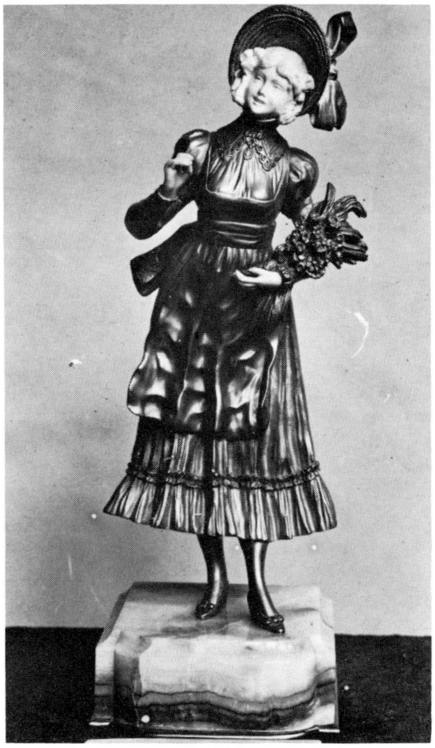

Sweetheart, 34cm: 13½in.

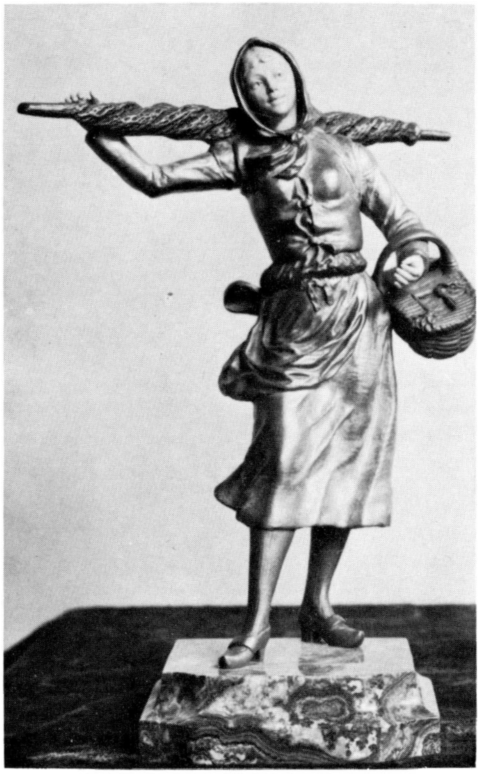

Farm Girl, 28cm: 11in.

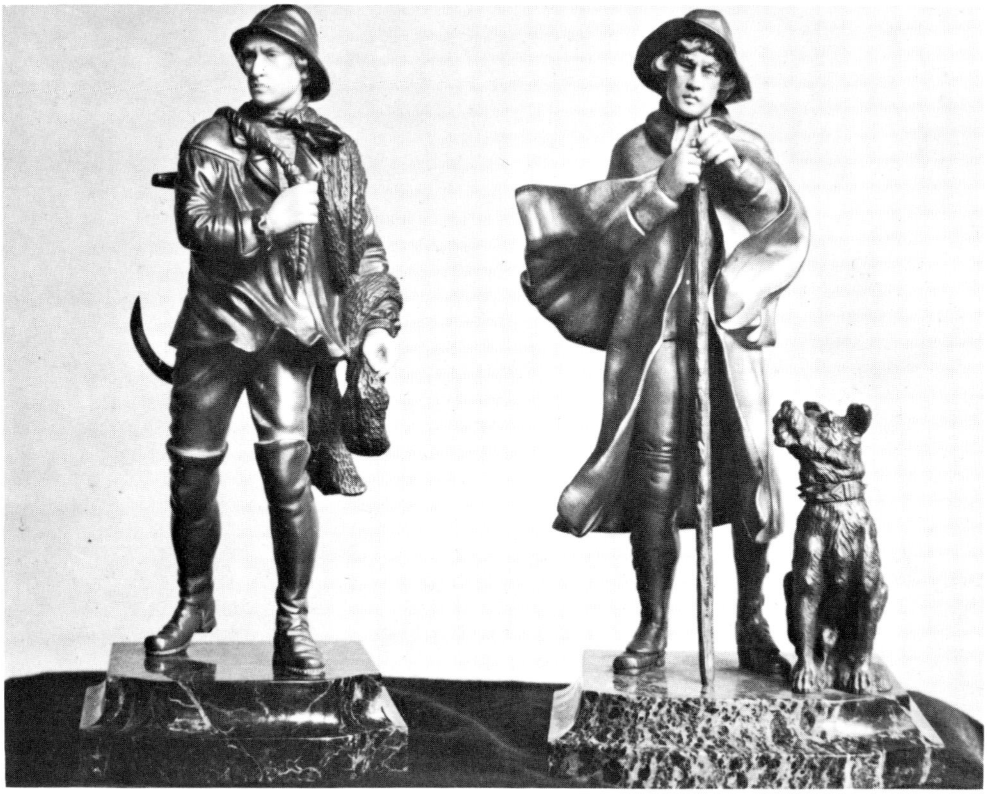

Old Fisherman
28cm: 11in.

Old Shepherd
28cm: 11in.

G. OMERTH

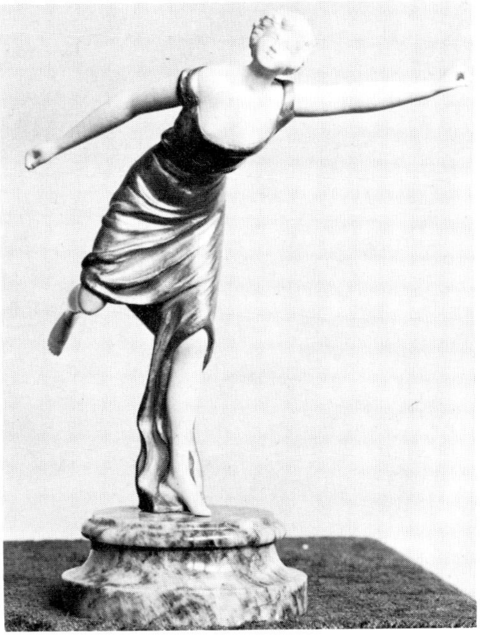

Little Bacchante
22cm: 8½in.

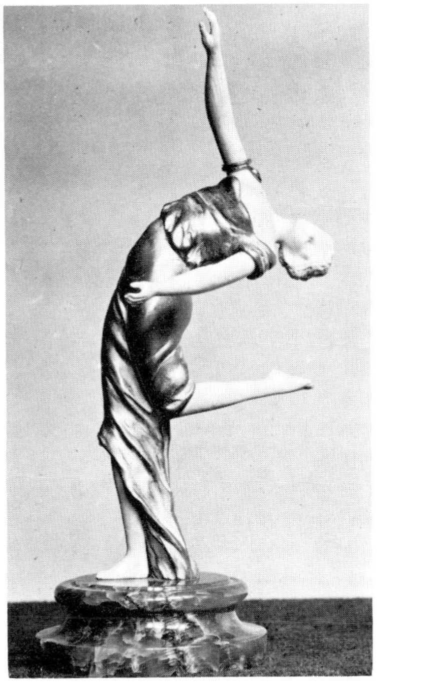

Little Bacchante
19cm: 7½in.

Mme. AURORE ONU

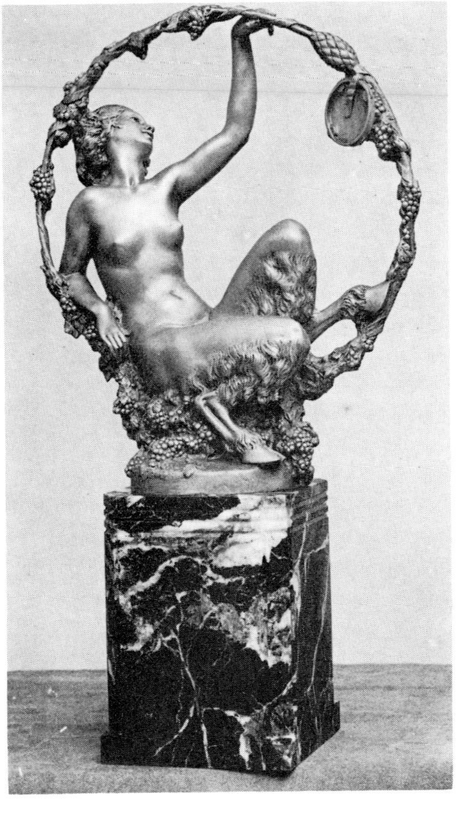

Bacchante with Thyrse, 60cm: 23½in.

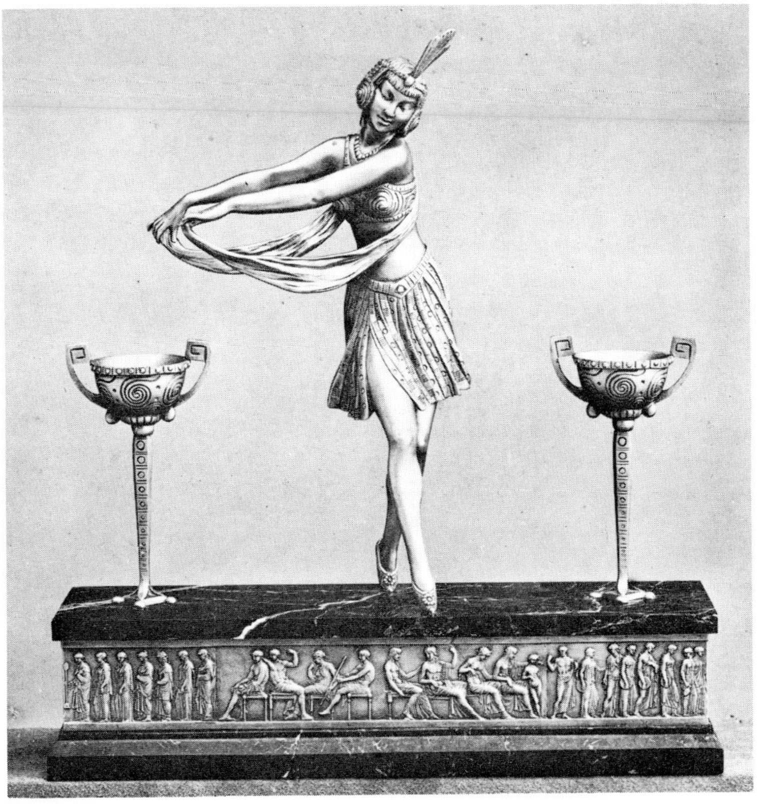

Incantation, 50cm: 19½in.

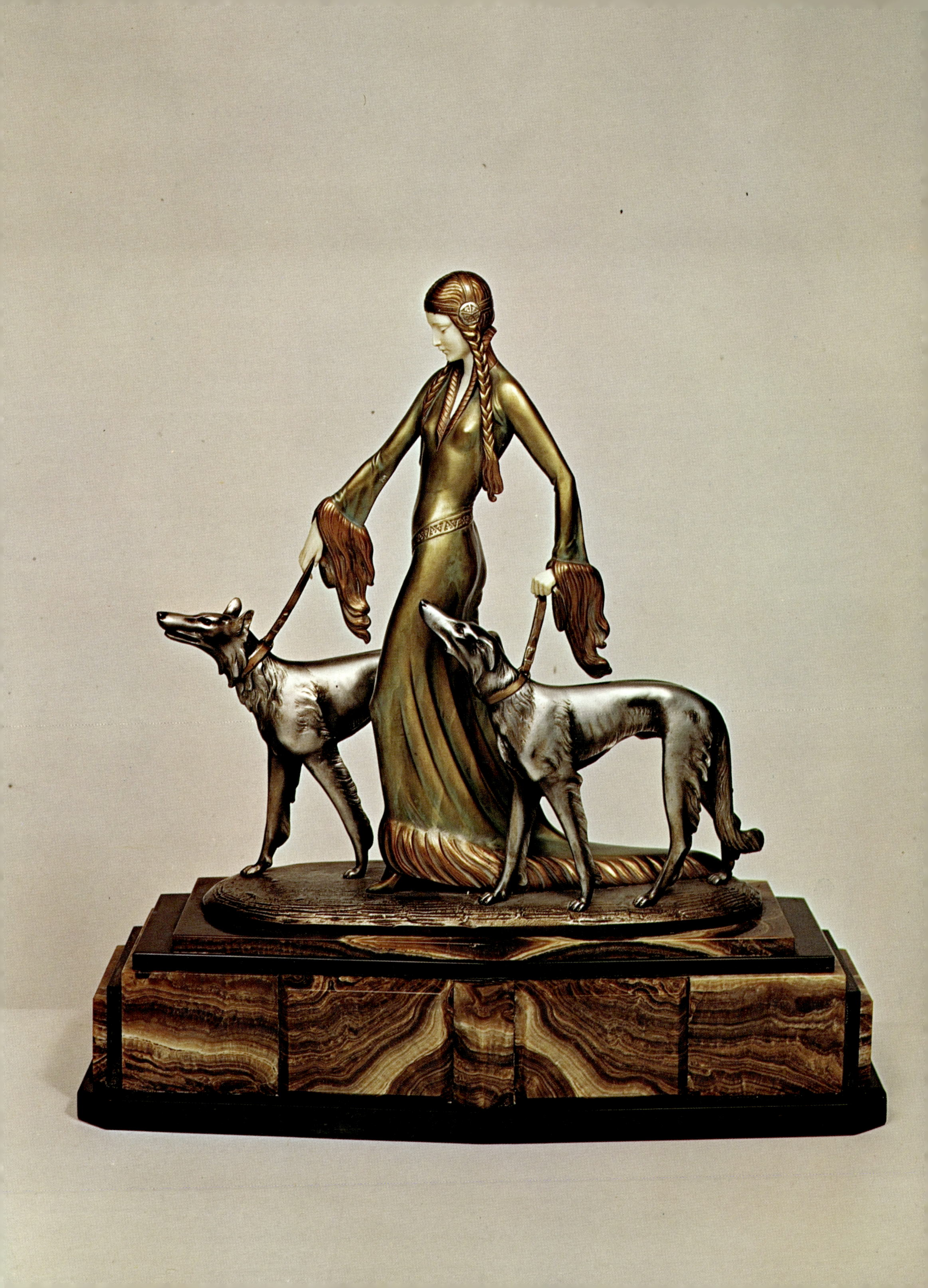

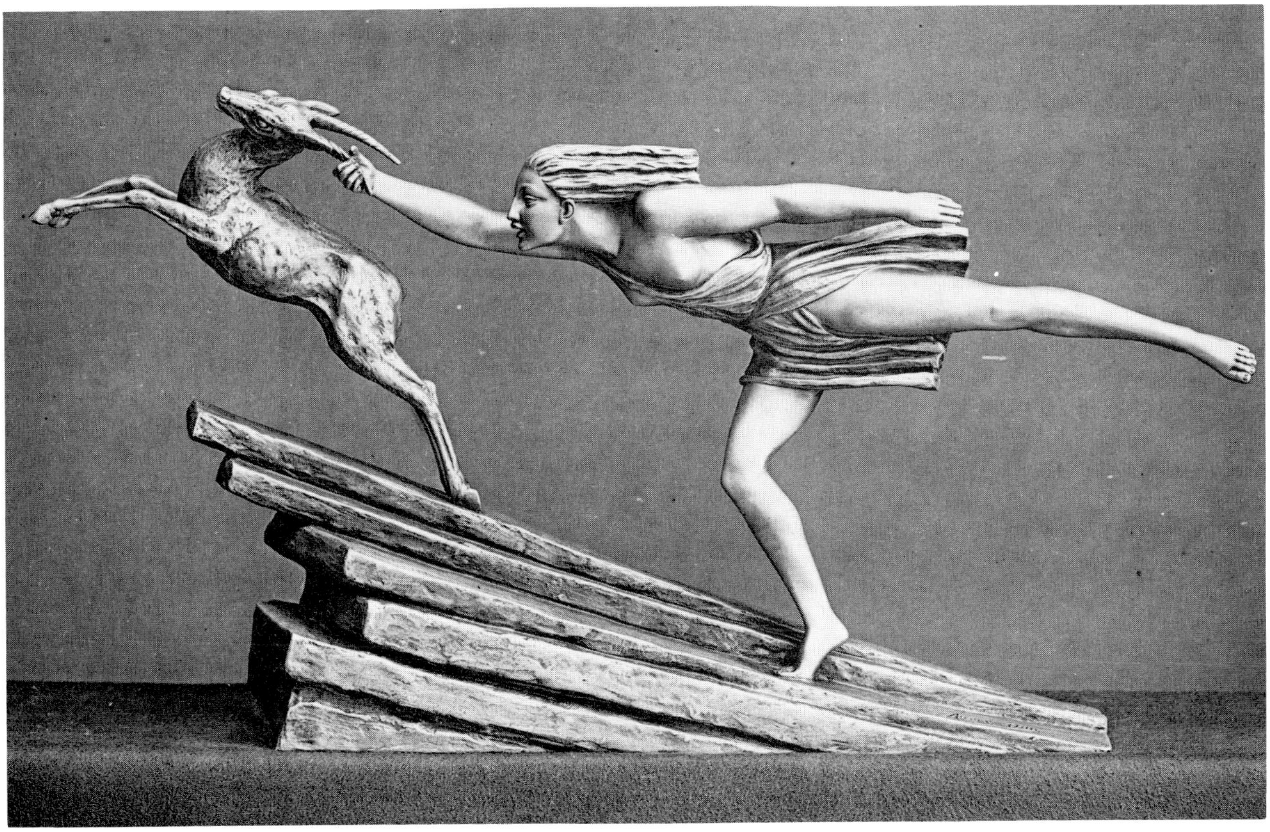

Above: Chasing the Hind, 35cm:13¾in.; 18cm:7in.
Right: The Mask Dance, 61cm:24in.

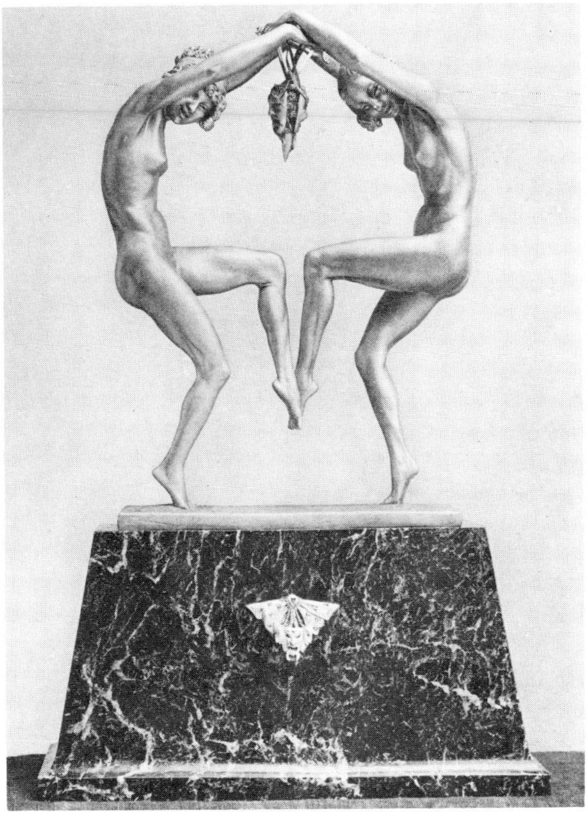

Left. The Aristocrats by Prof. Otto Poertzel, 49cm:19in. A similar figure was produced by F. Preiss. Original cost £50 in 1937.

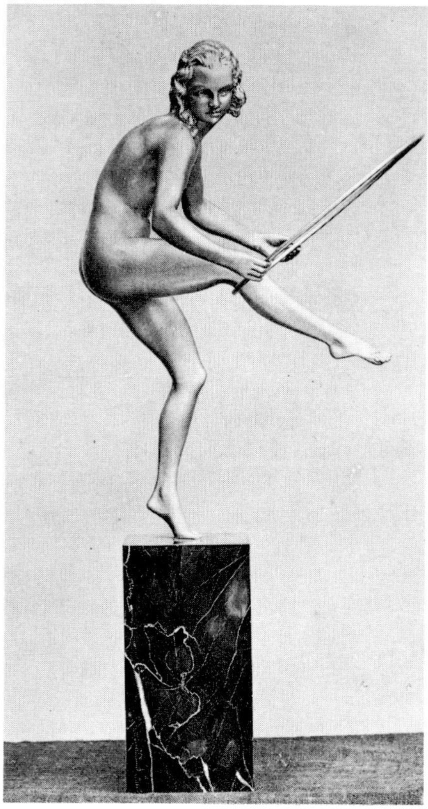

Hoop Dance
50cm:19½in.

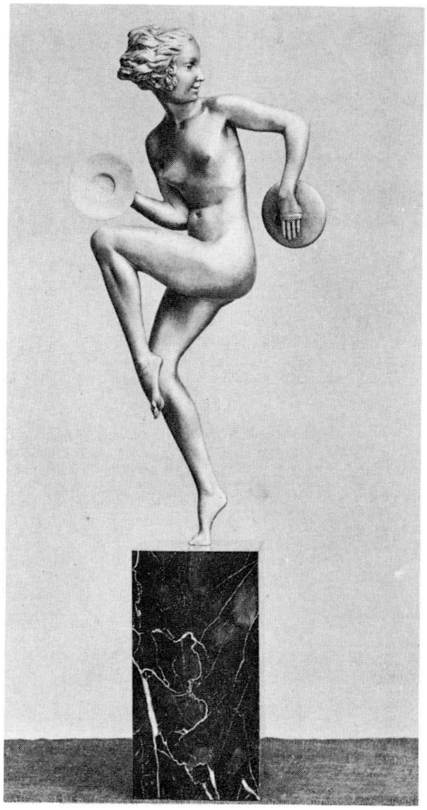

Dance of the Cymbals
50cm:19½in.

JEAN ORTIS

Innocence, 52cm:20½in.

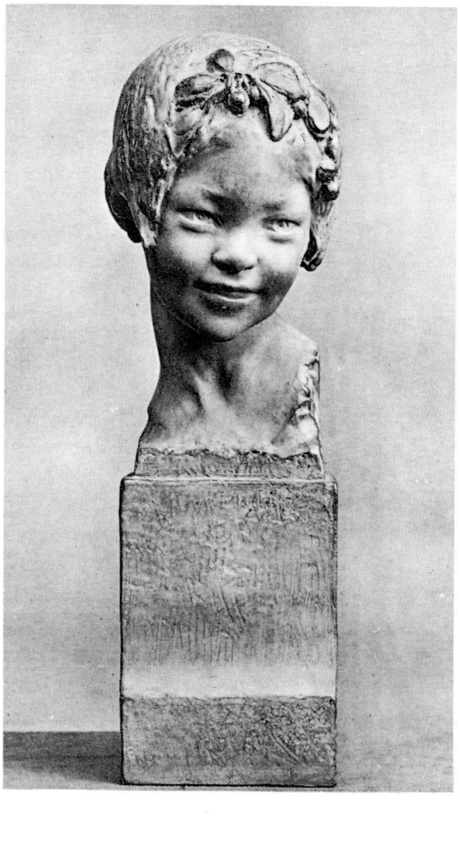

F. OUILLON-CARRÈRE

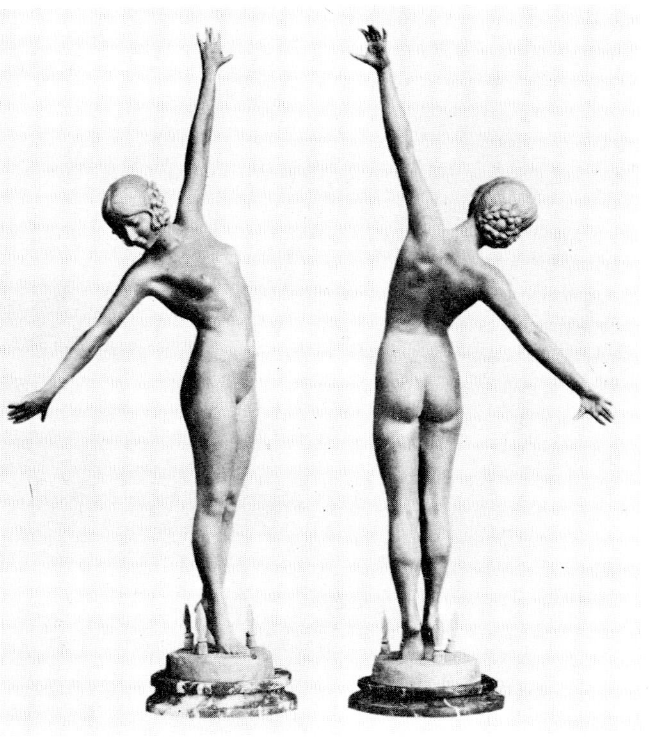

Sword Dance, 51cm: 20in.
36cm: 14¼in.; 26cm: 10¼in.
Exhibited 1919 in the Paris Salon

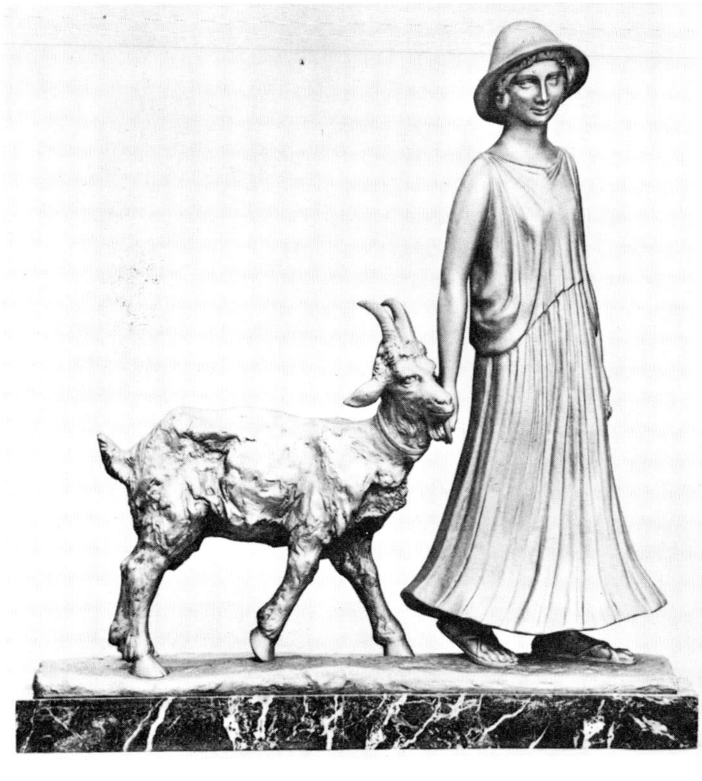

GERMAINE OURY

Spring Walk
43cm: 17in.

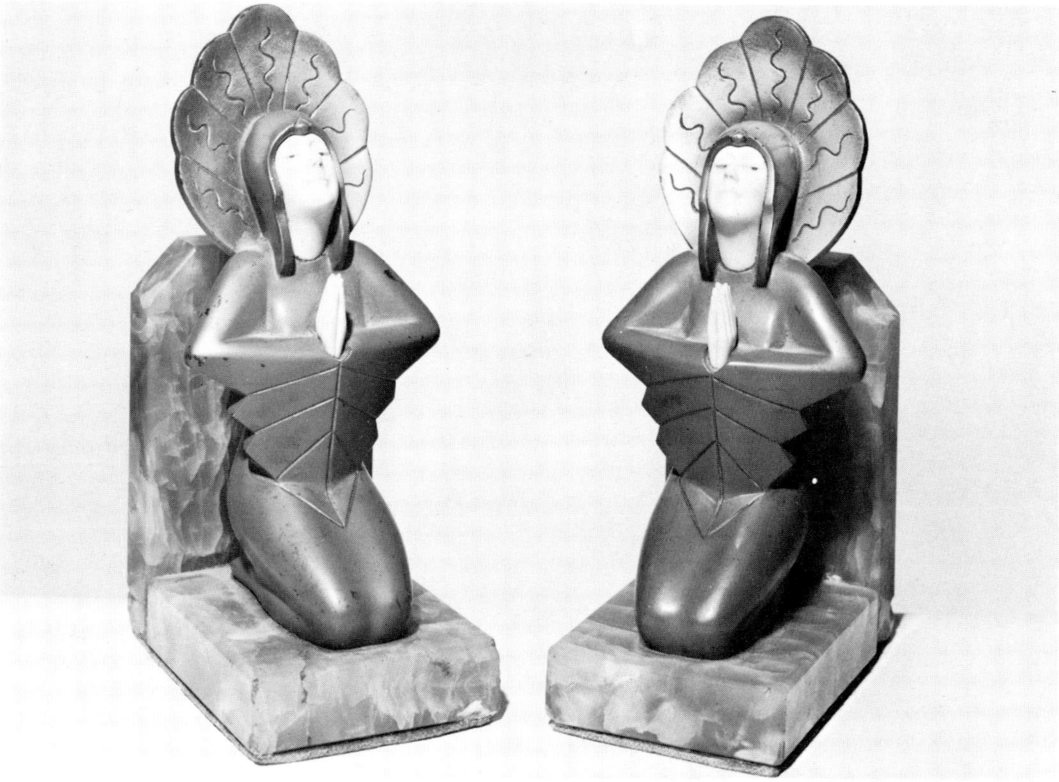

Pair of bookends, 19cm: 7½in.

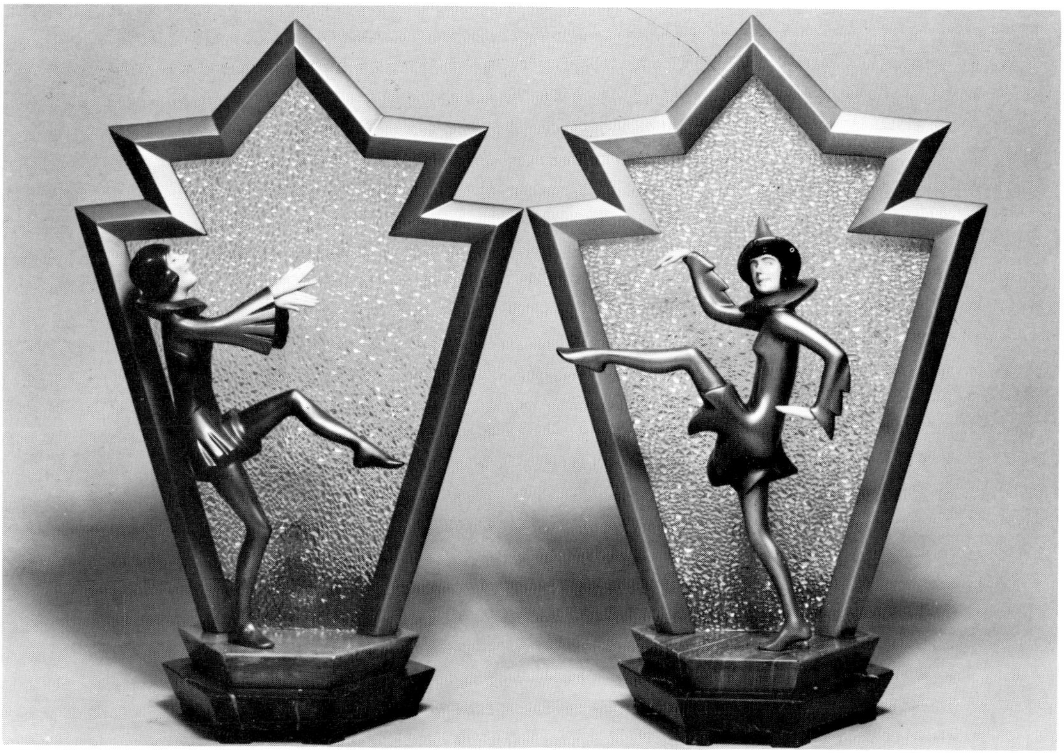

Pair of lamps, 41cm: 16in.

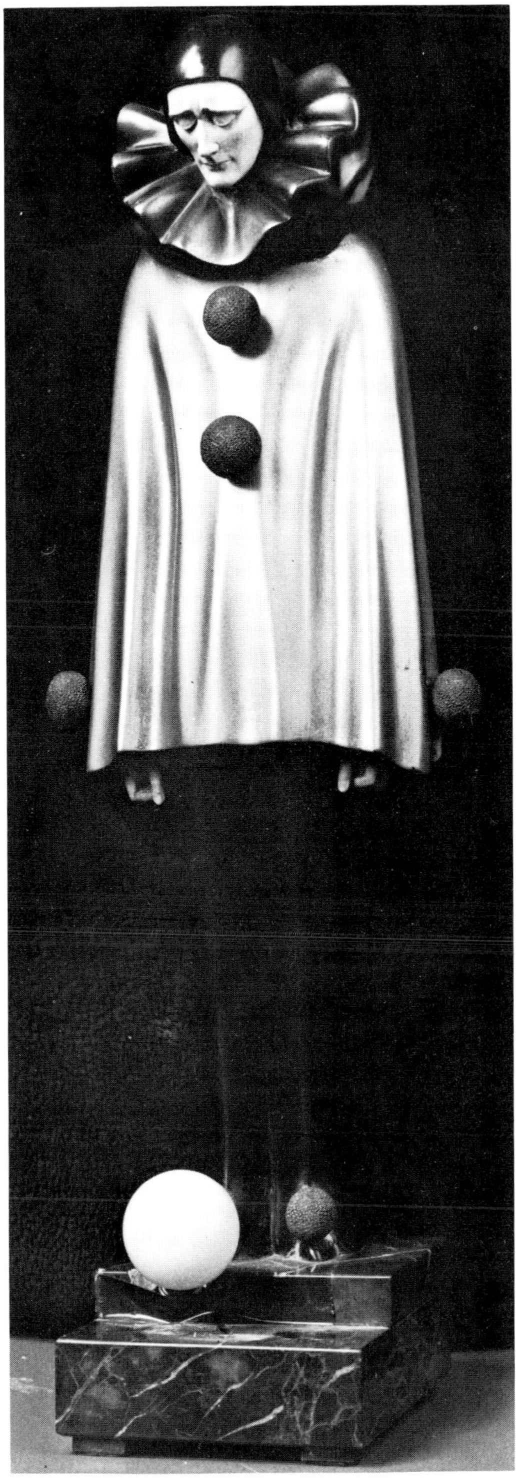

A Lamp, 56cm:22in.

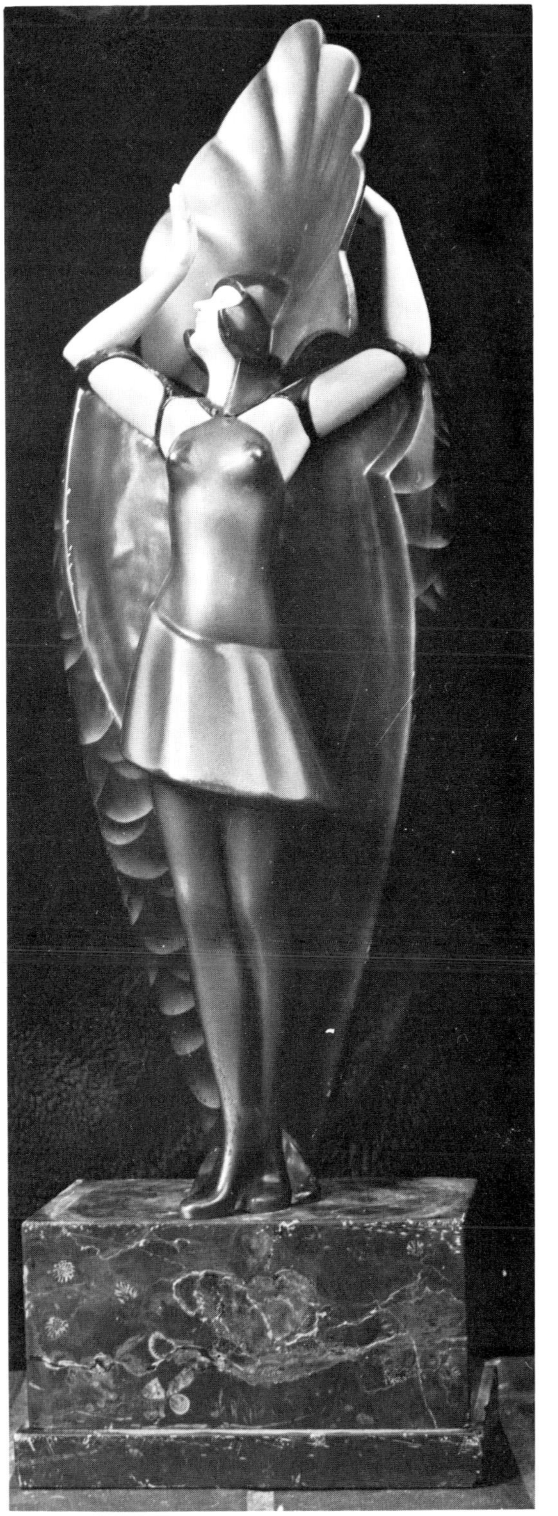

A Dancer, 58cm:23in.

CH. PERRON

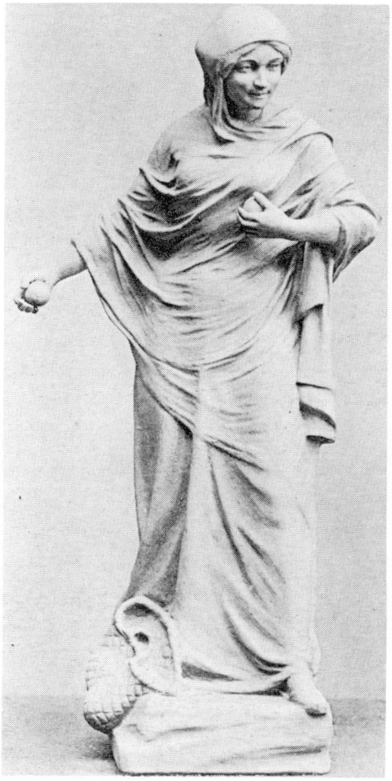

Girl with Spheres
74cm:29in.
33cm:13in.

RAPHAEL PEYRE

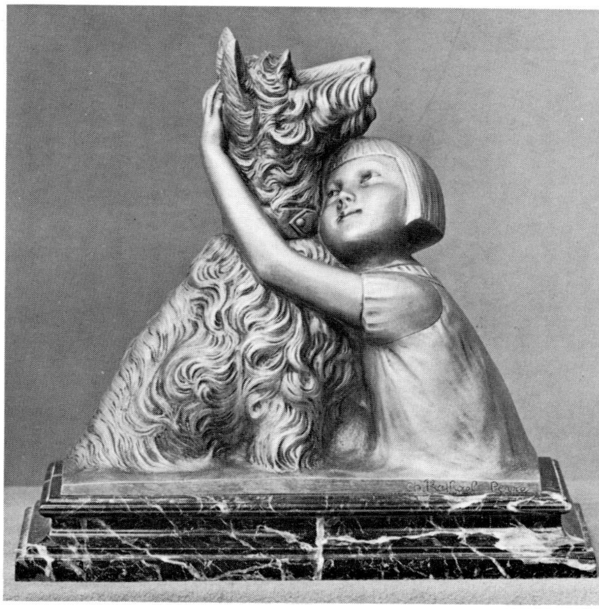

Good Friends, 23cm:9in.

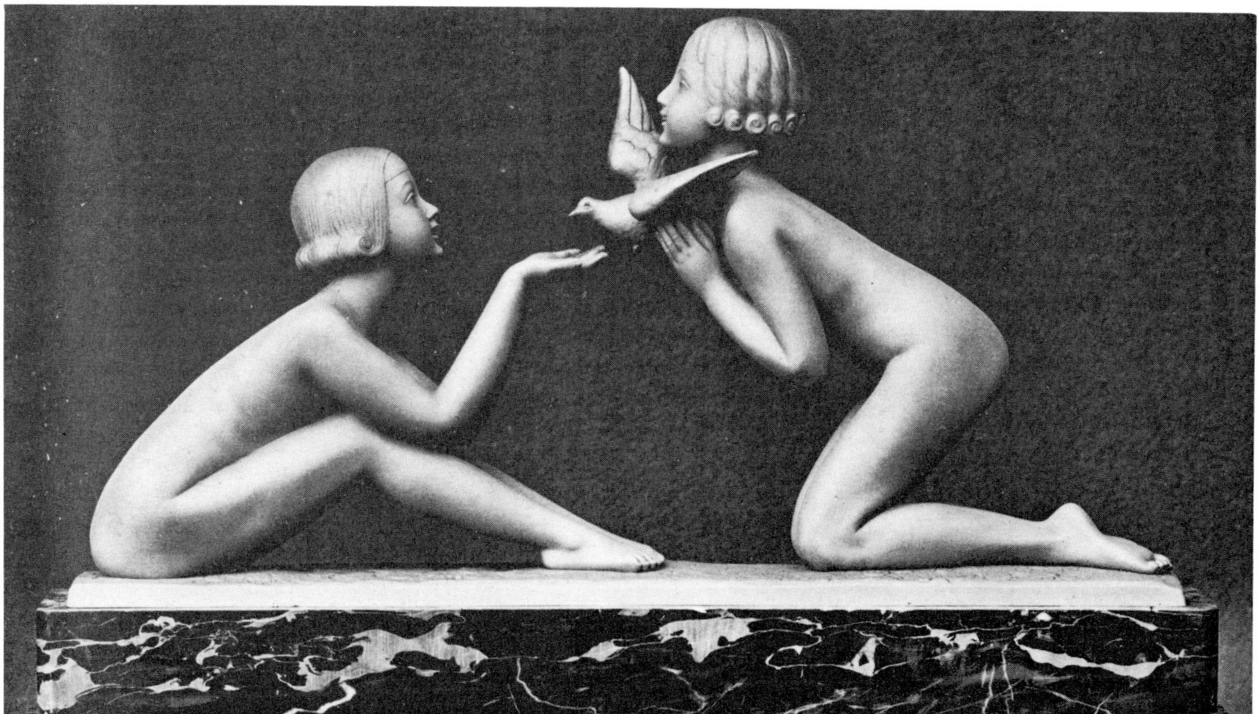

Children and the Dove, 38cm:15in.

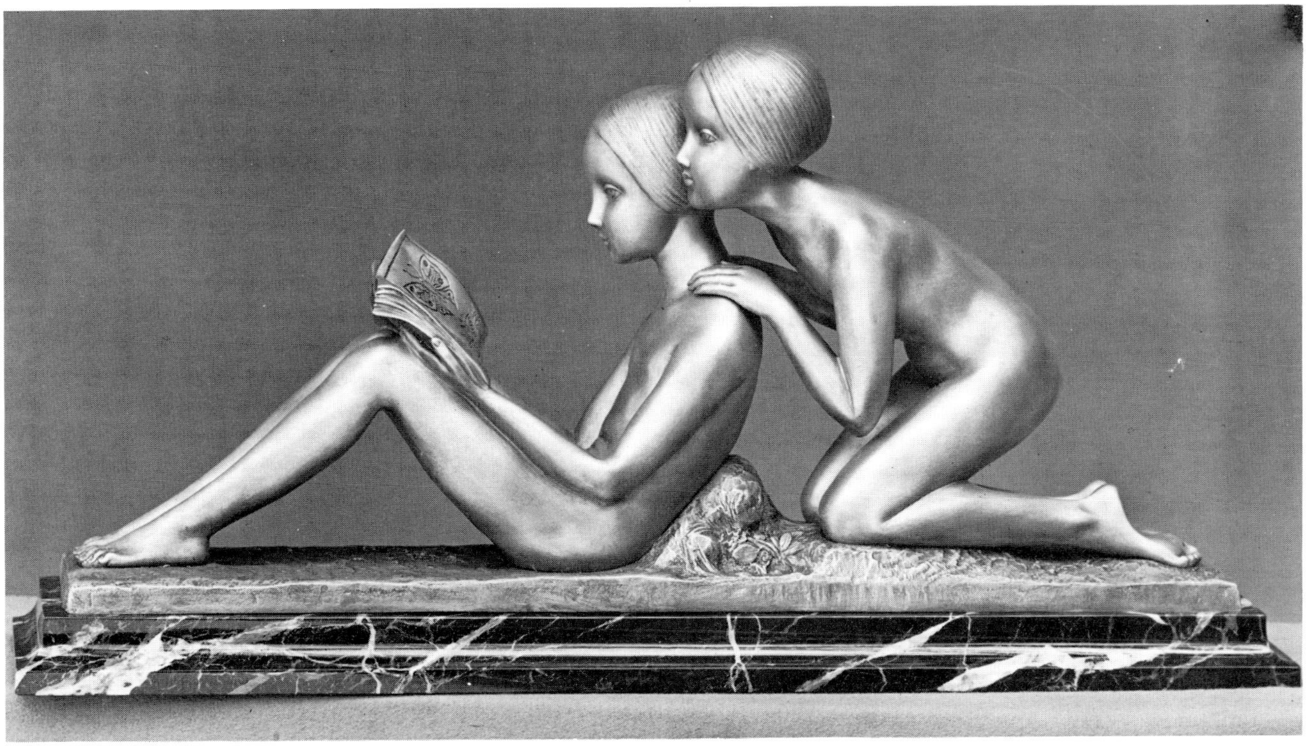

Reading, 32cm:12½in.

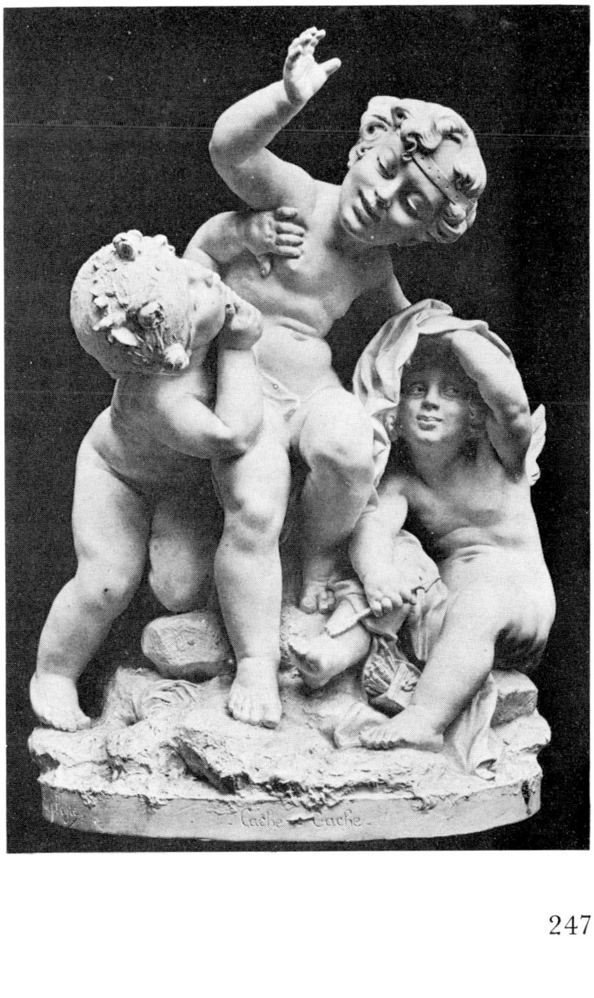

Hide and Seek, 70cm:27½in.

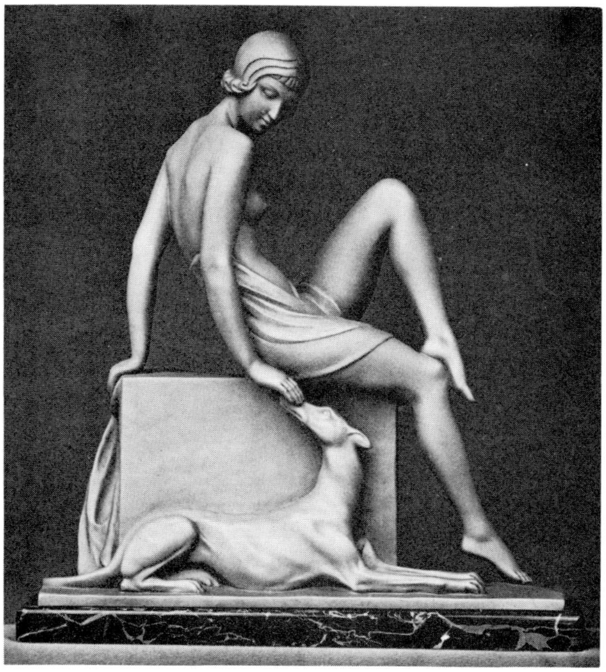

Companionship, 47cm:18½in.

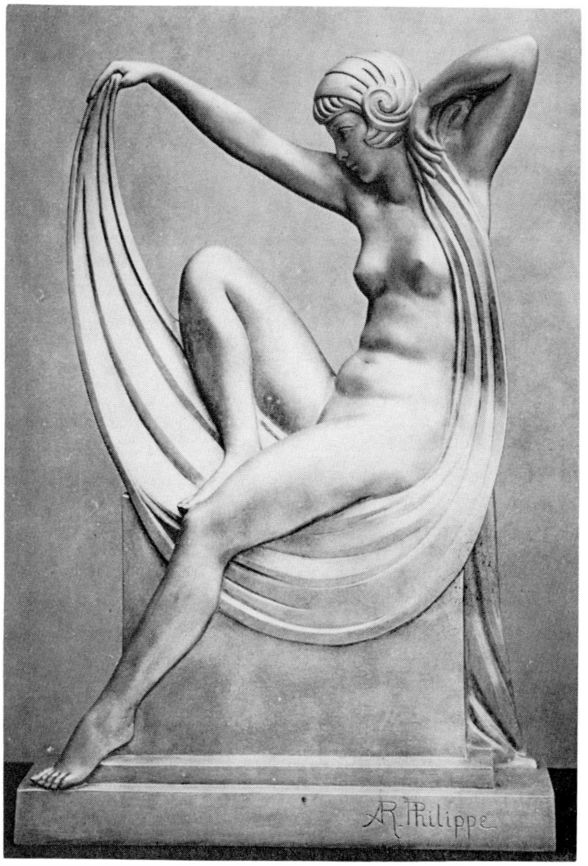

Before the Bath
53cm:21in.; 27cm:10½in.

The Bather
49cm:19¼in.
30cm:11¾in.

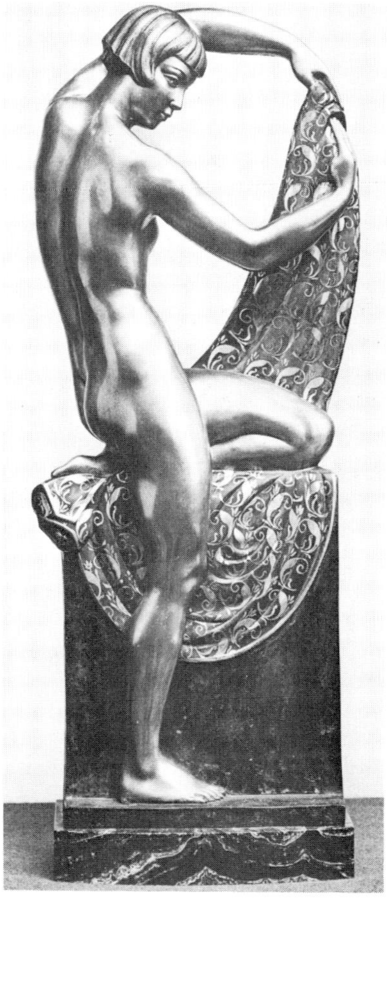

Right. P. Philippe
Girl with Parrot
61cm:24in.

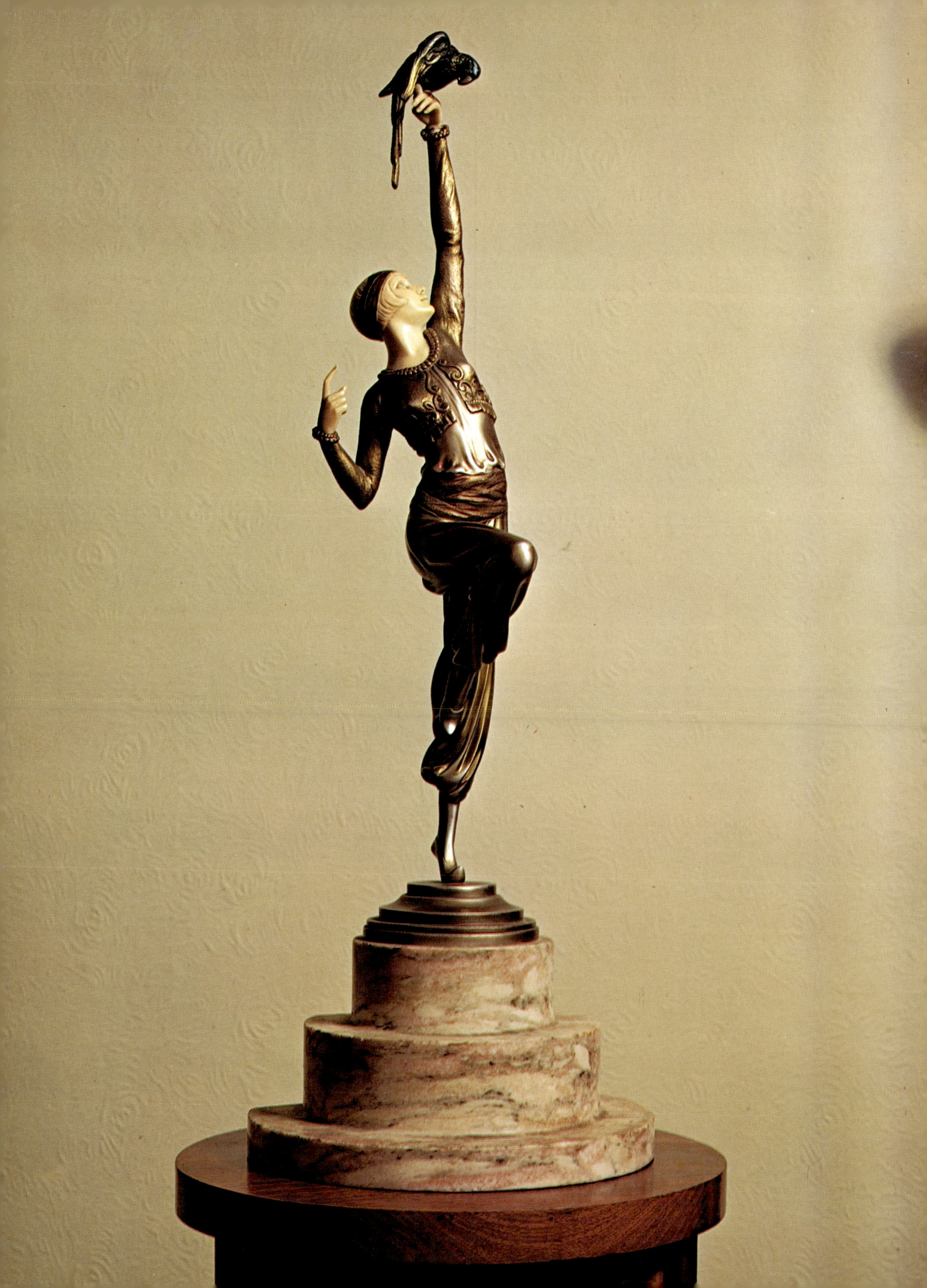

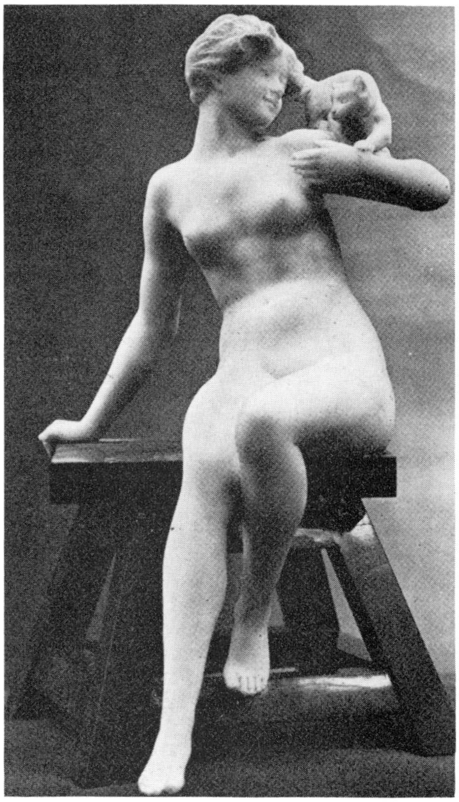

Left: Dainty, 32cm:12½in.
22cm:8½in.; 16cm:6¼in.

Right: Awakening
34cm:13½in.; 22cm:8¾in.
19cm:7½in.

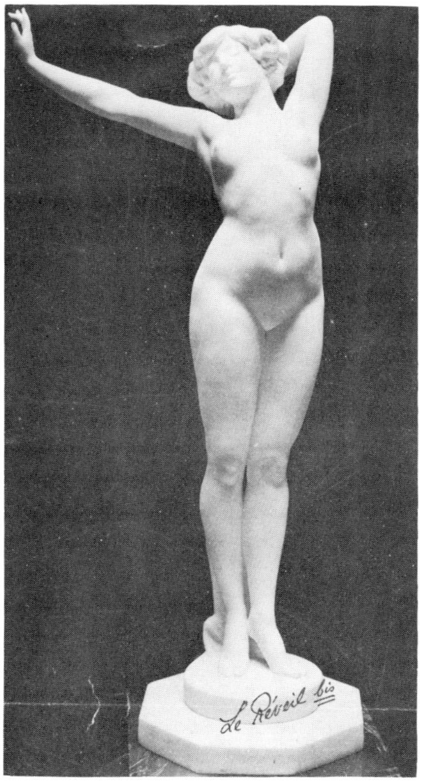

Below left: The Challenge
68cm:26¾in.; 48cm:19in.
31cm:12¼in.; 23cm:9in.
13cm:5in.

Below right: Mischievous
68cm:26¾in.; 40cm:15¾in.
24cm:9½in.

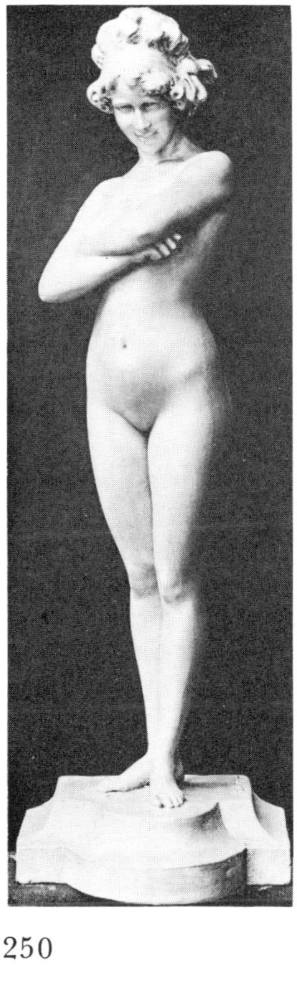

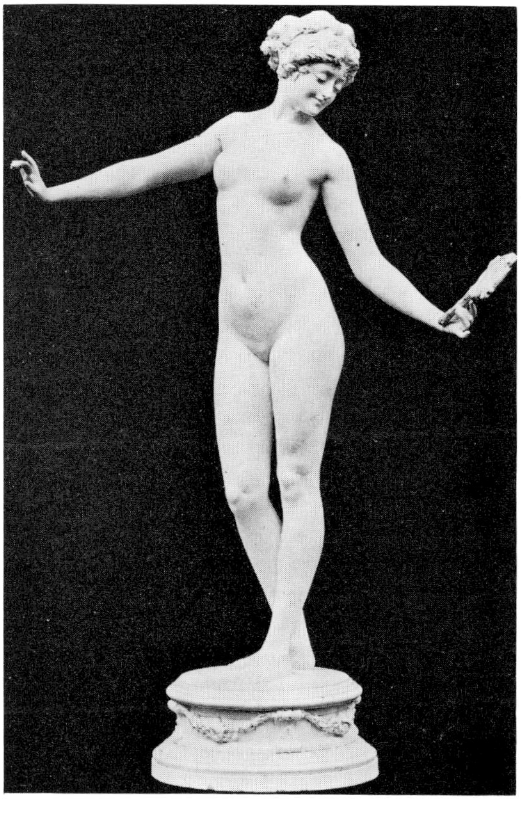

Girl and Mirror, 48cm:19in.
35cm:13¾in.; 25cm:10in.

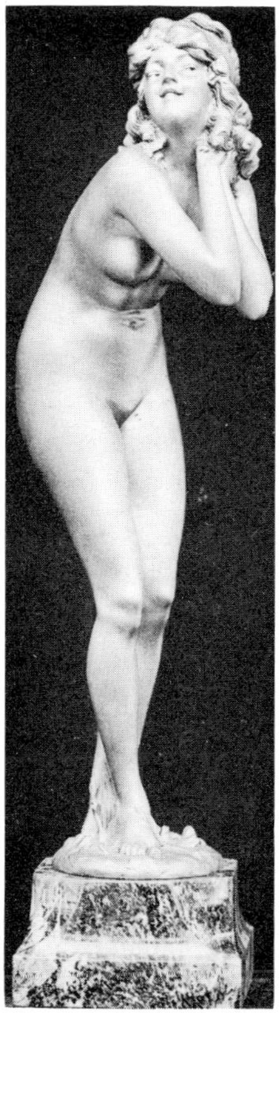

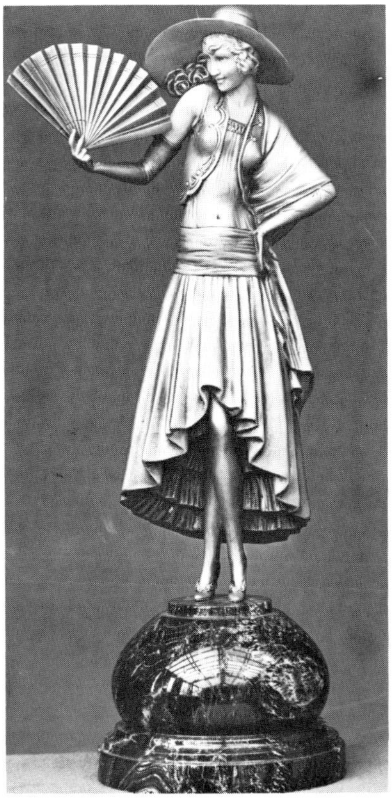

Longchamp, 43cm:17in.

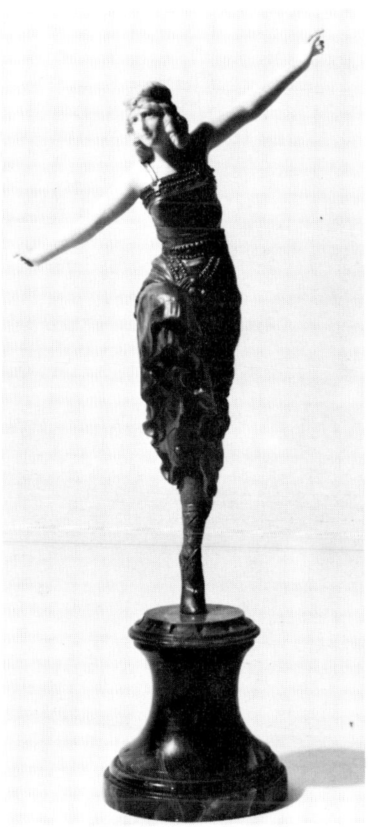

Russian Dancer
Several sizes and combinations of material

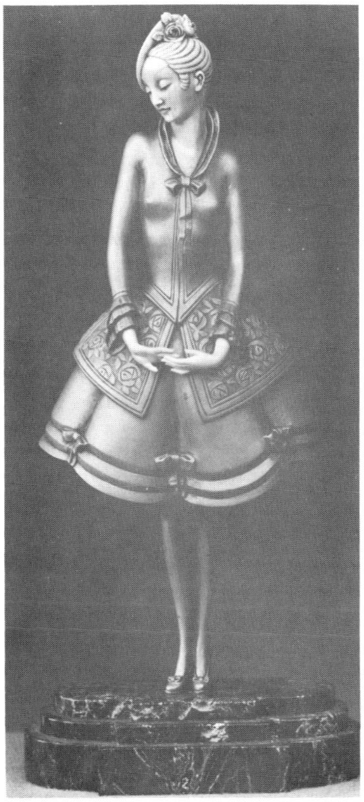

Simplicity, 40cm:15¾in.

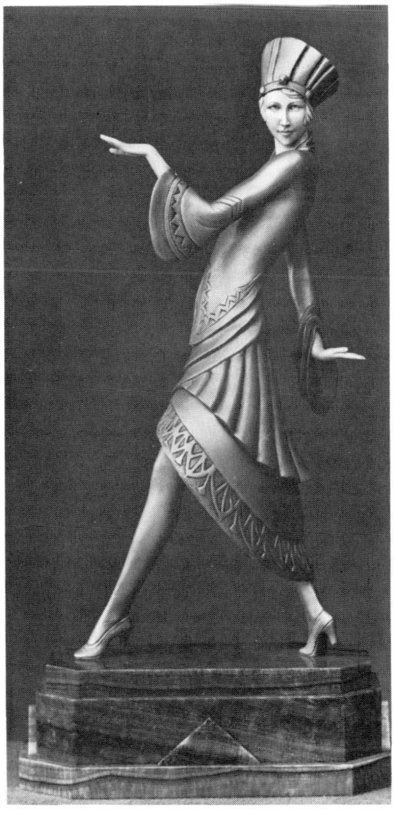

Miss Paris, 44cm:17¼in.

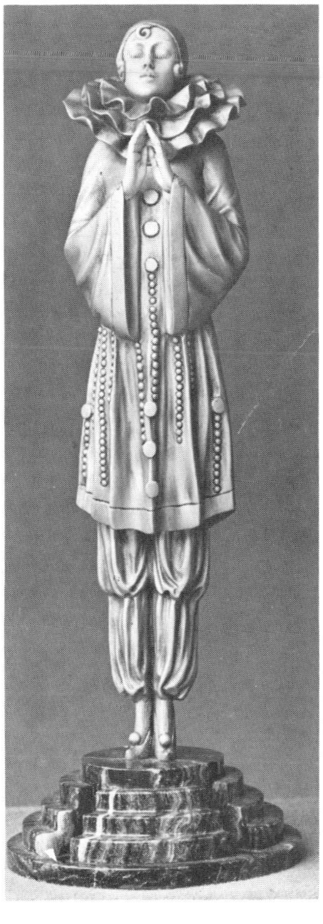

Adoration, 41cm:16in.

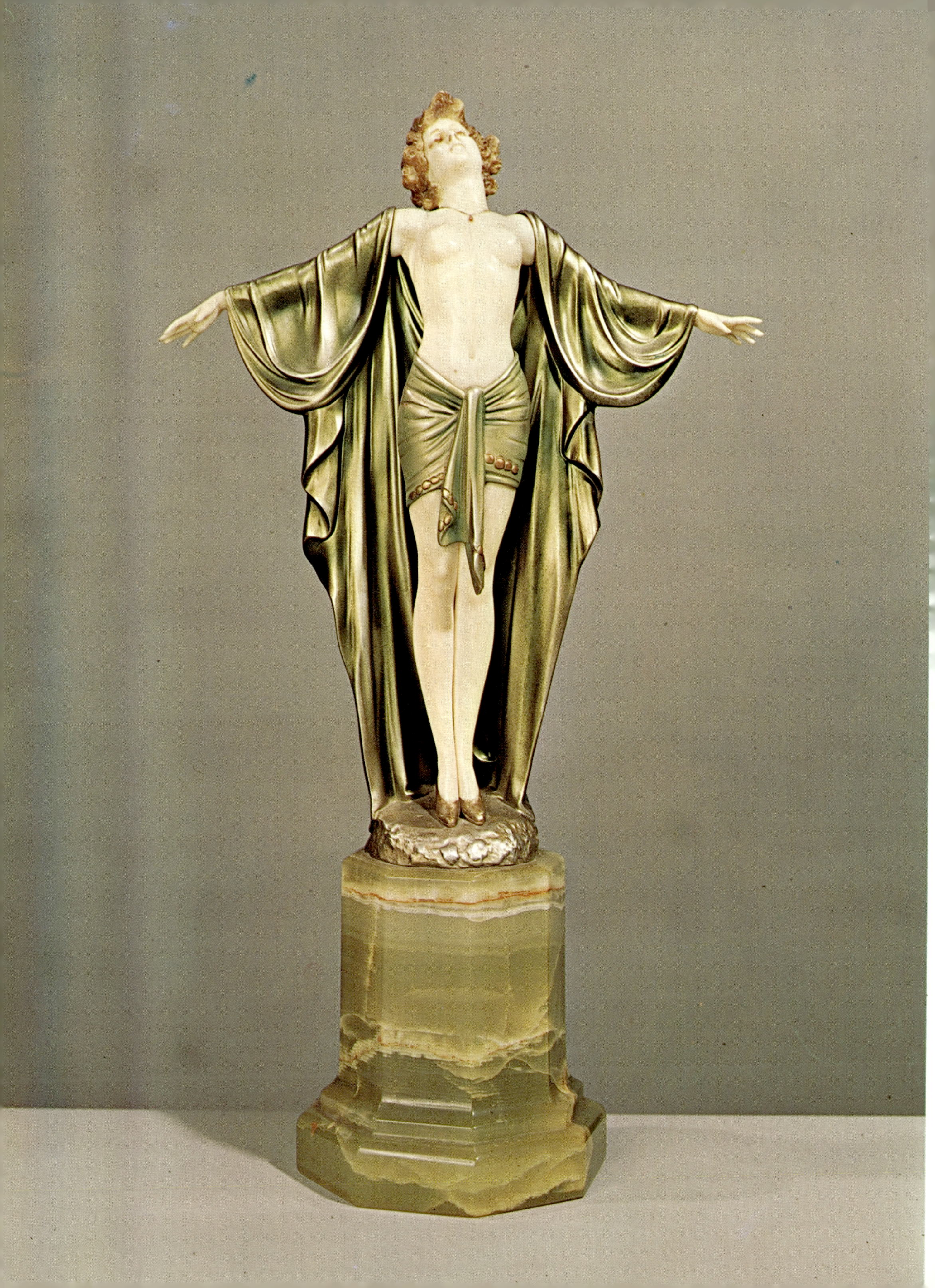

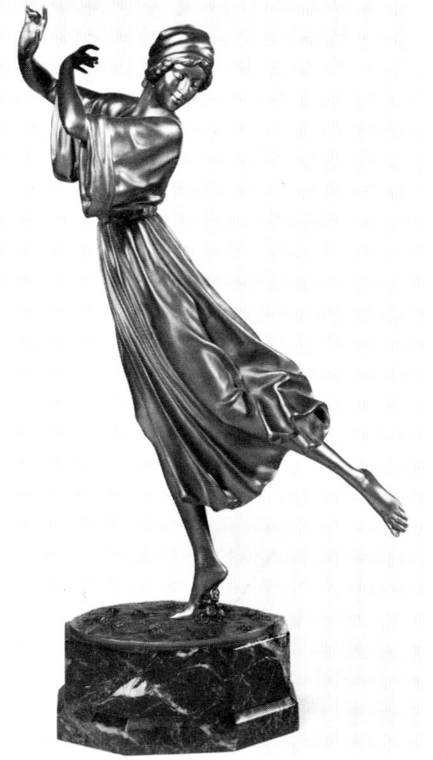

Dancer (draped)
56cm: 22in.

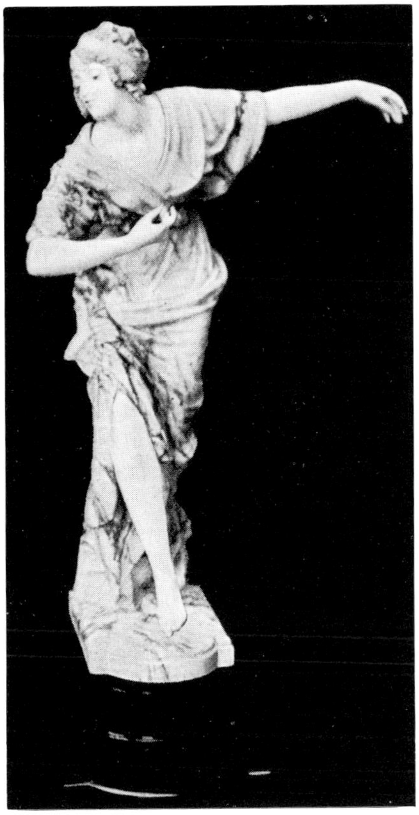

Grace
55cm: 21½in.; 39cm: 15¼in.

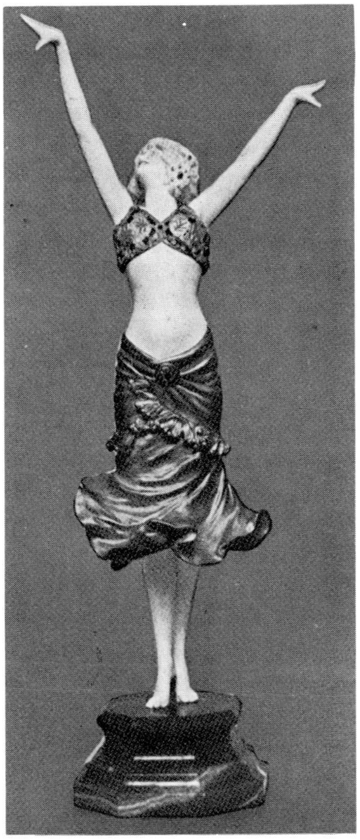

Radha, 58cm: 23in.
39cm: 15½in.; 23cm: 9in.

Group of Dancers
47cm: 18½in.

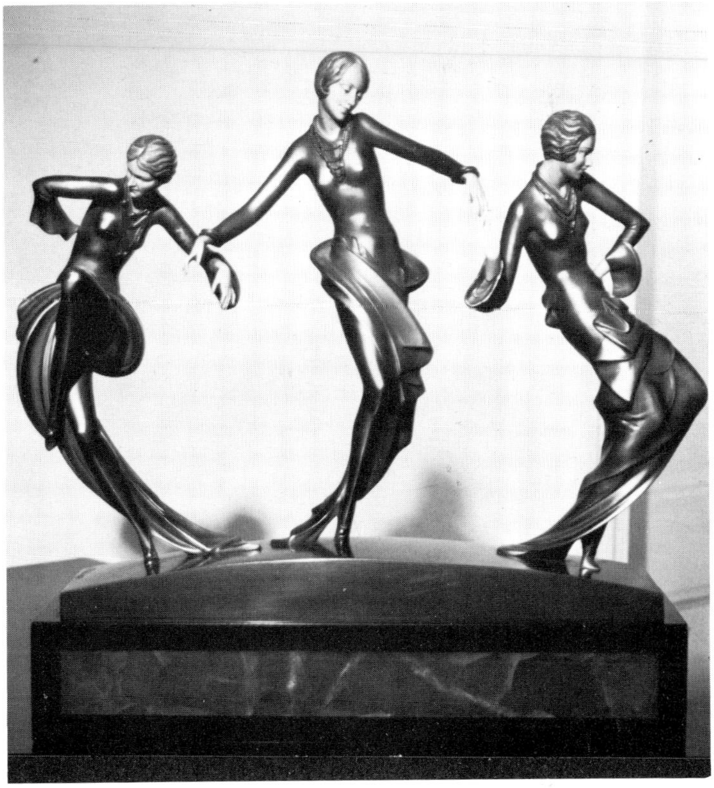

Left. Spring Awakening, F. Preiss. 37cm: 14¼in. Original cost in 1936 £22 in bronze and ivory, £13 in all bronze. Two different hairstyles are known for this work.

E. PICAULT

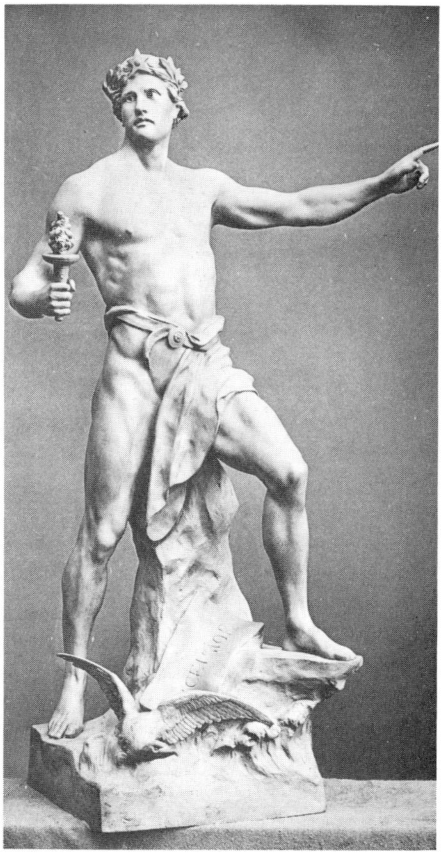

Excelsior, 85cm:33½in.
64cm:25in.; 41cm:16in.
Exhibited in the Salon des Artistes Français

LEON PILLET

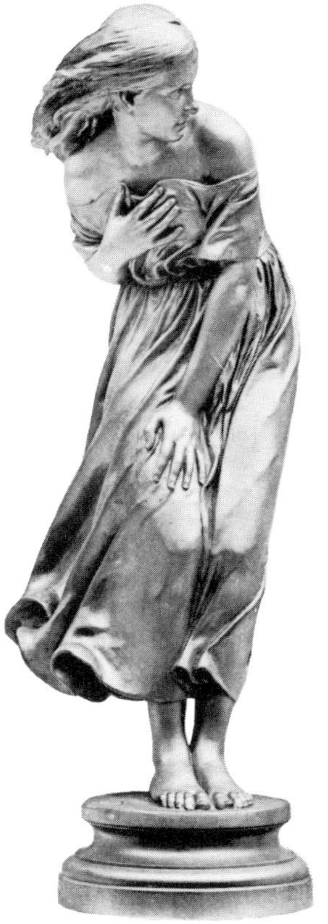

Windblown, 79cm:31in.
59cm:23¼in.; 29cm:11½in.

ALFRED PINA

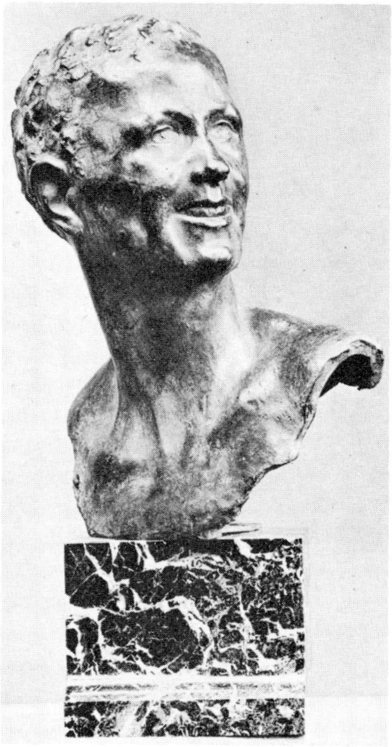

Happy Age
50cm:19½in.

OTTO POERTZEL

Group, 61cm:24in.

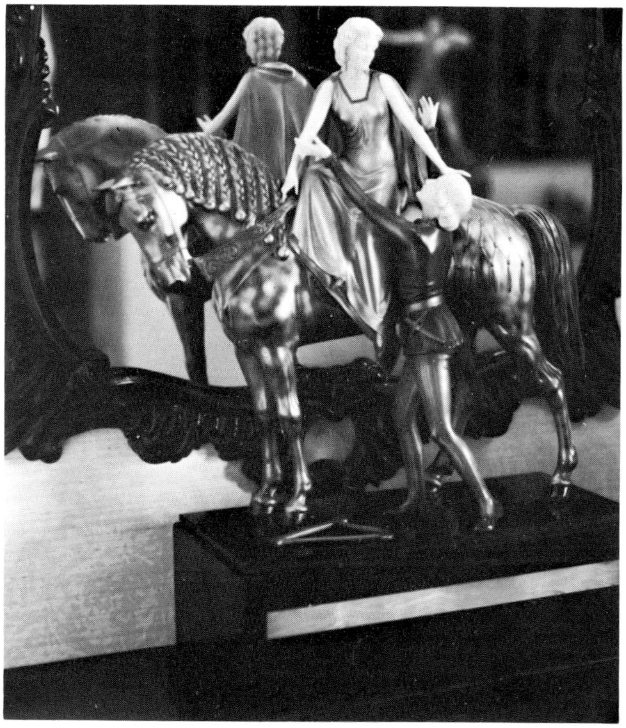

OTTO POERTZEL

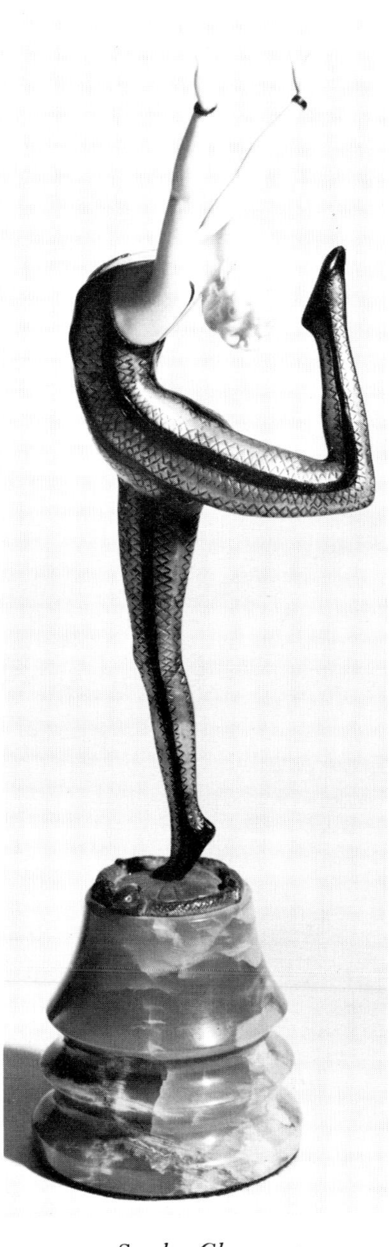

Snake Charmer
53cm:21in.: 27cm:10¾in.

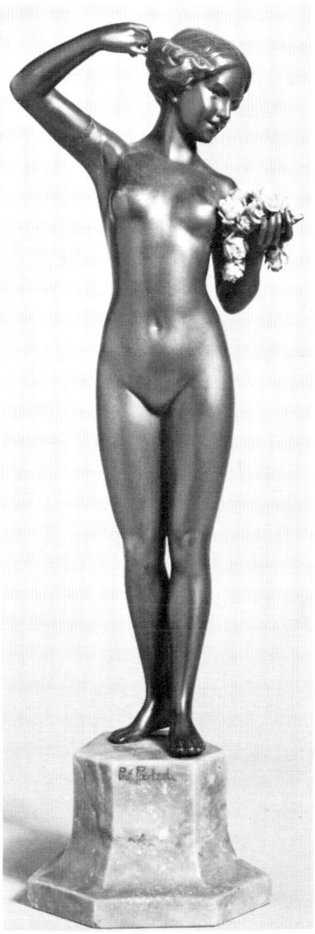

Nude with Flowers
43cm:17in.

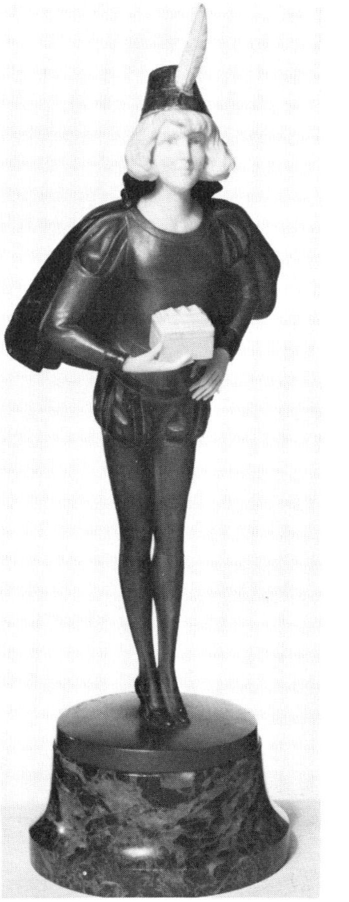

Page Boy
28cm:11in.

PAUL PONSARD

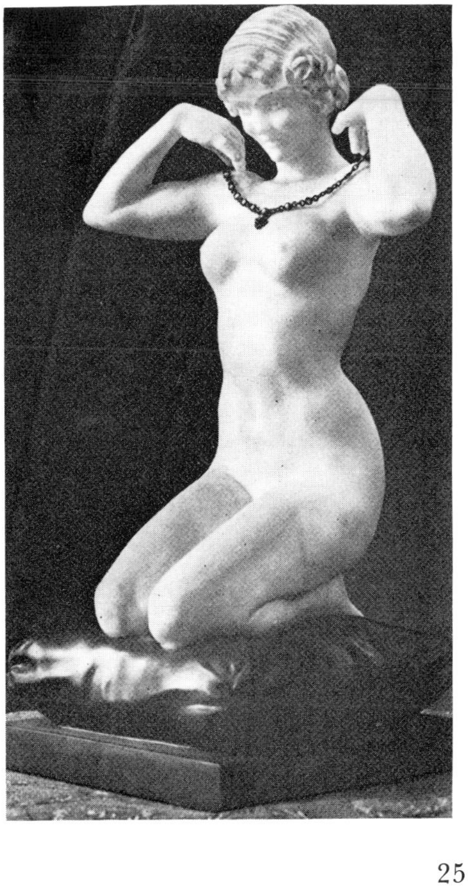

New Necklace, 60cm:23½in.
30cm:11¾in.; 14cm:5½in.

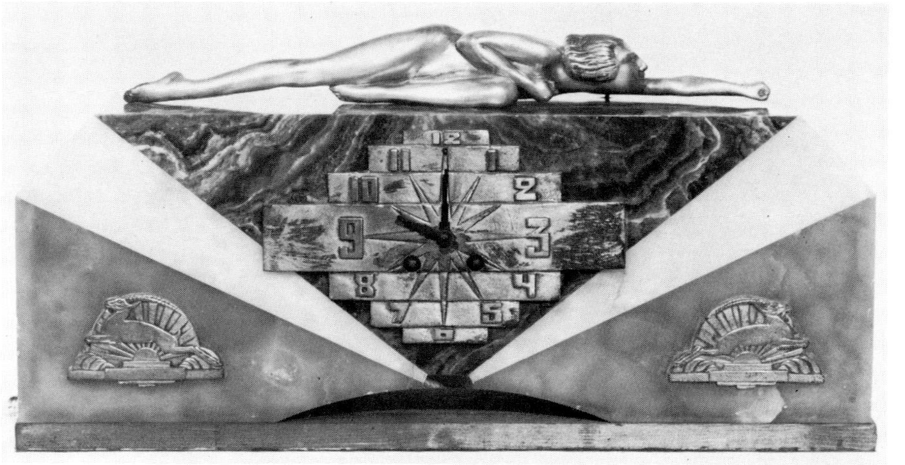

Where original costs are given for works by Preiss, these were for 1936/7.

Amazon Clock, 20cm: 7¾in.

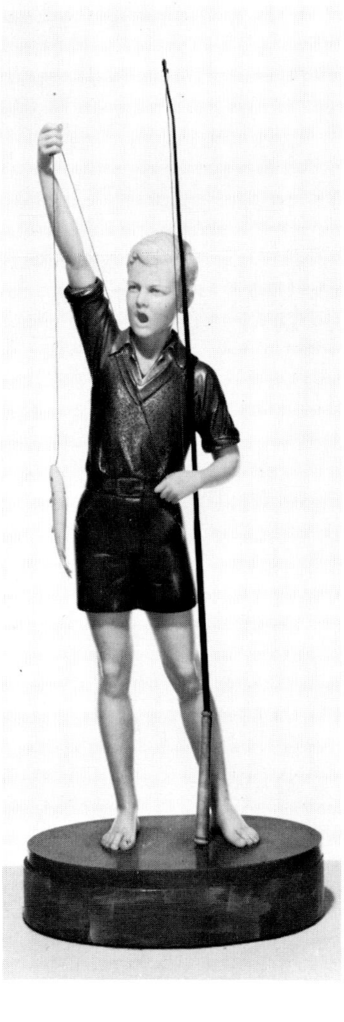

Fisher Boy 31cm: 12in.

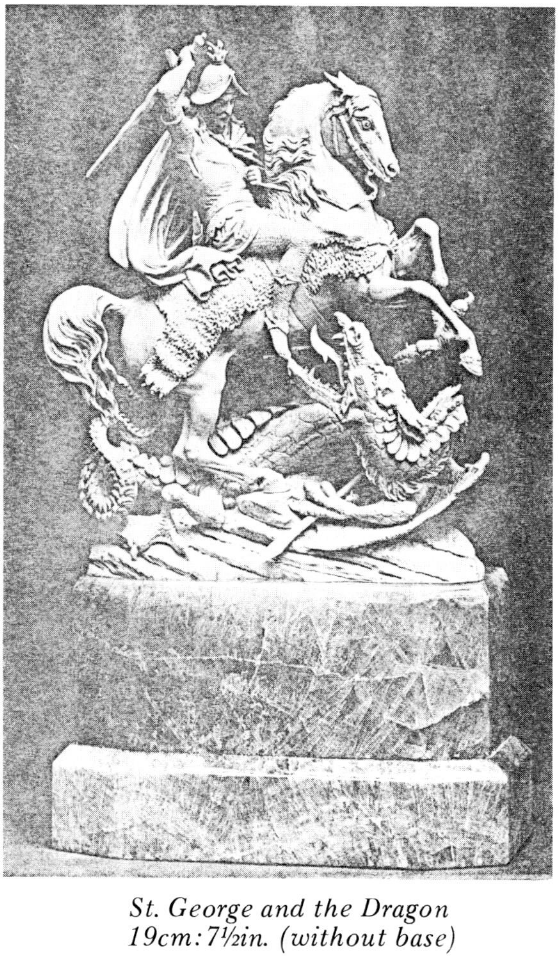

St. George and the Dragon 19cm: 7½in. (without base)

Right. A selection of figures by F. Preiss

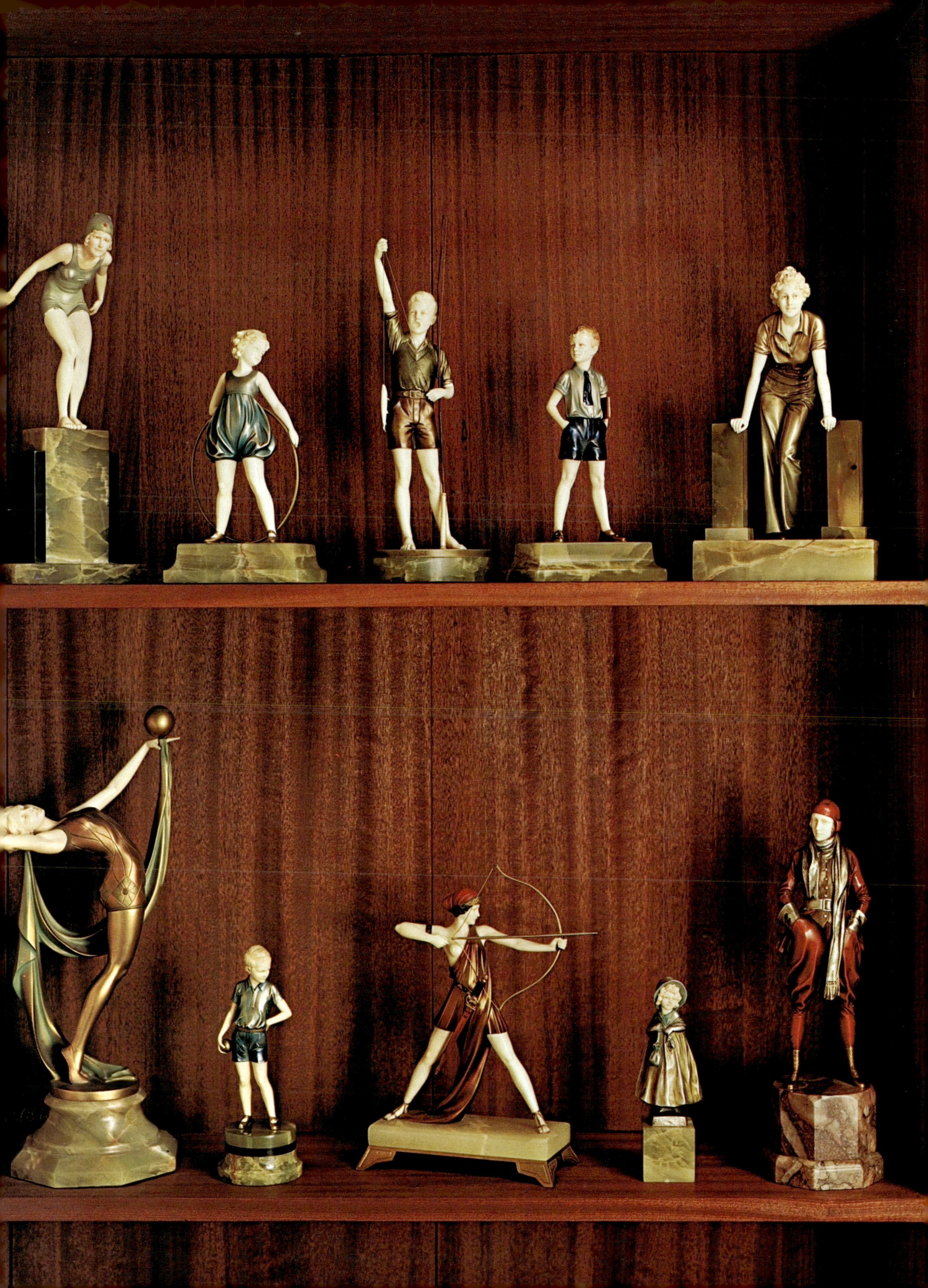

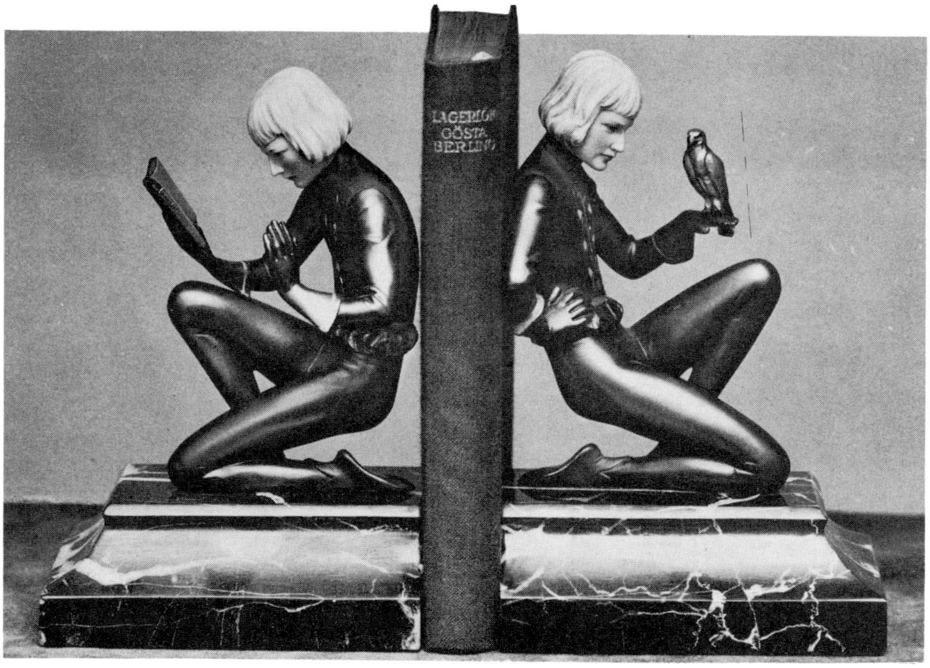

Pursuits of Youth, 14cm: 5½in.
Original cost £12

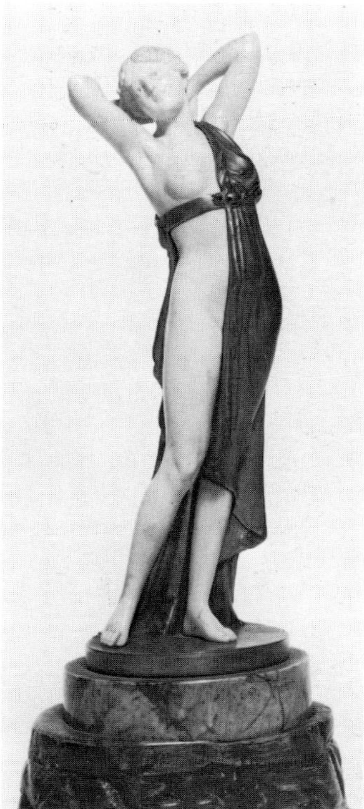

Aphrodite 25cm: 10in.

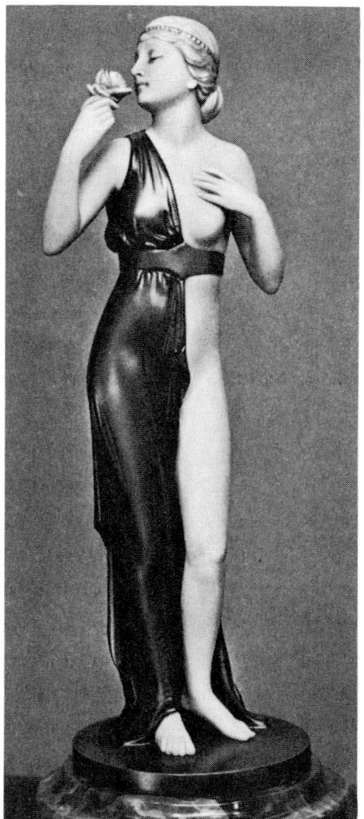

Aphrodite with Rose
22cm: 8½in.
Original cost £15

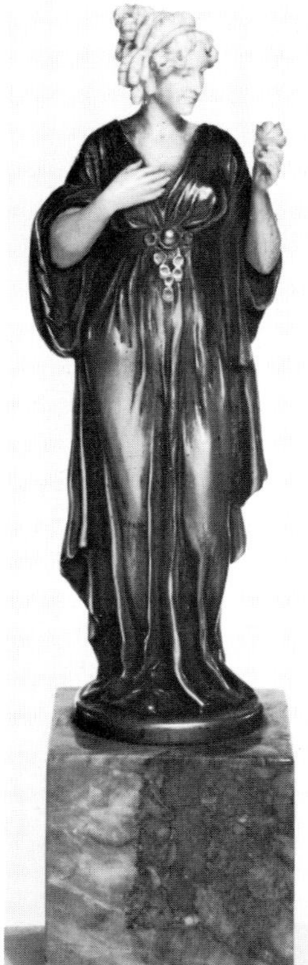

The Rose
22cm: 8½in.

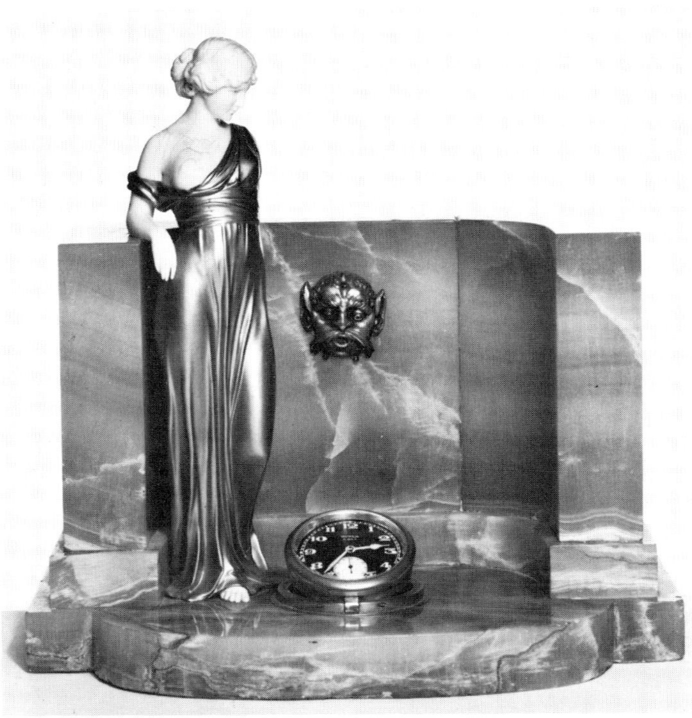

The Spring, 22cm:8½in.
Also made as an all ivory nude

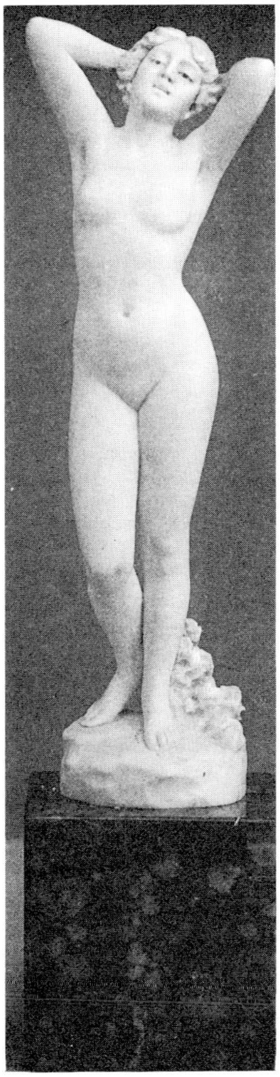

Nude, 18cm:7¾in.
Original cost £7

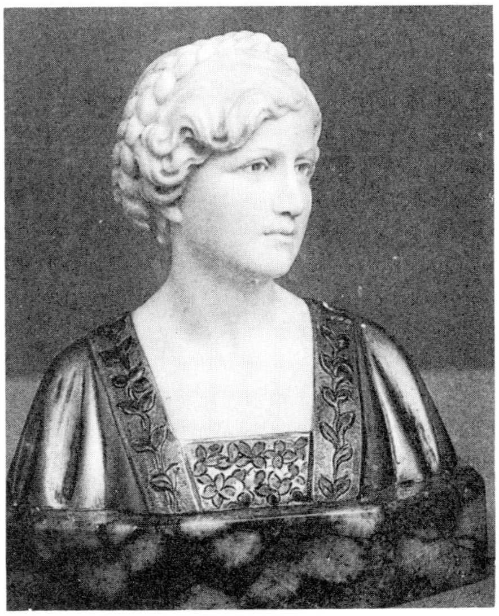

Bust, 9cm:3½in.
Original cost £6

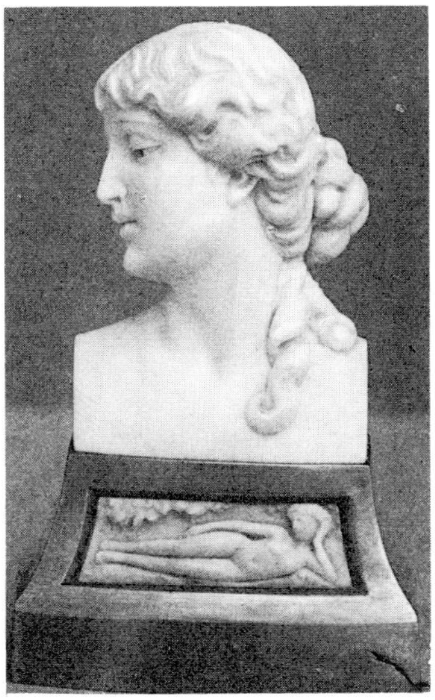

Bust, 10cm:3¾in.
Original cost £6

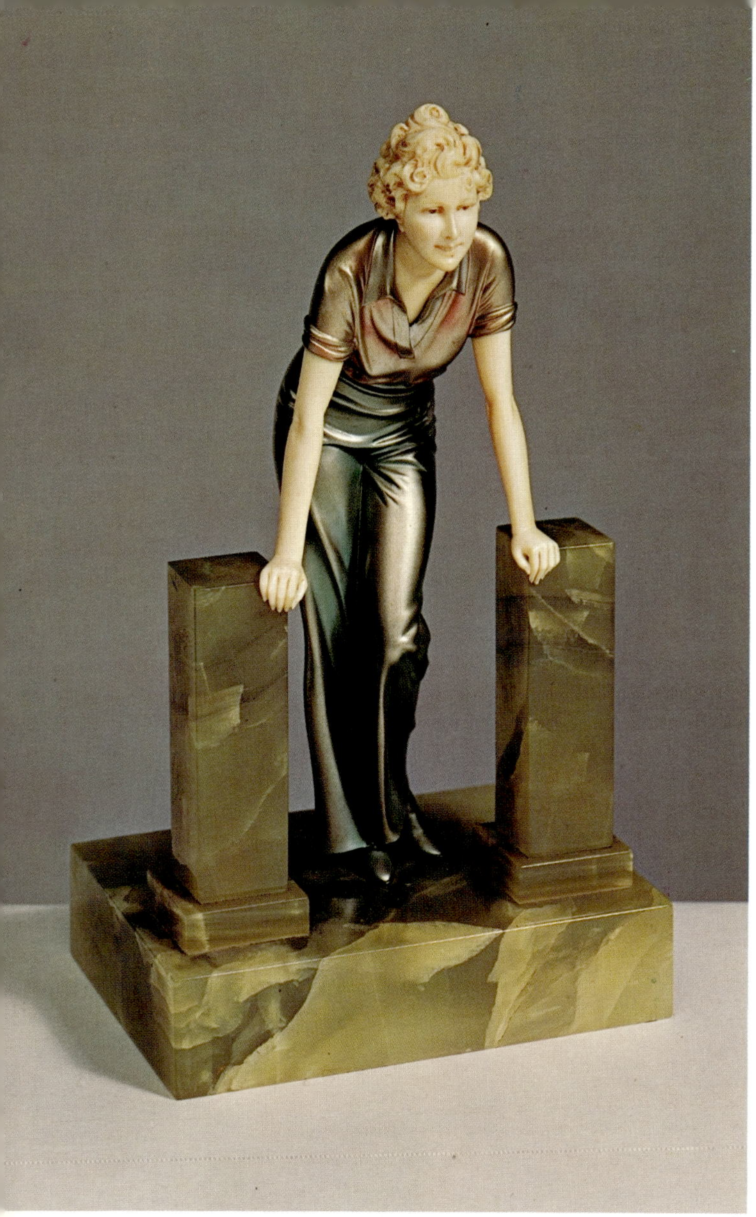

Right. F. Preiss
Airwoman
31cm:12in.
The figure is possibly modelled on Amy Johnson

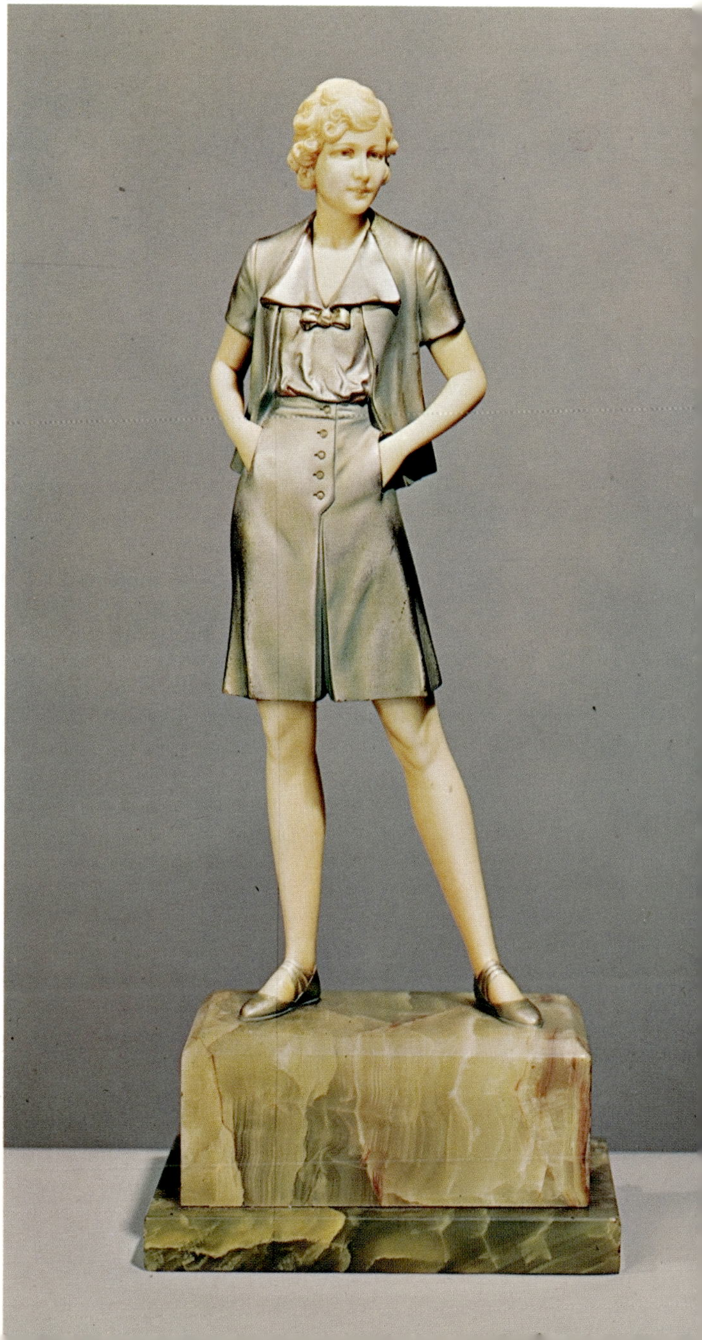

Two figures by F. Preiss
Above: *The Stile, 25cm:9¾in.*
Right: *Gamin, 34cm:13½in.; 25cm:9¾in.*

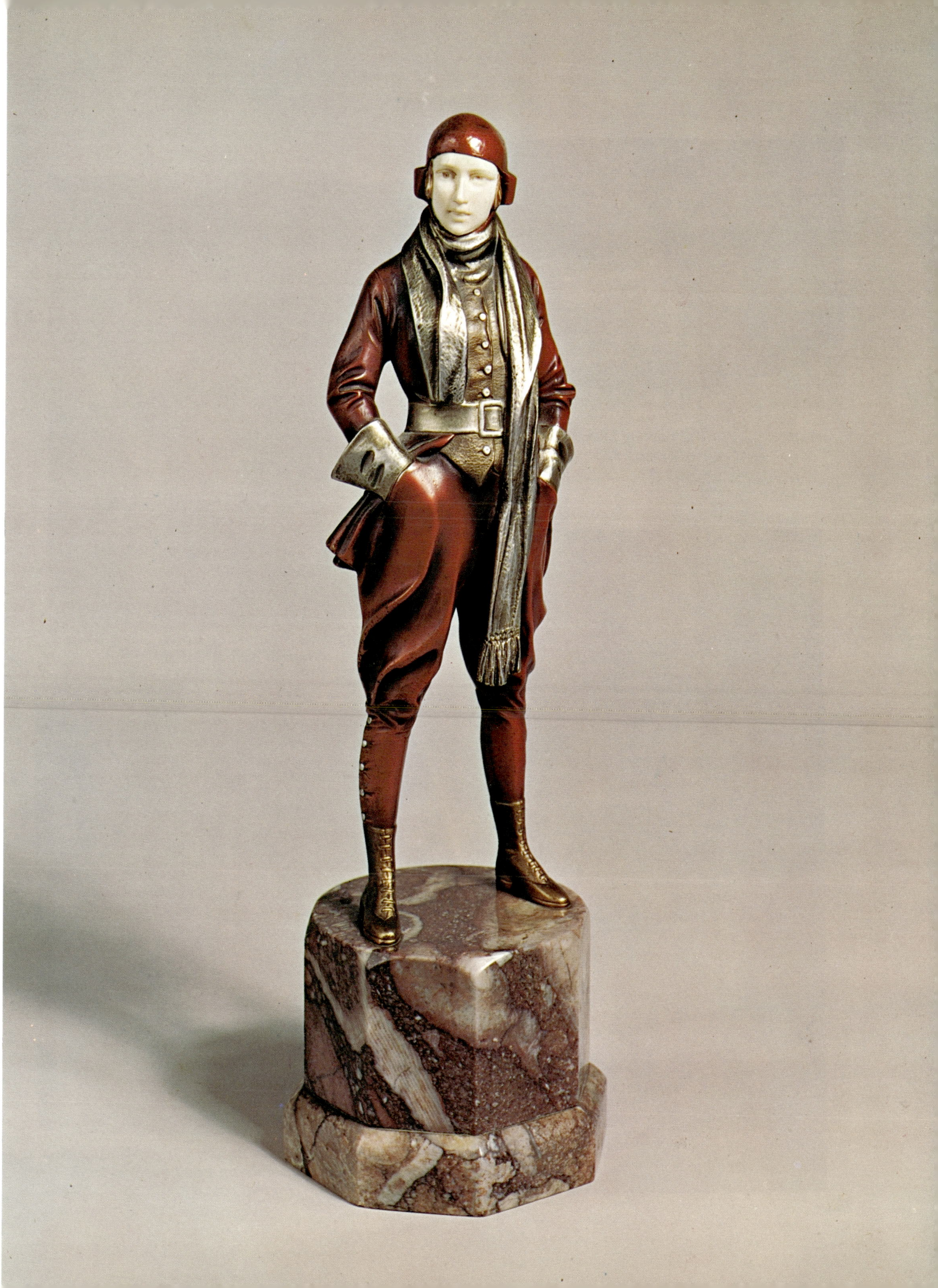

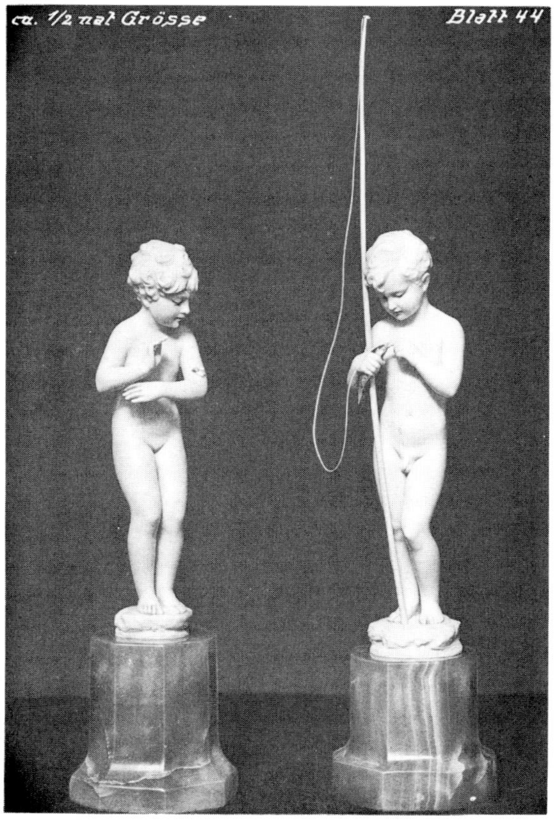

Girl with Fly *Fisher Boy*
Each measuring 18cm: 7in.; 14cm: 5½in.
Original cost £8 each

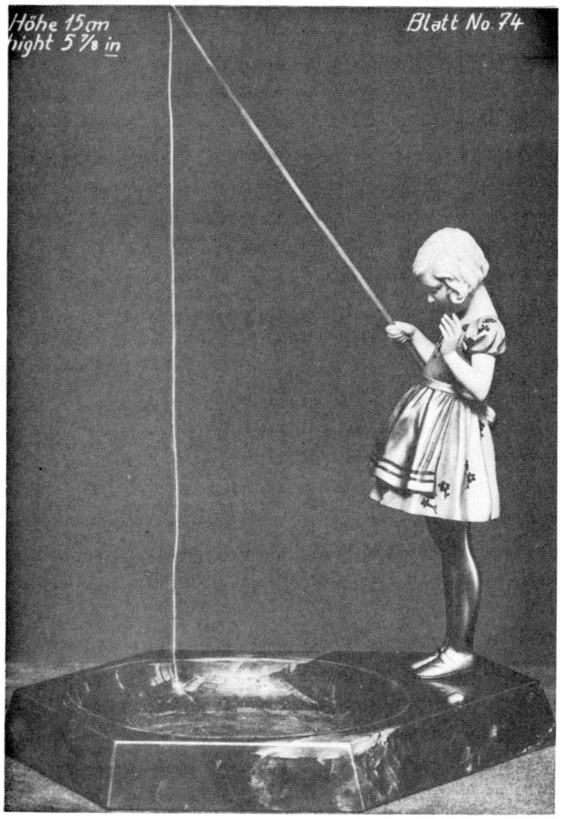

Girl Fishing, 15cm: 5¾in.
Original cost £6

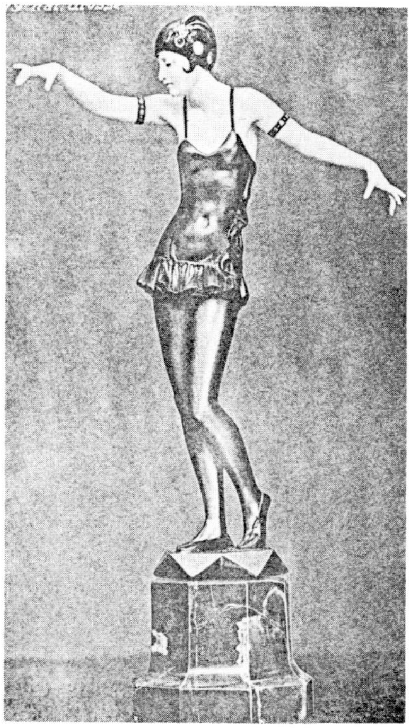

Dancer, 24cm: 9½in.

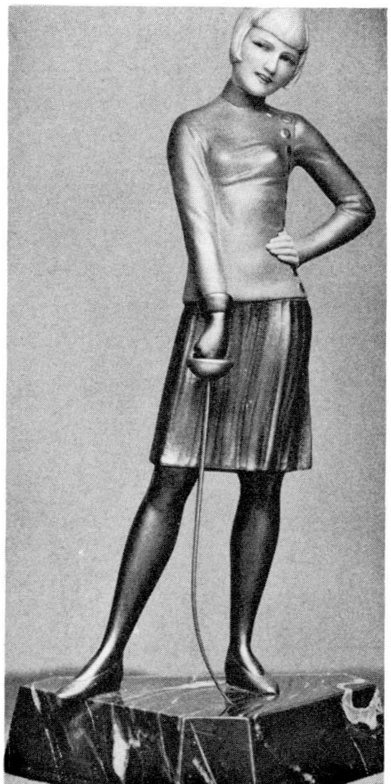

Girl Fencer
20cm: 7¾in.

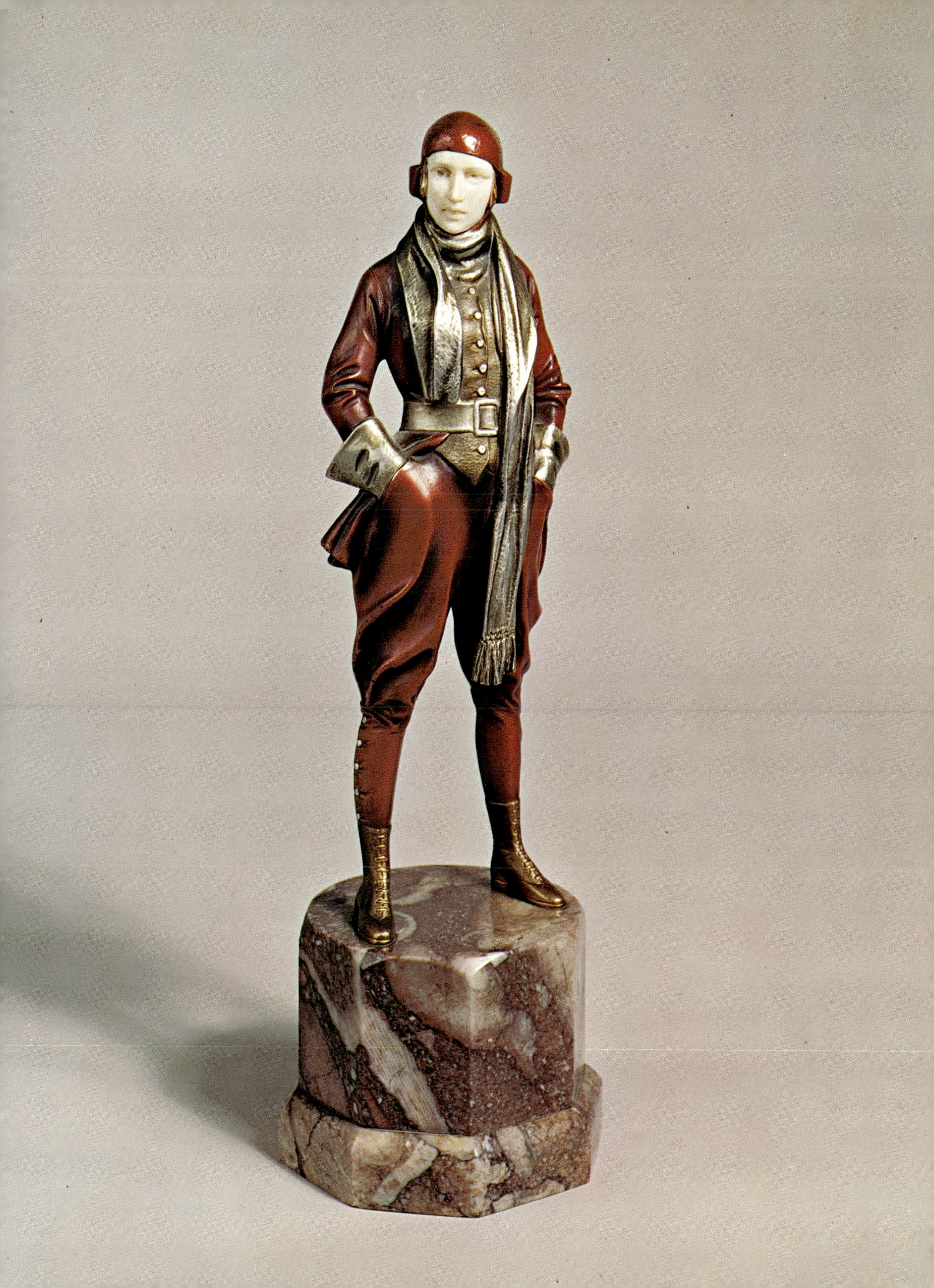

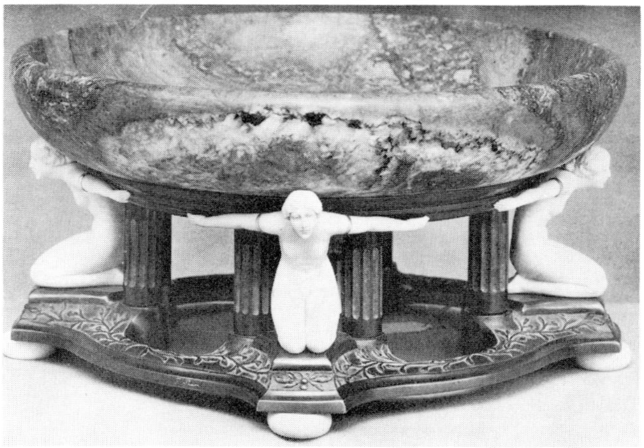

Grecian Maidens Supporting Dish, 15cm:5¾in.
Original cost £46

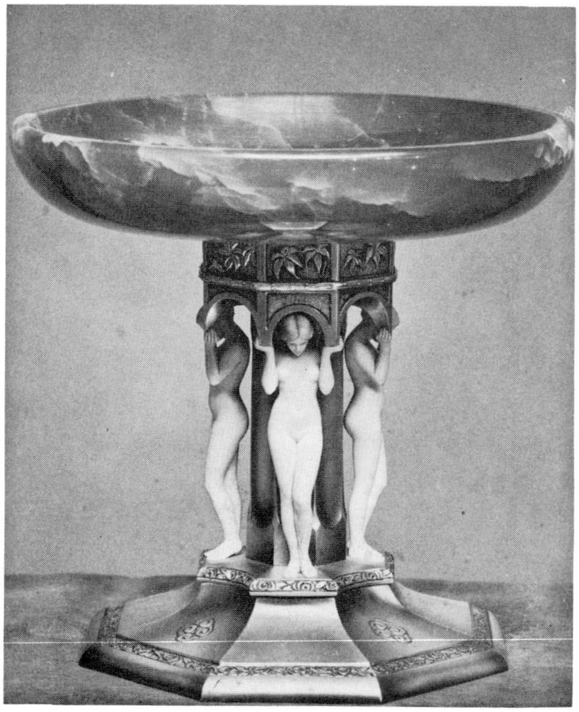

Grecian Maidens Supporting Bowl, 22cm:8¾in.
Original cost £32 10s.

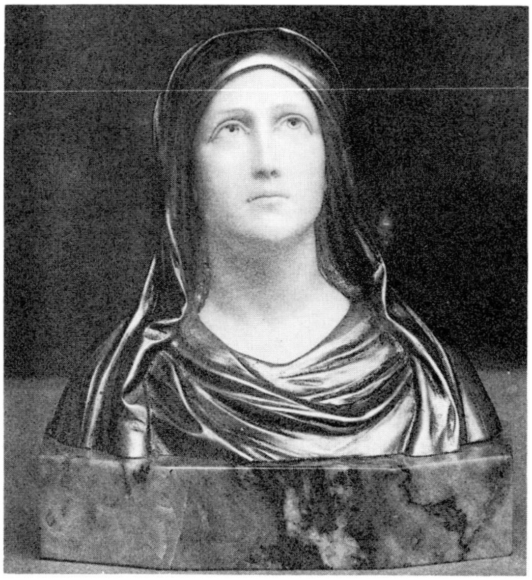

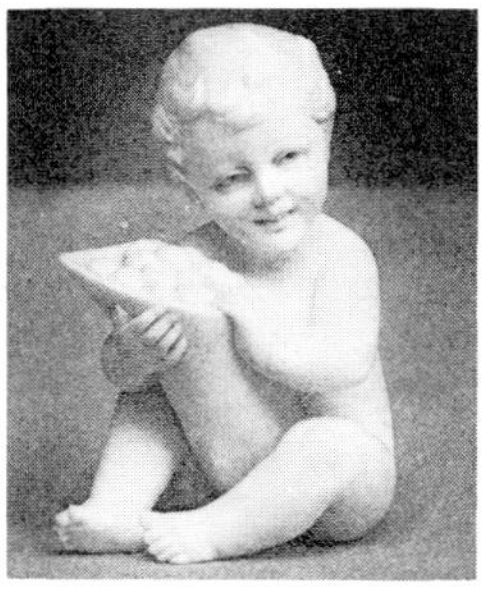

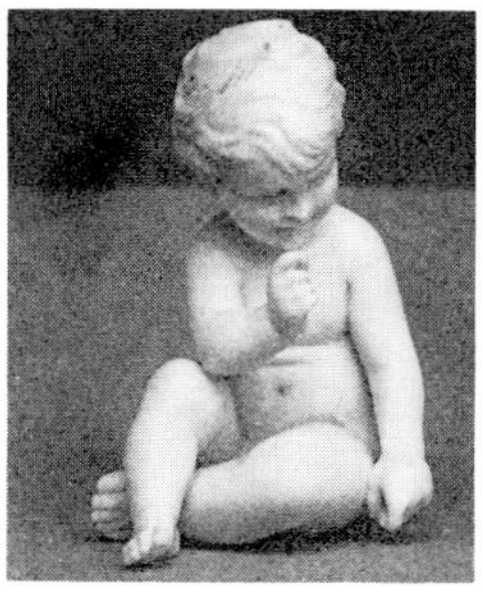

Bust with Two Ivory Children
10cm:4in. and 5cm:2in. Original cost £3—£5

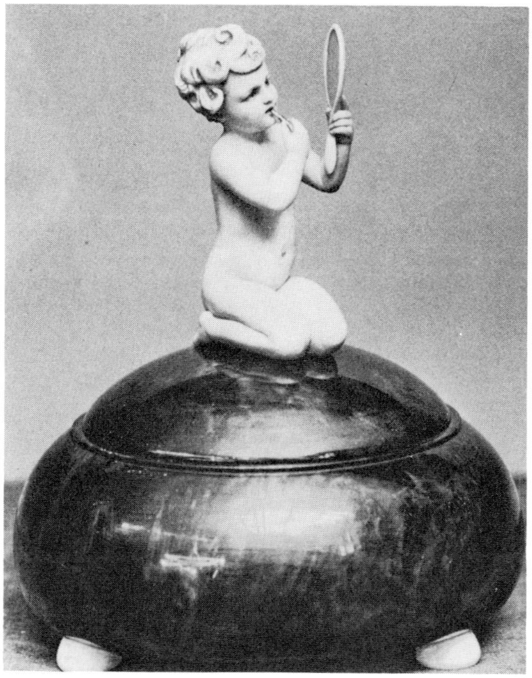

Lipstick (Powder Bowl), 13cm:5¼in.
Also available on small base
Original cost £7

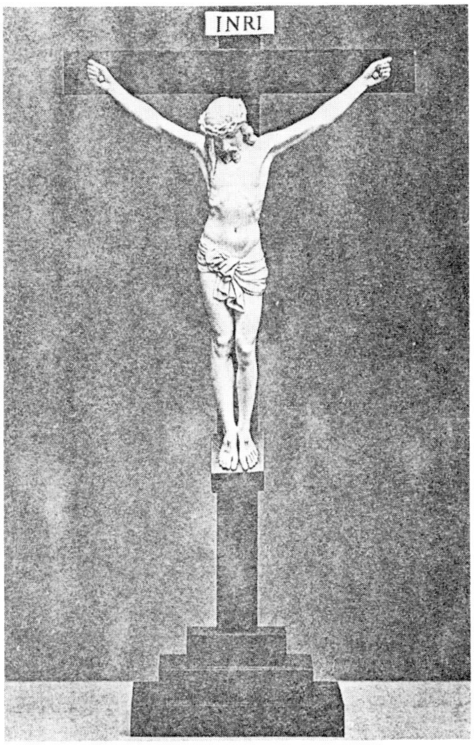

Crucifixion, 36cm:14in.

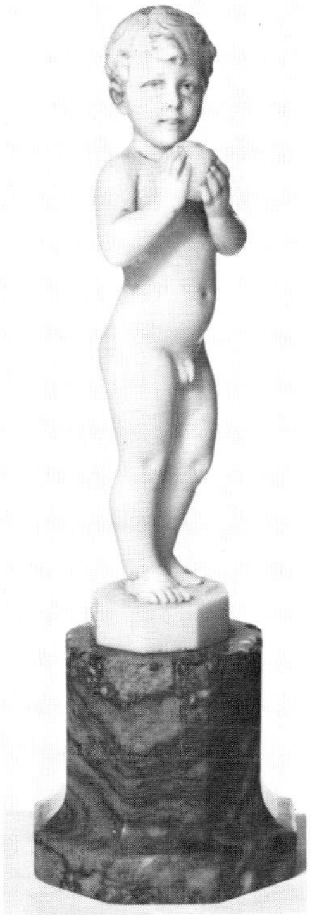

Boy with Apple
18cm:7in.; 15cm:5¾in.

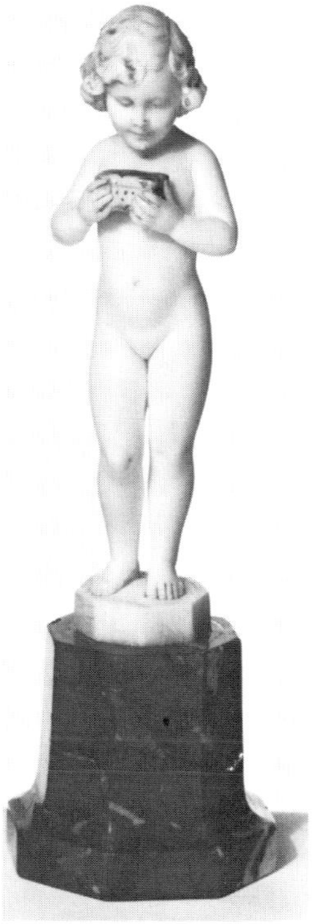

Girl with Casket
18cm:7in.; 15cm:5¾in.

Original cost £5–£8

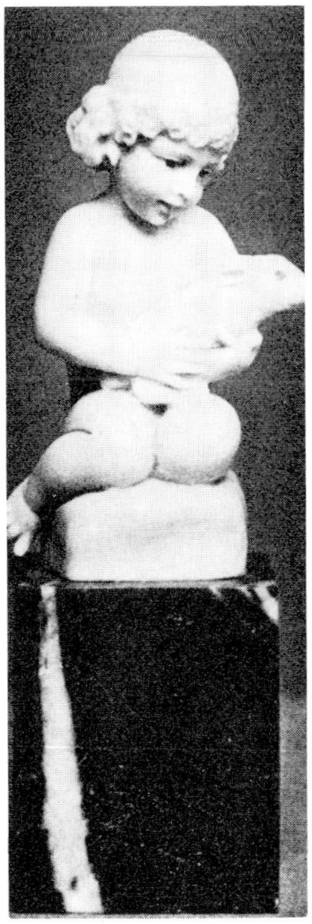

Girl and Rabbit
8cm:3in.
Original cost £3

Right,
from left to right:
Boy with Canary,
Girl with
Skipping Rope,
Boy with Trumpet.
Each measuring
14cm:5½in.
Original cost
£5 each

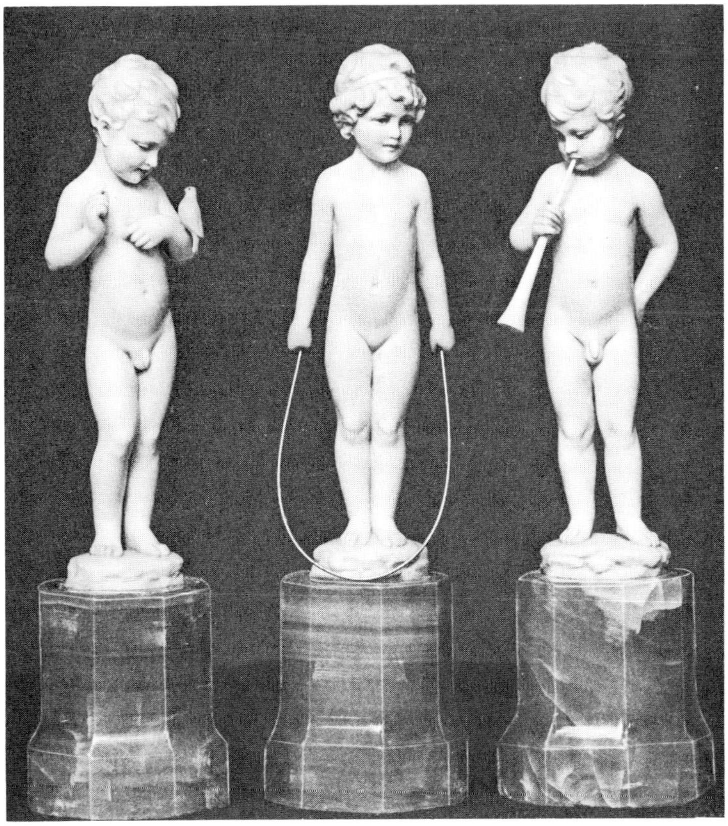

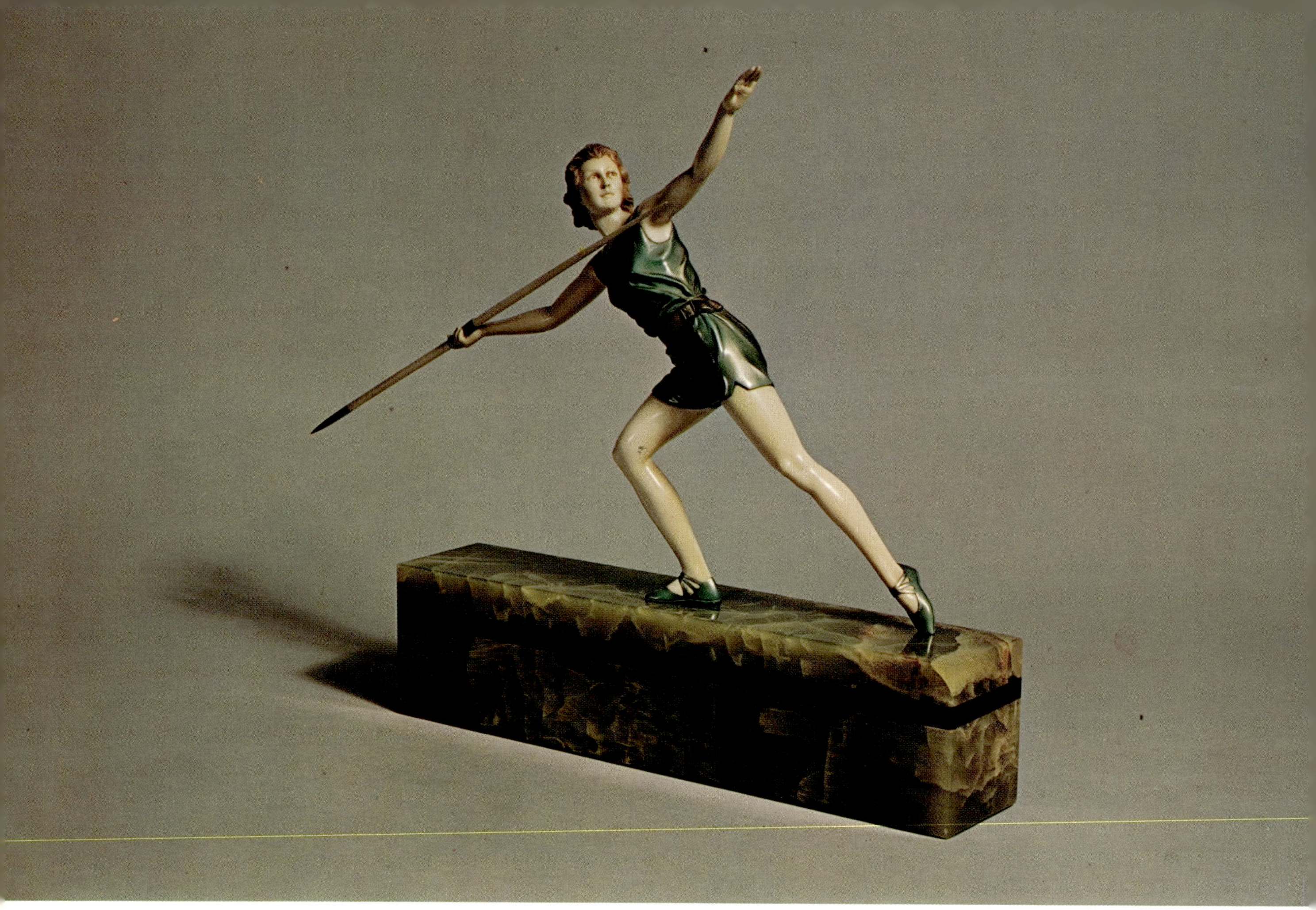

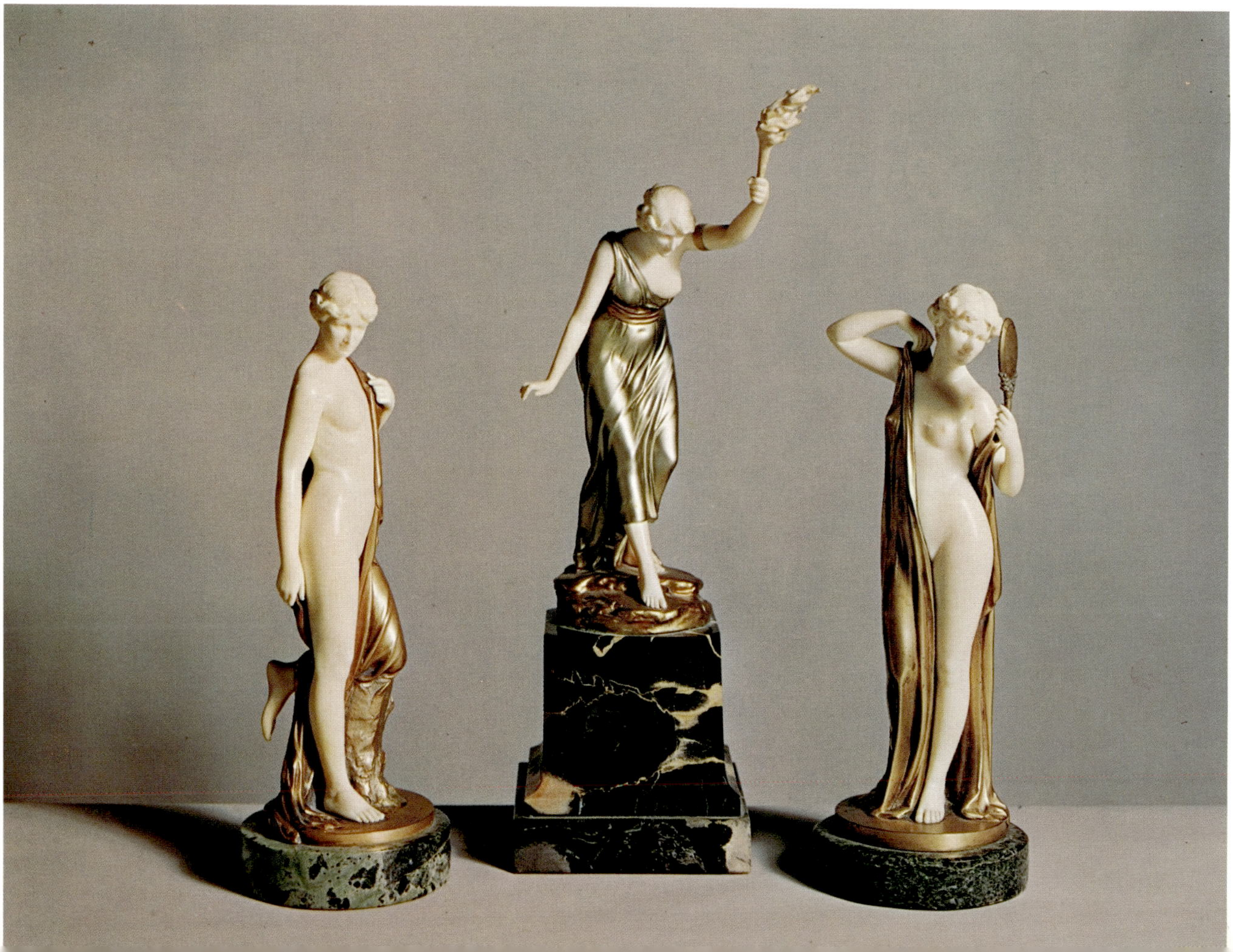

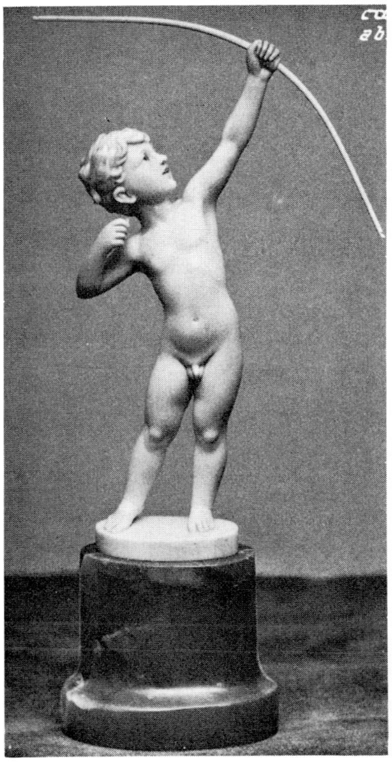

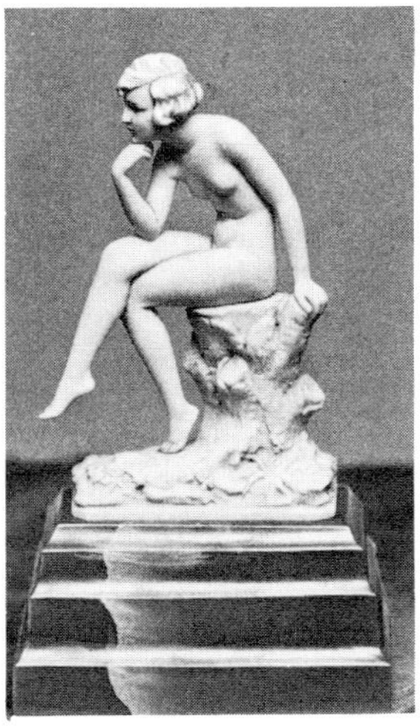

Contemplation
11cm:4½in.
Original cost £5–£7

Left: Archer, 18cm:7in. Original cost £5–£7

Right: Girl Feeding Bird, 18cm:7in.
Original cost £5–£7

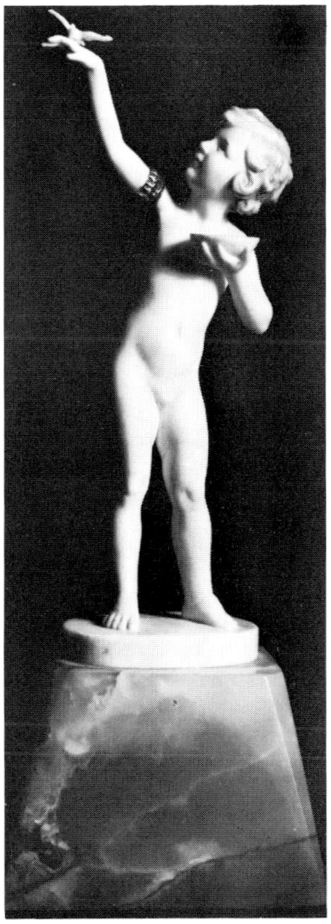

Above left. F. Preiss –
Javelin Thrower, 30cm:11¾in.
Left. Three figures by F. Preiss
Left to right: *Aphrodite, 22cm:8½in.*
Grecian with Torch, 28cm:11in.;
Vanity, 22cm:8½in.
Original cost for each figure £15

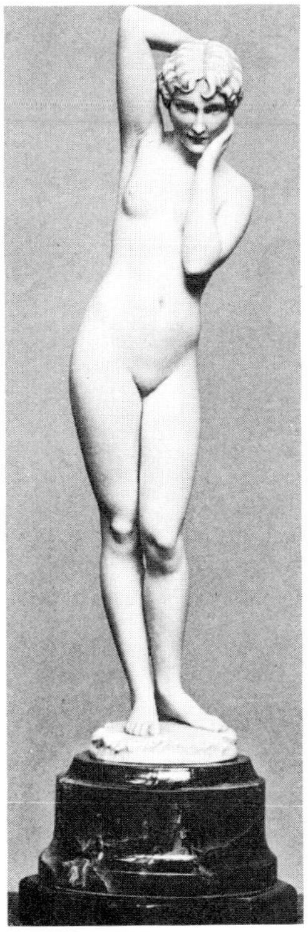

Posing, 22cm:8¾in.
Original cost £16

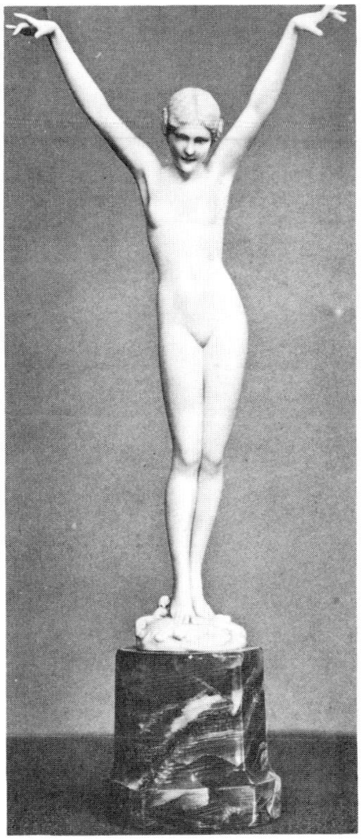

Ecstasy, 20cm:8in.
Original cost £8

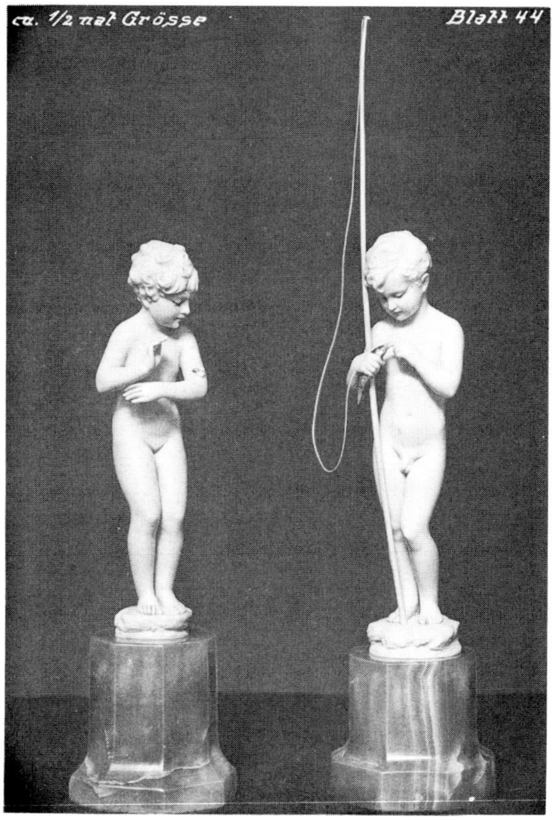

Girl with Fly *Fisher Boy*
Each measuring 18cm: 7in.; 14cm: 5½in.
Original cost £8 each

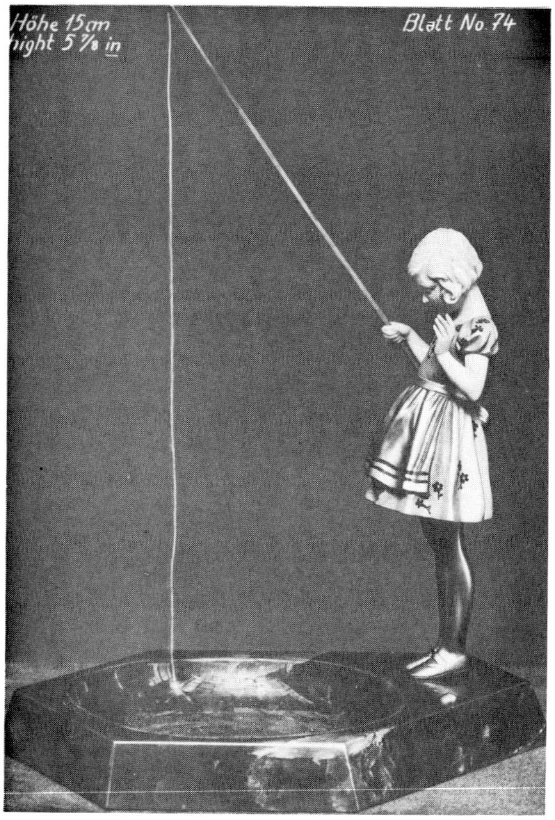

Girl Fishing, 15cm: 5¾in.
Original cost £6

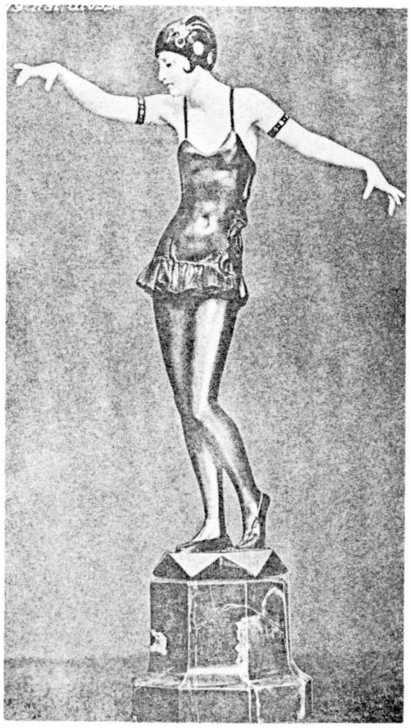

Dancer, 24cm: 9½in.

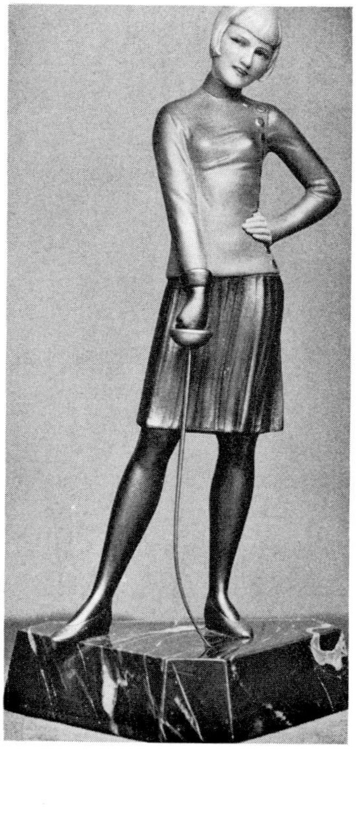

Girl Fencer
20cm: 7¾in.

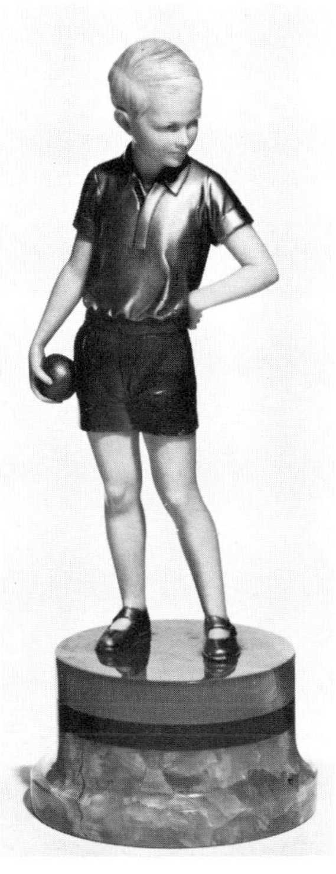

Little Cricketer
19cm: 7½in.

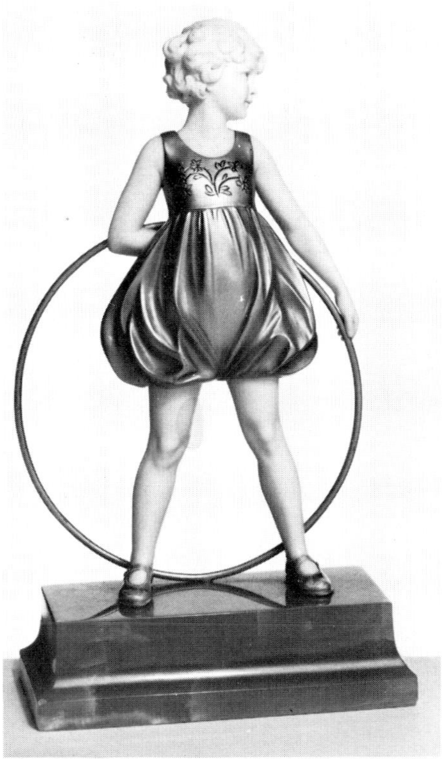

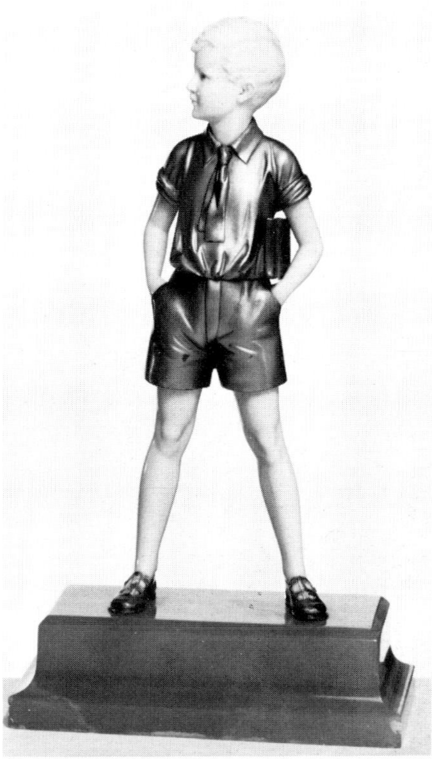

Hoop Girl and Sonny Boy. Each 31cm: 12in.; 20cm: 7¾in.

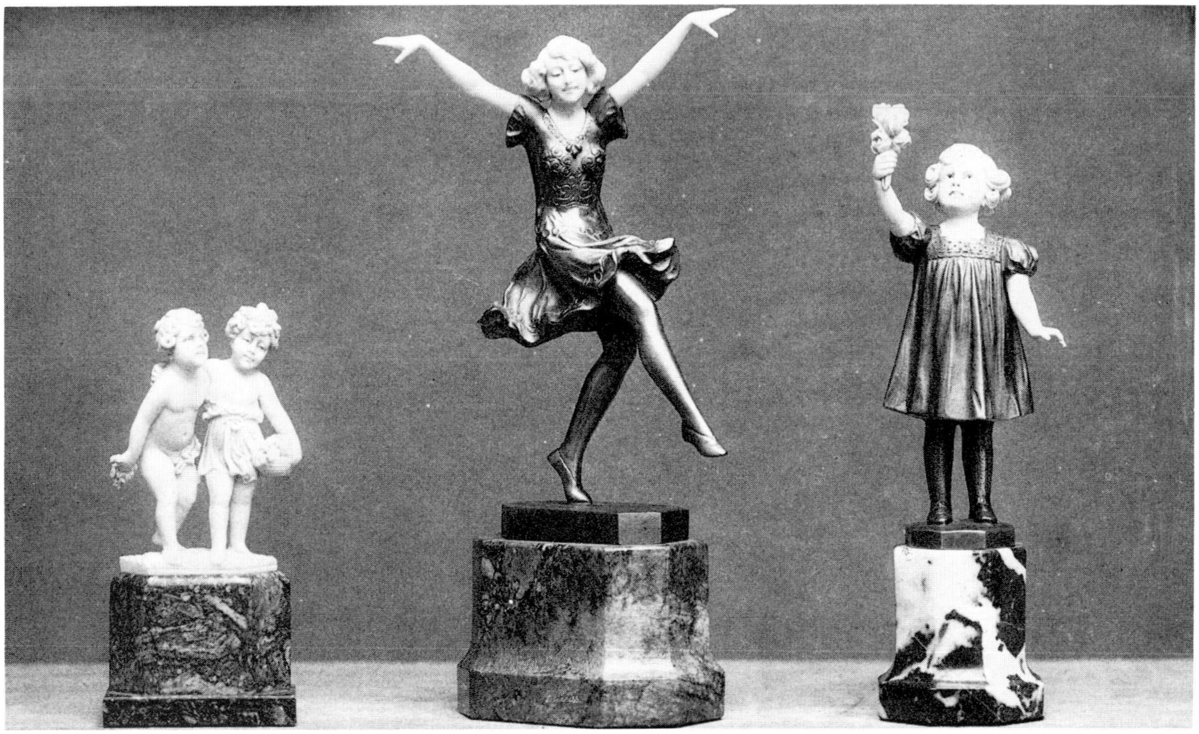

Left to right: Cherubs, 10cm: 4in. Original cost £7
Dancing Figure, 20cm: 8in. Original cost £7
The Posy, 18cm: 7in. Original cost £4 10s.

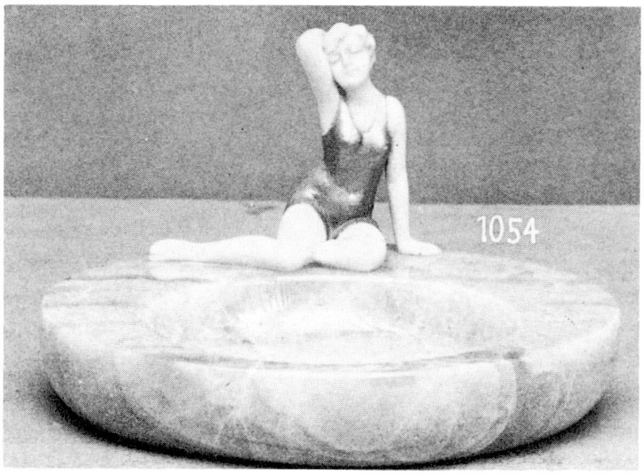

Sunshine, 10cm:4in. Original cost £3 3s.

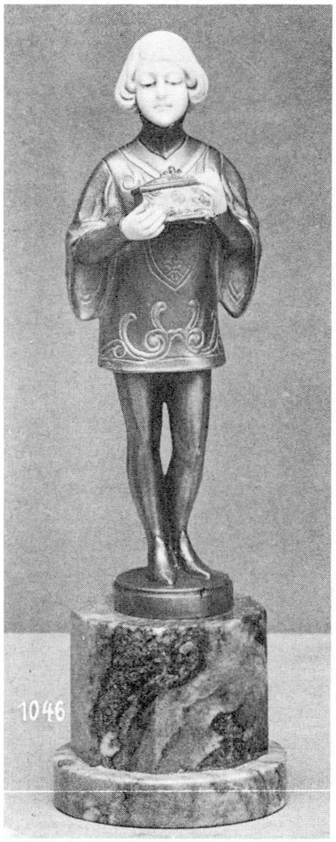

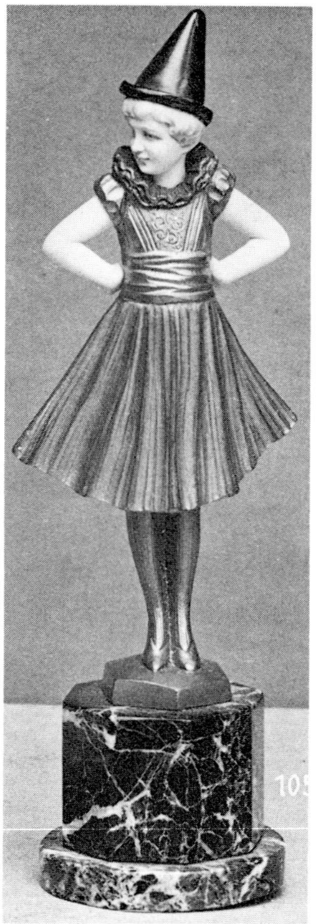

Left: Page Boy, 17cm:6½in. Original cost £4 45s.
Right: Pierrette, 18cm:7in. Original cost £5

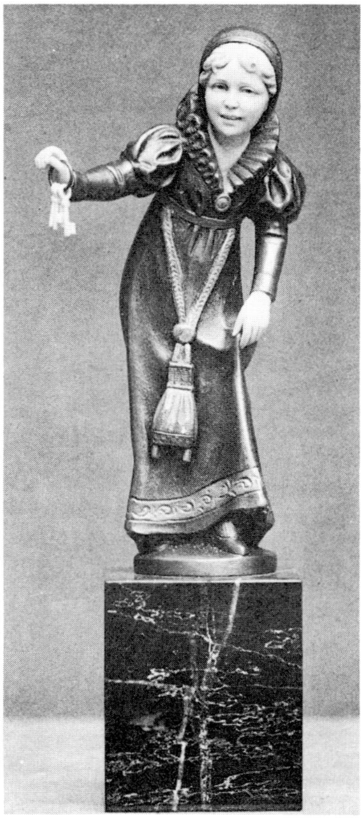

Child with Keys, 13cm:5in.
Original cost £3

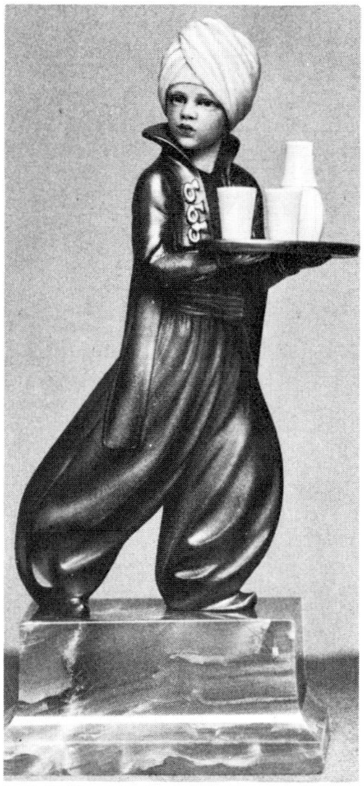

Oriental Waiter
18cm:7in.
A Girl was also
produced

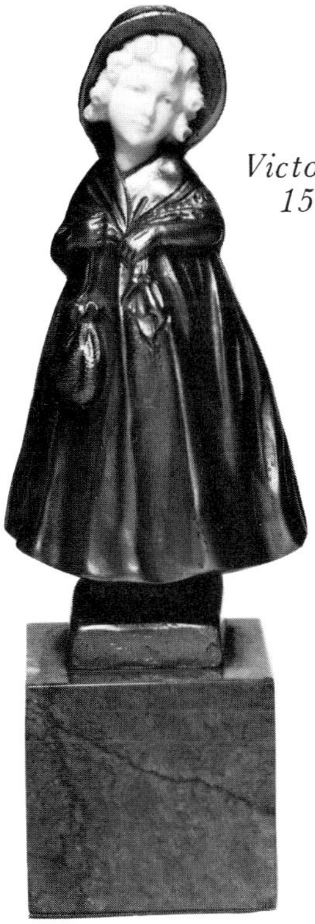

Victorian Child
15cm:6in.

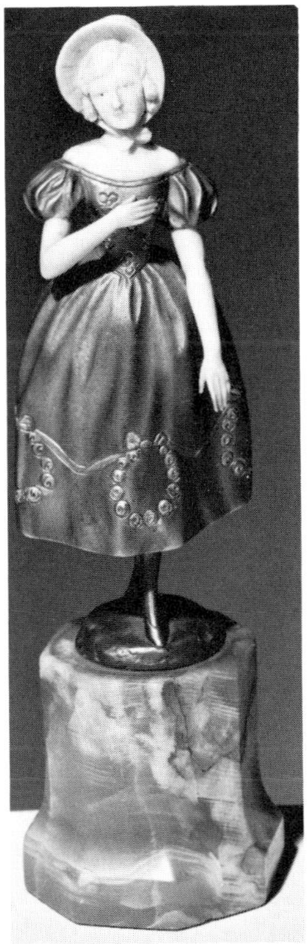

Victorian Lady
15cm:6in.
Original cost £3

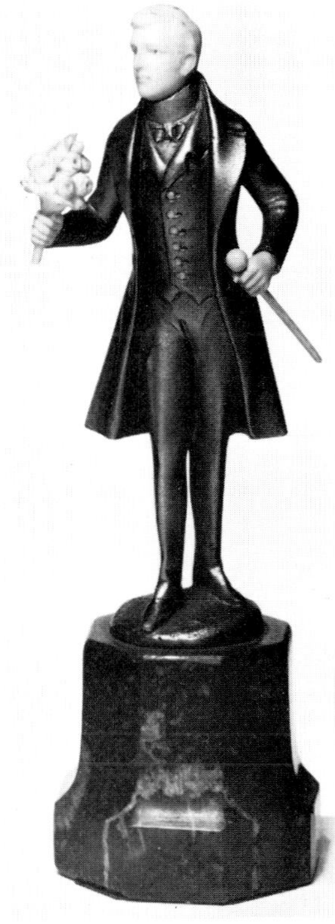

Victorian Gentleman
15cm:6in.
Original cost £3

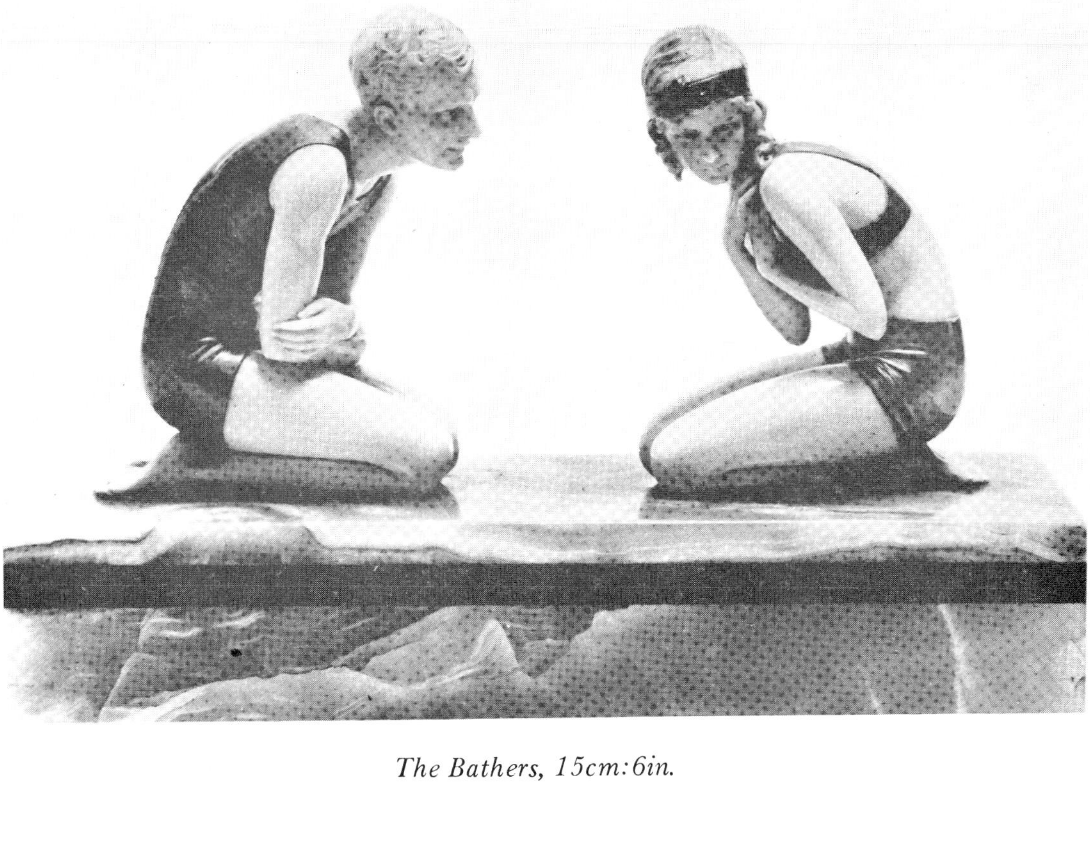

The Bathers, 15cm:6in.

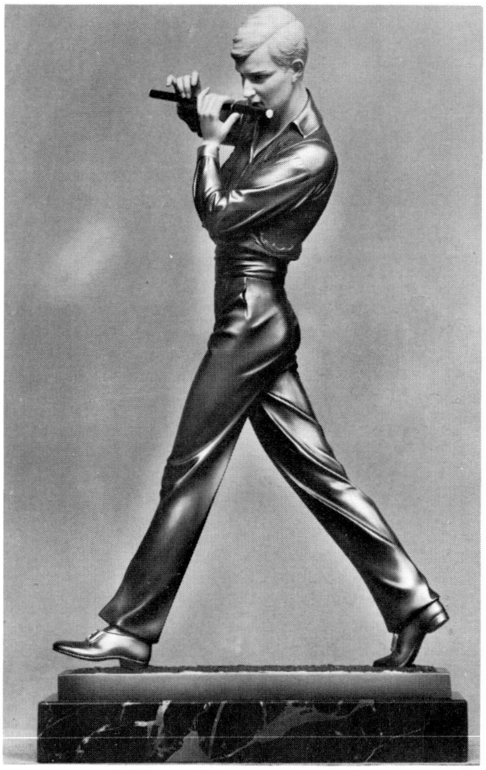

Flute Player, 43cm:17in.

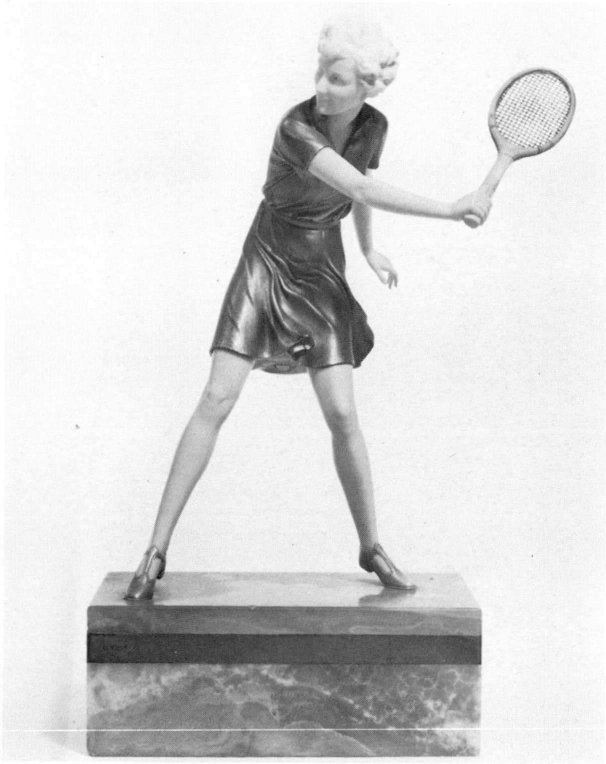

Girl Tennis Player, 29cm:11¼in.

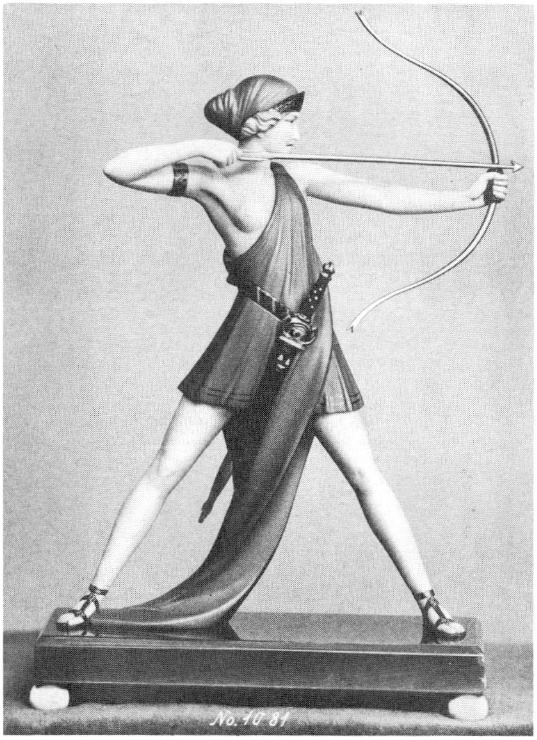

The Archer, 46cm:18in.; 20cm:9in.
Original cost £67 and £17 respectively

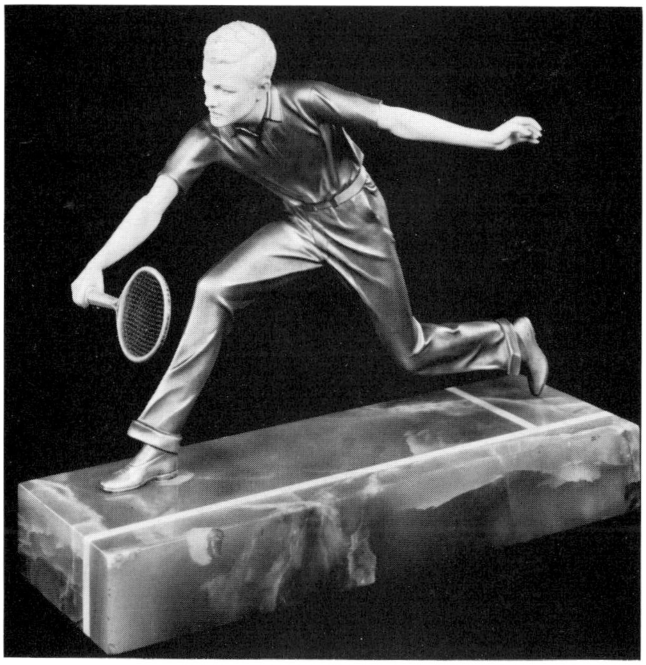

Male Tennis Player, 25cm:10in.

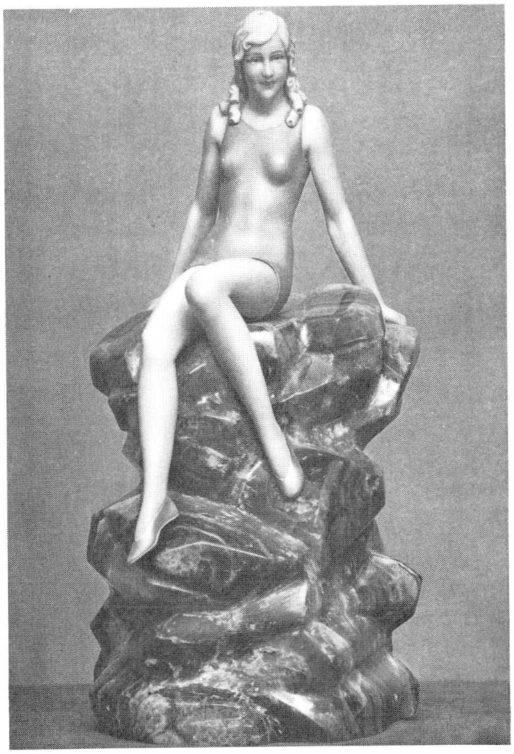

Bather on Rock, 24cm:9¼in.

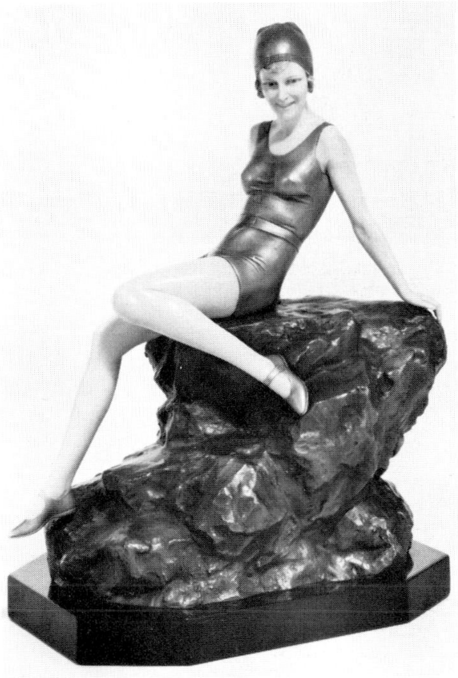

Bather with Cap on Rock 25cm:10in.

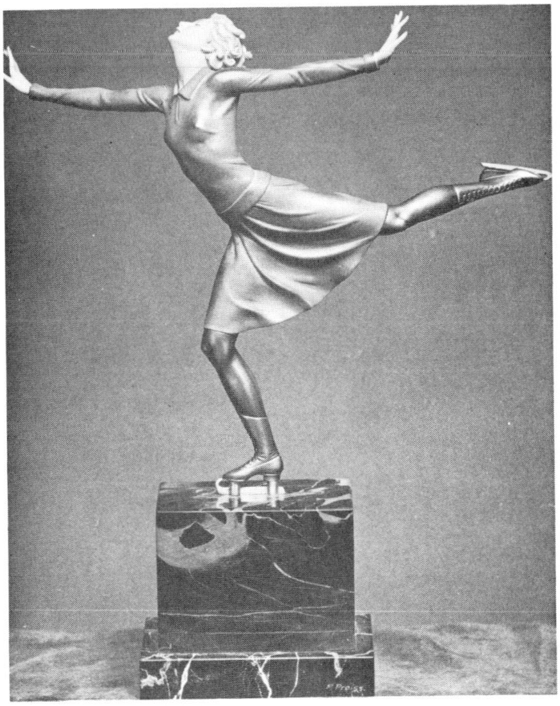

Skater, 35cm:13¾in. Another version is known with the girl wearing a cap

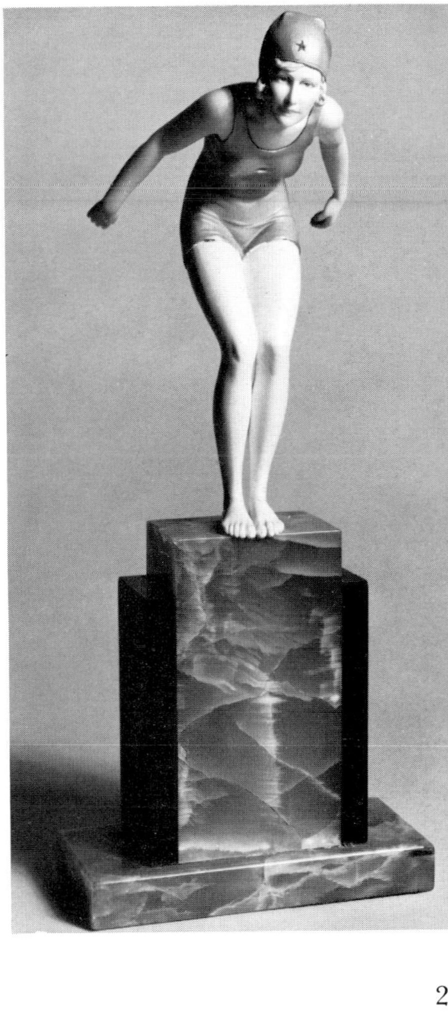

The Diver 30cm:11¾in.

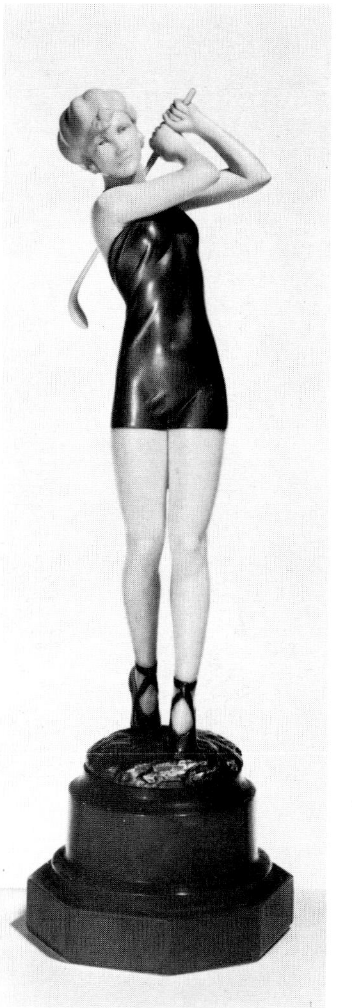

Golfer
34cm:13½in.
A similar figure, with a long skirt and bronze legs, was also produced

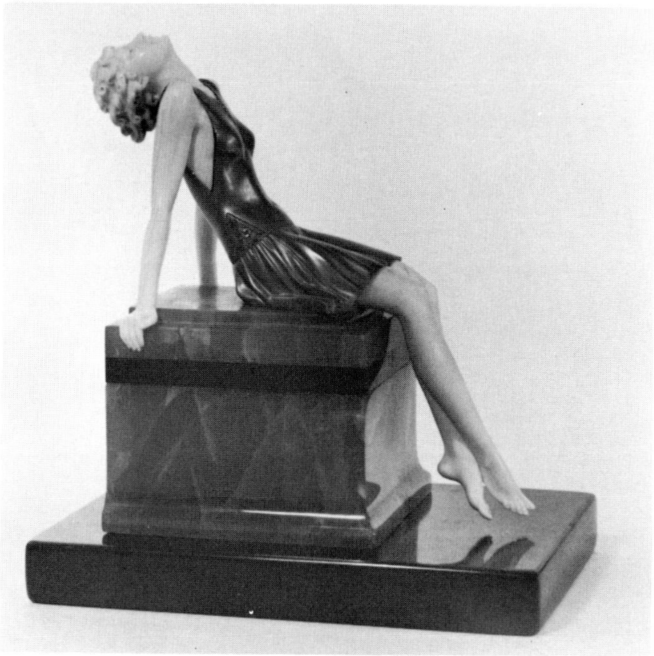

Sun Worshipper
20cm:7¾in.

Below: Breasting the Tape, 27cm:10½in.

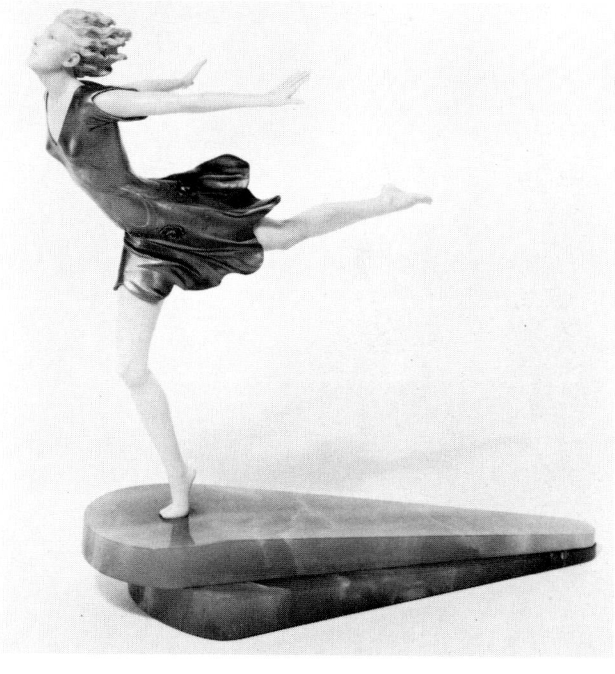

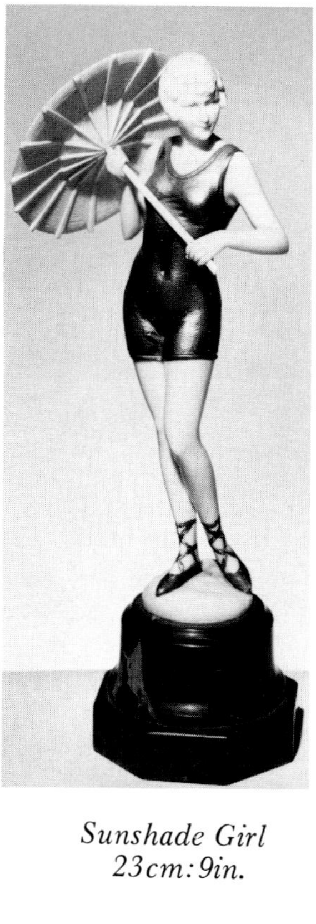

Sunshade Girl
23cm:9in.

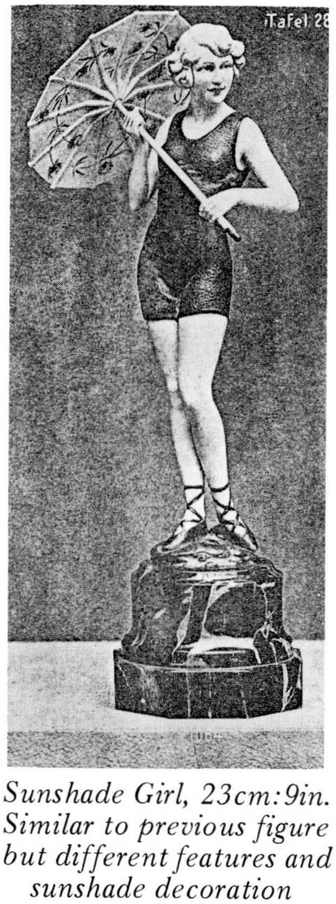

Sunshade Girl, 23cm:9in.
Similar to previous figure but different features and sunshade decoration
Original cost £10

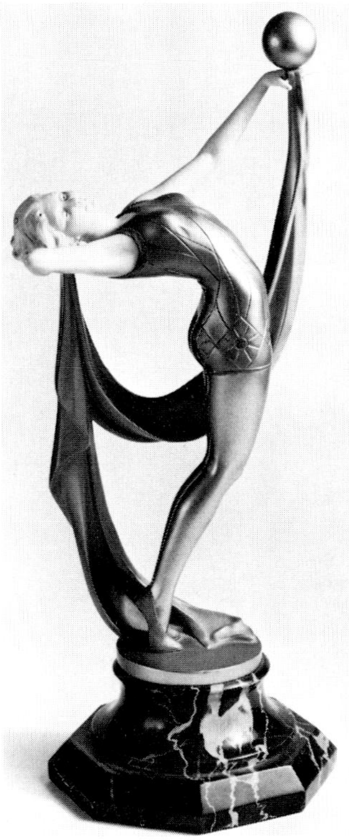

Balancing, 38cm:15in.

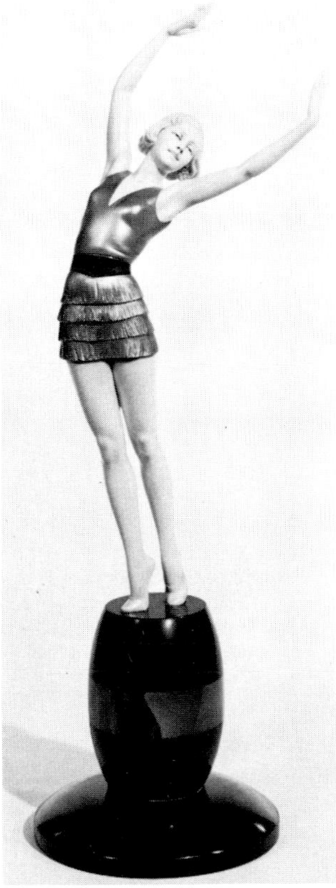

Beach Ball Girl
(ball missing)
38cm:15in.

Lighter than Air (Miss Ada May, taken from C.B. Cochran's 1930 Revue) 34cm: 13½in. Original cost £19

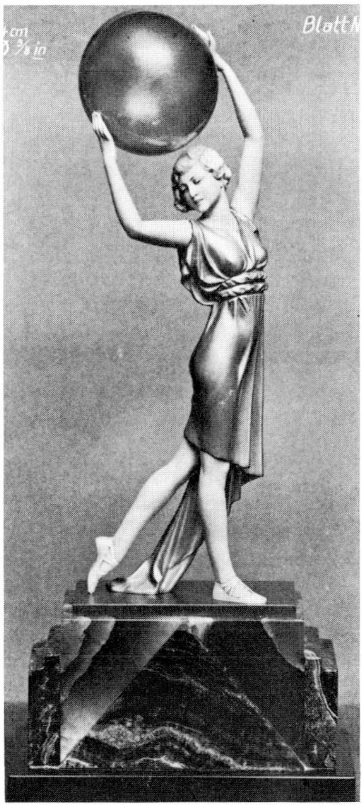

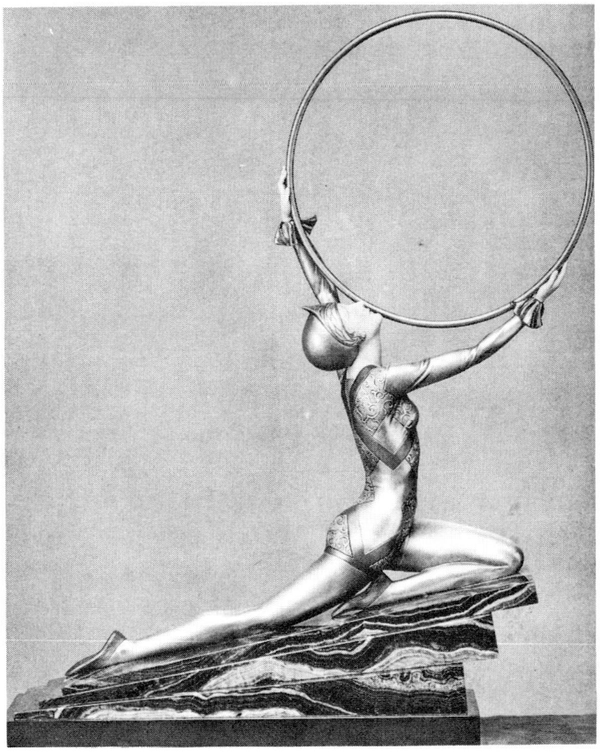

Ecstasy, 56cm:22in.
Figures also known holding a clock or mirror in place of the hoop

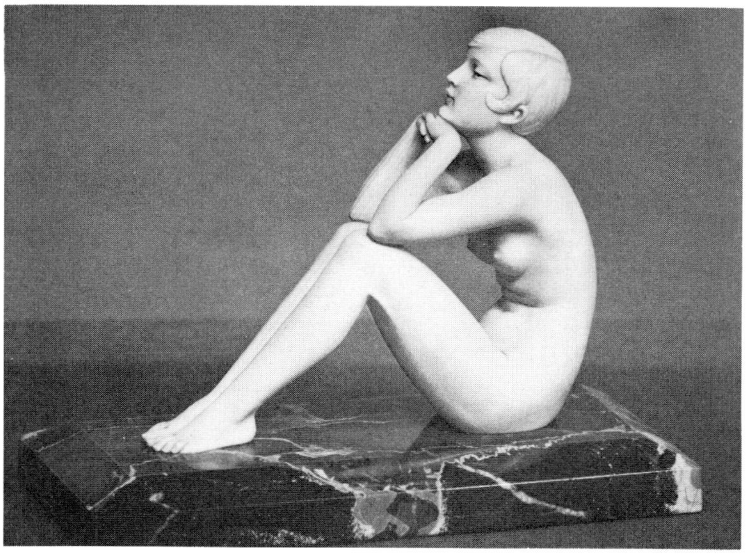

Thoughts, 10cm: 4in.

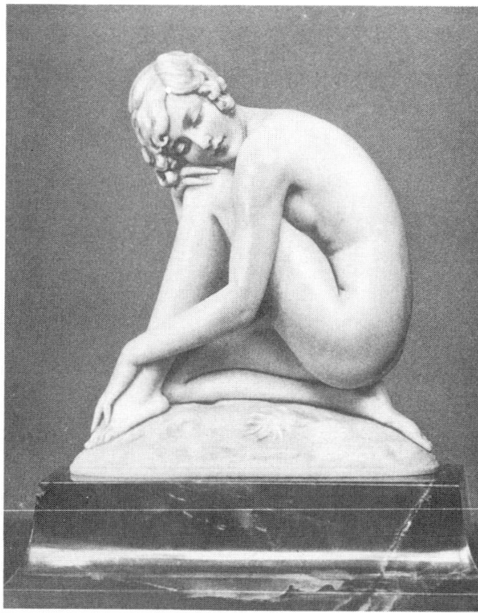

Dreaming, 13cm: 5¼in.
Original cost £16

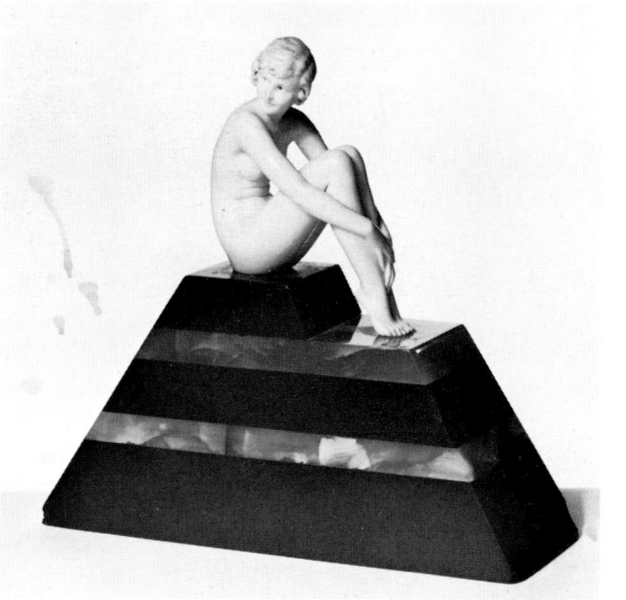

Ivory Nude, 15cm: 6in.
Same figure produced wearing bathing costume

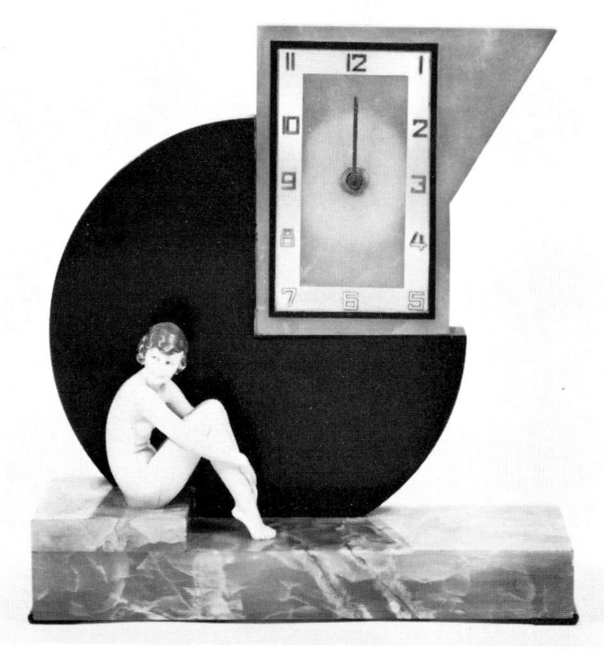

Ivory Nude with Clock, 25cm: 10in.

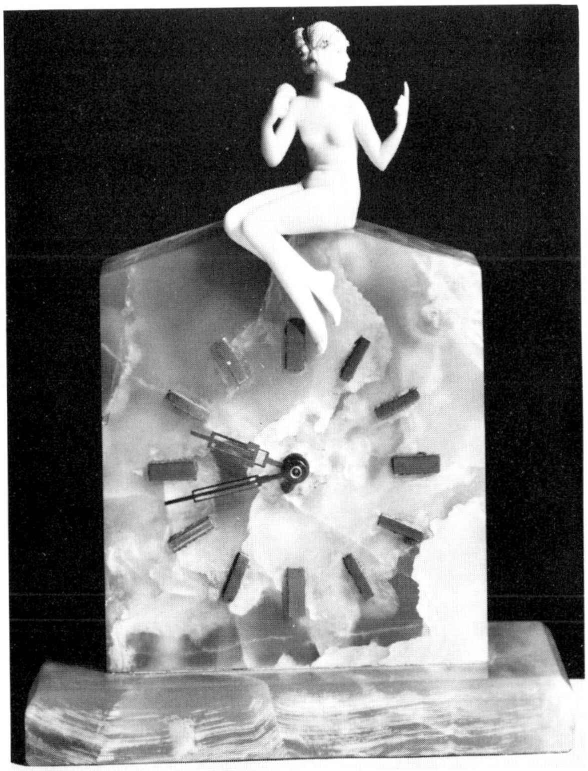

The Toilet, 15cm:6in.

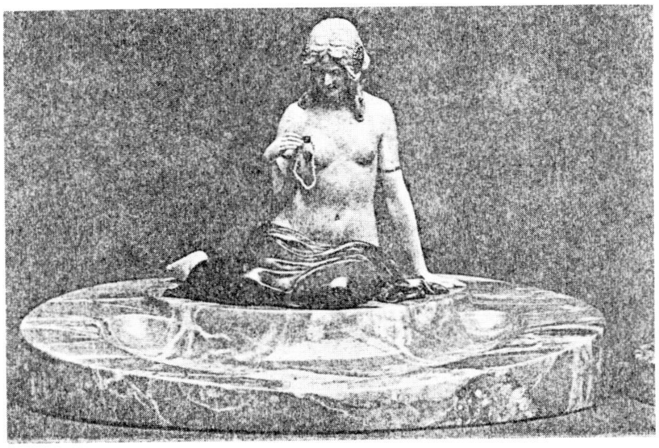

The Necklace, 25cm:10in.

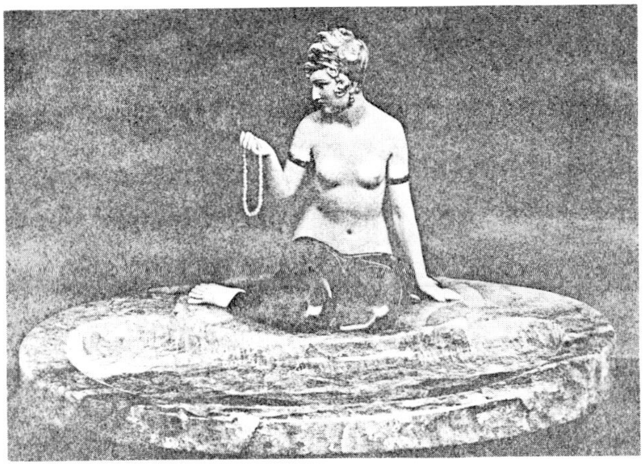

String of Pearls, 13cm:5in.

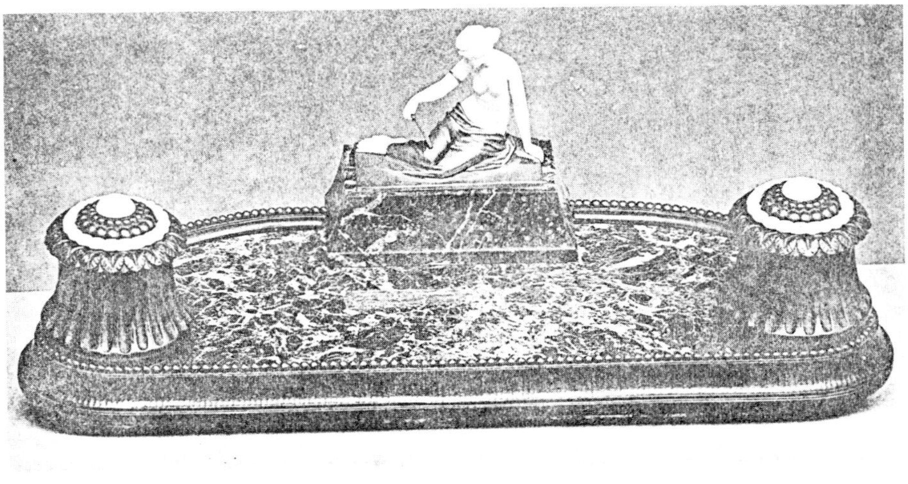

Inkstand, 13cm:5in.

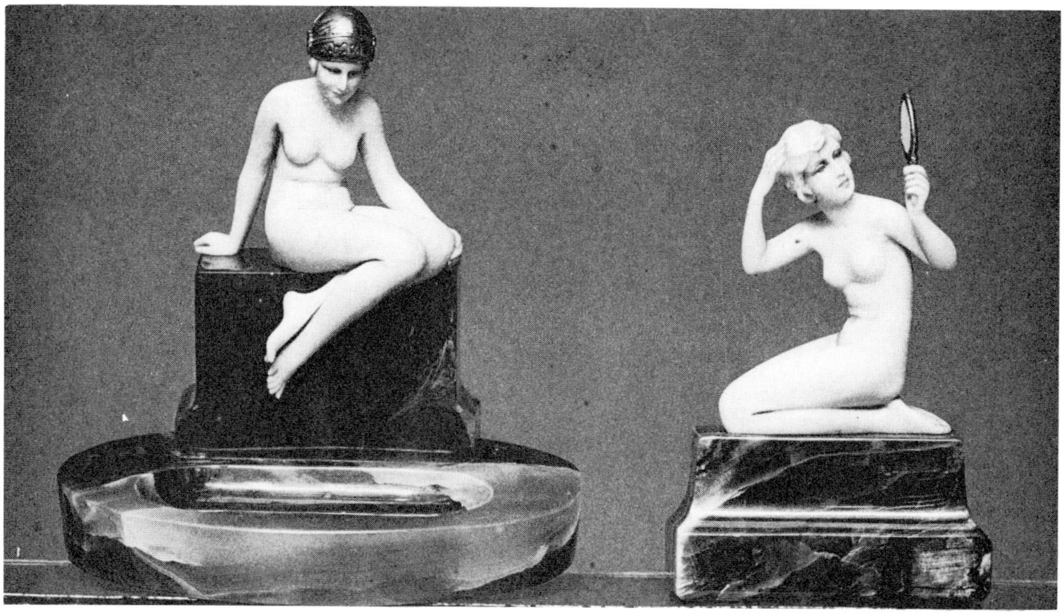

Reflection *Toilette*

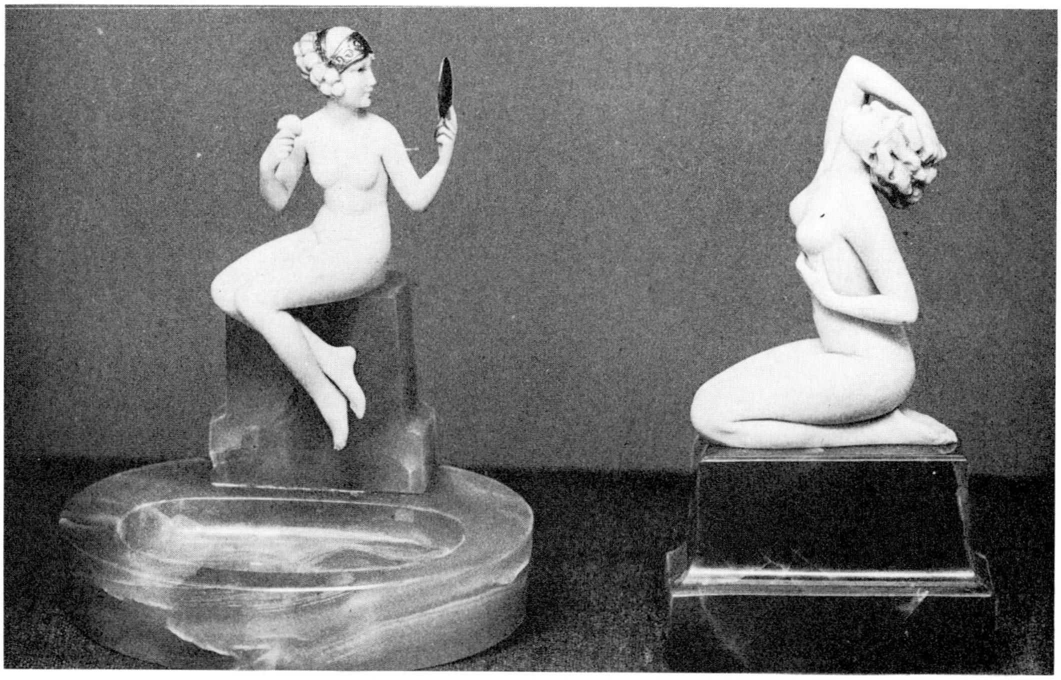

The Toilet *Posing*

All ivory, all about 9cm: 3½in. Original cost £4—£5 each

Right. F. Preiss
Flame Leaper, 34cm: 13½in.
Also known to be mounted as bookends without the supporting flame, as well as in front of a mirror.
Original cost £25

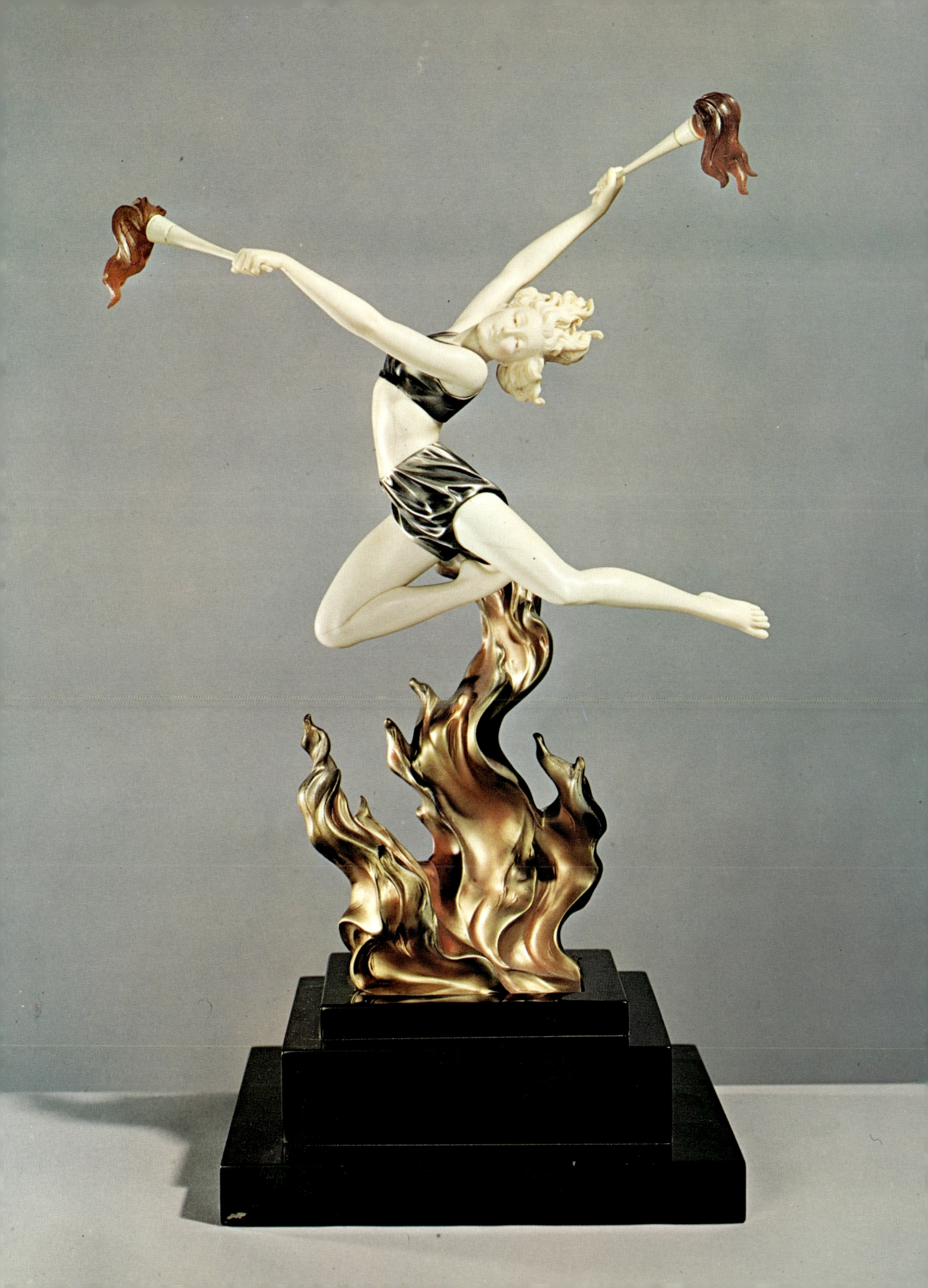

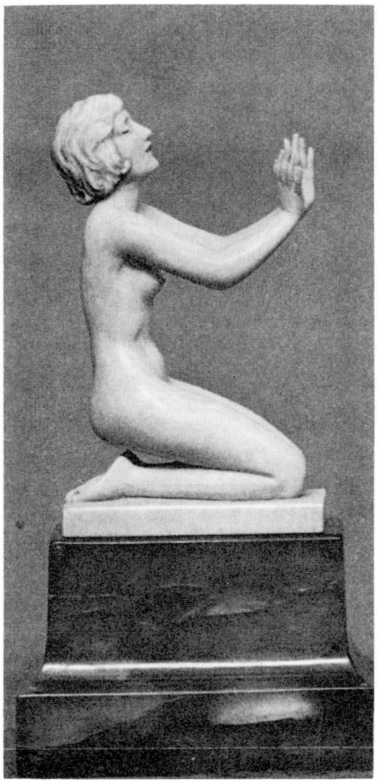

Ivory Nude, 18cm:7in.

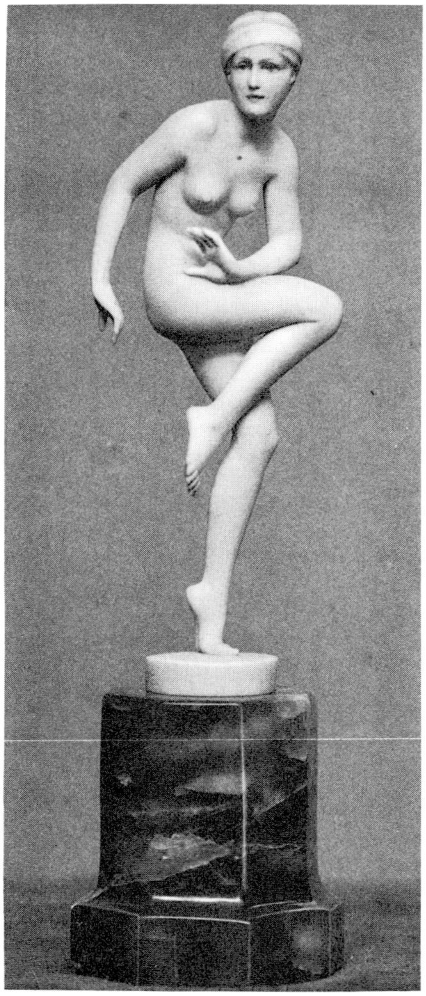

Ivory Nude, 25cm:10in.

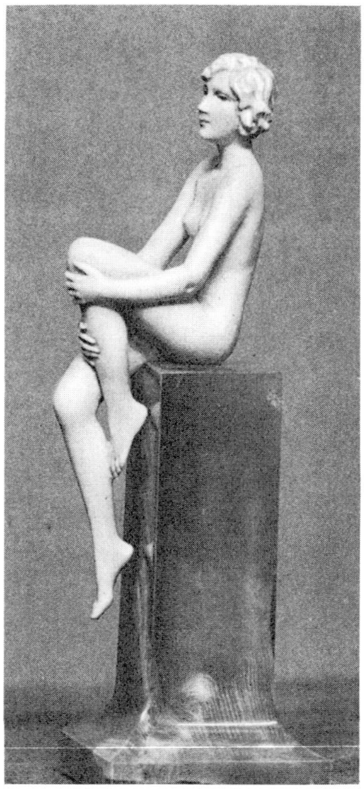

Ivory Nude, 18cm:7in.

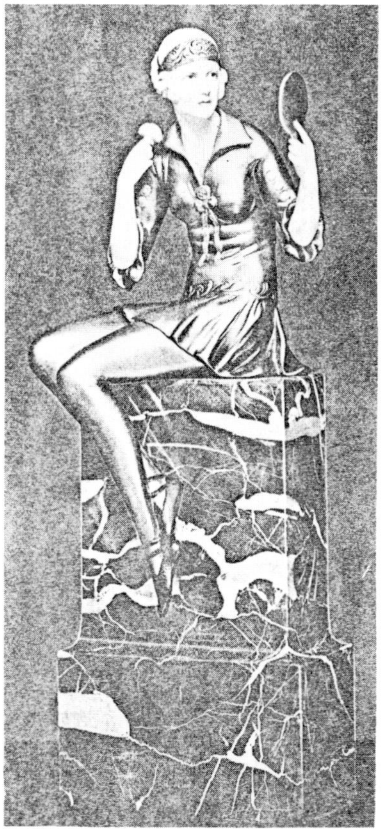

Powder Puff
33cm:13in.

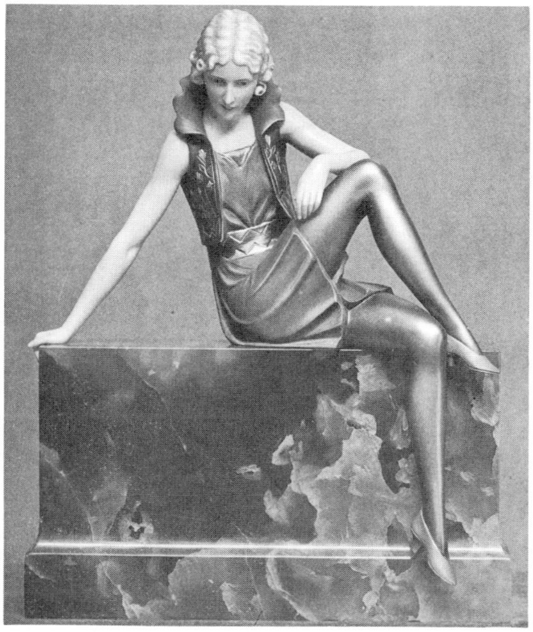

Girl on Wall, 23cm:9in.
Various hairstyles have
been used for this work

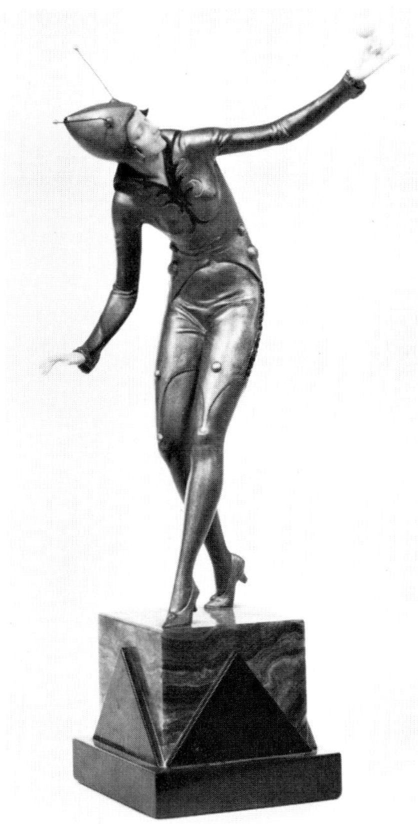

Moth Girl, 43cm:17in.
Original cost £16

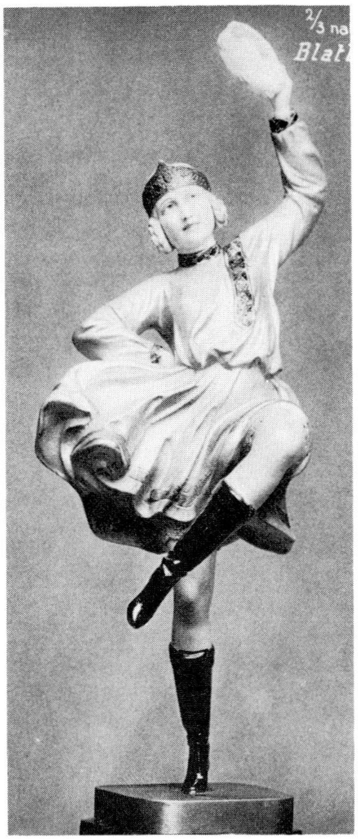

Russian Dancer
30cm:11¾in.

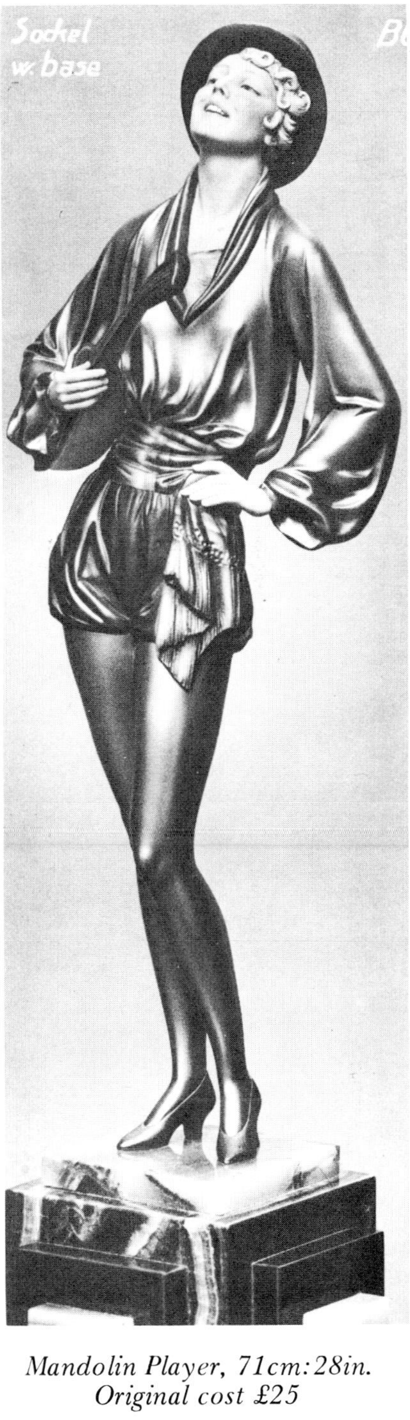

Mandolin Player, 71cm:28in.
Original cost £25

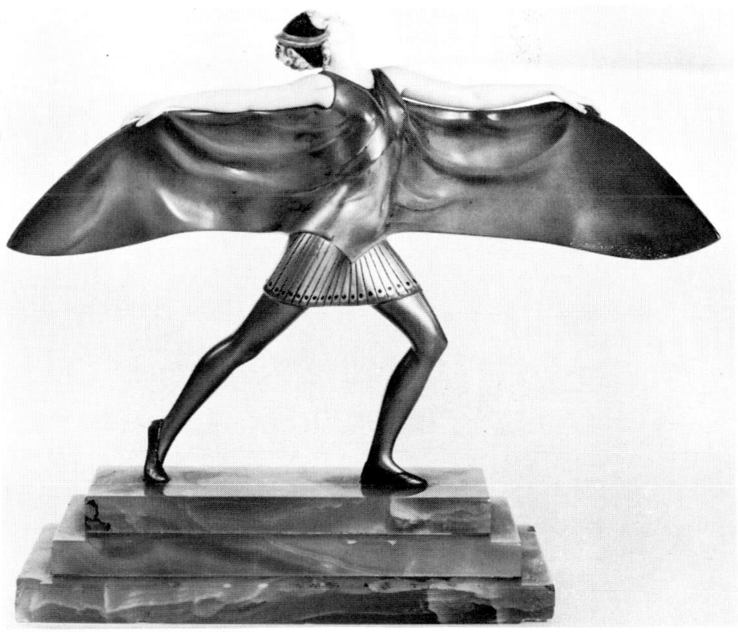

Bat Dancer, 24cm:9¼in.
Similar figures known to be mounted on various bases and as a decoration for clocks

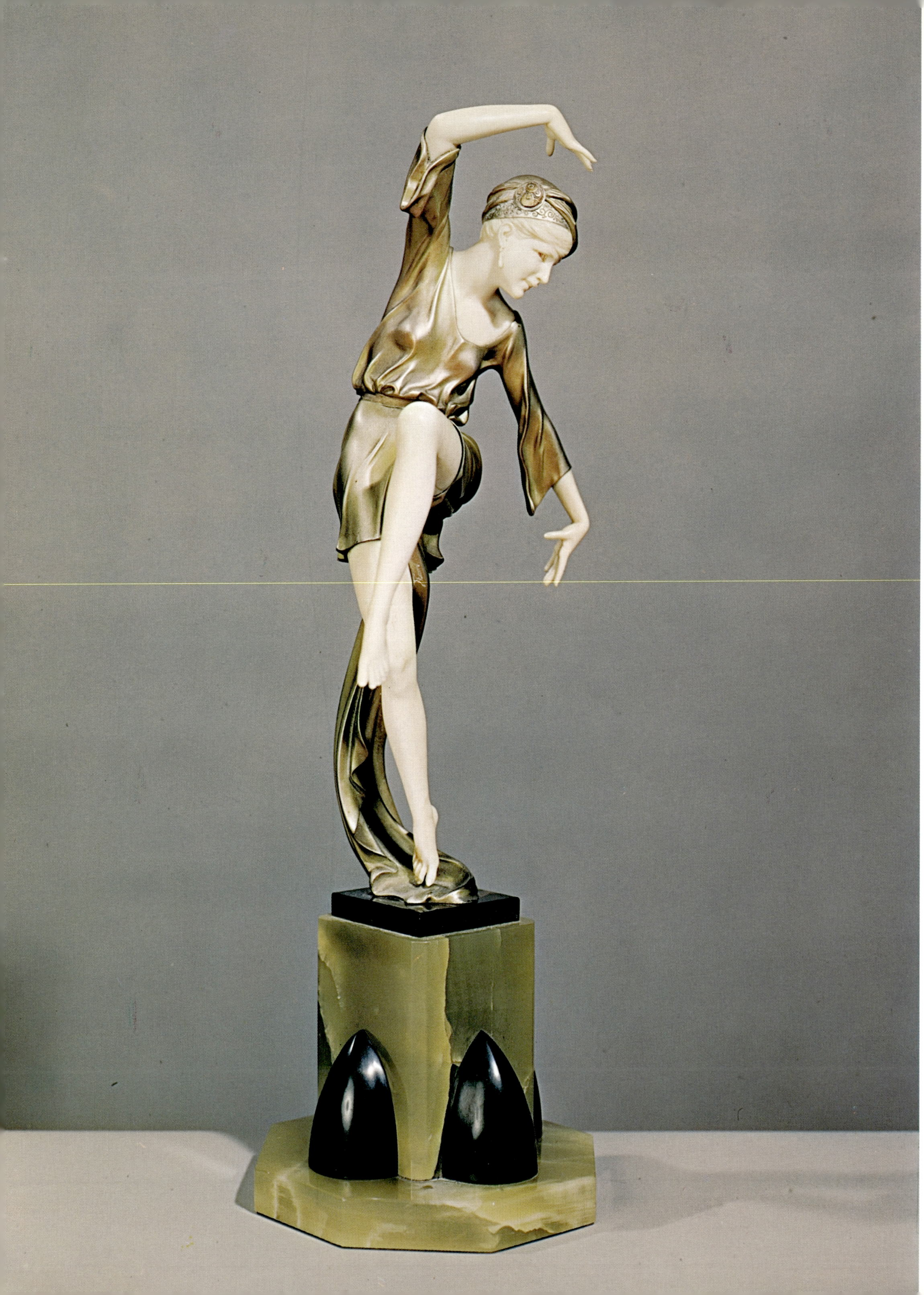

Right: Torch Dancer, 42cm:16½in.
on pedestal; 31cm:12in. on dish
Various bases used including pedestals and
various shaped onyx dishes
Original cost £25

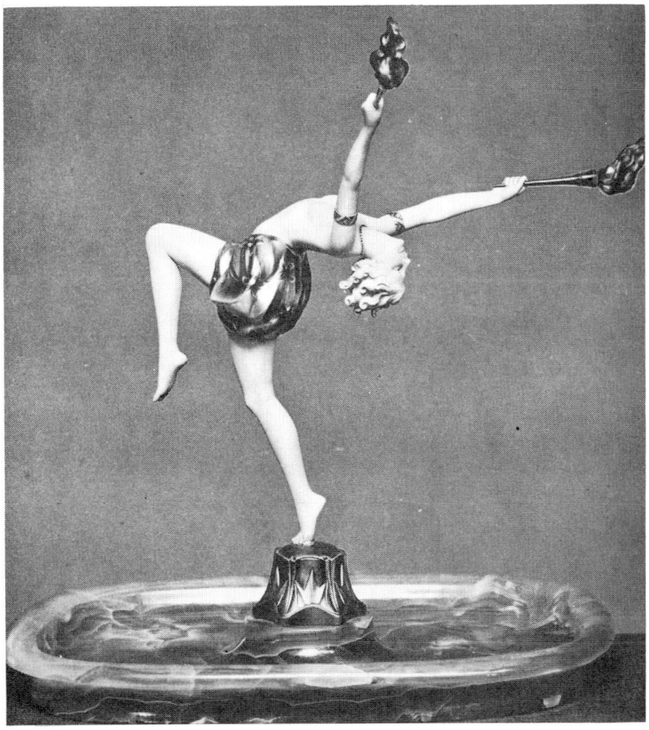

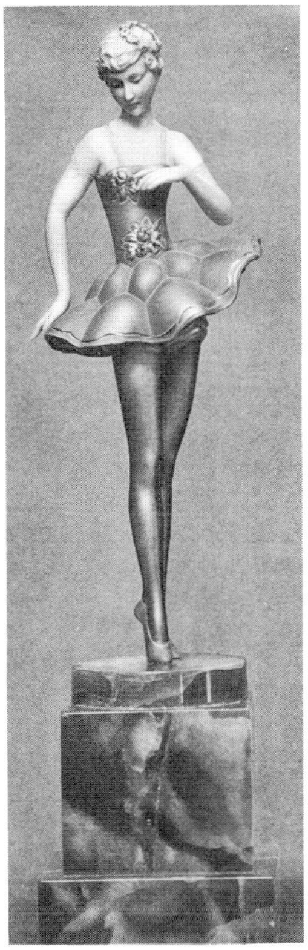

Ballet Dancer
23cm:9in.

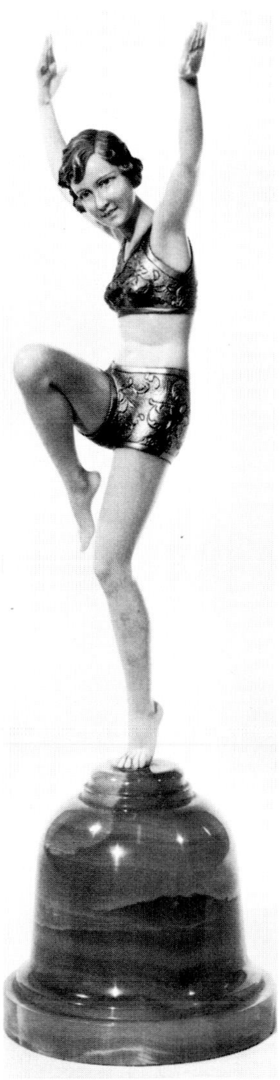

Right: Beach Dancer
39cm:15½in.

Right: Butterfly Dancers, 41cm:16in.
Single figures also available
This figure has been found signed Prof. O.
Poertzel and the author has seen one
signed by both artists
Original cost £30

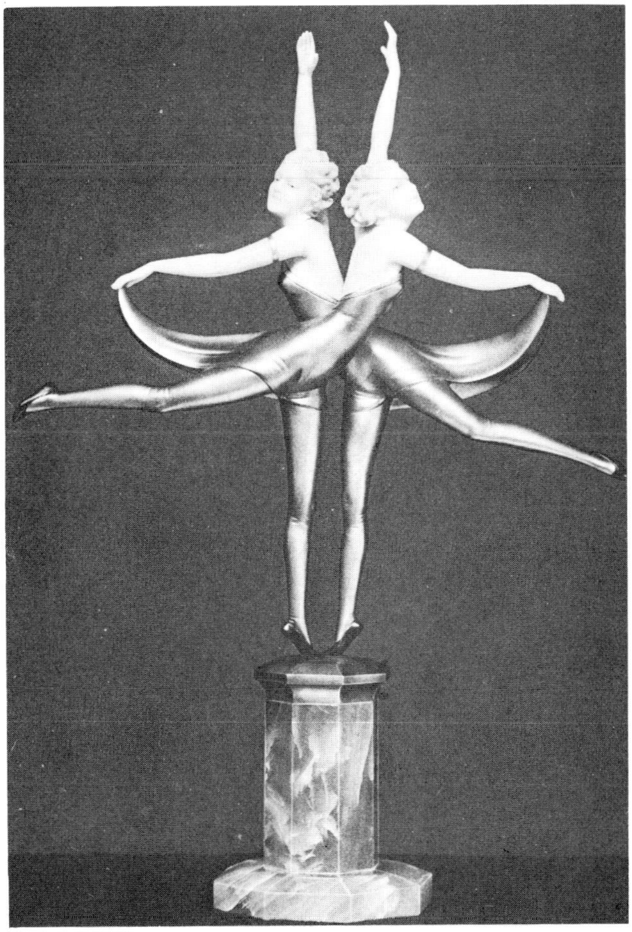

Left. F. Preiss
Autumn Dancer
38cm:15in.

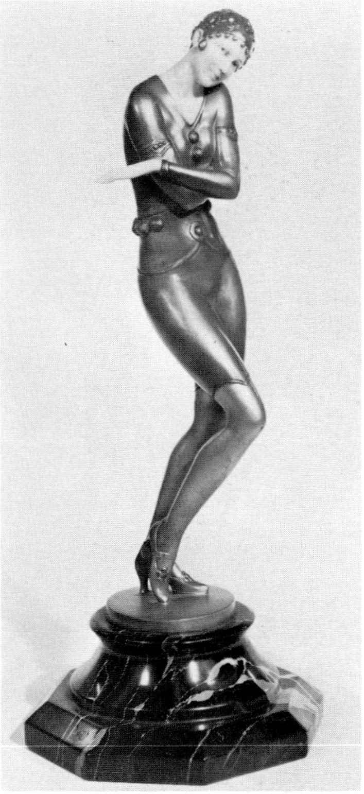

Coy Dancer, 39cm:15¼in.

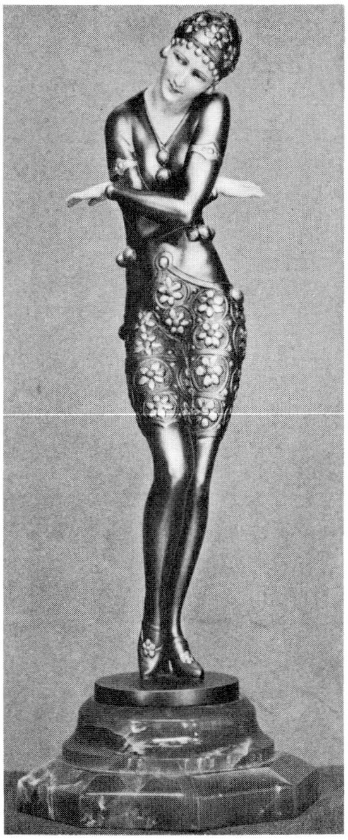

Coy Dancer, 39cm:15¼in. Similar to previous Coy Dancer but with different decoration Original cost £17

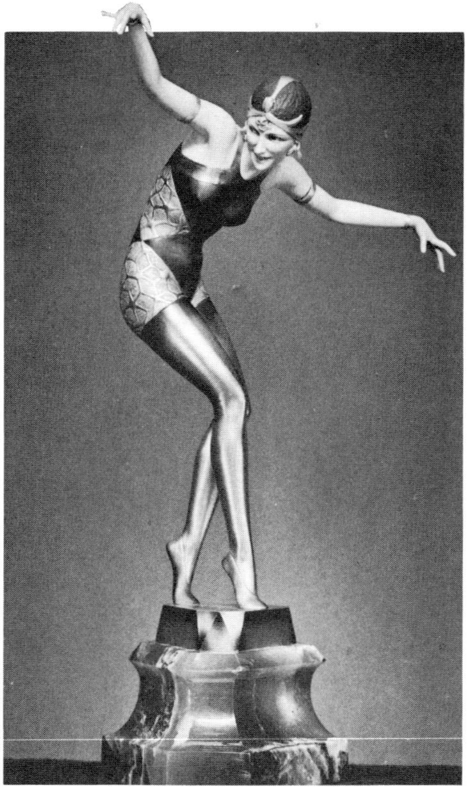

Cabaret Girl, 39cm:15¼in. Original cost £24

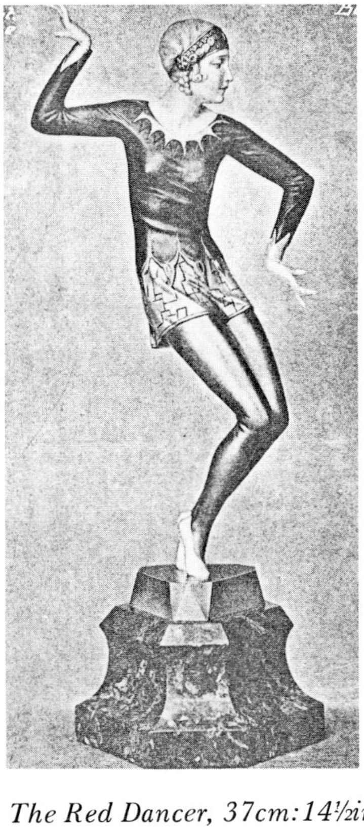

The Red Dancer, 37cm:14½in.

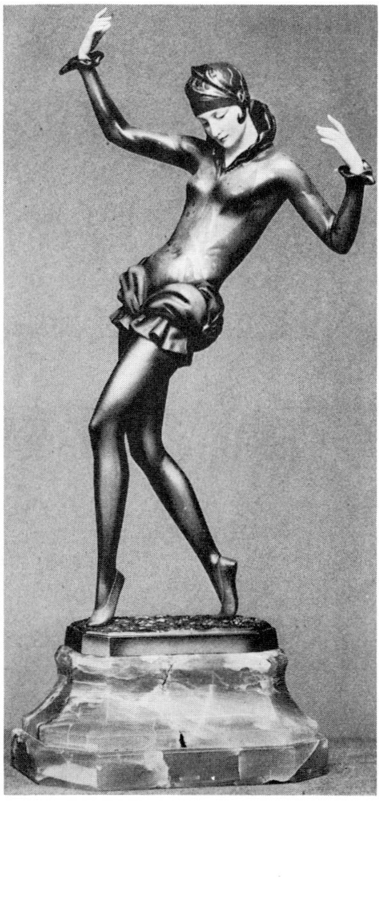

A Dancer, 38cm:14¾in. Original cost £16

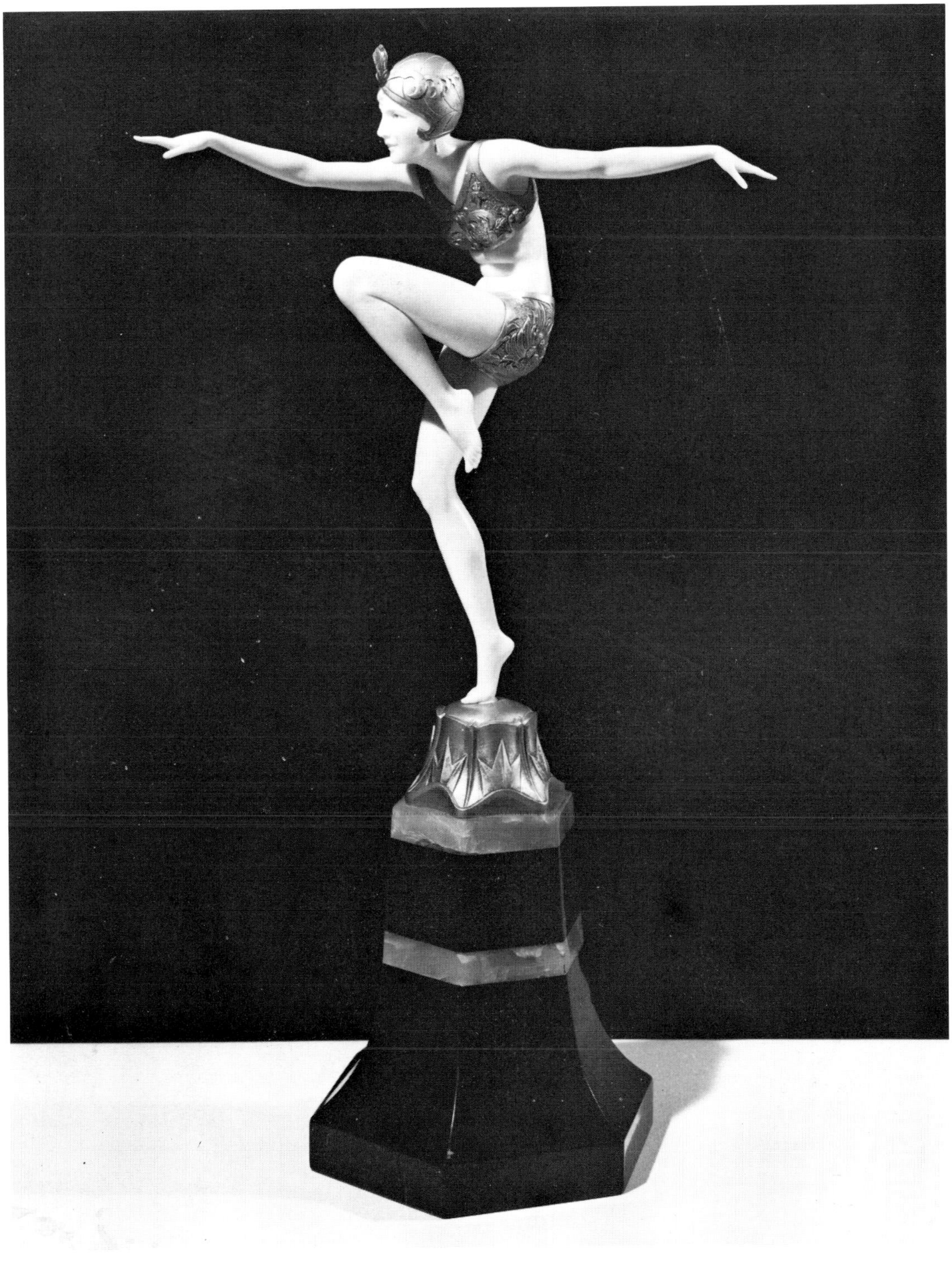

Con Brio, 37cm: 14½in.

Several different bases were used for mounting this work, the most popular being the one illustrated and an onyx dish

Original cost £25

REMONDOT

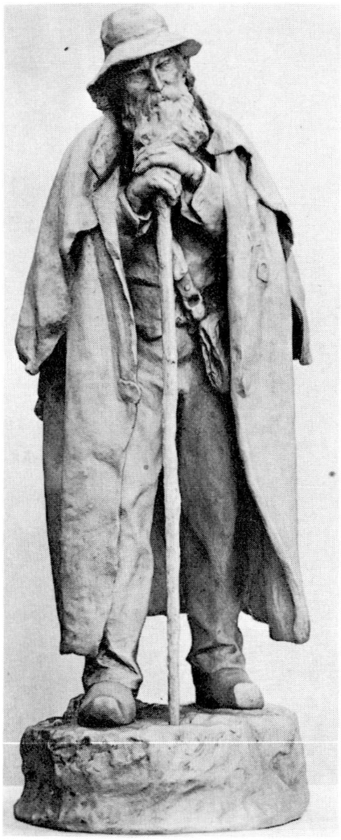

The Old Shepherd
60cm:23¾in.; 24cm:9½in.

P. RICHER

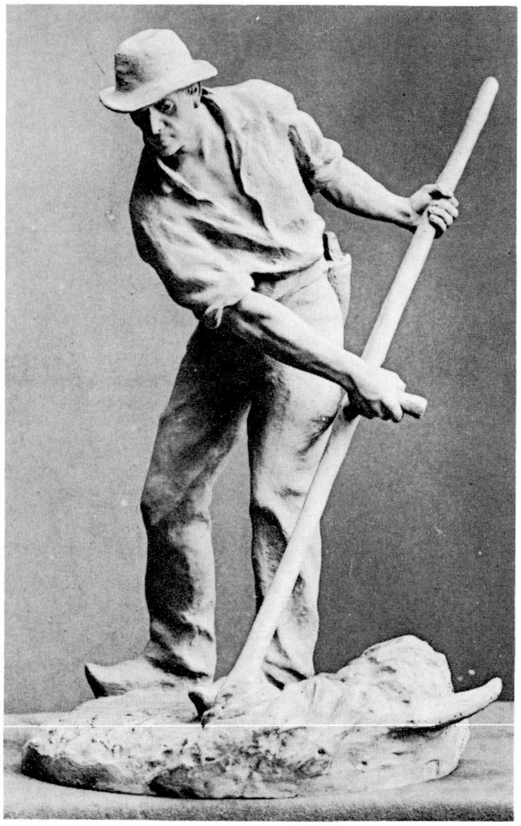

The Haymaker
55cm:21½in.; 35cm:13¾in.

RIGOT

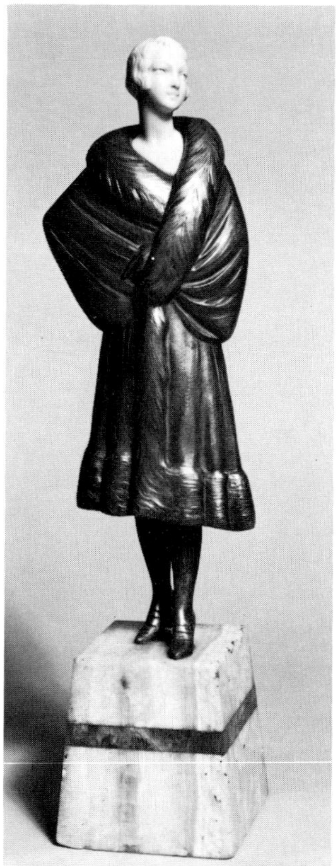

A Girl in a Fur Coat
28cm:11in.

ROSSI

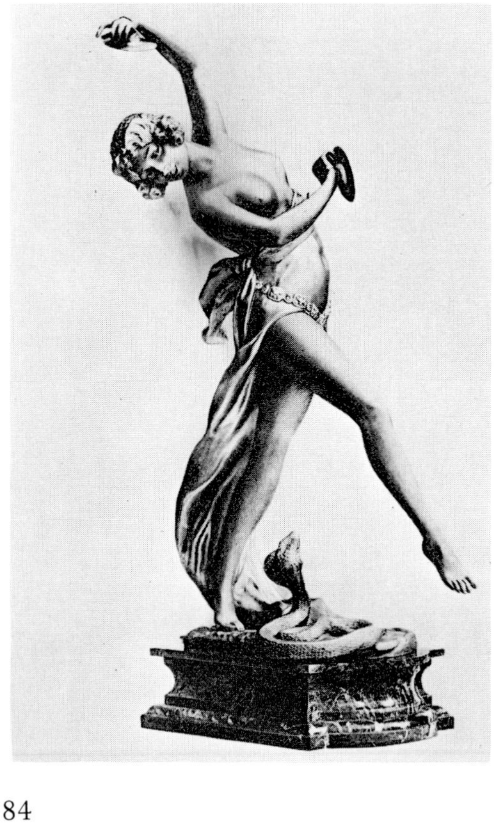

The Snake Charmer
61cm:24in.; 40cm:15¾in.

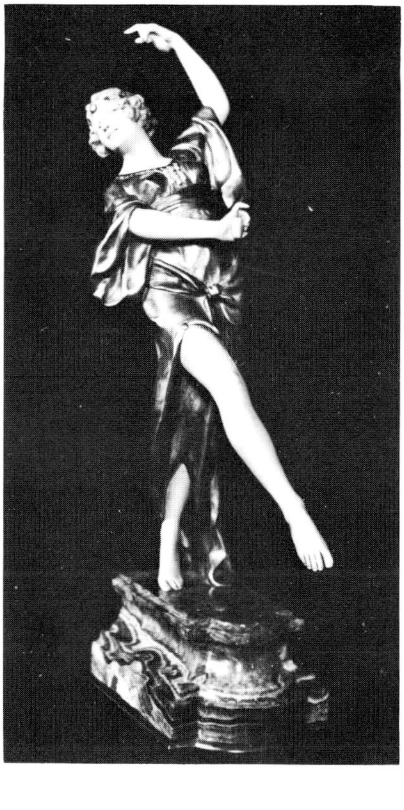

Oriental Dancer
45cm:17¾in.

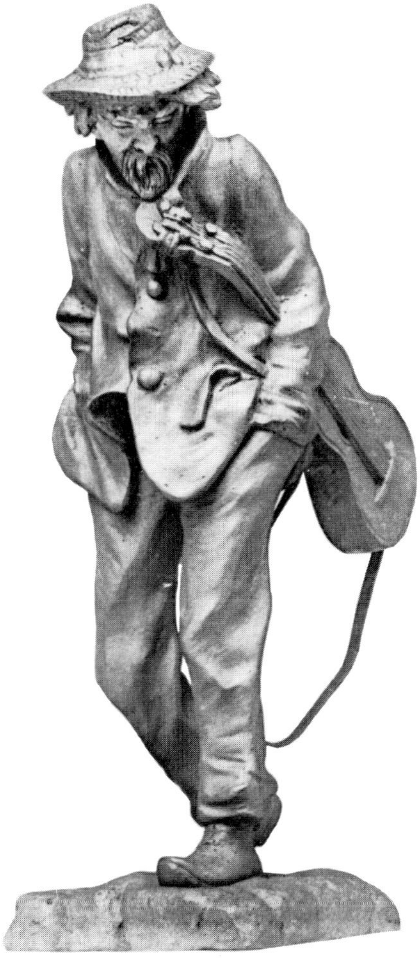

Unappreciated
27cm:10½in.; 20cm:8in.

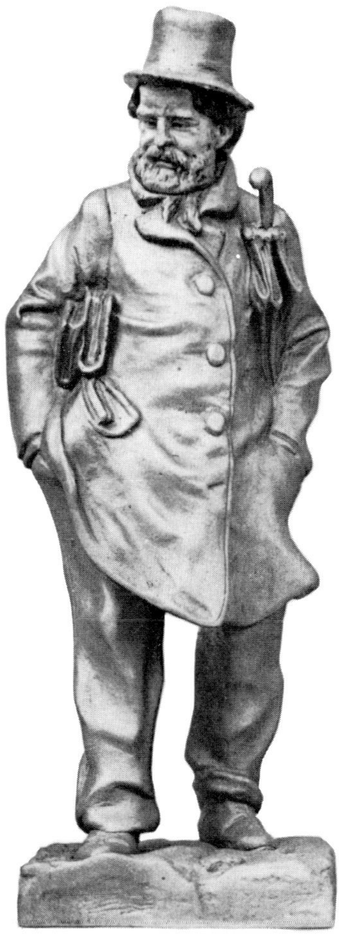

Second-hand Bookdealer
27cm:10½in.; 21cm:8¼in.

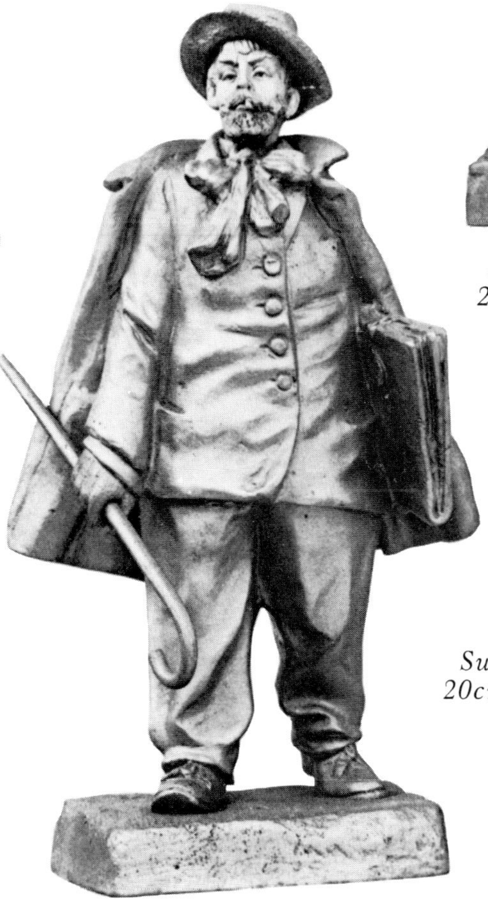

Success
20cm:8in.

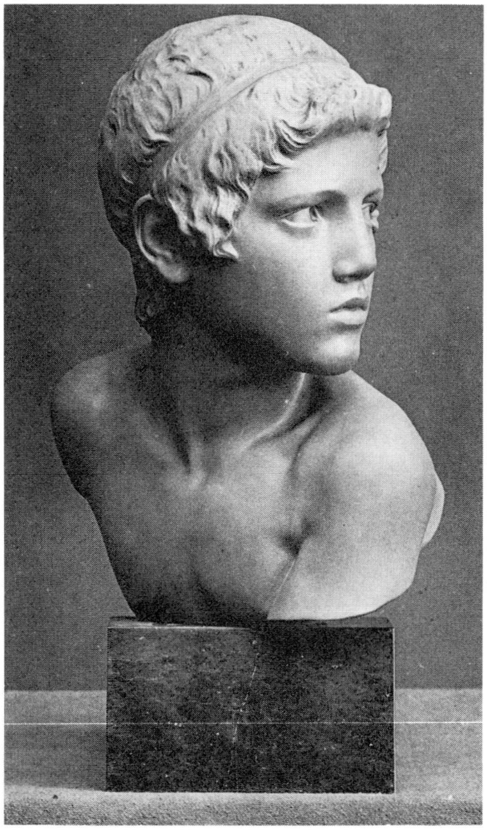

The Child Achilles
45cm:17¾in.; 30cm:11¾in.
25cm:10in.; 11cm:4½in.

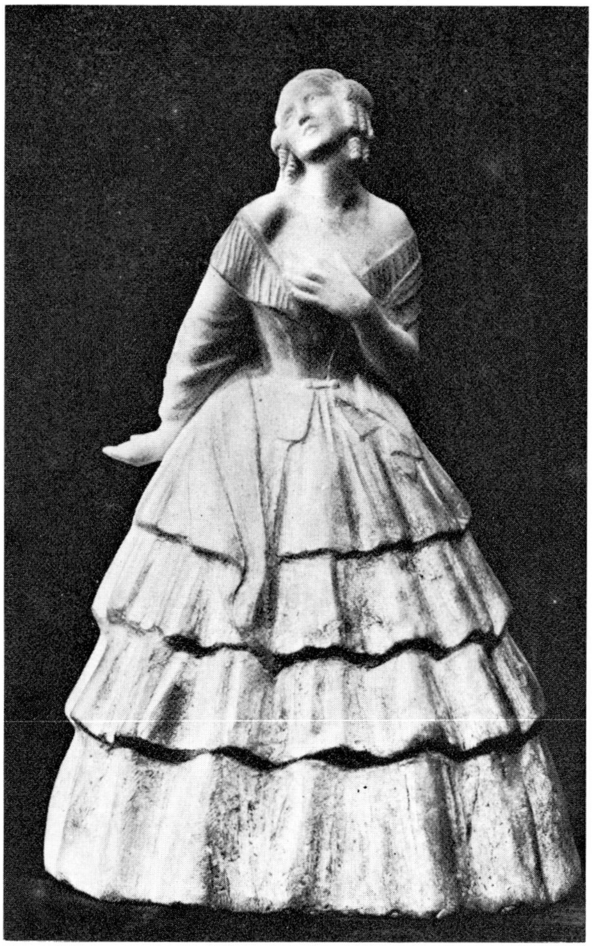

Low Note, 34cm:13¼in.; 30cm:11¾in.

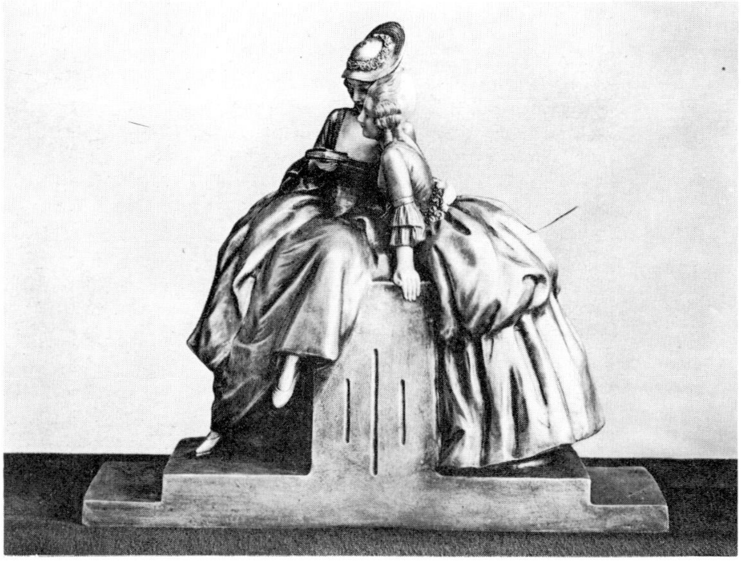

Sentimental Initiation, 31cm:12in.

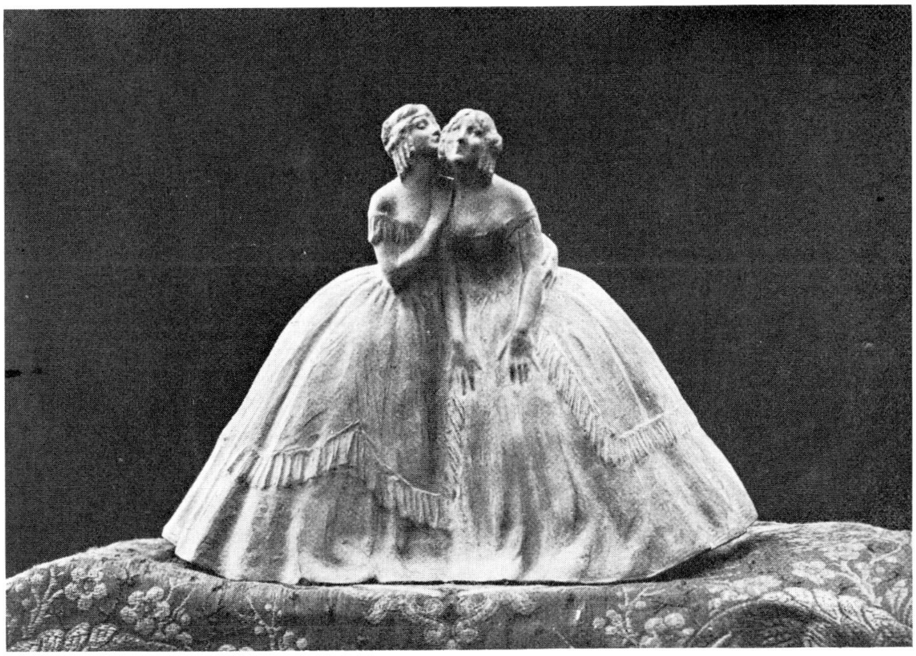

Secrets, 25cm:10in.

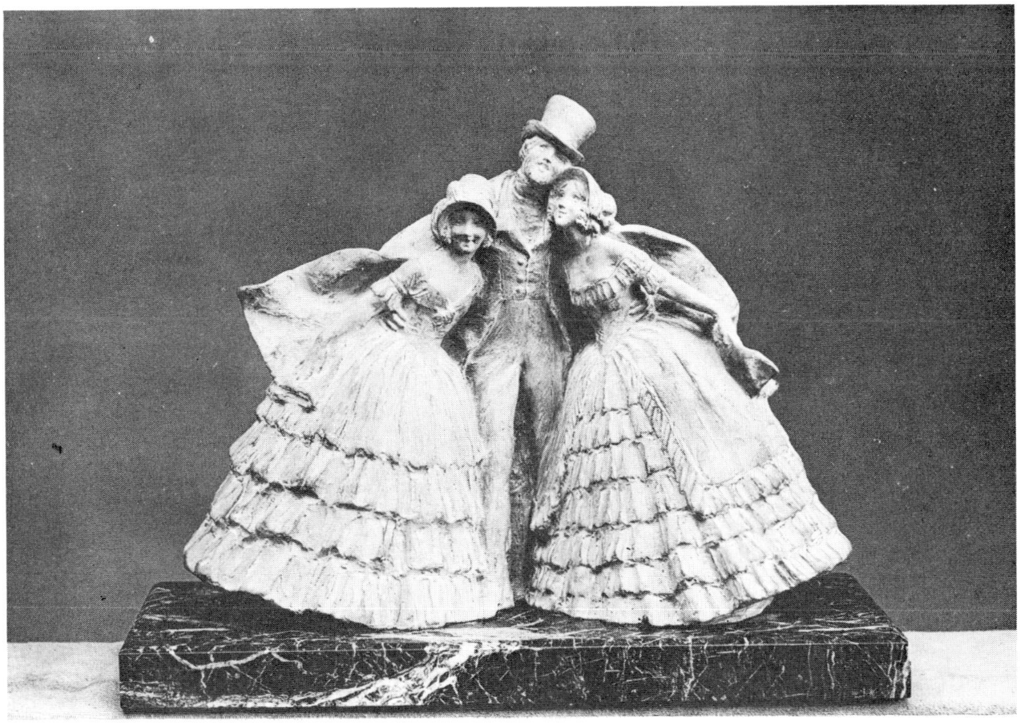

Old Time Dance, 34cm:13½in.

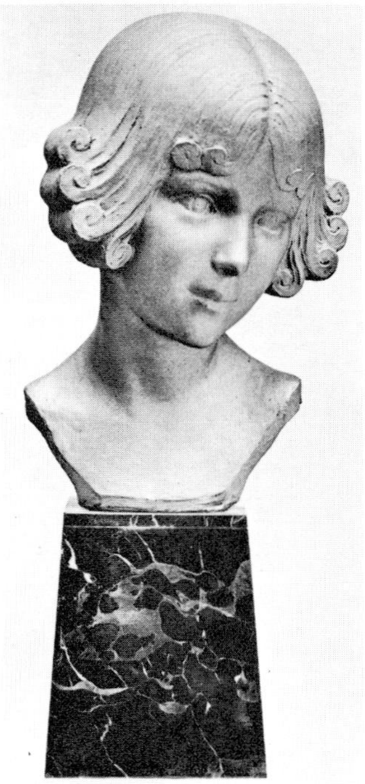

Daughter, 51cm:20in.

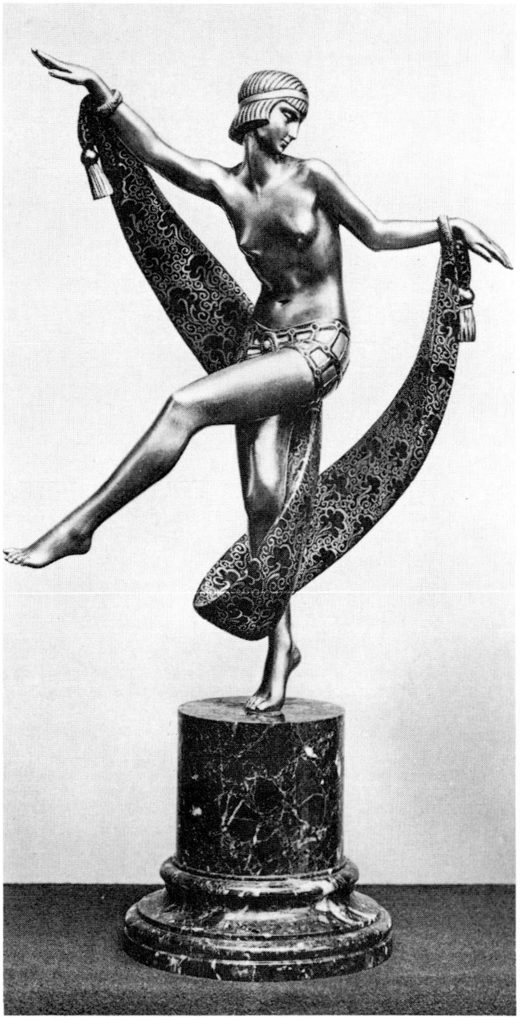

The Scarf Dance
47cm:18½in.; 31cm:12¼in.

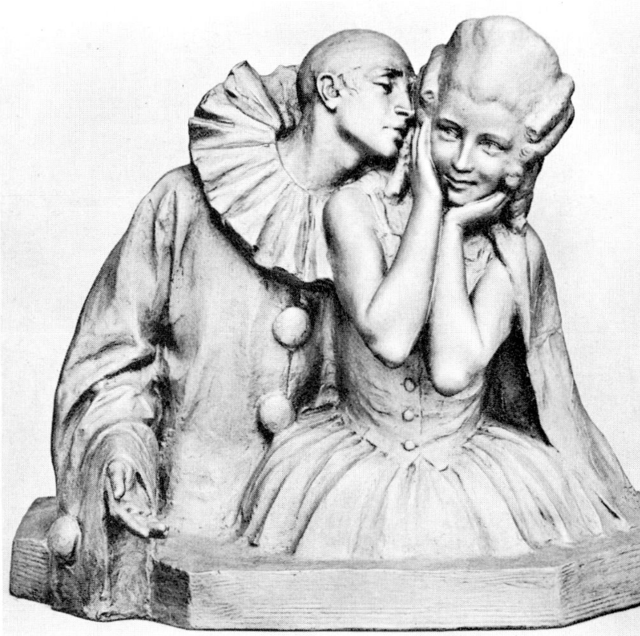

The Eternal Story, 46cm:18in.

Right. G. Schmidt-Cassel
Eastern Dancer
37cm:14½in.

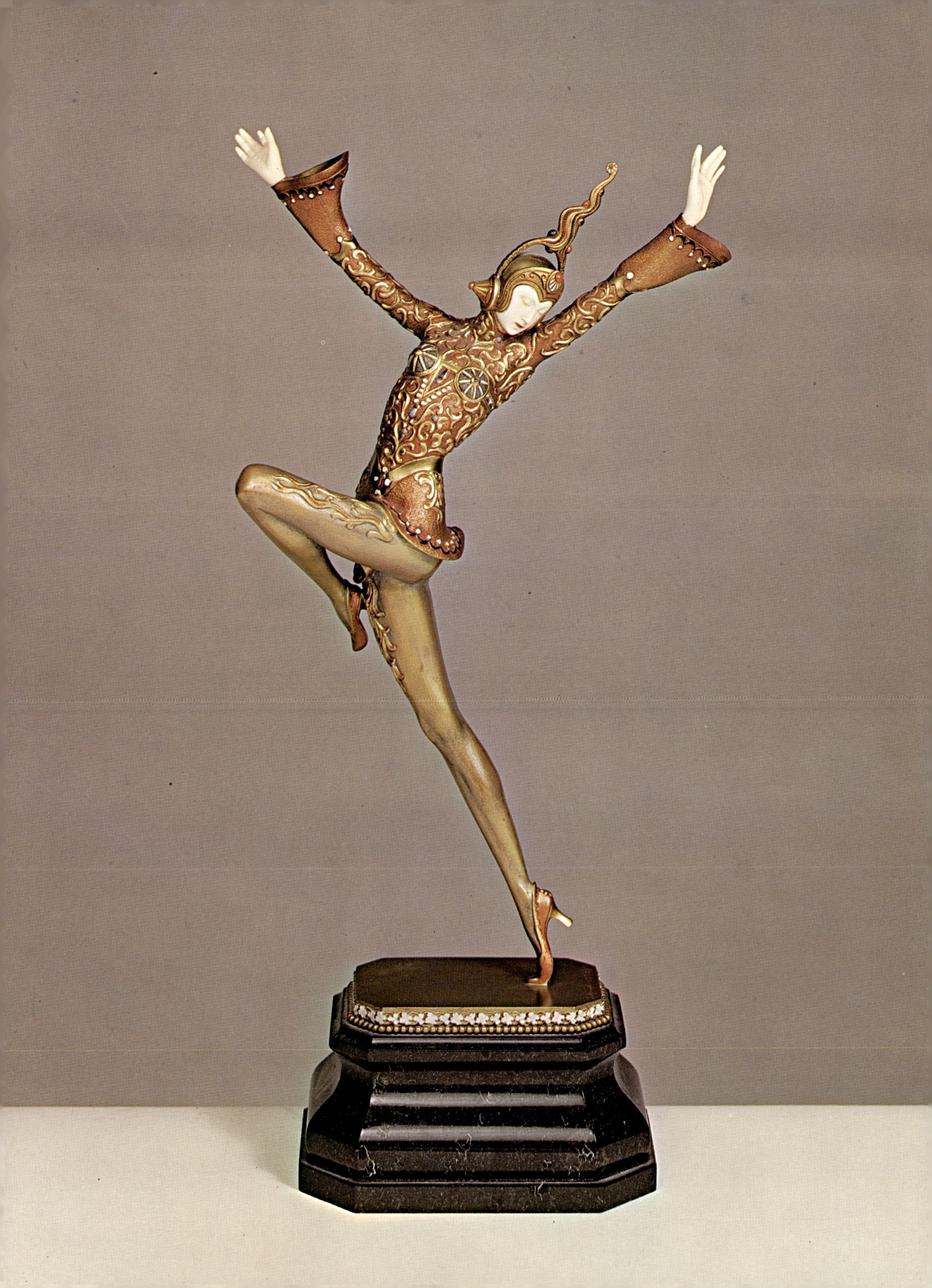

M.J. SAÏN

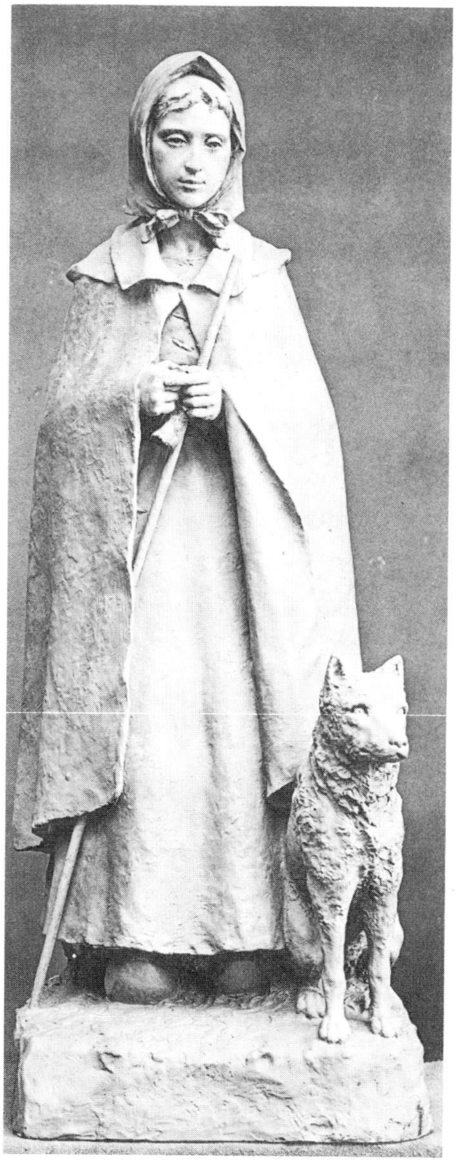

Shepherdess and Dog
72cm:28¼in.; 57cm:22½in.

SALAT

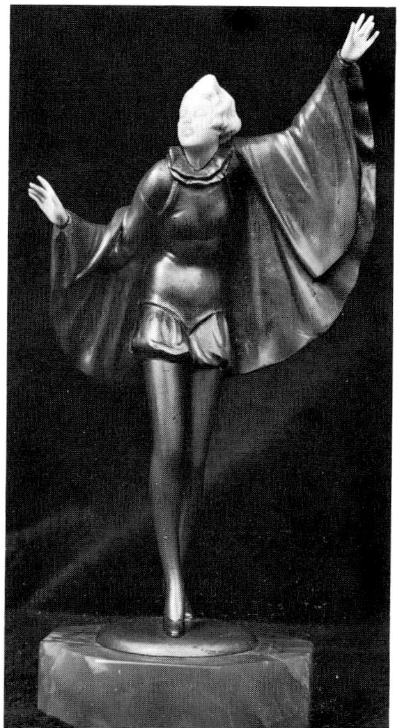

A Dancer
21cm:8¼in.

SALESIO

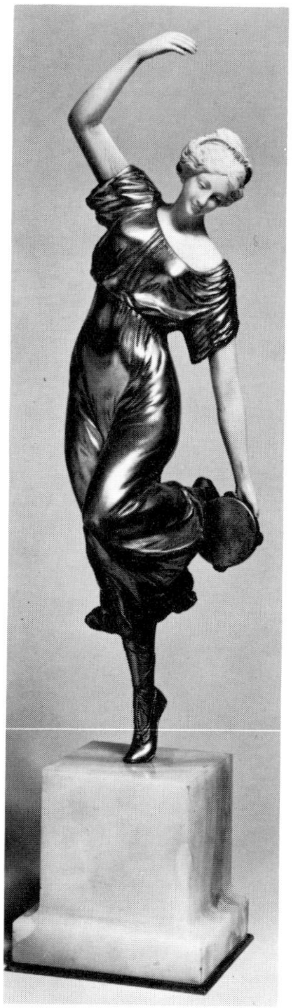

A Dancer
38cm:15in.

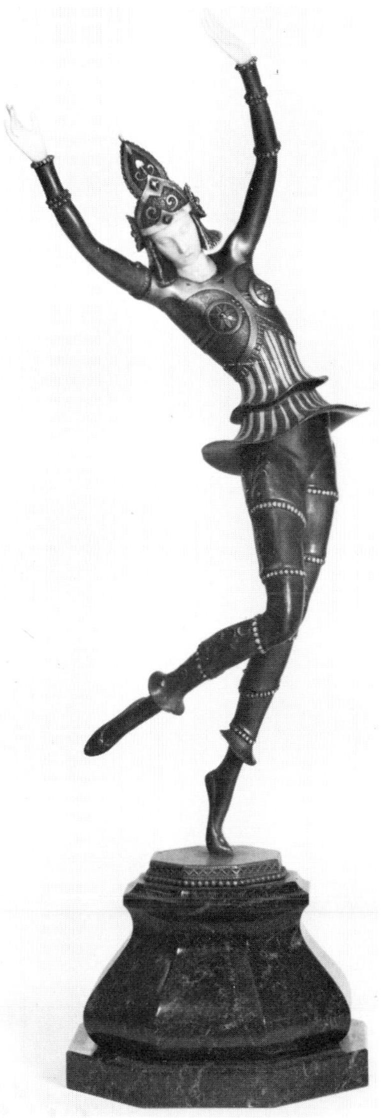

Dancer, 45cm:17½in.

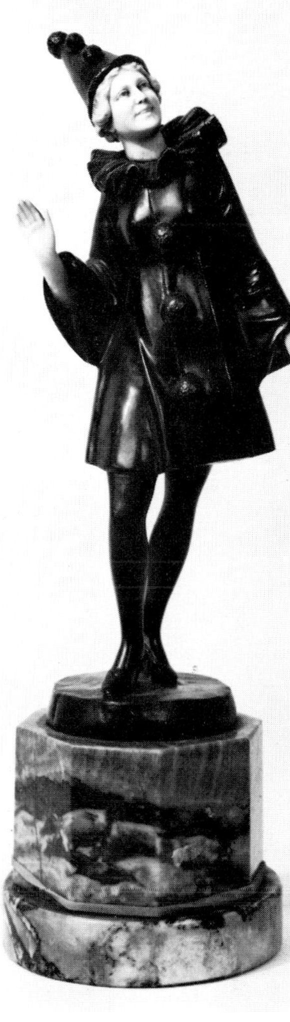

Pierrot, 25cm:10in.

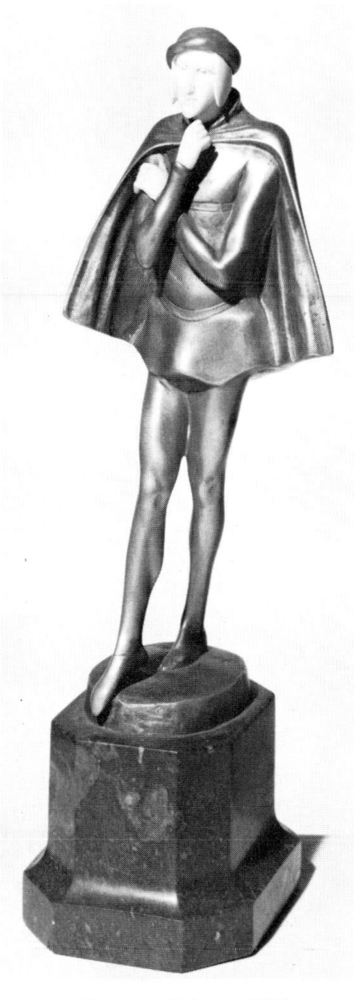

Dante, 24cm:9½in.

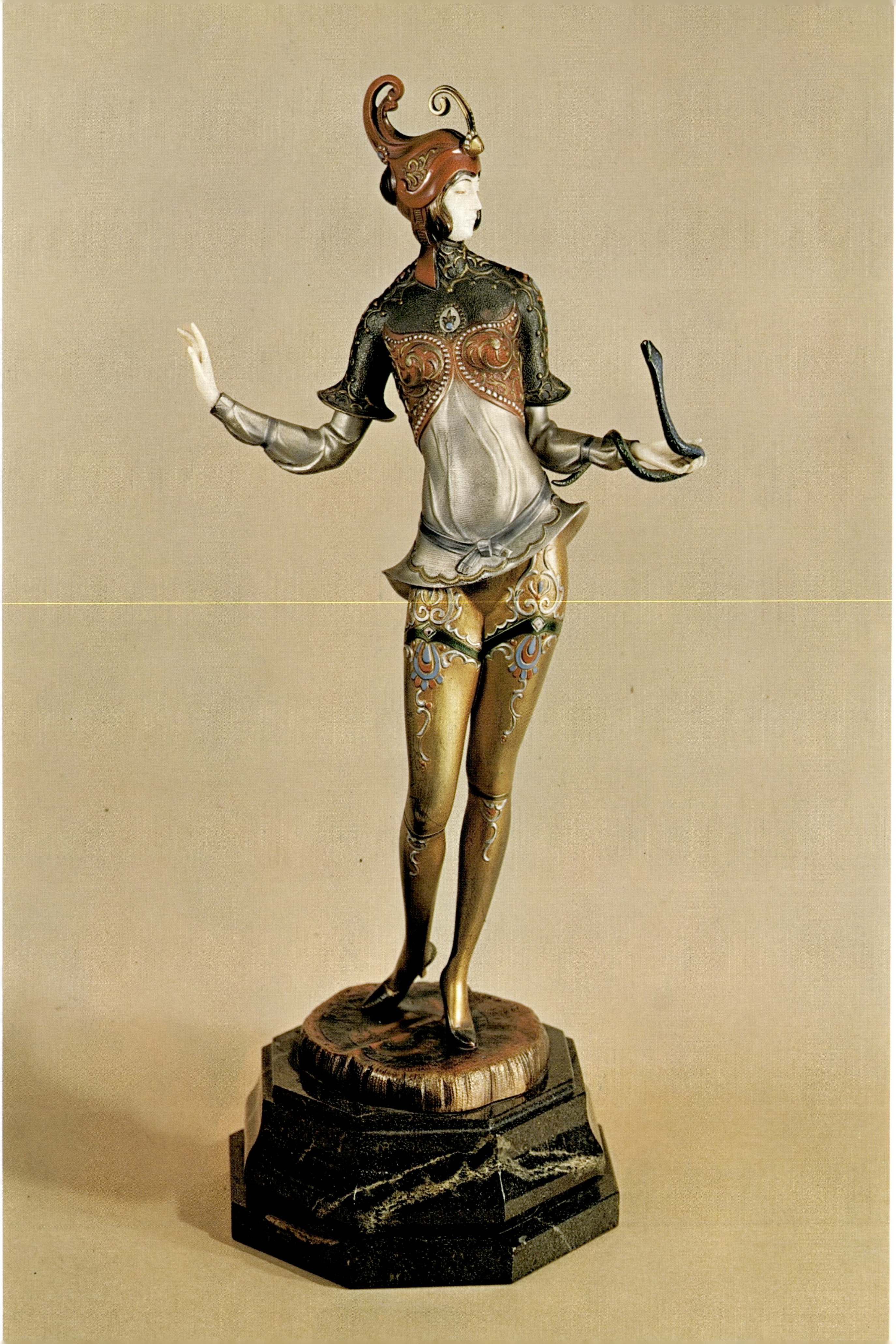

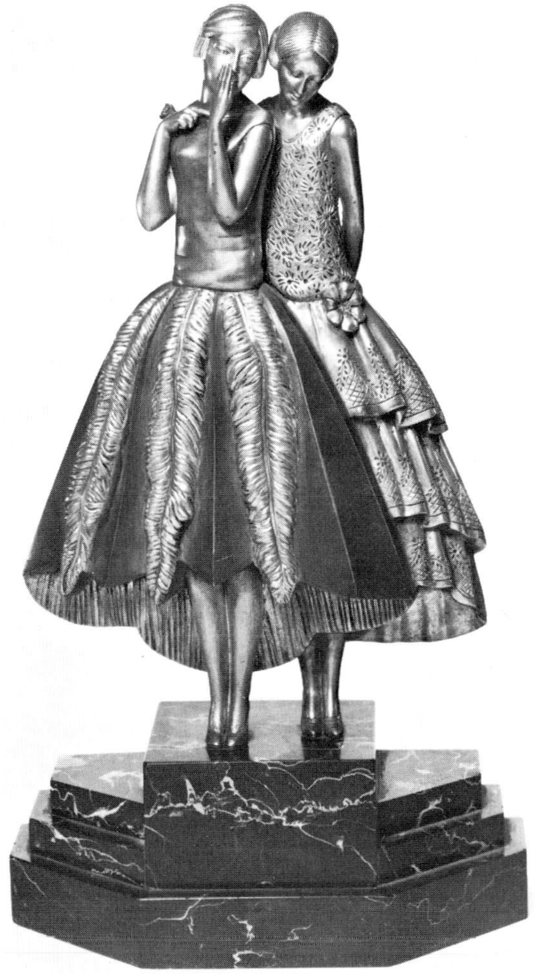

During the Dance, 36cm:14in.

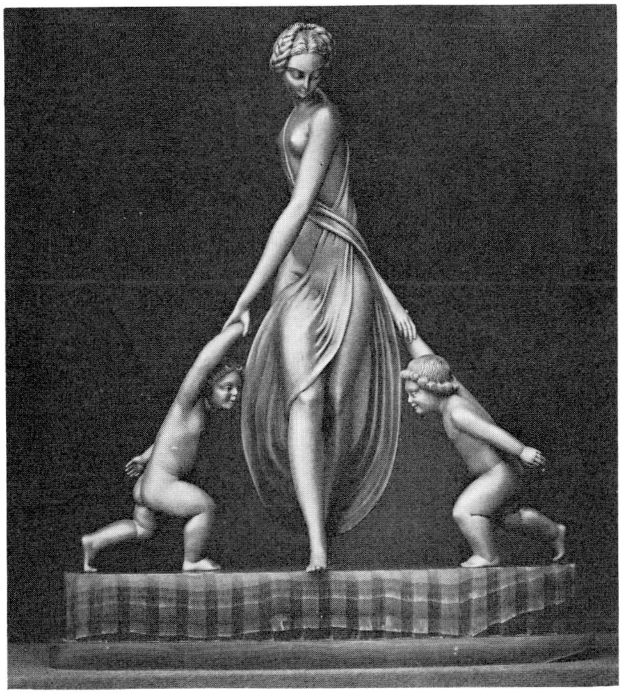

Happy Youth, 50cm:19½in.

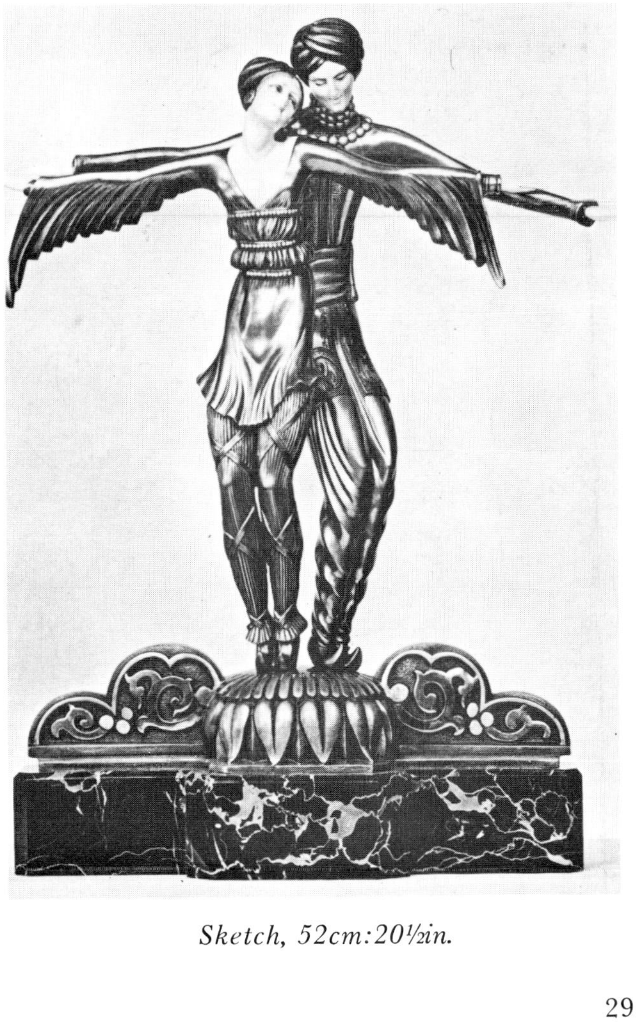

Sketch, 52cm:20½in.

Left. G. Schmidt-Cassel
Snake Charmer
43cm:17in.

SIMARD

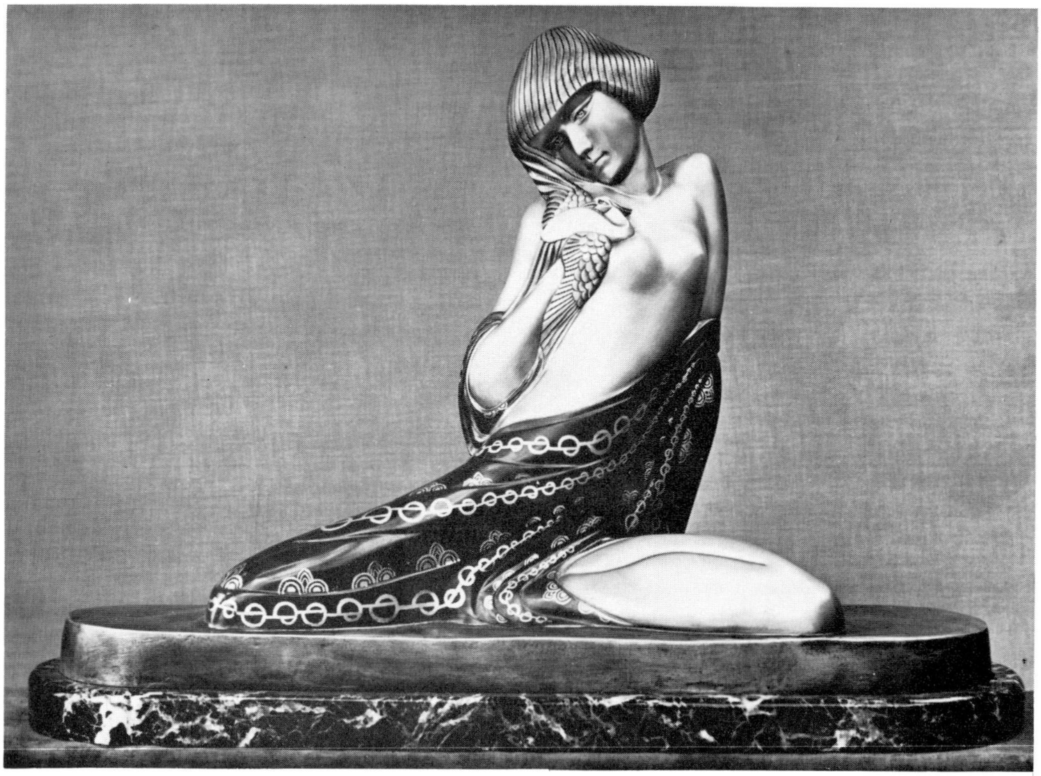

Blue Bird,
43cm:17in.

SIMON

Tambourine Dance
45cm:17¾in.
35cm:13¾in.
26cm:10¼in.

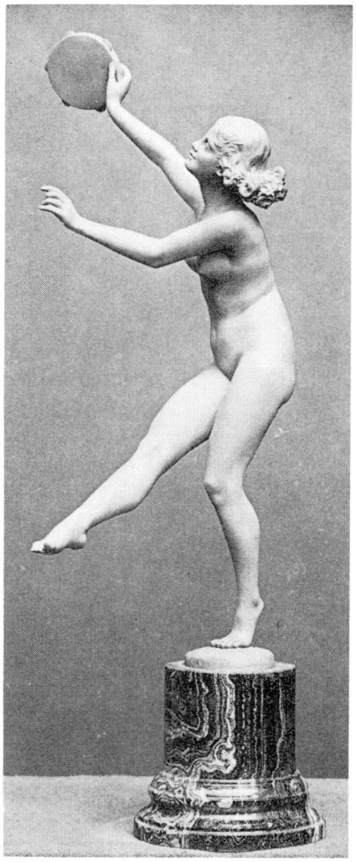

Spring, 51cm:20in.

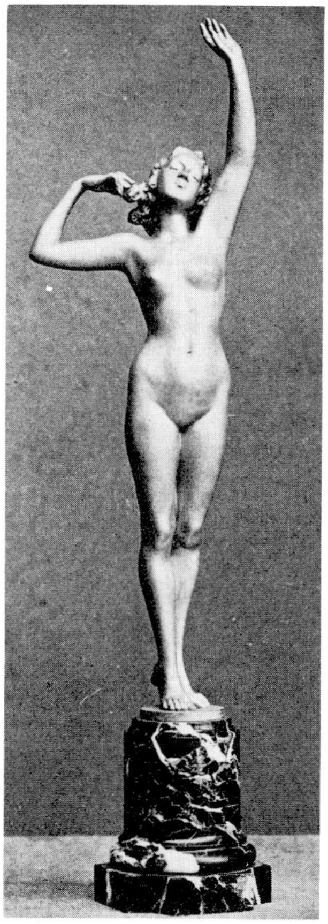

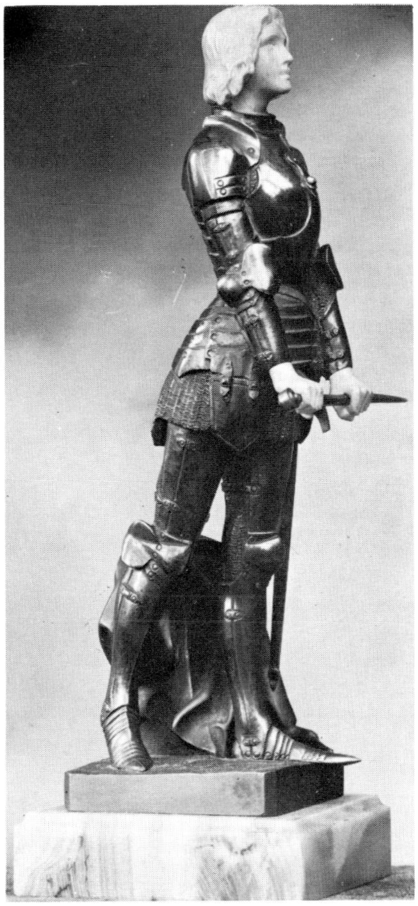

Joan of Arc
60cm:23½in.
40cm:15¾in.
30cm:11¾in.
15cm:6in.

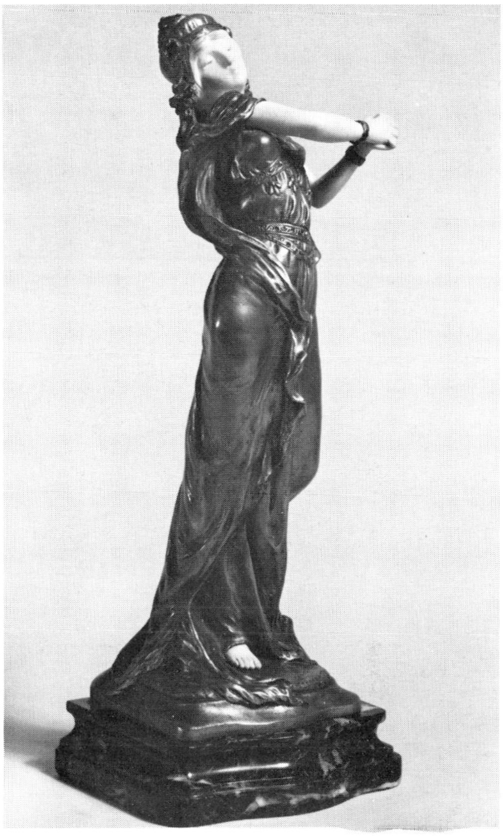

Heroine
32cm:12½in.

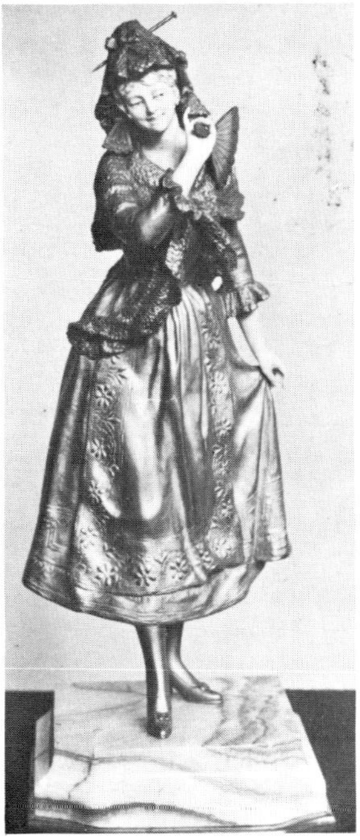

Carmen, 31cm:12¼in.

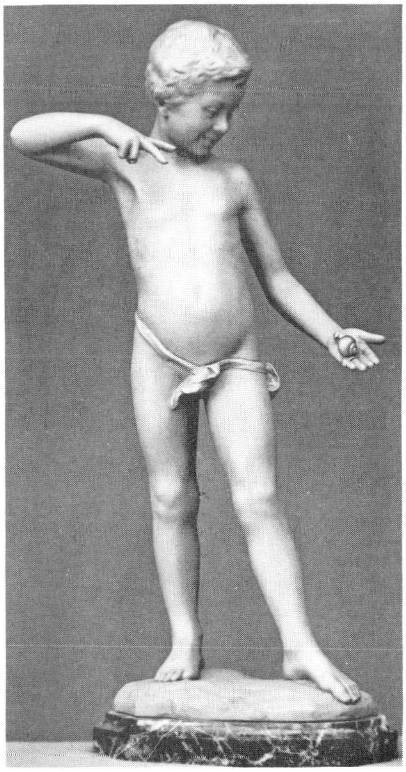

Urchin and Snail
55cm:21½in.

SOSSON

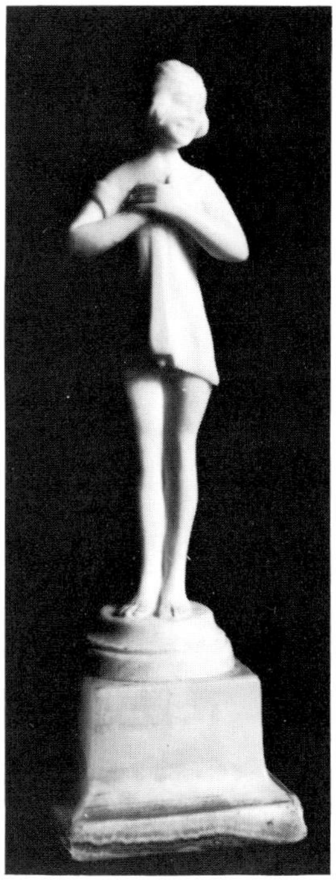

Ivory Nude
10cm:4in.

SPLIETH

Man on Horseback
41cm:16in.
Dated 1919

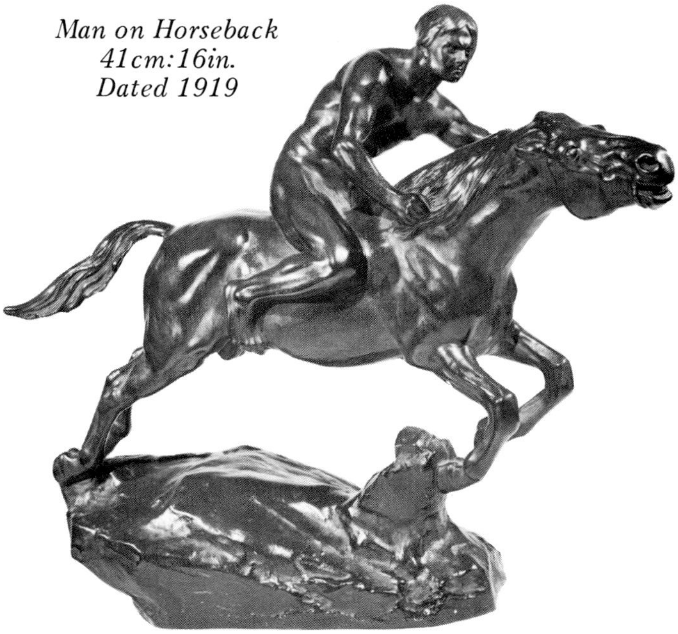

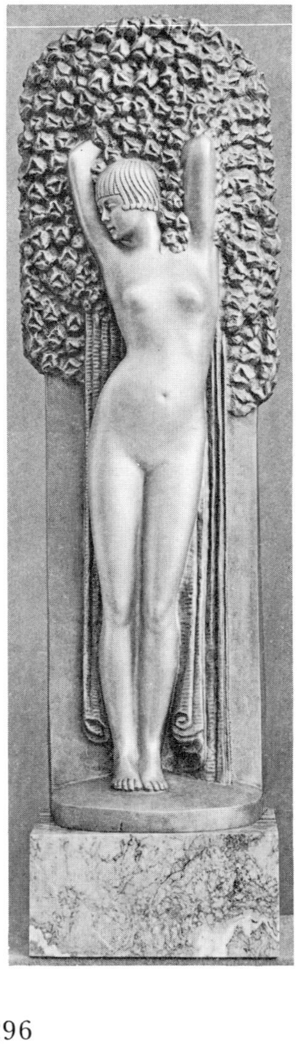

FREDY STOLL

Young Girl
95cm:37½in.

SUGGON

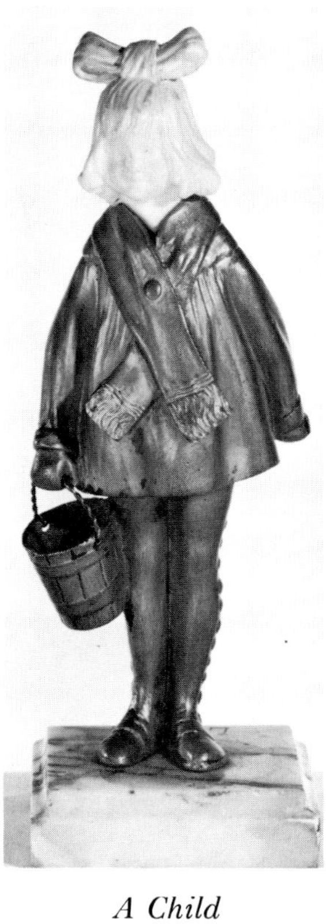

A Child
14cm:5½in.

THOMASSIN

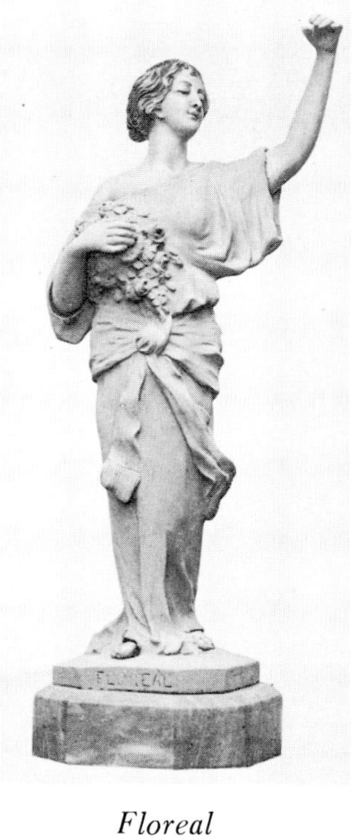

Floreal
26cm:10¼in.

ULRICH

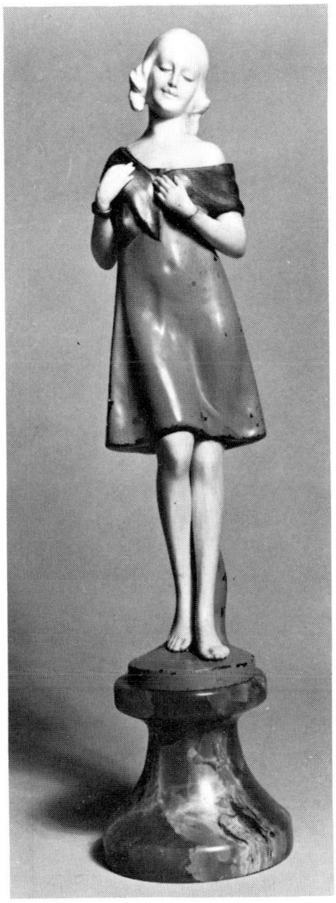

A Dancer
36cm:14in.

G. VACOSSIN

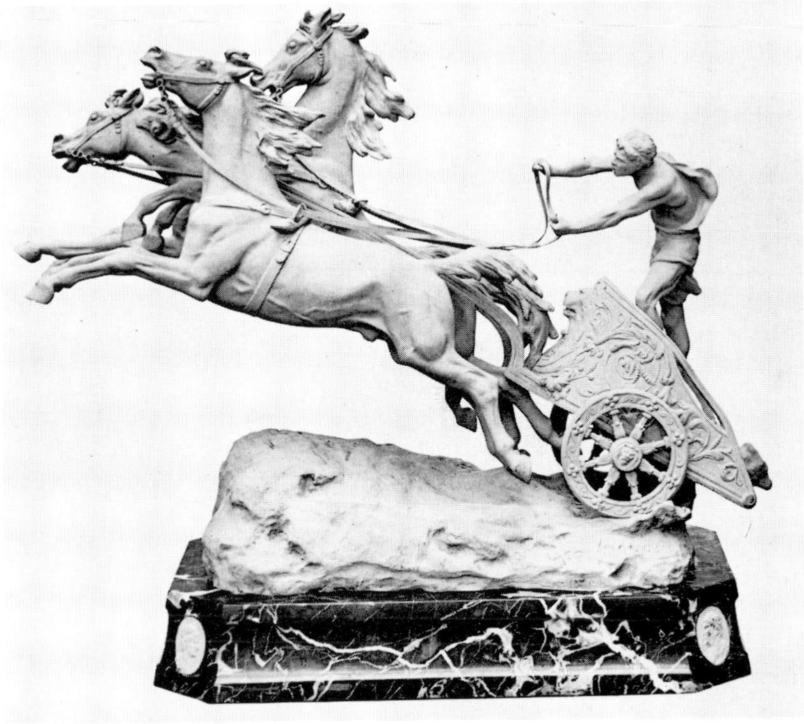

Roman Chariot, 54cm:21¼in.

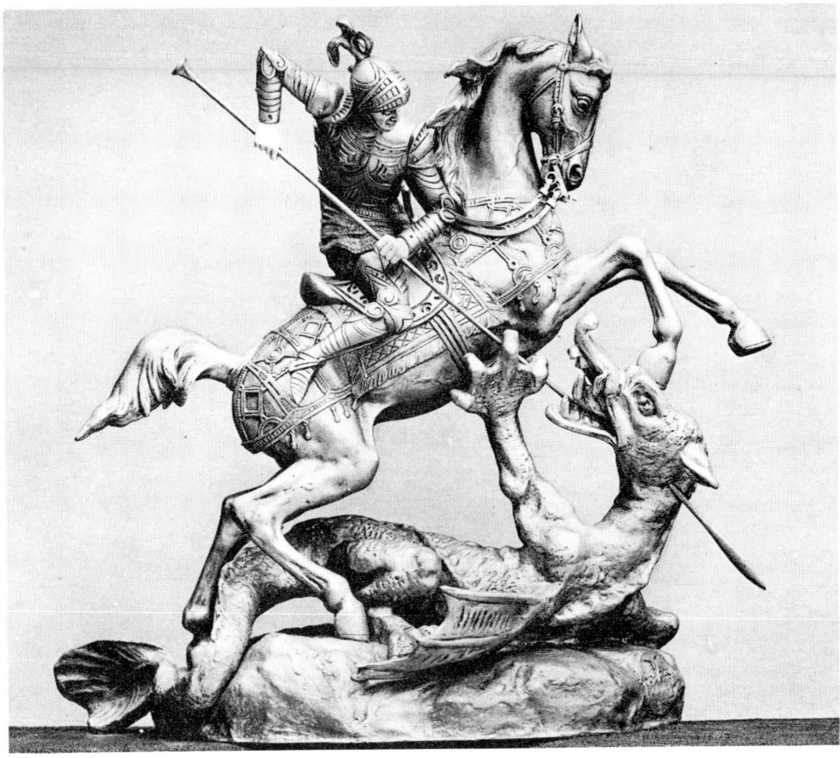

Saint George, 54cm:21¼in.

VAN DER STRAETEN

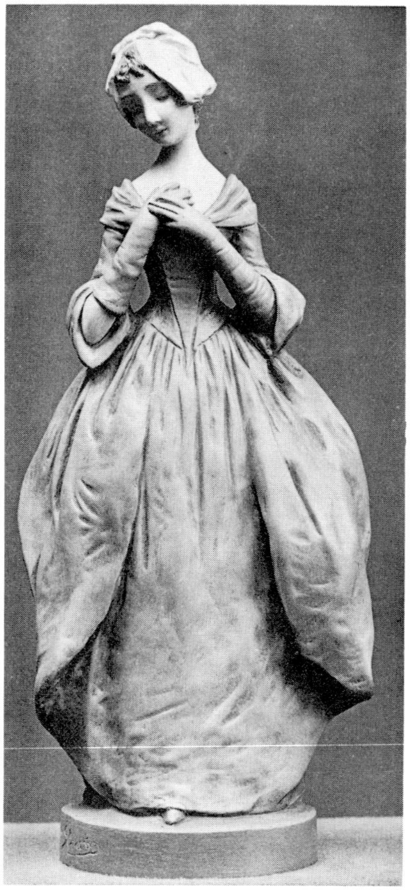

Flirting
35cm:13¾in.

Meditation
32cm:12½in.

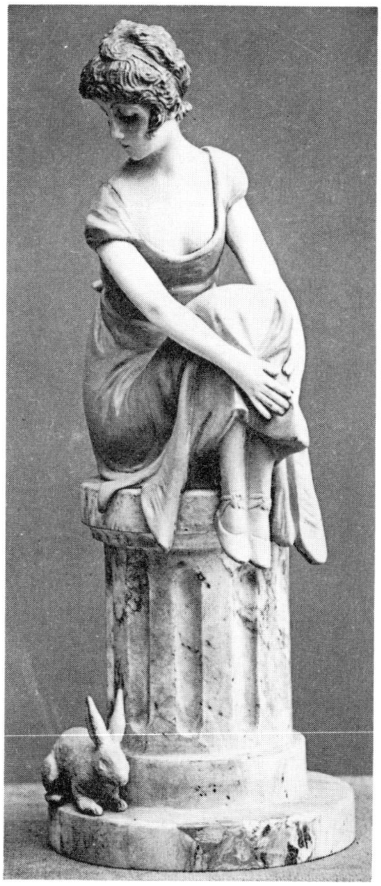

P. MAREAU VAN THIER

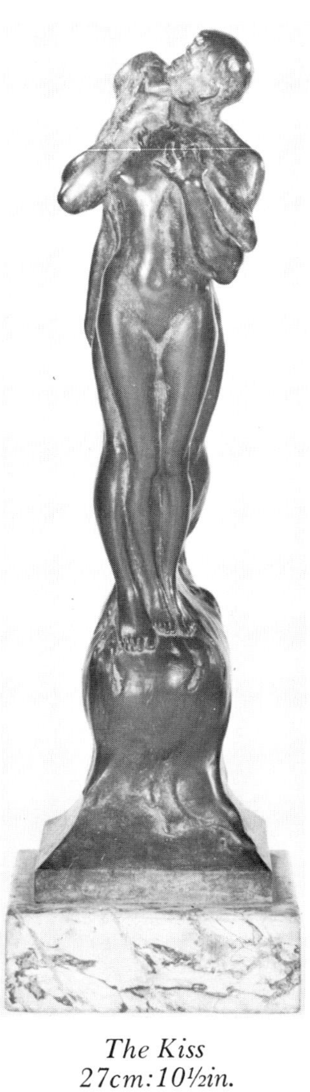

The Kiss
27cm:10½in.

E. VAX

JEAN VERSCHNEIDER

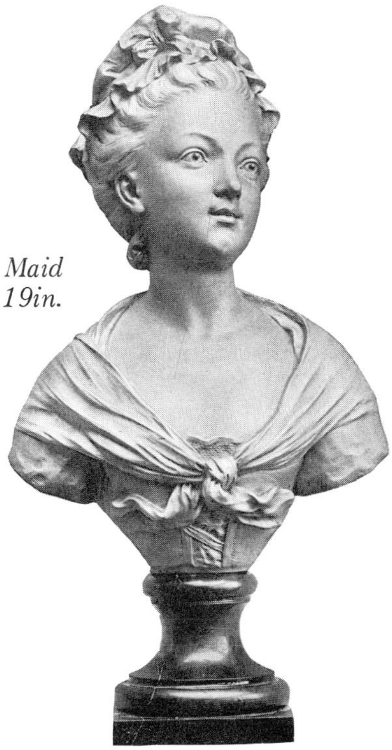

Lady's Maid
48cm:19in.

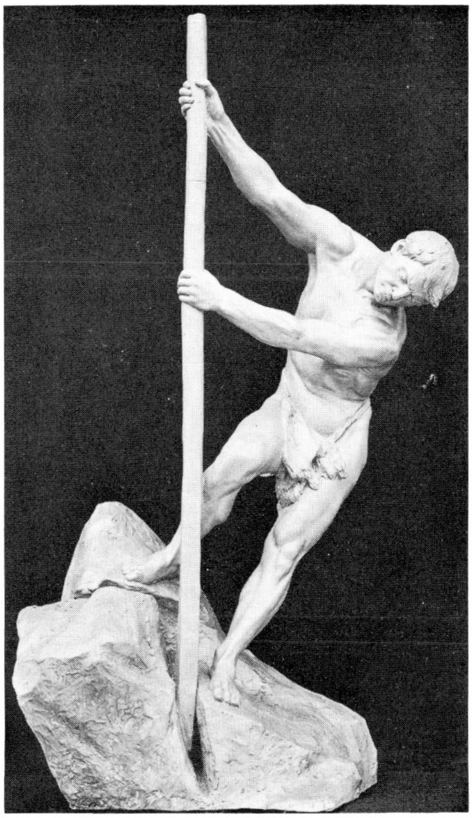

Force, 95cm:37½in.
65cm:25½in.; 45cm:17¾in.
Exhibited at the Salon des Artistes Français, 1913

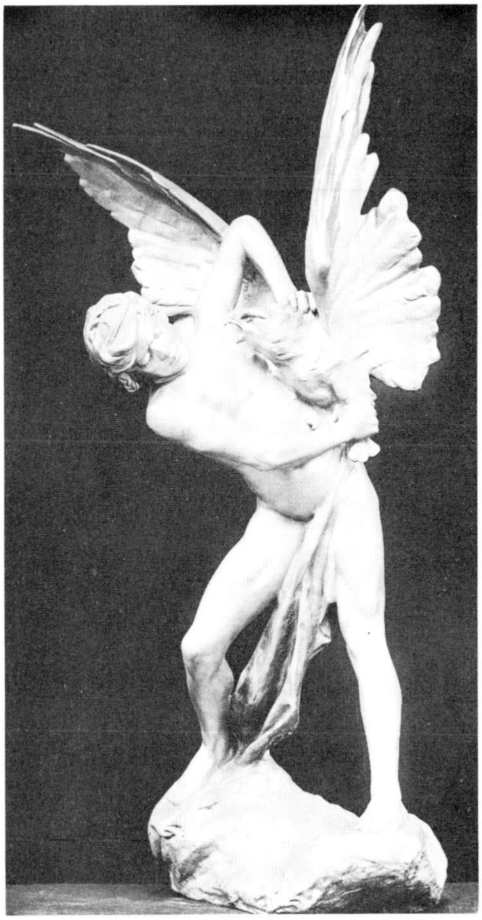

Son of Amilcar, 107cm:42in.
72cm:28¼in.; 36cm:14in.
Exhibited at the Salon des Artistes Français, 1908

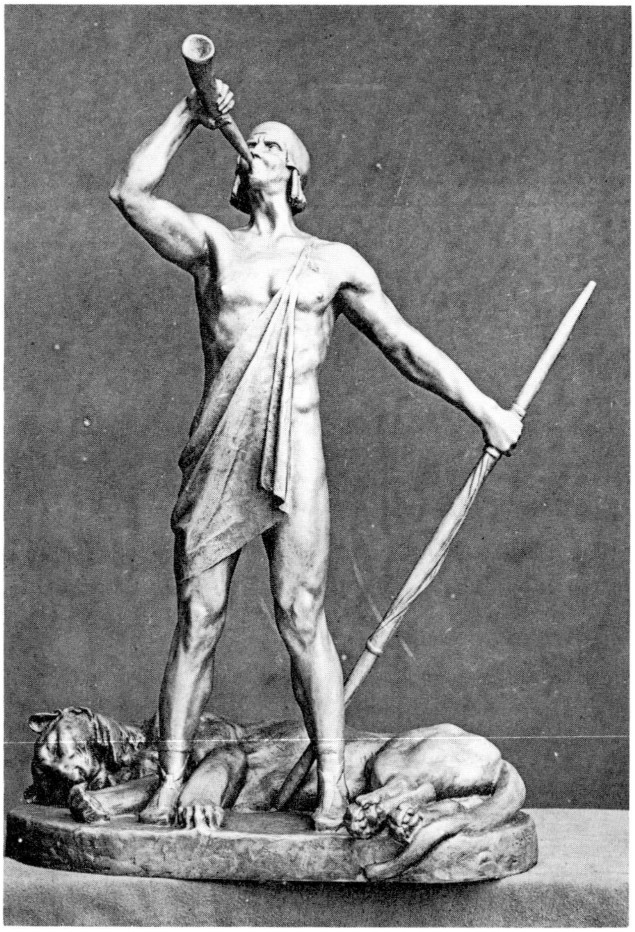

Death of the Beast, 79cm:31in.
Exhibited at the Salon des Artistes Français, 1923

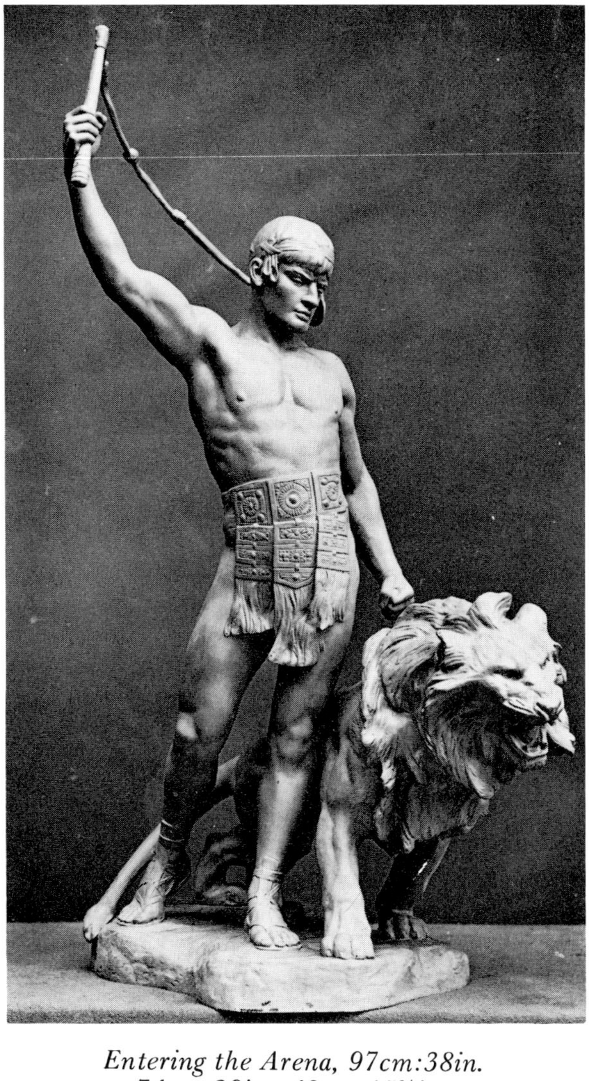

Entering the Arena, 97cm:38in.
74cm:29in.; 40cm:15¾in.

Right. Sosson
Dutch Boy
23cm:9in.

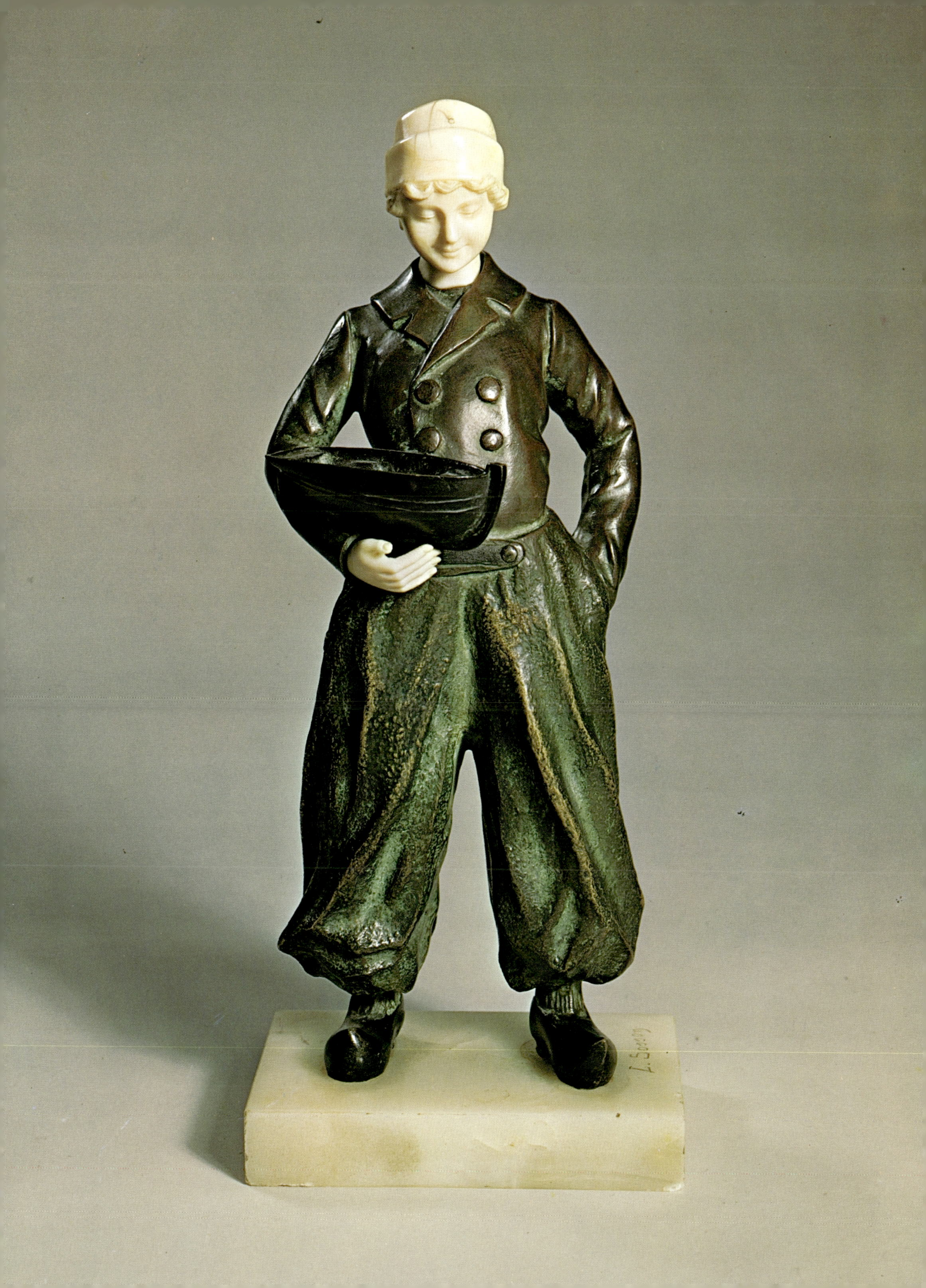

JEAN VERSCHNEIDER

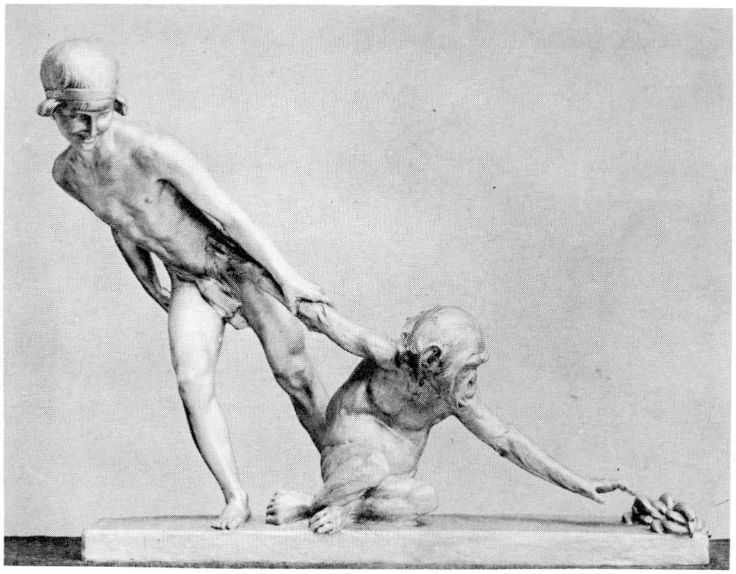

Forbidden Fruits, 58cm:23in.

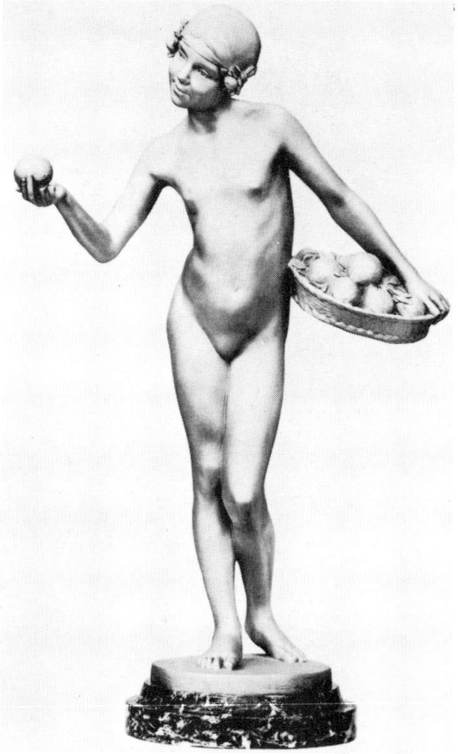

*Golden Apples, 57cm:22½in.
35cm:13¾in.; 15cm:6in.*

VICTOR

*Seated Figure
14cm:5½in.*

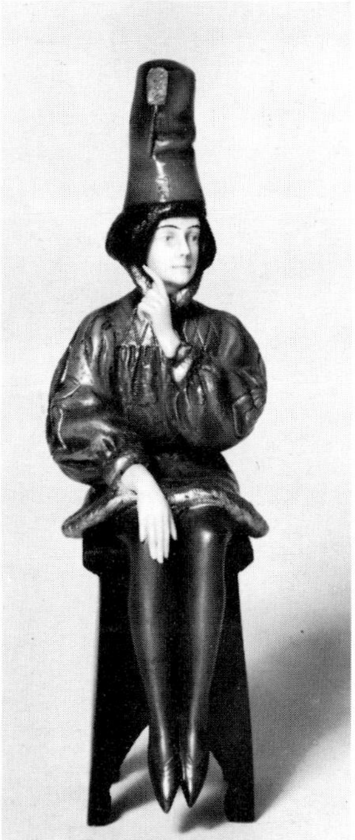

L. WALTHER

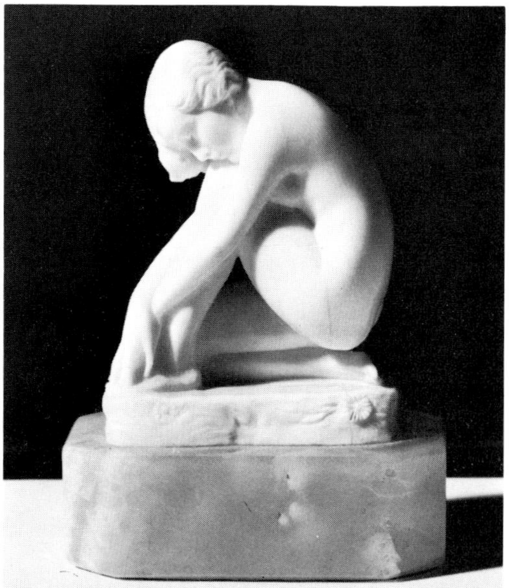

Ivory Nude, 9cm:3½in.

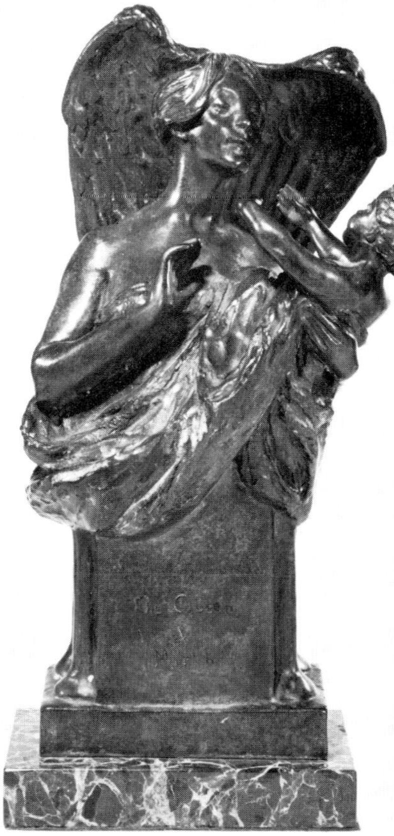

Queen of Mirth, 31cm:12in.

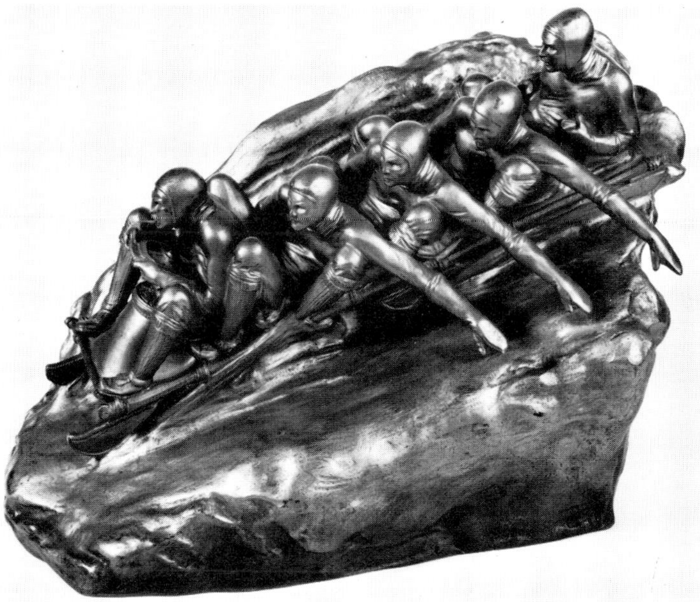

Bobsleigh, 27cm:10¾in.

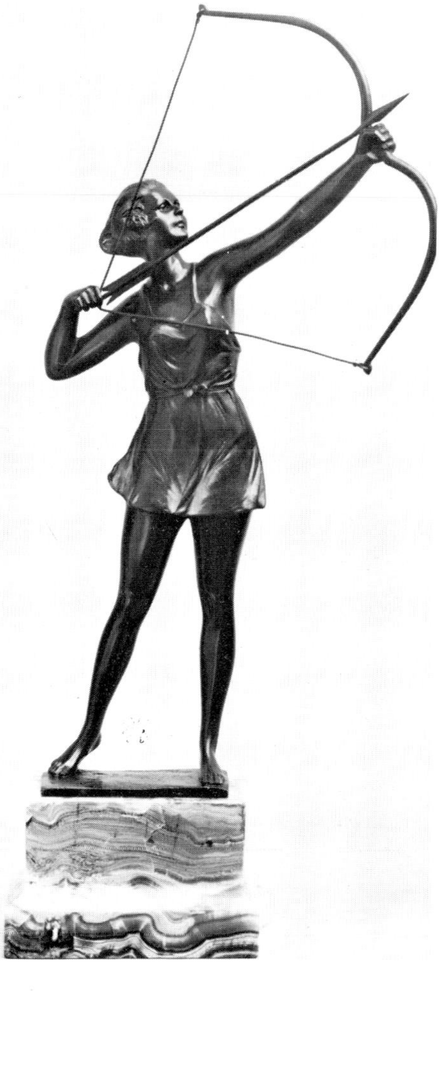

Girl with Bow
32cm:12½in.
Original price
in 1936 – £5

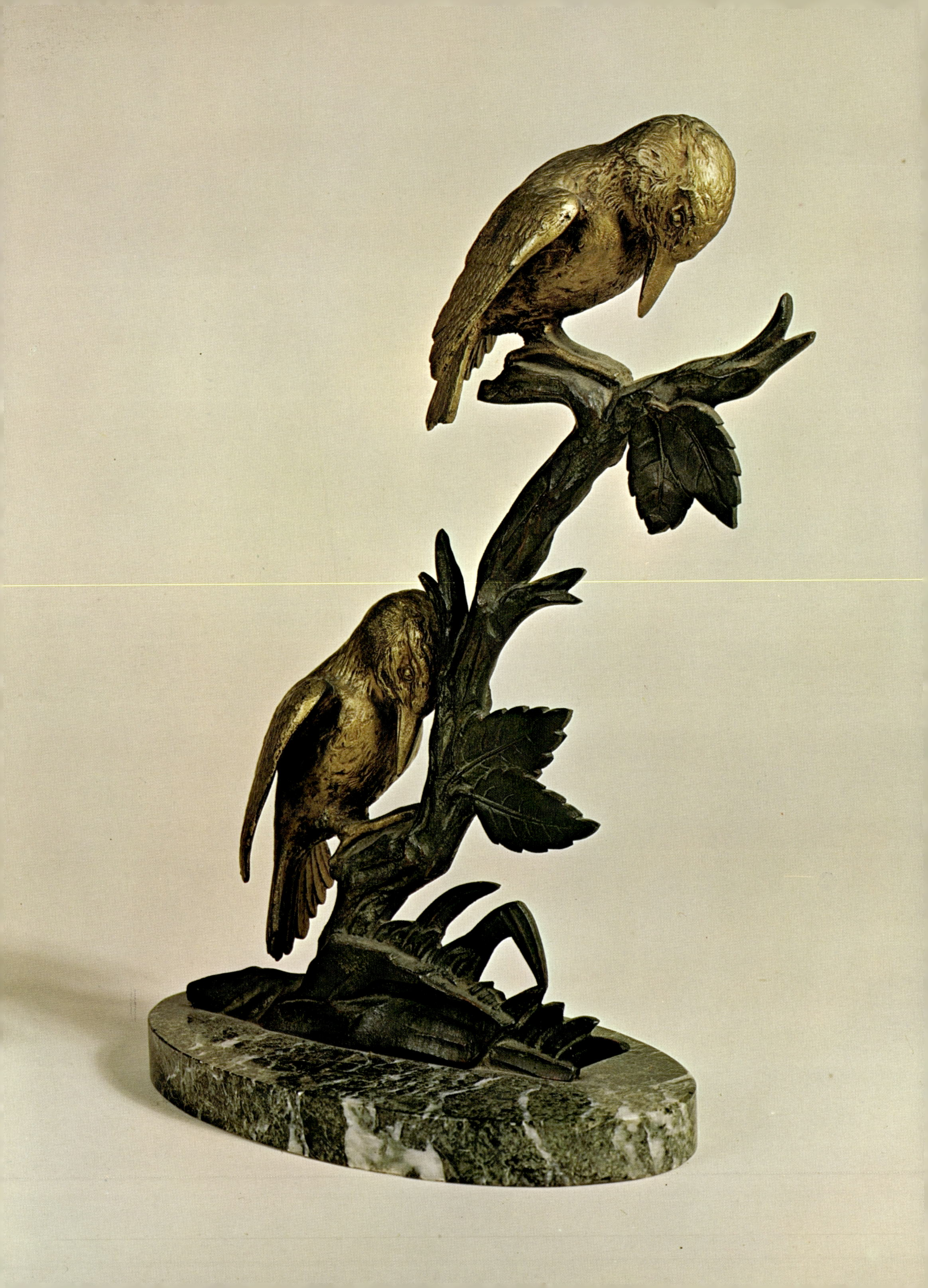

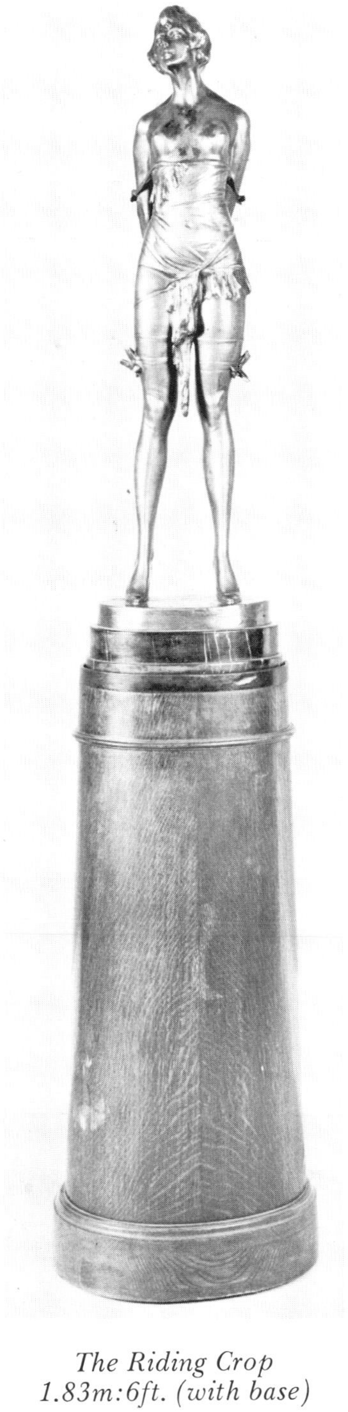

The Riding Crop
1.83m:6ft. (with base)

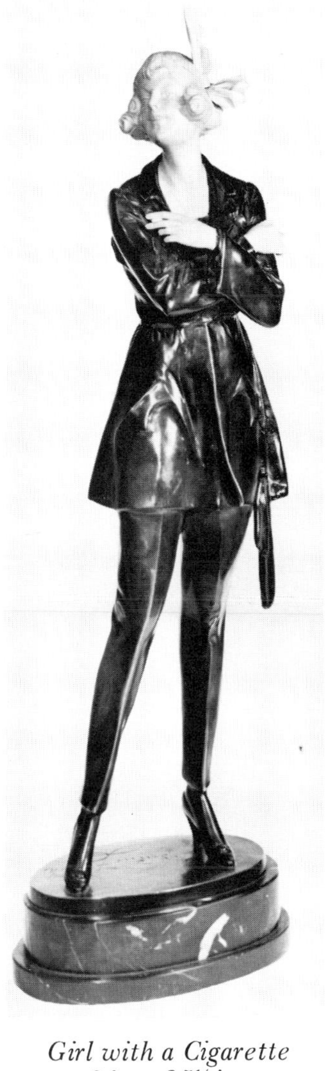

Girl with a Cigarette
64cm:25¼in.

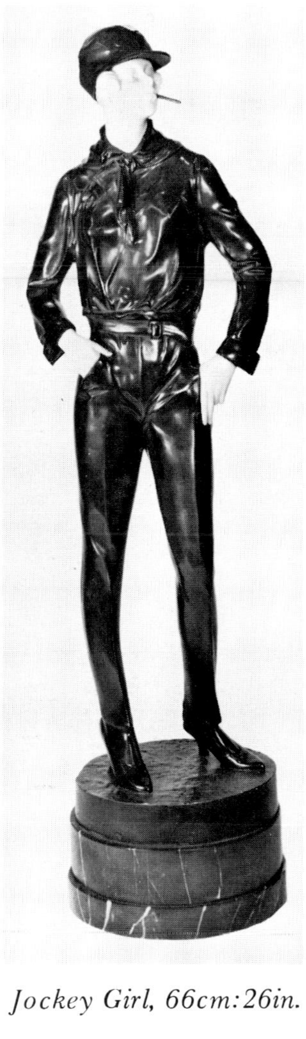

Jockey Girl, 66cm:26in.

Left. Unsigned figure of Two Birds on a Branch 41cm:16in.

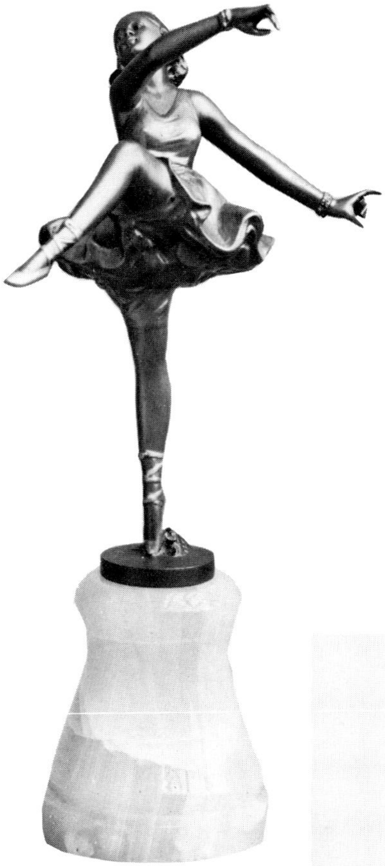

Dancer, 28cm:11in.

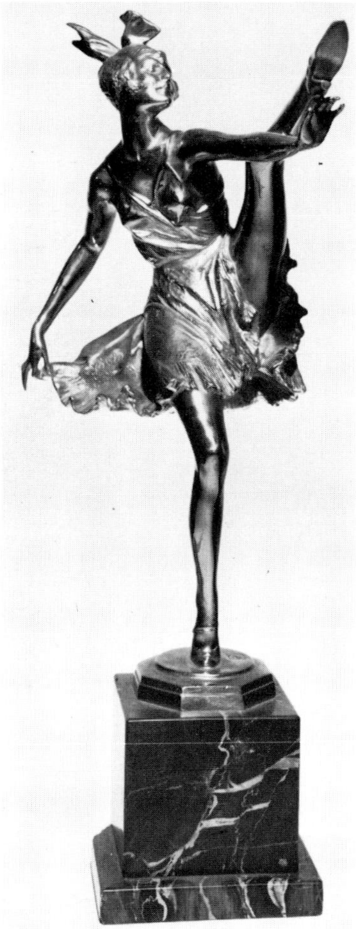

Kicking Girl
48cm:19in.

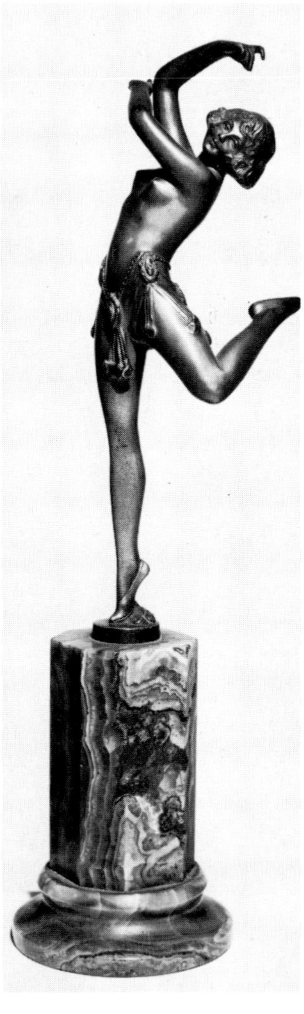

A Dancer, 38cm:15in.

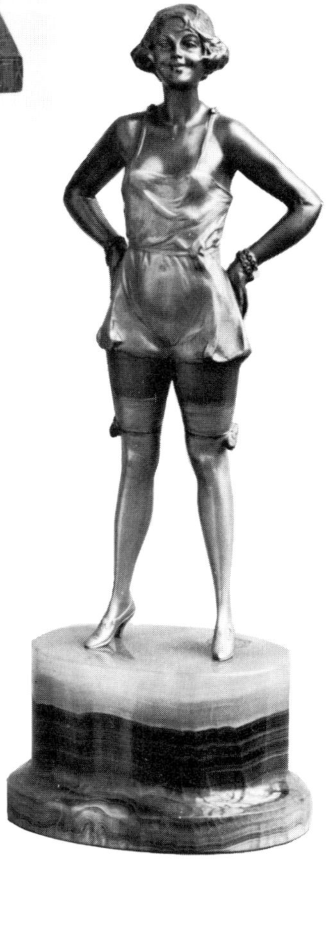

Girl, 28cm:11in.

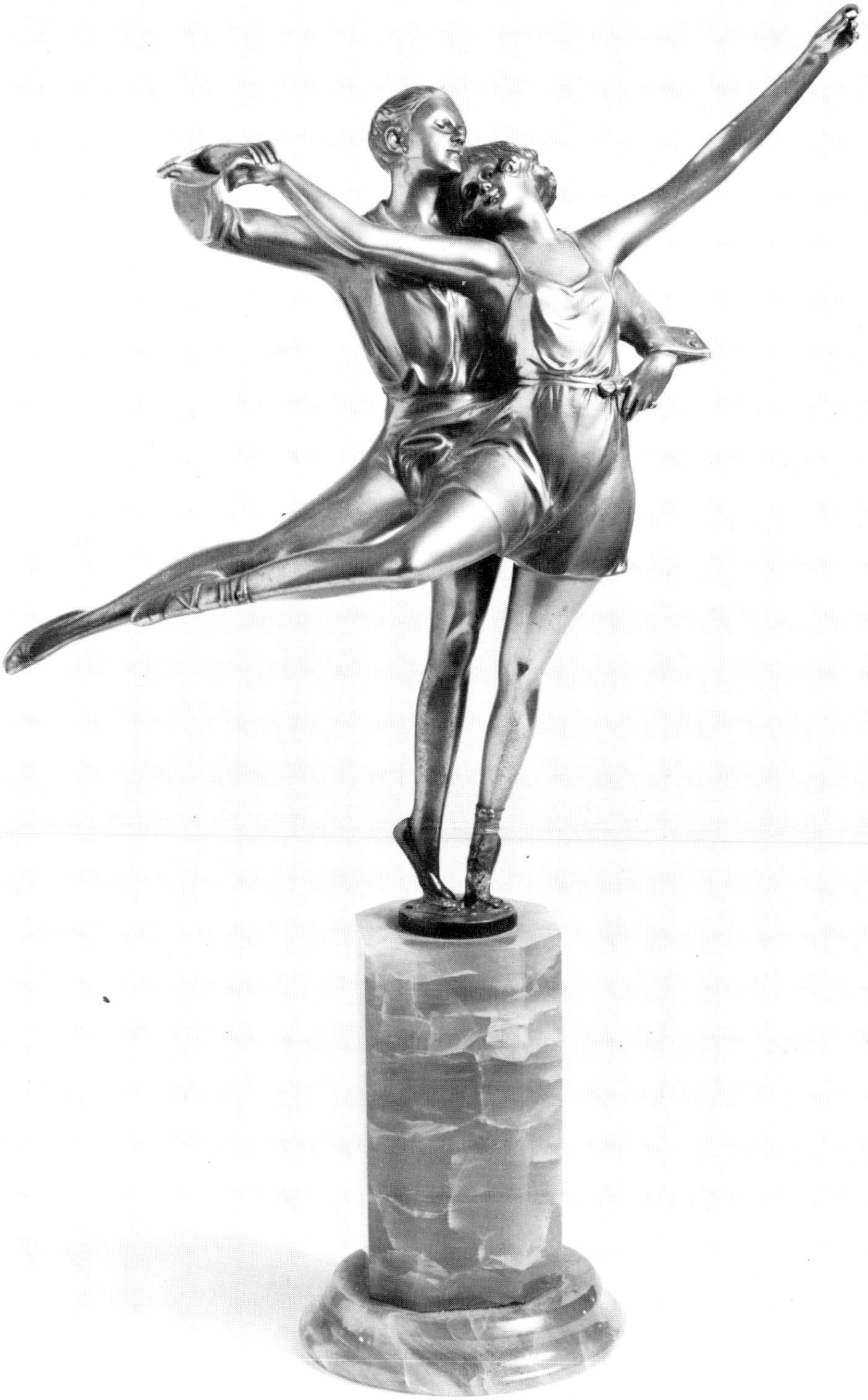

Pair of Dancers, 37cm: 14½in.
Original price in 1936 – £9

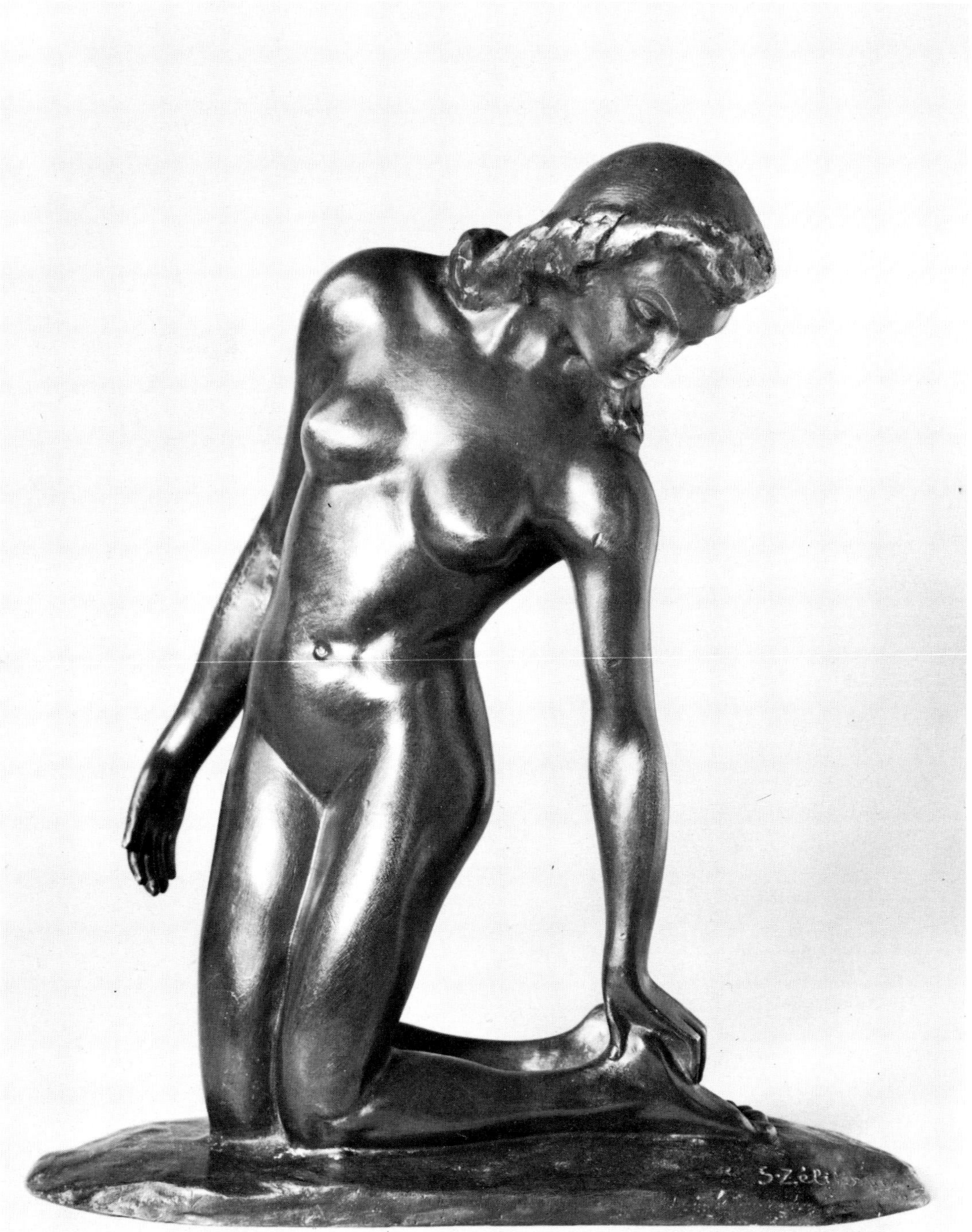

A Nude, 33cm:13in.

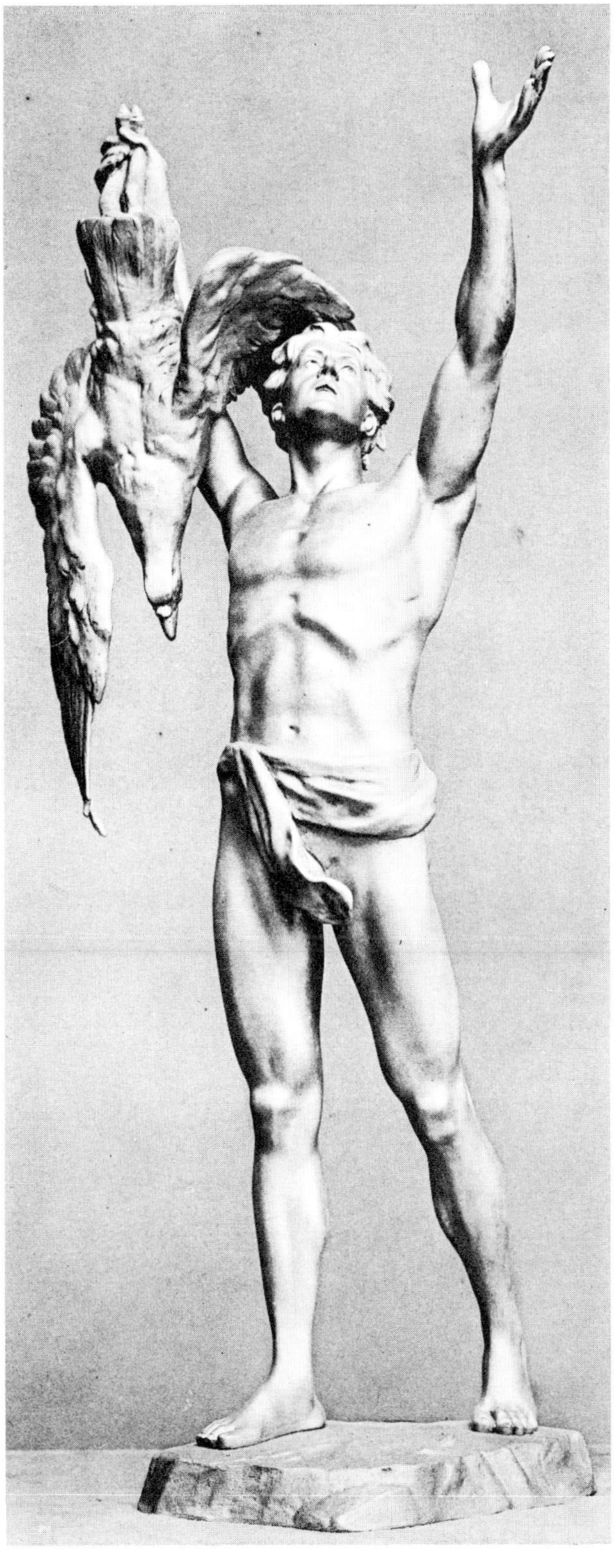

Eagle Hunter
84cm:33in.; 52cm:20½in.

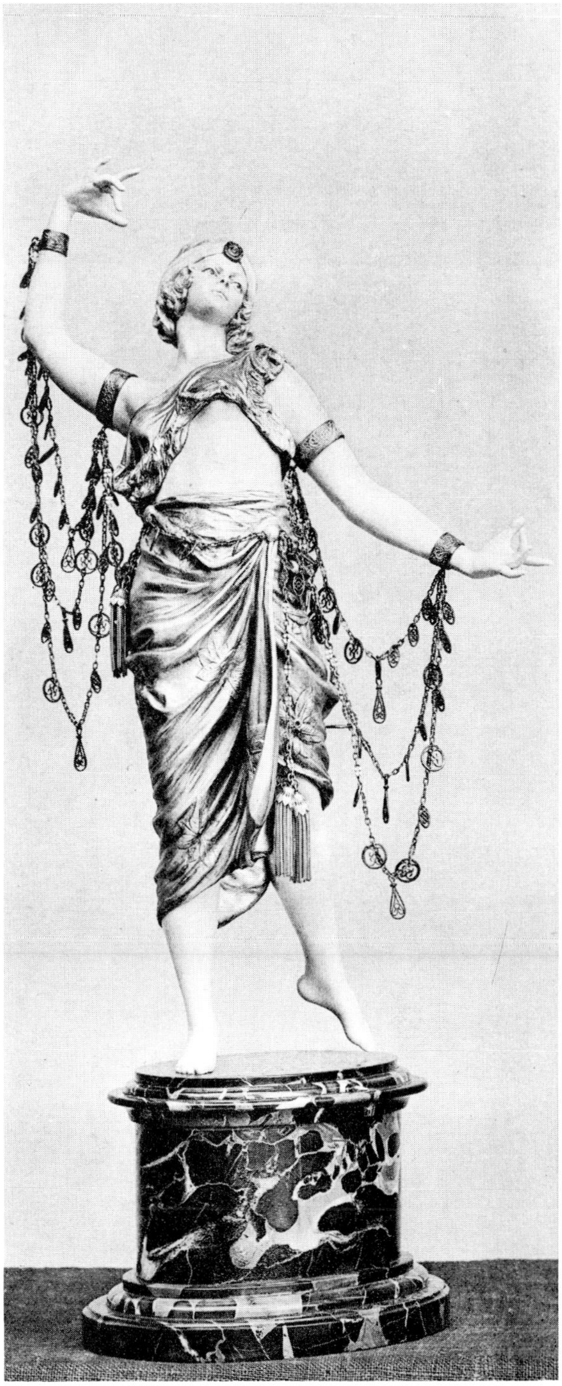

Dacia
51cm:20in.

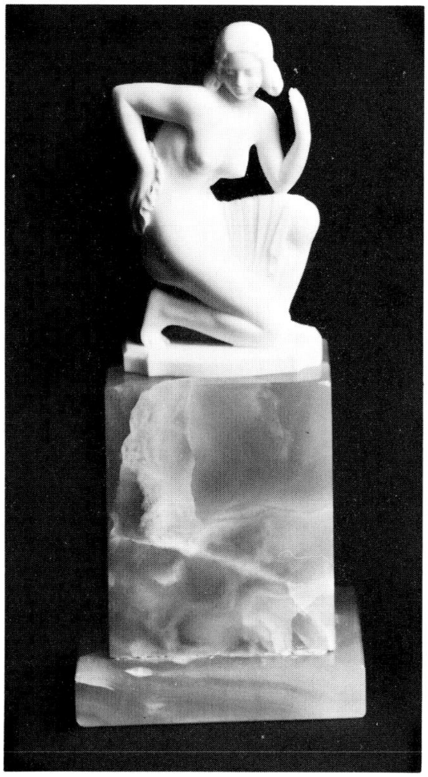

Pair of ivory nudes
13cm:5in.

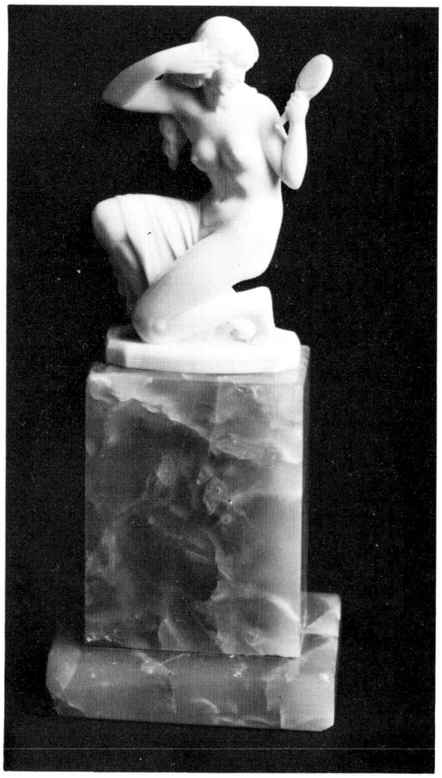

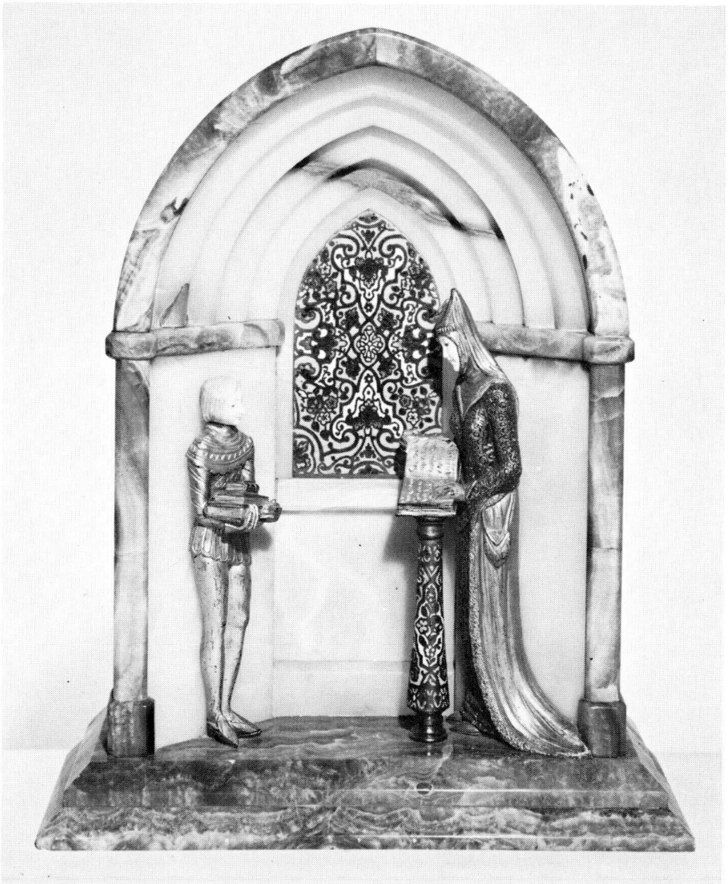

Reading
39cm:15¼in.

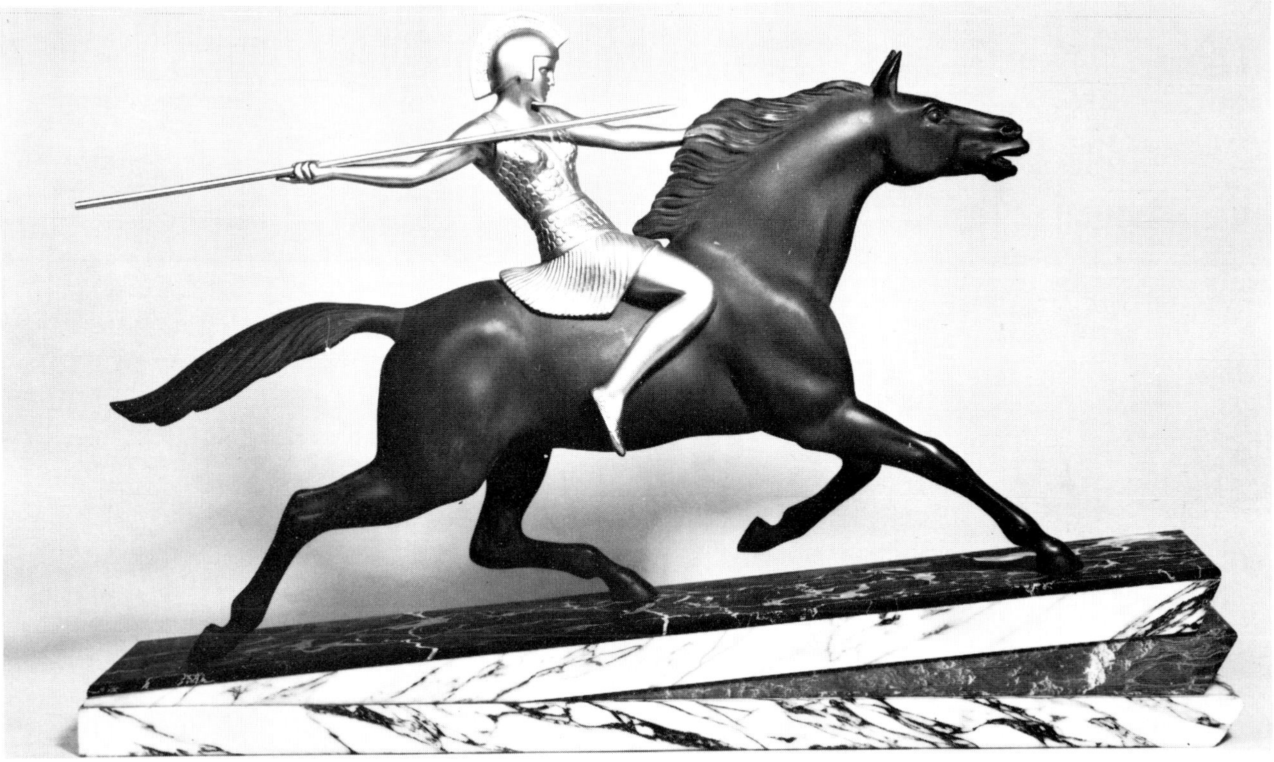

Roman Soldier, 38cm:15in.

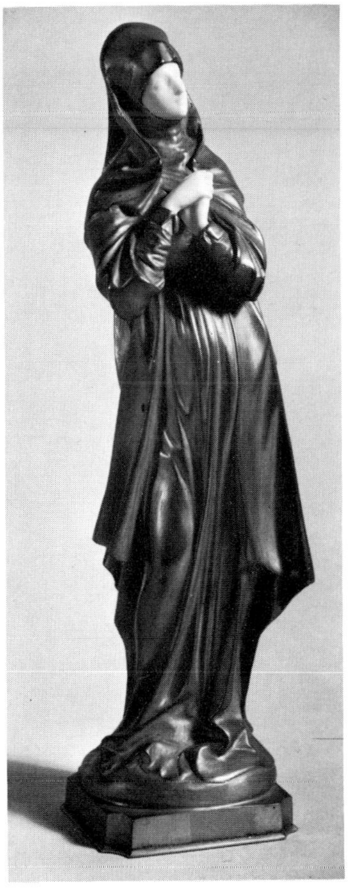

A Nun
26cm:10¼in.

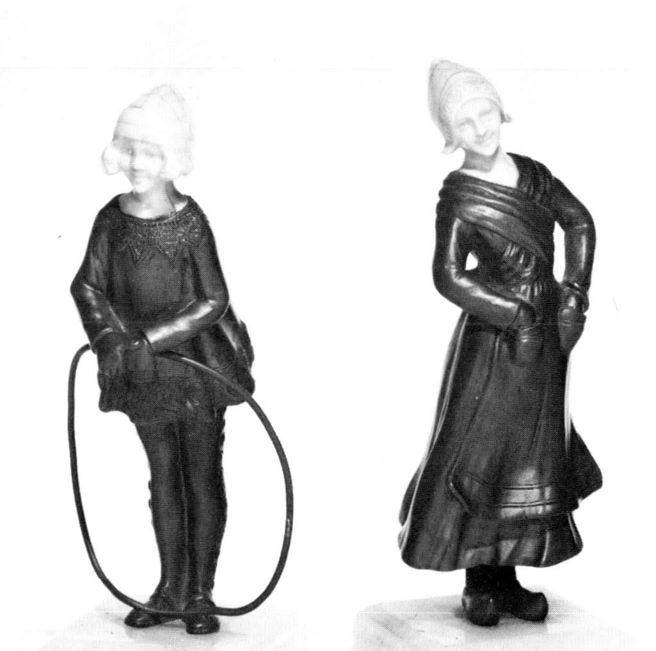

Two Children, 15cm:5¾in.
(possibly by Bertrand)

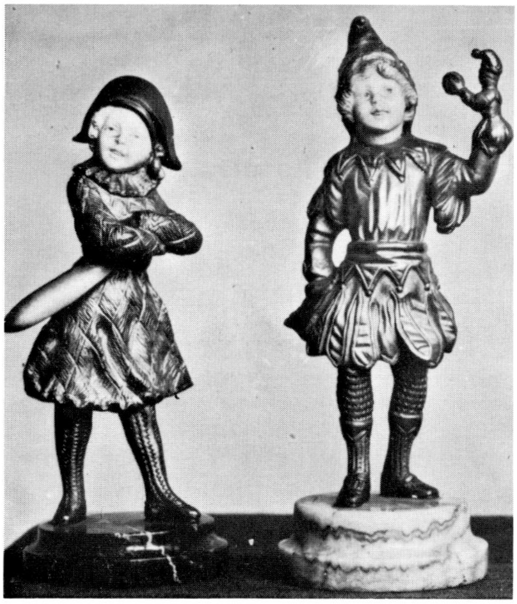

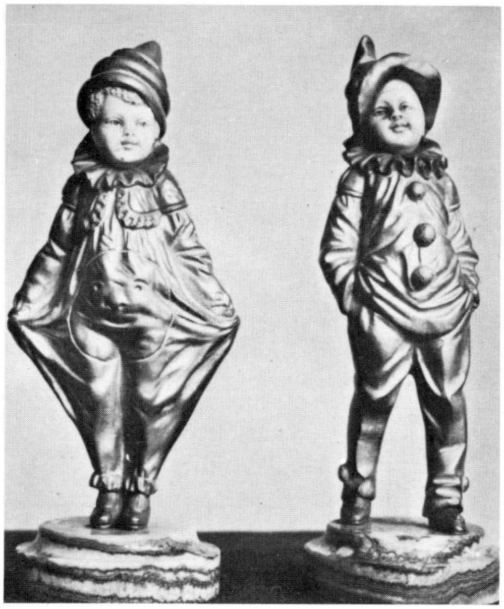

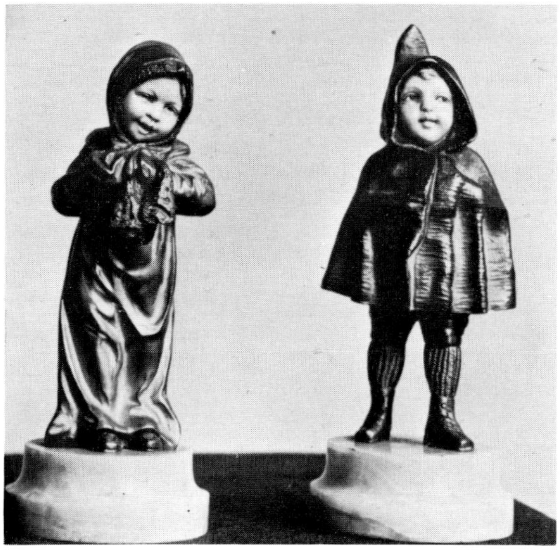

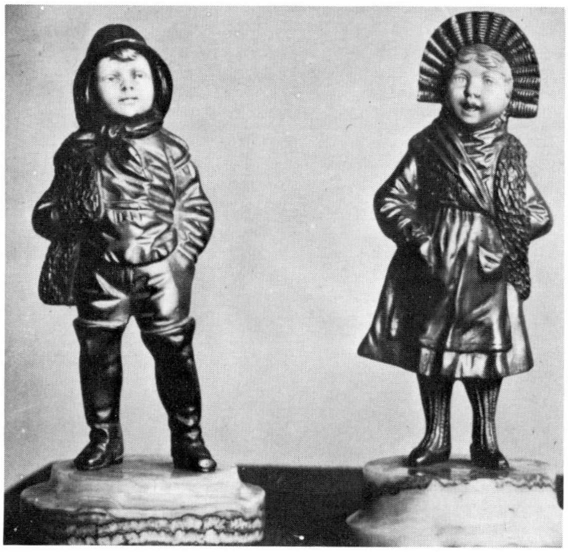

Series of Children
All between 16-20cm: 6¼-8in.

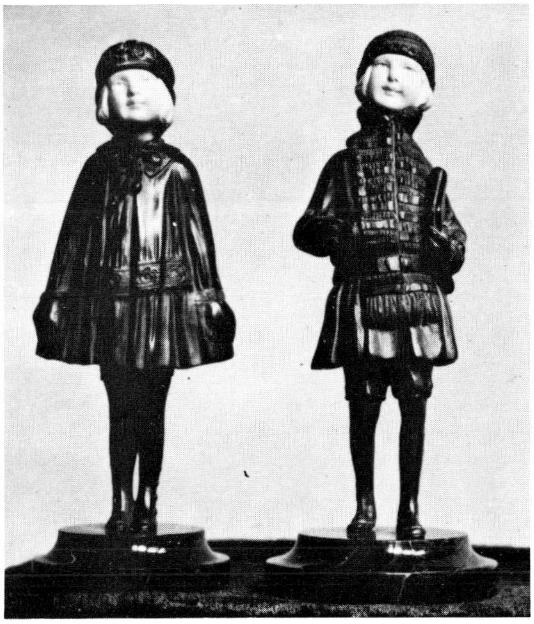

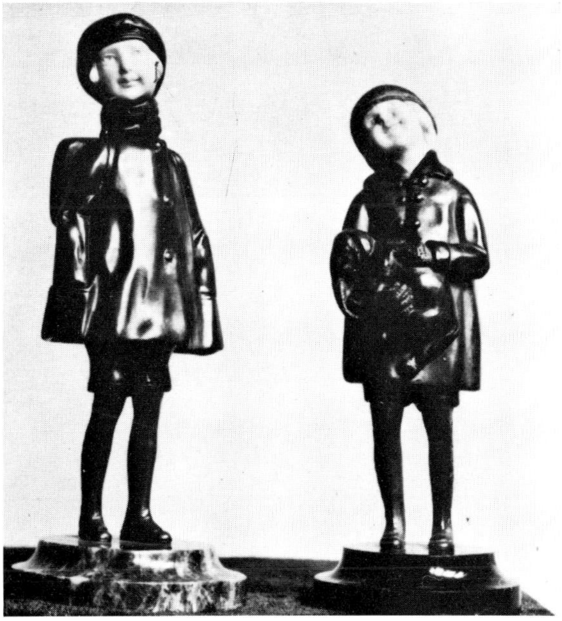

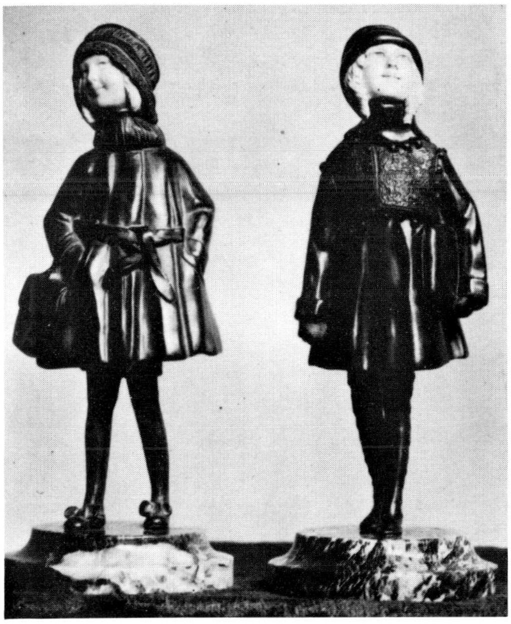

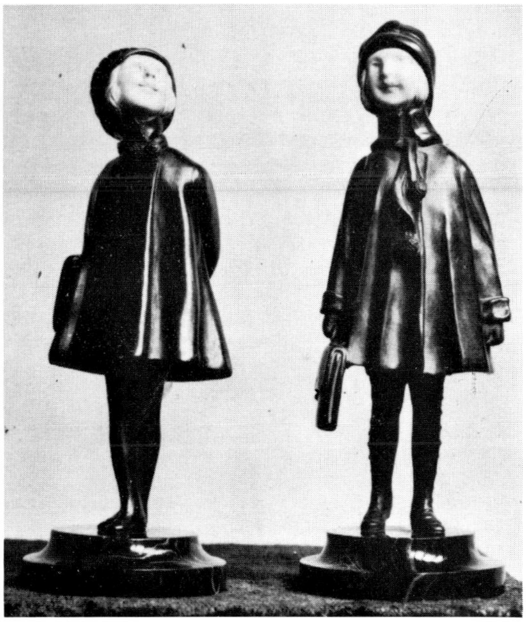

Series of Schoolchildren
16-20cm: 6¼-8in.

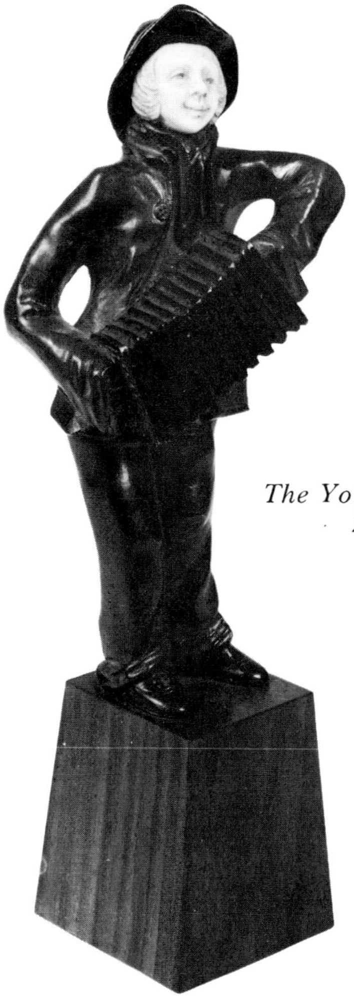

The Young Accordionist
23cm: 9in.

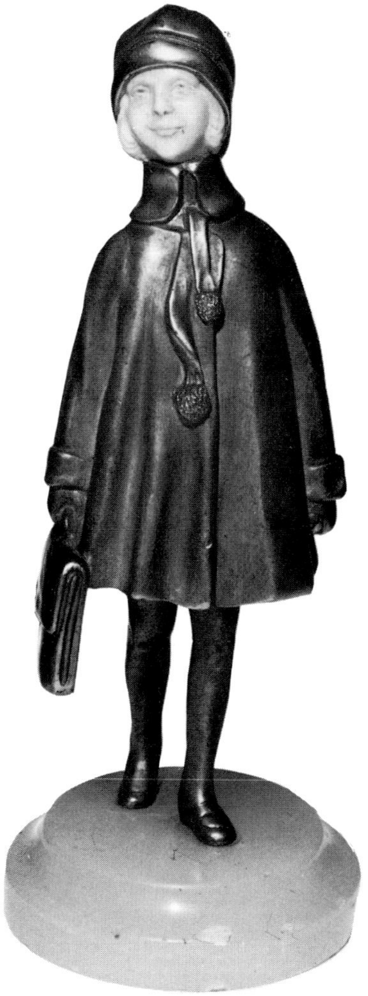

One of the Schoolchildren on page 313, with slight variations in details. Possibly by D.H. Chiparus.

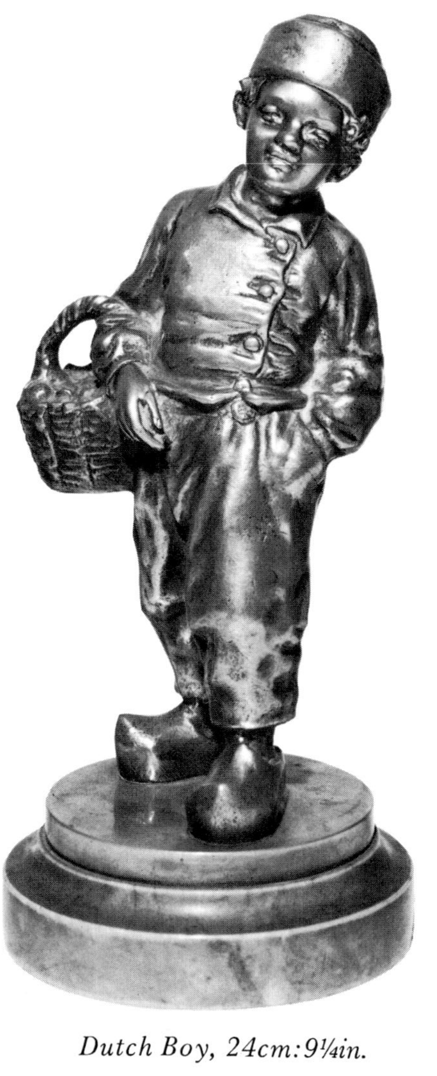

Dutch Boy, 24cm: 9¼in.

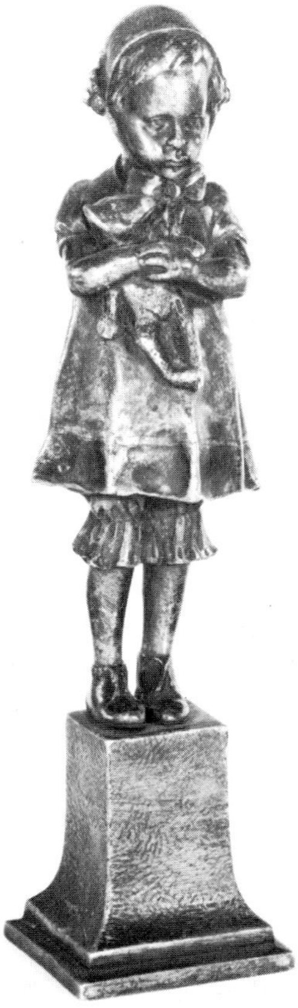

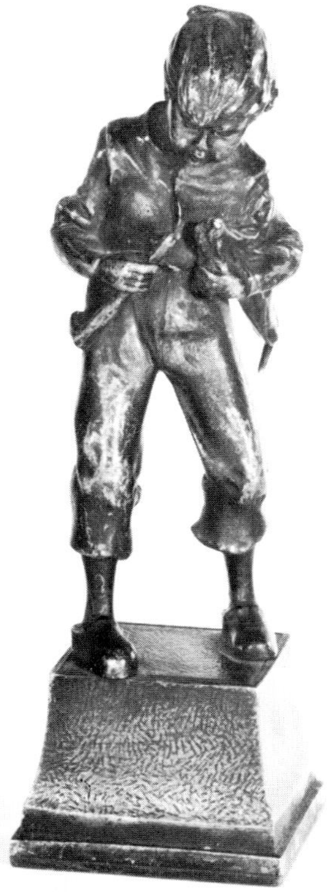

Girl, 13cm:5in., and Boy, 11cm:4½in.

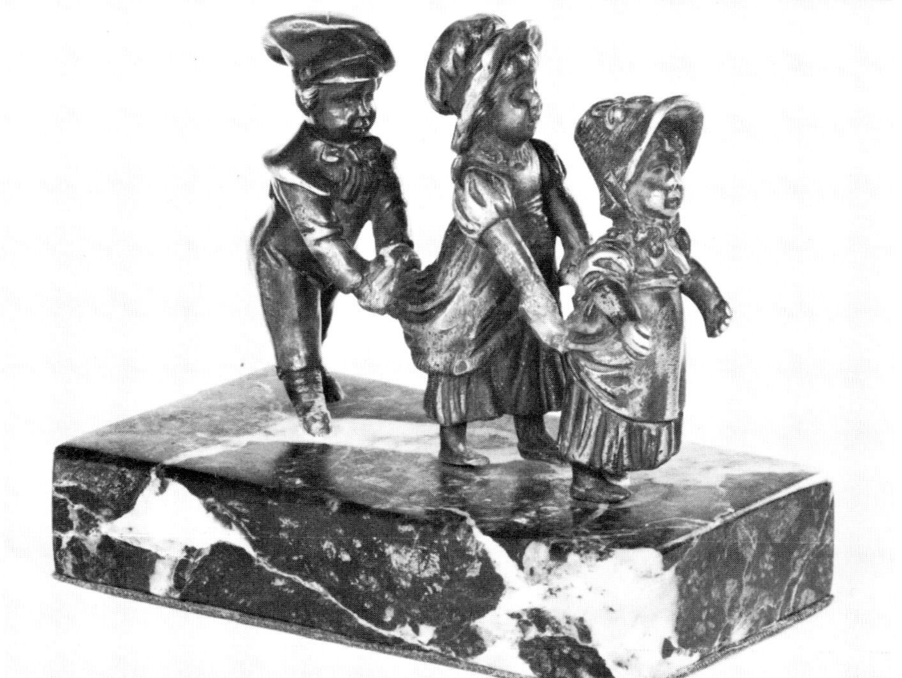

Three Children 11cm:4½in.

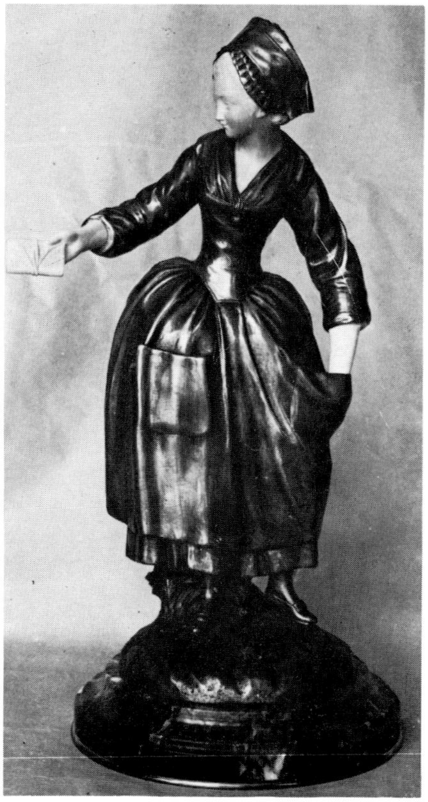

Left: Jeannette
37cm:14½in.

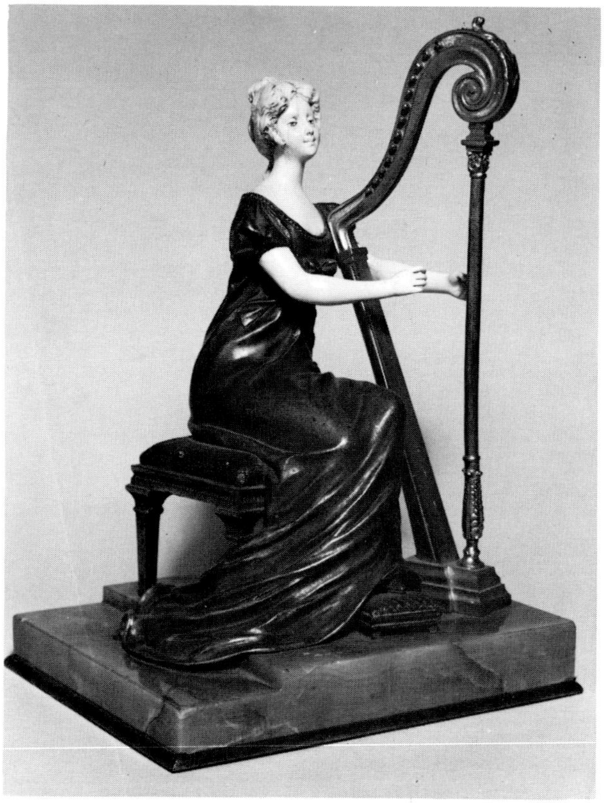

Right:
Girl with Harp
25cm:10in.

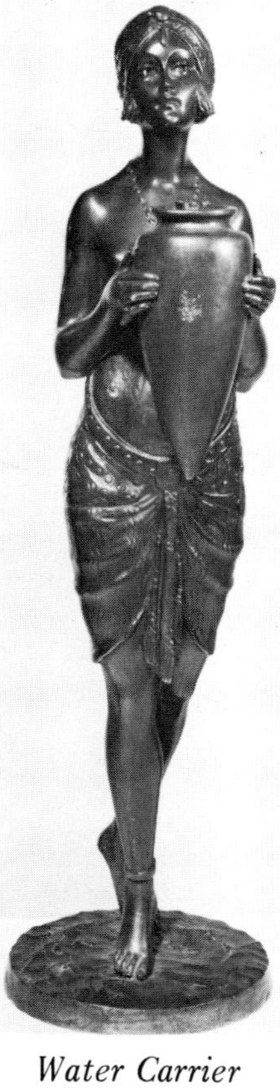

Water Carrier
31cm:12in.

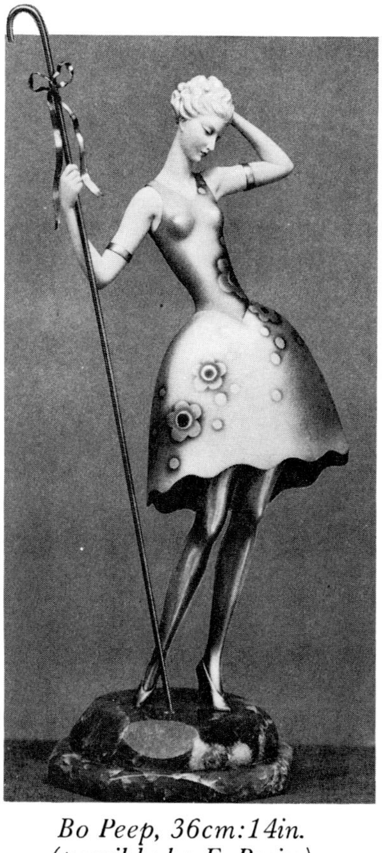

Bo Peep, 36cm:14in.
(possibly by F. Preiss)

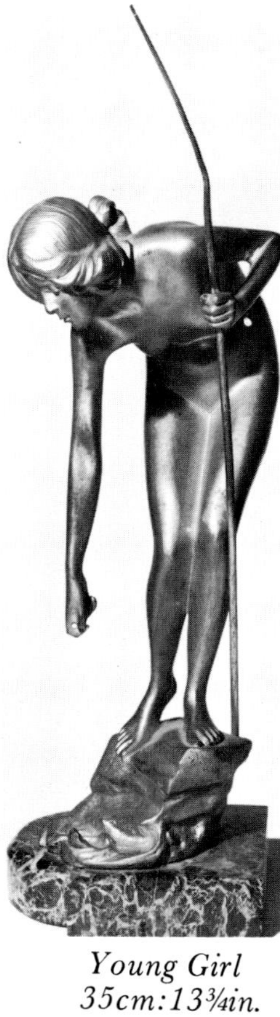

Young Girl
35cm:13¾in.

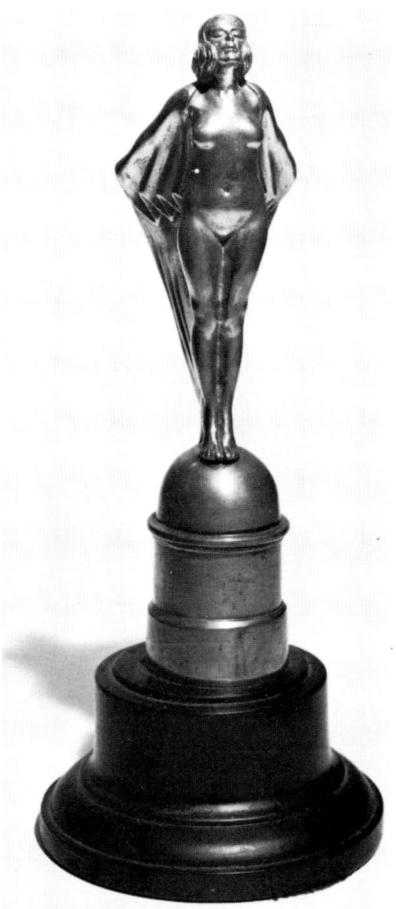

Nude, 27cm:10¾in.

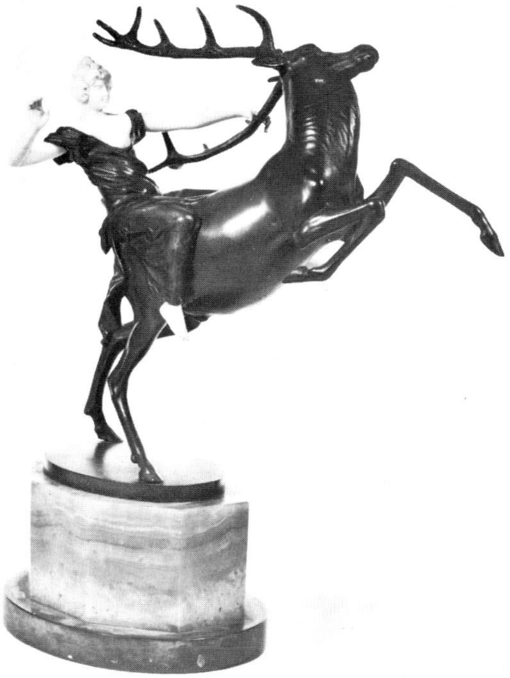

Girl and Stag
25cm:10in.

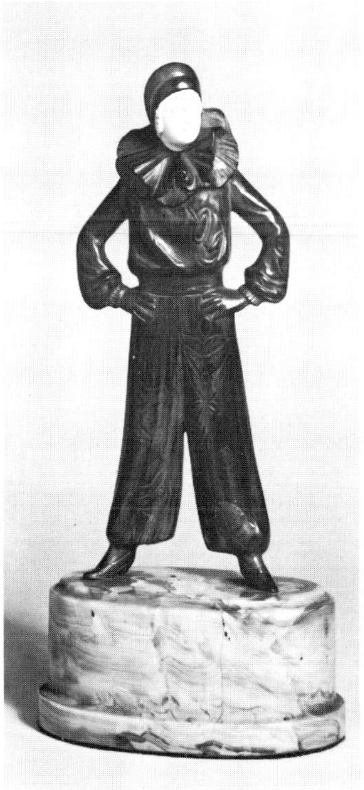

Pierrot, 28cm:11in.

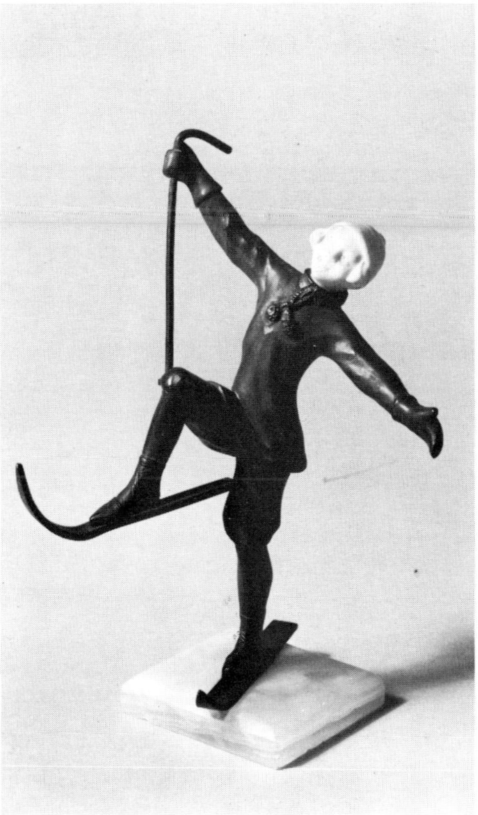

A Skier, 17cm:6½in.

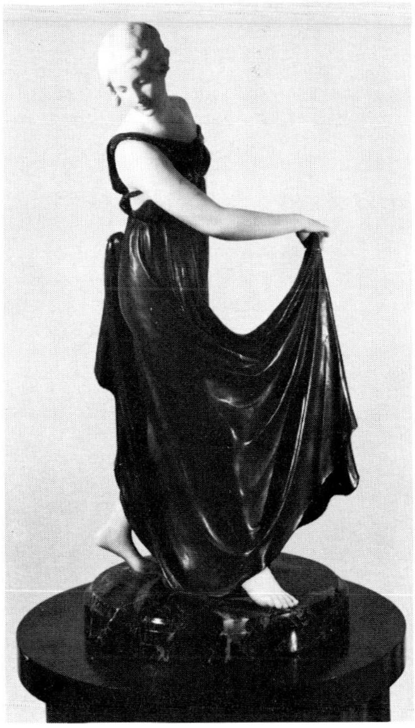

Young Girl, 42cm:16½in.
(bronze and marble)

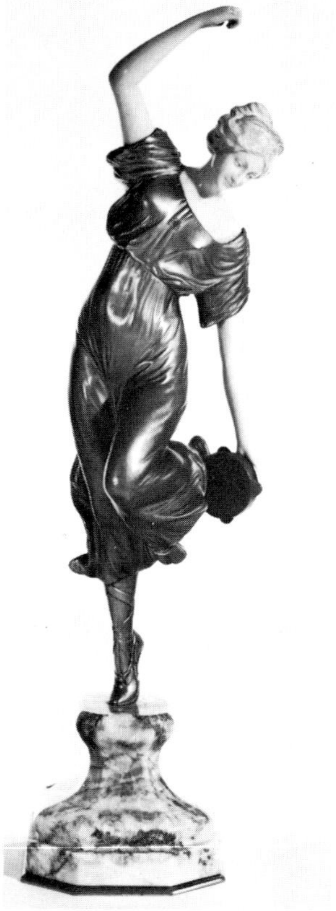

Dancer, 36cm:14in.

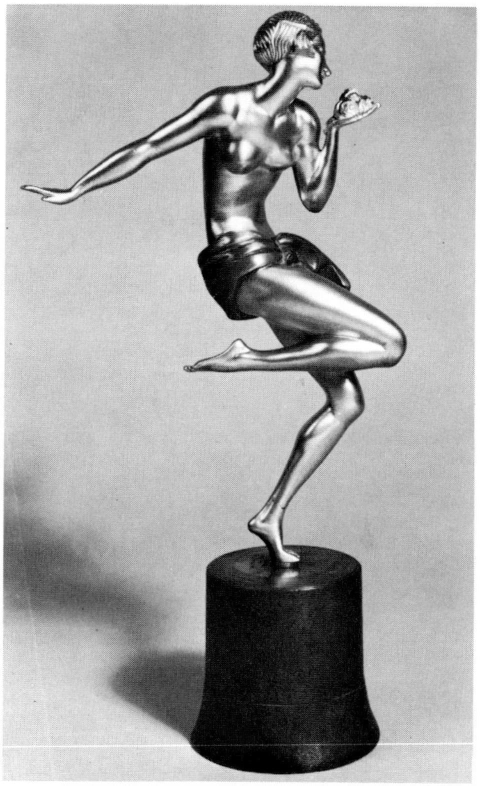

Dancer
36cm:14in.

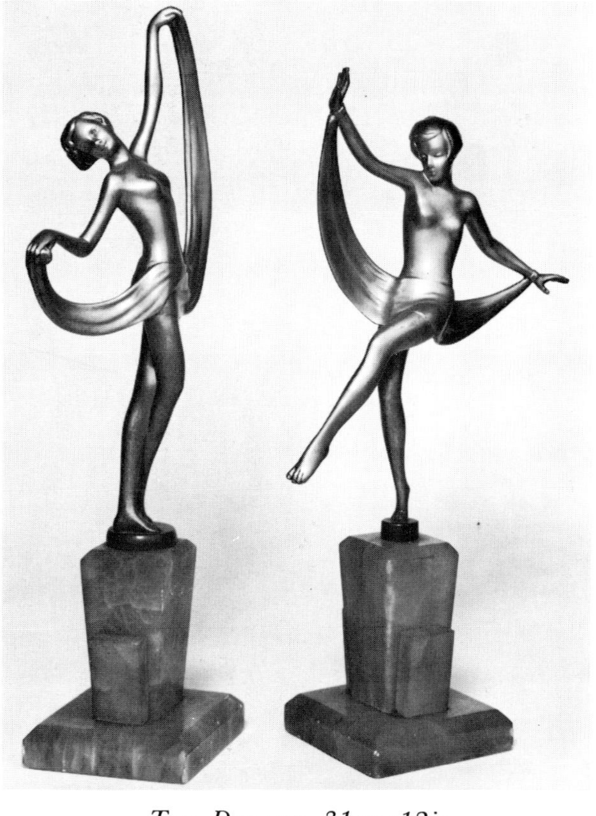

Two Dancers, 31cm:12in.

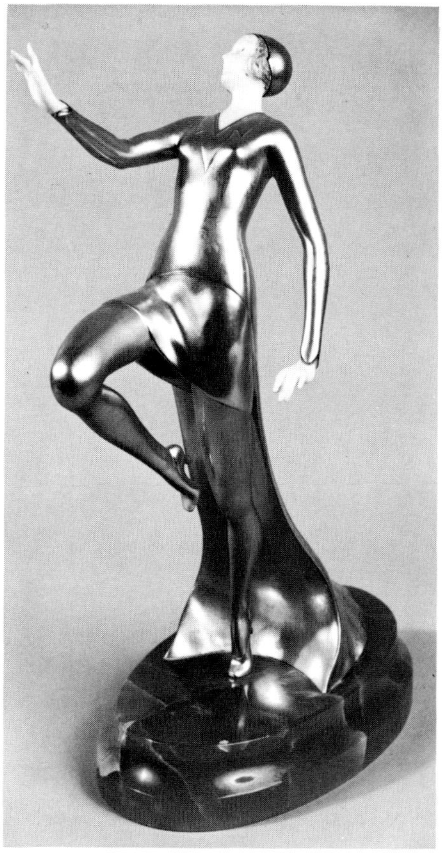

Dancer
25cm:10in.

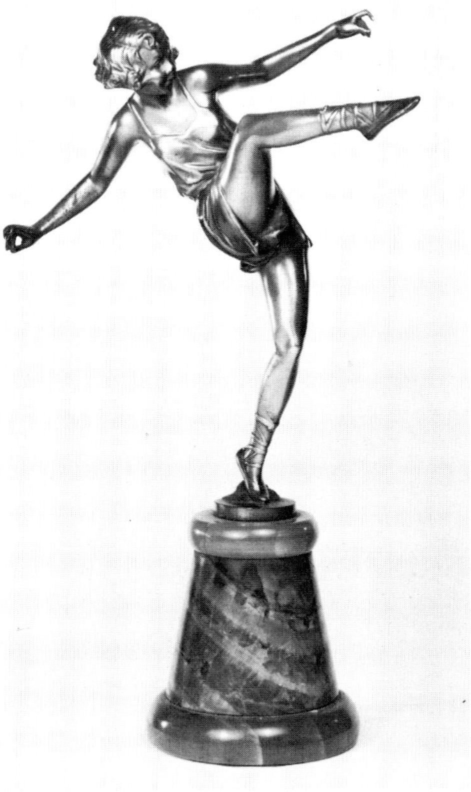

Dancer, 20cm:8in.

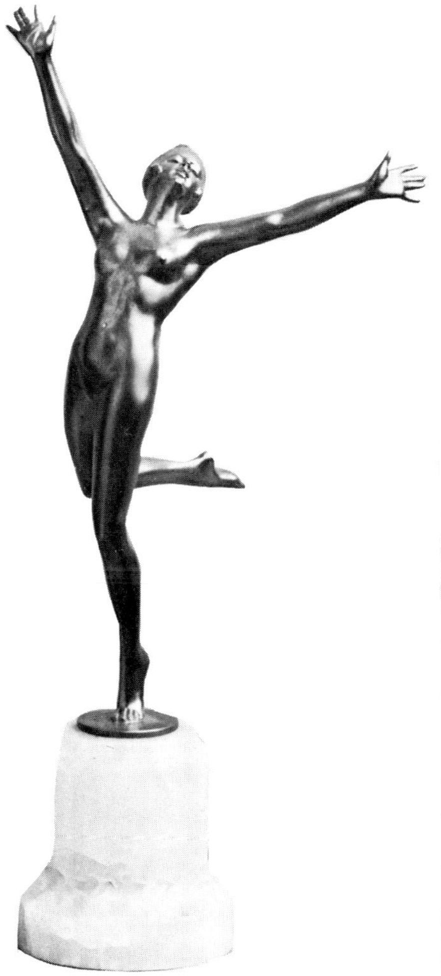

Dancer
32cm:12½in.

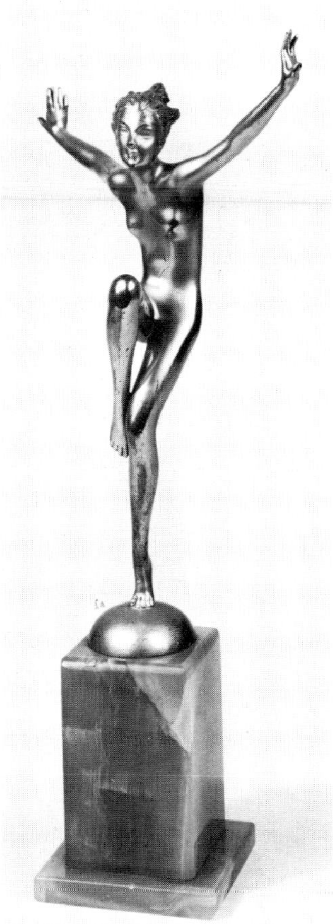

Dancer, various sizes
(possibly by Lorenzel or Dakon)

A SELECTION OF ART DECO FIGURES USED ON LAMPS
(in alphabetical order of artists)

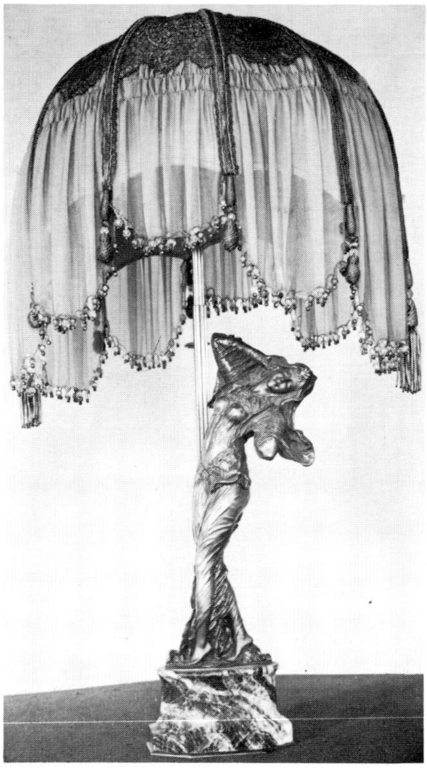

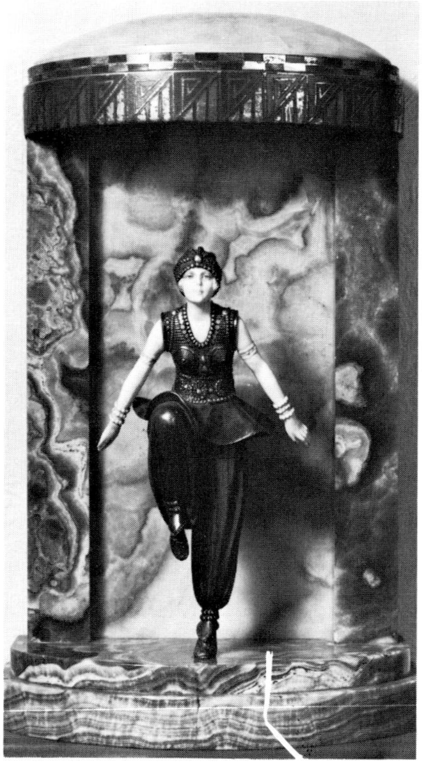

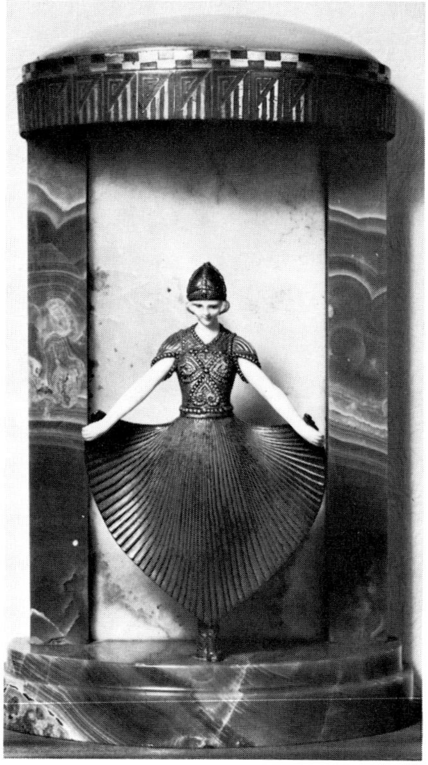

Three lamps incorporating figures by D.H. Chiparus (see pages 63, 19 and 96)

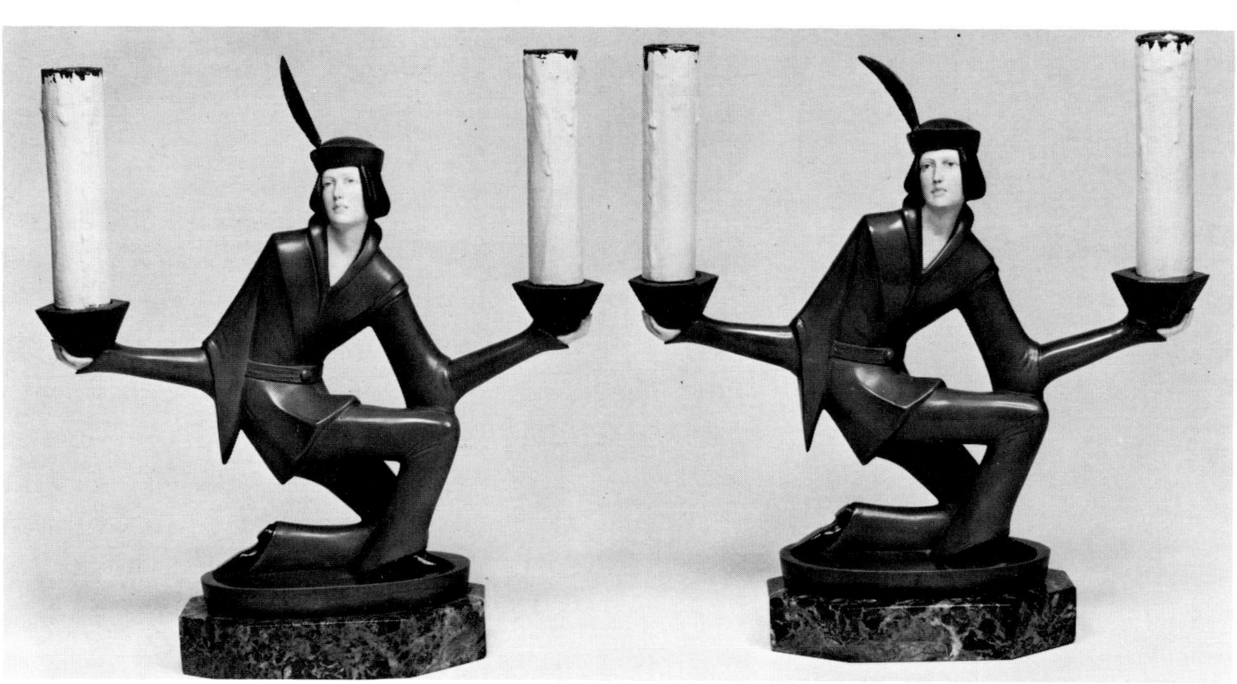

Pair of lamps by Harders

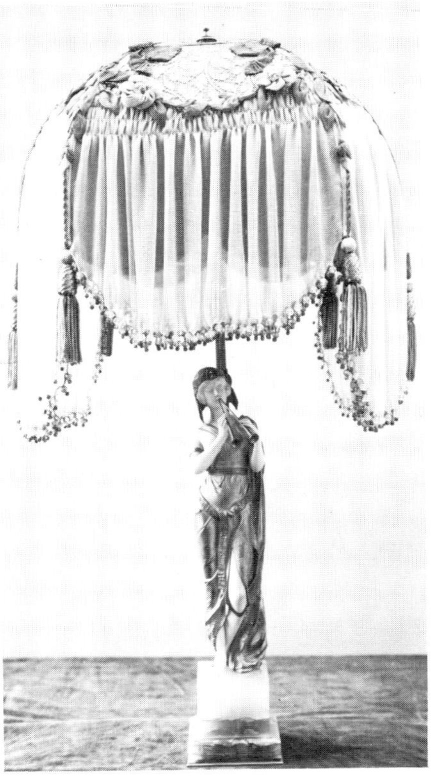

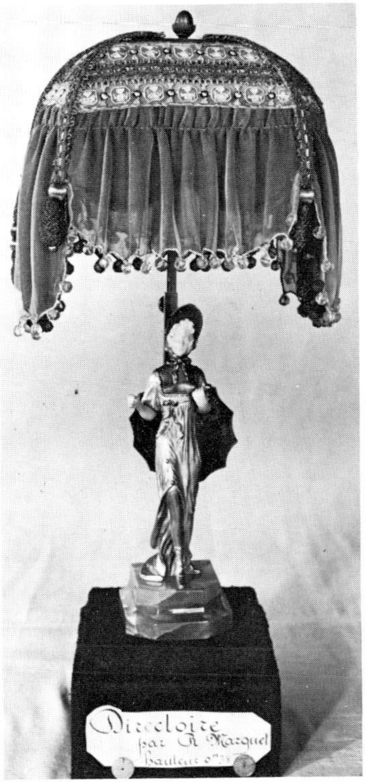

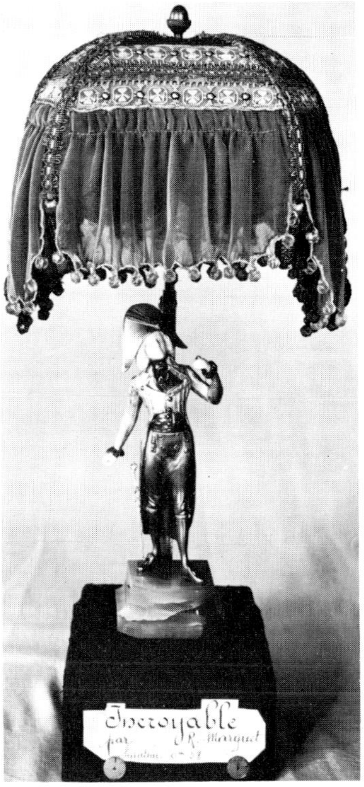

Lamps with figures by R. Marquet (see page 216)

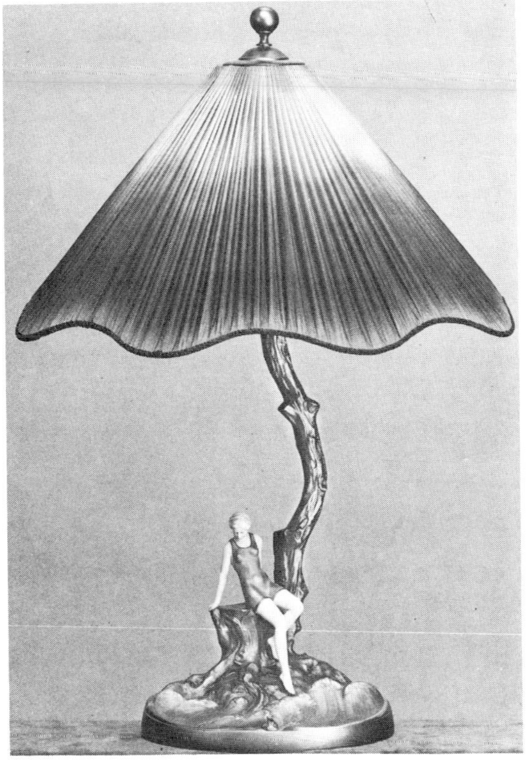

Bathing Girl on a lamp
by F. Preiss

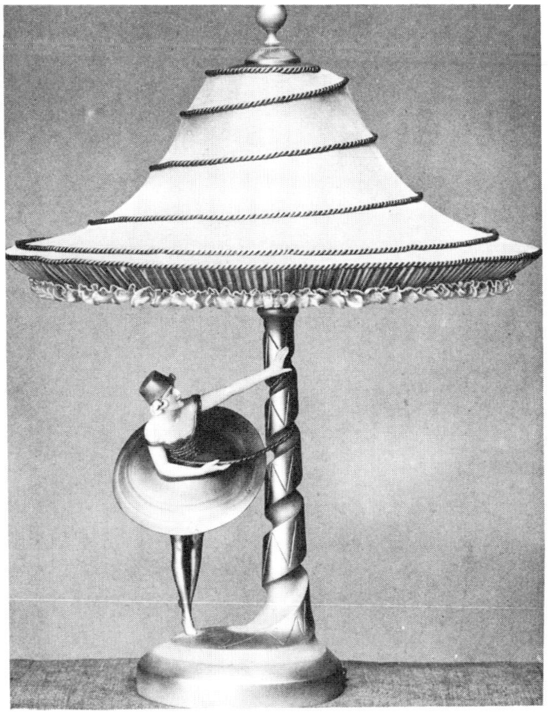

The Top,
Prof. Otto. Poertzel or F. Preiss

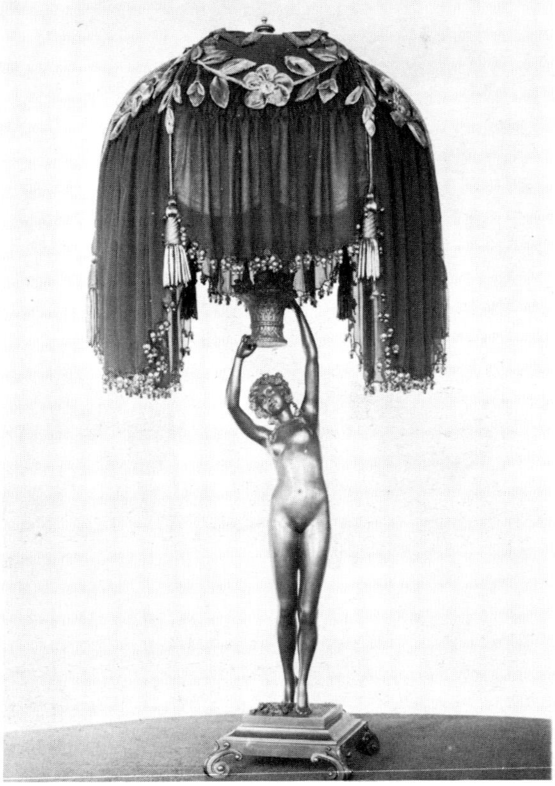

Rose of Mine, unsigned

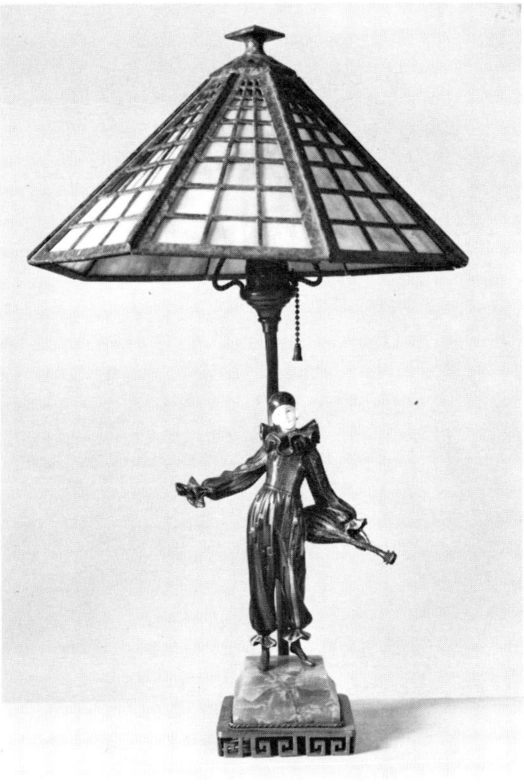

Mandolin Player, unsigned

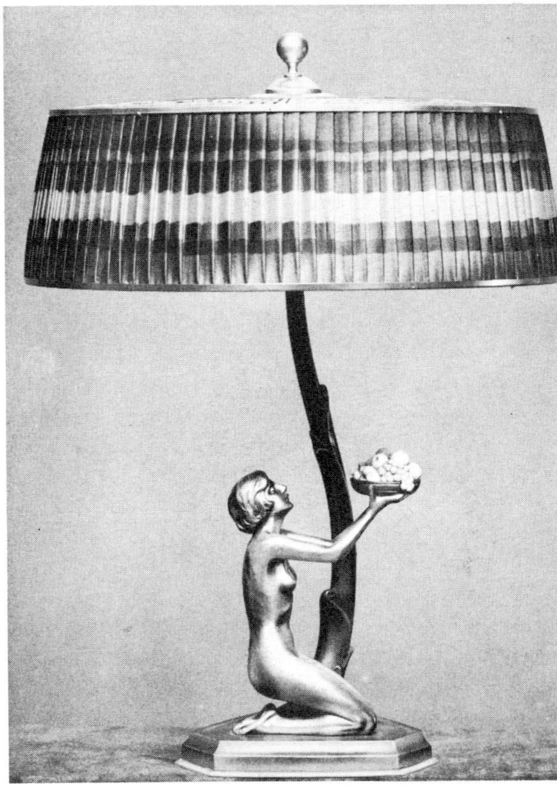

Bowl of Fruit,
unsigned (possibly by F. Preiss)

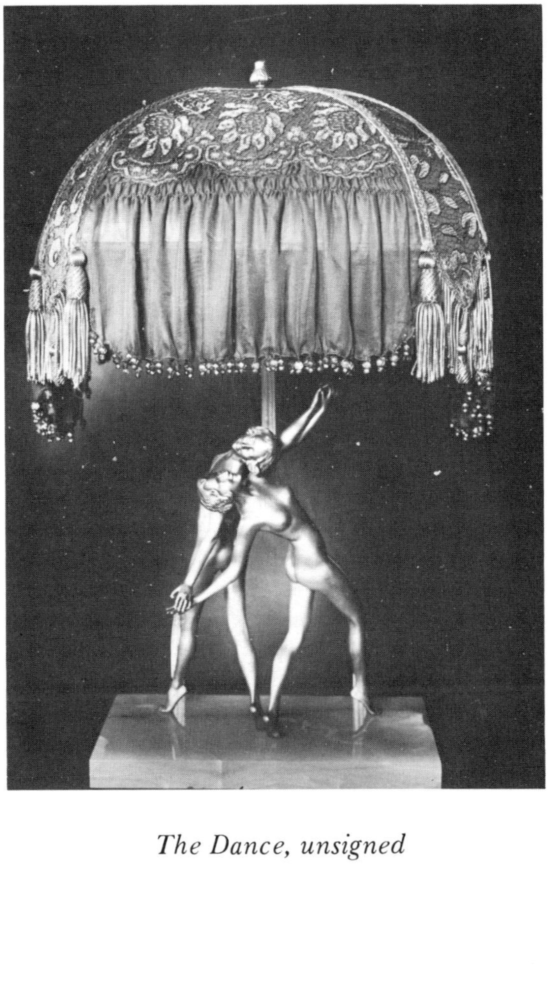

The Dance, unsigned

BOOKENDS WITH ART DECO SCULPTURES SHOW HOW EFFECTIVELY PAIRS OF FIGURES CAN BE USED
(in alphabetical order of artists)

Four pairs of bookends incorporating figures by Magd. Anthouard

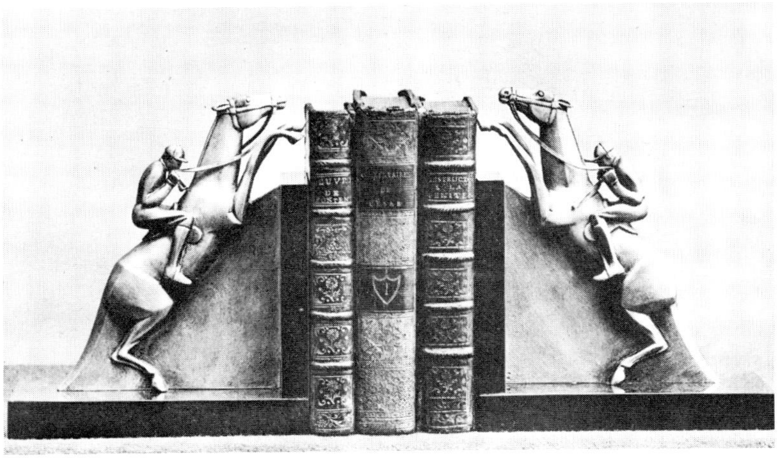

Obstacle

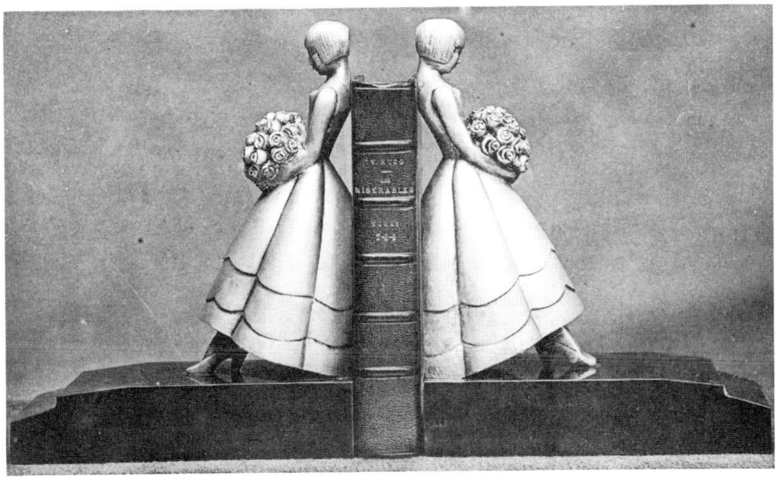

Spring

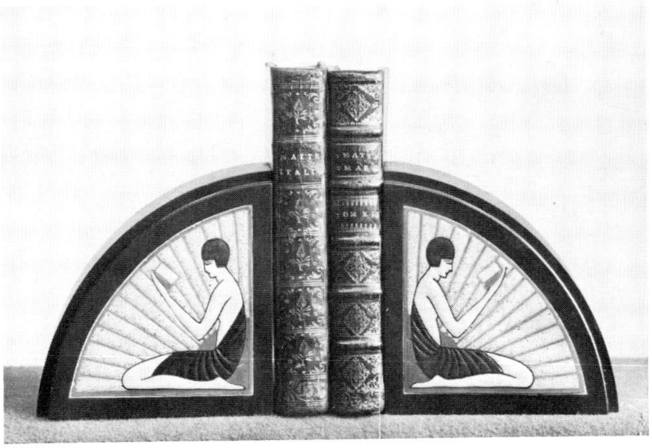

Poems

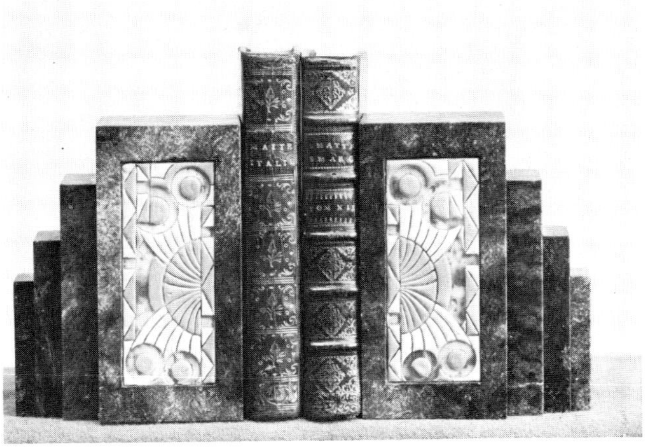

Butterflies

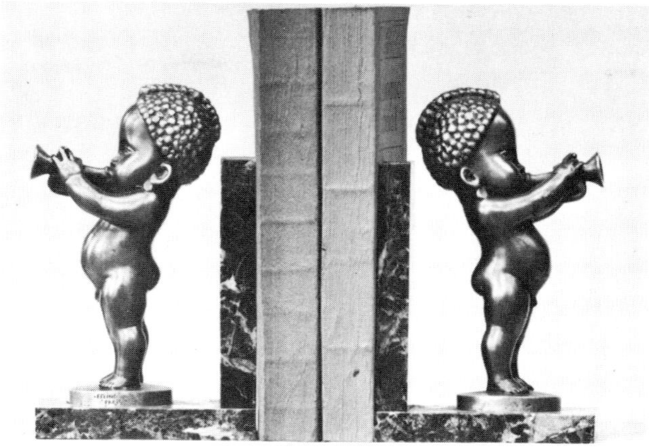

Jazz Band, A. Becquerel

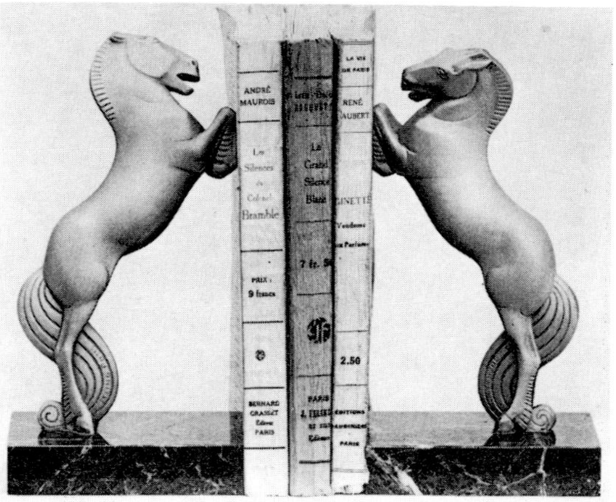

Ponies, A. Becquerel

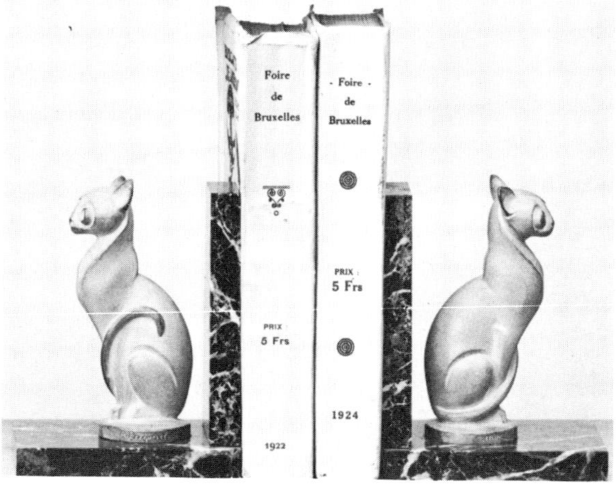

Cats, A. Becquerel

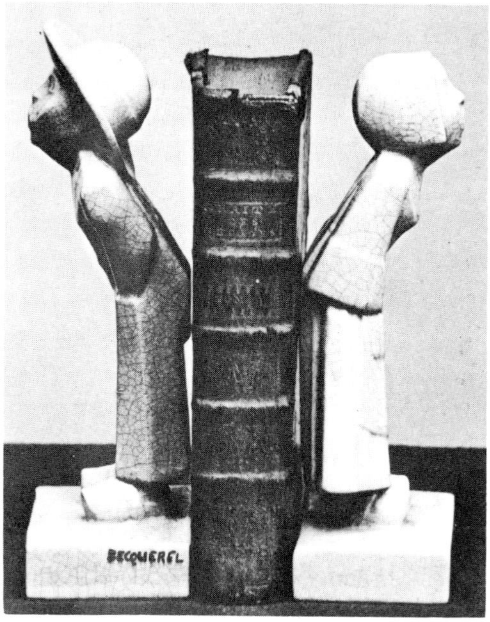

Back to Back, A. Becquerel

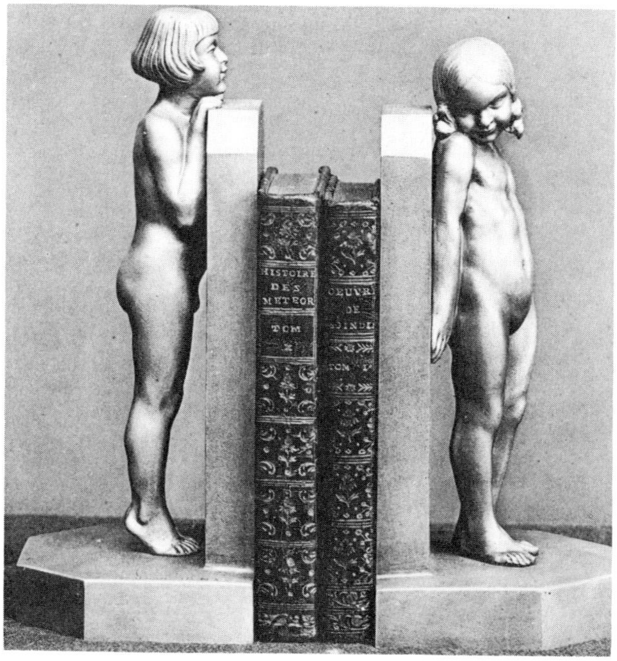

Simplicity, Raoul Bérnard

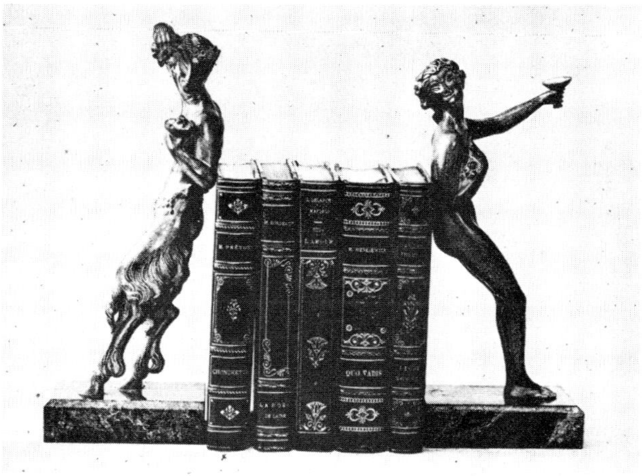

Drunkenness, Bouraine

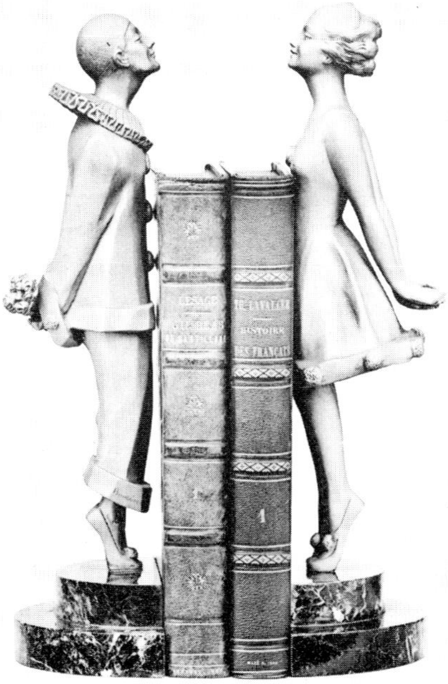

Flirt, Bouraine

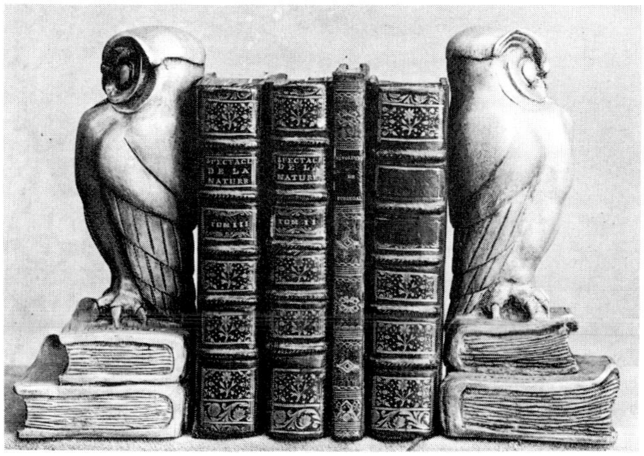

Meditation, Bouraine

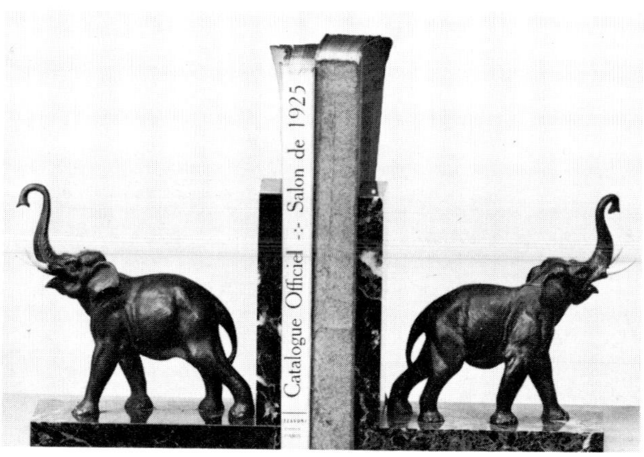

Above and below: Elephants by Carvin

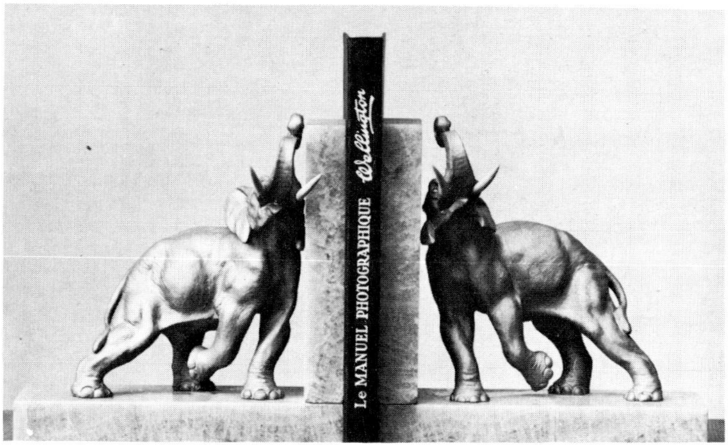

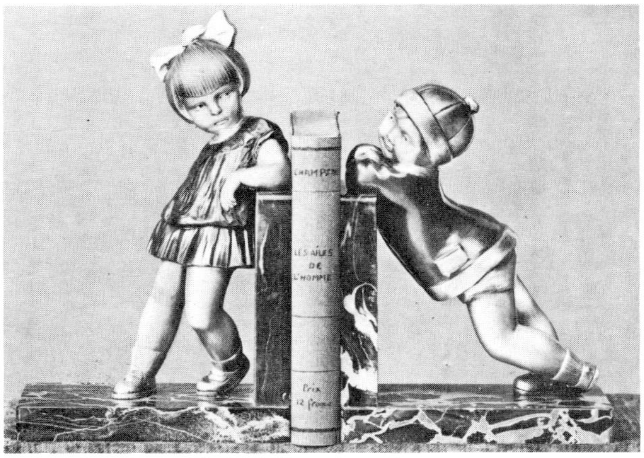

Sulks, Alex Kéléty

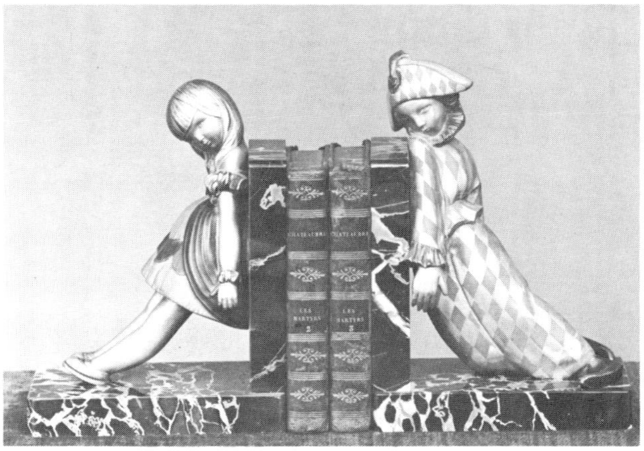

Dolls, Alex Kéléty

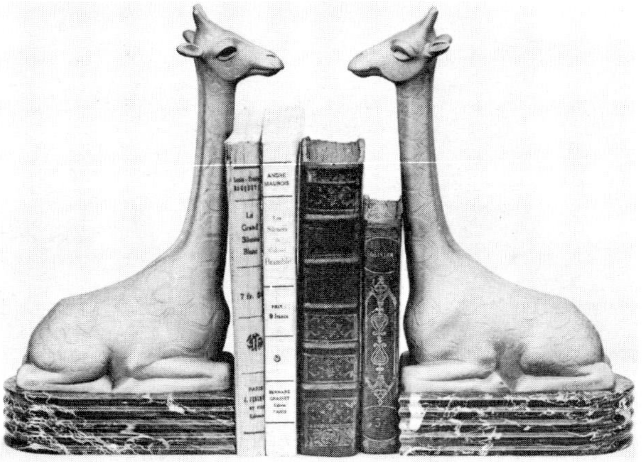

Giraffes, Alex Kéléty

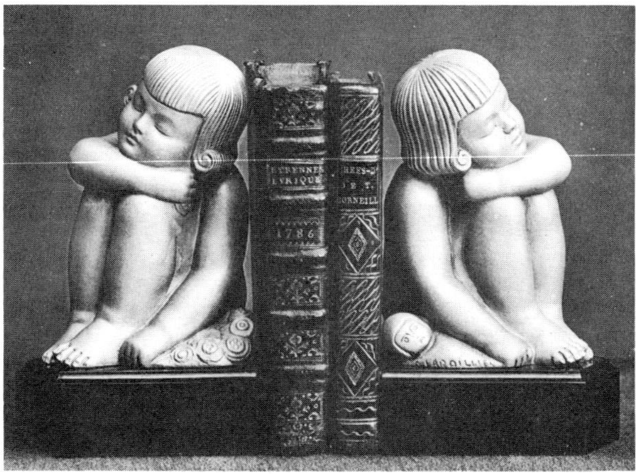

Sleep, Lardillier

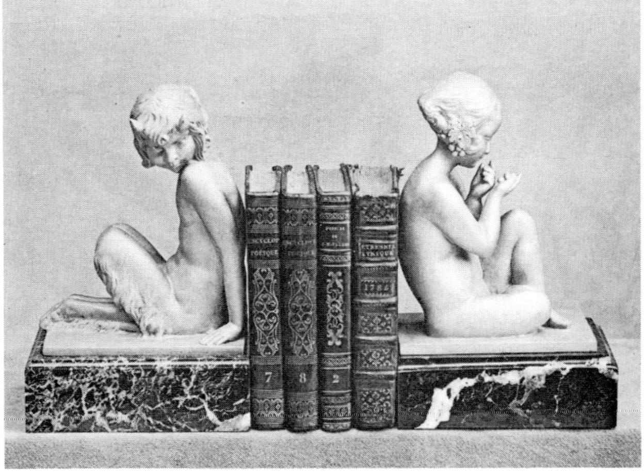

The Envious Faun and Girl with Grapes,
Pierre Laurel

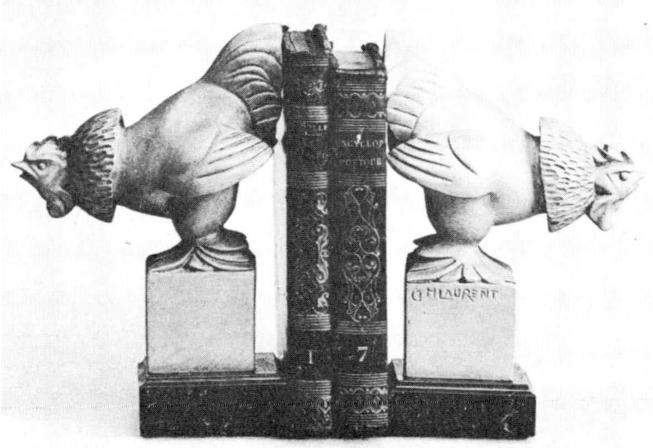

Cocks, G.H. Laurent

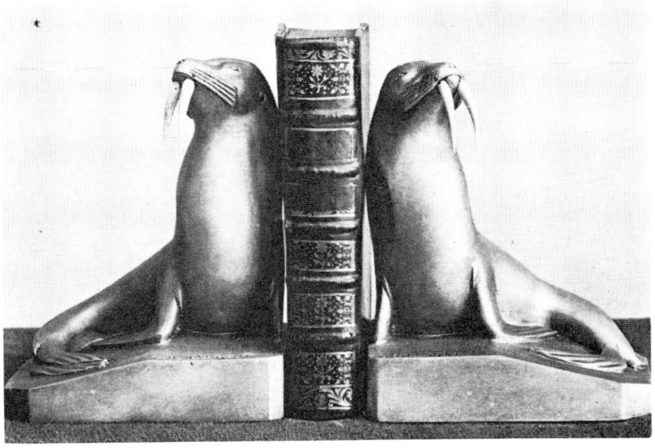

Walruses

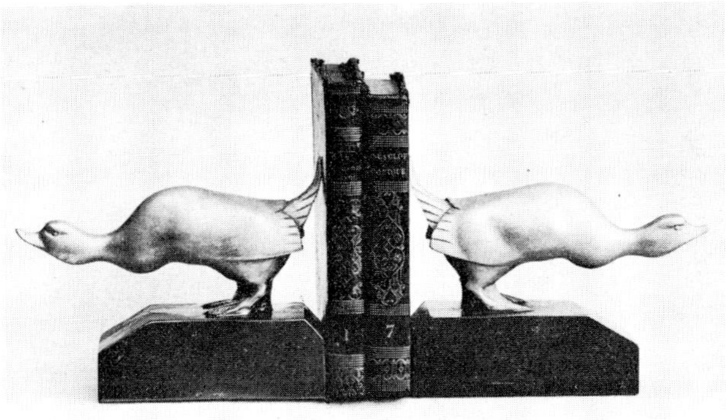

Ducks

Six pairs of bookends, incorporating animals, birds and fishes, by G.H. Laurent

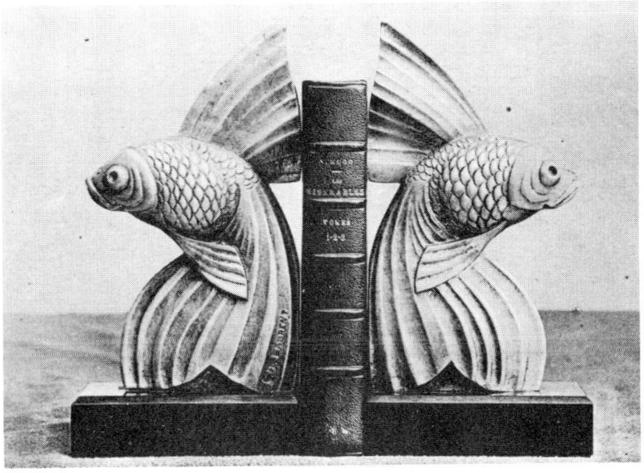

Japanese Fishes

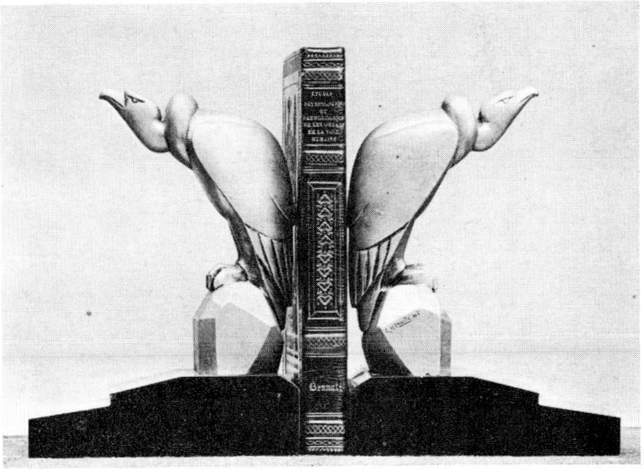

Vultures

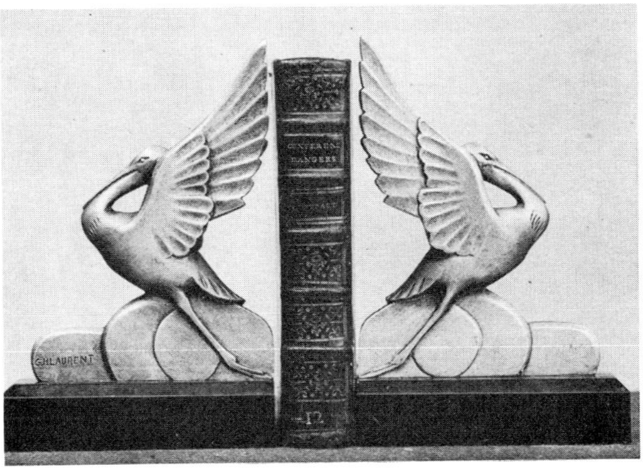

Storks

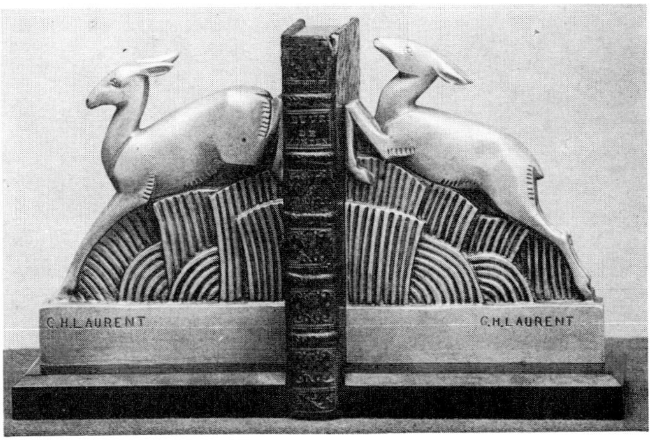

Russian Hinds

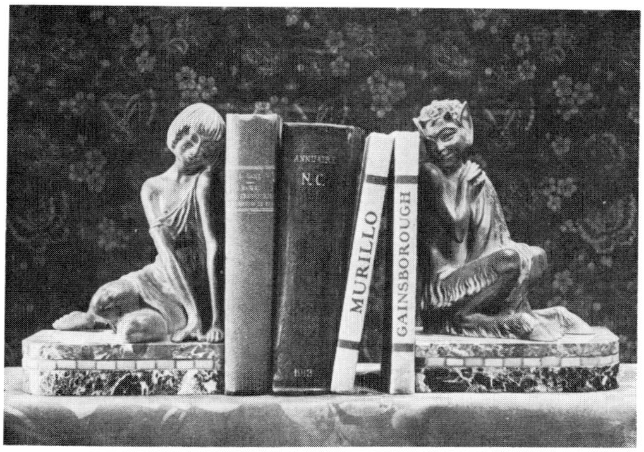

Faun and Nymph, Pierre Le Faguays

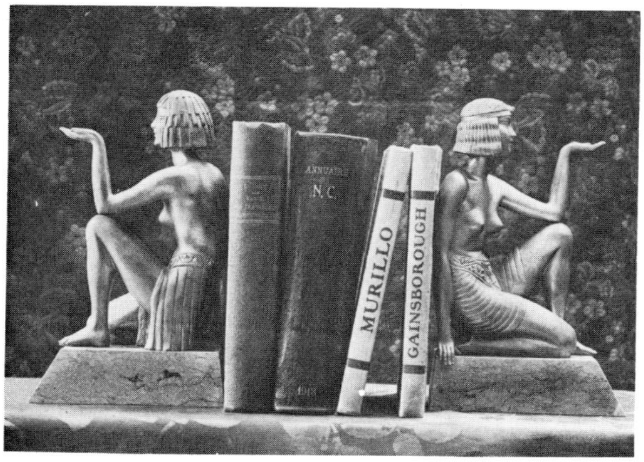

Offering, Pierre Le Faguays

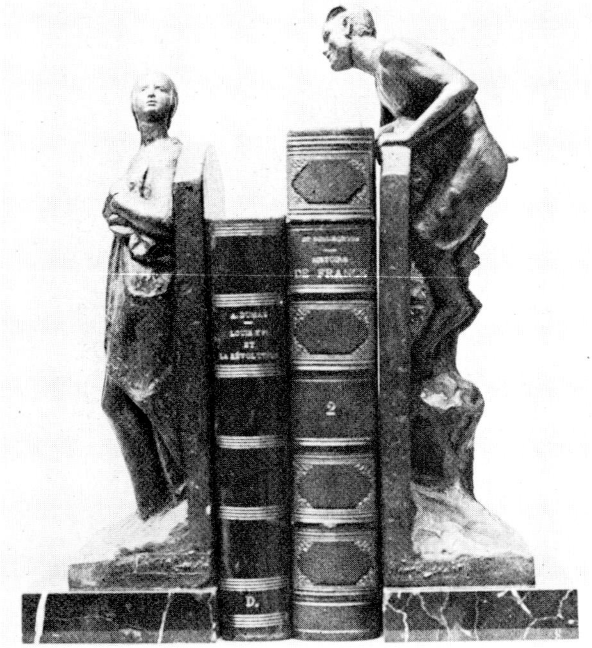

Bucolic, Pierre Lenoir

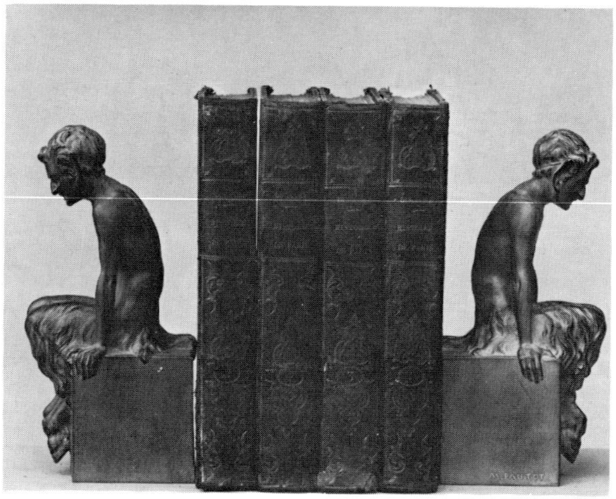

Fauns, M. Poeutot

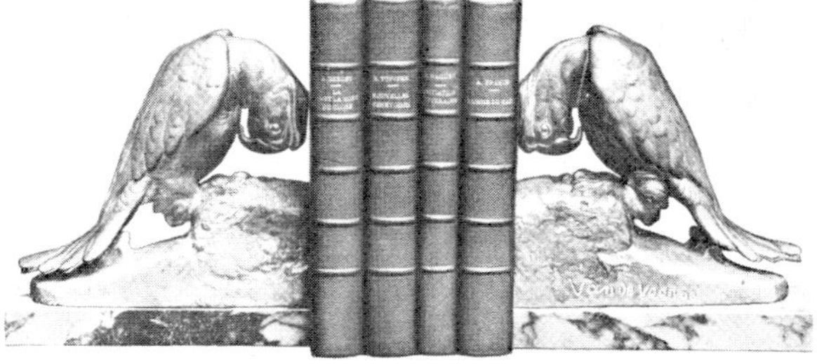

Parrots, Van de Voorde

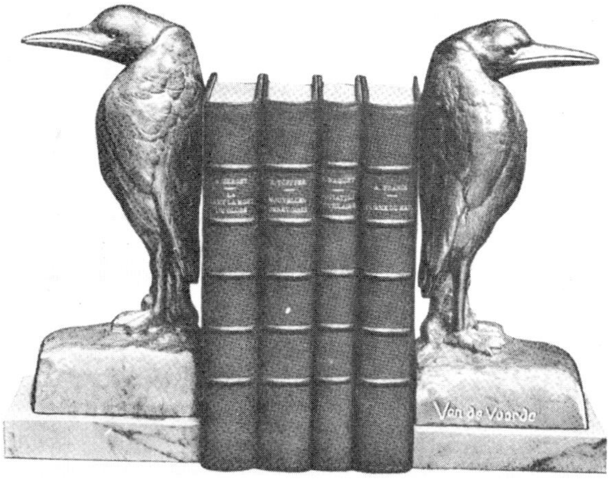

Marabou, Van de Voorde

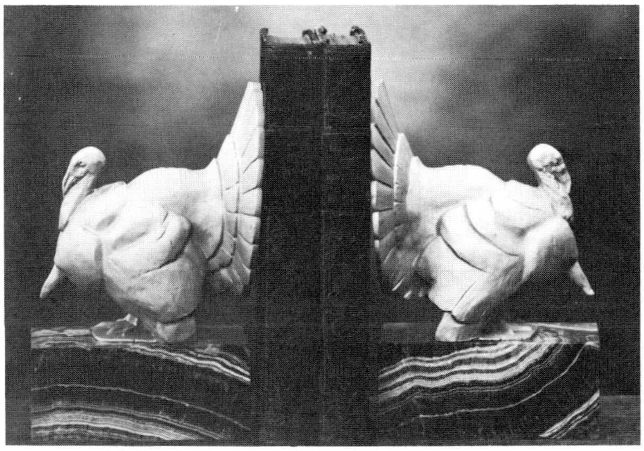

Turkeys

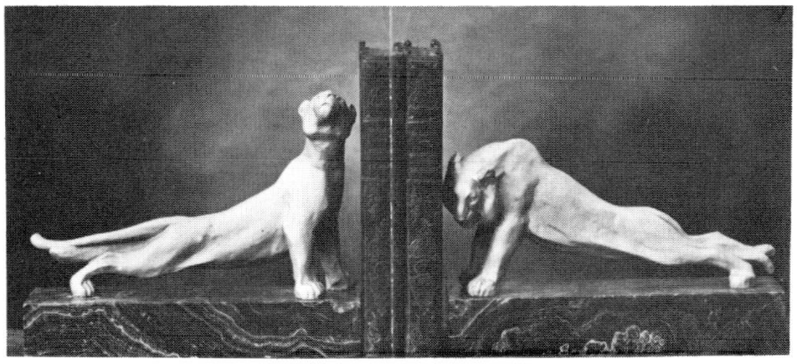

Panther and Tiger

Left, above and below: Three pairs of bookends by Waldman

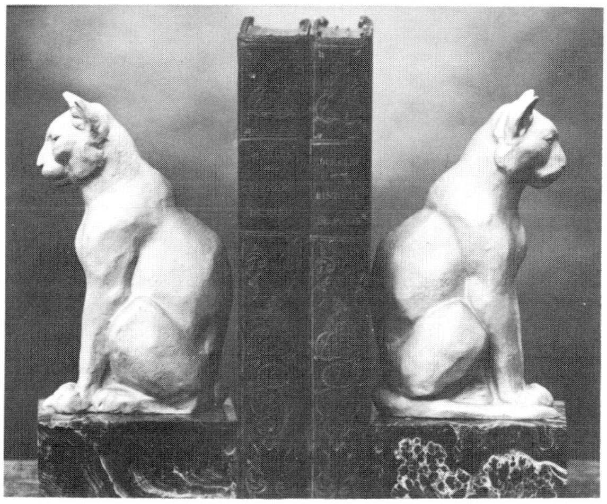

Sitting Cats

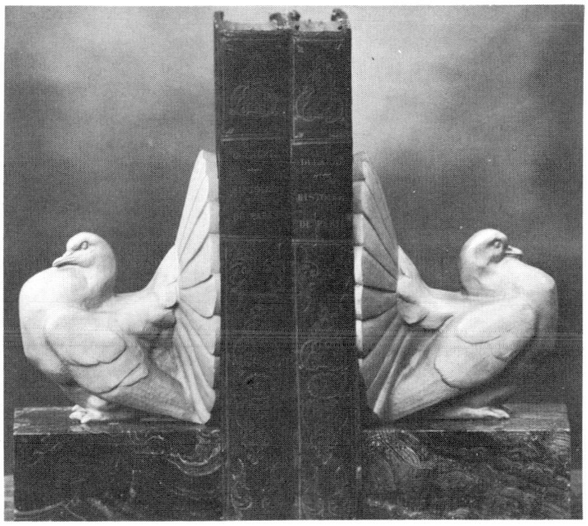

Fantail pigeons

Left and below: Fantail pigeons and frogs by Mlle. White

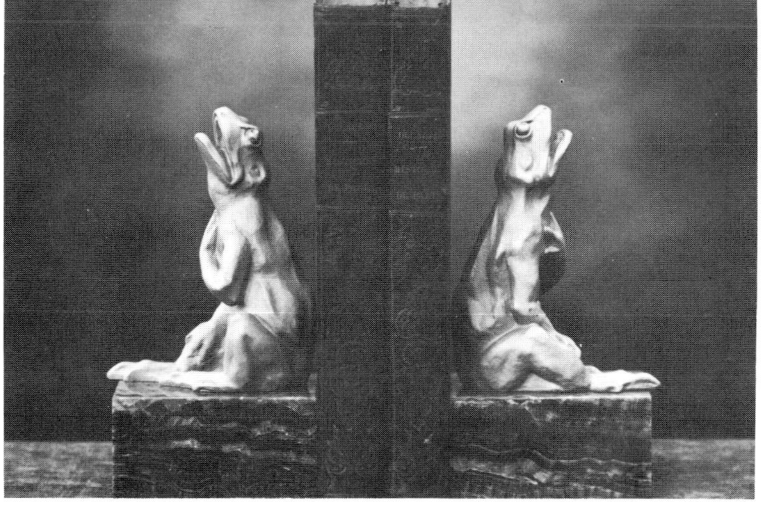

Frogs

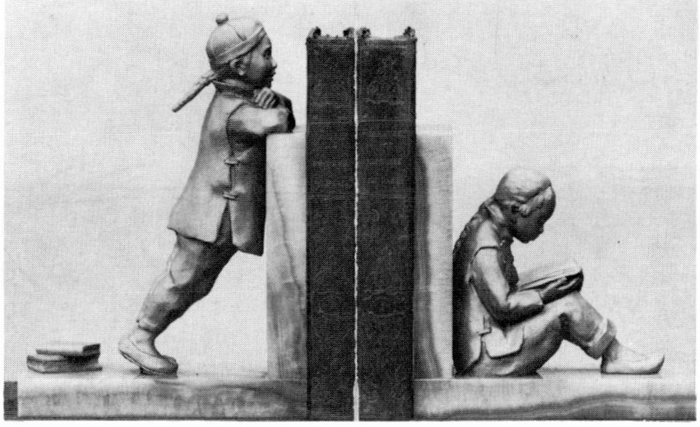

Chinese Students

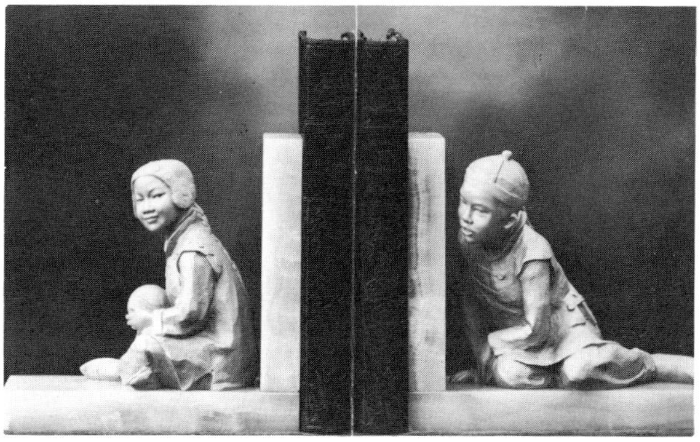

Chinese Children

Above, right and below: Three bookends using figures of children by Mlle White

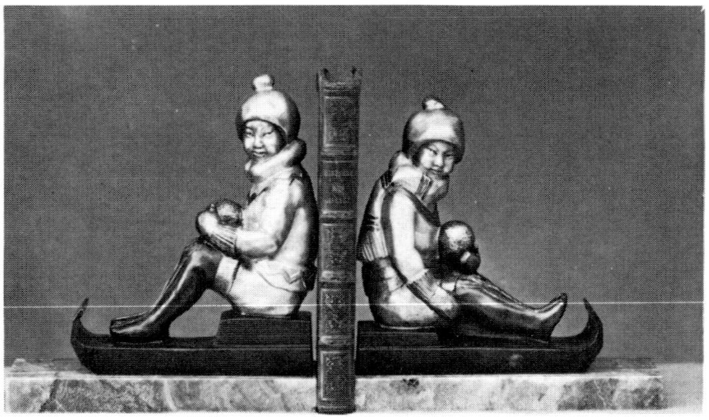

Snowballs

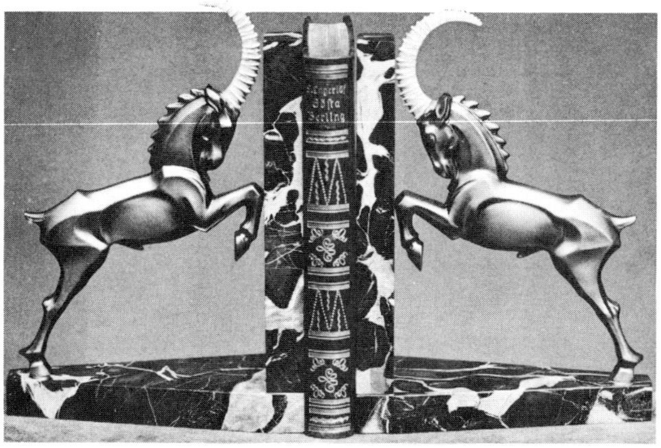

Unicorns, unsigned

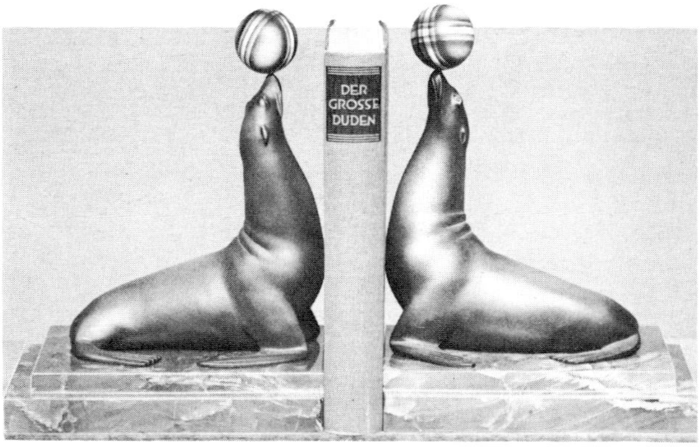

Seals, unsigned

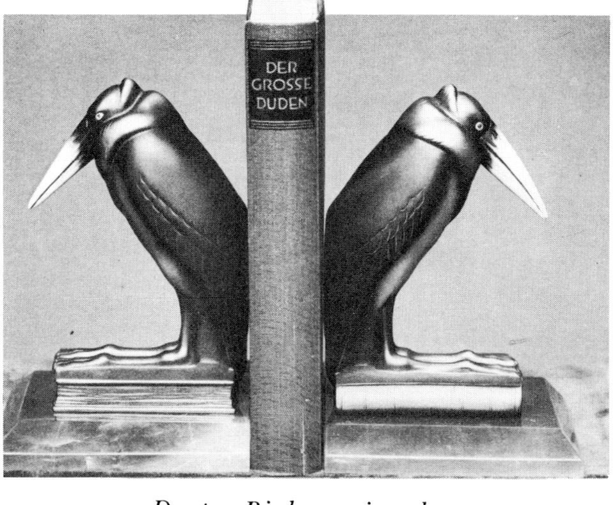

Doctor Birds, unsigned

A SELECTION OF ART DECO ANIMAL, BIRD AND FISH FIGURES
(in alphabetical order of artists)

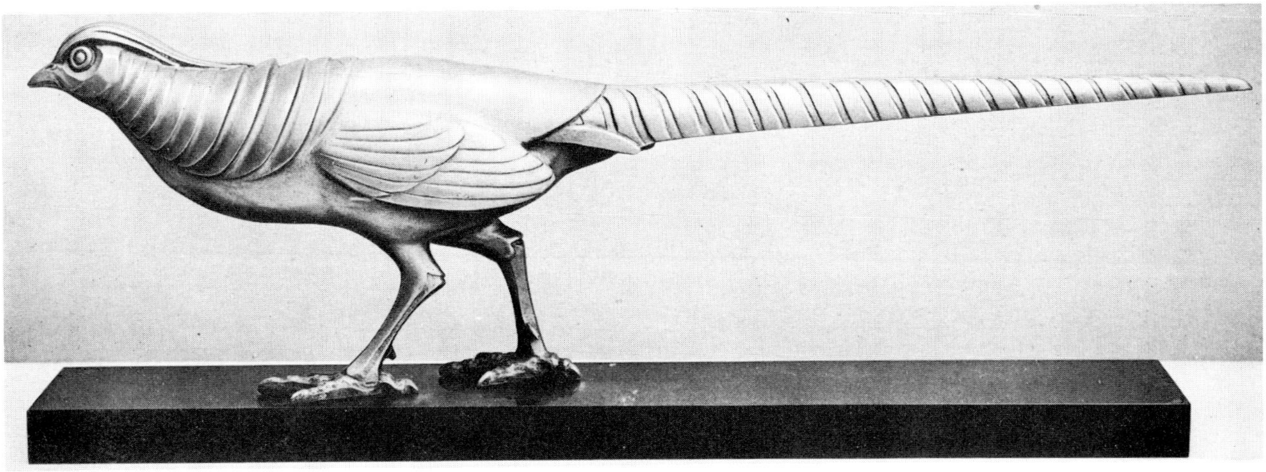

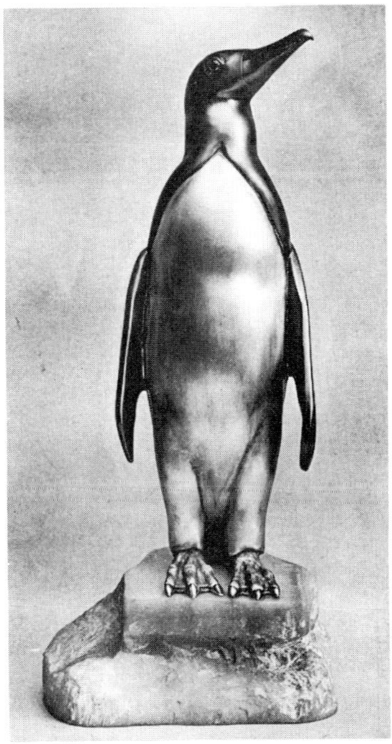

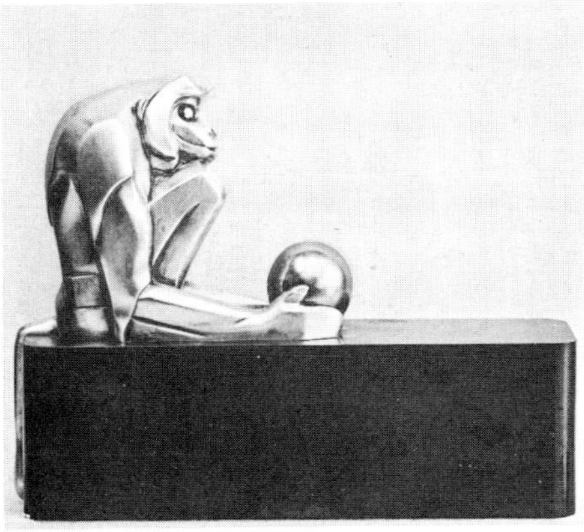

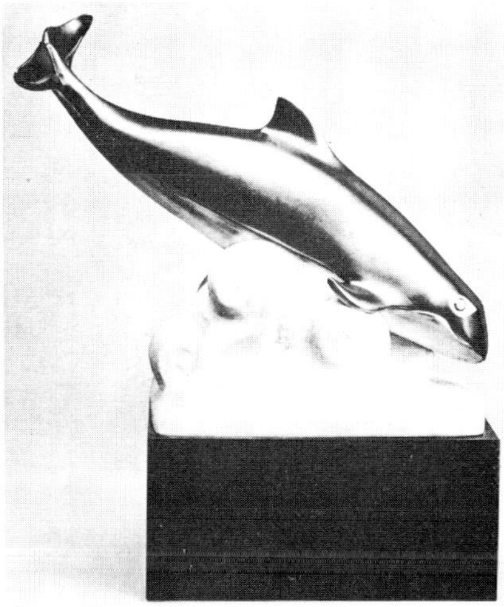

Bouraine

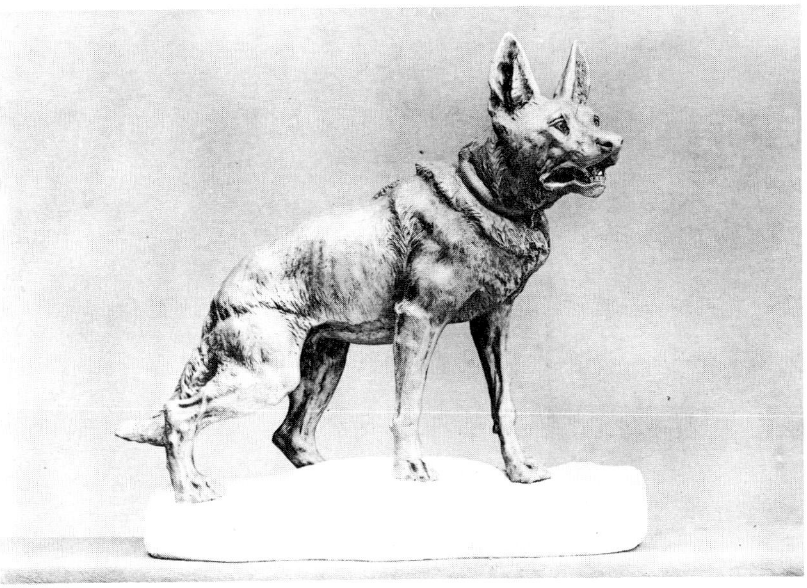

Th. Cartier

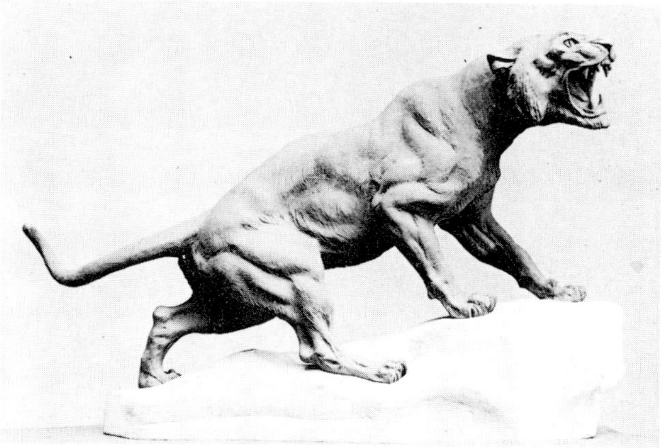

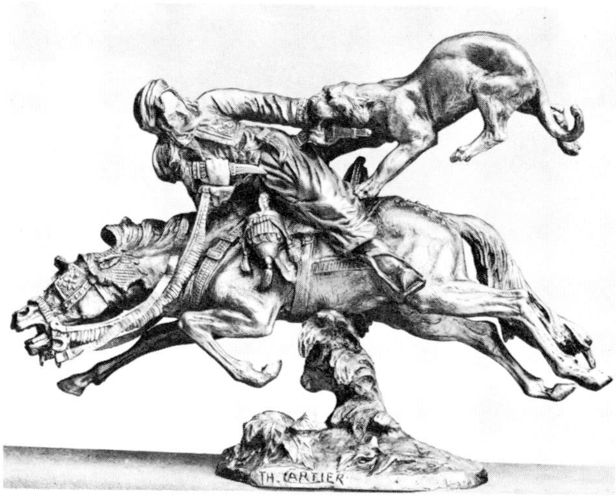

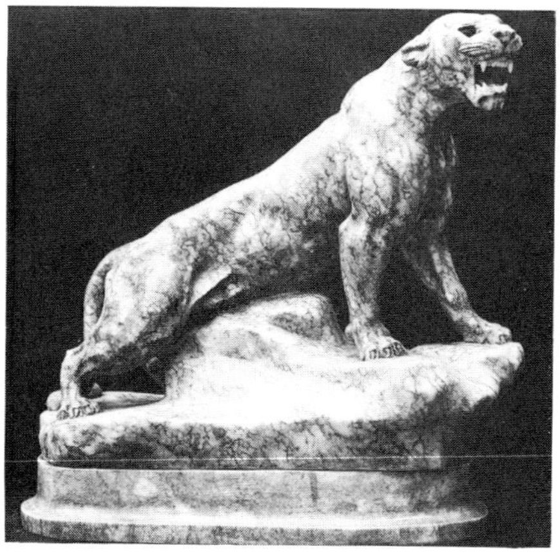

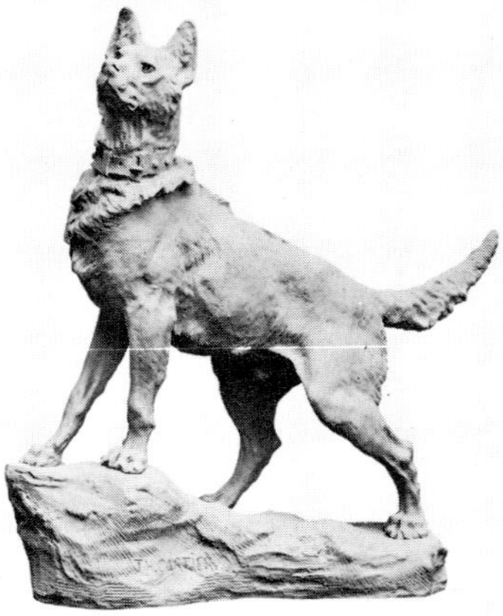

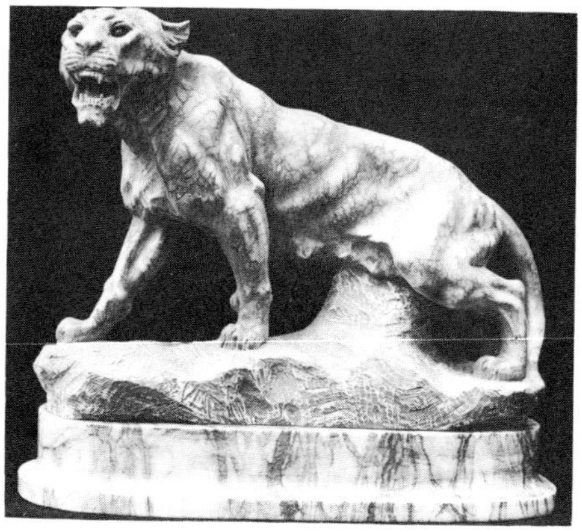

Th. Cartier

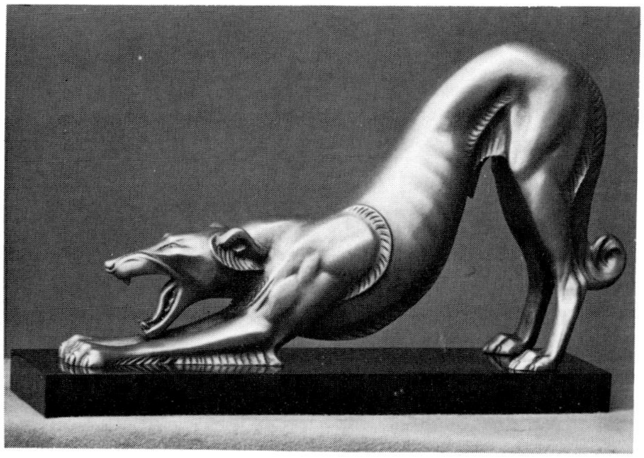

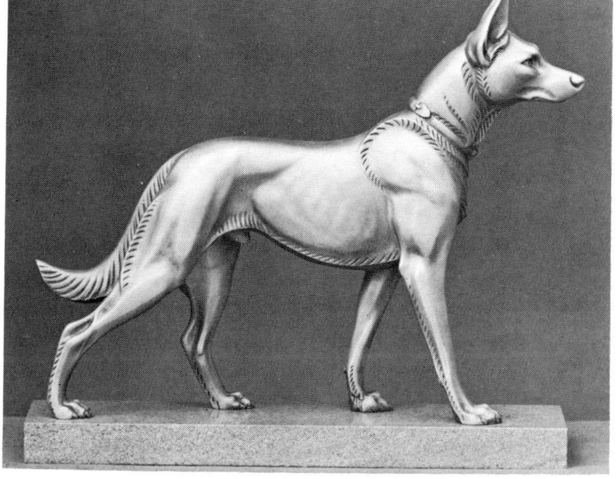

Carvin

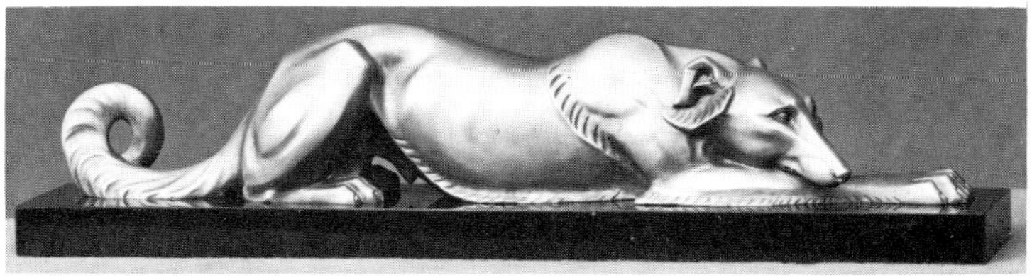

Carvin

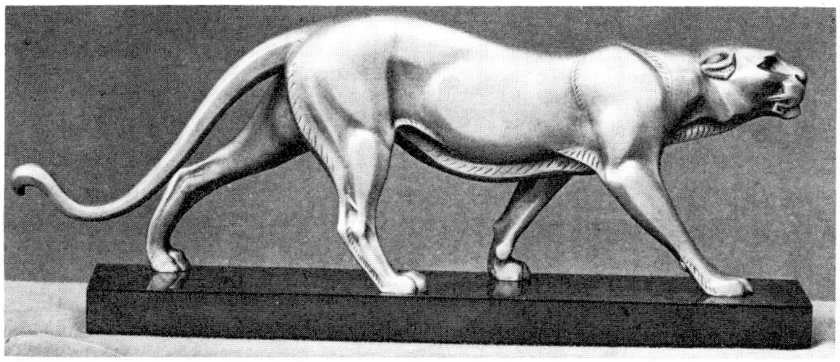

Carvin

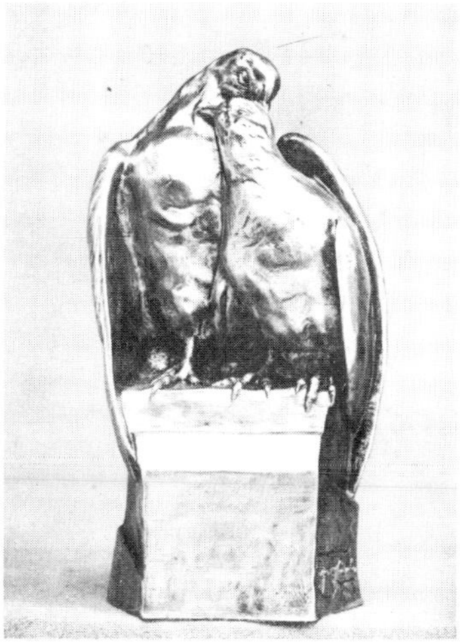

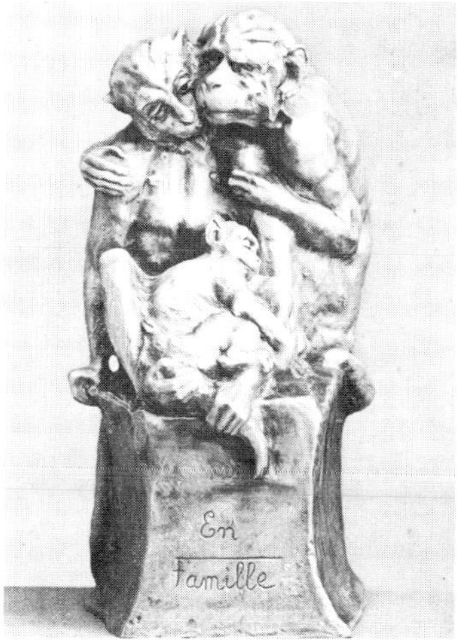

Ozanne Cederlund

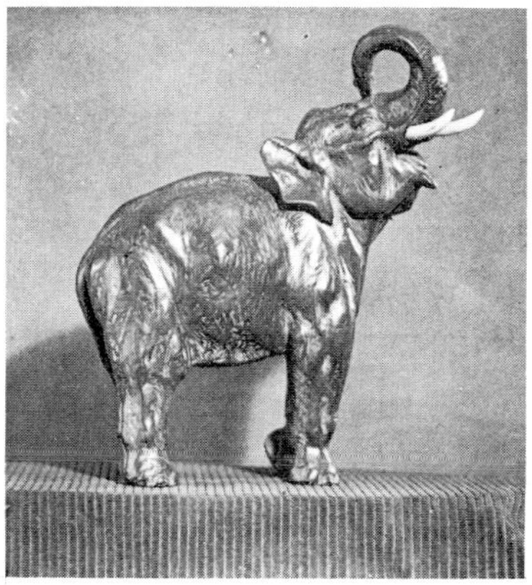

Cluzel

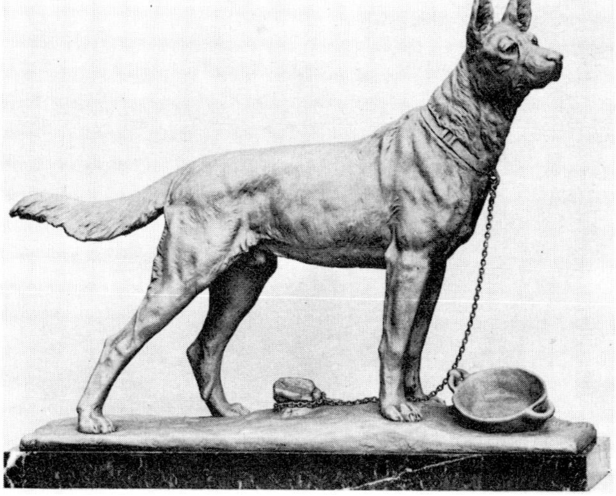

E. Drouot

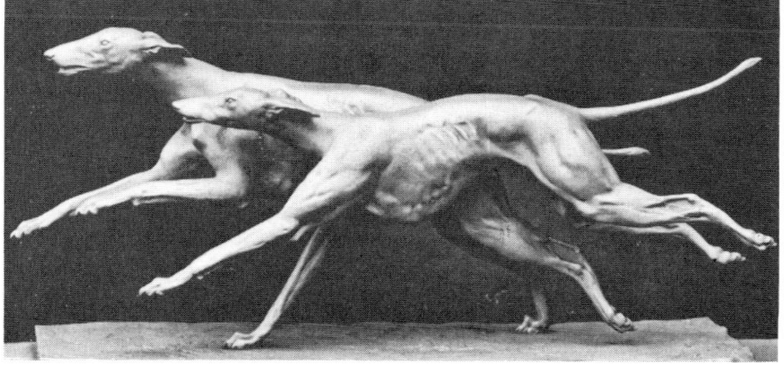

R. Fath

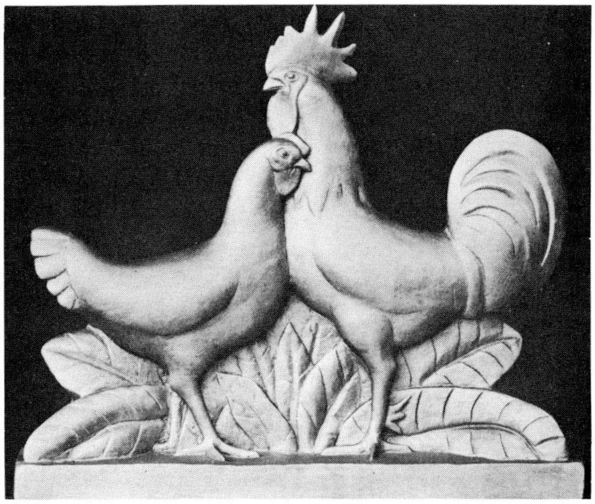

Geneviève Granger

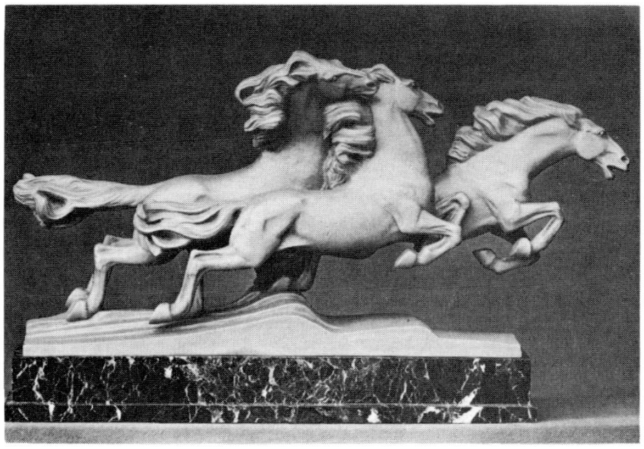

Alex Kéléty

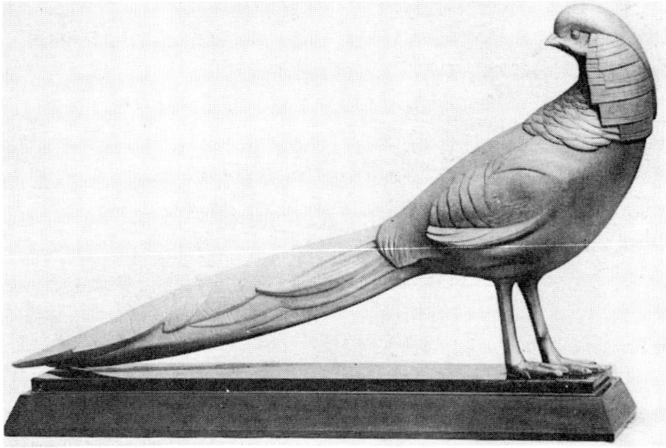

Alex Kéléty

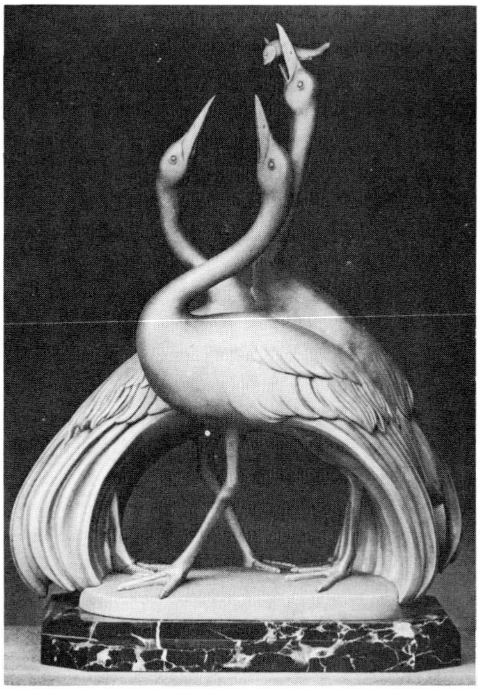

Alex Kéléty

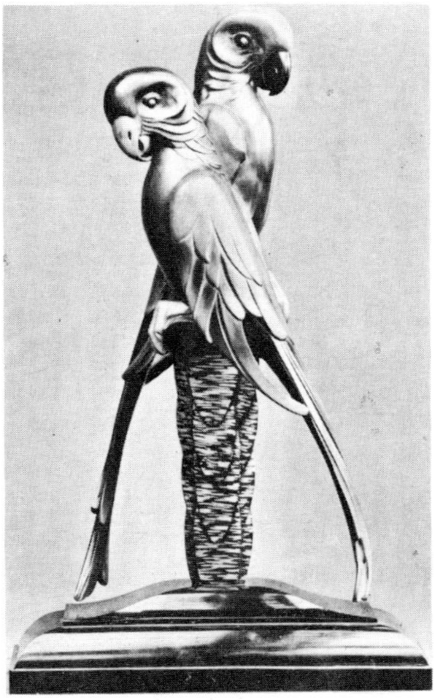

Alex Kéléty

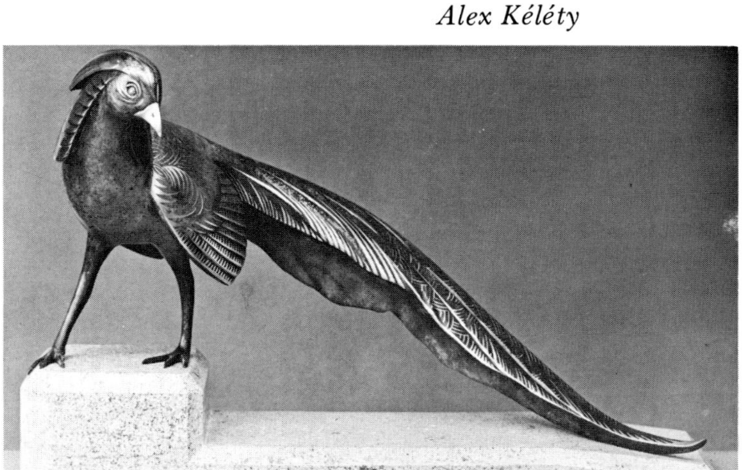

G.H. Laurent

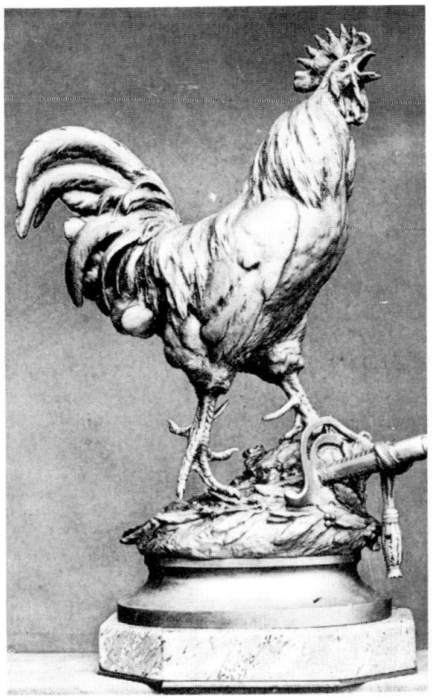

P. Lecourtier

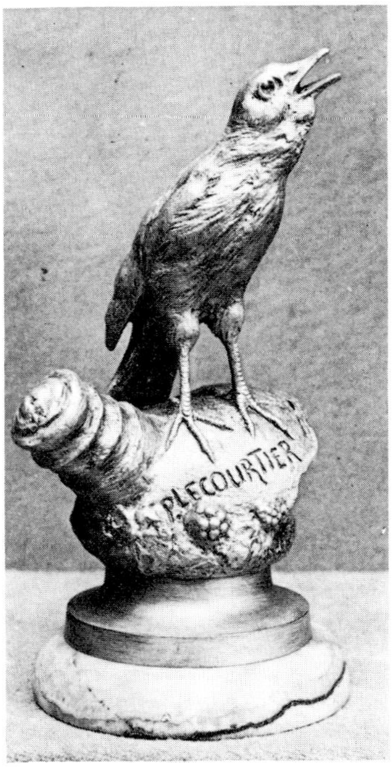

P. Lecourtier

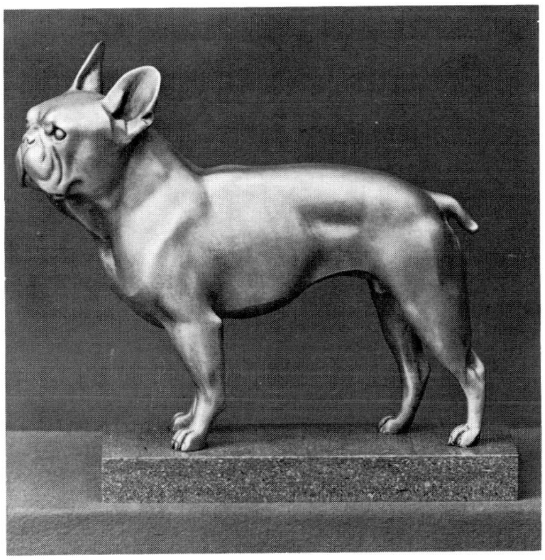

Linko

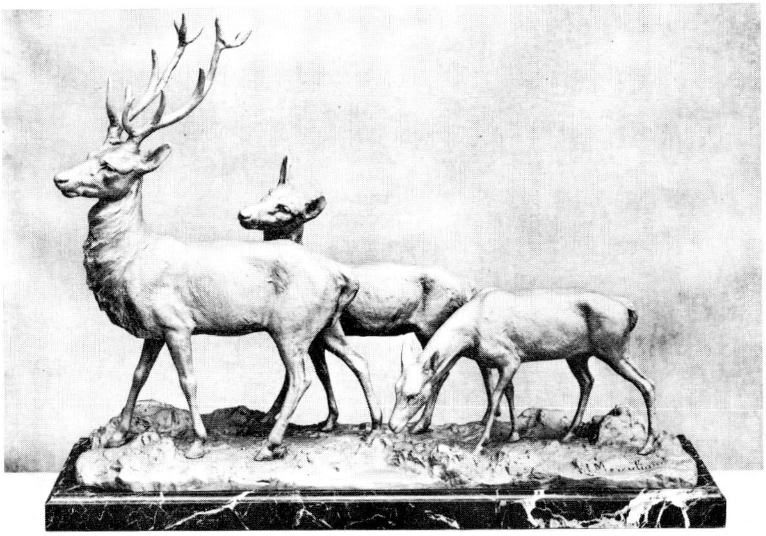

Merculiano

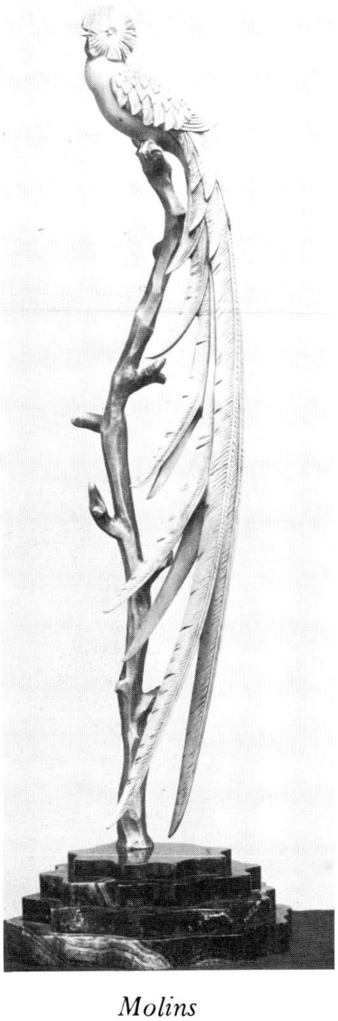

Molins

SELECTION OF ART DECO FIGURES USED AS CAR MASCOTS
(in alphabetical order of artists)

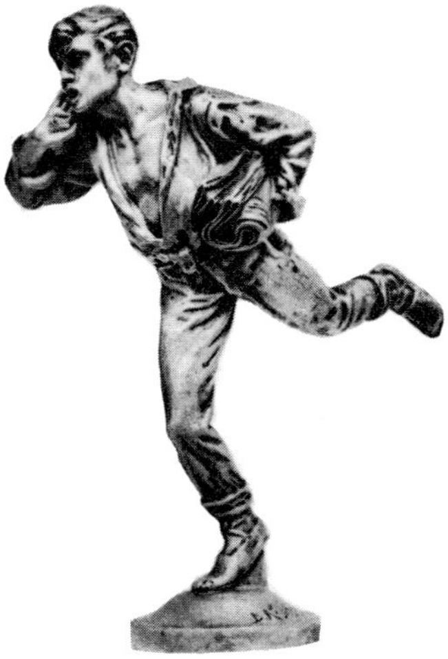

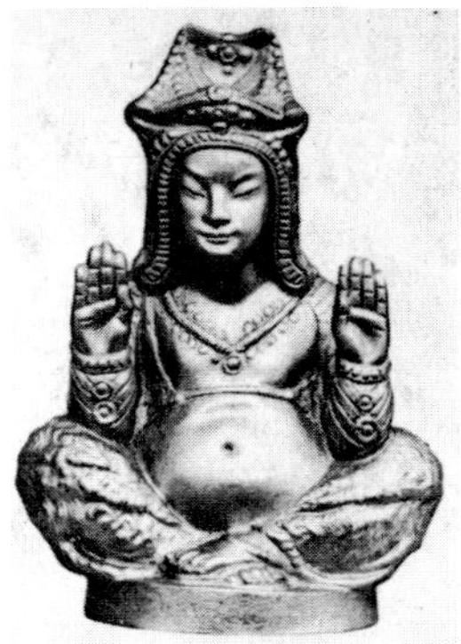

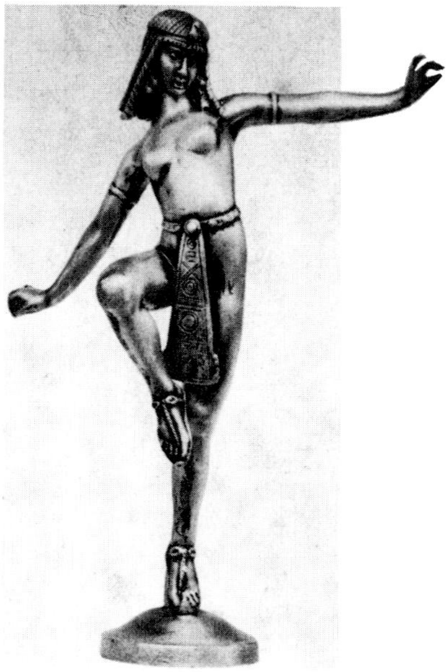

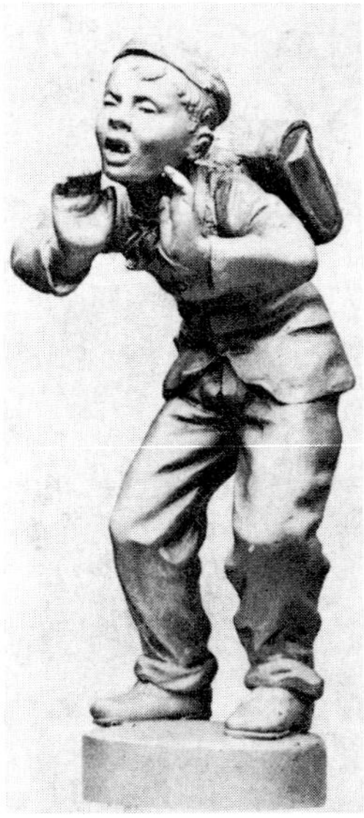

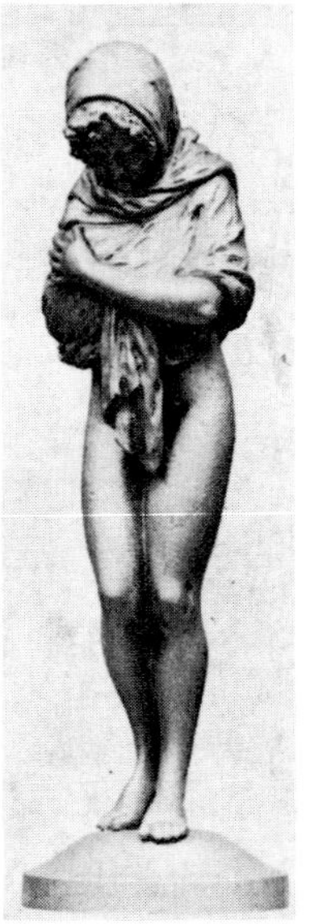

Five figures by D. Alonzo

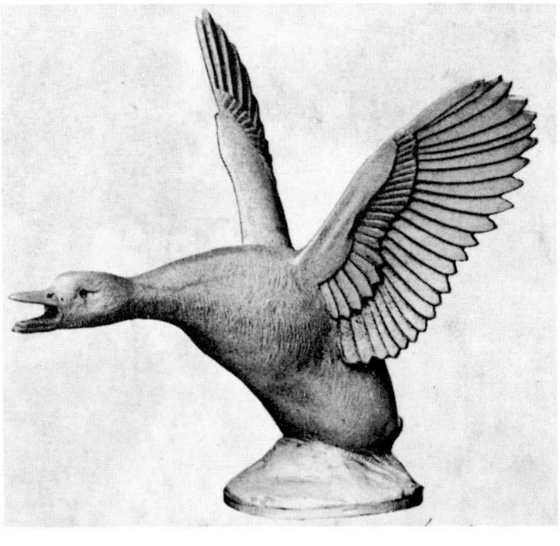

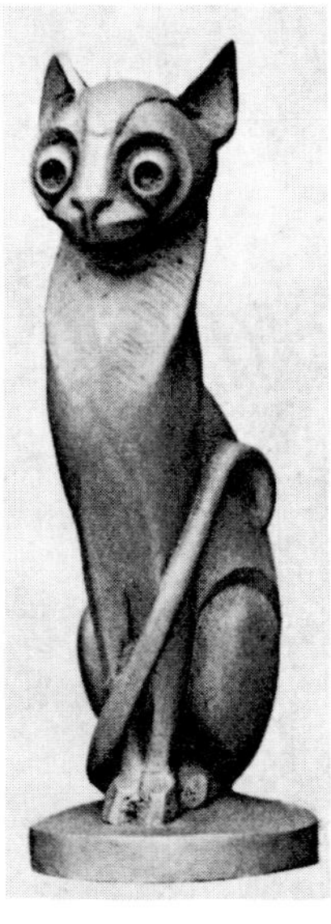

Becquerel

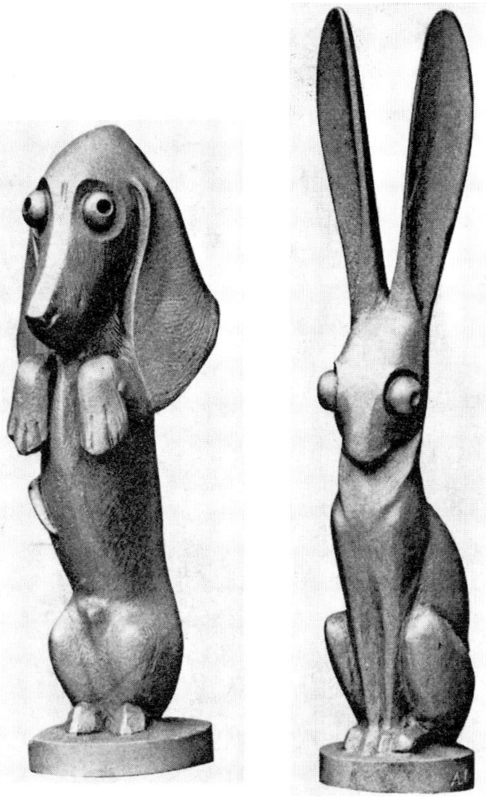

Becquerel

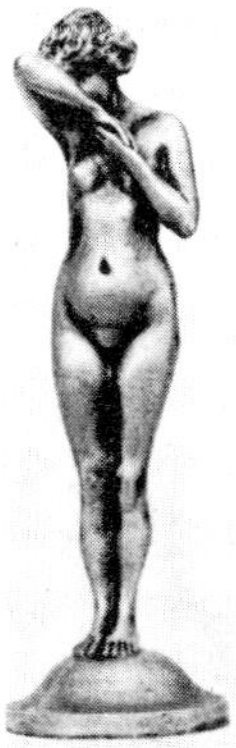

L. Betti

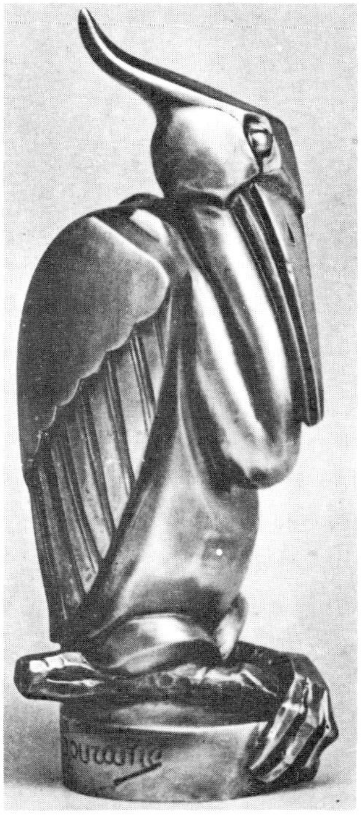

Bouraine

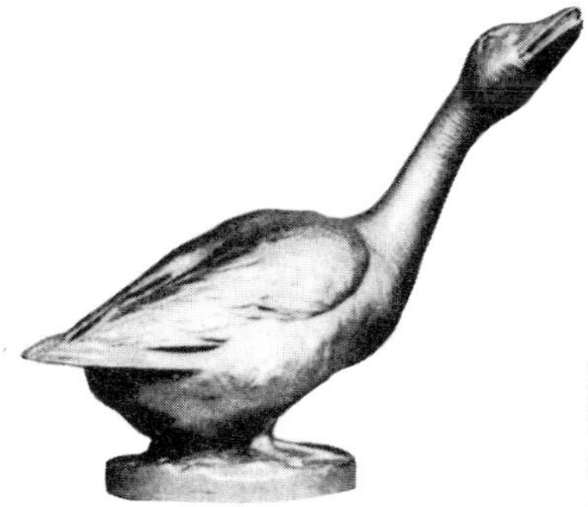

Caron

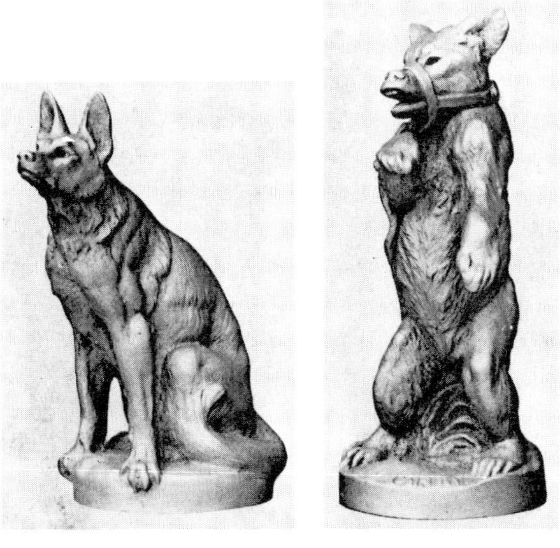

Carvin

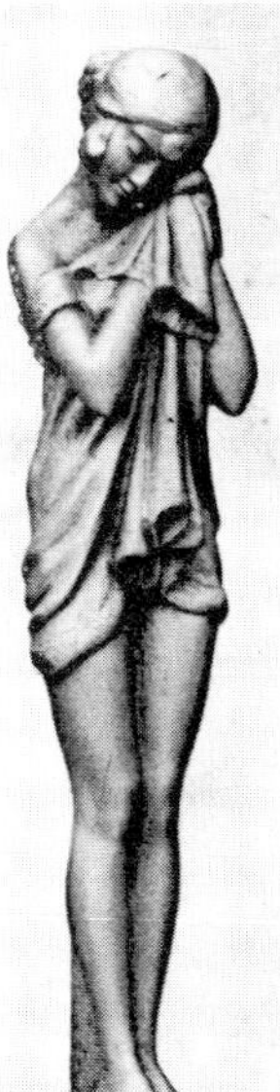

D.H. Chiparus

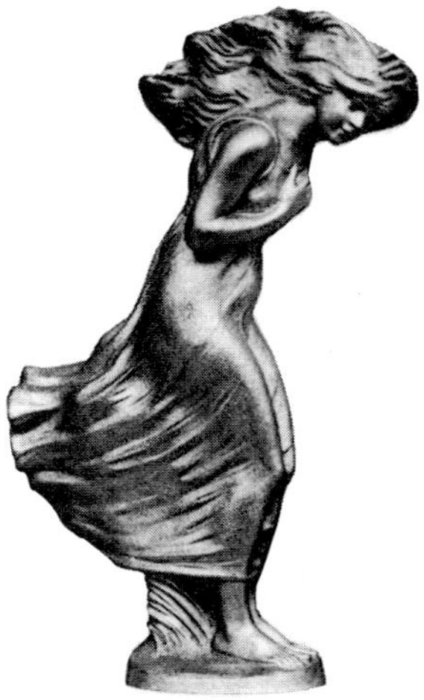

J. Descomps

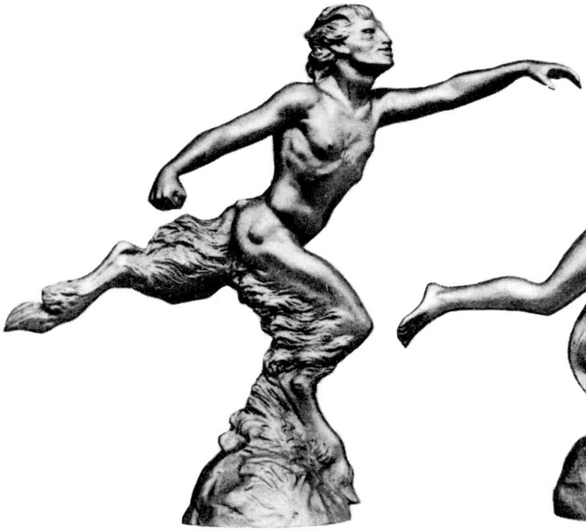

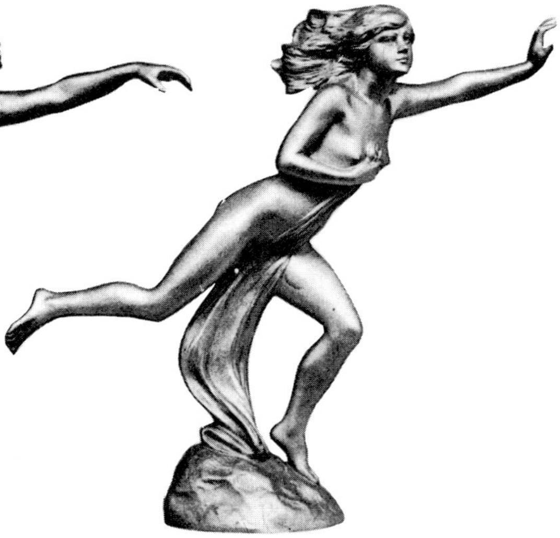

J. Descomps

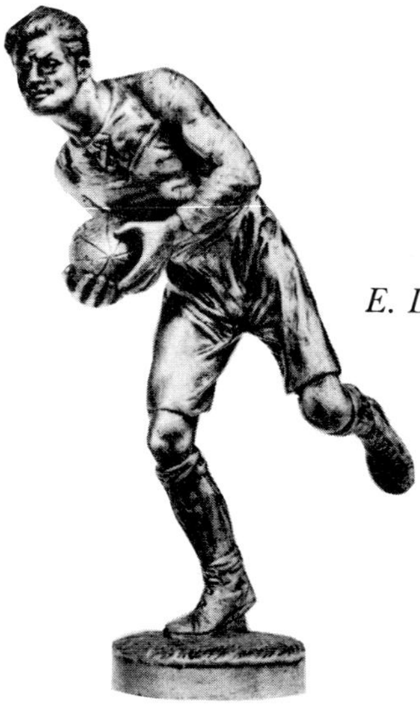

E. Drouot

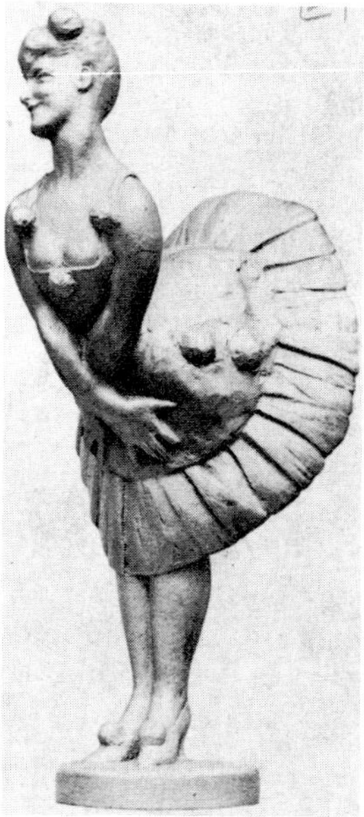

M. Guiraud Riviere

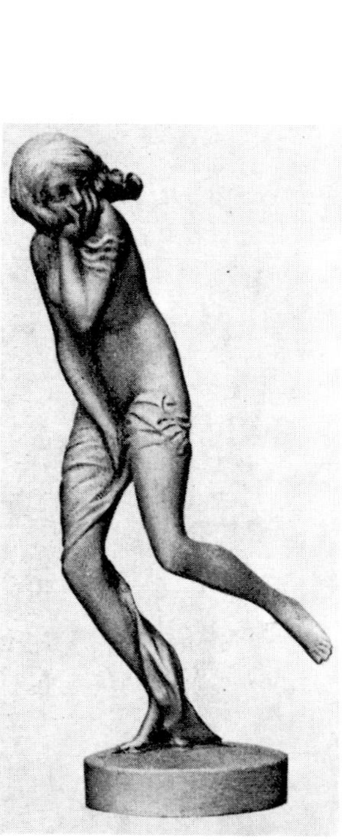

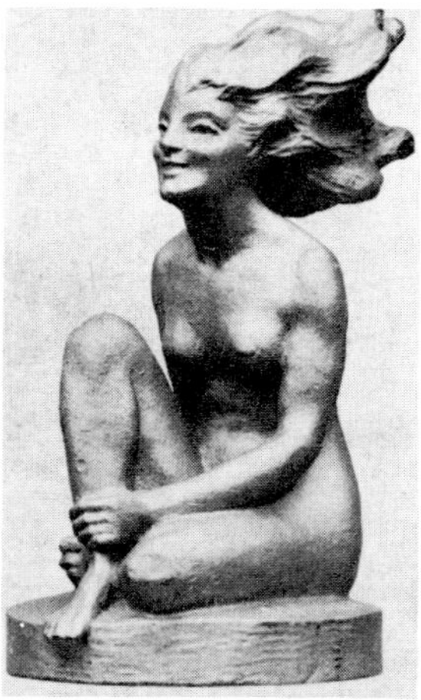

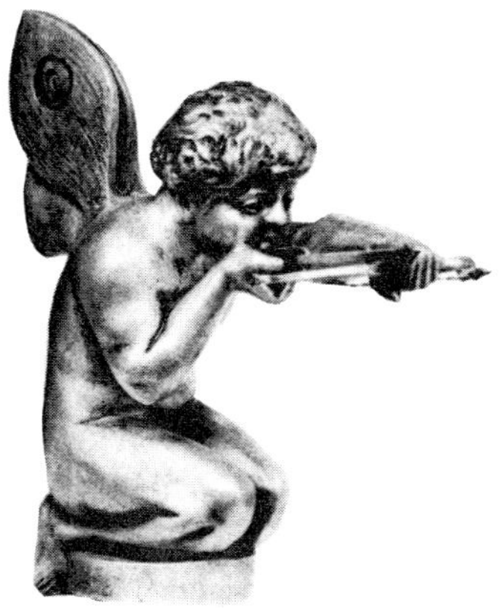

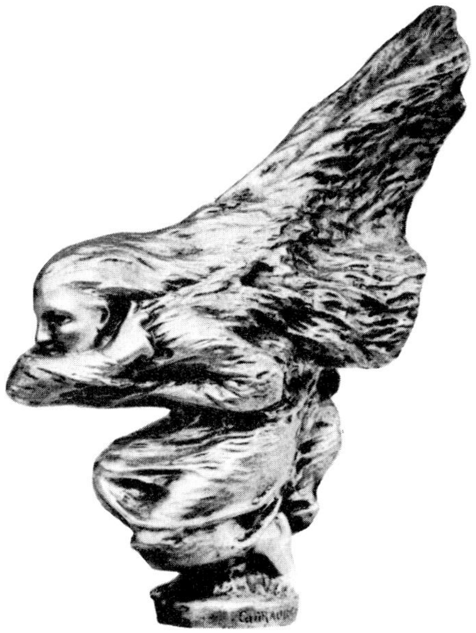

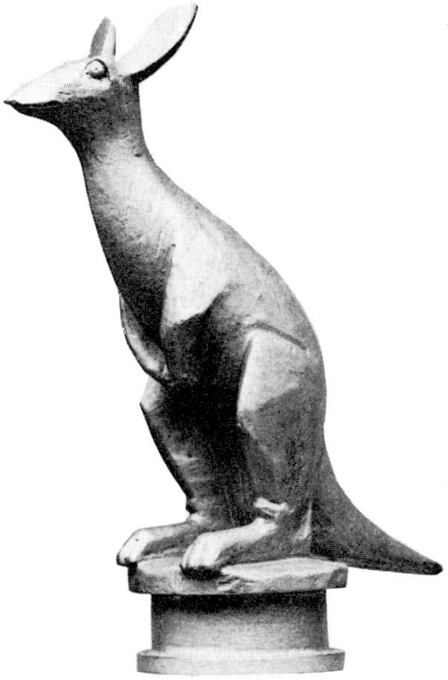

Page of mascot figures by M. Guiraud Riviere

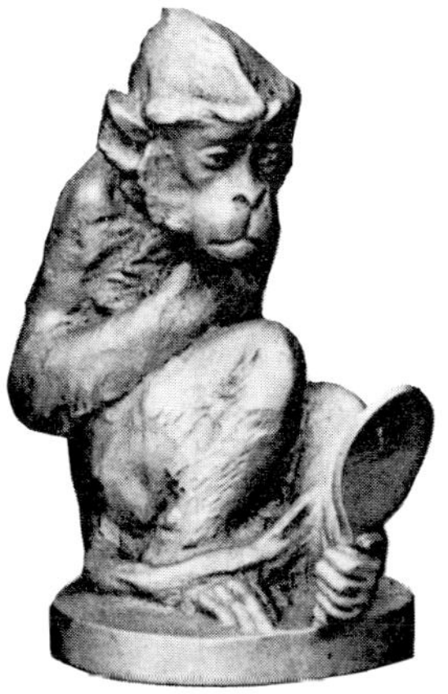

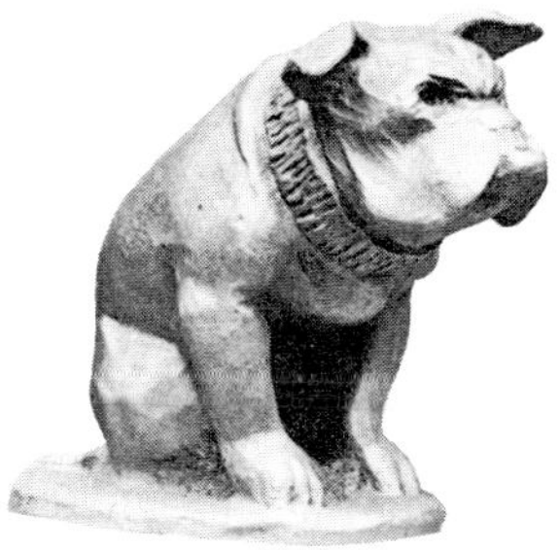

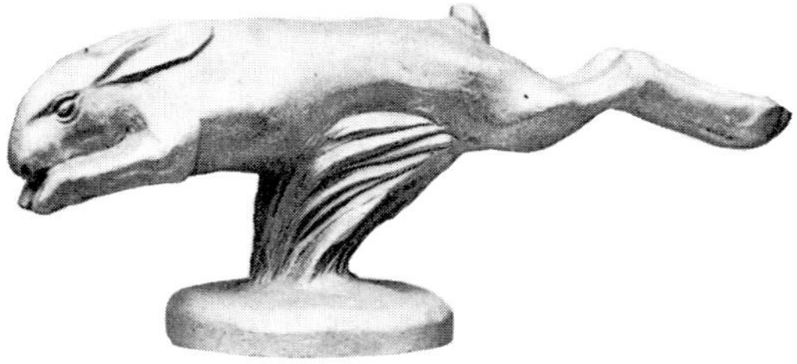

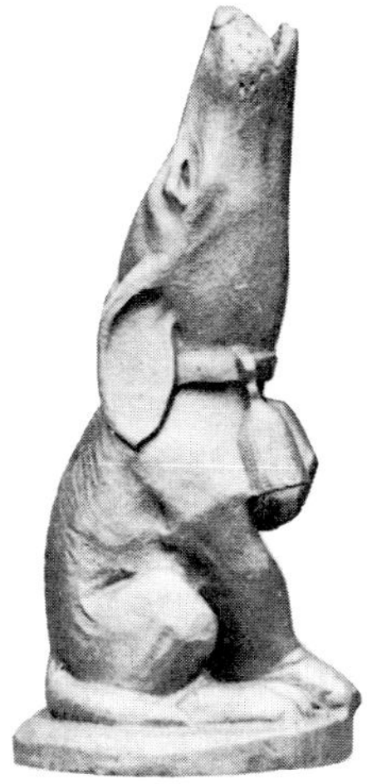

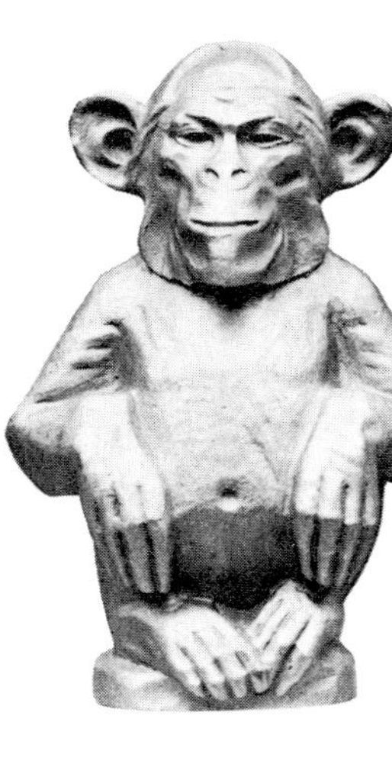

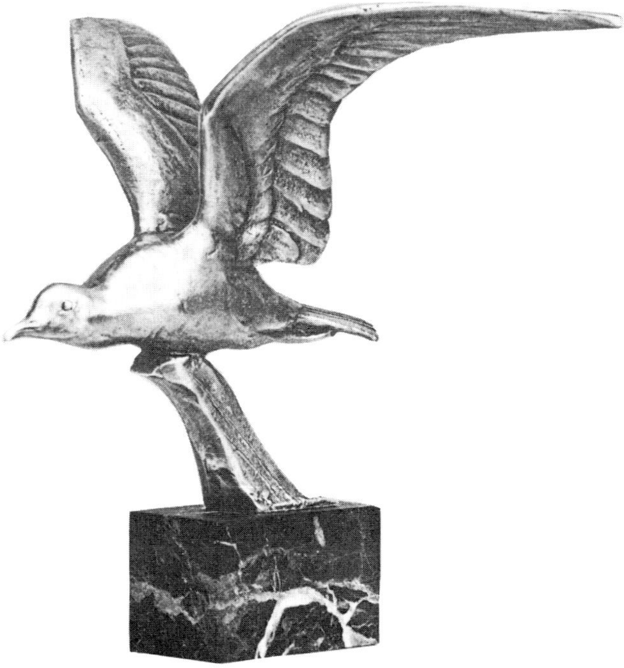

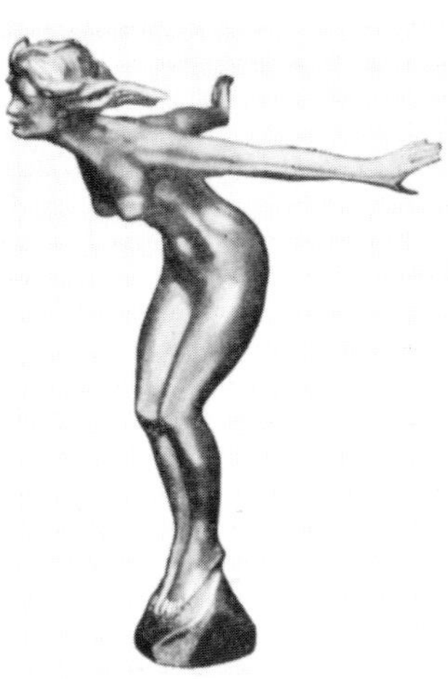

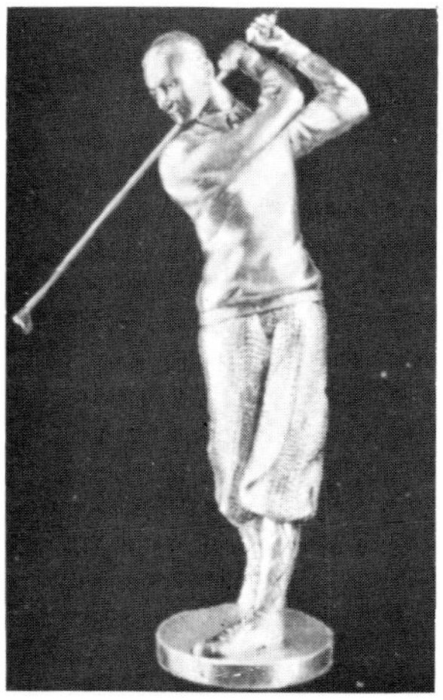

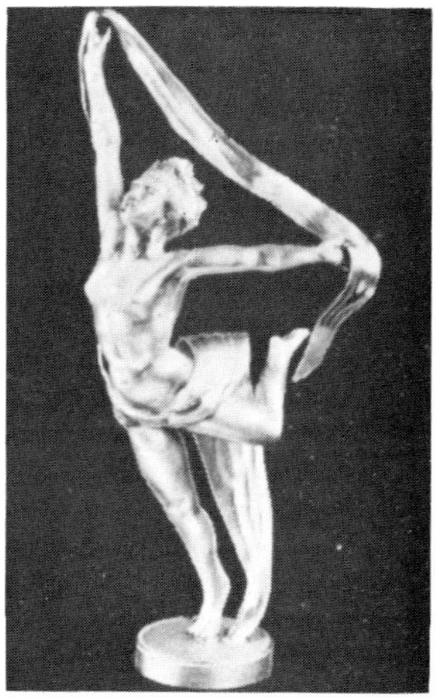

Pages 340-344 illustrate a selection of car mascots designed by Lejeune

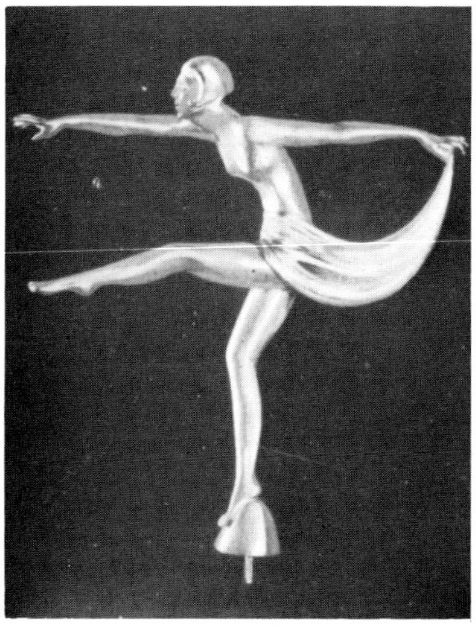

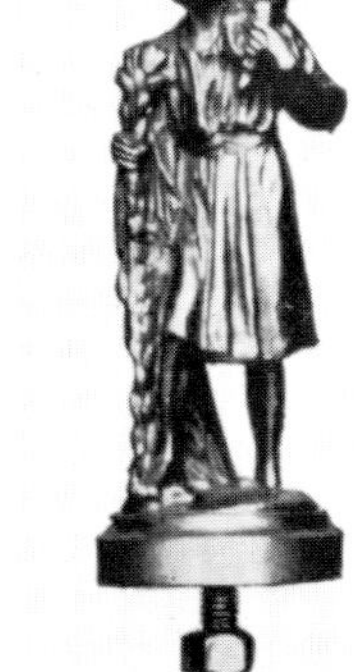

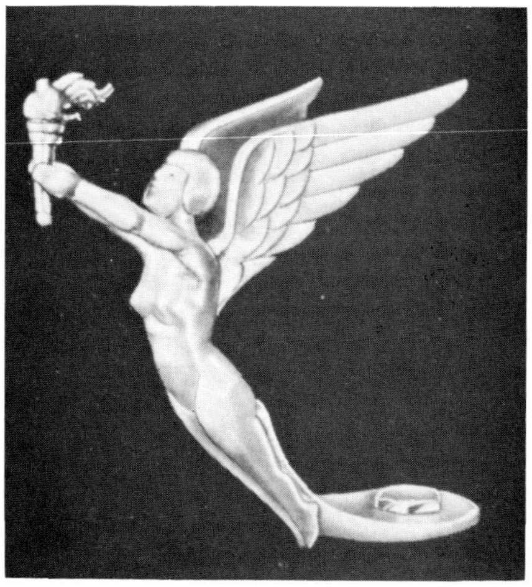

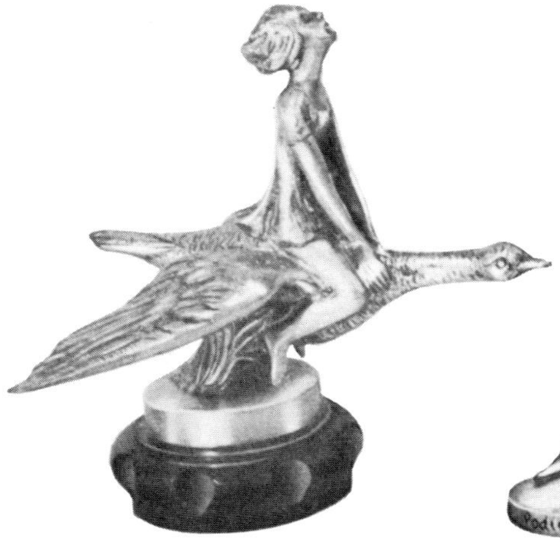

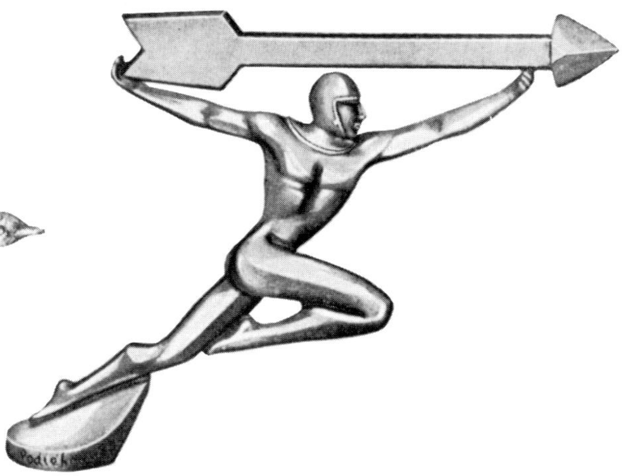

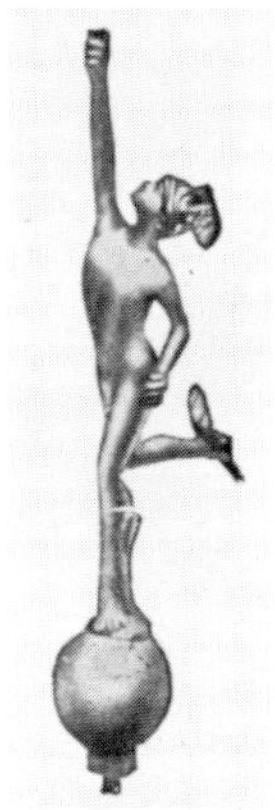

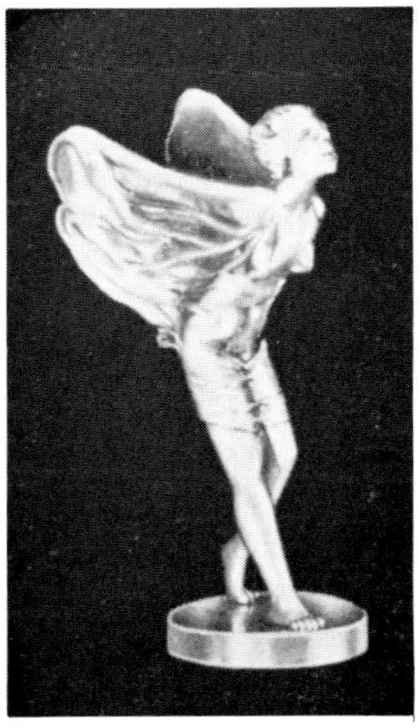

Lejeune

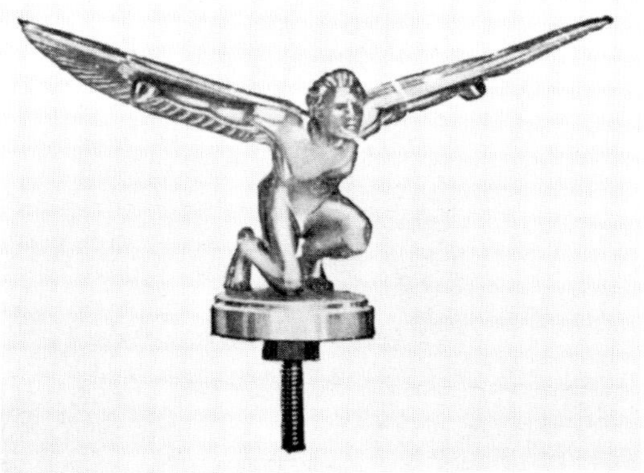

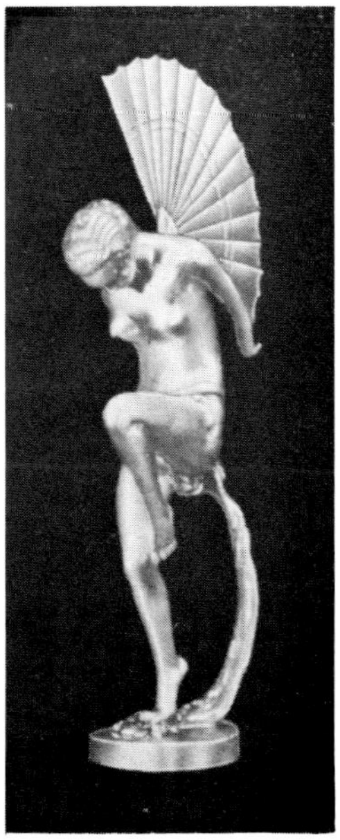

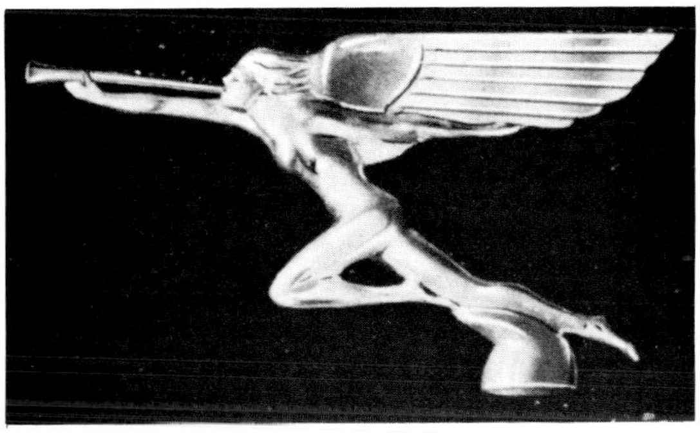

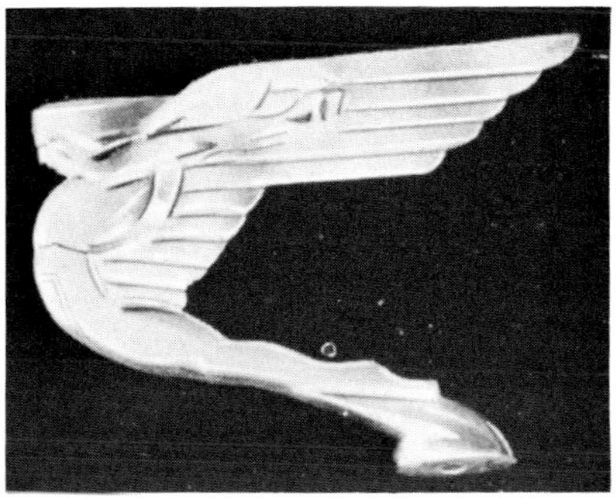

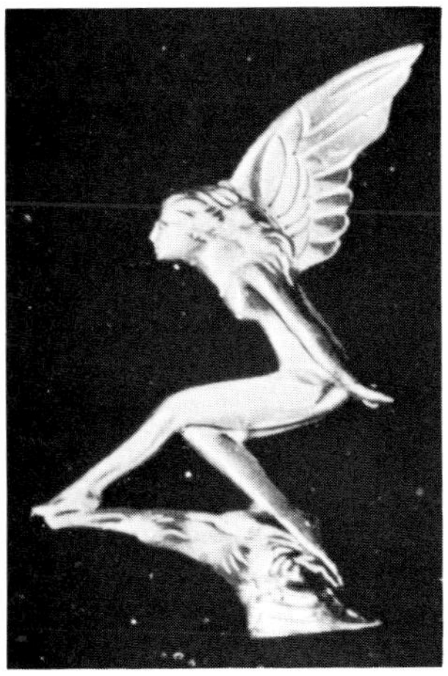

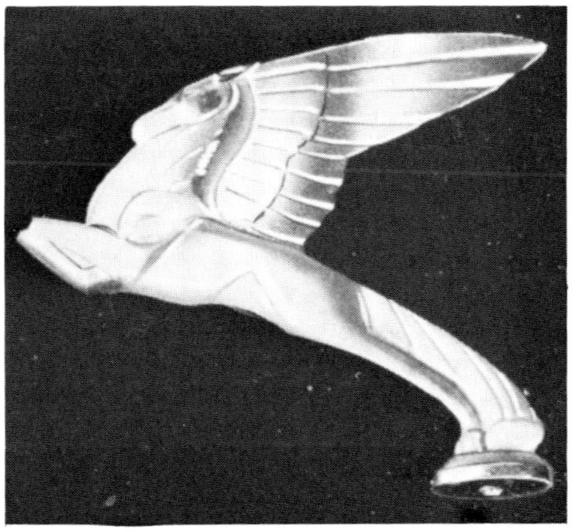

Lejeune

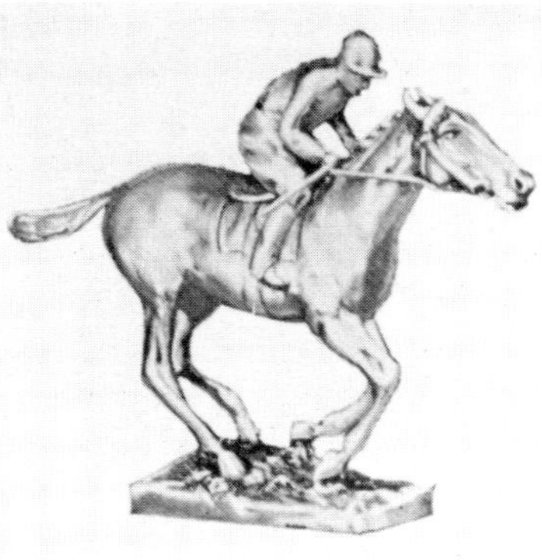

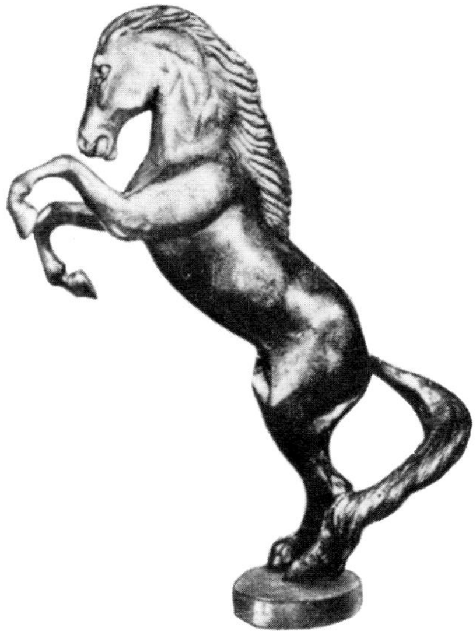

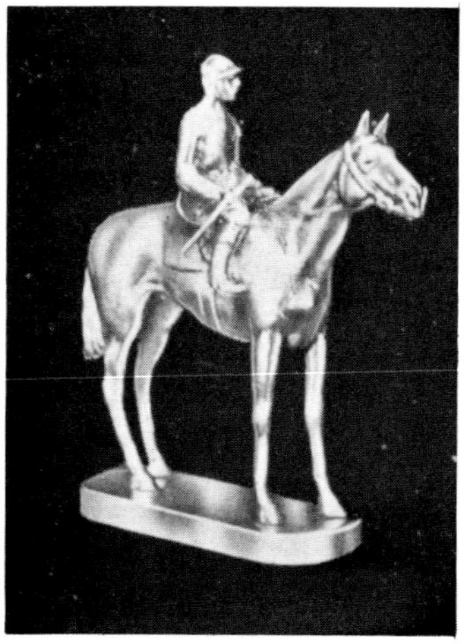

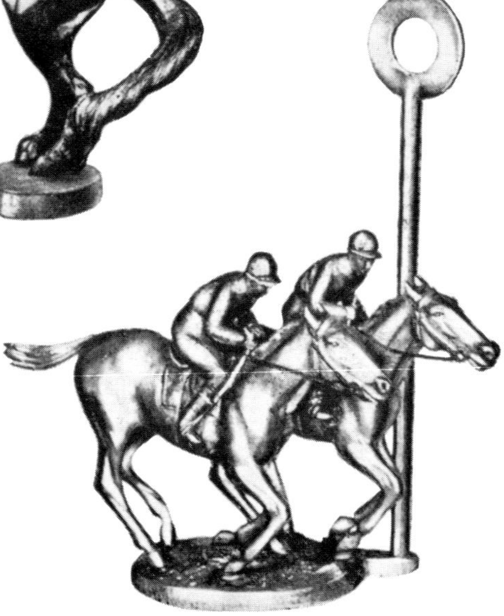

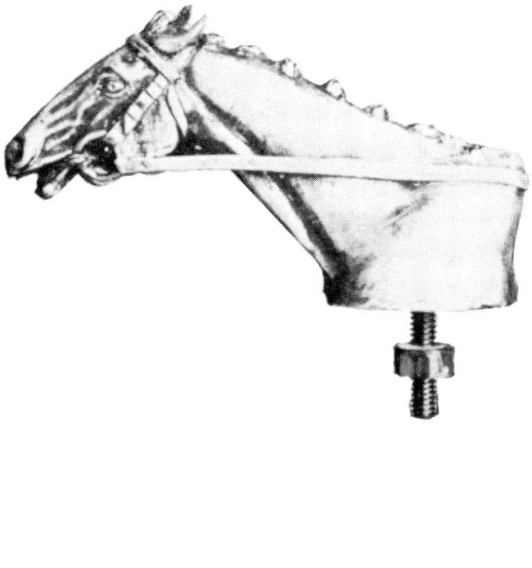

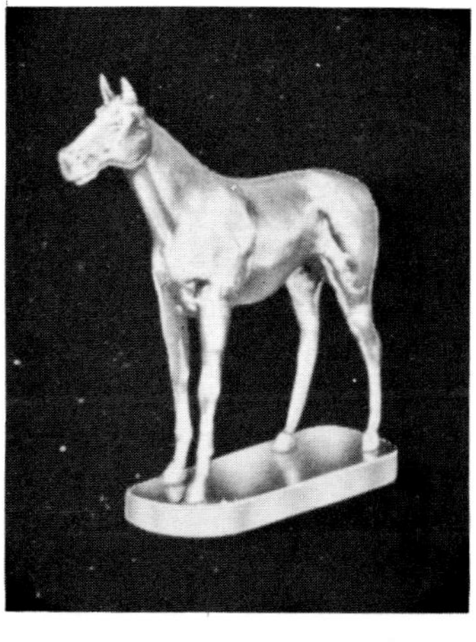

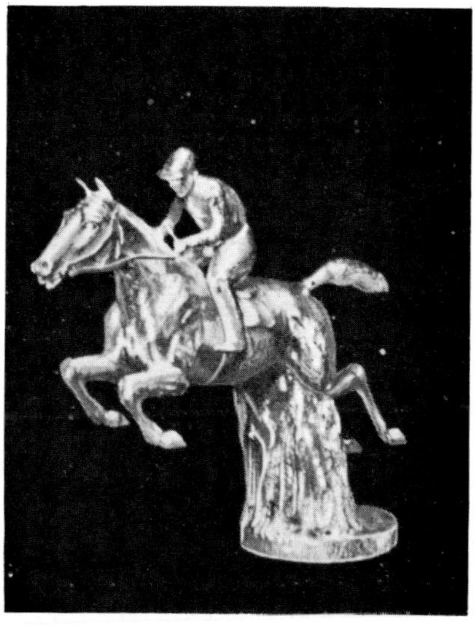

Lejeune

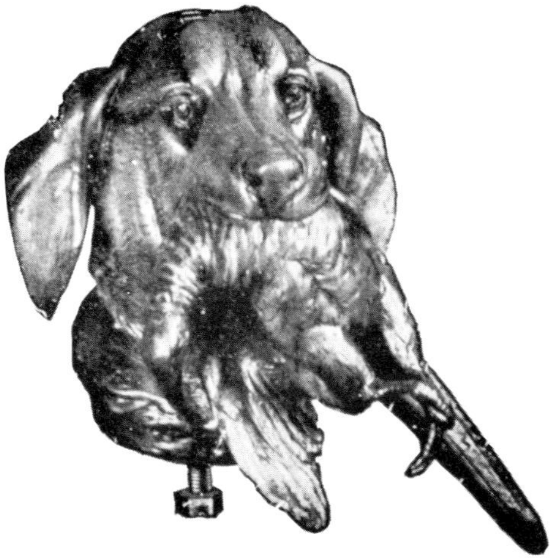

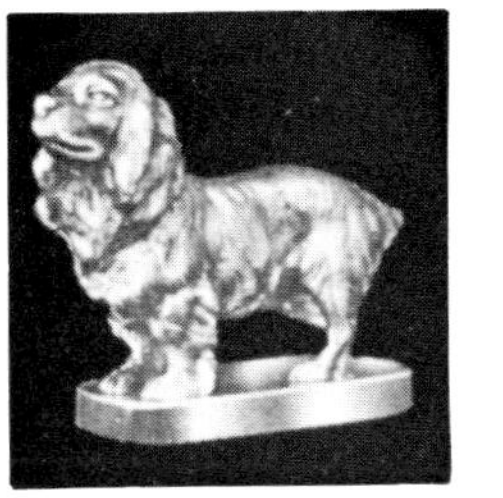

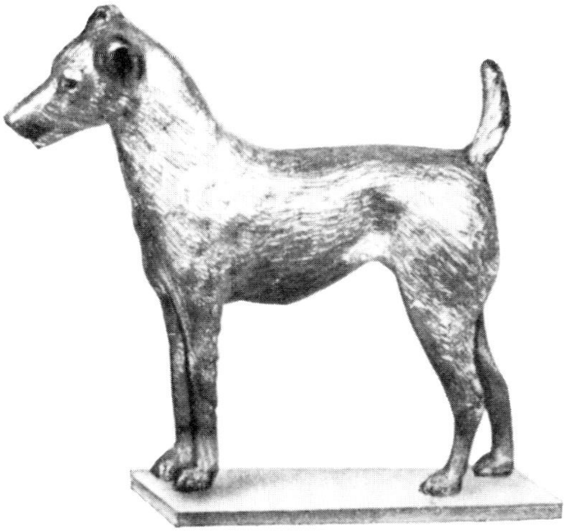

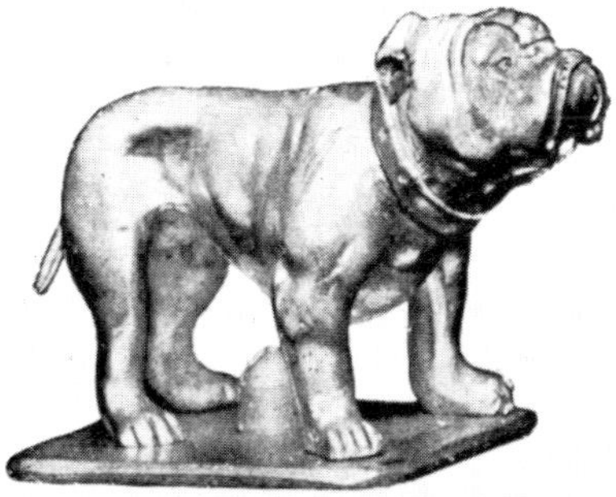

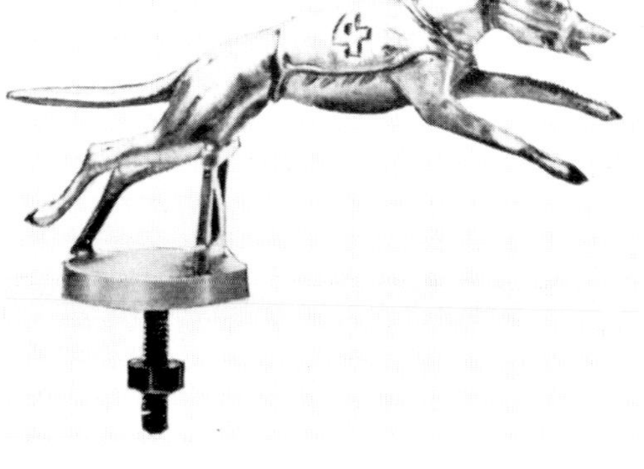

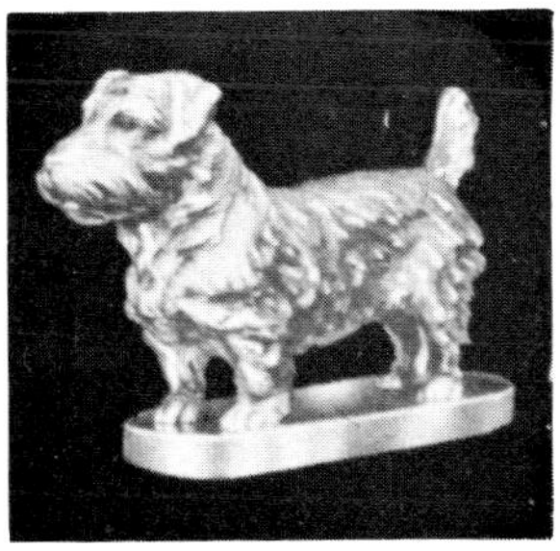

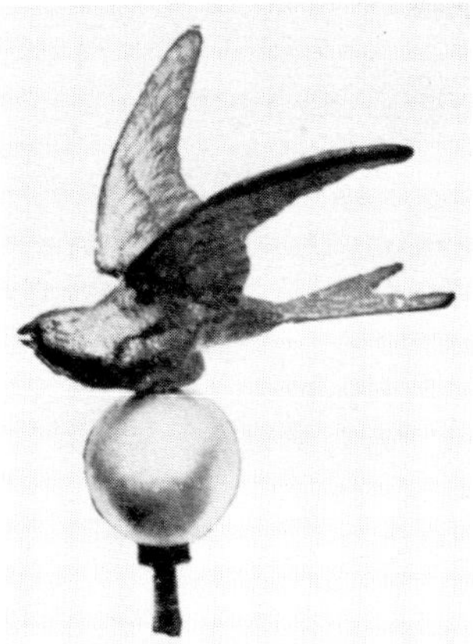

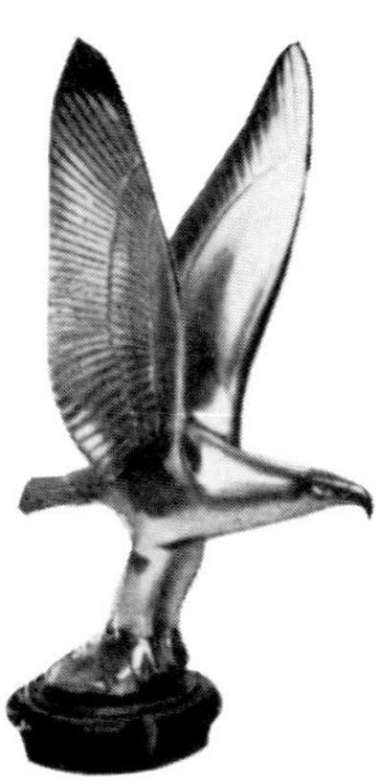

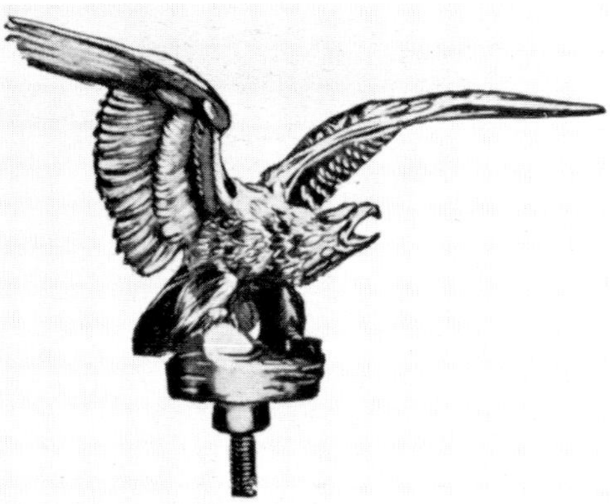

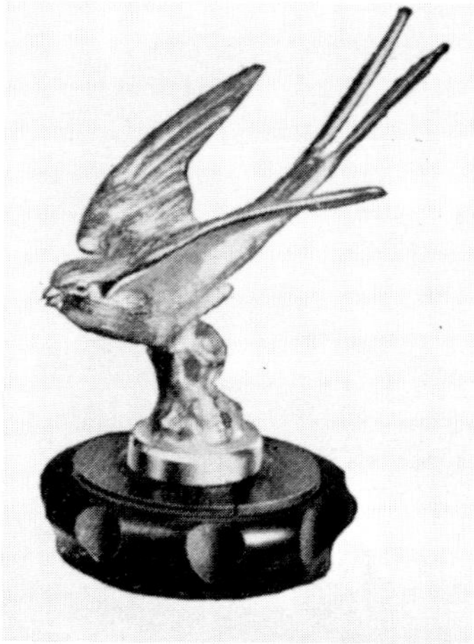
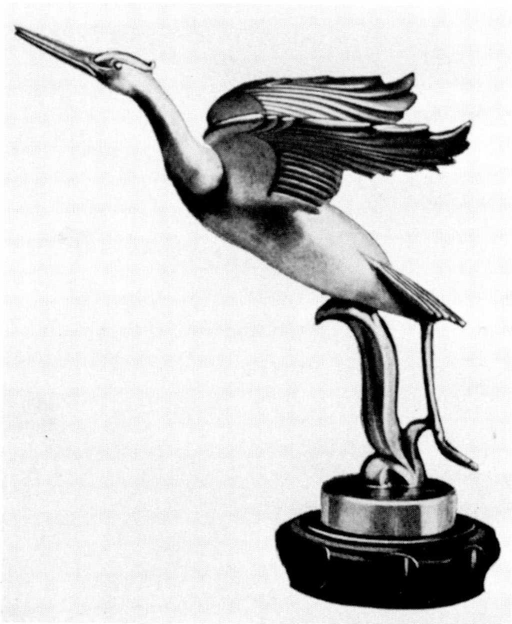
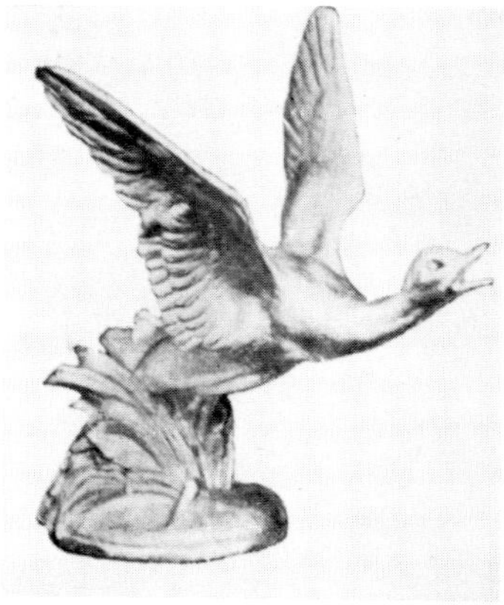

Lejeune

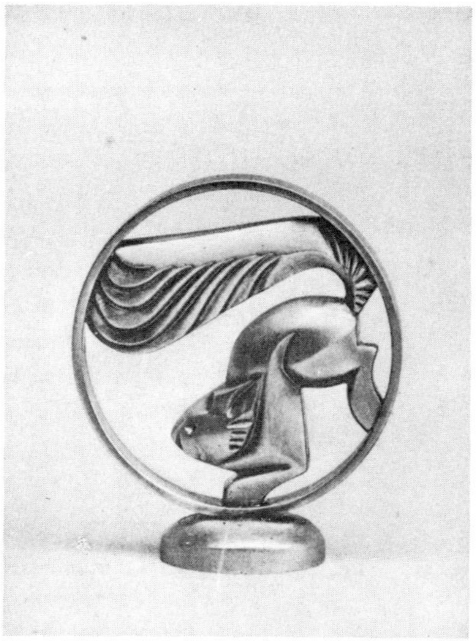

J.J. Martel

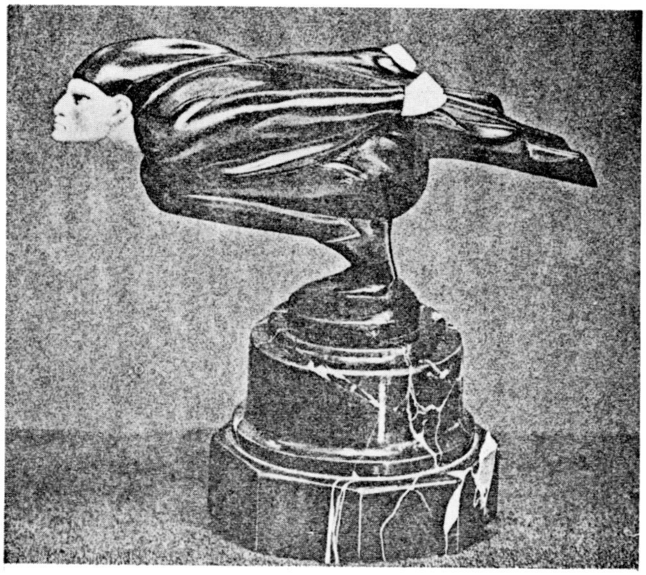

F. Preiss

SUPPLEMENT

Since this book went to press several more figures have come to light; these arc now included together with a Preiss figure of two ballet dancers.

ARDERS

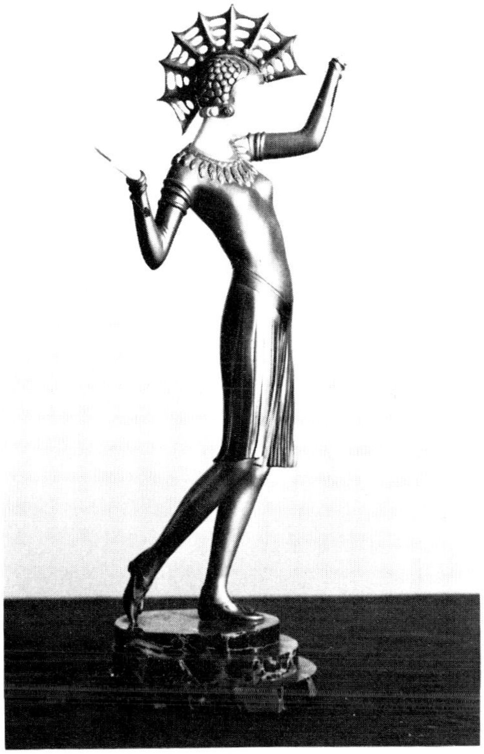

Brigitte Helm`as she was in the film 'Metropolis', 1926
51cm:20in.
(also known to be signed by Preiss)

JUVERNET

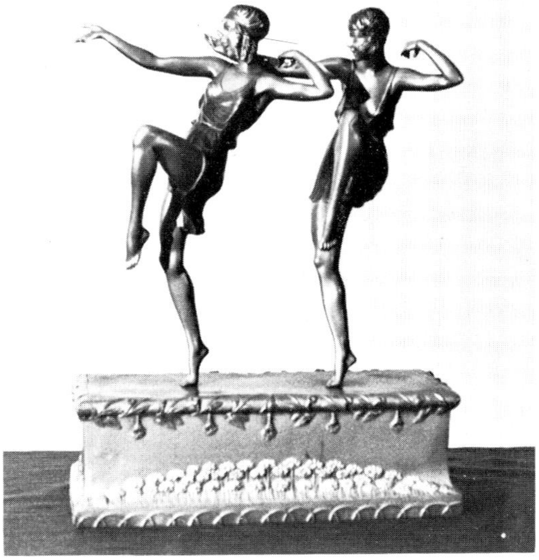

Two Dancers
48cm:18¾in.

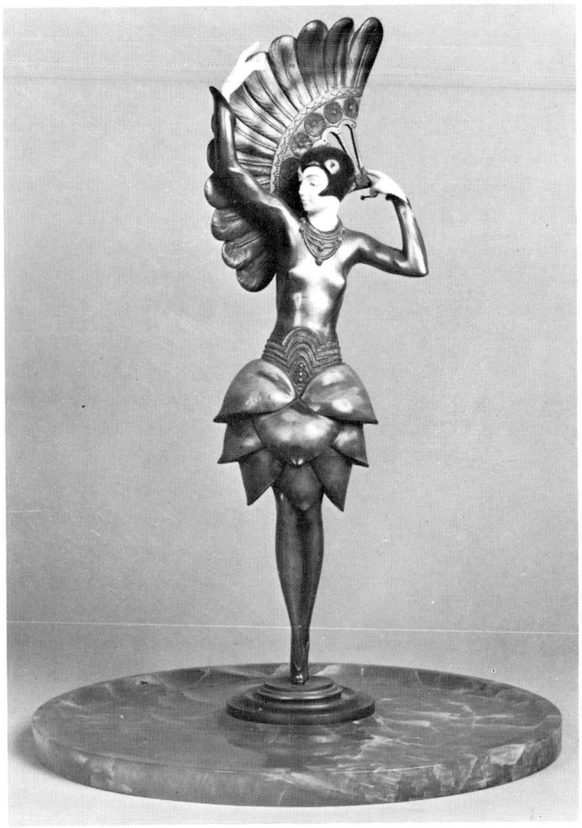

PHILIPPE

A Fan Dancer
47cm:18½in.

PHILIPPE

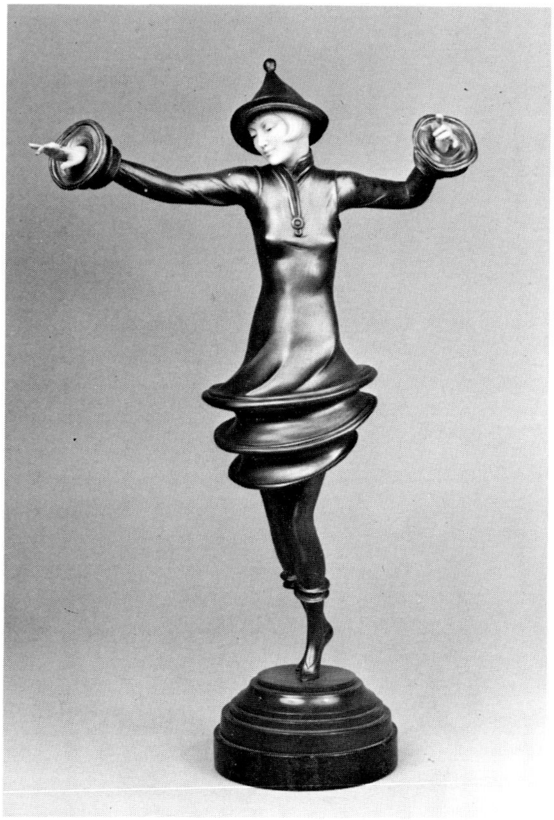

A Dancer, 41cm:16in.

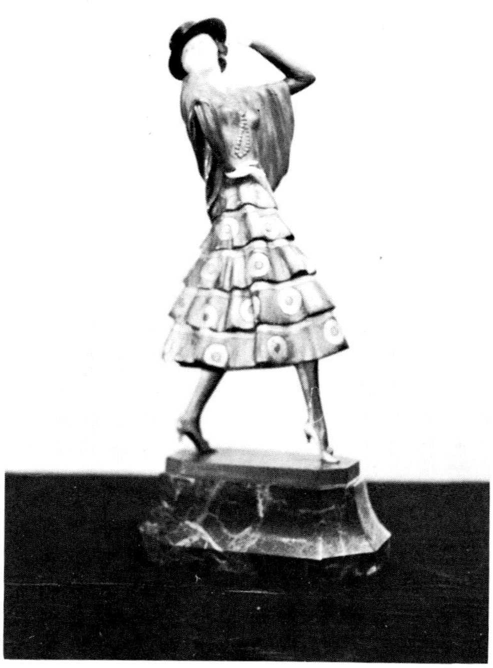

Spanish Dancer, 43cm:17in.

F. PREISS

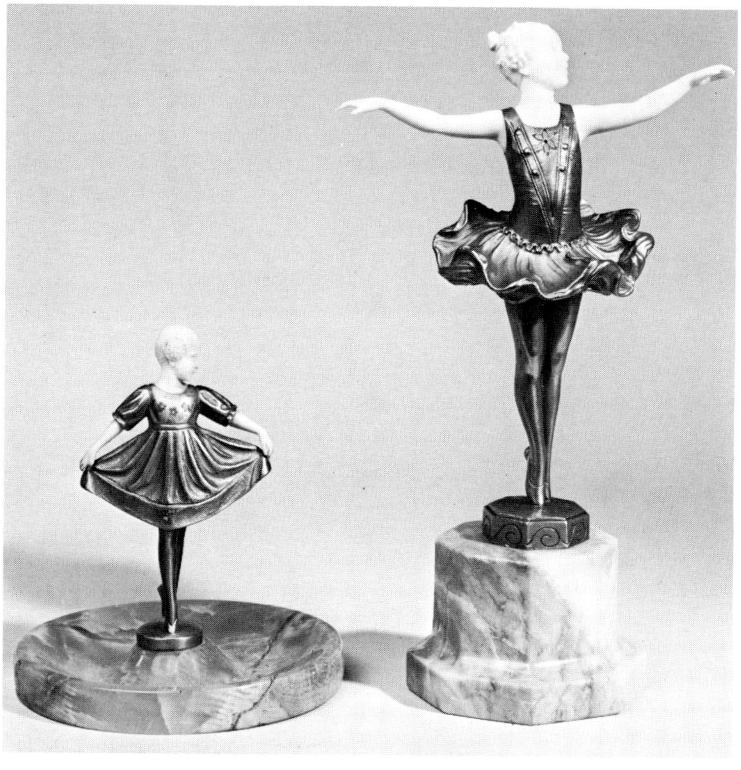

Two Ballet Dancers, Various sizes